Alfred
Lord Tennyson

Crossing the Bar

Sunset and evening star,
    And one clear call for me!
And may there be no moaning of the bar,
    When I put out to sea.

But such a tide as moving seems asleep,
    Too full for sound and foam,
When that which drew from out the boundless deep
    Turns again home.

Twilight and evening bell,
    And after that the dark!
And may there be no sadness of farewell,
    When I embark;

For tho' from out our bourne of Time and Place
    The flood may bear me far,
I hope to see my Pilot face to face
    When I have crost the bar.

Crossing the Bar was written by Alfred Tennyson in twenty minutes while crossing the Solent, a journey he often made to and from his home on the Isle of Wight.

The Works of
Alfred
Lord Tennyson

with an Introduction and Bibliography

Wordsworth Poetry Library

This edition published 1994 by Wordsworth Editions Ltd,
Cumberland House, Crib Street, Ware, Hertfordshire SG12 9ET

Copyright © Wordsworth Editions Ltd 1994

Wordsworth® is a registered trade mark of
Wordsworth Editions Ltd

ISBN 1-85326-414-8

Typeset by Antony Gray
Printed and bound in Great Britain by
Mackays of Chatham plc, Chatham, Kent

INTRODUCTION

At a late-Victorian dinner party the guest of honour admired the plate set before him. Turning it over to ascertain the maker's mark, he drenched himself with the soup it contained. This guest was the Poet Laureate, patriarchally bearded, admired by the Queen and, for many of his contemporaries, emblem of all that was best in the Victorian Age. But the unselfconscious oddity of his behaviour points to something stranger and more disturbing than is usually associated with this grand but apparently dated figure. While much of Tennyson's work, deadened for many of us by uninspired English teachers, speaks only faintly to the late twentieth century, attentive reading will reveal, even in his most familiar poems, the dark, sensuous, even morbid richness which is the underside of the nineteenth-century creative temper.

Alfred Tennyson was born in August 1809 at the rectory of Somersby, a pretty Lincolnshire village, the third surviving son of George Tennyson and his wife Elizabeth. Although the rector was the eldest son of a prosperous family, the considerable estate had been willed to his ambitious younger brother Charles, something which was to rankle increasingly with George and his family. George, depressive, violent and addictive, died in 1831, drunk and drugged, after a year-long estrangement from his wife and family, leaving an inheritance of dangerous melancholy: Alfred had long battles with depression and most of his siblings had histories of mental instability (often called 'hypochondria' in those days); in 1832 his brother Edward was committed to a lunatic asylum where he remained until his death.

Alfred's education, rigorously classical, came substantially from his father. By the age of sixteen he was writing, and in 1827 he published a volume of poetry with his elder brother. That year he went to Trinity College, Cambridge, but became happy there only after he won a prize with his poem 'Timbuctoo' and met Arthur Hallam. This friendship deepened when they were elected to the élite secret society, the

Apostles. Hallam was welcomed by the Somersby family and became engaged to Tennyson's sister, Emily. The two young men travelled abroad twice, journeys whose landscapes were a powerful influence on Tennyson's poetry. The year 1830 saw the publication of *Poems, Chiefly Lyrical*, and in 1832 two volumes of *Poems* appeared. In 1833 Hallam died suddenly, on a visit to Vienna with his father. This devastating bereavement was the inspiration for what is perhaps Tennyson's greatest poem, *In Memoriam*, published in 1850 and leading to the laureateship.

In 1835 Tennyson fell painfully in love with a rich beauty, Rosa Baring, whose rejection of him inspired some of his more painful poems and exacerbated the soreness about his social position which the earlier disinheritance had fostered. But in 1836 he met Emily Sellwood, sister of his brother Charles's bride. Before long they were planning to marry but her family insisted on their breaking off the engagement because of his financial problems (caused by unwise investments) and the 'black blood' of the Tennysons. Meanwhile, however, Tennyson was establishing his reputation with the 1842 publication of his collected poems and, in 1847, of *The Princess*. Emily remained staunch and in 1850, a month after the publication of *In Memoriam*, whose title she had suggested, they were married. After the stillbirth of their first baby, a son was born in 1852 whom his parents christened Hallam.

By now Tennyson's fame was firmly established. In 1854 the little family moved to the Isle of Wight, partly to escape the hordes of eager admirers who besieged their Twickenham house. Although still socially awkward, Tennyson enjoyed the sociability and lionising which accompanied his fame. And he was writing prolifically: *Maud and Other Poems* appeared in 1855, the first four *Idylls of the King* in 1859, *Enoch Arden Etc.* in 1864, *The Holy Grail and Other Poems* in 1869 and *Gareth and Lynette etc.* in 1872. By now he was also writing poetic dramas. Although these are difficult to read now, he had a great success with *Beckett*, in which Henry Irving and Ellen Terry appeared in 1893. In 1884 he was given his peerage and in 1885 he published *Tiresias, and Other Poems*. He died in October 1892, and was buried in Westminster Abbey, a fitting tribute to a poet whose productive life had commenced with the dawning of the Victorian Age, and lasted almost to its close.

While Tennyson's popularity flourished in anthologies and classrooms, critical opinion soon turned against him. He has been seen as sentimental, bombastic, boring and – thought T. S. Eliot – a deadening influence on succeeding poets. More recent critics, in predictable reaction, have seen how much passion and complexity there is in Tennyson's accomplished and mellifluous poetry. The early poem, 'Mariana', inspired by *Measure for Measure*'s Mariana in her moated grange (and inspiring Millais' famous picture of 1851), uses an obsessive cataloguing of decay and stasis to objectify the tragic *ennui* of the abandoned woman:

> With blackest moss the flower-plots
>   Were thickly crusted, one and all:
> The rusted nails fell from the knots
>   That held the pear to the garden-wall . . .
> All day within the dreamy house,
>   The doors upon the hinges creak'd;
> The blue fly sung in the pane; the mouse
>   Behind the mouldering wainscot shriek'd...

Its 'pendant' poem, 'Mariana in the South', uses a heat-parched landscape as correlative of the sterile wastes of longing. 'The Kraken' evokes an invisible sea-monster, whose form can only be inferred from the vastness of its surrounding sponges and 'enormous polypi', and which will never be seen 'Until the latter fire shall heat the deep' and the creature, rising and becoming visible, must die. The song, 'A spirit haunts the year's last hours', languishes with death-bed imagery, and 'The Two Voices' (suggestively written in three-line stanzas) is an extended account of suicidal depression and debate.

The poems collected in the 1842 volume show that Tennyson had achieved complete confidence in subject matter and prosody. Many of us have had 'The Lady of Shalott' spoiled for us by premature and simplistic reading. It is of course the narrative poem we know so well, but it can also be read as an allegory for the artist, toiling in seclusion, whose art withers in the face of reality. The skill of its construction, with The Lady evoked only in her absence in the first part, portrayed in her ghostly, enchanted room in the second, and, in the third, suffering the incursion of the bright world as she looks out to Lancelot and, beyond him, to the towers of Camelot, has powerful emotional impulsion, underlined by the chiming rhyme scheme. 'Locksley Hall', quite strange and difficult with its long, rolling couplets, gives us a bitter lover, jilted by a proud, rich woman – echoing the rejection by Rosa Baring – and has extraordinary visions of the future:

> Heard the heavens fill with shouting, and there rain'd a ghastly dew
>   From the nations' airy navies grappling in the central blue . . .

(Tennyson's clanging line, 'Let the great world spin for ever down the ringing grooves of change', arose from his mistaken idea that the new railway trains ran in grooves rather than on rails.)

'Ulysses', 'Tithonus' and 'The Lotos-Eaters', subjects arising from his profound classical knowledge, all deal with the temptations of idleness.

Tithonus was a young shepherd beloved of the goddess Aurora, who gave him eternal life but forgot to give him eternal youth. The poem depicts him withering in the goddess's maternal arms. The Lotos-eaters, seduced by the magical drug (fabled to be of dragging, neurotic sweetness), resist Ulysses's urgings, while 'Ulysses' shows the old war-leader bored with the peaceful life of 'an idle king', and longing for a last odyssey with his old companions –

> To sail beyond the sunset, and the baths
> Of all the western stars, until I die . . .
> One equal temper of heroic hearts,
> Made weak by time and fate, but strong in will
> To strive, to seek, to find, and not to yield.

The sentiments of the last line held a vital message for Tennyson. Will was all he had to set against his grief for Hallam and the lethargy of his depressions, and these poems are mimetic of the dull inertia which could so easily overpower him.

The Princess: A Medley presents problems for the modern reader. Its story of the Princess Ida (burlesqued in Gilbert and Sullivan's operetta) who sets up an all-female college, and banishes men on pain of death, but is restored to 'womanliness' by nursing her wounded prince after a battle, is not fashionable now. But in fact Tennyson felt a strong sympathy for women and their oppression by the conventions of the day, and his message is ultimately that 'woman is not undevelop'd man [as so many of his contemporaries felt]/ But diverse', that Love's 'dearest bond is this, / Not like to like, but like in difference, /. . . The man be more of woman, she of man'. The long poem is framed by a discussion initiated by the spirited Lilia, and the story is purportedly told by the men in the group, while the women intersperse the ravishing lyrics. Tennyson was aiming at the tone of Shakespearian festive comedy, particularly *Love's Labours Lost*, not always successfully. Nevertheless, reading this as if it were a novel is rewarding and interesting, and the lyrics (for example, 'Tears, idle tears', 'Ask me no more', O Swallow, Swallow, flying, flying south', 'The splendour falls on castle walls', 'Now sleeps the crimson petal, now the white'), while able triumphantly to stand alone, contribute subtly to the mood and atmosphere of the narrative.

Soon after Hallam's death Tennyson started writing individual elegies, of differing lengths but using the same rhyme scheme. These explored the death of his beloved friend and the fears and doubts it awoke. Each can stand alone, but gradually Tennyson built them into *In Memoriam*, a subtle but telling structure in which the mood moves from desolation, through a vision of the ship carrying Hallam's body back to England, memories of Hallam, a tormented debate about humanity's relationship with evolved nature and the godlessness and therefore meaninglessness it implies, dreams and hauntings and happier memories of Hallam in Cambridge and at Somersby, towards a gradual softening of the grief, and ultimate reconciliation with a family marriage. The calendar of bereavement provides a subsidiary structure: the first bleak Christmas without Hallam, the first anniversary of his death, the second Christmas, the second anniversary, a quiet third Christmas which modulates into a hopeful New Year ('Ring out, wild bells, to the wild sky') where 'Ring out the old, ring in the new' signals brightening hope.

Although fearing it 'half a sin/ To put in words the grief I feel', Tennyson needed 'the sad mechanic exercise'. Canto VII gives us the poet's desolation with terrible simplicity:

> Dark house, by which once more I stand
>   Here in the long unlovely street,
>   Doors where my heart was used to beat...
>
> And ghastly thro' the drizzling rain
> On the bald street breaks the blank day.

Much, much later in the poem (canto CXVIII) these lines are echoed and answered:

> Doors where my heart was used to beat
>   So quickly, not as one that weeps
>   I come once more; the city sleeps;
> I smell the meadow in the street.

The repeated (and unfortunately hackneyed) sentiment, ' 'Tis better to have loved and lost / Than never to have loved at all', leads us to the final message of the poem, that love is never lost, though it is possible to feel that the conclusion is more willed than achieved through the action of reason. (The introductory canto, 'Strong Son of God, immortal Love', was added once the poem was finished.)

Maud, which deepens and expands the neurotic atmosphere of Locksley Hall, is astonishing and telling for the modern reader. Tennyson called it a monodrama; its protagonist falls in love with the beautiful heiress of the man who has killed the narrator's father in a 'dreadful hollow'. The narrator is very far from reliable, as he progresses from hostility to Maud through an obsessive and rhapsodic love, to exile after killing her brother in a duel, and madness. Each section is different in mood and metre, and their many beauties are luridly enhanced by the realisation of the narrator's precarious sanity. The whole drama is pervaded by suggestive imagery of lilies, roses, a rivulet, and that red-ribbed hollow. The ecstasies of, 'Go not, happy day', and 'Come into the garden, Maud', are contrasted with the tenderly grave, 'I have led her home, my love, my only friend', and the hallucinations of the mad scene which is reminiscent of Poe's horror stories.

Idylls of the King are long poems about the knights of King Arthur's court, and the early *Morte d'Arthur* becomes the last of these. The death of an Arthur naturally had deep significance for Tennyson, and these poems ('idyll' signifies intimate rather than epic treatment, as in his early 'English Idyls' [sic]) allegorise the decline from idealism to decay which he believed he saw in contemporary life. The 'good' characters of Enid and Elaine are contrasted with the false Guinevere and Vivien, and Merlin is seen as the intelligence of Camelot ensnared by the enchantress, Vivien. Like *Enoch Arden* they are not easy to read, but they reward the dedicated student.

This brief introduction can do no more than indicate the 'lollipops'. But the *Collected Poems* are a treasury to be dipped into and explored. From the aching desolation of 'Break, break, break / On thy cold gray stones, O Sea', and the dizzy perception of height in 'The Eagle', to the long narrative poems, or the appealing dialect of 'Northern Farmer: Old Style'; from the angry and comic satire of 'St Simeon Stylites' to the futile gallop of 'The Charge of the Light Brigade', Tennyson shows his mastery of rhyme, metre, imagery and mood. And it is the tranquil and resigned 'Crossing the Bar' which is often seen as his epitaph:

> Sunset and evening star,
> And one clear call for me!
> And may there be no moaning of the bar,
> When I put out to sea.

FURTHER READING

Hallam Tennyson, *Alfred Lord Tennyson*, London, 1897

Christopher Ricks, *Tennyson*, New York and London, 1972

Jerome H. Buckley, *Tennyson: The Growth of a Poet*, Cambridge, Mass., 1960

A. Dwight Culler, *The Poetry of Tennyson*, New Haven & London, 1977

T. S. Eliot, *'In Memoriam': Selected Essays*, London, 1969

John Dixon Hunt, *Tennyson: 'In Memoriam': A Casebook*, London, 1970

Robert Bernard Martin, *The Unquiet Heart*, Oxford, 1970

F. E. L. Priestley, *Language and Structure in Tennyson's Poetry*, London, 1973

CONTENTS

To The Queen

Revered, beloved – O you that hold
   A nobler office upon earth
   Than arms, or power of brain, or birth
Could give the warrior kings of old,

Victoria, – since your Royal grace
   To one of less desert allows
   This laurel greener from the brows
Of him that utter'd nothing base;

And should your greatness, and the care
   That yokes with empire, yield you time
   To make demand of modern rhyme
If aught of ancient worth be there;

Then – while a sweeter music wakes,
   And thro' wild March the throstle calls,
   Where all about your palace-walls
The sun-lit almond-blossom shakes –

Take, Madam, this poor book of song,
   For tho' the faults were thick as dust
   In vacant chambers, I could trust
Your kindness. May you rule us long,

And leave us rulers of your blood
   As noble till the latest day!
   May children of our children say,
'She wrought her people lasting good;

'Her court was pure; her life serene;
   God gave her peace; her land reposed;
   A thousand claims to reverence closed
In her as Mother, Wife and Queen;

'And statesmen at her council met
   Who knew the seasons when to take
   Occasion by the hand, and make
The bounds of freedom wider yet

'By shaping some august decree,
   Which kept her throne unshaken still,
   Broad-based upon her people's will,
And compass'd by the inviolate sea.'

March 1851

POEMS, CHIEFLY LYRICAL

Claribel

A Melody

I

Where Claribel low-lieth
  The breezes pause and die,
    Letting the rose-leaves fall:
But the solemn oak-tree sigheth
    Thick-leaved, ambrosial,
  With an ancient melody
  Of an inward agony,
Where Claribel low-lieth.

II

At eve the beetle boometh
  Athwart the thicket lone:
At noon the wild bee hummeth
  About the moss'd headstone:
At midnight the moon cometh,
  And looketh down alone.
Her song the lintwhite swelleth,
The clear-voiced mavis dwelleth,
  The callow throstle lispeth,
The slumbrous wave outwelleth,
  The babbling runnel crispeth,
The hollow grot replieth
Where Claribel low-lieth.

Lilian

I

  Airy, fairy Lilian,
  Flitting, fairy Lilian,
When I ask her if she love me
Claps her tiny hands above me,
  Laughing all she can;
She'll not tell me if she love me,
  Cruel little Lilian.

II

When my passion seeks
Pleasance in love-sighs
She, looking thro' and thro' me
Thoroughly to undo me,
Smiling, never speaks:
So innocent-arch, so cunning-simple,
From beneath her gather'd wimple
Glancing with black-beaded eyes,
Till the lightning laughters dimple
The baby-roses in her cheeks;
Then away she flies.

III

Prythee weep, May Lilian!
Gaiety without eclipse
Wearieth me, May Lilian:
Thro' my very heart it thrilleth
When from crimson-threaded lips
Silver-treble laughter trilleth:
Prythee weep, May Lilian.

IV

Praying all I can
If prayers will not hush thee,
Airy Lilian
Like a rose-leaf I will crush thee,
Fairy Lilian.

Isabel

I

Eyes not down-dropt nor over-bright, but fed
With the clear-pointed flame of chastity,
Clear, without heat, undying, tended by
Pure vestal thoughts in the translucent fane
Of her still spirit; locks not wide-dispread,
Madonna-wise on either side her head;
Sweet lips whereon perpetually did reign
The summer calm of golden charity,
Were fixed shadows of thy fixed mood,
Revered Isabel, the crown and head,
The stately flower of female fortitude,
Of perfect wifehood and pure lowlihead.

II

The intuitive decision of a bright
   And thorough-edged intellect to part
      Error from crime a prudence to withhold;
      The laws of marriage character'd in gold
   Upon the blanched tablets of her heart;
A love still burning upward, giving light
   To read those laws; an accent very low
   In blandishment, but a most silver flow
      Of subtle-paced counsel in distress,
Right to the heart and brain, tho' undescried,
      Winning its way with extreme gentleness
Thro' all the outworks of suspicious pride;
A courage to endure and to obey,
A hate of gossip parlance, and of sway,
Crown'd Isabel, thro' all her placid life,
The queen of marriage, a most perfect wife.

III

The mellow'd reflex of a winter moon;
A clear stream flowing with a muddy one,
   Till in its onward current it absorbs
      With swifter movement and in purer light
      The vexed eddies of its wayward brother:
   A leaning and upbearing parasite,
   Clothing the stem, which else had fallen quite,
With cluster'd flower-bells and ambrosial orbs
      Of rich fruit-bunches leaning on each other –
      Shadow forth thee: – the world hath not another
(Tho' all her fairest forms are types of thee,
And thou of God in thy great charity)
Of such a finish'd chasten'd purity.

Elegiacs

Low-flowing breezes are roaming the broad valley dimm'd in the
    gloaming:
Thoro' the black-stemm'd pines only the far river shines.
Creeping through blossomy rushes and bowers of rose-blowing bushes,
Down by the poplar tall rivulets babble and fall.
Barketh the shepherd-dog cheerly; the grasshopper carolleth clearly;
Deeply the turtle coos; shrilly the owlet halloos;
Winds creep; dews fall chilly: in her first sleep earth breathes stilly:
Over the pools in the burn water-gnats murmur and mourn.
Sadly the far kine loweth: the glimmering water outfloweth:

Twin peaks shadow'd with pine slope to the dark hyaline.
Low-throned Hesper is stayed between the two peaks; but the Naiad
Throbbing in mild unrest holds him beneath in her breast.
The ancient poetess singeth, that Hesperus all things bringeth,
Smoothing the wearied mind: bring me my love, Rosalind.
Thou comest morning and even; she cometh not morning or even.
False-eyed Hesper, unkind, where is my sweet Rosalind?

Mariana

'Mariana in the moated grange' – *Measure for Measure*

With blackest moss the flower-plots
    Were thickly crusted, one and all:
The rusted nails fell from the knots
    That held the pear to the garden-wall.
The broken sheds look'd sad and strange:
    Unlifted was the clinking latch;
    Weeded and worn the ancient thatch
Upon the lonely moated grange.
    She only said, 'My life is dreary,
        He cometh not,' she said;
    She said, 'I am aweary, aweary,
        I would that I were dead!'

Her tears fell with the dews at even;
    Her tears fell ere the dews were dried;
She could not look on the sweet heaven,
    Either at morn or eventide.
After the flitting of the bats,
    When thickest dark did trance the sky,
    She drew her casement-curtain by,
And glanced athwart the glooming flats.
    She only said, 'The night is dreary,
        He cometh not,' she said;
    She said, 'I am aweary, aweary,
        I would that I were dead!'

Upon the middle of the night,
    Waking she heard the night-fowl crow:
The cock sung out an hour ere light:
    From the dark fen the oxen's low
Came to her: without hope of change,
    In sleep she seem'd to walk forlorn,
    Till cold winds woke the grey-eyed morn
About the lonely moated grange.

She only said, 'The day is dreary,
  He cometh not,' she said;
She said, 'I am aweary, aweary,
  I would that I were dead! '

About a stone-cast from the wall
  A sluice with blacken'd waters slept,
And o'er it many, round and small,
  The cluster'd marish-mosses crept.
Hard by a poplar shook alway,
  All silver-green with gnarled bark:
  For leagues no other tree did mark
The level waste, the rounding grey.
     She only said, 'My life is dreary,
       He cometh not,' she said;
     She said, 'I am aweary, aweary,
       I would that I were dead!'

And ever when the moon was low,
  And the shrill winds were up and away,
In the white curtain, to and fro,
  She saw the gusty shadow sway.
But when the moon was very low,
  And wild winds bound within their cell,
  The shadow of the poplar fell
Upon her bed, across her brow.
     She only said, 'The night is dreary,
       He cometh not,' she said;
     She said, 'I am aweary, aweary,
       I would that I were dead!'

All day within the dreamy house,
  The doors upon their hinges creak'd;
The blue fly sung in the pane; the mouse
  Behind the mouldering wainscot shriek'd,
Or from the crevice peer'd about.
  Old faces glimmer'd thro' the doors,
  Old footsteps trod the upper floors,
Old voices called her from without.
     She only said, 'My life is dreary,
       He cometh not,' she said;
     She said, 'I am aweary, aweary,
       I would that I were dead!'

The sparrow's chirrup on the roof,
  The slow clock ticking, and the sound

Which to the wooing wind aloof
   The poplar made, did all confound
Her sense; but most she loathed the hour
   When the thick-moted sunbeam lay
   Athwart the chambers, and the day
Was sloping toward his western bower.
     Then, said she, 'I am very dreary,
       He will not come,' she said;
     She wept, 'I am aweary, aweary,
       Oh God, that I were dead!'

To —

I

Clear-headed friend, whose joyful scorn,
   Edged with sharp laughter, cuts atwain
     The knots that tangle human creeds,
     The wounding cords that bind and strain
     The heart until it bleeds,
Ray-fringed eyelids of the morn
     Roof not a glance so keen as thine:
     If aught of prophecy be mine,
Thou wilt not live in vain.

II

Low-cowering shall the Sophist sit;
   Falsehood shall bare her plaited brow:
   Fair-fronted Truth shall droop not now
With shrilling shafts of subtle wit.
Nor martyr-flames, nor trenchant swords
   Can do away that ancient lie;
   A gentler death shall Falsehood die
Shot thro' and thro' with cunning words.

III

Weak Truth a-leaning on her crutch
   Wan, wasted Truth in her utmost need,
   Thy kingly intellect shall feed,
     Until she be an athlete bold,
And weary with a finger's touch
   Those writhed limbs of lightning speed;
     Like that strange angel which of old,
     Until the breaking of the light,
   Wrestled with wandering Israel
     Past Yabbok brook the livelong night,
And heaven's mazed signs stood still
In the dim tract of Penuel.

Madeline

I

Thou art not steep'd in golden languors,
   No tranced summer calm is thine,
      Ever varying Madeline.
   Thro' light and shadow thou dost range,
   Sudden glances, sweet and strange,
Delicious spites and darling angers,
   And airy forms of flitting change.

II

Smiling, frowning, evermore,
Thou art perfect in love-lore.
Revealings deep and clear are thine
Of wealthy smiles: but who may know
Whether smile or frown be fleeter?
Whether smile or frown be sweeter,
      Who may know?
Frowns perfect-sweet along the brow
Light-glooming over eyes divine,
Like little clouds sun-fringed, are thine,
      Ever varying Madeline.
  Thy smile and frown are not aloof
    From one another
    Each to each is dearest brother;
  Hues of the silken sheeny woof
    Momently shot into each other.
    All the mystery is thine;
Smiling, frowning, evermore,
Thou art perfect in love-lore,
      Ever varying Madeline.

III

A subtle, sudden flame,
  By veering passion fann'd,
    About thee breaks and dances;
  When I would kiss thy hand,
The flush of anger'd shame
    O'erflows thy calmer glances,
And o'er black brows drops down
A sudden-curved frown:
But when I turn away,
Thou, willing me to stay,
  Wooest not, nor vainly wranglest;
  But, looking fixedly the while,

All my bounding heart entanglest
    In a golden-netted smile;
Then in madness and in bliss,
If my lips should dare to kiss
Thy taper fingers amorously,
Again thou blushest angerly;
And o'er black brows drops down
A sudden-curved frown.

The Merman

I

Who would be
A merman bold,
Sitting alone,
Singing alone
Under the sea,
With a crown of gold,
On a throne?

II

I would be a merman bold;
I would sit and sing the whole of the day;
I would fill the sea-halls with a voice of power:
But at night I would roam abroad and play
With the mermaids in and out of the rocks,
Dressing their hair with the white sea-flower;
And holding them back by their flowing locks
I would kiss them often under the sea,
And kiss them again till they kiss'd me
    Laughingly, laughingly;
And then we would wander away, away
To the pale-green sea-groves straight and high,
    Chasing each other merrily.

III

There would be neither moon nor star;
But the wave would make music above us afar –
Low thunder and light in the magic night –
    Neither moon nor star.
We would call aloud in the dreamy dells,
Call to each other and whoop and cry
    All night, merrily, merrily;
They would pelt me with starry spangles and shells,
    Laughing and clapping their hands between,

All night, merrily, merrily:
But I would throw to them back in mine
Turkis and agate and almondine:
Then leaping out upon them unseen
I would kiss them often under the sea,
And kiss them again till they kiss'd me
  Laughingly, laughingly.
Oh! what a happy life were mine
Under the hollow-hung ocean green!
Soft are the moss-beds under the sea;
We would live merrily, merrily.

The Mermaid

I

Who would be
A mermaid fair,
Singing alone,
Combing her hair
Under the sea
In a golden curl
With a comb of pearl,
On a throne?

II

I would be a mermaid fair;
I would sing to myself the whole of the day;
With a comb of pearl I would comb my hair;
And still as I comb'd I would sing and say,
'Who is it loves me? who loves not me?'
I would comb my hair till my ringlets would fall,
  Low adown, low adown,
From under my starry sea-bud crown
  Low adown and around,
And I should look like a fountain of gold
  Springing alone
  With a shrill inner sound,
  Over the throne
  In the midst of the hall;
Till that great sea-snake under the sea
From his coiled sleeps in the central deeps
Would slowly trail himself sevenfold
Round the hall where I sate, and look in at the gate
With his large calm eyes for the love of me.
And all the mermen under the sea
Would feel their immortality
Die in their hearts for the love of me.

III

But at night I would wander away, away
   I would fling on each side my low-flowing locks,
And lightly vault from the throne and play
   With the mermen in and out of the rocks;
We would run to and fro, and hide and seek,
   On the broad sea-wolds in the crimson shells,
   Whose silvery spikes are nighest the sea.
But if any came near I would call, and shriek,
And adown the steep like a wave I would leap
   From the diamond-ledges that jut from the dells
For I would not be kiss'd by all who would list
Of the bold merry mermen under the sea;
They would sue me, and woo me, and flatter me,
In the purple twilights under the sea;
But the king of them all would carry me,
Woo me, and win me, and marry me,
In the branching jaspers under the sea;
Then all the dry pied things that be
In the hueless mosses under the sea
Would curl round my silver feet silently,
All looking up for the love of me.
And if I should carol aloud, from aloft
All things that are forked, and horned, and soft
Would lean out from the hollow sphere of the sea,
All looking down for the love of me.

Supposed Confessions
of a second-rate sensitive mind not in unity with itself

Oh God! my God! have mercy now.
I faint, I fall. Men say that
Thou Did'st die for me, for such as *me*,
Patient of ill, and death, and scorn,
And that my sin was as a thorn
Among the thorns that girt Thy brow,
Wounding Thy soul. – That even now,
In this extremest misery
Of ignorance, I should require
A sign! and if a bolt of fire
Would rive the slumbrous summer noon
While I do pray to Thee alone,
Think my belief would stronger grow!
Is not my human pride brought low?
The boastings of my spirit still?
The joy I had in my freewill

All cold, and dead, and corpse-like grown?
And what is left to me, but Thou,
And faith in Thee? Men pass me by;
Christians with happy countenances –
And children all seem full of Thee!
And women smile with saint-like glances
Like Thine own mother's when she bow'd
Above Thee, on that happy morn
When angels spake to men aloud,
And Thou and peace to earth were born.
Goodwill to me as well as all –
    I one of them: my brothers they:
Brothers in Christ – a world of peace
    And confidence, day after day;
And trust and hope till things should cease,
    And then one Heaven receive us all.

How sweet to have a common faith!
To hold a common scorn of death!
And at a burial to hear
    The creaking cords which wound and eat
Into my human heart, whene'er
Earth goes to earth, with grief, not fear,
    With hopeful grief, were passing sweet!
A grief not uninformed, and dull,
Hearted with hope, of hope as full
As is the blood with life, or night
And a dark cloud with rich moonlight.
To stand beside a grave, and see
The red small atoms wherewith we
Are built, and smile in calm, and say –
    'These little motes and grains shall be
    Clothed on with immortality
    More glorious than the noon of day.
        All that is pass'd into the flowers,
    And into beasts, and other men,
        And all the Norland whirlwind showers
    From open vaults, and all the sea
    O'erwashes with sharp salts, again
    Shall fleet together all, and be
    Indued with immortality.

Thrice happy state again to be
The trustful infant on the knee!
Who lets his waxen fingers play
About his mother's neck, and knows
    Nothing beyond his mother's eyes.

They comfort him by night and day;
They light his little life alway;
He hath no thought of coming woes;
He hath no care of life or death,
Scarce outward signs of joy arise,
Because the Spirit of happiness
And perfect rest so inward is;
And loveth so his innocent heart,
Her temple and her place of birth,
Where she would ever wish to dwell,
Life of the fountain there, beneath
Its salient springs, and far apart,
Hating to wander out on earth,
Or breathe into the hollow air
Whose chillness would make visible
Her subtil, warm, and golden breath,
Which mixing with the infant's blood,
Fulfils him with beatitude.
Oh! sure it is a special care
Of God, to fortify from doubt,
To arm in proof, and guard about
With triple-mailèd trust, and clear
Delight, the infant's dawning year.

Would that my gloomed fancy were
As thine, my mother, when with brows
Propped on thy knees, my hands upheld
In thine, I listen'd to thy vows,
For me outpour'd in holiest prayer –
For me unworthy! – and beheld
Thy mild deep eyes upraised, that knew
The beauty and repose of faith,
And the clear spirit shining through.
Oh! wherefore do we grow awry
From roots which strike so deep? why dare
Paths in the desert? Could not I
Bow myself down, where thou hast knelt,
To th' earth – until the ice would melt
Here, and I feel as thou hast felt?
What Devil had the heart to scathe
Flowers thou had'st reared – to brush the dew
From thine own lily, when thy grave
Was deep, my mother, in the clay?
Myself? Is it thus? Myself? Had I
So little love for thee? But why
Prevail'd not thy pure prayers? Why pray
To one who heeds not, who can save

But will not? Great in faith, and strong
Against the grief of circumstance
Wert thou, and yet unheard. What if
Thou pleadest still, and seest me drive
Through utter dark a full-sail'd skiff,
Unpiloted i' the echoing dance
Of reboant whirlwinds, stooping low
Unto the death, not sunk! I know
At matins and at evensong,
That thou, if thou wert yet alive
In deep and daily prayers would'st strive
To reconcile me with thy God.
Albeit, my hope is grey, and cold
At heart, thou wouldest murmur still —
'Bring this lamb back into Thy fold,
My Lord, if so it be Thy will.'
Would'st tell me I must brook the rod,
And chastisement of human pride;
That pride, the sin of devils, stood
Betwixt me and the light of God!
That hitherto I had defied,
And had rejected God — that grace
Would drop from his o'erbrimming love,
As manna on my wilderness,
If I would pray — that God would move
And strike the hard hard rock, and thence,
Sweet in their utmost bitterness,
Would issue tears of penitence
Which would keep green hope's life.
Alas! I think that pride hath now no place
Nor sojourn in me. I am void,
Dark, formless, utterly destroyed.

Why not believe then? Why not yet
Anchor thy frailty there, where man
Hath moor'd and rested? Ask the sea
At midnight, when the crisp slope waves
After a tempest, rib and fret
The broad-imbased beach, why he
Slumbers not like a mountain tarn?
Wherefore his ridges are not curls
And ripples of an inland mere?
Wherefore he moaneth thus, nor can
Draw down into his vexed pools
All that blue heaven which hues and paves
The other? I am too forlorn,
Too shaken: my own weakness fools

My judgement, and my spirit whirls
Moved from beneath with doubt and fear.

'Yet,' said I, in my morn of youth,
The unsunn'd freshness of my strength,
When I went forth in quest of truth,
'It is man's privilege to doubt,
If so be that from doubt at length,
Truth may stand forth unmoved of change,
An image with profulgent brows,
And perfect limbs, as from the storm
Of running fires and fluid range
Of lawless airs, at last stood out
This excellence and solid form
Of constant beauty. For the Ox
Feeds in the herb, and sleeps, or fills
The horned valleys all about,
And hollows of the fringed hills
In summer heats, with placid lows
Unfearing, till his own blood flows
About his hoof. And in the flocks
The lamb rejoiceth in the year,
And raceth freely with his fere
And answers to his mother's calls
From the flower'd furrow. In a time,
Of which he wots not, run short pains
Through his warm heart; and then, from whence
He knows not, on his light there falls
A shadow; and his native slope,
Where he was wont to leap and climb,
Floats from his sick and filmed eyes,
And something in the darkness draws
His forehead earthward, and he dies.
Shall man live thus, in joy and hope
As a young lamb, who cannot dream,
Living, but that he shall live on?
Shall we not look into the laws
Of life and death, and things that seem,
And things that be, and analyse
Our double nature, and compare
All creeds till we have found the one,
If one there be?' Ay me! I fear
All may not doubt, but everywhere
Some must clasp Idols. Yet, my God,
Whom call I Idol? Let Thy dove
Shadow me over, and my sins
Be unremember'd, and Thy love

Enlighten me. Oh teach me yet
Somewhat before the heavy clod
Weighs on me, and the busy fret
Of that sharp-headed worm begins
In the gross blackness underneath.

Oh weary life! oh weary death!
Oh spirit and heart made desolate!
Oh damned vacillating state!

Song. The Owl

I

When cats run home and light is come,
  And dew is cold upon the ground,
And the far-off stream is dumb,
  And the whirring sail goes round,
  And the whirring sail goes round;
    Alone and warming his five wits,
    The white owl in the belfry sits.

II

When merry milkmaids click the latch,
  And rarely smells the new-mown hay,
And the cock hath sung beneath the thatch
  Twice or thrice his roundelay,
  Twice or thrice his roundelay;
    Alone and warming his five wits,
    The white owl in the belfry sits.

Second Song to the Owl

I

Thy tuwhits are lull'd I wot,
  Thy tuwhoos of yesternight,
Which upon the dark afloat,
  So took echo with delight,
  So took echo with delight,
    That her voice untuneful grown,
    Wears all day a fainter tone.

II

I would mock thy chaunt anew;
  But I cannot mimick it;
Not a whit of thy tuwhoo,
  Thee to woo to thy tuwhit,
  Thee to woo to thy tuwhit,
    With a lengthen'd loud halloo,
    Tuwhoo, tuwhit, tuwhit, tuwhoo-o-o.

Recollections of the Arabian Nights

When the breeze of a joyful dawn blew free
In the silken sail of infancy,
    The tide of time flow'd back with me,
The forward-flowing tide of time;
And many a sheeny summer-morn,
Adown the Tigris I was borne,
By Bagdat's shrines of fretted gold,
High-walled gardens green and old;
True Mussulman was I and sworn,
     For it was in the golden prime
       Of good Haroun Alraschid.

Anight my shallop, rustling thro'
The low and bloomed foliage, drove
The fragrant, glistening deeps, and clove
The citron-shadows in the blue:
By garden porches on the brim,
The costly doors flung open wide,
Gold glittering thro' lamplight dim,
And broider'd sofas on each side:
    In sooth it was a goodly time,
     For it was in the golden prime
       Of good Haroun Alraschid.

Often, where clear-stemm'd platans guard
The outlet, did I turn away
The boat-head down a broad canal
From the main river sluiced, where all
The sloping of the moon-lit sward
Was damask-work, and deep inlay
Of braided blooms unmown, which crept
Adown to where the water slept.
    A goodly place, a goodly time,
     For it was in the golden prime
       Of good Haroun Alraschid.

A motion from the river won
Ridged the smooth level, bearing on
My shallop thro' the star-strown calm,
Until another night in night
I enter'd, from the clearer light,
Imbower'd vaults of pillar'd palm,
Imprisoning sweets, which, as they clomb
Heavenward, were stay'd beneath the dome
    Of hollow boughs. – A goodly time,
     For it was in the golden prime
       Of good Haroun Alraschid.

Still onward; and the clear canal
Is rounded to as clear a lake.
From the green rivage many a fall
Of diamond rillets musical
Thro' little crystal arches low
Down from the central fountain's flow
Fall'n silver-chiming, seem'd to shake
The sparkling flints beneath the prow.
   A goodly place, a goodly time,
    For it was in the golden prime
      Of good Haroun Alraschid.

Above thro' many a bowery turn
A walk with vary-colour'd shells
Wander'd engrain'd. On either side
All round about the fragrant marge
From fluted vase, and brazen urn
In order, eastern flowers large,
Some dropping low their crimson bells
Half-closed, and others studded wide
   With disks and tiars, fed the time
   With odour in the golden prime
     Of good Haroun Alraschid.

Far off, and where the lemon-grove
In closest coverture upsprung
The living airs of middle night
Died round the bulbul as he sung;
Not he: but something which possess'd
The darkness of the world, delight,
Life, anguish, death, immortal love,
Ceasing not, mingled, unrepress'd,
   Apart from place, withholding time
   But flattering the golden prime
     Of good Haroun Alraschid.

Black the garden-bowers and grots
Slumber'd: the solemn palms were ranged
Above, unwoo'd of summer wind:
A sudden splendour from behind
Flush'd all the leaves with rich gold-green,
And, flowing rapidly between
Their interspaces, counterchanged
The level lake with diamond-plots
   Of dark and bright. A lovely time
   For it was in the golden prime
     Of good Haroun Alraschid.

Dark-blue the deep sphere overhead,
Distinct with vivid stars inlaid
Grew darker from that under-flame:
So, leaping lightly from the boat,
With silver anchor left afloat,
In marvel whence that glory came
Upon me, as in sleep I sank
In cool soft turf upon the bank,
   Entranced with that place and time,
   So worthy of the golden prime
      Of good Haroun Alraschid.

Thence thro' the garden I was drawn –
A realm of pleasance, many a mound,
And many a shadow-chequer'd lawn
Full of the city's stilly sound,
And deep myrrh-thickets blowing round
The stately cedar, tamarisks,
Thick rosaries of scented thorn,
Tall orient shrubs, and obelisks
   Graven with emblems of the time,
   In honour of the golden prime
      Of good Haroun Alraschid.

With dazed vision unawares
From the long alley's latticed shade
Emerged, I came upon the great
Pavilion of the Caliphat.
Right to the carven cedarn doors,
Flung inward over spangled floors,
Broad-based flights of marble stairs
Ran up with golden balustrade,
   After the fashion of the time,
   And humour of the golden prime
      Of good Haroun Alraschid.

The fourscore windows all alight
As with the quintessence of flame,
A million tapers flaring bright
From twisted silvers look'd to shame
The hollow-vaulted dark, and stream'd
Upon the mooned domes aloof
In inmost Bagdat, till there seem'd
Hundreds of crescents on the roof
   Of night new-risen, that marvellous time,
   To celebrate the golden prime
      Of good Haroun Alraschid.

Then stole I up, and trancedly
Gazed on the Persian girl alone,
Serene with argent-lidded eyes
Amorous, and lashes like to rays
Of darkness, and a brow of pearl
Tressed with redolent ebony,
In many a dark delicious curl,
Flowing beneath her rose-hued zone;
   The sweetest lady of the time,
    Well worthy of the golden prime
      Of good Haroun Alraschid.

Six columns, three on either side,
Pure silver, underpropt a rich
Throne of the massive ore, from which
Down-droop'd, in many a floating fold,
Engarlanded and diaper'd
With inwrought flowers, a cloth of gold.
Thereon, his deep eye laughter-stirr'd
With merriment of kingly pride,
   Sole star of all that place and time,
    I saw him – in his golden prime,
      THE GOOD HAROUN ALRASCHID!

Ode to Memory

I

Thou who stealest fire,
From the fountains of the past,
To glorify the present; oh, haste
   Visit my low desire!
Strengthen me, enlighten me!
I faint in this obscurity,
Thou dewy dawn of memory.

II

Come not as thou camest of late,
Flinging the gloom of yesternight
On the white day; but robed in soften'd light
   Of orient state.
Whilome thou camest with the morning mist,
Even as a maid, whose stately brow
The dew-impearled winds of dawn have kiss'd,
   When she, as thou,
Stays on her floating locks the lovely freight
Of overflowing blooms, and earliest shoots

Of orient green, giving safe pledge of fruits,
Which in wintertide shall star
The black earth with brilliance rare.

III

Whilome thou camest with the morning mist,
    And with the evening cloud,
Showering thy gleaned wealth into my open breast
(Those peerless flowers which in the rudest wind
        Never grow sere,
When rooted in the garden of the mind,
  Because they are the earliest of the year).
    Nor was the night thy shroud.
In sweet dreams softer than unbroken rest
Thou leddest by the hand thine infant Hope.
The eddying of her garments caught from thee
The light of thy great presence; and the cope
  Of the half-attain'd futurity,
  Though deep not fathomless,
Was cloven with the million stars which tremble
O'er the deep mind of dauntless infancy.
Small thought was there of life's distress;
For sure she deem'd no mist of earth could dull
Those spirit-thrilling eyes so keen and beautiful:
Sure she was nigher to heaven's spheres,
Listening the lordly music flowing from
      The illimitable years.
  O strengthen me, enlighten me!
  I faint in this obscurity,
  Thou dewy dawn of memory.

IV

Come forth I charge thee, arise,
Thou of the many tongues, the myriad eyes!
Thou comest not with shows of flaunting vines
      Unto mine inner eye,
      Divinest Memory!
  Thou wert not nursed by the waterfall
Which ever sounds and shines
  A pillar of white light upon the wall
Of purple cliffs, aloof descried:
Come from the woods that belt the grey hill-side,
The seven elms, the poplars four
That stand beside my father's door,
And chiefly from the brook that loves
To purl o'er matted cress and ribbed sand,
Or dimple in the dark of rushy coves,

Drawing into his narrow earthen urn,
  In every elbow and turn,
The filter'd tribute of the rough woodland.
   O! hither lead thy feet!
Pour round mine ears the livelong bleat
Of the thick-fleeced sheep from wattled folds,
  Upon the ridged wolds,
When the first matin-song hath waken'd loud
Over the dark dewy earth forlorn,
What time the amber morn
Forth gushes from beneath a low-hung cloud.

V

Large dowries doth the raptured eye
 To the young spirit present
  When first she is wed;
   And like a bride of old
  In triumph led,
    With music and sweet showers
    Of festal flowers,
 Unto the dwelling she must sway.
Well hast thou done, great artist Memory,
 In setting round thy first experiment
  With royal frame-work of wrought gold;
Needs must thou dearly love thy first essay,
And foremost in thy various gallery
 Place it, where sweetest sunlight falls
 Upon the storied walls;
   For the discovery
And newness of thine art so pleased thee,
That all which thou hast drawn of fairest
 Or boldest since, but lightly weighs
With thee unto the love thou bearest
The first-born of thy genius. Artist-like,
Ever retiring thou dost gaze
On the prime labour of thine early days:
No matter what the sketch might be;
Whether the high field on the bushless Pike,
Or even a sand-built ridge
Of heaped hills that mound the sea,
Overblown with murmurs harsh,
Or even a lowly cottage whence we see
Stretch'd wide and wild the waste enormous marsh,
Where from the frequent bridge,
Like emblems of infinity,
The trenched waters run from sky to sky;
Or a garden bower'd close

With plaited alleys of the trailing rose,
Long alleys falling down to twilight grots,
Or opening upon level plots
Of crowned lilies, standing near
Purple-spiked lavender:
Whither in after life retired
From brawling storms,
From weary wind,
With youthful fancy reinspired,
We may hold converse with all forms
Of the many-sided mind,
And those whom passion hath not blinded,
Subtle-thoughted, myriad-minded.
My friend, with you to live alone,
Were how much better than to own
A crown, a sceptre, and a throne!
O strengthen me, enlighten me!
I faint in this obscurity,
Thou dewy dawn of memory.

Song

I

A spirit haunts the year's last hours
Dwelling amid these yellowing bowers:
　　　To himself he talks;
For at eventide, listening earnestly,
At his work you may hear him sob and sigh
　　　In the walks;
　　　Earthward he boweth the heavy stalks
Of the mouldering flowers:
　　Heavily hangs the broad sunflower
　　　Over its grave i' the earth so chilly;
　　Heavily hangs the hollyhock,
　　　Heavily hangs the tiger-lily.

II

The air is damp, and hush'd, and close,
As a sick man's room when he taketh repose
　　　An hour before death;
My very heart faints and my whole soul grieves
At the moist rich smell of the rotting leaves,
　　　And the breath
　　　Of the fading edges of box beneath,
And the year's last rose.
　　Heavily hangs the broad sunflower
　　　Over its grave i' the earth so chilly;
　　Heavily hangs the hollyhock,
　　　Heavily hangs the tiger-lily.

Adeline

I

Mystery of mysteries,
   Faintly smiling Adeline,
   Scarce of earth nor all divine,
     Nor unhappy, nor at rest,
      But beyond expression fair
      With thy floating flaxen hair;
Thy rose-lips and full blue eyes
     Take the heart from out my breast.
   Wherefore those dim looks of thine,
   Shadowy, dreaming Adeline?

II

Whence that aery bloom of thine,
   Like a lily which the sun
Looks thro' in his sad decline,
   And a rose-bush leans upon,
Thou that faintly smilest still,
   As a Naiad in a well,
   Looking at the set of day,
Or a phantom two hours old
   Of a maiden past away,
Ere the placid lips be cold?
Wherefore those faint smiles of thine,
   Spiritual Adeline?

III

What hope or fear or joy is thine?
Who talketh with thee, Adeline?
   For sure thou art not all alone:
     Do beating hearts of salient springs
   Keep measure with thine own?
      Hast thou heard the butterflies
     What they say betwixt their wings?
     Or in stillest evenings
With what voice the violet woos
To his heart the silver dews?
     Or when little airs arise,
   How the merry bluebell rings
      To the mosses underneath?
      Hast thou look'd upon the breath
     Of the lilies at sunrise?
Wherefore that faint smile of thine,
Shadowy, dreaming Adeline?

IV

Some honey-converse feeds thy mind
   Some spirit of a crimson rose
   In love with thee forgets to close
   His curtains, wasting odorous sighs
All night long on darkness blind.
What aileth thee? whom waitest thou
With thy soften'd, shadow'd brow,
      And those dew-lit eyes of thine,
      Thou faint smiler, Adeline?

V

Lovest thou the doleful wind
      When thou gazest at the skies?
Doth the low-tongued Orient
      Wander from the side of the morn,
        Dripping with Sabaean spice
On thy pillow, lowly bent
      With melodious airs lovelorn
Breathing Light against thy face,
While his locks a-dropping twined
      Round thy neck in subtle ring
Make a carcanet of rays,
      And ye talk together still,
     In the language wherewith Spring
      Letters cowslips on the hill?
Hence that look and smile of thine,
      Spiritual Adeline.

A Character

With a half-glance upon the sky
At night he said, 'The wanderings
Of this most intricate Universe
Teach me the nothingness of things.'
Yet could not all creation pierce
Beyond the bottom of his eye.

He spake of beauty: that the dull
Saw no divinity in grass,
Life in dead stones, or spirit in air;
Then looking as 'twere in a glass,
He smooth'd his chin and sleek'd his hair,
And said the earth was beautiful.

He spake of virtue: not the gods
More purely, when they wish to charm
Pallas and Juno sitting by:
And with a sweeping of the arm,
And a lack-lustre dead-blue eye,
Devolved his rounded periods.

Most delicately hour by hour
He canvass'd human mysteries
And trod on silk, as if the winds
Blew his own praises in his eyes,
And stood aloof from other minds
In impotence of fancied power.

With lips depress'd as he were meek,
Himself unto himself he sold:
Upon himself himself did feed:
Quiet, dispassionate, and cold,
And other than his form of creed,
With chisell'd features clear and sleek.

The Poet

The poet in a golden clime was born,
    With golden stars above;
Dower'd with the hate of hate, the scorn of scorn,
    The love of love.

He saw thro' life and death, thro' good and ill,
    He saw thro' his own soul.
The marvel of the everlasting will,
    An open scroll,

Before him lay: with echoing feet he threaded
    The secretest walks of fame:
The viewless arrows of his thoughts were headed
    And wing'd with flame,

Like Indian reeds blown from his silver tongue,
    And of so fierce a flight,
From Calpe unto Caucasus they sung,
    Filling with light

And vagrant melodies the winds which bore
    Them earthward till they lit;
Then, like the arrow-seeds of the field flower,
    The fruitful wit

Cleaving, took root, and springing forth anew
    Where'er they fell, behold,
Like to the mother plant in semblance, grew
    A flower all gold,

And bravely furnish'd all abroad to fling
    The winged shafts of truth,
To throng with stately blooms the breathing spring
    Of Hope and Youth.

So many minds did gird their orbs with beams,
    Tho' one did fling the fire.
Heaven flow'd upon the soul in many dreams
    Of high desire.

Thus truth was multiplied on truth, the world
    Like one great garden show'd
And thro' the wreaths of floating dark upcurl'd,
    Rare sunrise flow'd.

And Freedom rear'd in that august sunrise
    Her beautiful bold brow,
When rites and forms before his burning eyes
    Melted like snow.

There was no blood upon her maiden robes
    Sunn'd by those orient skies;
But round about the circles of the globes
    Of her keen eyes

And in her raiment's hem was traced in flame
    WISDOM, a name to shake
All evil dreams of power – a sacred name.
    And when she spake,

Her words did gather thunder as they ran,
    And as the lightning to the thunder
Which follows it, riving the spirit of man,
    Making earth wonder,

So was their meaning to her words. No sword
    Of wrath her right arm whirl'd,
But one poor poet's scroll, and with *his* word
    She shook the world.

The Poet's Mind

I

Vex not thou the poet's mind
   With thy shallow wit:
Vex not thou the poet's mind;
      For thou canst not fathom it.
   Clear and bright it should be ever,
   Flowing like a crystal river;
   Bright as light, and clear as wind.

II

   Dark-brow'd sophist, come not anear;
      All the place is holy ground;
   Hollow smile and frozen sneer
            Come not here.
   Holy water kill I pour
   Into every spicy flower
Of the laurel-shrubs that hedge it around.
The flowers would faint at your cruel cheer.
   In your eye there is death,
   There is frost in your breath
   Which would blight the plants.
      Where you stand you cannot hear
         From the groves within
         The wild-bird's din.
In the heart of the garden the merry bird chants,
It would fall to the ground if you came in.
   In the middle leaps a fountain
      Like sheet lightning,
      Ever brightening
   With a low melodious thunder;
All day and all night it is ever drawn
   From the brain of the purple mountain
   Which stands in the distance yonder:
It springs on a level of bowery lawn,
And the mountain draws it from Heaven above,
And it sings a song of undying love;
And yet, tho' its voice be so clear and full,
You never would hear it; your ears are so dull,
So keep where you are: you are foul with sin;
It would shrink to the earth if you came in.

Nothing Will Die

When will the stream be aweary of flowing
          Under my eye?
When will the wind be aweary of blowing
          Over the sky?
When will the clouds be aweary of fleeting?
When will the heart be aweary of beating?
          And nature die?
Never, oh! never, nothing will die;
          The stream flows,
          The wind blows,
          The cloud fleets,
          The heart beats,
             Nothing will die.

Nothing will die;
   All things will change
Through eternity.
   'Tis the world's winter;
      Autumn and summer
         Are gone long ago.
   Earth is dry to the centre,
      But spring a new comer —
      A spring rich and strange,
   Shall make the winds blow
Round and round,
   Through and through,
      Here and there,
      Till the air
And the ground
   Shall be filled with life anew.

The world was never made;
   It will change, but it will not fade.
So let the wind range;
   For even and morn
      Ever will be
      Through eternity.
Nothing was born;
   Nothing will die,
All things will change.

All Things Will Die

Clearly the blue river chimes in its flowing
          Under my eye;
Warmly and broadly the south winds are blowing
          Over the sky.
One after another the white clouds are fleeting;
Every heart this May morning in joyance is beating
          Full merrily;
    Yet all things must die.
  The stream will cease to flow;
  The wind will cease to blow;
  The clouds will cease to fleet;
  The heart will cease to beat;
    For all things must die.

      All things must die.
Spring will come never more.
    Oh! vanity!
Death waits at the door.
See! our friends are all forsaking
The wine and the merrymaking.
We are called – we must go.
Laid low, very low,
In the dark we must lie.
The merry glees are still;
    The voice of the bird
    Shall no more be heard,
    Nor the wind on the hill.
      Oh! misery!
Hark! death is calling
While I speak to ye,
The jaw is falling,
The red cheek paling,
The strong limbs failing;
Ice with the warm blood mixing,
The eyeballs fixing.
Nine times goes the passing bell:
Ye merry souls, farewell.

    The old earth
    Had a birth,
    As all men know
      Long ago.
And the old earth must die.
So let the warm winds range,

And the blue wave beat the shore;
For even and morn
Ye will never see
Through eternity.
All things were born.
Ye will come never more,
For all things must die.

The Dying Swan

I

The plain was grassy, wild and bare,
Wide, wild, and open to the air,
Which had built up everywhere
    An under-roof of doleful grey.
With an inner voice the river ran,
Adown it floated a dying swan,
        And loudly did lament.
    It was the middle of the day.
Ever the weary wind went on,
        And took the reed-tops as it went.

II

Some blue peaks in the distance rose,
And white against the cold-white sky,
Shone out their crowning snows.
    One willow over the river wept,
And shook the wave as the wind did sigh;
Above in the wind was the swallow,
    Chasing itself at its own wild will
    And far thro' the marish green and still
    The tangled water-courses slept,
Shot over with purple, and green, and yellow.

III

The wild swan's death-hymn took the soul
Of that waste place with joy
Hidden in sorrow: at first to the ear
The warble was low, and full and clear;
And floating about the under-sky,
Prevailing in weakness, the coronach stole
Sometimes afar, and sometimes anear
But anon her awful jubilant voice,
With a music strange and manifold,
Flow'd forth on a carol free and bold;

As when a mighty people rejoice
With shawms, and with cymbals, and harps of gold,
And the tumult of their acclaim is roll'd
Thro' the open gates of the city afar,
To the shepherd who watcheth the evening star.
And the creeping mosses and clambering weeds,
And the willow-branches hoar and dank,
And the wavy swell of the soughing reeds,
And the wave-worn horns of the echoing bank,
And the silvery marish-flowers that throng
The desolate creeks and pools among,
Were flooded over with eddying song.

A Dirge

I

Now is done thy long day's work;
Fold thy palms across thy breast,
Fold thine arms, turn to thy rest.
    Let them rave.
Shadows of the silver birk
Sweep the green that folds thy grave
    Let them rave.

II

Thee nor carketh care nor slander;
Nothing but the small cold worm
Fretteth thine enshrouded form.
    Let them rave.
Light and shadow ever wander
O'er the green that folds thy grave.
    Let them rave.

III

Thou wilt not turn upon thy bed;
Chaunteth not the brooding bee
Sweeter tones than calumny?
    Let them rave.
Thou wilt never raise thine head
From the green that folds thy grave.
    Let them rave.

IV

Crocodiles wept tears for thee;
The woodbine and eglatere

Drip sweeter dews than traitor's tear.
       Let them rave.
Rain makes music in the tree
O'er the green that folds thy grave.
       Let them rave.

V

Round thee blow, self-pleached deep,
Bramble-roses, faint and pale,
And long purples of the dale.
       Let them rave.
These in every shower creep
Thro' the green that folds thy grave.
       Let them rave.

VI

The gold-eyed kingcups fine;
The frail bluebell peereth over
Rare broidry of the purple clover.
       Let them rave.
Kings have no such couch as thine,
As the green that folds thy grave.
       Let them rave.

VII

Wild words wander here and there;
God's great gift of speech abused
Makes thy memory confused:
       But let them rave.
The balm-cricket carols clear
In the green that folds thy grave
       Let them rave.

The Deserted House

I

Life and Thought have gone away
  Side by side,
   Leaving door and windows wide:
Careless tenants they!

II

All within is dark as night:
In the windows is no light;
And no murmur at the door,
So frequent on its hinge before.

III

Close the door, the shutters close,
  Or thro' the windows we shall see
  The nakedness and vacancy
Of the dark deserted house.

IV

Come away: no more of mirth
  Is here or merry-making sound.
The house was builded of the earth
  And shall fall again to ground.

V

Come away: for Life and Thought
    Here no longer dwell;
  But in a city glorious –
A great and distant city – have bought
    A mansion incorruptible.
    Would they could have stayed with us!

Love and Death

What time the mighty moon was gathering light
Love paced the thymy plots of Paradise,
And all about him roll'd his lustrous eyes;
When, turning round a cassia, full in view
Death, walking all alone beneath a yew,
And talking to himself, first met his sight:
'You must begone,' said Death, 'these walks are mine.'
Love wept and spread his sheeny vans for flight;
Yet ere he parted said, 'This hour is thine:
Thou art the shadow of life, and as the tree
Stands in the sun and shadows all beneath,
So in the light of great eternity
Life eminent creates the shade of death;
The shadow passeth when the tree shall fall,
But I shall reign for ever over all.'

The Kraken

Below the thunders of the upper deep;
Far far beneath in the abysmal sea,
His ancient, dreamless, uninvaded sleep
The Kraken sleepeth: faintest sunlights flee
About his shadowy sides: above him swell
Huge sponges of millennial growth and height;
And far away into the sickly light,
From many a wondrous grot and secret cell
Unnumber'd and enormous polypi
Winnow with giant fins the slumbering green.
There hath he lain for ages and will lie
Battening upon huge seaworms in his sleep,
Until the latter fire shall heat the deep;
Then once by men and angels to be seen
In roaring he shall rise and on the surface die.

The Ballad of Oriana

My heart is wasted with my woe,
           Oriana.
There is no rest for me below,
           Oriana.
When the long dun wolds are ribb'd with snow,
And loud the Norland whirlwinds blow,
           Oriana,
Alone I wander to and fro,
           Oriana.

Ere the light on dark was growing,
           Oriana,
At midnight the cock was crowing,
           Oriana:
Winds were blowing, waters flowing,
We heard the steeds to battle going,
           Oriana;
Aloud the hollow bugle blowing,
           Oriana.

In the yew-wood black as night,
           Oriana,
Ere I rode into the fight,
           Oriana
While blissful tears blinded my sight

By star-shine and by moonlight,
          Oriana,
I to thee my troth did plight,
          Oriana.

She stood upon the castle wall,
          Oriana:
She watch'd my crest among them all,
          Oriana:
She saw me fight, she heard me call,
When forth there stept a foeman tall,
          Oriana
Atween me and the castle wall,
          Oriana.

The bitter arrow went aside,
          Oriana:
The false, false arrow went aside,
          Oriana:
The damned arrow glanced aside,
And pierced thy heart, my love, my bride,
          Oriana!
Thy heart, my life, my love, my bride,
          Oriana!

Oh! narrow, narrow was the space,
          Oriana.
Loud, loud rung out the bugle's brays,
          Oriana.
Oh! deathful stabs were dealt apace,
The battle deepen'd in its place,
          Oriana
But I was down upon my face,
          Oriana.

They should have stabb'd me where I lay,
          Oriana!
How could I rise and come away,
          Oriana?
How could I look upon the day?
They should have stabb'd me where I lay,
          Oriana –
They should have trod me into clay,
          Oriana.

O breaking heart that will not break,
        Oriana!
O pale, pale face so sweet and meek,
        Oriana!
Thou smilest, but thou dost not speak,
And then the tears run down my cheek,
        Oriana:
What wantest thou? whom dost thou seek,
        Oriana?

I cry aloud: none hear my cries,
        Oriana.
Thou comest atween me and the skies,
        Oriana.
I feel the tears of blood arise
Up from my heart unto my eyes,
        Oriana.
Within thy heart my arrow lies,
        Oriana.

O cursed hand! O cursed blow!
        Oriana!
O happy thou that liest low,
        Oriana!
All night the silence seems to flow
Beside me in my utter woe,
        Oriana.
A weary, weary way I go,
        Oriana.

When Norland winds pipe down the sea,
        Oriana,
I walk, I dare not think of thee,
        Oriana.
Thou liest beneath the greenwood true,
I dare not die and come to thee,
        Oriana.
I hear the roaring of the sea,
        Oriana.

Circumstance

Two children in two neighbour villages
Playing mad pranks along the heathy leas;
Two strangers meeting at a festival
Two lovers whispering by an orchard wall;
Two lives bound fast in one with golden ease;
Two graves grass-green beside a grey church-tower,
Wash'd with still rains and daisy-blossomed;
Two children in one hamlet born and bred;
So runs the round of life from hour to hour.

We Are Free

The winds, as at their hour of birth,
   Leaning upon the ridged sea,
Breathed low around the rolling earth
   With mellow preludes, 'We are free.'
The streams through many a lilied row
   Down-carolling to the crisped sea,
Low-tinkled with a bell-like flow
   Atween the blossoms, 'We are free.'

The Sea-Fairies

Slow sail'd the weary mariners and saw,
Betwixt the green brink and the running foam,
Sweet faces, rounded arms, and bosoms prest
To little harps of gold; and while they mused,
Whispering to each other half in fear,
Shrill music reach'd them on the middle sea.

Whither away, whither away, whither away? fly no more.
Whither away from the high green field, and the happy
   blossoming shore?
 Day and night to the billow the fountain calls;
Down shower the gambolling waterfalls
From wandering over the lea:
Out of the live-green heart of the dells
They freshen the silvery-crimson shells,
And thick with white bells the clover-hill swells
High over the full-toned sea:
O hither, come hither and furl your sails,
Come hither to me and to me:
Either, come hither and frolic and play;
Here it is only the mew that wails;

We will sing to you all the day:
Mariner, mariner, furl your sails
For here are the blissful downs and dales,
And merrily merrily carol the gales,
And the spangle dances in bight and bay
And the rainbow forms and flies on the land
Over the islands free;
And the rainbow lives in the curve of the sand;
Hither, come hither and see;
And the rainbow hangs on the poising wave,
And sweet is the colour of cove and cave
And sweet shall your welcome be:
O hither, come hither, and be our lords,
For merry brides are we:
We will kiss sweet kisses, and speak sweet words:
O listen, listen, your eyes shall glisten
With pleasure and love and jubilee:
O listen, listen, your eyes shall glisten
When the sharp clear twang of the golden chords
Runs up the ridged sea.
Who can light on as happy a shore
All the world o'er, all the world o'er?
Whither away? listen and stay: mariner, mariner, fly no
    more.

Sonnet to J. M. K.

My hope and heart is with thee – thou wilt be
A latter Luther, and a soldier-priest
To scare church-harpies from the master's feast;
Our dusted velvets have much need of thee:
Thou art no sabbath-drawler of old saws
Distill'd from some worm-canker'd homily;
But spurr'd at heart with fieriest energy
To embattail and to wall about thy cause
With iron-worded proof, hating to hark
The humming of the drowsy pulpit-drone
Half God's good sabbath, while the worn-out clerk
Brow-beats his desk below. Thou from a throne
Mounted in heaven wilt shoot into the dark
Arrows of lightnings. I will stand and mark.

POEMS

Sonnet

Mine be the strength of spirit fierce and free,
Like some broad river rushing down alone,
With the selfsame impulse wherewith he was thrown
From his loud fount upon the echoing lea: –
Which with increasing might doth forward flee
By town, and tower, and hill, and cape, and isle,
And in the middle of the green salt sea
Keeps his blue waters fresh for many a mile.
Mine be the Power which ever to its sway
Will win the wise at once, and by degrees
May into uncongenial spirits flow;
Even as the great gulf-stream of Florida
Floats far away into the Northern seas
The lavish growths of southern Mexico.

To —

I

My life is full of weary days
   But good things have not kept aloof,
Nor wander'd into other ways:
   I have not lack'd thy mild reproof,
Nor golden largess of thy praise.

II

And now shake hands across the brink
   Of that deep grave to which I go:
Shake hands once more: I cannot sink
   So far – far down, but I shall know
   Thy voice, and answer from below.

III

When in the darkness over me,
   The four-handed mole shall scrape,
Plant thou no dusky cypress-tree,
   Nor wreathe thy cap with doleful crape,
   But pledge me in the flowing grape.

IV

And when the sappy field and wood
  Grow green beneath the showery grey,
And rugged barks begin to bud
  And through damp holts, new-flush'd with may
  Ring sudden laughters of the Jay;

V

Then let wise Nature work her will
  And on my clay her darnels grow.
Come only, when the days are still,
  And at my headstone whisper low,
  And tell me if the woodbines blow,

VII

If thou art blest, my mother's smile
  Undimmed, if bees are on the wing:
Then cease, my friend, a little while,
  That I may hear the throstle sing
  His bridal song, the boast of spring.

VII

Sweet as the noise in parchèd plains
  Of bubbling wells that fret the stones,
(If any sense in me remains)
  Thy words will be; thy cheerful tones
  As welcome to my crumbling bones.

Buonaparte

He thought to quell the stubborn hearts of oak,
Madman! – to chain with chains, and bind with bands
That island queen that sways the floods and lands
From Ind to Ind, but in fair daylight woke,
When from her wooden walls, lit by sure hands,
With thunders, and with lightnings, and with smoke,
Peal after peal, the British battle broke,
Lulling the brine against the Coptic sands.
We taught him lowlier moods, when Elsinore
Heard the war moan along the distant sea,
Rocking with shattered spars, with sudden fires
Flamed over: at Trafalgar yet once more
We taught him: late he learned humility
Perforce, like those whom Gideon school'd with briers.

Sonnet

But were I loved, as I desire to be
What is there in the great sphere of the earth
And range of evil between death and birth,
That I should fear, – if I were loved by thee?
All the inner, all the outer world of pain
Clear Love would pierce and cleave, if thou wert mine,
As I have heard that, somewhere in the main,
Fresh-water springs come up through bitter brine.
'Twere joy, not fear, clasped hand-in-hand with thee,
To wait for death – mute – careless of all ills,
Apart upon a mountain, tho' the surge
Of some new deluge from a thousand hills
Flung leagues of roaring foam into the gorge
Below us, as far on as eye could see.

The Lady of Shalott

Part 1

On either side the river lie
Long fields of barley and of rye,
That clothe the wold and meet the sky;
And thro' the field the road runs by
      To many-tower'd Camelot;
And up and down the people go,
Gazing where the lilies blow
Round an island there below,
      The island of Shalott.

Willows whiten, aspens quiver,
Little breezes dusk and shiver
Thro' the wave that runs for ever
By the island in the river
      Flowing down to Camelot.
Four grey walls, and four grey towers,
Overlook a space of flowers,
And the silent isle imbowers
      The Lady of Shalott.

By the margin, willow-veil'd,
Slide the heavy barges trail'd
By slow horses; and unhail'd
The shallop flitteth silken-sail'd
      Skimming down to Camelot:

But who hath seen her wave her hand?
Or at the casement seen her stand?
Or is she known in all the land
      The Lady of Shalott?

Only reapers, reaping early
In among the bearded barley,
Hear a song that echoes cheerly
From the river winding clearly,
      Down to tower'd Camelot:
And by the moon the reaper weary,
Piling sheaves in uplands airy,
Listening, whispers ' 'Tis the fairy
      Lady of Shalott.'

Part 2

There she weaves by night and day
A magic web with colours gay.
She has heard a whisper say,
A curse is on her if she stay
      To look down to Camelot.
She knows not what the curse may be,
And so she weaveth steadily,
And little other care hath she,
      The Lady of Shalott.

And moving thro' a mirror clear
That hangs before her all the year
Shadows of the world appear.
There she sees the highway near
      Winding down to Camelot:
There the river eddy whirls
And there the surly village-churls,
And the red cloaks of market girls
      Pass onward from Shalott.

Sometimes a troop of damsels glad,
An abbot on an ambling pad,
Sometimes a curly shepherd-lad,
Or long-hair'd page in crimson clad,
      Goes by to tower'd Camelot;
And sometimes thro' the mirror blue
The knights come riding two and two:
She hath no loyal knight and true,
      The Lady of Shalott.

But in her web she still delights
To weave the mirror's magic sights,
For often thro' the silent nights
A funeral, with plumes and lights,
   And music, went to Camelot:
Or when the moon was overhead,
Came two young lovers lately wed.
'I am half sick of shadows,' said
   The Lady of Shalott.

Part 3

A bow shot from her bower-eaves,
He rode between the barley-sheaves,
The sun came dazzling thro' the leaves
And flamed upon the brazen greaves
   Of bold Sir Lancelot.
A red-cross knight for ever kneel'd
To a lady in his shield
That sparkled on the yellow field,
   Beside remote Shalott.

The gemmy bridle glitter'd free,
Like to some branch of stars we see
Hung in the golden Galaxy.
The bridle bells rang merrily
   As he rode down to Camelot:
And from his blazon'd baldric slung
A mighty silver bugle hung,
And as he rode his armour rung,
   Beside remote Shalott.

All in the blue unclouded weather
Thick-jewell'd shone the saddle-leather,
The helmet and the helmet-feather
Burn'd like one burning flame together,
   As he rode down to Camelot.
As often thro' the purple night,
Below the starry clusters bright,
Some bearded meteor, trailing light,
   Moves over still Shalott.

His broad clear brow in sunlight glow'd;
On burnish'd hooves his war-horse trode;
From underneath his helmet flow'd
His coal-black curls as on he rode
   As he rode down to Camelot.

From the bank and from the river
He flash'd into the crystal mirror,
'Tirra lirra,' by the river
        Sang Sir Lancelot.

She left the web, she left the loom,
She made three paces thro' the room,
She saw the water-lily bloom,
She saw the helmet and the plume,
        She look'd down to Camelot.
Out flew the web and floated wide;
The mirror crack'd from side to side;
'The curse is come upon me,' cried
        The Lady of Shalott.

Part 4
In the stormy east-wind straining,
The pale yellow woods were waning,
The broad stream in his banks complaining,
Heavily the low sky raining
        Over tower'd Camelot;
Down she came and found a boat
Beneath a willow left afloat,
And round about the prow she wrote
        The Lady of Shalott.

And down the river's dim expanse –
Like some bold seër in a trance,
Seeing all his own mischance –
With a glassy countenance
        Did she look to Camelot.
And at the closing of the day
She loosed the chain, and down she lay;
The broad stream bore her far away,
        The Lady of Shalott.

Lying robed in snowy white
That loosely flew to left and right –
The leaves upon her falling light –
Thro' the noises of the night
        She floated down to Camelot:
And as the boat-head wound along
The willowy hills and fields among,
They heard her singing her last song,
        The Lady of Shalott.

Heard a carol, mournful, holy
Chanted loudly, chanted lowly,
Till her blood was frozen slowly,
And her eyes were darken'd wholly,
   Turn'd to tower'd Camelot.
For ere she reach'd upon the tide
The first house by the water-side,
Singing in her song she died,
   The Lady of Shalott.

Under tower and balcony,
By garden-wall and gallery,
A gleaming shape she floated by,
Dead-pale between the houses high,
   Silent into Camelot.
Out upon the wharfs they came,
Knight and burgher, lord and dame,
And round the prow they read her name,
   The Lady of Shalott.

Who is this? and what is here?
And in the lighted palace near
Died the sound of royal cheer;
And they cross'd themselves for fear,
   All the knights at Camelot:
But Lancelot mused a little space;
He said, 'She has a lovely face;
God in his mercy lend her grace,
   The Lady of Shalott.'

Mariana in the South

With one black shadow at its feet,
 The house thro' all the level shines,
Close-latticed to the brooding heat,
 And silent in its dusty vines:
A faint-blue ridge upon the right,
 An empty river-bed before,
 And shallows on a distant shore,
In glaring sand and inlets bright.
  But 'Ave Mary,' made she moan,
   And 'Ave Mary,' night and morn,
   And 'Ah,' she sang, 'to be all alone,
    To live forgotten, and love forlorn.'

She, as her carol sadder grew,
  From brow and bosom slowly down
Thro' rosy taper fingers drew
  Her streaming curls of deepest brown
To left and right, and made appear,
  Still-lighted in a secret shrine,
  Her melancholy eyes divine,
The home of woe without a tear.
    And 'Ave Mary,' was her moan,
      'Madonna, sad is night and morn;'
    And 'Ah,' she sang, 'to be all alone,
      To live forgotten, and love forlorn.'

Till all the crimson changed, and past
  Into deep orange o'er the sea,
Low on her knees herself she cast,
  Before Our Lady murmur'd she;
Complaining, 'Mother, give me grace
  To help me of my weary load.'
  And on the liquid mirror glow'd
The clear perfection of her face.
    'Is this the form,' she made her moan,
      'That won his praises night and morn?'
    And 'Ah,' she said, 'but I wake alone,
      I sleep forgotten, I wake forlorn.'

Nor bird would sing, nor lamb would bleat,
  Nor any cloud would cross the vault,
But day increased from heat to heat,
  On stony drought and steaming salt;
Till now at noon she slept again,
  And seem'd knee-deep in mountain grass,
  And heard her native breezes pass
And runlets babbling down the glen.
    She breathed in sleep a lower moan,
      And murmuring, as at night and morn,
    She thought, 'My spirit is here alone,
      Walks forgotten, and is forlorn.'

Dreaming, she knew it was a dream:
  She felt he was and was not there.
She woke: the babble of the stream
  Fell, and, without, the steady glare
Shrank one sick willow sere and small.
  The river-bed was dusty-white;
  And all the furnace of the light

Struck up against the blinding wall.
    She whisper'd, with a stifled moan
  More inward than at night or morn,
     'Sweet Mother, let me not here alone
  Live forgotten and die forlorn.'

And, rising, from her bosom drew
  Old letters, breathing of her worth,
For 'Love' they said, 'must needs be true,
  To what is loveliest upon earth.'
An image seem'd to pass the door,
  To look at her with slight, and say
  'But now thy beauty flows away,
So be alone for evermore.'
     'O cruel heart,' she changed her tone,
      'And cruel love, whose end is scorn,
    Is this the end to be left alone,
     To live forgotten, and die forlorn?'

But sometimes in the falling day
  An image seem'd to pass the door,
To look into her eyes and say,
  'But thou shalt be alone no more.'
And flaming downward over all
  From heat to heat the day decreased,
  And slowly rounded to the east
The one black shadow from the wall.
     'The day to night,' she made her moan,
      'The day to night, the night to morn,
    And day and night I am left alone
     To live forgotten, and love forlorn.'

At eve a dry cicala sung,
  There came a sound as of the sea;
Backward the lattice-blind she flung,
  And lean'd upon the balcony.
There all in spaces rosy-bright
  Large Hesper glitter'd on her tears,
  And deepening thro' the silent spheres,
Heaven over Heaven rose the night.
     And weeping then she made her moan,
      'The night comes on that knows not morn
    When I shall cease to be all alone,
     To live forgotten, and love forlorn.'

Eleänore

I

Thy dark eyes open'd not,
        Nor first reveal'd themselves to English air,
            For there is nothing here,
Which, from the outward to the inward brought,
Moulded thy baby thought.
Far off from human neighbourhood,
        Thou wert born, on a summer morn,
A mile beneath the cedar-wood.
Thy bounteous forehead was not fann'd
        With breezes from our oaken glades
But thou wert nursed in some delicious land
        Of lavish lights, and floating shades:
And fluttering thy childish thought
        The oriental fairy brought,
            At the moment of thy birth,
From old well-heads of haunted rills,
And the hearts of purple hills,
        And shadow'd coves on a sunny shore,
            The choicest wealth of all the earth,
        Jewel or shell, or starry ore,
        To deck thy cradle, Eleänore.

II

Or the yellow-banded bees,
Thro' half-open lattices
Coming in the scented breeze,
        Fed thee, a child, lying alone,
            With whitest honey in fairy gardens cull'd –
        A glorious child, dreaming alone,
        In silk-soft folds, upon yielding down,
With the hum of swarming bees
        Into dreamful slumber lull'd.

III

Who may minister to thee?
Summer herself should minister
        To thee, with fruitage golden-rinded
        On golden salvers, or it may be,
Youngest Autumn, in a bower
Grape-thicken'd from the light, and blinded
        With many a deep-hued bell-like flower
Of fragrant trailers, when the air
        Sleepeth over all the heaven,

And the crag that fronts the Even,
    All along the shadowing shore,
Crimsons over an inland mere,
      Eleänore!

IV

How may full-sail'd verse express,
    How may measured words adore
      The full-flowing harmony
Of thy swan-like stateliness,
      Eleänore?
      The luxuriant symmetry
Of thy floating gracefulness,
      Eleänore?
        Every turn and glance of thine,
        Every lineament divine,
          Eleänore,
      And the steady sunset glow,
      That stays upon thee? For in thee
        Is nothing sudden, nothing single;
      Like two streams of incense free
        From one censer, in one shrine,
        Thought and motion mingle,
      Mingle ever. Motions flow
      To one another, even as tho'
      They were modulated so
        To an unheard melody,
Which lives about thee, and a sweep
    Of richest pauses, evermore
Drawn from each other mellow-deep;
    Who may express thee, Eleänore?

V

I stand before thee, Eleänore;
    I see thy beauty gradually unfold,
Daily and hourly, more and more.
I muse, as in a trance, the while
    Slowly, as from a cloud of gold,
Comes out thy deep ambrosial smile.
I muse, as in a trance, whene'er
    The languors of thy love-deep eyes
Float on to me. I would I were
    So tranced, so rapt in ecstasies,
To stand apart, and to adore,
Gazing on thee for evermore,
Serene, imperial Eleänore!

VI

Sometimes, with most intensity
Gazing, I seem to see
Thought folded over thought, smiling asleep,
Slowly awaken'd, grow so full and deep
In thy large eyes, that, overpower'd quite.
I cannot veil, or droop my sight,
But am as nothing in its light:
As tho' a star, in inmost heaven set,
Ev'n while we gaze on it,
Should slowly round his orb, and slowly grow
To a full face, there like a sun remain
Fix'd – then as slowly fade again,
    And draw itself to what it was before;
      So full, so deep, so slow,
        Thought seems to come and go
    In thy large eyes, imperial Eleänore.

VII

As thunder-clouds that, hung on high,
    Roof'd the world with doubt and fear,
Floating thro' an evening atmosphere,
Grow golden all about the sky;
In thee all passion becomes passionless
Touch'd by thy spirit's mellowness,
Losing his fire and active might
    In a silent meditation,
Falling into a still delight,
    And luxury of contemplation
As waves that up a quiet cove
    Rolling slide, and lying still
      Shadow forth the banks at will:
Or sometimes they swell and move,
    Pressing up against the land,
    With motions of the outer sea:
      And the self-same influence
      Controlleth all the soul and sense
Of Passion gazing upon thee.
His bow-string slacken'd, languid Love
    Leaning his cheek upon his hand,
    Droops both his wings, regarding thee,
      And so would languish evermore,
      Serene, imperial Eleänore.

VIII

But when I see thee roam, with tresses unconfined,
While the amorous, odorous wind
    Breathes low between the sunset and the moon;
        Or, in a shadowy saloon,
On silken cushions half reclined;
            I watch thy grace; and in its place
        My heart a charmed slumber keeps,
            While I muse upon thy face;
        And a languid fire creeps
            Thro' my veins to all my frame,
    Dissolvingly and slowly: soon
            From thy rose-red lips MY name
    Floweth; and then, as in a swoon,
        With dinning sound my ears are rife,
        My tremulous tongue faltereth,
        I lose my colour, I lose my breath,
        I drink the cup of a costly death,
Brimm'd with delirious draughts of warmest life.
        I die with my delight, before
            I hear what I would hear from thee;
            Yet tell my name again to me,
        I *would* be dying evermore,
        So dying ever, Eleänore.

The Miller's Daughter

I see the wealthy miller yet,
    His double chin, his portly size,
And who that knew him could forget
    The busy wrinkles round his eyes?
The slow wise smile that, round about
    His dusty forehead dryly curl'd,
Seem'd half-within and half-without,
    And full of dealings with the world?

In yonder chair I see him sit,
    Three fingers round the old silver cup —
I see his grey eyes twinkle yet
    At his own jest — grey eyes lit up
With summer lightnings of a soul
    So full of summer warmth, so glad,
So healthy, sound, and clear and whole,
    His memory scarce can make me sad.

Yet fill my glass: give me one kiss:
   My own sweet Alice, we must die.
There's somewhat in this world amiss
   Shall be unriddled by and by.
There's somewhat flows to us in life,
   But more is taken quite away.
Pray, Alice, pray, my darling wife,
   That we may die the self-same day.

Have I not found a happy earth?
   I least should breathe a thought of pain.
Would God renew me from my birth
   I'd almost live my life again.
So sweet it seems with thee to walk,
   And once again to woo thee mine –
It seems in after-dinner talk
   Across the walnuts and the wine –

To be the long and listless boy
   Late-left an orphan of the squire,
Where this old mansion mounted high
   Looks down upon the village spire:
For even here, where I and you
   Have lived and loved alone so long,
Each morn my sleep was broken thro'
   By some wild skylark's matin song.

And oft I heard the tender dove
   In firry woodlands making moan;
But ere I saw your eyes, my love,
   I had no motion of my own.
For scarce my life with fancy play'd
   Before I dream'd that pleasant dream –
Still hither thither idly sway'd
   Like those long mosses in the stream.

Or from the bridge I lean'd to hear
   The milldam rushing down with noise,
And see the minnows everywhere
   In crystal eddies glance and poise,
The tall flag-flowers when they sprung
   Below the range of stepping-stones,
Or those three chestnuts near, that hung
   In masses thick with milky cones.

But, Alice, what an hour was that,
    When after roving in the woods
('Twas April then), I came and sat
    Below the chestnuts, when their buds
Were glistening to the breezy blue;
    And on the slope, an absent fool,
I cast me down, nor thought of you,
    But angled in the higher pool.

A love-song I had somewhere read,
    An echo from a measured strain,
Beat time to nothing in my head
    From some odd corner of the brain.
It haunted me, the morning long,
    With weary sameness in the rhymes,
The phantom of a silent song,
    That went and came a thousand times.

Then leapt a trout. In lazy mood
    I watch'd the little circles die;
They past into the level flood,
    And there a vision caught my eye;
The reflex of a beauteous form,
    A glowing arm, a gleaming neck,
As when a sunbeam wavers warm
    Within the dark and dimpled beck.

For you remember, you had set,
    That morning, on the casement's edge
A long green box of mignonette,
    And you were leaning from the ledge:
And when I raised my eyes, above
    They met with two so full and bright –
Such eyes! I swear to you, my love,
    That these have never lost their light.

I loved, and love dispell'd the fear
    That I should die an early death:
For love possess'd the atmosphere,
    And fill'd the breast with purer breath.
My mother thought, What ails the boy?
    For I war alter'd, and began
To move about the house with joy,
    And with the certain step of man.

I loved the brimming wave that swam
Thro' quiet meadows, round the mill,
The sleepy pool above the dam,
The pool beneath it never still,
The meal-sacks, on the whiten'd floor,
The dark round of the dripping wheel,
The very air about the door
Made misty with the floating meal.

And oft in ramblings on the wold,
When April nights began to blow,
And April's crescent glimmer'd cold,
I saw the village lights below;
I knew your taper far away,
And full at heart of trembling hope
From off the wold I came, and lay
Upon the freshly-flower'd slope.

The deep brook groan'd beneath the mill;
And 'by that lamp,' I thought, 'she sits!'
The white chalk-quarry from the hill
Gleam'd to the flying moon by fits.
'O that I were beside her now!
O will she answer if I call?
O would she give me vow for vow,
Sweet Alice, if I told her all?'

Sometimes I saw you sit and spin;
And, in the pauses of the wind,
Sometimes I heard you sing within;
Sometimes your shadow cross'd the blind.
At last you rose and moved the light,'
And the long shadow of the chair
Flitted across into the night,
And all the casement darken'd there.

But when at last I dared to speak,
The lanes, you know, were white with may,
Your ripe lips moved not, but your cheek
Flush'd like the coming of the day;
And so it was – half-sly, half-shy,
You would, and would not, little one!
Although I pleaded tenderly,
And you and I were all alone.

And slowly was my mother brought
    To yield consent to my desire:
She wish'd me happy, but she thought
    I might have look'd a little higher;
And I was young – too young to wed:
    'Yet must I love her for your sake;
Go fetch your Alice here,' she said:
    Her eyelid quiver'd as she spake.

And down I went to fetch my bride:
    But, Alice, you were ill at ease;
This dress and that by turns you tried,
    Too fearful that you should not please.
I loved you better for your fears,
    I knew you could not look but well;
And dews, that would have fall'n in tears,
    I kiss'd away before they fell.

I watch'd the little flutterings,
    The doubt my mother would not see;
She spoke at large of many things,
And at the last she spoke of me;
And turning look'd upon your face,
As near this door you sat apart,
And rose, and, with a silent grace
Approaching, press'd you heart to heart.

Ah, well – but sing the foolish song
I gave you, Alice, on the day
When, arm in arm, we went along,
A pensive pair, and you were gay
With bridal flowers – that I may seem,
As in the nights of old, to lie
Beside the mill-wheel in the stream,
While those full chestnuts whisper by.

> *It is the miller's daughter,*
>   *And she is grown so dear, so dear,*
> *That I would be the jewel*
>   *That trembles at her ear:*
> *For hid in ringlets day and night,*
>   *I'd touch her neck so warm and white.*
>
> *And I would be the girdle*
>   *About her dainty dainty waist,*
> *And her heart would beat against me,*
>   *In sorrow and in rest:*
> *And I should know if it beat right,*
>   *I'd clasp it round so close and tight.*

And I would be the necklace,
*   And all day long to fall and rise*
Upon her balmy bosom,
*   With her laughter or her sighs,*
And I would lie so light, so light,
*   I scarce should be unclasp'd at night.*

A trifle, sweet! which true love spells –
    True love interprets – right alone.
His light upon the letter dwells,
    For all the spirit is his own.
So, if I waste words now, in truth
    You must blame Love. His early rage
Had force to make me rhyme in youth,
    And makes me talk too much in age.

And now those vivid hours are gone,
    Like mine own life to me thou art,
Where Past and Present, wound in one,
    Do make a garland for the heart:
So sing that other song I made,
    Half-anger'd with my happy lot,
The day, when in the chestnut shade
    I found the blue Forget-me-not.

Love that hath us in the net,
Can he pass, and we forget?
Many suns arise and set.
Many a chance the years beget.
Love the gift is Love the debt.
*   Even so.*
Love is hurt with jar and fret.
Love is made a vague regret.
Eyes with idle tears are wet.
Idle habit links us yet.
What is love? for we forget:
*   Ah, no! no!*

Look thro' mine eyes with thine. True wife,
    Round my true heart thine arms entwine;
My other dearer life in life,
    Look thro' my very soul with thine!
Untouch'd with any shade of years,
    May those kind eyes for ever dwell!
They have not shed a many tears,
    Dear eyes, since first I knew them well.

Yet tears they shed: they had their part
   Of sorrow: for when time was ripe,
The still affection of the heart
   Became an outward breathing type,
That into stillness past again,
   And left a want unknown before;
Although the loss that brought us pain,
   That loss but made us love the more,

With farther lookings on. The kiss,
   The woven arms, seem but to be
Weak symbols of the settled bliss,
   The comfort, I have found in thee:
But that God bless thee, dear – who wrought
   Two spirits to one equal mind –
With blessings beyond hope or thought,
   With blessings which no words can find.

Arise, and let us wander forth,
   To yon old mill across the wolds;
For look, the sunset, south and north,
   Winds all the vale in rosy folds,
And fires your narrow casement glass,
   Touching the sullen pool below:
On the chalk-hill the bearded grass
   Is dry and dewless. Let us go.

Fatima

O Love, Love, Love! O withering might!
O sun, that from thy noonday height
Shudderest when I strain my sight,
Throbbing thro' all thy heat and light,
   Lo, falling from my constant mind,
   Lo, parch'd and wither'd, deaf and blind,
   I whirl like leaves in roaring wind.

Last night I wasted hateful hours
Below the city's eastern towers:
I thirsted for the brooks, the showers:
I roll'd among the tender flowers:
   I crush'd them on my breast, my mouth:
   I look'd athwart the burning drouth
   Of that long desert to the south.

Last night, when some one spoke his name,
From my swift blood that went and came
A thousand little shafts of flame
Were shiver'd in my narrow frame.
    O Love, O fire! once he drew
    With one long kiss my whole soul thro'
    My lips, as sunlight drinketh dew.

Before he mounts the hill, I know
He cometh quickly: from below
Sweet gales, as from deep gardens, blow
Before him, striking on my brow.
    In my dry brain my spirit soon,
    Down-deepening from swoon to swoon,
    Faints like a dazzled morning moon.

The wind sounds like a silver wire,
And from beyond the noon a fire
Is pour'd upon the hills, and nigher
The skies stoop down in their desire;
    And, isled in sudden seas of light,
    My heart, pierced thro' with fierce delight,
    Bursts into blossom in his sight.

My whole soul waiting silently,
All naked in a sultry sky,
Droops blinded with his shining eye:
    I *will* possess him or will die.
    I will grow round him in his place,
    Grow, live, die looking on his face,
Die, dying clasp'd in his embrace.

Oenone

There lies a vale in Ida, lovelier
Than all the valleys of Ionian hills.
The swimming vapour slopes athwart the glen,
Puts forth an arm, and creeps from pine to pine,
And loiters, slowly drawn. On either hand
The lawns and meadow-ledges midway down
Hang rich in flowers, and far below them roars
The long brook falling thro' the clov'n ravine
In cataract after cataract to the sea.
Behind the valley topmost Gargarus
Stands up and takes the morning: but in front

The gorges, opening wide apart, reveal
Troas and Ilion's column'd citadel,
The crown of Troas.
                              Hither came at noon
Mournful Oenone, wandering forlorn
Of Paris, once her playmate on the hills.
Her cheek had lost the rose, and round her neck
Floated her hair or seem'd to float in rest.
She, leaning on a fragment twined with vine,
Sang to the stillness, till the mountain-shade
Sloped downward to her seat from the upper cliff.

  'O mother Ida, many-fountain'd Ida,
Dear mother Ida, hearken ere I die.
For now the noonday quiet holds the hill:
The grasshopper is silent in the grass:
The lizard, with his shadow on the stone,
Rests like a shadow, and the cicala sleeps.
The purple flowers droop: the golden bee
Is lily-cradled: I alone awake.
My eyes are full of tears, my heart of love,
My heart is breaking, and my eyes are dim,
And I am all aweary of my life.

  'O mother Ida, many-fountain'd Ida,
Dear mother Ida, hearken ere I die.
Hear me O Earth, hear me O Hills, O Caves
That house the cold crown'd snake! O mountain brooks
 I am the daughter of a River-God
Hear me, for I will speak, and build up all
My sorrow with my song, as yonder walls
Rose slowly to a music slowly breathed,
A cloud that gather'd shape: for it may be
That, while I speak of it, a little while
My heart may wander from its deeper woe.

  'O mother Ida, many-fountain'd Ida,
Dear mother Ida, hearken ere I die.
I waited underneath the dawning hills,
Aloft the mountain lawn was dewy-dark,
And dewy-dark aloft the mountain pine:
Beautiful Paris, evil-hearted Paris,
Leading a jet-black goat white-horn'd, white-hooved,
Came up from reedy Simois all alone.

  'O mother Ida, hearken ere I die.
Far-off the torrent call'd me from the cleft:
Far up the solitary morning smote

The streaks of virgin snow. With down-dropt eyes
I sat alone: white-breasted like a star
Fronting the dawn he moved; a leopard skin
Droop'd from his shoulder, but his sunny hair
Cluster'd about his temples like a God's;
And his cheek brighten'd as the foam-bow brightens
When the wind blows the foam, and all my heart
Went forth to embrace him coming ere he came.

'Dear mother Ida, hearken ere I die.
He smiled, and opening out his milk-white palm
Disclosed a fruit of pure Hesperian gold,
That smelt ambrosially, and while I look'd
And listen'd, the full-flowing river of speech
Came down upon my heart.

' "My own Oenone,
Beautiful-brow'd Oenone, my own soul,
Behold this fruit, whose gleaming rind ingrav'n
'For the most fair,' would seem to award it thine,
As lovelier than whatever Oread haunt
The knolls of Ida, loveliest in all grace
Of movement, and the charm of married brows."

'Dear mother Ida, hearken ere I die.
He prest the blossom of his lips to mine,
And added "This was cast upon the board,
When all the full-faced presence of the Gods
Ranged in the halls of Peleus; whereupon
Rose feud, with question unto whom 'twere due:
But light-foot Iris brought it yester-eve,
Delivering, that to me, by common voice
Elected umpire, Herè comes to-day,
Pallas and Aphrodite, claiming each
This meed of fairest. Thou, within the cave
Behind yon whispering tuft of oldest pine,
Mayst well behold them unbeheld, unheard
Hear all, and see thy Paris judge of Gods."

'Dear mother Ida, hearken ere I die.
It was the deep midnoon: one silvery cloud
Had lost his way between the piney sides
Of this long glen. Then to the bower they came,
Naked they came to that smooth-swarded bower,
And at their feet the crocus brake like fire,
Violet, amaracus, and asphodel,

Lotos and lilies: and a wind arose,
And overhead the wandering ivy and vine
This way and that, in many a wild festoon
Ran riot, garlanding the gnarled boughs
With bunch and berry and flower thro' and thro'.

'O mother Ida, hearken ere I die.
On the tree-tops a crested peacock lit,
And o'er him flow'd a golden cloud, and lean'd
Upon him, slowly dropping fragrant dew.
Then first I heard the voice of her, to whom
Coming thro' Heaven, like a light that grows
Larger and clearer, with one mind the Gods
Rise up for reverence. She to Paris made
Proffer of royal power, ample rule
Unquestion'd, overflowing revenue
Wherewith to embellish state, "from many a vale
And river-sunder'd champaign clothed with corn,
Or labour'd mines undrainable of ore.
Honour," she said, "and homage, tax and toll,
From many an inland town and haven large,
Mast-throng'd beneath her shadowing citadel
In glassy bays among her tallest towers."

'O mother Ida, hearken ere I die.
Still she spake on and still she spake of power,
"Which in all action is the end of all;
Power fitted to the season; wisdom-bred
And throned of wisdom – from all neighbour crowns
Alliance and allegiance, till thy hand
Fail from the sceptre-staff. Such boon from me,
From me, Heaven's Queen, Paris, to thee king-born,
A shepherd all thy life but yet king-born,
Should come most welcome, seeing men, in power
Only, are likest gods, who have attain'd
Rest in a happy place and quiet seats
Above the thunder, with undying bliss
In knowledge of their own supremacy."

'Dear mother Ida, hearken ere I die.
She ceased, and Paris held the costly fruit
Out at arm's-length, so much the thought of power
Flatter'd his spirit; but Pallas where she stood
Somewhat apart, her clear and bared limbs
O'erthwarted with the brazen-headed spear
Upon her pearly shoulder leaning cold,

The while, above, her full and earnest eye
Over her snow-cold breast and angry cheek
Kept watch, waiting decision, made reply.

 ' "Self-reverence, self-knowledge, self-control,
These three alone lead life to sovereign power.
Yet not for power (power of herself
Would come uncall'd for), but to live by law,
Acting the law we live by without fear;
And, because right is right, to follow right
Were wisdom in the scorn of consequence."

 'Dear mother Ida, hearken ere I die.
Again she said: "I woo thee not with gifts.
Sequel of guerdon could not alter me
To fairer. Judge thou me by what I am,
So shalt thou find me fairest.
      Yet, indeed,
If gazing on divinity disrobed
Thy mortal eyes are frail to judge of fair,
Unbiass'd by self-profit, oh! rest thee sure
That I shall love thee well and cleave to thee,
So that my vigour, wedded to thy blood
Shall strike within thy pulses, like a God's,
To push thee forward thro' a life of shocks,
Dangers, and deeds, until endurance grow
Sinew'd with action, and the full-grown will,
Circled thro' all experiences, pure law,
Commeasure perfect freedom."
      'Here she ceased,
And Paris ponder'd, and I cried, "O Paris,
Give it to Pallas!" but he heard me not,
Or hearing would not hear me, woe is me!

 'O mother Ida, many-fountain'd Ida,
Dear mother Ida, hearken ere I die.
Idalian Aphrodite beautiful,
Fresh as the foam, new-bathed in Paphian wells,
With rosy slender fingers backward drew
From her warm brows and bosom her deep hair
Ambrosial, golden round her lucid throat
And shoulder: from the violets her light foot
Shone rosy-white, and o'er her rounded form
Between the shadows of the vine-bunches
Floated the glowing sunlights, as she moved.

'Dear mother Ida, hearken ere I die.
She with a subtle smile in her mild eyes,
The herald of her triumph, drawing nigh
Half-whisper'd in his ear, "I promise thee
The fairest and most loving wife in Greece,"
She spoke and laugh'd: I shut my sight for fear:
But when I look'd, Paris had raised his arm
And I beheld great Herè's angry eyes,
As she withdrew into the golden cloud,
And I was left alone within the bower;
And from that time to this I am alone,
And I shall be alone until I die.

'Yet, mother Ida, hearken ere I die.
Fairest – why fairest wife? am I not fair?
My love hath told me so a thousand times.
Methinks I must be fair, for yesterday,
When I past by, a wild and wanton pard,
Eyed like the evening star, with playful tail
Crouch'd fawning in the weed. Most loving is she?
Ah me, my mountain shepherd, that my arms
Were wound about thee, and my hot lips prest
Close, close to thine in that quick-falling dew
Of fruitful kisses, thick as Autumn rains
Flash in the pools of whirling Simois.

'O mother, hear me yet before I die.
They came, they cut away my tallest pines,
My dark tall pines, that plumed the craggy ledge
High over the blue gorge, and all between
The snowy peak and snow-white cataract
Foster'd the callow eaglet – from beneath
Whose thick mysterious boughs in the dark morn
The panther's roar came muffled, while I sat
Low in the valley. Never, never more
Shall lone Oenone see the morning mist
Sweep thro' them; never see them overlaid
With narrow moon-lit slips of silver cloud,
Between the loud stream and the trembling stars.

'O mother, hear me yet before I die.
I wish that somewhere in the ruin'd folds,
Among the fragments tumbled from the glens,
Or the dry thickets, I could meet with her,
The Abominable, that uninvited came
Into the fair Peleïan banquet-hall,

And cast the golden fruit upon the board,
And bred this change; that I might speak my mind,
And tell her to her face how much I hate
Her presence, hated both of Gods and men.

'O mother, hear me yet before I die.
Hath he not sworn his love a thousand times,
In this green valley, under this green hill,
Ev'n on this hand, and sitting on this stone?
Seal'd it with kisses? water'd it with tears?
O happy tears, and how unlike to these!
O happy Heaven, how canst thou see my face?
O happy earth, how canst thou bear my weight?
O death, death, death, thou ever-floating cloud,
There are enough unhappy on this earth,
Pass by the happy souls, that love to live:
I pray thee, pass before my light of life,
And shadow all my soul, that I may die.
Thou weighest heavy on the heart within,
Weigh heavy on my eyelids: let me die.

'O mother, hear me yet before I die.
I will not die alone, for fiery thoughts
Do shape themselves within me, more and more,
Whereof I catch the issue, as I hear
Dead sounds at night come from the inmost hills,
Like footsteps upon wool. I dimly see
My far-off doubtful purpose, as a mother
Conjectures of the features of her child
Ere it is born: her child! – a shudder comes
Across me: never child be born of me,
Unblest, to vex me with his father's eyes!

'O mother, hear me yet before I die.
Hear me O earth. I will not die alone,
Lest their shrill happy laughter come to me
Walking the cold and starless road of Death
Uncomforted, leaving my ancient love
With the Greek woman. I will rise and go
Down into Troy, and ere the stars come forth
Talk with the wild Cassandra, for she says
A fire dances before her, and a sound
Rings ever in her ears of armed men.
What this may be I know not, but I know
That, wheresoe'er I am by night and day,
All earth and air seem only burning fire.'

The Sisters

We were two daughters of one race:
She was the fairest in the face:
   The wind is blowing in turret and tree.
They were together, and she fell;
Therefore revenge became me well.
   O the Earl was fair to see!

She died: she went to burning flame:
She mix'd her ancient blood with shame.
   The wind is howling in turret and tree.
Whole weeks and months, and early and late,
To win his love I lay in wait:
   O the Earl was fair to see!

I made a feast; I bad him come;
I won his love, I brought him home.
   The wind is roaring in turret and tree.
And after supper, on a bed,
Upon my lap he laid his head:
   O the Earl was fair to see!

I kiss'd his eyelids into rest:
His ruddy cheek upon my breast.
   The wind is raging in turret and tree.
I hated him with the hate of hell,
But I loved his beauty passing well.
   O the Earl was fair to see!

I rose up in the silent night:
I made my dagger sharp and bright.
   The wind is raving in turret and tree.
As half-asleep his breath he drew,
Three times I stabb'd him thro' and thro'.
   O the Earl was fair to see!

I curl'd and comb'd his comely head.
He look'd so grand when he was dead.
   The wind is blowing in turret and tree.
I wrapt his body in the sheet,
And laid him at his mother's feet.
   O the Earl was fair to see!

To —

with the following poem

I send you here a sort of allegory,
(For you will understand it) of a soul,
A sinful soul possess'd of many gifts,
A spacious garden full of flowering weeds,
A glorious Devil, large in heart and brain,
That did love Beauty only, (Beauty seen
In all varieties of mould and mind)
And Knowledge for its beauty; or if Good,
Good only for its beauty, seeing not
That Beauty, Good, and Knowledge, are three sisters
That doat upon each other, friends to man,
Living together under the same roof,
And never can be sunder'd without tears.
And he that shuts Love out, in turn shall be
Shut out from Love, and on her threshold lie
Howling in outer darkness. Not for this
Was common clay ta'en from the common earth,
Moulded by God, and temper'd with the tears
Of angels to the perfect shape of man.

The Palace of Art

I built my soul a lordly pleasure-house,
     Wherein at ease for ay to dwell.
I said, 'O Soul, make merry and carouse,
     Dear soul, for all is well.'

A huge crag-platform, smooth as burnish'd brass,
     I chose. The ranged ramparts bright
From level meadow-bases of deep grass
     Suddenly scaled the light.

Thereon I built it firm. Of ledge or shelf
     The rock rose clear, or winding stair.
My soul would live alone unto herself
     In her high palace there.

And 'while the world runs round and round,' I said,
     'Reign thou apart, a quiet king
Still as, while Saturn whirls, his steadfast shade
     Sleeps on his luminous ring.'

To which my soul made answer readily.
  'Trust me, in bliss I shall abide
In this great mansion, that is built for me,
    So royal-rich and wide.'

*

Four courts I made, East, West and South and North,
  In each a squared lawn, wherefrom
The golden gorge of dragons spouted forth
    A flood of fountain-foam.

And round the cool green courts there ran a row
  Of cloisters, branch'd like mighty woods,
Echoing all night to that sonorous flow
    Of spouted fountain-floods.

And round the roofs a gilded gallery
  That lent broad verge to distant lands,
Far as the wild swan wings, to where the sky
    Dipt down to sea and sands.

From those four jets four currents in one swell
  Across the mountain stream'd below
In misty folds, that floating as they fell
    Lit up a torrent-bow.

And high on every peak a statue seem'd
  To hang on tiptoe, tossing up
A cloud of incense of all odour steam'd
    From out a golden cup.

So that she thought, 'And who shall gaze upon
  My palace with unblinded eyes,
While this great bow will waver in the sun
    And that sweet incense rise?'

For that sweet incense rose and never fail'd,
  And, while day sank or mounted higher,
The light aërial gallery, golden-rail'd,
    Burnt like a fringe of fire.

Likewise the deep-set windows, stain'd and traced,
  Would seem slow-flaming crimson fires
From shadow'd grots of arches interlaced,
    And tipt with frost-like spires.

*

Full of long-sounding corridors it was,
    That over-vaulted grateful gloom,
Thro' which the livelong day my soul did pass,
        Well-pleased, from room to room.

Full of great rooms and small the palace stood,
    All various, each a perfect whole
From living Nature, fit for every mood
        And change of my still soul.

For some were hung with arras green and blue,
    Showing a gaudy summer-morn,
Where with puff'd cheek the belted hunter blew
        His wreathed bugle-horn.

One seem'd all dark and red – a tract of sand,
    And some one pacing there alone,
Who paced for ever in a glimmering land,
        Lit with a low large moon.

One show'd an iron coast and angry waves.
    You seem'd to hear them climb and fall
And roar rock-thwarted under bellowing caves
        Beneath the windy wall.

And one, a full-fed river winding slow
    By herds upon an endless plain,
The ragged rims of thunder brooding low
        With shadow-streaks of rain.

And one, the reapers at their sultry toil.
    In front they bound the sheaves. Behind
Were realms of upland, prodigal in oil,
        And hoary to the wind.

And one, a foreground black with stones and slags,
    Beyond, a line of heights, and higher
All barr'd with long white cloud the scornful crags,
        And highest, snow and fire.

And one, an English home – grey twilight pour'd
    On dewy pastures, dewy trees,
Softer than sleep – all things in order stored,
        A haunt of ancient Peace.

Nor these alone, but every landscape fair,
   As fit for every mood of mind,
Or gay, or grave, or sweet, or stern, was there,
    Not less than truth design'd.

*

Or the maid-mother by a crucifix,
   In tracts of pasture sunny-warm,
Beneath branch-work of costly sardonyx
    Sat smiling, babe in arm.

Or in a clear-wall'd city on the sea,
   Near gilded organ-pipes, her hair
Wound with white roses, slept St. Cecily;
    An angel look'd at her.

Or thronging all one porch of Paradise,
   A group of Houris bow'd to see
The dying Islamite, with hands and eyes
    That said, We wait for thee.

Or mythic Uther's deeply-wounded son
   In some fair space of sloping greens
Lay, dozing in the vale of Avalon,
    And watch'd by weeping queens.

Or hollowing one hand against his ear,
   To list a foot-fall, ere he saw
The wood-nymph, stay'd the Ausonian king to hear
    Of wisdom and of law.

Or over hills with peaky tops engrail'd,
   And many a tract of palm and rice,
The throne of Indian Cama slowly sail'd
    A summer fann'd with spice.

Or sweet Europa's mantle blew unclasp'd,
   From off her shoulder backward bourne:
From one hand droop'd a crocus: one hand grasp'd
    The mild bull's golden horn.

Or else flush'd Ganymede, his rosy thigh
   Half-buried in the Eagle's down
Sole as a flying star shot thro' the sky
    Above the pillar'd town.

Nor these alone: but every legend fair
   Which the supreme Caucasian mind
Carved out of Nature for itself, was there,
    Not less than life, design'd.

*

Then in the towers I placed great bells that swung,
   Moved of themselves, with silver sound;
And with choice paintings of wise men I hung
    The royal dais round.

For there was Milton like a seraph strong,
   Beside him Shakespeare bland and mild;
And there the world-worn Dante grasp'd his song,
    And somewhat grimly smiled.

And there the Ionian father of the rest;
   A million wrinkles carved his skin;
A hundred winters snow'd upon his breast,
    From cheek and throat and chin.

Above, the fair hall-ceiling stately-set
   Many an arch high up did lift,
And angels rising and descending met
    With interchange of gift.

Below was all mosaic choicely plann'd
   With cycles of the human tale
Of this wide world, the times of every land
    So wrought, they will not fail.

The people here, a beast of burden slow,
   Toil'd onward, prick'd with goads and stings;
Here play'd, a tiger, rolling to and fro
    The heads and crowns of kings;

Here rose, an athlete, strong to break or bind
   All force in bonds that might endure,
And here once more like some sick man declined
    And trusted any cure.

But over these she trod: and those great bells
   Began to chime. She took her throne:
She sat betwixt the shining Oriels,
    To sing her songs alone.

And thro' the topmost Oriels' colour'd flame
   Two godlike faces gazed below;
Plato the wise, and large-brow'd Verulam,
    The first of those who know.

And all those names, that in their motion were
   Full-welling fountain-heads of change,
Betwixt the slender shafts were blazon'd fair
    In diverse raiment strange:

Thro' which the lights, rose, amber, emerald, blue,
   Flush'd in her temples and her eyes,
And from her lips, as morn from Memnon, drew
    Rivers of melodies.

No nightingale delighteth to prolong
   Her low preamble all alone
More than my soul to hear her echo'd song
    Throb thro' the ribbed stone;

Singing and murmuring in her feastful mirth,
   Joying to feel herself alive,
Lord over Nature, Lord of the visible earth,
    Lord of the senses five;

Communing with herself: 'All these are mine,
   And let the world have peace or wars,
'Tis one to me.' She – when young night divine
    Crown'd dying day with stars,

Making sweet close of his delicious toils –
   Lit light in wreaths and anadems,
And pure quintessences of precious oils
    In hollow'd moons of gems,

To mimic heaven; and clapt her hands and cried,
   'I marvel if my still delight
In this great house so royal-rich, and wide,
    Be flatter'd to the height.

'O all things fair to sate my various eyes!
   O shapes and hues that please me well!
O silent faces of the Great and Wise,
    My Gods, with whom I dwell!

'O God-like isolation which art mine,
    I can but count thee perfect gain,
What time I watch the darkening droves of swine
      That range on yonder plain.

'In filthy sloughs they roll a prurient skin,
    They graze and wallow, breed and sleep;
And oft some brainless devil enters in,
      And drives them to the deep.'

Then of the moral instinct would she prate,
    And of the rising from the dead,
As hers by right of full-accomplish'd Fate;
      And at the last she said:

'I take possession of man's mind and deed.
    I care not what the sects may brawl.
I sit as God holding no form of creed,
      But contemplating all.'

*

Full oft the riddle of the painful earth
    Flash'd thro' her as she sat alone,
Yet not the less held she her solemn mirth,
      And intellectual throne.

And so she throve and prosper'd: so three years
    She prosper'd: on the fourth she fell
Like Herod, when the shout was in his ears,
      Struck thro' with pangs of hell.

Lest she should fail and perish utterly,
    God, before whom ever lie bare
The abysmal deeps of Personality,
      Plagued her with sore despair.

When she would think, where'er she turn'd her sight,
    The airy hand confusion wrought,
Wrote 'Mene, mene,' and divided quite
      The kingdom of her thought.

Deep dread and loathing of her solitude
    Fell on her, from which mood was born
Scorn of herself; again, from out that mood
      Laughter at her self-scorn.

'What! is not this my place of strength,' she said,
   'My spacious mansion built for me,
Whereof the strong foundation-stones were laid
     Since my first memory?'

But in dark corners of her palace stood
   Uncertain shapes; and unawares
On white-eyed phantasms weeping tears of blood,
     And horrible nightmares,

And hollow shades enclosing hearts of flame,
   And, with dim fretted foreheads all,
On corpses three-months-old at noon she came,
     That stood against the wall.

A spot of dull stagnation, without light
   Or power of movement, seem'd my soul,
'Mid onward-sloping motions infinite
     Making for one sure goal.

A still salt pool, lock'd in with bars of sand;
   Left on the shore; that hears all night
The plunging seas draw backward from the land
     Their moon-led waters white.

A star that with the choral starry dance
   Join'd not, but stood, and standing saw
The hollow orb of moving Circumstance
     Roll'd round by one fix'd law.

Back on herself her serpent pride had curl'd.
   'No voice,' she shriek'd in that lone hall,
'No voice breaks thro' the stillness of this world:
     One deep, deep silence all!'

She, mouldering with the dull earth's mouldering sod,
   Inwrapt tenfold in slothful shame,
Lay there exiled from eternal God,
     Lost to her place and name;

And death and life she hated equally,
   And nothing saw, for her despair,
But dreadful time, dreadful eternity,
     No comfort anywhere;

Remaining utterly confused with fears,
    And ever worse with growing time,
And ever unrelieved by dismal tears,
     And all alone in crime:

Shut up as in a crumbling tomb, girt round
    With blackness as a solid wall,
Far off she seem'd to hear the dully sound
     Of human footsteps fall.

As in strange lands a traveller walking slow,
    In doubt and great perplexity,
A little before moon-rise hears the low
     Moan of an unknown sea;

And knows not if it be thunder, or a sound
    Of rocks thrown down, or one deep cry
Of great wild beasts; then thinketh, 'I have found
     A new land, but I die.'

She howl'd aloud, 'I am on fire within.
    There comes no murmur of reply.
What is it that will take away my sin,
     And save me lest I die?'

So when four years were wholly finished,
    She threw her royal robes away.
'Make me a cottage in the vale,' she said,
     Where I may mourn and pray.

'Yet pull not down my palace towers, that are
    So lightly, beautifully built:
Perchance I may return with others there
     When I have purged my guilt.'

The May Queen

ou must wake and call me early, call me early, mother dear;
o-morrow 'ill be the happiest time of all the glad New-year;
f all the glad New-year, mother, the maddest merriest day;
or I'm to be Queen o' the May, mother, I'm to be Queen o' the May.

here's many a black black eye, they say, but none so bright as mine;
here's Margaret and Mary, there's Kate and Caroline:
ut none so fair as little Alice in all the land they say,
 I'm to be Queen o' the May, mother, I'm to be Queen o' the May.

leep so sound all night, mother, that I shall never wake,
you do not call me loud when the day begins to break:
ut I must gather knots of flowers, and buds and garlands gay,
or I'm to be Queen o' the May, mother, I'm to be Queen o' the May.

 I came up the valley whom think ye should I see,
ut Robin leaning on the bridge beneath the hazel-tree?
e thought of that sharp look, mother, I gave him yesterday, –
ut I'm to be Queen o' the May, mother, I'm to be Queen o' the May.

e thought I was a ghost, mother, for I was all in white,
nd I ran by him without speaking, like a flash of light.
hey call me cruel-hearted, but I care not what they say,
or I'm to be Queen o' the May, mother, I'm to be Queen o' the May.

hey say he's dying all for love, but that can never be:
hey say his heart is breaking, mother – what is that to me?
here's many a bolder lad 'ill woo me any summer day,
nd I'm to be Queen o' the May, mother, I'm to be Queen o' the May.

ttle Effie shall go with me to-morrow to the green,
nd you'll be there, too, mother, to see me made the Queen;
r the shepherd lads on every side 'ill come from far away,
nd I'm to be Queen o' the May, mother, I'm to be Queen o' the May.

e honeysuckle round the porch has wov'n its wavy bowers,
nd by the meadow-trenches blow the faint sweet cuckoo-flowers;
nd the wild marsh-marigold shines like fire in swamps and hollows grey,
nd I'm to be Queen o' the May, mother, I'm to be Queen o' the May.

e night-winds come and go, mother, upon the meadowgrass,
nd the happy stars above them seem to brighten as they pass;
ere will not be a drop of rain the whole of the livelong day,
nd I'm to be Queen o' the May, mother, I'm to be Queen o' the May.

All the valley, mother, 'ill be fresh and green and still,
And the cowslip and the crowfoot are over all the hill,
And the rivulet in the flowery dale 'ill merrily glance and play,
For I'm to be Queen o' the May, mother, I'm to be Queen o' the May.

So you must wake and call me early, call me early, mother dear,
To-morrow 'ill be the happiest time of all the glad New-year:
To-morrow 'ill be of all the year the maddest merriest day,
For I'm to be Queen o' the May, mother, I'm to be Queen o' the May.

New Year's Eve

If you're waking call me early, call me early, mother dear,
For I would see the sun rise upon the glad New-year.
It is the last New-year that I shall ever see,
Then you may lay me low i' the mould and think no more of me.

To-night I saw the sun set: he set and left behind
The good old year, the dear old time, and all my peace of mind;
And the New-year's coming up, mother, but I shall never see
The blossom on the blackthorn, the leaf upon the tree.

Last May we made a crown of flowers: we had a merry day;
Beneath the hawthorn on the green they made me Queen of May;
And we danced about the may-pole and in the hazel copse,
Till Charles's Wain came out above the tall white chimney-tops.

There's not a flower on all the hills: the frost is on the pane:
I only wish to live till the snowdrops come again:
I wish the snow would melt and the sun come out on high:
I long to see a flower so before the day I die.

The building rook 'ill caw from the windy tall elm-tree
And the tufted plover pipe along the fallow lea,
And the swallow 'ill come back again with summer o'er the wave,
But I shall lie alone, mother, within the mouldering grave.

Upon the chancel-casement, and upon that grave of mine,
In the early early morning the summer sun 'ill shine,
Before the red cock crows from the farm upon the hill,
When you are warm-asleep, mother, and all the world is still.

When the flowers come again, mother, beneath the waning light
You'll never see me more in the long grey fields at night;
When from the dry dark wold the summer airs blow cool
On the oat-grass and the sword-grass, and the bulrush in the pool

You'll bury me, my mother, just beneath the hawthorn shade,
And you'll come sometimes and see me where I am lowly laid.
I shall not forget you, mother, I shall hear you when you pass,
With your feet above my head in the long and pleasant grass.

I have been wild and wayward, but you'll forgive me now;
You'll kiss me, my own mother, and forgive me ere I go;
Nay, nay, you must not weep, nor let your grief be wild,
You should not fret for me, mother, you have another child.

If I can I'll come again, mother, from out my resting-place;
Tho' you'll not see me, mother, I shall look upon your face;
Tho' I cannot speak a word, I shall hearken what you say,
And be often, often with you when you think I'm far away.

Goodnight, goodnight, when I have said goodnight for evermore,
And you see me carried out from the threshold of the door;
Don't let Effie come to see me till my grave be growing green:
She'll be a better child to you than ever I have been.

She'll find my garden-tools upon the granary floor:
Let her take 'em: they are hers: I shall never garden more:
But tell her, when I'm gone, to train the rose-bush that I set
About the parlour-window and the box of mignonette.

Goodnight, sweet mother: call me before the day is born.
All night I lie awake, but I fall asleep at morn;
But I would see the sun rise upon the glad New-year,
So, if you're waking, call me, call me early, mother dear.

Conclusion

I thought to pass away before, and yet alive I am;
And in the fields all round I hear the bleating of the lamb.
How sadly, I remember, rose the morning of the year!
To die before the snowdrop came, and now the violet's here.

O sweet is the new violet, that comes beneath the skies,
And sweeter is the young lamb's voice to me that cannot rise,
And sweet is all the land about, and all the flowers that blow,
And sweeter far is death than life to me that long to go.

It seem'd so hard at first, mother, to leave the blessed sun,
And now it seems as hard to stay, and yet His will be done!
But still I think it can't be long before I find release;
And that good man, the clergyman, has told me words of peace.

O blessings on his kindly voice and on his silver hair!
And blessings on his whole life long, until he meet me there!
O blessings on his kindly heart and on his silver head!
A thousand times I blest him, as he knelt beside my bed.

He taught me all the mercy, for he show'd me all the sin.
Now, tho' my lamp was lighted late, there's One will let me in:
Nor would I now be well, mother, again if that could be,
For my desire is but to pass to Him that died for me.

I did not hear the dog howl, mother, or the deathwatch beat,
There came a sweeter token when the night and morning meet:
But sit beside my bed, mother, and put your hand in mine,
And Effie on the other side, and I will tell the sign.

All in the wild March-morning I heard the angels call;
It was when the moon was setting, and the dark was over all;
The trees began to whisper, and the wind began to roll,
And in the wild March-morning I heard them call my soul.

For lying broad awake I thought of you and Effie dear;
I saw you sitting in the house, and I no longer here;
With all my strength I pray'd for both, and so I felt resign'd,
And up the valley came a swell of music on the wind.

I thought that it was fancy, and I listen'd in my bed,
And then did something speak to me – I know not what was said;
For great delight and shuddering took hold of all my mind,
And up the valley came again the music on the wind.

But you were sleeping; and I said, 'It's not for them: it's mine.'
And if it comes three times, I thought, I take it for a sign.
And once again it came, and close beside the window-bars,
Then seem'd to go right up to Heaven and die among the stars.

So now I think my time is near. I trust it is. I know
The blessed music went that way my soul will have to go.
And for myself, indeed, I care not if I go to-day.
But, Effie, you must comfort *her* when I am past away.

And say to Robin a kind word, and tell him not to fret;
There's many worthier than I, would make him happy yet.
If I had lived – I cannot tell – I might have been his wife;
But all these things have ceased to be, with my desire of life.

O look! the sun begins to rise, the heavens are in a glow;
He shines upon a hundred fields, and all of them I know.
And there I move no longer now, and there his light may shine –
Wild flowers in the valley for other hands than mine.

O sweet and strange it seems to me, that ere this day is done
The voice, that now is speaking, may be beyond the sun –
For ever and for ever with those just souls and true –
And what is life, that we should moan? why make we such ado?

For ever and for ever, all in a blessed home –
And there to wait a little while till you and Effie come –
To lie within the light of God, as I lie upon your breast –
And the wicked cease from troubling, and the weary are at rest.

The Lotos-Eaters

'Courage!' he said, and pointed toward the land,
'This mounting wave will roll us shoreward soon.'
In the afternoon they came unto a land
In which it seemed always afternoon.
All round the coast the languid air did swoon,
Breathing like one that hath a weary dream.
Full-faced above the valley stood the moon;
And like a downward smoke, the slender stream
Along the cliff to fall and pause and fall did seem.

A land of streams! some, like a downward smoke,
Slow-dropping veils of thinnest lawn, did go;
And some thro' wavering lights and shadows broke,
Rolling a slumbrous sheet of foam below.
They saw the gleaming river seaward flow
From the inner land: far off, three mountain-tops,
Three silent pinnacles of aged snow,
Stood sunset-flush'd: and, dew'd with showery drops,
Up-clomb the shadowy pine above the woven copse.

The charmed sunset linger'd low adown
In the red West: thro' mountain clefts the dale
Was seen far inland, and the yellow down
Border'd with palm, and many a winding vale
And meadow, set with slender galingale;
A land where all things always seem'd the same!
And round about the keel with faces pale,
Dark faces pale against that rosy flame,
The mild-eyed melancholy Lotos-eaters came.

Branches they bore of that enchanted stem,
Laden with flower and fruit, whereof they gave
To each, but whoso did receive of them,
And taste, to him the gushing of the wave
Far far away did seem to mourn and rave
On alien shores; and if his fellow spake,
His voice was thin, as voices from the grave;
And deep-asleep he seem'd, yet all awake,
And music in his ears his beating heart did make.

They sat them down upon the yellow sand,
Between the sun and moon upon the shore;
And sweet it was to dream of Fatherland,
Of child, and wife, and slave; but evermore
Most weary seem'd the sea, weary the oar,
Weary the wandering fields of barren foam.
Then some one said, 'We will return no more;'
And all at once they sang, 'Our island home
Is far beyond the wave; we will no longer roam.'

Choric Song

I

There is sweet music here that softer falls
Than petals from blown roses on the grass,
Or night-dews on still waters between walls
Of shadowy granite, in a gleaming pass;
Music that gentlier on the spirit lies,
Than tir'd eyelids upon tir'd eyes;
Music that brings sweet sleep down from the blissful skies.
Here are cool mosses deep,
And thro' the moss the ivies creep,
And in the stream the long-leaved flowers weep,
And from the craggy ledge the poppy hangs in sleep.

II

Why are we weigh'd upon with heaviness,
And utterly consumed with sharp distress,
While all things else have rest from weariness?
All things have rest: why should we toil alone,
We only toil, who are the first of things,
And make perpetual moan,
Still from one sorrow to another thrown:
Nor ever fold our wings,
And cease from wanderings,

Nor steep our brows in slumber's holy balm;
Nor hearken what the inner spirit sings,
'There is no joy but calm!'
Why should we only toil, the roof and crown of things?

III

Lo! in the middle of the wood,
The folded leaf is woo'd from out the bud
With winds upon the branch, and there
Grows green and broad, and takes no care
Sun-steep'd at noon, and in the moon
Nightly dew-fed; and turning yellow
Falls, and floats adown the air.
Lo! sweeten'd with the summer light,
The full-juiced apple, waxing over-mellow,
Drops in a silent autumn night.
All its allotted length of days,
The flower ripens in its place,
Ripens and fades, and falls, and hath no toil,
Fast-rooted in the fruitful soil.

IV

Hateful is the dark-blue sky,
Vaulted o'er the dark-blue sea.
Death is the end of life; ah, why
Should life all labour be?
Let us alone. Time driveth onward fast,
And in a little while our lips are dumb.
Let us alone. What is it that will last?
All things are taken from us, and become
Portions and parcels of the dreadfulPast.
Let us alone. What pleasure can we have
To war with evil? Is there any peace
In ever climbing up the climbing wave?
All things have rest, and ripen toward the grave
In silence; ripen, fall and cease:
Give us long rest or death, dark death, or dreamful ease.

V

How sweet it were, hearing the downward stream,
With half-shut eyes ever to seem
Falling asleep in a half-dream!
To dream and dream, like yonder amber light,
Which will not leave the myrrh-bush on the height;
To hear each other's whisper'd speech;
Eating the Lotos day by day,

To watch the crisping ripples on the beach,
And tender curving lines of creamy spray;
To lend our hearts and spirits wholly
To the influence of mild-minded melancholy;
To muse and brood and live again in memory,
With those old faces of our infancy
Heap'd over with a mound of grass,
Two handfuls of white dust, shut in an urn of brass!

VI

Dear is the memory of our wedded lives,
And dear the last embraces of our wives
And their warm tears: but all hath suffer'd change;
For surely now our household hearths are cold:
Our sons inherit us: our looks are strange:
And we should come like ghosts to trouble joy.
Or else the island princes over-bold
Have eat our substance, and the minstrel sings
Before them of the ten-years' war in Troy,
And our great deeds, as half-forgotten things.
Is there confusion in the little isle?
Let what is broken so remain.
The Gods are hard to reconcile:
'Tis hard to settle order once again.
There is confusion worse than death,
Trouble on trouble, pain on pain,
Long labour unto aged breath,
Sore task to hearts worn out with many wars
And eyes grown dim with gazing on the pilot-stars.

VII

But, propt on beds of amaranth and moly,
How sweet (while warm airs lull us, blowing lowly)
With half-dropt eyelids still,
Beneath a heaven dark and holy,
To watch the long bright river drawing slowly
His waters from the purple hill –
To hear the dewy echoes calling
From cave to cave thro' the thick-twined vine –
To watch the emerald-colour'd water falling
Thro' many a wov'n acanthus-wreath divine!
Only to hear and see the far-off sparkling brine,
Only to hear were sweet, stretch'd out beneath the pine.

VIII

The Lotos blooms below the barren peak:
The Lotos blows by every winding creek:
All day the wind breathes low with mellower tone:
Thro' every hollow cave and alley lone
Round and round the spicy downs the yellow Lotos-dust is blown.
We have had enough of action, and of motion we.
Roll'd to starboard, roll'd to larboard, when the surge was seething
    free,
Where the wallowing monster spouted his foam-fountains in the
    sea.
Let us swear an oath, and keep it with an equal mind,
In the hollow Lotos-land to live and lie reclined
On the hills like Gods together, careless of mankind.
For they lie beside their nectar, and the bolts are hurl'd
Far below them in the valleys, and the clouds are lightly curl'd
Round their golden houses, girdled with the gleaming world:
Where they smile in secret, looking over wasted lands,
Blight and famine, plague and earthquake, roaring deeps and fiery
    sands,
Clanging fights, and flaming towns, and sinking ships, and praying
    hands.
But they smile, they find a music centred in a doleful song
Steaming up, a lamentation and an ancient tale of wrong,
Like a tale of little meaning tho' the words are strong;
Chanted from an ill-used race of men that cleave the soil,
Sow the seed, and reap the harvest with enduring toil,
Storing yearly little dues of wheat, and wine and oil;
Till they perish and they suffer – some, 'tis whisper'd – down in
    hell
Suffer endless anguish, others in Elysian valleys dwell
Resting weary limbs at last on beds of asphodel.
Surely, surely, slumber is more sweet than toil, the shore
Than labour in the deep mid-ocean, wind and wave and oar;
Oh rest ye, brother mariners, we will not wander more.

Rosalind

I

My Rosalind, my Rosalind,
My frolic falcon, with bright eyes,
Whose free delight, from any height of rapid flight,
Stoops at all game that wing the skies,
My Rosalind, my Rosalind,
My bright-eyed, wild-eyed falcon, whither.
Careless both of wind and weather,
Whither fly ye, what game spy ye,
Up or down the streaming wind?

II

The quick lark's closest-caroll'd strains,
The shadow rushing up the sea,
The lightning-flash atween the rains,
The sunlight driving down the lea,
The leaping stream, the very wind,
That will not stay, upon his way,
To stoop the cowslip to the plains,
Is not so clear and bold and free
As you, my falcon Rosalind.
You care not for another's pains,
Because you are the soul of joy,
Bright metal all without alloy.
Life shoots and glances thro' your veins,
And flashes off a thousand ways,
Through lips and eyes in subtle rays.
Your hawk-eyes are keen and bright,
Keen with triumph, watching still
To pierce me through with pointed light;
But oftentimes they flash and glitter
Like sunshine on a dancing rill,
And your words are seeming-bitter,
Sharp and few, but seeming-bitter
From excess of swift delight.

III

Come down, come home, my Rosalind,
My gay young hawk, my Rosalind:
Too long you keep the upper skies;
Too long you roam and wheel at will;
But we must hood your random eyes,
That care not whom they kill,
And your cheek, whose brilliant hue
Is so sparkling-fresh to view,

Some red heath-flower in the dew,
Touched with sunrise. We must bind
And keep you fast, my Rosalind,
Fast, fast, my wild-eyed Rosalind,
And clip your wings, and make you love:
When we have lured you from above,
And that delight of frolic flight, by day or night,
From North to South;
We'll bind you fast in silken cords,
And kiss away the bitter words
From off your rosy mouth.

A Dream of Fair Women

I read, before my eyelids dropt their shade,
    '*The Legend of Good Women*,' long ago
Sung by the morning star of song, who made
    His music heard below;

Dan Chaucer, the first warbler, whose sweet breath
    Preluded those melodious bursts that fill
The spacious times of great Elizabeth
    With sounds that echo still.

And, for a while, the knowledge of his art
    Held me above the subject, as strong gales
Hold swollen clouds from raining, tho' my heart,
    Brimful of those wild tales,

Charged both mine eyes with tears. In every land
    I saw, wherever light illumineth,
Beauty and anguish walking hand in hand
    The downward slope to death

Those far-renowned brides of ancient song
    Peopled the hollow dark, like burning stars,
And I heard sounds of insult, shame, and wrong,
    And trumpets blown for wars;

And clattering flints batter'd with clanging hoofs:
    And I saw crowds in column'd sanctuaries;
And forms that pass'd at windows and on roofs
    Of marble palaces;

Corpses across the threshold; heroes tall
    Dislodging pinnacle and parapet
Upon the tortoise creeping to the wall;
    Lances in ambush set;

And high shrine-doors burst thro' with heated blasts
    That run before the fluttering tongues of fire;
White surf wind-scatter'd over sails and masts,
       And ever climbing higher;

Squadrons and squares of men in brazen plates,
    Scaffolds, still sheets of water, divers woes,
Ranges of glimmering vaults with iron grates,
       And hush'd seraglios.

So shape chased shape as swift as, when to land
    Bluster the winds and tides the self-same way,
Crisp foam-flakes scud along the level sand,
       Torn from the fringe of spray.

I started once, or seem'd to start in pain,
    Resolved on noble things, and strove to speak,
As when a great thought strikes along the brain,
       And flushes all the cheek.

And once my arm was lifted to hew down
    A cavalier from off his saddle-bow,
That bore a lady from a leaguer'd town;
       And then, I know not how,

All those sharp fancies, by down-lapsing thought
    Stream'd onward, lost their edges, and did creep
Roll'd on each other, rounded, smooth'd, and brought
       Into the gulfs of sleep.

At last methought that I had wander'd far
    In an old wood: fresh-wash'd in coolest dew,
The maiden splendours of the morning star
       Shook in the steadfast blue.

Enormous elm-tree-boles did stoop and lean
    Upon the dusky brushwood underneath
Their broad curved branches, fledged with clearest green,
       New from its silken sheath.

The dim red morn had died, her journey done,
    And with dead lips smiled at the twilight plain,
Half-fall'n across the threshold of the sun,
       Never to rise again.

There was no motion in the dumb dead air,
    Not any song of bird or sound of rill;
Gross darkness of the inner sepulchre
       Is not so deadly still

As that wide forest. Growths of jasmine turn'd
 Their humid arms festooning tree to tree,
And at the root thro' lush green grasses burn'd
  The red anemone.

I knew the flowers, I knew the leaves, I knew
 The tearful glimmer of the languid dawn
On those long, rank, dark wood-walks drench'd in dew,
 Leading from lawn to lawn.

The smell of violets, hidden in the green,
 Pour'd back into my empty soul and frame
The times when I remember to have been
 Joyful and free from blame.

And from within me a clear under-tone
 Thrill'd thro' mine ears in that unblissful clime,
'Pass freely thro': the wood is all thine own,
 Until the end of time.'

At length I saw a lady with call,
 Stiller than chisell'd marble, standing there;
A daughter of the gods, divinely tall,
 And most divinely fair.

Her loveliness with shame and with surprise
 Froze my swift speech: she turning on my face
The star-like sorrows of immortal eyes,
 Spoke slowly in her place.

'I had great beauty: ask thou not my name:
 No one can be more wise than destiny.
Many drew swords and died. Where'er I came
 I brought calamity.'

'No marvel, sovereign lady: in fair field
 Myself for such a face had boldly died,'
I answer'd free; and turning I appeal'd
 To one that stood beside.

But she, with sick and scornful looks averse,
 To her full height her stately stature draws;
'My youth,' she said, 'was blasted with a curse:
 This woman was the cause.

'I was cut off from hope in that sad place,
 Which yet to name my spirit loathes and fears:
My father held his hand upon his face;
 I, blinded with my tears,

'Still strove to speak: my voice was thick with sighs
    As in a dream. Dimly I could descry
The stern black-bearded kings with wolfish eyes,
    Waiting to see me die.

'The high masts flicker'd as they lay afloat;
    The crowds, the temples, waver'd, and the shore;
The bright death quiver'd at the victim's throat;
    Touch'd; and I knew no more.'

Whereto the other with a downward brow:
    'I would the white cold heavy-plunging foam,
Whirl'd by the wind, had roll'd me deep below,
    Then when I left my home.'

Her slow full words sank thro' the silence drear,
    As thunder-drops fall on a sleeping sea:
Sudden I heard a voice that cried, 'Come here,
    That I may look on thee.'

I turning saw, throned on a flowery rise,
    One sitting on a crimson scarf unroll'd;
A queen, with swarthy cheeks and bold black eyes,
    Brow-bound with burning gold.

She, flashing forth a haughty smile, began:
    'I govern'd men by change, and so I sway'd
All moods. 'Tis long since I have seen a man.
    Once, like the moon, I made

'The ever-shifting currents of the blood
    According to my humour ebb and flow.
I have no men to govern in this wood:
    That makes my only woe.

'Nay – yet it chafes me that I could not bend
    One will; nor tame and tutor with mine eye
That dull cold-blooded Caesar. Prythee, friend,
    Where is Mark Antony?

'The man, my lover, with whom I rode sublime
    On Fortune's neck: we sat as God by God:
The Nilus would have risen before his time
    And flooded at our nod.

'We drank the Libyan Sun to sleep, and lit
    Lamps which outburn'd Canopus. O my life
In Egypt! O the dalliance and the wit,
    The flattery and the strife,

'And the wild kiss, when fresh from war's alarms.
    My Hercules, my Roman Antony,
My mailed Bacchus leapt into my arms,
    Contented there to die!

'And there he died: and when I heard my name
    Sigh'd forth with life I would not brook my fear
Of the other: with a worm I balk'd his fame.
    What else was left? look here!'

(With that she tore her robe apart, and half
    The polish'd argent of her breast to sight
Laid bare. Thereto she pointed with a laugh,
    Showing the aspick's bite.)

'I died a Queen. The Roman soldier found
    Me lying dead, my crown about my brows,
A name for ever! – lying robed and crown'd,
    Worthy a Roman spouse.'

Her warbling voice, a lyre of widest range
    Struck by all passion, did fall down and glance
From tone to tone, and glided thro' all change
    Of liveliest utterance.

When she made pause I knew not for delight;
    Because with sudden motion from the ground
She raised her piercing orbs, and fill'd with light
    The interval of sound.

Still with their fires Love tipt his keenest darts;
    As once they drew into two burning rings
All beams of Love, melting the mighty hearts
    Of captains and of kings.

Slowly my sense undazzled. Then I heard
    A noise of some one coming thro' the lawn,
And singing clearer than the crested bird,
    That claps his wings at dawn.

'The torrent brooks of hallow'd Israel
    From craggy hollows pouring, late and soon,
Sound all night long, in falling thro' the dell,
    Far-heard beneath the moon.

'The balmy moon of blessed Israel
    Floods all the deep-blue gloom with beams divine:
All night the splinter'd crags that wall the dell
    With spires of silver shine.'

As one that museth where broad sunshine laves
    The lawn by some cathedral, thro' the door
Hearing the holy organ rolling waves
    Of sound on roof and floor

Within, and anthem sung, is charm'd and tied
    To where he stands, – so stood I, when that flow
Of music left the lips of her that died
    To save her father's vow;

The daughter of the warrior Gileadite,
    A maiden pure; as when she went along
From Mizpeh's tower'd gate with welcome light,
    With timbrel and with song.

My words leapt forth: 'Heaven heads the count of crimes
    With that wild oath.' She render'd answer high:
'Not so, nor once alone; a thousand times
    I would be born and die.

'Single I grew, like some green plant, whose root
    Creeps to the garden water-pipes beneath,
Feeding the flower; but ere my flower to fruit
    Changed, I was ripe for death.

'My God, my land, my father – these did move
    Me from my bliss of life, that Nature gave,
Lower'd softly with a threefold cord of love
    Down to a silent grave.

'And I went mourning, "No fair Hebrew boy
    Shall smile away my maiden blame among
The Hebrew mothers" – emptied of all joy,
    Leaving the dance and song,

'Leaving the olive-gardens far below,
    Leaving the promise of my bridal bower,
The valleys of grape-loaded vines that glow
    Beneath the battled tower.

'The light white cloud swam over us. Anon
    We heard the lion roaring from his den;
We saw the large white stars rise one by one,
    Or, from the darken'd glen,

'Saw God divide the night with flying flame,
    And thunder on the everlasting hills.
I heard Him, for He spake, and grief became
    A solemn scorn of ills.

'When the next moon was roll'd into the sky,
        Strength came to me that equall'd my desire.
How beautiful a thing it was to die
        For God and for my sire!

'It comforts me in this one thought to dwell,
        That I subdued me to my father's will;
Because the kiss he gave me, ere I fell,
        Sweetens the spirit still.

'Moreover it is written that my race
        Hew'd Ammon, hip and thigh, from Aroer
On Arnon unto Minneth.' Here her face
        Glow'd, as I look'd at her.

She lock'd her lips: she left me where I stood:
        'Glory to God,' she sang, and past afar,
Thridding the sombre boskage of the wood,
        Toward the morning-star.

Losing her carol I stood pensively,
        As one that from a casement leans his head,
When midnight bells cease ringing suddenly,
        And the old year is dead.

'Alas! alas!' a low voice, full of care
        Murmur'd beside me: 'Turn and look on me:
I am that Rosamond, whom men call fair,
        If what I was I be.

'Would I had been some maiden coarse and poor!
        O me, that I should ever see the light!
Those dragon eyes of anger'd Eleänor
        Do hunt me, day and night.'

She ceased in tears, fallen from hope and trust:
        To whom the Egyptian: 'O, you tamely died!
You should have clung to Fulvia's waist, and thrust
        The dagger thro' her side.'

With that sharp sound the white dawn's creeping beams,
        Stol'n to my brain, dissolved the mystery
Of folded sleep. The captain of my dreams
        Ruled in the eastern sky.

Morn broaden'd on the borders of the dark,
        Ere I saw her, who clasp'd in her last trance
Her murder'd father's head, or Joan of Arc,
        A light of ancient France;

Or her, who knew that Love can vanquish Death,
    Who kneeling, with one arm about her king,
Drew forth the poison with her balmy breath,
    Sweet as new buds in Spring.

No memory labours longer from the deep
    Gold-mines of thought to lift the hidden ore
That glimpses, moving up, than I from sleep
    To gather and tell o'er

Each little sound and sight. With what dull pain
    Compass'd, how eagerly I sought to strike
Into that wondrous track of dreams again!
    But no two dreams are like.

As when a soul laments, which hath been blest,
    Desiring what is mingled with past years,
In yearnings that can never be exprest
    By signs or groans or tears;

Because all words, tho' cull'd with choicest art,
    Failing to give the bitter of the sweet
Wither beneath the palate, and the heart
    Faints, faded by its heat.

Margaret

I

O sweet pale Margaret,
O rare pale Margaret,
What lit your eyes with tearful power,
Like moonlight on a falling shower?
Who lent you, love, your mortal dower
    Of pensive thought and aspect pale,
    Your melancholy sweet and frail
As perfume of the cuckoo-flower?
From the westward-winding flood,
From the evening-lighted wood,
    From all things outward you have won
A tearful grace, as tho' you stood
    Between the rainbow and the sun.
The very smile before you speak,
That dimples your transparent cheek,
    Encircles all the heart, and feedeth
The senses with a still delight

Of dainty sorrow without sound,
Like the tender amber round,
Which the moon about her spreadeth,
Moving thro' a fleecy night.

II

You love, remaining peacefully,
To hear the murmur of the strife,
But enter not the toil of life.
Your spirit is the calmed sea,
Laid by the tumult of the fight.
You are the evening star, alway
Remaining betwixt dark and bright:
Lull'd echoes of laborious day
Come to you, gleams of mellow light
Float by you on the verge of night.

III

What can it matter, Margaret
What songs below the waning stars
The lion-heart, Plantagenet,
Sang looking thro' his prison bars?
Exquisite Margaret, who can tell
The last wild thought of Chatelet,
Just ere the falling axe did part
The burning brain from the true heart,
Even in her sight he loved so well?

IV

A fairy shield your Genius made
And gave you on your natal day.
Your sorrow, only sorrow's shade,
Keeps real sorrow far away.
You move not in such solitudes,
You are not less divine,
But more human in your moods,
Than your twin-sister, Adeline.
Your hair is darker, and your eyes
Touch'd with a somewhat darker hue,
And less aërially blue
But ever trembling thro' the dew
Of dainty-woeful sympathies.

V

O sweet pale Margaret,
O rare pale Margaret,
Come down, come down, and hear me speak:
Tie up the ringlets on your cheek:

The sun is just about to set,
The arching limes are tall and shady,
    And faint, rainy lights are seen,
        Moving in the leavy beech.
Rise from the feast of sorrow, lady,
        Where all day long you sit between
            Joy and woe, and whisper each.
Or only look across the lawn,
    Look out below your bower-eaves,
Look down, and let your blue eyes dawn
    Upon me thro' the jasmine-leaves.

Kate

I know her by her angry air,
Her bright black eyes, her bright black hair,
    Her rapid laughters wild and shrill,
As laughter of the woodpecker
    From the bosom of a hill.
    'Tis Kate – she sayeth what she will:
For Kate hath an unbridled tongue,
    Clear as the twanging of a harp.
        Her heart is like a throbbing star.
Kate hath a spirit ever strung
        Like a new bow, and bright and sharp
            As edges of the scymetar.
Whence shall she take a fitting mate?
    For Kate no common love will feel;
My woman-soldier, gallant Kate,
    As pure and true as blades of steel.

Kate saith 'the world is void of might.'
        Kate saith 'the men are gilded flies.'
            Kate snaps her fingers at my vows;
        Kate will not hear of lover's sighs.
I would I were an armèd knight,
        Far-famed for well-won enterprise,
            And wearing on my swarthy brows
        The garland of new-wreathed emprise
            For in a moment I would pierce
The blackest files of clanging fight,
And strongly strike to left and right,
    In dreaming of my lady's eyes.
        Oh! Kate loves well the bold and fierce;
    But none are bold enough for Kate,
    She cannot find a fitting mate.

Sonnet
on the result of the late Russian invasion of Poland

How long, O God, shall men be ridden down,
And trampled under by the last and least
Of men? The heart of Poland hath not ceased
To quiver, though her sacred blood doth drown
The fields; and out of every smouldering town
Cries to Thee, lest brute Power be increased,
Till that o'ergrown Barbarian in the East
Transgress his ample bound to some new crown: —
Cries to Thee, 'Lord, how long shall these things be?
How long shall the icy-hearted Muscovite
Oppress the region?' Us, O Just and Good,
Forgive, who smiled when she was torn in three;
Us, who stand *now,* when we should aid the right —
A matter to be wept with tears of blood!

Sonnet

As when with downcast eyes we muse and brood,
And ebb into a former life, or seem
To lapse far back in a confused dream
To states of mystical similitude;
If one but speaks or hems or stirs his chair,
Ever the wonder waxeth more and more,
So that we say, 'All this hath been before,
All this *hath* been, I know not when or where.'
So, friend, when first I look'd upon your face,
Our thought gave answer, each to each, so true,
Opposed mirrors each reflecting each —
Altho' I knew not in what time or place,
Methought that I had often met with you,
And each had lived in the other's mind and speech.

The Death of the Old Year

Full knee-deep lies the winter snow,
And the winter winds are wearily sighing:
Toll ye the church-bell sad and slow,
And tread softly and speak low,
For the old year lies a-dying.
　　　Old year, you must not die;
　　　You came to us so readily,
　　　You lived with us so steadily,
　　　Old year, you shall not die.

He lieth still: he doth not move:
He will not see the dawn of day.
He hath no other life above.
He gave me a friend, and a true true-love,
And the New-year will take 'em away.
> Old year, you must not go;
> O long as you have been with us,
> Such joy as you have seen with us,
> Old year, you shall not go.

He froth'd his bumpers to the brim;
A jollier year we shall not see.
But tho' his eyes are waxing dim,
And tho' his foes speak ill of him,
He was a friend to me.
> Old year, you shall not die;
> We did so laugh and cry with you,
> I've half a mind to die with you,
> Old year, if you must die.

He was full of joke and jest,
But all his merry quips are o'er.
To see him die, across the waste
His son and heir doth ride post-haste,
But he'll be dead before.
> Every one for his own.
> The night is starry and cold, my friend,
> And the New-year blithe and bold, my friend,
> Comes up to take his own.

How hard he breathes! over the snow
I heard just now the crowing cock.
The shadows flicker to and fro:
The cricket chirps: the light burns low:
'Tis nearly twelve o'clock.
> Shake hands, before you die.
> Old year, we'll dearly rue for you:
> What is it we can do for you?
> Speak out before you die.

His face is growing sharp and thin.
Alack! our friend is gone.
Close up his eyes: tie up his chin:
Step from the corpse, and let him in
That standeth there alone,
> And waiteth at the door.
> There's a new foot on the floor, my friend,
> And a new face at the door, my friend,
> A new face at the door.

To J. S.

The wind, that beats the mountain, blows
    More softly round the open wold,
And gently comes the world to those
    That are cast in gentle mould.

And me this knowledge bolder made,
    Or else I had not dared to flow
In these words toward you, and invade
    Even with a verse your holy woe.

'Tis strange that those we lean on most,
    Those in whose laps our limbs are nursed,
Fall into shadow, soonest lost:
    Those we love first are taken first.

God gives us love. Something to love
    He lends us; but, when love is grown
To ripeness, that on which it throve
    Falls off, and love is left alone.

This is the curse of time. Alas!
    In grief I am not all unlearn'd:
Once thro' mine own doors Death did pass;
    One went, who never hath return'd.

He will not smile – not speak to me
    Once more. Two years his chair is seen
Empty before us. That was he
    Without whose life I had not been.

Your loss is rarer; for this star
    Rose with you thro' a little arc
Of heaven, nor having wander'd far
    Shot on the sudden into dark.

I knew your brother: his mute dust
    I honour and his living worth:
A man more pure and bold and just
    Was never born into the earth.

I have not look'd upon you nigh,
    Since that dear soul hath fall'n asleep.
Great Nature is more wise than I:
    I will not tell you not to weep.

And tho' mine own eyes fill with dew,
    Drawn from the spirit thro' the brain,
I will not even preach to you,
    'Weep, weeping dulls the inward pain.'

Let Grief be her own mistress still.
        She loveth her own anguish deep
More than much pleasure. Let her will
        Be done — to weep or not to weep.

I will not say 'God's ordinance
        Of Death is blown in every wind;'
For that is not a common chance
        That takes away a noble mind.

His memory long, will live alone
        In all our hearts, as mournful light
That broods above the fallen sun,
        And dwells in heaven half the night.

Vain solace! Memory standing near
        Cast down her eyes, and in her throat
Her voice seem'd distant, and a tear
        Dropt on the letters as I wrote.

I wrote I know not what. In truth,
        How *should* I soothe you anyway,
Who miss the brother of your youth?
        Yet something I did wish to say:

For he too was a friend to me:
        Both are my friends, and my true breast
Bleedeth for both; yet it may be
        That only silence suiteth best.

Words weaker than your grief would make
        Grief more.'Twere better I should cease;
Although myself could almost take
        The place of him that sleeps in peace.

Sleep sweetly, tender heart, in peace:
        Sleep, holy spirit, blessed soul,
While the stars burn, the moons increase,
        And the great ages onward roll.

Sleep till the end, true soul and sweet.
        Nothing comes to thee new or strange.
Sleep full of rest from head to feet;
        Lie still, dry dust, secure of change.

St Agnes' Eve

Deep on the convent-roof the snows
   Are sparkling to the moon:
My breath to heaven like vapour goes:
   May my soul follow soon!
The shadows of the convent-towers
   Slant down the snowy sward,
Still creeping with the creeping hours
   That lead me to my Lord:
Make Thou my spirit pure and clear
   As are the frosty skies,
Or this first snowdrop of the year
   That in my bosom lies.

As these white robes are soil'd and dark,
   To yonder shining ground;
As this pale taper's earthly spark,
   To yonder argent round;
So shows my soul before the Lamb,
   My spirit before Thee;
So in mine earthly house I am,
   To that I hope to be.
Break up the heavens, O Lord! and far,
   Thro' all yon starlight keen,
Draw me, thy bride, a glittering star,
   In raiment white and clean.

He lifts me to the golden doors;
   The flashes come and go;
All heaven bursts her starry floors,
   And strows her lights below,
And deepens on and up! the gates
   Roll back, and far within
For me the Heavenly Bridegroom waits,
   To make me pure of sin.
The sabbaths of Eternity,
   One sabbath deep and wide –
A light upon the shining sea –
   The Bridegroom with his bride!

POEMS

Lady Clara Vere de Vere

Lady Clara Vere de Vere,
    Of me you shall not win renown:
You thought to break a country heart
    For pastime, ere you went to town.
At me you smiled, but unbeguiled
    I saw the snare, and I retired:
The daughter of a hundred Earls,
    You are not one to be desired.

Lady Clara Vere de Vere,
    I know you proud to bear your name,
Your pride is yet no mate for mine,
    Too proud to care from whence I came.
Nor would I break for your sweet sake
    A heart that doats on truer charms.
A simple maiden in her flower
    Is worth a hundred coats-of-arms.

Lady Clara Vere de Vere,
    Some meeker pupil you must find,
For were you queen of all that is,
    I could not stoop to such a mind.
You sought to prove how I could love,
    And my disdain is my reply.
The lion on your old stone gates
    Is not more cold to you than I.

Lady Clara Vere de Vere,
    You put strange memories in my head.
Not thrice your branching limes have blown
    Since I beheld young Laurence dead.
Oh your sweet eyes, your low replies:
    A great enchantress you may be;
But there was that across his throat
    Which you had hardly cared to see.

Lady Clara Vere de Vere,
    When thus he met his mother's view,
She had the passions of her kind,

She spake some certain truths of you.
Indeed I heard one bitter word
    That scarce is fit for you to hear;
Her manners had not that repose
    Which stamps the caste of Vere de Vere.

Lady Clara Vere de Vere,
    There stands a spectre in your hall:
The guilt of blood is at your door:
    You changed a wholesome heart to gall.
You held your course without remorse,
    To make him trust his modest worth,
And, last, you fix'd a vacant stare,
    And slew him with your noble birth.

Trust me, Clara Vere de Vere,
    From yon blue heavens above us bent
The grand old gardener and his wife
    Smile at the claims of long descent.
Howe'er it be, it seems to me,
    'Tis only noble to be good.
Kind hearts are more than coronets,
    And simple faith than Norman blood.

I know you, Clara Vere de Vere:
    You pine among your halls and towers:
The languid light of your proud eyes
    Is wearied of the rolling hours.
In glowing health, with boundless wealth,
    But sickening of a vague disease,
You know so ill to deal with time,
    You needs must play such pranks as these.

Clara, Clara Vere de Vere,
    If time be heavy on your hands,
Are there no beggars at your gate,
    Nor any poor about your lands?
Oh! teach the orphan-boy to read,
    Or teach the orphan-girl to sew,
Pray Heaven for a human heart,
    And let the foolish yeoman go.

The Blackbird

O Blackbird! sing me something well:
   While all the neighbours shoot thee round,
   I keep smooth plats of fruitful ground,
Where thou may'st warble, eat and dwell.

The espaliers and the standards all
   Are thine; the range of lawn and park:
   The unnetted black-hearts ripen dark,
All thine, against the garden wall.

Yet, tho' I spared thee all the spring,
   Thy sole delight is, sitting still,
   With that gold dagger of thy bill
To fret the summer jenneting.

A golden bill! the silver tongue,
   Cold February loved, is dry:
   Plenty corrupts the melody
That made thee famous once, when young:

And in the sultry garden-squares,
   Now thy flute-notes are changed to coarse,
   I hear thee not at all, or hoarse
As when a hawker hawks his wares.

Take warning! he that will not sing
   While yon sun prospers in the blue,
   Shall sing for want, ere leaves are new,
Caught in the frozen palms of Spring.

You ask Me, Why, tho' Ill at Ease

You ask me, why, tho' ill at ease,
   Within this region I subsist,
   Whose spirits falter in the mist,
And languish for the purple seas.

It is the land that freemen till,
   That sober-suited Freedom chose,
   The land, where girt with friends or foes
A man may speak the thing he will;

A land of settled government,
   A land of just and old renown,
   Where Freedom broadens slowly down
From precedent to precedent:

Where faction seldom gathers head,
    But by degrees to fullness wrought,
    The strength of some diffusive thought
Hath time and space to work and spread.

Should banded unions persecute
    Opinion, and induce a time
    When single thought is civil crime,
And individual freedom mute;

Tho' Power should make from land to land
    The name of Britain trebly great –
    Tho' every channel of the State
Should fill and choke with golden sand –

Yet waft me from the harbour-mouth,
    Wild wind! I seek a warmer sky,
    And I will see before I die
The palms and temples of the South.

Of Old sat Freedom on the Heights

Of old sat Freedom on the heights,
    The thunders breaking at her feet:
Above her shook the starry lights:
    She heard the torrents meet.

There in her place she did rejoice,
    Self-gather'd in her prophet-mind,
But fragments of her mighty voice
    Came rolling on the wind.

Then stept she down thro' town and field
    To mingle with the human race,
And part by part to men reveal'd
    The fullness of her face –

Grave mother of majestic works,
    From her isle-altar gazing down,
Who, God-like, grasps the triple forks,
    And, King-like, wears the crown:

Her open eyes desire the truth.
    The wisdom of a thousand years
Is in them. May perpetual youth
    Keep dry their light from tears;

That her fair form may stand and shine,
   Make bright our days and light our dreams,
Turning to scorn with lips divine
   The falsehood of extremes!

Love Thou thy Land, with Love far Brought

Love thou thy land, with love far-brought
   From out the storied Past, and used
   Within the Present, but transfused
Thro' future time by power of thought.

True love turn'd round on fixed poles,
   Love, that endures not sordid ends,
   For English natures, freemen, friends,
Thy brothers and immortal souls.

But pamper not a hasty time,
   Nor feed with crude imaginings
   The herd, wild hearts and feeble wings,
That every sophister can lime.

Deliver not the tasks of might
   To weakness, neither hide the ray
   From those, not blind, who wait for day,
Tho' sitting girt with doubtful light.

Make knowledge circle with the winds;
   But let her herald, Reverence, fly
   Before her to whatever sky
Bear seed of men and growth of minds.

Watch what main-currents draw the years:
   Cut Prejudice against the grain:
   But gentle words are always gain:
Regard the weakness of thy peers:

Nor toil for title, place, or touch
   Of pension, neither count on praise:
   It grows to guerdon after-days:
Nor deal in watch-words overmuch;

Not clinging to some ancient saw;
   Not master'd by some modern term;
   Not swift nor slow to change, but firm
And in its season bring the law;

That from Discussion's lip may fall
    With Life, that, working strongly, binds –
    Set in all lights by many minds,
To close the interests of all.

For Nature also, cold and warm,
    And moist and dry, devising long,
    Thro' many agents making strong,
Matures the individual form.

Meet is it changes should control
    Our being, lest we rust in ease.
    We all are changed by still degrees
All but the basis of the soul.

So let the change which comes be free
    To ingroove itself with that which flies,
    And work, a joint of state, that plies
Its office, moved with sympathy.

A saying, hard to shape in act;
    For all the past of Time reveals
    A bridal dawn of thunder-peals,
Wherever Thought hath wedded Fact.

Ev'n now we hear with inward strife
    A motion toiling in the gloom –
    The Spirit of the years to come
Yearning to mix himself with Life.

A slow-develop'd strength awaits
    Completion in a painful school;
    Phantoms of other forms of rule,
New Majesties of mighty States –

The warders of the growing hour,
    But vague in vapour, hard to mark;
    And round them sea and air are dark
With great contrivances of Power.

Of many changes, aptly join'd,
    Is bodied forth the second whole.
    Regard gradation, lest the soul
Of Discord race the rising wind;

A wind to puff your idol-fires,
    And heap their ashes on the head;
    To shame the boast so often made,
That we are wiser than our sires.

Oh yet, if Nature's evil star
   Drive men in manhood, as in youth,
   To follow flying steps of Truth
Across the brazen bridge of war —

If New and Old, disastrous feud,
   Must ever shock, like armed foes,
   And this be true, till Time shall close
That Principles are rain'd in blood;

Not yet the wise of heart would cease
   To hold his hope thro' shame and guilt,
   But with his hand against the hilt,
Would pace the troubled land, like Peace;

Not less, tho' dogs of Faction bay,
   Would serve his kind in deed and word,
   Certain, if knowledge bring the sword,
That knowledge takes the sword away —

Would love the gleams of good that broke
   From either side, nor veil his eyes
   And if some dreadful need should rise
Would strike, and firmly, and one stroke:

To-morrow yet would reap to-day,
   As we bear blossom of the dead;
   Earn well the thrifty months, nor wed
Raw Haste, half-sister to Delay.

The Goose

I knew an old wife lean and poor,
   Her rags scarce held together;
There strode a stranger to the door,
   And it was windy weather.

He held a goose upon his arm,
   He utter'd rhyme and reason,
'Here, take the goose, and keep you warm,
   It is a stormy season.'

She caught the white goose by the leg,
   A goose — 'twas no great matter.
The goose let fall a golden egg
   With cackle and with clatter.

She dropt the goose, and caught the pelf,
 And ran to tell her neighbours;
And bless'd herself, and cursed herself
 And rested from her labours.

And feeding high, and living soft,
 Grew plump and able-bodied;
Until the grave churchwarden doff'd,
 The parson smirk'd and nodded.

So sitting, served by man and maid,
 She felt her heart grow prouder:
But ah! the more the white goose laid
 It clack'd and cackled louder.

It clutter'd here, it chuckled there;
 It stirr'd the old wife's mettle:
She shifted in her elbow-chair,
 And hurl'd the pan and kettle.

'A quinsy choke thy cursed note!'
 Then wax'd her anger stronger.
'Go, take the goose, and wring her throat,
 I will not bear it longer.'

Then yelp'd the cur, and yawl'd the cat;
 Ran Gaffer, stumbled Gammer.
The goose flew this way and flew that,
 And fill'd the house with clamour.

As head and heels upon the floor
 They flounder'd all together,
There strode a stranger to the door
 And it was windy weather:

He took the goose upon his arm,
 He utter'd words of scorning;
'So keep you cold, or keep you warm,
 It is a stormy morning.'

The wild wind rang from park and plain,
 And round the attics rumbled,
Till all the tables danced again,
 And half the chimneys tumbled.

The glass blew in, the fire blew out,
 The blast was hard and harder.
Her cap blew off, her gown blew up,
 And a whirlwind clear'd the larder;

And while on all sides breaking loose
   Her household fled the danger,
Quoth she, 'The Devil take the goose,
   And God forget the stranger!'

The Epic

At Francis Allen's on the Christmas-eve –
The game of forfeits done – the girls all kiss'd
Beneath the sacred bush and past away –
The parson Holmes, the poet Everard Hall,
The host, and I sat round the wassail-bowl,
Then half-way ebb'd: and there we held a talk,
How all the old honour had from Christmas gone,
Or gone, or dwindled down to some odd games
In some odd nooks like this; till I, tired out
With cutting eights that day upon the pond,
Where, three times slipping from the outer edge,
I bump'd the ice into three several stars,
Fell in a doze; and half-awake I heard
The parson taking wide and wider sweeps,
Now harping on the church-commissioners,
Now hawking at Geology and schism;
Until I woke, and found him settled down
Upon the general decay of faith
Right thro' the world, 'at home was little left,
And none abroad: there was no anchor, none,
To hold by.' Francis, laughing, clapt his hand
On Everard's shoulder, with 'I hold by him.'
'And I,' quoth Everard, 'by the wassail-bowl.'
'Why yes,' I said, 'we knew your gift that way
At college: but another which you had,
I mean of verse (for so we held it then),
What came of that?' 'You know,' said Frank, 'he burnt
His epic, his King Arthur, some twelve books'–
And then to me demanding why? 'Oh, sir,
He thought that nothing new was said, or else
Something so said 'twas nothing – that a truth
Looks freshest in the fashion of the day:
God knows: he has a mint of reasons: ask.
It pleased me well enough.' 'Nay, nay,' said Hall,
'Why take the style of those heroic times?
For nature brings not back the Mastodon,
Nor we those times; and why should any man
Remodel models? these twelve books of mine

Were faint Homeric echoes, nothing-worth,
Mere chaff and draff, much better burnt.' 'But I,'
Said Francis, 'pick'd the eleventh from this hearth,
And have it: keep a thing, its use will come.
I hoard it as a sugar-plum for Holmes.'
He laugh'd, and I, though sleepy, like a horse
That hears the corn-bin open, prick'd my ears;
For I remember'd Everard's college fame
When we were Freshmen: then at my request
He brought it; and the poet little urged,
But with some prelude of disparagement,
Read, mouthing out his hollow oes and aes,
Deep-chested music, and to this result.

Morte d'Arthur

So all day long the noise of battle roll'd
Among the mountains by the winter sea;
Until King Arthur's table, man by man,
Had fall'n in Lyonnesse about their Lord,
King Arthur: then, because his wound was deep,
The bold Sir Bedivere uplifted him,
Sir Bedivere, the last of all his knights,
And bore him to a chapel nigh the field,
A broken chancel with a broken cross,
That stood on a dark strait of barren land.
On one side lay the Ocean, and on one
Lay a great water, and the moon was full.
   Then spake King Arthur to Sir Bedivere:
'The sequel of to-day unsolders all
The goodliest fellowship of famous knights
Whereof this world holds record. Such a sleep
They sleep — the men I loved. I think that we
Shall never more, at any future time,
Delight our souls with talk of knightly deeds,
Walking about the gardens and the halls
Of Camelot, as in the days that were.
I perish by this people which I made, —
Tho' Merlin sware that I should come again
To rule once more — but let what will be, be,
I am so deeply smitten thro' the helm
That without help I cannot last till morn.
Thou therefore take my brand Excalibur,
Which was my pride: for thou rememberest how
In those old days, one summer noon, an arm

Rose up from out the bosom of the lake,
Clothed in white samite, mystic, wonderful,
Holding the sword – and how I row'd across
And took it, and have worn it, like a king:
And, wheresoever I am sung or told
In aftertime this also shall be known:
But now delay not: take Excalibur,
And fling him far into the middle mere:
Watch what thou seëst, and lightly bring me word.'

   To him replied the bold Sir Bedivere:
'It is not meet, Sir King, to leave thee thus,
Aidless, alone, and smitten thro' the helm.
A little thing may harm a wounded man.
Yet I thy hest will all perform at full,
Watch what I see, and lightly bring thee wold.'

   So saying, from the ruin'd shrine he stept
And in the moon athwart the place of tombs,
Where lay the mighty bones of ancient men,
Old knights, and over them the sea-wind sang
Shrill, chill, with flakes of foam. He, stepping down
By zig-zag paths, and juts of pointed rock,
Came on the shining levels of the lake.

   There drew he forth the brand Excalibur,
And o'er him, drawing it, the winter moon,
Brightening the skirts of a long cloud, ran forth
And sparkled keen with frost against the hilt:
For all the haft twinkled with diamond sparks,
Myriads of topaz-lights, and jacinth-work
Of subtlest jewellery. He gazed so long
That both his eyes were dazzled, as he stood,
This way and that dividing the swift mind,
In act to throw: but at the last it seem'd
Better to leave Excalibur conceal'd
There in the many-knotted waterflags,
That whistled stiff and dry about the marge.
So strode he back slow to the wounded King.

   Then spake King Arthur to Sir Bedivere:
'Hast thou perform'd my mission which I gave?
What is it thou hast seen? or what hast heard?'

   And answer made the bold Sir Bedivere:
'I heard the ripple washing in the reeds,
And the wild water lapping on the crag.'

   To whom replied King Arthur, faint and pale:
'Thou hast betray'd thy nature and thy name,
Not rendering true answer, as beseem'd
Thy fëalty, nor like a noble knight:

For surer sign had follow'd, either hand,
Or voice, or else a motion of the mere.
This is a shameful thing for men to lie.
Yet now, I charge thee, quickly go again
As thou art lief and dear, and do the thing
I bad thee, watch, and lightly bring me word.'

   Then went Sir Bedivere the second time
Across the ridge, and paced beside the mere,
Counting the dewy pebbles, fix'd in thought;
But when he saw the wonder of the hilt,
How curiously and strangely chased, he smote
His palms together, and he cried aloud,

   'And if indeed I cast the brand away,
Surely a precious thing, one worthy note,
Should thus be lost for ever from the earth,
Which might have pleased the eyes of many men.
What good should follow this, if this were done?
What harm, undone? deep harm to disobey,
Seeing obedience is the bond of rule.
Were it well to obey then, if a king demand
An act unprofitable, against himself?
The King is sick, and knows not what he does.
What record, or what relic of my lord
Should be to aftertime, but empty breath
And rumours of a doubt? but were this kept,
Stored in some treasure-house of mighty kings,
Some one might show it at a joust of arms,
Saying, "King Arthur's sword, Excalibur
Wrought by the lonely maiden of the Lake.
Nine years she wrought it, sitting in the deeps
Upon the hidden bases of the hills."
So might some old man speak in the aftertime
To all the people, winning reverence.
But now much honour and much fame were lost.'

   So spake he, clouded with his own conceit,
And hid Excalibur the second time,
And so strode back slow to the wounded King.

   Then spoke King Arthur, breathing heavily:
'What is it thou hast seen? or what hast heard?

   And answer made the bold Sir Bedivere:
'I heard the water lapping on the crag,
And the long ripple washing in the reeds.'

   To whom replied King Arthur, much in wrath:
'Ah, miserable and unkind, untrue,
Unknightly, traitor-hearted! Woe is me!
Authority forgets a dying king,

Laid widow'd of the power in his eye
That bow'd the will. I see thee what thou art,
For thou, the latest-left of all my knights,
In whom should meet the offices of all,
Thou wouldst betray me for the precious hilt;
Either from lust of gold, or like a girl
Valuing the giddy pleasure of the eyes.
Yet, for a man may fail in duty twice,
And the third time may prosper, get thee hence:
But, if thou spare to fling Excalibur,
I will arise and slay thee with my hands.'

    Then quickly rose Sir Bedivere, and ran,
And, leaping down the ridges lightly, plunged
Among the bulrush-beds, and clutch'd the sword,
And strongly wheel'd and threw it. The great brand
Made lightnings in the splendour of the moon,
And flashing round and round, and whirl'd in an arch,
Shot like a streamer of the northern morn,
Seen where the moving isles of winter shock
By night, with noises of the northern sea.
So flash'd and fell the brand Excalibur:
But ere he dipt the surface, rose an arm
Clothed in white samite, mystic, wonderful
And caught him by the hilt, and brandish'd him
Three times, and drew him under in the mere.
And lightly went the other to the King.

    Then spoke King Arthur, drawing thicker breath:
'Now see I by thine eyes that this is done.
Speak out: what is it thou hast heard, or seen?'

    And answer made the bold Sir Bedivere:
'Sir King, I closed mine eyelids, lest the gems
Should blind my purpose, for I never saw,
Nor shall see, here or elsewhere, till I die,
Not tho' I live three lives of mortal men,
So great a miracle as yonder hilt.
Then with both hands I flung him, wheeling him;
But when I look'd again, behold an arm,
Clothed in white samite, mystic, wonderful,
That caught him by the hilt, and brandish'd him
Three times, and drew him under in the mere.'

    And answer made King Arthur, breathing hard:
'My end draws nigh; 'tis time that I were gone.
Make broad thy shoulders to receive my weight,
And bear me to the margin; yet I fear
My wound hath taken cold, and I shall die.'

    So saying, from the pavement he half rose,

Slowly, with pain, reclining on his arm,
And looking wistfully with wide blue eyes
As in a picture. Him Sir Bedivere
Remorsefully regarded thro' his tears,
And would have spoken, but he found not words,
Then took with care, and kneeling on one knee,
O'er both his shoulders drew the languid hands,
And rising bore him thro' the place of tombs.

But, as he walk'd, King Arthur panted hard,
Like one that feels a nightmare on his bed
When all the house is mute. So sigh'd the King,
Muttering and murmuring at his ear, 'Quick, quick!
I fear it is too late, and I shall die.'
But the other swiftly strode from ridge to ridge,
Clothed with his breath, and looking, as he walk'd,
Larger than human on the frozen hills.
He heard the deep behind him, and a cry
Before. His own thought drove him like a goad.
Dry clash'd his harness in the icy caves
And barren chasms, and all to left and right
The bare black cliff clang'd round him, as he based
His feet on juts of slippery crag that rang
Sharp-smitten with the dint of armed heels —
And on a sudden, lo! the level lake,
And the long glories of the winter moon.

Then saw they how there hove a dusky barge,
Dark as a funeral scarf from stem to stern,
Beneath them; and descending they were ware
That all the decks were dense with stately forms
Black-stoled, black-hooded, like a dream — by these
Three Queens with crowns of gold — and from them rose
A cry that shiver'd to the tingling stars,
And, as it were one voice, an agony
Of lamentation, like a wind, that shrills
All night in a waste land, where no one comes,
Or hath come, since the making of the world.

Then murmur'd Arthur, 'Place me in the barge,'
And to the barge they came. There those three Queens
Put forth their hands, and took the King, and wept.
But she, that rose the tallest of them all
And fairest, laid his head upon her lap,
And loosed the shatter'd casque, and chafed his hands,
And call'd him by his name, complaining loud,
And dropping bitter tears against his brow
Striped with dark blood: for all his face was white
And colourless, and like the wither'd moon

Smote by the fresh beam of the springing east;
And all his greaves and cuisses dash'd with drops
Of onset; and the light and lustrous curls –
That made his forehead like a rising sun
High from the dais-throne – were parch'd with dust;
Or, clotted into points and hanging loose,
Mix'd with the knightly growth that fringed his lips.
So like a shatter'd column lay the King;
Not like that Arthur who, with lance in rest,
From spur to plume a star of tournament,
Shot thro' the lists at Camelot, and charged
Before the eyes of ladies and of kings.

    Then loudly cried the bold Sir Bedivere,
'Ah! my Lord Arthur, whither shall I go?
Where shall I hide my forehead and my eyes?
For now I see the true old times are dead,
When every morning brought a noble chance,
And every chance brought out a noble knight.
Such times have been not since the light that led
The holy Elders with the gift of myrrh.
But now the whole ROUND TABLE is dissolved
Which was an image of the mighty world;
And I, the last, go forth companionless,
And the days darken round me, and the years,
Among new men, strange faces, other minds.'

    And slowly answered Arthur from the barge:
'The old order changeth, yielding place to new,
And God fulfils Himself in many ways,
Lest one good custom should corrupt the world.
Comfort thyself: what comfort is in me?
I have lived my life, and that which I have done
May He within Himself make pure! but thou,
If thou shouldst never see my face again,
Pray for my soul. More things are wrought by prayer
Than this world dreams of. Wherefore, let thy voice
Rise like a fountain for me night and day.
For what are men better than sheep or goats
That nourish a blind life within the brain,
If, knowing God, they lift not hands of prayer
Both for themselves and those who call them friend?
For so the whole round earth is every way
Bound by gold chains about the feet of God.
But now farewell. I am going a long way
With these thou seëst – if indeed I go –
(For all my mind is clouded with a doubt)
To the island-valley of Avilion;

Where falls not hail, or rain, or any snow,
Nor ever wind blows loudly, but it lies
Deep-meadow'd, happy, fair with orchard-lawns
And bowery hollows crown'd with summer sea,
Where I will heal me of my grievous wound.'
   So said he, and the barge with oar and sail
Moved from the brink, like some full-breasted swan
That, fluting a wild carol ere her death,
Ruffles her pure cold plume, and takes the flood
With swarthy webs. Long stood Sir Bedivere
Revolving many memories, till the hull
Look'd one black dot against the verge of dawn,
And on the mere the wailing died away.

                        *

   Here ended Hall, and our last light, that long
Had wink'd and threaten'd darkness, flared and fell:
At which the Parson, sent to sleep with sound,
And waked with silence, grunted 'Good!' but we
Sat rapt: it was the tone with which he read —
Perhaps some modern touches here and there
Redeem'd it from the charge of nothingness —
Or else we loved the man and prized his work;
I know not: but we sitting, as I said,
The cock crew loud; as at that time of year
The lusty bird takes every hour for dawn:
Then Francis, muttering, like a man ill-used,
'There now — that's nothing!' drew a little back,
And drove his heel into the smoulder'd log
That sent a blast of sparkles up the flue
And so to bed; where yet in sleep I seem'd
To sail with Arthur under looming shores,
Point after point; till on to dawn, when dreams
Begin to feel the truth and stir of day,
To me, methought, who waited with a crowd,
There came a bark that, blowing forward, bore
King Arthur, like a modern gentleman
Of stateliest port; and all the people cried
'Arthur is come again: he cannot die.'
Then those that stood upon the hills behind
Repeated — 'Come again and thrice as fair;'
And, further inland, voices echoed — 'Come
With all good things, and war shall be no more.'
At this a hundred bells began to peal,
That with the sound I woke, and heard indeed
The clear church-bells ring in the Christmas morn.

The Gardener's Daughter; or the Pictures

This morning is the morning of the day,
When I and Eustace from the city went
To see the Gardener's Daughter; I and he,
Brothers in Art; a friendship so complete
Portion'd in halves between us, that we grew
The fable of the city where we dwelt.

   My Eustace might have sat for Hercules;
So muscular he spread, so broad of breast.
He, by some law that holds in love, and draws
The greater to the lesser, long desired
A certain miracle of symmetry,
A miniature of loveliness, all grace
Summ'd up and closed in little, – Juliet she
So light of foot, so light of spirit – oh, she
To me myself, for some three careless moons,
The summer pilot of an empty heart
Unto the shores of nothing! Know you not
Such touches are but embassies of love,
To tamper with the feelings, ere he found
Empire for life? but Eustace painted her,
And said to me, she sitting with us then,
'When will *you* paint like this?' and I replied,
(My words were half in earnest, half in jest,)
' 'Tis not your work, but Love's. Love, unperceived,
A more ideal Artist he than all,
Came, drew your pencil from you, made those eyes
Darker than darkest pansies, and that hair
More black than ashbuds in the front of March.'
And Juliet answer'd laughing, 'Go and see
The Gardener's daughter: trust me, after that
You scarce can fail to match his masterpiece.'
And up we rose, and on the spur we went.

   Not wholly in the busy world, nor quite
Beyond it, blooms the garden that I love.
News from the humming city comes to it
In sound of funeral or of marriage bells;
And, sitting muffled in dark leaves, you hear
The windy clanging of the minster clock;
Although between it and the garden lies
A league of grass, wash'd by a slow broad stream,
That, stirr'd with languid pulses of the oar,
Waves all its lazy lilies, and creeps on,
Barge-laden, to three arches of a bridge
Crown'd with the minster-towers.
                   The fields between

Are dewy-fresh, browsed by deep-udder'd kine,
And all about the large lime feathers low,
The lime a summer home of murmurous wings.

In that still place she, hoarded in herself,
Grew, seldom seen: not less among us lived
Her fame from lip to lip. Who had not heard
Of Rose, the Gardener's daughter? Where was he,
So blunt in memory, so old at heart,
At such a distance from his youth in grief,
That, having seen, forgot? The common mouth,
So gross to express delight, in praise of her
Grew oratory. Such a lord is Love,
And Beauty such a mistress of the world.

And if I said that Fancy, led by Love,
Would play with flying forms and images,
Yet this is also true, that, long before
I look'd upon her, when I heard her name
My heart was like a prophet to my heart,
And told me I should love. A crowd of hopes,
That sought to sow themselves like winged seeds,
Born out of everything I heard and saw,
Flutter'd about my senses and my soul;
And vague desires, like fitful blasts of balm
To one that travels quickly, made the air
Of Life delicious, and all kinds of thought,
That verged upon them, sweeter than the dream
Dream'd by a happy man, when the dark East,
Unseen, is brightening to his bridal morn.

And sure this orbit of the memory folds
For ever in itself the day we went
To see her. All the land in flowery squares,
Beneath a broad and equal-blowing wind,
Smelt of the coming summer, as one large cloud
Drew downward: but all else of Heaven was pure
Up to the Sun, and May from verge to verge,
And May with me from head to heel. And now,
As tho' 'twere yesterday, as tho' it were
The hour just flown, that morn with all its sound,
(For those old Mays had thrice the life of these,)
Rings in mine ears. The steer forgot to graze,
And, where the hedge-row cuts the pathway, stood,
Leaning his horns into the neighbour field,
And lowing to his fellows. From the woods
Came voices of the well-contented doves.
The lark could scarce get out his notes for joy,
But shook his song together as he near'd
His happy home, the ground. To left and right,

The cuckoo told his name to all the hills;
The mellow ouzel fluted in the elm;
The redcap whistled; and the nightingale
Sang loud, as tho' he were the bird of day.

    And Eustace turn'd, and smiling said to me,
'Hear how the bushes echo! by my life,
These birds have joyful thoughts. Think you they sing
Like poets, from the vanity of song?
Or have they any sense of why they sing?
And would they praise the heavens for what they have?'
And I made answer, 'Were there nothing else
For which to praise the heavens but only love,
That only love were cause enough for praise.'

    Lightly he laugh'd, as one that read my thought,
And on we went; but ere an hour had pass'd
We reach'd a meadow slanting to the North;
Down which a well-worn pathway courted us
To one green wicket in a privet hedge;
This, yielding, gave into a grassy walk
Thro' crowded lilac-ambush trimly pruned;
And one warm gust, full-fed with perfume, blew
Beyond us, as we enter'd in the cool.
The garden stretches southward. In the midst
A cedar spread his dark-green layers of shade.
The garden-glasses shone, and momently
The twinkling laurel scatter'd silver lights.

    'Eustace,' I said, 'this wonder keeps the house.'
He nodded, but a moment afterwards
He cried, 'Look! look!' Before he ceased I turn'd,
And, ere a star can wink, beheld her there.

    For up the porch there grew an Eastern rose,
That, flowering high, the last night's gale had caught,
And blown across the walk. One arm aloft –
Gown'd in pure white, that fitted to the shape –
Holding the bush, to fix it back, she stood.
A single stream of all her soft brown hair
Pour'd on one side: the shadow of the flowers
Stole all the golden gloss, and, wavering
Lovingly lower, trembled on her waist –
Ah, happy shade – and still went wavering down,
But, ere it touch'd a foot, that might have danced
The greensward into greener circles, dipt,
And mix'd with shadows of the common ground!
But the full day dwelt on her brows, and sunn'd
Her violet eyes, and all her Hebe bloom,
And doubled his own warmth against her lips,
And on the bounteous wave of such a breast

As never pencil drew. Half light, half shade,
She stood, a sight to make an old man young.
   So rapt, we near'd the house, but she, a Rose
In roses, mingled with her fragrant toil,
Nor heard us come, nor from her tendance turn'd
Into the world without; till close at hand,
And almost ere I knew mine own intent,
This murmur broke the stillness of that air
Which brooded round about her:
                                        'Ah, one rose,
One rose, but one, by those fair fingers cull'd,
Were worth a hundred kisses press'd on lips
Less exquisite than thine.'
                              She look'd: but all
Suffused with blushes – neither self-possess'd
Nor startled, but betwixt this mood and that,
Divided in a graceful quiet – paused,
And dropt the branch she held, and turning, wound
Her looser hair in braid, and stirr'd her lips
For some sweet answer, tho' no answer came,
Nor yet refused the rose, but granted it,
And moved away, and left me, statue-like,
In act to render thanks.
                          I, that whole day
Saw her no more, altho' I linger'd there
Till every daisy slept, and Love's white star
Beam'd thro' the thicken'd cedar in the dusk.
   So home we went, and all the livelong way
With solemn gibe did Eustace banter me.
'Now,' said he, 'will you climb the top of Art.
You cannot fail but work in hues to dim
The Titianic Flora. Will you match
My Juliet? you, not you, – the Master, Love,
A more ideal Artist he than all.'
   So home I went, but could not sleep for joy,
Reading her perfect features in the gloom,
Kissing the rose she gave me o'er and o'er,
And shaping faithful record of the glance
That graced the giving – such a noise of life
Swarm'd in the golden present, such a voice
Call'd to me from the years to come, and such
A length of bright horizon rimm'd the dark.
And all that night I heard the watchman peal
The sliding season: all that night I heard
The heavy clocks knolling the drowsy hours.
The drowsy hours, dispensers of all good,
O'er the mute city stole with folded wings,

Distilling odours on me as they went
To greet their fairer sisters of the East.
  Love at first sight, first-born, and heir to all,
Made this night thus. Henceforward squall nor storm
Could keep me from that Eden where she dwelt.
Light pretexts drew me: sometimes a Dutch love
For tulips; then for roses, moss or musk
To grace my city-rooms; or fruits and cream
Served in the weeping elm; and more and more
A word could bring the colour to my cheek;
A thought would fill my eyes with happy dew;
Love trebled life within me, and with each
The year increased.
              The daughters of the year,
One after one, thro' that still garden pass'd:
Each garlanded with her peculiar flower
Danced into light, and died into the shade;
And each in passing touch'd with some new grace
Or seem'd to touch her, so that day by day,
Like one that never can be wholly known,
Her beauty grew; till Autumn brought an hour
For Eustace, when I heard his deep 'I will',
Breathed, like the covenant of a God, to hold
From thence thro' all the worlds: but I rose up
Full of his bliss, and following her dark eyes
Felt earth as air beneath me, till I reach'd
The wicket-gate, and found her standing there.
  There sat we down upon a garden mound,
Two mutually enfolded; Love, the third,
Between us, in the circle of his arms
Enwound us both; and over many a range
Of waning lime the grey cathedral towers,
Across a hazy glimmer of the west,
Reveal'd their shining windows: from them clash'd
The bells; we listen'd; with the time we play'd;
We spoke of other things; we coursed about
The subject most at heart, more near and near,
Like doves about a dovecote, wheeling round
The central wish, until we settled there.
  Then, in that time and place, I spoke to her,
Requiring, tho' I knew it was mine own,
Yet for the pleasure that I took to hear,
Requiring at her hand the greatest gift,
A woman's heart, the heart of her I loved;
And in that time and place she answer'd me,
And in the compass of three little words,
More musical than ever came in one,

The silver fragments of a broken voice,
Made me most happy, faltering 'I am thine.'
   Shall I cease here? Is this enough to say
That my desire, like all strongest hopes
By its own energy fulfill'd itself,
Merged in completion? Would you learn at full
How passion rose thro' circumstantial grades
Beyond all grades develop'd? and indeed
I had not staid so long to tell you all,
But while I mused came Memory with sad eyes,
Holding the folded annals of my youth;
And while I mused, Love with knit brows went by,
And with a flying finger swept my lips,
And spake, 'Be wise: not easily forgiven
Are those, who setting wide the doors, that bar
The secret bridal chambers of the heart,
Let in the day.' Here, then, my words have end.
      Yet might I tell of meetings, of farewells –
Of that which came between, more sweet than each,
In whispers like the whispers of the leaves
That tremble round a nightingale – in sighs
Which perfect Joy, perplex'd for utterance,
Stole from her sister Sorrow. Might I not tell
Of difference, reconcilement, pledges given,
And vows, where there was never need of vows,
And kisses, where the heart on one wild leap
Hung tranced from all pulsation, as above
The heavens between their fairy fleeces pale
Sow'd all their mystic gulfs with fleeting stars;
Or while the balmy glooming, crescent-lit,
Spread the light haze along the river-shores,
And in the hollows; or as once we met
Unheedful, tho' beneath a whispering rain
Night slid down one long stream of sighing wind,
And in her bosom bore the baby, Sleep.
   But this whole hour your eyes have been intent
On that veil'd picture – veil'd, for what it holds
May not be dwelt on by the common day.
This prelude has prepared thee. Raise thy soul;
Make thine heart ready with thine eyes: the time
Is come to raise the veil.
                              Behold her there,
As I beheld her ere she knew my heart,
My first, last love; the idol of my youth,
The darling of my manhood, and, alas!
Now the most blessed memory of mine age.

Dora

With farmer Allan at the farm abode
William and Dora. William was his son,
And she his niece. He often look'd at them,
And often thought 'I'll make them man and wife.'
Now Dora felt her uncle's will in all,
And yearn'd towards William; but the youth, because
He had been always with her in the house,
Thought not of Dora.
            Then there came a day
When Allan call'd his son, and said,
'My son: I married late, but I would wish to see
My grandchild on my knees before I die:
And I have set my heart upon a match.
Now therefore look to Dora; she is well
To look to; thrifty too beyond her age.
She is my brother's daughter: he and I
Had once hard words, and parted, and he died
In foreign lands; but for his sake I bred
His daughter Dora: take her for your wife;
For I have wish'd this marriage, night and day,
For many years.' But William answer'd short;
'I cannot marry Dora; by my life,
I will not marry Dora.' Then the old man
Was wroth, and doubled up his hands, and said:
'You will not, boy! you dare to answer thus!
But in my time a father's word was law,
And so it shall be now for me. Look to it;
Consider, William: take a month to think,
And let me have an answer to my wish;
Or, by the Lord that made me, you shall pack,
And never more darken my doors again.'
But William answer'd madly; bit his lips,
And broke away. The more he look'd at her
The less he liked her; and his ways were harsh;
But Dora bore them meekly. Then before
The month was out he left his father's house,
And hired himself to work within the fields;
And half in love, half spite, he woo'd and wed
A labourer's daughter, Mary Morrison.

Then, when the bells were ringing, Allan call'd
His niece and said: 'My girl, I love you well;
But if you speak with him that was my son,
Or change a word with her he calls his wife,
My home is none of yours. My will is law.'

And Dora promised, being meek. She thought,
'It cannot be: my uncle's mind will change!'
   And days went on, and there was born a boy
To William; then distresses came on him;
And day by day he pass'd his father's gate,
Heart-broken, and his father help'd him not.
But Dora stored what little she could save,
And sent it them by stealth, nor did they know
Who sent it; till at last a fever seized
On William, and in harvest time he died.
   Then Dora went to Mary. Mary sat
And look'd with tears upon her boy, and thought
Hard things of Dora. Dora came and said:
   'I have obey'd my uncle until now,
And I have sinn'd, for it was all thro' me
This evil came on William at the first.
But, Mary, for the sake of him that's gone,
And for your sake, the woman that he chose,
And for this orphan, I am come to you:
You know there has not been for these five years
So full a harvest: let me take the boy,
And I will set him in my uncle's eye
Among the wheat; that when his heart is glad
Of the full harvest, he may see the boy,
And bless him for the sake of him that's gone.'
   And Dora took the child, and went her way
Across the wheat, and sat upon a mound
That was unsown, where many poppies grew.
Far off the farmer came into the field
And spied her not; for none of all his men
Dare tell him Dora waited with the child;
And Dora would have risen and gone to him
But her heart fail'd her; and the reapers reap'd,
And the sun fell, and all the land was dark.
   But when the morrow came, she rose and took
The child once more, and sat upon the mound;
And made a little wreath of all the flowers
That grew about, and tied it round his hat
To make him pleasing in her uncle's eye.
Then when the farmer pass'd into the field
He spied her, and he left his men at work,
And came and said; 'Where were you yesterday?
Whose child is that? What are you doing here?'
So Dora cast her eyes upon the ground,
And answer'd softly, 'This is William's child!'
'And did I not,' said Allan, 'did I not

Forbid you, Dora?' Dora said again;
'Do with me as you will, but take the child
And bless him for the sake of him that's gone!'
And Allan said, 'I see it is a trick
Got up betwixt you and the woman there.
I must be taught my duty, and by you!
You knew my word was law, and yet you dared
To slight it. Well – for I will take the boy;
But go you hence, and never see me more.'

So saying, he took the boy, that cried aloud
And struggled hard. The wreath of flowers fell
At Dora's feet. She bow'd upon her hands,
And the boy's cry came to her from the field,
More and more distant. She bow'd down her head,
Remembering the day when first she came
And all the things that had been. She bow'd down
And wept in secret; and the reapers reap'd,
And the sun fell, and all the land was dark.

Then Dora went to Mary's house, and stood
Upon the threshold. Mary saw the boy
Was not with Dora. She broke out in praise
To God, that help'd her in her widowhood
And Dora said, 'My uncle took the boy;
But, Mary, let me live and work with you:
He says that he will never see me more.'
Then answer'd Mary, 'This shall never be,
That thou shouldst take my trouble on thyself
And, now I think, he shall not have the boy,
For he will teach him hardness, and to slight
His mother; therefore thou and I will go,
And I will have my boy, and bring him home;
And I will beg of him to take thee back:
But if he will not take thee back again,
Then thou and I will live within one house,
And work for William's child, until he grows
Of age to help us.'
               So the women kiss'd
Each other, and set out, and reach'd the farm
The door was off the latch they peep'd, and saw
The boy set up betwixt his grandsire's knees,
Who thrust him in the hollows of his arm,
And clapt him on the hands and on the cheeks,
Like one that loved him: and the lad stretch'd out
And babbled for the golden seal, that hung
From Allan's watch, and sparkled by the fire.
Then they came in: but when the boy beheld

His mother, he cried out to come to her:
And Allan set him down, and Mary said:
  'O Father! – if you let me call you so –
I never came a-begging for myself,
Or William, or this child; but now I come
For Dora: take her back; she loves you well.
O Sir, when William died, he died at peace
With all men; for I ask'd him, and he said,
He could not ever rue his marrying me –
I had been a patient wife but, Sir, he said
That he was wrong to cross his father thus:
"God bless him!" he said, "and may he never know
The troubles I have gone thro'!" Then he turn'd
His face and pass'd – unhappy that I am!
But now, Sir, let me have my boy, for you
Will make him hard, and he will learn to slight
His father's memory, and take Dora back,
And let all this be as it was before.'
  So Mary said, and Dora hid her face
By Mary. There was silence in the room;
And all at once the old man burst in sobs: –
  'I have been to blame – to blame. I have kill'd my son.
I have kill'd him – but I loved him – my dear son.
May God forgive me! – I have been to blame.
Kiss me, my children.'
               Then they clung about
The old man's neck, and kiss'd him many times.
And all the man was broken with remorse;
And all his love came back a hundredfold;
And for three hours he sobb'd o'er William's child,
Thinking of William.
              So those four abode
Within one house together; and as years
Went forward, Mary took another mate;
But Dora lived unmarried till her death.

Audley Court

'The Bull, the Fleece are cramm'd, and not a room
For love or money. Let us picnic there
At Audley Court.'
        I spoke, while Audley feast
Humm'd like a hive all round the narrow quay,
To Francis, with a basket on his arm,
To Francis just alighted from the boat,
And breathing of the sea. 'With all my heart,'
Said Francis. Then we shoulder'd thro' the swarm,
And rounded by the stillness of the beach
To where the bay runs up its latest horn.

We left the dying ebb that faintly lipp'd
The flat red granite; so by many a sweep
Of meadow smooth from aftermath we reach'd
The griffin-guarded gates, and pass'd thro' all
The pillar'd dusk of sounding sycamores,
And cross'd the garden to the gardener's lodge,
With all its casements bedded, and its walls
And chimneys muffled in the leafy vine.

There, on a slope of orchard, Francis laid
A damask napkin wrought with horse and hound,
Brought out a dusky loaf that smelt of home,
And, half-cut-down, a pasty costly-made,
Where quail and pigeon, lark and leveret lay,
Like fossils of the rock, with golden yolks
Imbedded and injellied; last, with these,
A flask of cider from his father's vats,
Prime, which I knew; and so we sat and eat
And talk'd old matters over; who was dead,
Who married, who was like to be, and how
The races went, and who would rent the hall:
Then touch'd upon the game, how scarce it was
This season; glancing thence, discuss'd the farm,
The four-field system, and the price of grain;
And struck upon the corn-laws, where we split,
And came again together on the king
With heated faces; till he laugh'd aloud;
And, while the blackbird on the pippin hung
To hear him, clapt his hand in mine and sang –

'Oh! who would fight and march and countermarch,
Be shot for sixpence in a battle-field,
And shovell'd up into a bloody trench
Where no one knows? but let me live my life.

'Oh! who would cast and balance at a desk,

Perch'd like a crow upon a three-legg'd stool,
Till all his juice is dried, and all his joints
Are full of chalk? but let me live my life.

  'Who'd serve the state? for if I carved my name
Upon the cliffs that guard my native land,
I might as well have traced it in the sands
The sea wastes all: but let me live my life.

  'Oh! who would love? I woo'd a woman once,
But she was sharper than an eastern wind,
And all my heart turn'd from her, as a thorn
Turns from the sea: but let me live my life.'

  He sang his song, and I replied with mine:
I found it in a volume, all of songs
Knock'd down to me, when old Sir Robert's pride,
His books – the more the pity, so I said –
Came to the hammer here in March – and this –
I set the words, and added names I knew.

  'Sleep, Ellen Aubrey, sleep, and dream of me:
Sleep, Ellen, folded in thy sister's arm,
And sleeping, haply dream her arm is mine.

  'Sleep, Ellen, folded in Emilia's arm;
Emilia, fairer than all else but thou,
For thou art fairer than all else that is.

  'Sleep, breathing health and peace upon her breast:
Sleep breathing love and trust against her lip:
I go to-night: I come to-morrow morn.

  'I go, but I return: I would I were
The pilot of the darkness and the dream.
Sleep, Ellen Aubrey, love and dream of me.'

  So sang we each to either, Francis Hale,
The farmer's son, who lived across the bay
My friend; and I, that having wherewithal,
And in the fallow leisure of my life
A rolling stone of here and everywhere,
Did what I would; but ere the night we rose
And saunter'd home beneath a moon, that, just
In crescent, dimly rain'd about the leaf
Twilights of airy silver, till we reach'd
The limit of the hills, and as we sank
From rock to rock upon the glooming quay,
The town was hush'd beneath us: lower down
The bay was oily-calm; the harbour-buoy
With one green sparkle ever and anon
Dipt by itself, and we were glad at heart.

Walking to the Mail

John. I'm glad I walk'd. How fresh the meadows look
Above the river, and, but a month ago,
The whole hill-side was redder than a fox.
Is yon plantation where this byway joins
The turnpike?
     James. Yes.
           John. And when does this come by?
James. The mail? At one o'clock.
               John. What is it now?
James. A quarter to.
           John. Whose house is that I see?
No, not the County Member's with the vane:
Up higher with the yew-tree by it, and half
A score of gables.
     James. That? Sir Edward Head's:
But he's abroad: the place is to be sold.
  John. Oh, his. He was not broken.
             James. No, sir, he,
Vex'd with a morbid devil in his blood
That veil'd the world with jaundice, hid his face
From all men, and commercing with himself,
He lost the sense that handles daily life –
That keeps us all in order more or less –
And sick of home went overseas for change.
  John. And whither?
    James. Nay, who knows? he's here and there.
But let him go; his devil goes with him,
As well as with his tenant, Jocky Dawes.
John. What's that?
    James. You saw the man – on Monday, was it? –
There by the humpback'd willow; half stands up
And bristles; half has fall'n and made a bridge;
And there he caught the younker tickling trout –
Caught *in flagrante* – what's the Latin word? –
Delicto: but his house, for so they say,
Was haunted with a jolly ghost, that shook
The curtains, whined in lobbies, tapt at doors
And rummaged like a rat: no servant stay'd:
The farmer vext packs up his beds and chairs,
And all his household stuff; and with his boy
Betwixt his knees, his wife upon the tilt,
Sets out, and meets a friend who hails him, 'What!
You're flitting!' 'Yes, we're flitting,' says the ghost
(For they had pack'd the thing among the beds,)

'Oh well,' says he, 'you flitting with us too –
Jack, turn the horses' heads and home again.'
   John. He left *his* wife behind; for so I heard.
   James. He left her, yes. I met my lady once:
A woman like a butt, and harsh as crabs.
John. Oh yet but I remember, ten years back –
'Tis now at least ten years – and then she was –
You could not light upon a sweeter thing:
A body slight and round, and like a pear
In growing, modest eyes, a hand, a foot,
Lessening in perfect cadence, and a skin
As clean and white as privet when it flowers.
   James. Aye, aye, the blossom fades, and they that loved
At first like dove and dove were cat and dog.
She was the daughter of a cottager
Out of her sphere. What betwixt shame and pride,
New things and old, himself and her, she sour'd
To what she is: a nature never kind!
Like men, like manners: like breeds like, they say.
Kind nature is the best: those manners next
That fit us like a nature second-hand;
Which are indeed the manners of the great.
   John. But I had heard it was this bill that past,
And fear of change at home, that drove him hence.
   James. That was the last drop in the cup of gall.
I once was near him, when his bailiff brought
A Chartist pike. You should have seen him wince
As from a venomous thing: he thought himself
A mark for all, and shudder'd, lest a cry
Should break his sleep by night, and his nice eyes
Should see the raw mechanic's bloody thumbs
Sweat on his blazon'd chairs; but, sir, you know
That these two parties still divide the world –
Of those that want, and those that have: and still
The same old sore breaks out from age to age
With much the same result. Now I myself,
A Tory to the quick, was as a boy
Destructive, when I had not what I would.
I was at school – a college in the South:
There lived a flayflint near; we stole his fruit,
His hens, his eggs; but there was law for us;
We paid in person. He had a sow, sir. She,
With meditative grunts of much content,
Lay great with pig, wallowing in sun and mud.
By night we dragg'd her to the college tower
From her warm bed, and up the corkscrew stair

With hand and rope we haled the groaning sow,
And on the leads we kept her till she pigg'd.
Large range of prospect had the mother sow,
And but for daily loss of one she loved,
As one by one we took them – but for this –
As never sow was higher in this world –
Might have been happy: but what lot is pure?
We took them all, till she was left alone
Upon her tower, the Niobe of swine,
And so return'd unfarrow'd to her sty.
  John. They found you out?
      James. Not they.
         John. Well – after all –
What know we of the secret of a man?
His nerves were wrong. What ails us, who are sound,
That we should mimic this raw fool the world,
Which charts us all in its coarse blacks or whites,
As ruthless as a baby with a worm
As cruel as a schoolboy ere he grows
To Pity – more from ignorance than will.
  But put your best foot forward, or I fear
That we shall miss the mail: and here it comes
With five at top: as quaint a four-in-hand
As you shall see – three piebalds and a roan.

St Simeon Stylites

Altho' I be the basest of mankind,
From scalp to sole one slough and crust of sin,
Unfit for earth, unfit for heaven, scarce meet
For troops of devils, mad with blasphemy,
I will not cease to grasp the hope I hold
Of saintdom, and to clamour, mourn and sob,
Battering the gates of heaven with storms of prayer,
Have mercy, Lord, and take away my sin.
  Let this avail, just, dreadful, mighty God,
This not be all in vain, that thrice ten years,
Thrice multiplied by superhuman pangs,
In hungers and in thirsts, fevers and cold,
In coughs, aches, stitches, ulcerous throes and cramps,
A sign betwixt the meadow and the cloud,
Patient on this tall pillar I have borne
Rain, wind, frost, heat, hail, damp, and sleet, and snow;
And I had hoped that ere this period closed
Thou wouldst have caught me up into thy rest,

Denying not these weather-beaten limbs
The meed of saints, the white robe and the palm.
    O take the meaning, Lord: I do not breathe,
Not whisper, any murmur of complaint.
Pain heap'd ten-hundred-fold to this, were still
Less burthen, by ten-hundred-fold, to bear,
Than were those lead-like tons of sin, that crush'd
My spirit flat before thee.
                                    O Lord, Lord,
Thou knowest I bore this better at the first,
For I was strong and hale of body then;
And tho' my teeth, which now are dropt away,
Would chatter with the cold, and all my beard
Was tagg'd with icy fringes in the moon,
I drown'd the whoopings of the owl with sound
Of pious hymns and psalms, and sometimes saw
An angel stand and watch me, as I sang.
Now am I feeble grown; my end draws nigh;
I hope my end draws nigh: half deaf I am,
So that I scarce can hear the people hum
About the column's base, and almost blind
And scarce can recognize the fields I know,
And both my thighs are rotted with the dew;
Yet cease I not to clamour and to cry,
While my stiff spine can hold my weary head,
Till all my limbs drop piecemeal from the stone,
Have mercy, mercy: take away my sin.
    O Jesus, if thou wilt not save my soul,
Who may be saved? who is it may be saved?
Who may be made a saint, if I fail here?
Show me the man hath suffer'd more than I.
For did not all thy martyrs die one death?
For either they were stoned or crucified
Or burn'd in fire, or boil'd in oil, or sawn
In twain beneath the ribs; but I die here
To-day, and whole years long, a life of death.
Bear witness, if I could have found a way
(And heedfully I sifted all my thought)
More slowly-painful to subdue this home
Of sin, my flesh, which I despise and hate,
I had not stinted practice, O my God.
    For not alone this pillar-punishment,
Not this alone I bore: but while I lived
In the white convent down the valley there,
For many weeks about my loins I wore
The rope that haled the buckets from the well,

Twisted as tight as I could knot the noose;
And spake not of it to a single soul,
Until the ulcer, eating thro' my skin,
Betray'd my secret penance, so that all
My brethren marvell'd greatly. More than this
I bore, whereof, O God, thou knowest all.

　　Three winters, that my soul might grow to thee,
I lived up there on yonder mountain side.
My right leg chain'd into the crag, I lay
Pent in a roofless close of ragged stones;
Inswathed sometimes in wandering mist, and twice
Black'd with thy branding thunder, and sometimes
Sucking the damps for drink, and eating not,
Except the spare chance-gift of those that came
To touch my body and be heal'd, and live:
And they say then that I work'd miracles,
Whereof my fame is loud amongst mankind,
Cured lameness, palsies, cancers. Thou, O God,
Knowest alone whether this was or no.
Have mercy, mercy; cover all my sin.

　　Then, that I might be more alone with thee,
Three years I lived upon a pillar, high
Six cubits, and three years on one of twelve;
And twice three years I crouch'd on one that rose
Twenty by measure; last of all, I grew
Twice ten long weary weary years to this,
That numbers forty cubits from the soil.

　　I think that I have borne as much as this –
Or else I dream – and for so long a time,
If I may measure time by yon slow light,
And this high dial, which my sorrow crowns –
So much – even so.
　　　　　　　　　And yet I know not well,
For that the evil ones come here, and say,
'Fall down, O Simeon: thou hast suffer'd long
For ages and for ages!' then they prate
Of penances I cannot have gone thro',
Perplexing me with lies; and oft I fall,
Maybe for months, in such blind lethargies
That Heaven, and Earth, and Time are choked.
　　　　　　　　　　　　　　But yet
Bethink thee, Lord, while thou and all the saints
Enjoy themselves in heaven, and men on earth
House in the shade of comfortable roofs
Sit with their wives by fires, eat wholesome food
And wear warm clothes, and even beasts have stalls,

I,'tween the spring and downfall of the light
Bow down one thousand and two hundred times,
To Christ, the Virgin Mother, and the, Saints;
Or in the night, after a little sleep,
I wake: the chill stars sparkle; I am wet
With drenching dews, or stiff with crackling frost.
I wear an undress'd goatskin on my back;
A grazing iron collar grinds my neck;
And in my weak, lean arms I lift the cross,
And strive and wrestle with thee till I die:
O mercy, mercy! wash away my sin.

   O Lord, thou knowest what a man I am;
A sinful man, conceived and born in sin:
'Tis their own doing; this is none of mine;
Lay it not to me. Am I to blame for this,
That here come those that worship me? Ha! ha!
They think that I am somewhat. What am I?
The silly people take me for a saint,
And bring me offerings of fruit and flowers:
And I, in truth (thou wilt bear witness here)
Have all in all endured as much, and more
Than many just and holy men, whose names
Are register'd and calendar'd for saints.

   Good people, you do ill to kneel to me.
What is it I can have done to merit this?
I am a sinner viler than you all.
It may be I have wrought some miracles
And cured some halt and maim'd, but what of that?
It may be, no one, even among the saints,
May match his pains with mine; but what of that?
Yet do not rise: for you may look on me,
And in your looking you may kneel to God.
Speak! is there any of you halt or maim'd?
I think you know I have some power with Heaven
From my long penance: let him speak his wish.

   Yes, I can heal him. Power goes forth from me.
They say that they are heal'd. Ah, hark! they shout
'St. Simeon Stylites.' Why, if so,
God reaps a harvest in me. O my soul,
God reaps a harvest in thee. If this be,
Can I work miracles and not be saved?
This is not told of any. They were saints.
It cannot be but that I shall be saved;
Yea, crown'd a saint. They shout, 'Behold a saint!',
And lower voices saint me from above.
Courage, St. Simeon! This dull chrysalis

Cracks into shining wings, and hope ere death
Spreads more and more and more, that God hath now
Sponged and made blank of crimeful record all
My mortal archives.
              O my sons, my sons,
I, Simeon of the pillar, by surname
Stylites, among men; I, Simeon,
The watcher on the column till the end;
I, Simeon, whose brain the sunshine bakes;
I, whose bald brows in silent hours become
Unnaturally hoar with rime, do now
From my high nest of penance here proclaim
That Pontius and Iscariot by my side
Show'd like fair seraphs. On the coals I lay,
A vessel full of sin: all hell beneath
Made me boil over. Devils pluck'd my sleeve;
Abaddon and Asmodeus caught at me.
I smote them with the cross; they swarm'd again.
In bed like monstrous apes they crush'd my chest:
They flapp'd my light out as I read: I saw
Their faces grow between me and my book:
With colt-like whinny and with hoggish whine
They burst my prayer. Yet this way was left,
And by this way I 'scaped them. Mortify
Your flesh, like me, with scourges and with thorns;
Smite, shrink not, spare not. If it may be, fast
Whole Lents, and pray. I hardly, with slow steps,
With slow, faint steps, and much exceeding pain,
Have scrambled past those pits of fire, that still
Sing in mine ears. But yield not me the praise:
God only thro' his bounty hath thought fit,
Among the powers and princes of this world,
To make me an example to mankind,
Which few can reach to. Yet I do not say
But that a time may come — yea, even now,
Now, now, his footsteps smite the threshold stairs
Of life — I say, that time is at the doors
When you may worship me without reproach;
For I will leave my relics in your land,
And you may carve a shrine about my dust,
And burn a fragrant lamp before my bones,
When I am gather'd to the glorious saints.
  While I spake then, a sting of shrewdest pain
Ran shrivelling thro' me, and a cloudlike change,
In passing, with a grosser film made thick
These heavy, horny eyes. The end! the end!

Surely the end! What's here? a shape, a shade,
A flash of light. Is that the angel there
That holds a crown? Come, blessed brother, come.
I know thy glittering face. I waited long;
My brows are ready. What! deny it now?
Nay, draw, draw, draw nigh. So I clutch it. Christ!
'Tis gone: 'tis here again; the crown! the crown!
So now 'tis fitted on and grows to me,
And from it melt the dews of Paradise,
Sweet! sweet! spikenard, and balm, and frankincense.
Ah! let me not be fool'd, sweet saints: I trust
That I am whole, and clean, and meet for Heaven.
   Speak, if there be a priest, a man of God
Among you there, and let him presently
Approach, and lean a ladder on the shaft,
And climbing up into my airy home,
Deliver me the blessed sacrament.
For by the warning of the Holy Ghost,
I prophesy that I shall die to-night,
A quarter before twelve.
               Put thou, O Lord,
Aid all this foolish people; let them take
Example, pattern: lead them to thy light.

The Talking Oak

Once more the gate behind me falls;
   Once more before my face
I see the moulder'd Abbey-walls,
   That stand within the chace.

Beyond the lodge the city lies,
   Beneath its drift of smoke;
And ah! with what delighted eyes
   I turn to yonder oak.

For when my passion first began,
   Ere that, which in me burn'd,
The love, that makes me thrice a man,
   Could hope itself return'd;

To yonder oak within the field
   I spoke without restraint,
And with a larger faith appeal'd
   Than Papist unto Saint.

For oft I talk'd with him apart,
   And told him of my choice,
Until he plagiarized a heart,
   And answer'd with a voice.

Tho' what he whisper'd, under Heaven
   None else could understand;
I found him garrulously given,
   A babbler in the land.

But since I heard him make reply
   Is many a weary hour;
'Twere well to question him, and try
   If yet he keeps the power.

Hail, hidden to the knees in fern,
   Broad Oak of Sumner-chace,
Whose topmost branches can discern
   The roofs of Sumner-place!

Say thou, whereon I carved her name,
   If ever maid or spouse,
As fair as my Olivia, came
   To rest beneath thy boughs. —

'O Walter, I have shelter'd here
   Whatever maiden grace
The good old Summers, year by year,
   Made ripe in Sumner-chace:

'Old Summers, when the monk was fat,
   And, issuing shorn and sleek,
Would twist his girdle tight, and pat
   The girls upon the cheek,

'Ere yet, in scorn of Peter's-pence,
   And number'd bead, and shrift,
Bluff Harry broke into the spence,
   And turn'd the cowls adrift:

'And I have seen some score of those
   Fresh faces, that would thrive
When his man-minded offset rose
   To chase the deer at five;

'And all that from the town would stroll
   Till that wild wind made work
In which the gloomy brewer's soul
   Went by me, like a stork:

'The slight she-slips of loyal blood,
 And others, passing praise,
Strait-laced, but all-too-full in bud
 For puritanic stays:

'And I have shadow'd many a group
 Of beauties, that were born
In teacup-times of hood and hoop,
 Or while the patch was worn;

'And, leg and arm with love-knots gay,
 About me leap'd and laugh'd
The modish Cupid of the day,
 And shrill'd his tinsel shaft.

'I swear (and else may insects prick
 Each leaf into a gall)
This girl, for whom your heart is sick,
 Is three times worth them all;

'For those and theirs, by Nature's law,
 Have faded long ago;
But in these latter springs I saw
 Your own Olivia blow,

'From when she gamboll'd on the greens,
 A baby-germ, to when
The maiden blossoms of her teens
 Could number five from ten.

'I swear, by leaf, and wind, and rain,
 (And hear me with thine ears,)
That, tho' I circle in the grain
 Five hundred rings of years —

'Yet, since I first could cast a shade,
 Did never creature pass
So slightly, musically made,
 So light upon the grass:

'For as to fairies, that will flit
 To make the greensward fresh,
I hold them exquisitely knit,
 But far too spare of flesh.'

Oh, hide thy knotted knees in fern,
 And overlook the chace;
And from thy topmost branch discern
 The roofs of Sumner-place.

But thou, whereon I carved her name,
   That oft hast heard my vows,
Declare when last Olivia came
   To sport beneath thy boughs.

'O yesterday, you know, the fair
   Was holden at the town;
Her father left his good arm-chair,
   And rode his hunter down.

'And with him Albert came on his.
   I look'd at him with joy:
As cowslip unto oxlip is,
   So seems she to the boy.

'An hour had past – and, sitting straight
   Within the low-wheel'd chaise,
Her mother trundled to the gate
   Behind the dappled greys.

'But, as for her, she stay'd at home,
   And on the roof she went,
And down the way you use to come,
   She look'd with discontent.

'She left the novel half-uncut
   Upon the rosewood shelf;
She left the new piano shut:
   She could not please herself.

'Then ran she, gamesome as the colt,
   And livelier than a lark
She sent her voice thro' all the holt
   Before her, and the park.

'A light wind chased her on the wing,
   And in the chase grew wild,
As close as might be would he cling
   About the darling child:

'But light as any wind that blows
   So fleetly did she stir,
The flower, she touch'd on, dipt and rose,
   And turn'd to look at her.

'And here she came, and round me play'd,
   And sang to me the whole
Of those three stanzas that you made
   About my "giant bole";

'And in a fit of frolic mirth
   She strove to span my waist:
Alas, I was so broad of girth,
   I could not be embraced.

'I wish'd myself the fair young beech
   That here beside me stands,
That round me, clasping each in each,
   She might have lock'd her hands.

'Yet seem'd the pressure thrice as sweet
   As woodbine's fragile hold
Or when I feel about my feet
   The berried briony fold.'

O muffle round thy knees with fern,
   And shadow Sumner-chace!
Long may thy topmost branch discern
   The roofs of Sumner-place!

But tell me, did she read the name
   I carved with many vows
When last with throbbing heart I came
   To rest beneath thy boughs?

'O yes, she wander'd round and round
   These knotted knees of mine,
And found, and kiss'd the name she found,
   And sweetly murmur'd thine.

'A teardrop trembled from its source,
   And down my surface crept.
My sense of touch is something coarse,
   But I believe she wept.

'Then flush'd her cheek with rosy light,
   She glanced across the plain;
But not a creature was in sight:
   She kiss'd me once again.

'Her kisses were so close and kind,
   That, trust me on my word,
Hard wood I am, and wrinkled rind,
   But yet my sap was stirr'd:

'And even into my inmost ring
   A pleasure I discern'd,
Like those blind motions of the Spring,
   That show the year is turn'd.

'Thrice-happy he that may caress
    The ringlet's waving balm –
The cushions of whose touch may press
    The maiden's tender palm.

'I, rooted here among the groves,
    But languidly adjust
My vapid vegetable loves
    With anthers and with dust:

'For ah! my friend, the days were brief
    Whereof the poets talk,
When that, which breathes within the leaf,
    Could slip its bark and walk.

'But could I, as in times foregone,
    From spray, and branch, and stem,
Have suck'd and gather'd into one
    The life that spreads in them,

'She had not found me so remiss;
    But lightly issuing thro',
I would have paid her kiss for kiss
    With usury thereto.'

O flourish high, with leafy towers,
    And overlook the lea,
Pursue thy loves among the bowers,
    But leave thou mine to me.

O flourish, hidden deep in fern,
    Old oak, I love thee well
A thousand thanks for what I learn
    And what remains to tell.

' 'Tis little more: the day was warm;
    At last, tired out with play,
She sank her head upon her arm,
    And at my feet she lay.

'Her eyelids dropp'd their silken eaves.
    I breathed upon her eyes
Thro' all the summer of my leaves
    A welcome mix'd with sighs.

'I took the swarming sound of life –
    The music from the town –
The murmurs of the drum and fife
    And lull'd them in my own.

'Sometimes I let a sunbeam slip,
    To light her shaded eye;
A second flutter'd round her lip
    Like a golden butterfly;

'A third would glimmer on her neck
    To make the necklace shine;
Another slid, a sunny fleck,
    From head to ankle fine,

'Then close and dark my arms I spread,
    And shadow'd all her rest –
Dropt dews upon her golden head,
    An acorn in her breast.

'But in a pet she started up,
    And pluck'd it out, and drew
My little oakling from the cup,
    And flung him in the dew.

'And yet it was a graceful gift –
    I felt a pang within
As when I see the woodman lift
    His axe to slay my kin.

'I shook him down because he was
    The finest on the tree.
He lies beside thee on the grass.
    O kiss him once for me.

'O kiss him twice and thrice for me,
    That have no lips to kiss,
For never yet was oak on lea
    Shall grow so fair as this.'

Step deeper yet in herb and fern,
    Look further thro' the chace
Spread upward till thy boughs discern
    The front of Sumner-place.

This fruit of thine by Love is blest,
    That but a moment lay
Where fairer fruit of Love may rest
    Some happy future day.

I kiss it twice, I kiss it thrice,
    The warmth it thence shall win
To riper life may magnetize
    The baby-oak within.

But thou, while kingdoms overset,
   Or lapse from hand to hand,
Thy leaf shall never fail, nor yet
   Thine acorn in the land.

May never saw dismember thee,
   Nor wielded axe disjoint,
That art the fairest-spoken tree
   From here to Lizard-point.

O rock upon thy towery top
   All throats that gurgle sweet!
All starry culmination drop
   Balm-dews to bathe thy feet!

All grass of silky feather grow –
   And while he sinks or swells
The full south-breeze around thee blow
   The sound of minster bells.

The fat earth feed thy branchy root,
   That under deeply strikes!
The northern morning o'er thee shoot,
   High up, in silver spikes!

Nor ever lightning char thy grain,
   But, rolling as in sleep
Low thunders bring the mellow rain,
   That makes thee broad and deep!

And hear me swear a solemn oath,
   That only by thy side
Will I to Olive plight my troth,
   And gain her for my bride.

And when my marriage morn may fall,
   She, Dryad-like, shall wear
Alternate leaf and acorn-ball
   In wreath about her hair.

And I will work in prose and rhyme,
   And praise thee more in both
Than bard has honour'd beech or lime,
   Or that Thessalian growth,

In which the swarthy ringdove sat,
   And mystic sentence spoke;
And more than England honours that,
   Thy famous brother-oak,

Wherein the younger Charles abode
   Till all the paths were dim,
And far below the Roundhead rode,
   And humm'd a surly hymn.

Love and Duty

Of love that never found his earthly close,
What sequel? Streaming eyes and breaking hearts?
Or all the same as if he had not been?
   Not so. Shall Error in the round of time
Still father Truth? O shall the braggart shout
For some blind glimpse of freedom work itself
Thro' madness, hated by the wise, to law
System and empire? Sin itself be found
The cloudy porch oft opening on the Sun?
And only he, this wonder, dead, become
Mere highway dust? or year by year alone
Sit brooding in the ruins of a life,
Nightmare of youth, the spectre of himself?
   If this were thus, if this, indeed, were all,
Better the narrow brain, the stony heart,
The staring eye glazed o'er with sapless days,
The long mechanic pacings to and fro,
The set grey life, and apathetic end.
But am I not the nobler thro' thy love?
O three times less unworthy! likewise thou
Art more thro' Love, and greater than thy years.
The Sun will run his orbit, and the Moon
Her circle. Wait, and Love himself will bring
The drooping flower of knowledge changed to fruit
Of wisdom. Wait: my faith is large in Time,
And that which shapes it to some perfect end.
   Will some one say, then why not ill for good?
Why took ye not your pastime? To that man
My work shall answer, since I knew the right
And did it; for a man is not as God,
But then most Godlike being most a man.
– So let me think 'tis well for thee and me –
Ill-fated that I am, what lot is mine
Whose foresight preaches peace, my heart so slow
To feel it! For how hard it seem'd to me,
When eyes, love-languid thro' half-tears, would dwell
One earnest, earnest moment upon mine,
Then not to dare to see! when thy low voice,

Faltering, would break its syllables, to keep
My own full-tuned, – hold passion in a leash,
And not leap forth and fall about thy neck,
And on thy bosom (deep-desired relief!)
Rain out the heavy mist of tears, that weigh'd
Upon my brain, my senses and my soul!
   For Love himself took part against himself
To warn us off, and Duty loved of Love –
O this world's curse, – beloved but hated – came
Like Death betwixt thy dear embrace and mine,
And crying, 'Who is this? behold thy bride,'
She push'd me from thee.
               If the sense is hard
To alien ears, I did not speak to these –
No, not to thee, but to thyself in me:
Hard is my doom and thine: thou knowest it all.
   Could Love part thus? was it not well to speak,
To have spoken once? It could not but be well.
The slow sweet hours that bring us all things good,
The slow sad hours that bring us all things ill,
And all good things from evil, brought the night
In which we sat together and alone,
And to the want, that hollow'd all the heart,
Gave utterance by the yearning of an eye,
That burn'd upon its object thro' such tears
As flow but once a life.
             The trance gave way
To those caresses, when a hundred times
In that last kiss, which never was the last,
Farewell, like endless welcome, lived and died.
Then follow'd counsel, comfort, and the words
That make a man feel strong in speaking truth;
Till now the dark was worn, and overhead
The lights of sunset and of sunrise mix'd
In that brief night; the summer night, that paused
Among her stars to hear us; stars that hung
Love-charmed to listen: all the wheels of Time
Spun round in station, but the end had come.
   O then like those, who clench their nerves to rush
Upon their dissolution, we two rose,
There – closing like an individual life –
In one blind cry of passion and of pain,
Like bitter accusation ev'n to death,
Caught up the whole of love and utter'd it,
And bade adieu for ever.
             Live – yet live –

Shall sharpest pathos blight us, knowing all
Life needs for life is possible to will –
Live happy; tend thy flowers; be tended by
My blessing! Should my Shadow cross thy thoughts
Too sadly for their peace, remand it thou
For calmer hours to Memory's darkest hold,
If not to be forgotten – not at once –
Not all forgotten. Should it cross thy dreams,
O might it come like one that looks content,
With quiet eyes unfaithful to the truth,
And point thee forward to a distant light
Or seem to lift a burthen from thy heart
And leave thee freër, till thou wake refresh'd,
Then when the first low matin-chirp hath grown
Full quire, and morning driv'n her plow of pearl
Far furrowing into light the mounded rack,
Beyond the fair green field and eastern sea.

Ulysses

It little profits that an idle king,
By this still hearth, among these barren crags,
Match'd with an aged wife, I mete and dole
Unequal laws unto a savage race,
That hoard, and sleep, and feed, and know not me.
I cannot rest from travel: I will drink
Life to the lees: all times I have enjoy'd
Greatly, have suffer'd greatly, both with those
That loved me, and alone; on shore, and when
Thro' scudding drifts the rainy Hyades
Vext the dim sea: I am become a name;
For always roaming with a hungry heart
Much have I seen and known; cities of men
And manners, climates, councils, governments,
Myself not least, but honour'd of them all;
And drunk delight of battle with my peers,
Far on the ringing plains of windy Troy.
I am a part of all that I have met;
Yet all experience is an arch wherethro'
Gleams that untravell'd world, whose margin fades
For ever and for ever when I move.
How dull it is to pause, to make an end,
To rust unburnish'd, not to shine in use!
As tho' to breathe were life. Life piled on life
Were all too little, and of one to me

Little remains: but every hour is saved
From that eternal silence, something more,
A bringer of new things; and vile it were
For some three suns to store and hoard myself,
And this grey spirit yearning in desire
To follow knowledge, like a sinking star,
Beyond the utmost bound of human thought.
    This is my son, mine own Telemachus,
To whom I leave the sceptre and the isle –
Well-loved of me, discerning to fulfil
This labour, by slow prudence to make mild
A rugged people, and thro' soft degrees
Subdue them to the useful and the good.
Most blameless is he, centred in the sphere
Of common duties, decent not to fail
In offices of tenderness, and pay
Meet adoration to my household gods,
When I am gone. He works his work, I mine.
    There lies the port: the vessel puffs her sail:
There gloom the dark broad seas. My mariners,
Souls that have toil'd, and wrought, and thought with me –
That ever with a frolic welcome took
The thunder and the sunshine, and opposed
Free hearts, free foreheads – you and I are old;
Old age hath yet his honour and his toil;
Death closes all: but something ere the end,
Some work of noble note, may yet be done,
Not unbecoming men that strove with Gods.
The lights begin to twinkle from the rocks:
The long day wanes: the slow moon climbs: the deep
Moans round with many voices. Come, my friends,
'Tis not too late to seek a newer world.
Push off, and sitting well in order smite
The sounding furrows; for my purpose holds
To sail beyond the sunset, and the baths
Of all the western stars, until I die.
It may be that the gulfs will wash us down:
It may be we shall touch the Happy Isles,
And see the great Achilles, whom we knew.
Tho' much is taken, much abides; and tho'
We are not now that strength which in old days
Moved earth and heaven; that which we are, we are;
One equal temper of heroic hearts,
Made weak by time and fate, but strong in will
To strive, to seek, to find, and not to yield.

Locksley Hall

Comrades, leave me here a little, while as yet 'tis early morn:
Leave me here, and when you want me, sound upon the bugle horn.

'Tis the place, and all around it, as of old, the curlews call,
Dreary gleams about the moorland flying over Locksley Hall;

Locksley Hall, that in the distance overlooks the sandy tracts,
And the hollow ocean-ridges roaring into cataracts.

Many a night from yonder ivied casement, ere I went to rest,
Did I look on great Orion sloping slowly to the West.

Many a night I saw the Pleiads, rising thro' the mellow shade,
Glitter like a swarm of fire-flies tangled in a silver braid.

Here about the beach I wander'd, nourishing a youth sublime
With the fairy tales of science, and the long result of Time;

When the centuries behind me like a fruitful land reposed;
When I clung to all the present for the promise that it closed:

When I dipt into the future far as human eye could see;
Saw the Vision of the world, and all the wonder that would be. –

In the Spring a fuller crimson comes upon the robin's breast;
In the Spring the wanton lapwing gets himself another crest;

In the Spring a livelier iris changes on the burnish'd dove;
In the Spring a young man's fancy lightly turns to thoughts of love.

Then her cheek was pale and thinner than should be for one so young,
And her eyes on all my motions with a mute observance hung.

And I said, 'My cousin Amy, speak, and speak the truth to me,
Trust me, cousin, all the current of my being sets to thee.'

On her pallid cheek and forehead came a colour and a light,
As I have seen the rosy red flushing in the northern night.

And she turn'd – her bosom shaken with a sudden storm of sighs –
All the spirit deeply dawning in the dark of hazel eyes –

Saying, 'I have hid my feelings, fearing they should do me wrong;'
Saying, 'Dost thou love me, cousin?' weeping, 'I have loved thee long.'

Love took up the glass of Time, and turn'd it in his glowing hands;
Every moment, lightly shaken, ran itself in golden sands.

Love took up the harp of Life, and smote on all the chords with might;
Smote the chord of Self, that, trembling, pass'd in music out of sight.

Many a morning on the moorland did we hear the copses ring,
And her whisper throng'd my pulses with the fullness of the Spring.

Many an evening by the waters did we watch the stately ships,
And our spirits rush'd together at the touching of the lips.

O my cousin, shallow-hearted! O my Amy, mine no more!
O the dreary, dreary moorland! O the barren, barren shore!

Falser than all fancy fathoms, falser than all songs have sung
Puppet to a father's threat, and servile to a shrewish tongue!

Is it well to wish thee happy? – having known me – to decline
On a range of lower feelings and a narrower heart than mine!

Yet it shall be: thou shalt lower to his level day by day,
What is fine within thee growing coarse to sympathize with clay.

As the husband is, the wife is: thou art mated with a clown,
And the grossness of his nature will have weight to drag thee down.

He will hold thee, when his passion shall have spent its novel force,
Something better than his dog, a little dearer than his horse.

What is this? his eyes are heavy: think not they are glazed with wine.
Go to him: it is thy duty: kiss him: take his hand in thine.

It may be my lord is weary, that his brain is overwrought:
Soothe him with thy finer fancies, touch him with thy lighter thought.

He will answer to the purpose, easy things to understand –
Better thou wert dead before me, tho' I slew thee with my hand!

Better thou and I were lying, hidden from the heart's disgrace,
Roll'd in one anothers arms, and silent in a last embrace.

Cursed be the social wants that sin against the strength of youth!
Cursed be the social lies that warp us from the living truth!

Cursed be the sickly forms that err from honest Nature's rule!
Cursed be the gold that gilds the straiten'd forehead of the fool!

Well – 'tis well that I should bluster! – Hadst thou less unworthy
  proved –
Would to God – for I had loved thee more than ever wife was loved.

Am I mad, that I should cherish that which bears but bitter fruit?
I will pluck it from my bosom, tho' my heart be at the root.

Never, tho' my mortal summers to such length of years should come
As the many-winter'd crow that leads the clanging rookery home.

Where is comfort? in division of the records of the mind?
Can I part her from herself, and love her, as I knew her, kind?

I remember one that perish'd: sweetly did she speak and move:
Such a one do I remember, whom to look at was to love.

Can I think of her as dead, and love her for the love she bore?
No – she never loved me truly: love is love for evermore.

Comfort? comfort scorn'd of devils! this is truth the poet sings,
That a sorrow's crown of sorrow is remembering happier things.

Drug thy memories, lest thou learn it, lest thy heart be put to proof,
In the dead unhappy night, and when the rain is on the roof.

Like a dog, he hunts in dreams, and thou art staring at the wall,
Where the dying night-lamp flickers, and the shadows rise and fall.

Then a hand shall pass before thee, pointing to his drunken sleep,
To thy widow'd marriage-pillows, to the tears that thou wilt weep.

Thou shalt hear the 'Never, never,' whisper'd by the phantom years,
And a song from out the distance in the ringing of thine ears;

And an eye shall vex thee, looking ancient kindness on thy pain.
Turn thee, turn thee on thy pillow: get thee to thy rest again.

Nay, but Nature brings thee solace; for a tender voice will cry.
'Tis a purer life than thine; a lip to drain thy trouble dry.

Baby lips will laugh me down: my latest rival brings thee rest.
Baby fingers, waxen touches, press me from the mother's breast.

O, the child too clothes the father with a dearness not his due.
Half is thine and half is his: it will be worthy of the two.

O, I see thee old and formal, fitted to thy petty part,
With a little hoard of maxims preaching down a daughter's heart.

'They were dangerous guides the feelings – she herself was not exempt –
Truly, she herself had suffer'd'– Perish in thy self contempt!

Overlive it – lower yet – be happy! wherefore should I care?
I myself must mix with action, lest I wither by despair.

What is that which I should turn to, lighting upon days like these?
Every door is barr'd with gold, and opens but to golden keys.

Every gate is throng'd with suitors, all the markets overflow.
I have but an angry fancy: what is that which I should do?

I had been content to perish, falling on the foeman's ground
When the ranks are roll'd in vapour, and the winds are laid with
        sound.

But the jingling of the guinea helps the hurt that Honour feels,
And the nations do but murmur, snarling at each other's heels.

Can I but relive in sadness? I will turn that earlier page.
Hide me from my deep emotion, O thou wondrous Mother-Age!

Make me feel the wild pulsation that I felt before the strife,
When I heard my days before me, and the tumult of my life;

Yearning for the large excitement that the coming years would yield,
Eager-hearted as a boy when first he leaves his father's field,

And at night along the dusky highway near and nearer drawn,
Sees in heaven the light of London flaring like a dreary dawn;

And his spirit leaps within him to be gone before him then,
Underneath the light he looks at, in among the throngs of men;

Men, my brothers, men the workers, ever reaping something new:
That which they have done but earnest of the things that they shall do:

For I dipt into the future, far as human eye could see,
Saw the Vision of the world, and all the wonder that would be;

Saw the heavens fill with commerce, argosies of magic sails,
Pilots of the purple twilight, dropping down with costly bales;

Heard the heavens fill with shouting, and there rain'd a ghostly dew
From the nations' airy navies grappling in the central blue;

Far along the world-wide whisper of the south-wind rushing warm,
With the standards of the peoples plunging thro' the thunder-storm;

Till the war-drum throbb'd no longer, and the battleflags were furl'd
In the Parliament of man, the Federation of the world.

There the common sense of most shall hold a fretful realm in awe,
And the kindly earth shall slumber, lapt in universal law.

So I triumph'd ere my passion sweeping thro' me left me dry,
Left me with the palsied heart, and left me with the jaundiced eye;

Eye, to which all order festers, all things here are out of joint:
Science moves, but slowly slowly, creeping on from point to point:

Slowly comes a hungry people, as a lion, creeping nigher,
Glares at one that nods and winks behind a slowly-dying fire.

Yet I doubt not thro' the ages one increasing purpose runs,
And the thoughts of men are widen'd with the process of the suns.

What is that to him that reaps not harvest of his youthful joys,
Tho' the deep heart of existence beat for ever like a boy's?

Knowledge comes, but wisdom lingers, and I linger on the shore,
And the individual withers, and the world is more and more.

Knowledge comes, but wisdom lingers, and he bears a laden breast,
Full of sad experience, moving toward the stillness of his rest.

Hark, my merry comrades call me, sounding on the bugle-horn,
They to whom my foolish passion were a target for their scorn:

Shall it not be scorn to me to harp on such a moulder'd string?
I am shamed thro' all my nature to have loved so slight a thing.

Weakness to be wroth with weakness! woman's pleasure, woman's
        pain –
Nature made them blinder motions bounded in a shallower brain:

Woman is the lesser man, and all thy passions, match'd with mine,
Are as moonlight unto sunlight, and as water unto wine –

Here at least, where nature sickens, nothing. Ah, for some retreat
Deep in yonder shining Orient, where my life began to beat;

Where in wild Mahratta-battle fell my father evil-starr'd; –
I was left a trampled orphan, and a selfish uncle's ward.

Or to burst all links of habit – there to wander far away,
On from island unto island at the gateways of the day.

Larger constellations burning, mellow moons and happy skies,
Breadths of tropic shade and palms in cluster, knots of Paradise.

Never comes the trader, never floats an European flag,
Slides the bird o'er lustrous woodland, swings the trailer from the crag;

Droops the heavy-blossom'd bower, hangs the heavy-fruited tree –
Summer isles of Eden lying in dark-purple spheres of sea.

There methinks would be enjoyment more than in this march of mind,
In the steamship, in the railway, in the thoughts that shake mankind.

There the passions cramp'd no longer shall have scope and breathing-
    space;
I will take some savage woman, she shall rear my dusky race.

Iron-jointed, supple-sinew'd, they shall dive, and they shall run,
Catch the wild goat by the hair, and hurl their lances in the sun;

Whistle back the parrot's call, and leap the rainbows of the brooks,
Not with blinded eyesight poring over miserable books –

Fool, again the dream, the fancy! but I *know* my words are wild,
But I count the grey barbarian lower than the Christian child.

I, to herd with narrow foreheads, vacant of our glorious gains,
Like a beast with lower pleasures, like a beast with lower pains!

Mated with a squalid savage – what to me were sun or clime?
I the heir of all the ages, in the foremost files of time –

I that rather held it better men should perish one by one,
Than that earth should stand at gaze like Joshua's moon in Ajalon!

Not in vain the distance beacons Forward, forward let us range
Let the great world spin for ever down the ringing grooves of change

Thro' the shadow of the globe we sweep into the younger day:
Better fifty years of Europe than a cycle of Cathay.

Mother-Age (for mine I knew not) help me as when life begun:
Rift the hills, and roll the waters, flash the lightnings, weigh the Sun —

O, I see the crescent promise of my spirit hath not set.
Ancient founts of inspiration well thro' all my fancy yet.

Howsoever these things be, a long farewell to Locksley Hall!
Now for me the woods may wither, now for me the roof-tree fall.

Comes a vapour from the margin, blackening over heath and holt,
Cramming all the blast before it, in its breast a thunderbolt.

Let it fall on Locksley Hall, with rain or hail, or fire or snow;
For the mighty wind arises, roaring seaward, and I go.

Godiva

I waited for the train at Coventry;
I hung with grooms and porters on the bridge,
To watch the three tall spires; and there I shaped
The city's ancient legend into this: —
   Not only we, the latest seed of Time,
New men, that in the flying of a wheel
Cry down the past, not only we, that prate
Of rights and wrongs, have loved the people well,
And loathed to see them overtax'd; but she
Did more, and underwent, and overcame,
The woman of a thousand summers back,
Godiva, wife to that grim Earl, who ruled
In Coventry: for when he laid a tax
Upon his town, and all the mothers brought
Their children, clamouring, 'If we pay, we starve!'
She sought her lord, and found him, where he strode
About the hall, among his dogs, alone,
His beard a foot before him, and his hair
A yard behind. She told him of their tears,
And pray'd him, 'If they pay this tax, they starve.'
Whereat he stared, replying, half-amazed,
'You would not let your little finger ache
For such as *these?*' — 'But I would die,' said she.
He laugh'd, and swore by Peter and by Paul:
Then fillip'd at the diamond in her ear;

'O aye, aye, aye, you talk!'– 'Alas!' she said,
'But prove me what it is I would not do.'
And from a heart as rough as Esau's hand,
He answer'd, 'Ride you naked thro' the town,
And I repeal it;' and nodding, as in scorn,
He parted, with great strides among his dogs.

   So left alone, the passions of her mind,
As winds from all the compass shift and blow,
Made war upon each other for an hour,
Till pity won. She sent a herald forth,
And bade him cry, with sound of trumpet, all
The hard condition; but that she would loose
The people: therefore, as they loved her well,
From then till noon no foot should pace the street,
No eye look down, she passing; but that all
Should keep within, door shut, and window barr'd.

   Then fled she to her inmost bower, and there
Unclasp'd the wedded eagles of her belt,
The grim Earl's gift; but ever at a breath
She linger'd, looking like a summer moon
Half-dipt in cloud: anon she shook her head
And shower'd the rippled ringlets to her knee,
Unclad herself in haste; adown the stair
Stole on; and, like a creeping sunbeam, slid
From pillar unto pillar, until she reach'd
The gateway; there she found her palfrey trapt
In purple blazon'd with armorial gold.

   Then she rode forth, clothed on with chastity:
The deep air listen'd round her as she rode,
And all the low wind hardly breathed for fear.
The little wide-mouth'd heads upon the spout
Had cunning eyes to see: the barking cur
Made her cheek flame: her palfrey's footfall shot
Light horrors thro' her pulses: the blind walls
Were full of chinks and holes; and overhead
Fantastic gables, crowding, stared: but she
Not less thro' all bore up, till, last, she saw
The white-flower'd elder-thicket from the field
Gleam thro' the Gothic archways in the wall.

   Then she rode back, clothed on with chastity:
And one low churl, compact of thankless earth,
The fatal byword of all years to come,
Boring a little auger-hole in fear
Peep'd – but his eyes, before they had their will,
Were shrivell'd into darkness in his head,
And dropt before him. So the Powers, who wait

On noble deeds, cancell'd a sense misused;
And she, that knew not, pass'd: and all at once,
With twelve great shocks of sound, the shameless noon
Was clash'd and hammer'd from a hundred towers,
One after one: but even then she gain'd
Her bower; whence reissuing, robed and crown'd,
To meet her lord, she took the tax away,
And built herself an everlasting name.

The Two Voices

A still small voice spake unto me,
'Thou art so full of misery,
Were it not better not to be?'

Then to the still small voice I said
'Let me not cast in endless shade
What is so wonderfully made.'

To which the voice did urge reply;
'To-day I saw the dragon-fly
Come from the wells where he did lie.

'An inner impulse rent the veil
Of his old husk: from head to tail
Came out clear plates of sapphire mail.

'He dried his wings: like gauze they grew:
Thro' crofts and pastures wet with dew
A living flash of light he flew.'

I said, 'When first the world began,
Young Nature thro' five cycles ran,
And in the sixth she moulded man.

'She gave him mind, the lordliest
Proportion, and, above the rest,
Dominion in the head and breast.'

Thereto the silent voice replied;
'Self-blinded are you by your pride:
Look up thro' night: the world is wide.

'This truth within thy mind rehearse,
That in a boundless universe
Is boundless better, boundless worse.

'Think you this mould of hopes and fears
Could find no statelier than his peers
In yonder hundred million spheres?'

It spake, moreover, in my mind:
'Tho' thou wert scatter'd to the wind,
Yet is there plenty of the kind.'

Then did my response clearer fall:
'No compound of this earthly ball
Is like another, all in all.'

To which he answer'd scoffingly;
'Good soul! suppose I grant it thee,
Who'll weep for thy deficiency?

'Or will one beam be less intense,
When thy peculiar difference
Is cancell'd in the world of sense?'

I would have said, 'Thou canst not know,'
But my full heart, that work'd below,
Rain'd thro' my sight its overflow.

Again the voice spake unto me:
'Thou art so steep'd in misery,
Surely 'twere better not to be.

'Thine anguish will not let thee sleep,
Nor any train of reason keep:
Thou canst not think, but thou wilt weep.'

I said, 'The years with change advance:
If I make dark my countenance,
I shut my life from happier chance.

'Some turn this sickness yet might take,
Ev'n yet.' But he: 'What drug can make
A wither'd palsy cease to shake?'

I wept, 'Tho' I should die, I know
That ail about the thorn will blow
In tufts of rosy-tinted snow;

'And men, thro' novel spheres of thought
Still moving after truth long sought,
Will learn new things when I am not.'

'Yet,' said the secret voice, 'some time,
Sooner or later, will grey prime
Make thy grass hoar with early rime.

'Not less swift souls that yearn for light,
Rapt after heaven's starry flight,
Would sweep the tracts of day and night.

'Not less the bee would range her cells,
The furzy prickle fire the dells,
The foxglove cluster dappled bells.'

I said that 'all the years invent;
Each month is various to present
The world with some development.

'Were this not well, to bide mine hour,
Tho' watching from a ruin'd tower
How grows the day of human power?'

'The highest-mounted mind,' he said,
'Still sees the sacred morning spread
The silent summit overhead.

'Will thirty seasons render plain
Those lonely lights that still remain,
Just breaking over land and main?

'Or make that morn, from his cold crown
And crystal silence creeping down,
Flood with full daylight glebe and town?

'Forerun thy peers, thy time, and let
Thy feet, millenniums hence, be set
In midst of knowledge, dream'd not yet.

'Thou hast not gain'd a real height,
Nor art thou nearer to the light,
Because the scale is infinite.

' 'Twere better not to breathe or speak,
Than cry for strength, remaining weak,
And seem to find, but still to seek.

'Moreover, but to seem to find
Asks what thou lackest, thought resign'd,
A healthy frame, a quiet mind.'

I said, 'When I am gone away,
"He dared not tarry," men will say,
Doing dishonour to my clay.'

'This is more vile,' he made reply
'To breathe and loathe, to live and sigh,
Than once from dread of pain to die.

'Sick art thou – a divided will
Still heaping on the fear of ill
The fear of men, a coward still.

'Do men love thee? Art thou so bound
To men, that how thy name may sound
Will vex thee lying underground?

'The memory of the wither'd leaf
In endless time is scarce more brief
Than of the garner'd Autumn-sheaf.

'Go, vexed Spirit, sleep in trust;
The right ear, that is fill'd with dust,
Hears little of the false or just.'

'Hard task, to pluck resolve,' I cried,
'From emptiness and the waste wide
Of that abyss, or scornful pride!

'Nay – rather yet that I could raise
One hope that warm'd me in the days
While still I yearn'd for human praise.

'When, wide in soul and bold of tongue,
Among the tents I paused and sung,
The distant battle flash'd and rung.

'I sung the joyful Paean clear,
And, sitting, burnish'd without fear
The brand, the buckler, and the spear –

'Waiting to strive a happy strife,
To war with falsehood to the knife,
And not to lose the good of life –

'Some hidden principle to move,
To put together, part and prove,
And mete the bounds of hate and love –

'As far as might be, to carve out
Free space for every human doubt,
That the whole mind might orb about –

'To search thro' all I felt or saw,
The springs of life, the depths of awe,
And reach the law within the law:

'At least, not rotting like a weed,
But, having sown some generous seed,
Fruitful of further thought and deed,

'To pass, when Life her light withdraws,
Not void of righteous self-applause,
Nor in a merely selfish cause –

'In some good cause, not in mine own,
To perish, wept for, honour'd, known,
And like a warrior overthrown;

'Whose eyes are dim with glorious tears,
When, soil'd with noble dust, he hears
His country's war-song thrill his ears:

'Then dying of a mortal stroke,
That time the foeman's line is broke,
And all the war is roll'd in smoke.'

'Yea!' said the voice, 'thy dream was good,
While thou abodest in the bud.
It was the stirring of the blood.

'If Nature put not forth her power
About the opening of the flower,
Who is it that could live an hour?

'Then comes the check, the change, the fall
Pain rises up, old pleasures pall.
There is one remedy for all.

'Yet hadst thou, thro' enduring pain,
Link'd month to month with such a chain
Of knitted purport, all were vain.

'Thou hadst not between death and birth
Dissolved the riddle of the earth.
So were thy labour little-worth.

'That men with knowledge merely play'd,
I told thee – hardly nigher made,
Tho' scaling slow from grade to grade;

'Much less this dreamer, deaf and blind
Named man, may hope some truth to find
That bears relation to the mind.

'For every worm beneath the moon
Draws different threads, and late and soon
Spins, toiling out his own cocoon.

'Cry, faint not: either Truth is born
Beyond the polar gleam forlorn,
Or in the gateways of the morn.

'Cry, faint not, climb: the summits slope
Beyond the furthest flights of hope,
Wrapt in dense cloud from base to cope.

'Sometimes a little corner shines,
As over rainy mist inclines
A gleaming crag with belts of pines.

'I will go forward, sayest thou,
I shall not fail to find her now.
Look up, the fold is on her brow.

'If straight thy track, or if oblique,
Thou know'st not. Shadows thou dost strike,
Embracing cloud, Ixion-like;

'And owning but a little more
Than beasts, abidest lame and poor,
Calling thyself a little lower

'Than angels. Cease to wail and brawl!
Why inch by inch to darkness crawl?
There is one remedy for all.'

'O dull, one-sided voice,' said I,
Wilt thou make everything a lie,
To flatter me that I may die?

'I know that age to age succeeds,
Blowing a noise of tongues and deeds,
A dust of systems and of creeds.

'I cannot hide that some have striven,
Achieving calm, to whom was given
The joy that mixes man with Heaven:

'Who, rowing hard against the stream,
Saw distant gates of Eden gleam,
And did not dream it was a dream;

'But heard, by secret transport led,
Ev'n in the charnels of the dead,
The murmur of the fountain-head –

'Which did accomplish their desire,
Bore and forbore, and did not tire,
Like Stephen, an unquenched fire.

'He heeded not reviling tones,
Nor sold his heart to idle moans,
Tho' cursed and scorn'd, and bruised with stones:

'But looking upward, full of grace,
He pray'd, and from a happy place
God's glory smote him on the face.'

The sullen answer slid betwixt:
Not that the grounds of hope were fix'd,
The elements were kindlier mix'd.'

I said, 'I toil beneath the curse,
But, knowing not the universe,
I fear to slide from bad to worse.

'And that, in seeking to undo
One riddle, and to find the true,
I knit a hundred others new:

'Or that this anguish fleeting hence,
Unmanacled from bonds of sense,
Be fix'd and froz'n to permanence:

'For I go, weak from suffering here;
Naked I go, and void of cheer:
What is it that I may not fear?'

'Consider well,' the voice replied,
'His face, that two hours since hath died
Wilt thou find passion, pain or pride?

'Will he obey when one commands?
Or answer should one press his hands?
He answers not, nor understands.

'His palms are folded on his breast:
There is no other thing express'd
But long disquiet merged in rest.

'His lips are very mild and meek:
Tho' one should smite him on the cheek,
And on the mouth, he will not speak.

'His little daughter, whose sweet face
He kiss'd, taking his last embrace,
Becomes dishonour to her race –

'His sons grow up that bear his name,
Some grow to honour some to shame, –
But he is chill to praise or blame.

'He will not hear the north-wind rave,
Nor, moaning, household shelter crave
From winter rains that beat his grave.

'High up the vapours fold and swim:
About him broods the twilight dim:
The place he knew forgetteth him.'

'If all be dark, vague voice,' I said,
'These things are wrapt in doubt and dread,
Nor canst thou show the dead are dead.

'The sap dries up: the plant declines.
A deeper tale my heart divines.
Know I not Death? the outward signs?

'I found him when my years were few;
A shadow on the graves I knew,
And darkness in the village yew.

'From grave to grave the shadow crept:
In her still place the morning wept:
Touch'd by his feet the daisy slept.

'The simple senses crown'd his head:
"Omega! thou art Lord," they said,
"We find no motion in the dead."

'Why, if man rot in dreamless ease,
Should that plain fact, as taught by these,
Not make him sure that he shall cease?

'Who forged that other influence,
That heat of inward evidence,
By which he doubts against the sense?

'He owns the fatal gift of eyes,
That read his spirit blindly wise,
Not simple as a thing that dies.

'Here sits he shaping wings to fly:
His heart forebodes a mystery:
He names the name Eternity.

'That type of Perfect in his mind
In Nature can he nowhere find.
He sows himself on every wind.

'He seems to hear a Heavenly Friend,
And thro' thick veils to apprehend
A labour working to an end.

'The end and the beginning vex
His reason: many things perplex,
With motions, checks, and counterchecks.

'He knows a baseness in his blood
At such strange war with something good,
He may not do the thing he would.

'Heaven opens inward, chasms yawn,
Vast images in glimmering dawn,
Half shown, are broken and withdrawn.

'Ah! sure within him and without,
Could his dark wisdom find it out,
There must be answer to his doubt.

'But thou canst answer not again.
With thine own weapon art thou slain,
Or thou wilt answer but in vain.

'The doubt would rest, I dare not solve.
In the same circle we revolve.
Assurance only breeds resolve.'

As when a billow, blown against,
Falls back, the voice with which I fenced
A little ceased, but recommenced.

'Where wert thou when thy father play'd
In his free field, and pastime made,
A merry boy in sun and shade?

'A merry boy they called him then.
He sat upon the knees of men
In days that never come again.

'Before the little ducts began
To feed thy bones with lime, and ran
Their course, till thou wert also man:

'Who took a wife, who rear'd his race,
Whose wrinkles gather'd on his face,
Whose troubles number with his days:

'A life of nothings, nothing-worth,
From that first nothing ere his birth
To that last nothing under earth!'

'These words,' I said, 'are like the rest,
No certain clearness, but at best
A vague suspicion of the breast:

'But if I grant, thou might'st defend
The thesis which thy words intend –
That to begin implies to end;

'Yet how should I for certain hold,
Because my memory is so cold,
That I first was in human mould?

'I cannot make this matter plain,
But I would shoot, howe'er in vain,
A random arrow from the brain.

'It may be that no life is found,
Which only to one engine bound
Falls off, but cycles always round.

'As old mythologies relate,
Some draught of Lethe might await
The slipping thro' from state to state.

'As here we find in trances, men
Forget the dream that happens then,
Until they fall in trance again.

'So might we, if our state were such
As one before, remember much,
For those two likes might meet and touch

'But, if I lapsed from nobler place,
Some legend of a fallen race
Alone might hint of my disgrace;

'Some vague emotion of delight
In gazing up an Alpine height,
Some yearning toward the lamps of night.

'Or if thro' lower lives I came –
Tho' all experience past became
Consolidate in mind and frame –

'I might forget my weaker lot;
For is not our first year forgot?
The haunts of memory echo not.

'And men, whose reason long was blind,
From cells of madness unconfined,
Oft lose whole years of darker mind.

'Much more, if first I floated free,
As naked essence, must I be
Incompetent of memory:

'For memory dealing but with time,
And he with matter, could she climb
Beyond her own material prime?

'Moreover, something is or seems,
That touches me with mystic gleams,
Like glimpses of forgotten dreams –

'Of something felt, like something here;
Of something done, I know not where;
Such as no language may declare.'

The still voice laugh'd. 'I talk,' said he,
'Not with thy dreams. Suffice it thee
Thy pain is a reality.'

'But thou,' said I, 'hast miss'd thy mark,
Who sought'st to wreck my mortal ark,
By making all the horizon dark.

'Why not set forth, if I should do
This rashness, that which might ensue
With this old soul in organs new?

'Whatever crazy sorrow saith,
No life that breathes with human breath
Has ever truly long'd for death.

' 'Tis life, whereof our nerves are scant,
Oh life, not death, for which we pant;
More life, and fuller, that I want.'

I ceased, and sat as one forlorn.
Then said the voice, in quiet scorn,
'Behold, it is the Sabbath morn.'

And I arose, and I released
The casement, and the light increased
With freshness in the dawning east.

Like soften'd airs that blowing steal,
When meres begin to uncongeal,
The sweet church bells began to peal.

On to God's house the people prest:
Passing the place where each must rest,
Each enter'd like a welcome guest.

One walk'd between his wife and child,
With measur'd footfall firm and mild
And now and then he gravely smiled.

The prudent partner of his blood
Lean'd on him, faithful, gentle, good,
Wearing the rose of womanhood.

And in their double love secure
The little maiden walk'd demure
Pacing with downward eyelids pure.

These three made unity so sweet,
My frozen heart began to beat,
Remembering its ancient heat.

I blest them, and they wander'd on:
I spoke, but answer came there none:
The dull and bitter voice was gone.

A second voice was at mine ear,
A little whisper silver-clear,
A murmur, 'Be of better cheer.'

As from some blissful neighbourhood
A notice faintly understood,
'I see the end, and know the good.'

A little hint to solace woe,
A hint, a whisper breathing low
'I may not speak of what I know.'

Like an Aeolian harp that wakes
No certain air, but overtakes
Far thought with music that it makes

Such seem'd the whisper at my side:
'What is it thou knowest, sweet voice?' I cried.
'A hidden hope,' the voice replied:

So heavenly-toned, that in that hour
From out my sullen heart a power
Broke, like the rainbow from the shower,

To feel, altho' no tongue can prove,
That every cloud, that spreads above
And veileth love, itself is love.

And forth into the fields I went,
And Nature's living motion lent
The pulse of hope to discontent.

I wonder'd at the bounteous hours,
The slow result of winter showers:
You scarce could see the grass for flowers.

I wonder'd, while I paced along:
The woods were fill'd so full with song,
There seem'd no room for sense of wrong.

So variously seem'd all things wrought,
I marvell'd how the mind was brought
To anchor by one gloomy thought;

And wherefore rather I made choice
To commune with that barren voice,
Than him that said, 'Rejoice! rejoice!'

The Day-Dream

Prologue

O Lady Flora, let me speak:
   A pleasant hour has past away
While, dreaming on your damask cheek,
   The dewy sister-eyelids lay.
As by the lattice you reclined,
   I went thro' many wayward moods
To see you dreaming – and, behind,
   A summer crisp with shining woods.
And I too dream'd, until at last
   Across my fancy, brooding warm,
The reflex of a legend past,
   And loosely settled into form.
And would you have the thought I had,
   And see the vision that I saw,
Then take the broidery-frame, and add
   A crimson to the quaint Macaw,
And I will tell it. Turn your face,
   Nor look with that too-earnest eye –
The rhymes are dazzled from their place,
   And order'd words asunder fly.

The Sleeping Palace

I

The varying year with blade and sheaf
   Clothes and reclothes the happy plains;
Here rests the sap within the leaf,
   Here stays the blood along the veins.
Faint shadows, vapours lightly curl'd,
   Faint murmurs from the meadows come,
Like hints and echoes of the world
   To spirits folded in the womb.

II

Soft lustre bathes the range of urns
   On every slanting terrace-lawn.
The fountain to his place returns
   Deep in the garden lake withdrawn.

Here droops the banner on the tower,
   On the hall-hearths the festal fires,
The peacock in his laurel bower,
   The parrot in his gilded wires.

III

Roof-haunting martins warm their eggs:
   In these, in those the life is stay'd.
The mantles from the golden pegs
   Droop sleepily: no sound is made,
Not even of a gnat that sings.
   More like a picture seemeth all
Than those old portraits of old kings,
   That watch the sleepers from the wall.

IV

Here sits the Butler with a flask
   Between his knees, half-drain'd; and there
The wrinkled steward at his task,
   The maid-of-honour blooming fair:
The page has caught her hand in his:
   Her lips are sever'd as to speak:
His own are pouted to a kiss:
   The blush is fix'd upon her cheek.

V

Till all the hundred summers pass,
   The beams, that thro' the Oriel shine,
Make prisms in every carven glass,
   And beaker brimm'd with noble wine.
Each baron at the banquet sleeps,
   Grave faces gather'd in a ring.
His state the king reposing keeps.
   He must have been a jovial king.

VI

All round a hedge upshoots, and shows
   At distance like a little wood;
Thorns, ivies, woodbine, mistletoes,
   And grapes with bunches red as blood;
All creeping plants, a wall of green
   Close-matted, bur and brake and brier,
And glimpsing over these, just seen,
   High up, the topmost palace-spire.

VII

When will the hundred summers die,
   And thought and time be born again,
And newer knowledge, drawing nigh,
   Bring truth that sways the soul of men?
Here all things in their place remain,
   As all were order'd, ages since.
Come, Care and Pleasure, Hope and Pain,
   And bring the fated fairy Prince.

The Sleeping Beauty

I

Year after year unto her feet,
   She lying on her couch alone,
Across the purpled coverlet,
   The maiden's jet-black hair has grown,
On either side her tranced form
   Forth streaming from a braid of pearl:
The slumbrous light is rich and warm,
   And moves not on the rounded curl.

II

The silk star-broider'd coverlid
   Unto her limbs itself doth mould
Languidly ever; and, amid
   Her full black ringlets downward roll'd,
Glows forth each softly-shadow'd arm
   With bracelets of the diamond bright:
Her constant beauty doth inform
   Stillness with love, and day with light.

III

She sleeps: her breathings are not heard
   In palace chambers far apart.
The fragrant tresses are not stirr'd
   That lie upon her charmed heart
She sleeps: on either hand upswells
   The gold-fringed pillow lightly prest:
She sleeps, nor dreams, but ever dwells
   A perfect form in perfect rest.

The Arrival

I

All precious things, discover'd late,
　To those that seek them issue forth;
For love in sequel works with fate,
　And draws the veil from hidden worth.
He travels far from other skies —
　His mantle glitters on the rocks —
A fairy Prince, with joyful eyes
　And lighter-footed than the foe.

II

The bodies and the bones of those
　That strove in other days to pass,
Are wither'd in the thorny close,
　Or scatter'd blanching on the grass.
He gazes on the silent dead:
　'They perish'd in their daring deeds.'
This proverb flashes thro' his head
　'The many fail: the one succeeds.'

III

He comes, scarce knowing what he seeks:
　He breaks the hedge: he enters there:
The colour flies into his cheeks:
　He trusts to light on something fair;
For all his life the charm did talk
　About his path, and hover near
With words of promise in his walk,
　And whisper'd voices at his ear.

IV

More close and close his footsteps wind;
　The Magic Music in his heart
Beats quick and quicker, till he find
　The quiet chamber far apart.
His spirit flutters like a lark,
　He stoops — to kiss her — on his knee.
'Love, if thy tresses be so dark,
　How dark those hidden eyes must be!'

The Revival

I

A touch, a kiss! the charm was snapt.
   There rose a noise of striking clocks,
And feet that ran, and doors that clapt,
   And barking dogs, and crowing cocks;
A fuller light illumined all,
   A breeze thro' all the garden swept,
A sudden hubbub shook the hall
   And sixty feet the fountain leapt.

II

The hedge broke in, the banner blew,
   The butler drank, the steward scrawl'd,
The fire shot up, the martin flew,
   The parrot scream'd, the peacock squall'd,
The maid and page renew'd their strife,
   The palace bang'd, and buzz'd and clackt,
And all the long-pent stream of life
   Dash'd downward in a cataract.

III

And last with these the king awoke,
   And in his chair himself uprear'd,
And yawn'd, and rubb'd his face, and spoke,
   'By holy rood, a royal beard!
How say you? we have slept, my lords.
   My beard has grown into my lap.'
The barons swore, with many words,
   'Twas but an after-dinner's nap.

IV

'Pardy,' return'd the king, 'but still
   My joints are something stiff or so.
My lord, and shall we pass the bill
   I mention'd half an hour ago?'
The chancellor, sedate and vain,
   In courteous words return'd reply:
But dallied with his golden chain,
   And, smiling, put the question by.

The Departure

I

And on her lover's arm she leant,
    And round her waist she felt it fold,
And far across the hills they went
    In that new world which is the old:
Across the hills, and far away
    Beyond their utmost purple rim,
And deep into the dying day
    The happy princess follow'd him.

II

'I'd sleep another hundred years,
    O love, for such another kiss;'
'O wake for ever, love,' she hears,
    'O love, 'twas such as this and this.'
And o'er them many a sliding star,
    And many a merry wind was borne,
And, stream'd thro' many a golden bar,
    The twilight melted into morn.

III

'O eyes long laid in happy sleep!'
    'O happy sleep, that lightly fled!'
'O happy kiss, that woke thy sleep!'
    'O love, thy kiss would wake the dead!'
And o'er them many a flowing range
    Of vapour buoy'd the crescent-bark,
And, rapt thro' many a rosy change,
    The twilight died into the dark.

'A hundred summers! can it be?
    And whither goest thou, tell me where?'
'O seek my father's court with me,
    For there are greater wonders there.'
And o'er the hills, and far away
    Beyond their utmost purple rim,
Beyond the night, across the day
    Thro' all the world she follow'd him.

Moral

I

So, Lady Flora, take my lay,
    And if you find no moral there,
Go, look in any glass and say,
    What moral is in being fair.
Oh, to what uses shall we put
    The wildweed-flower that simply blows?
And is there any moral shut
    Within the bosom of the rose?

II

But any man that walks the mead
    In bud or blade, or bloom, may find,
According as his humours lead
    A meaning suited to his mind.
And liberal applications lie
    In Art like Nature, dearest friend;
So 'twere to cramp its use, if I
    Should hook it to some useful end.

L'Envoi

I

You shake your head. A random string
    Your finer female sense offends.
Well – were it not a pleasant thing
    To fall asleep with all one's friends;
To pass with all our social ties
    To silence from the paths of men;
And every hundred years to rise
    And learn the world, and sleep again;
To sleep thro' terms of mighty wars,
    And wake on science grown to more,
On secrets of the brain, the stars,
    As wild as aught of fairy lore;
And all that else the years will show,
    The Poet-forms of stronger hours,
The vast Republics that may grow,
    The Federations and the Powers;
Titanic forces taking birth
    In divers seasons, divers climes;
For we are Ancients of the earth,
    And in the morning of the times.

II

So sleeping, so aroused from sleep
   Thro' sunny decads new and strange,
Or gay quinquenniads would we reap
   The flower and quintessence of change.

III

Ah, yet would I – and would I might!
   So much your eyes my fancy take –
Be still the first to leap to light
   That I might kiss those eyes awake!
For, am I right or am I wrong,
   To choose your own you did not care;
You'd have *my* moral from the song,
   And I will take my pleasure there:

And, am I right or am I wrong,
   My fancy, ranging thro' and thro',
To search a meaning for the song,
   Perforce will still revert to you;
Nor finds a closer truth than this
   All-graceful head, so richly curl'd,
And evermore a costly kiss
   The prelude to some brighter world.

IV

For since the time when Adam first
   Embraced his Eve in happy hour,
And every bird of Eden burst
   In carol, every bud to flower,
What eyes, like thine, have waken'd hopes?
   What lips, like thine, so sweetly join'd?
Where on the double rosebud droops
   The fullness of the pensive mind;
Which all too dearly self-involved,
   Yet sleeps a dreamless sleep to me;
A sleep by kisses undissolved,
   That lets thee neither hear nor see:
But break it. In the name of wife,
   And in the rights that name may give,
Are clasp'd the moral of thy life,
   And that for which I care to live.

Epilogue

So, Lady Flora, take my lay,
   And, if you find a meaning there,
O whisper to your glass, and say,
   'What wonder, if he thinks me fair?'
What wonder I was all unwise,
   To shape the song for your delight
Like long-tail'd birds of Paradise,
   That float thro' Heaven, and cannot light?
Or old-world trains, upheld at court
   By Cupid-boys of blooming hue –
But take it – earnest wed with sport,
   And either sacred unto you.

Amphion

My father left a park to me,
   But it is wild and barren,
A garden too with scarce a tree
   And waster than a warren:
Yet say the neighbours when they call,
   It is not bad but good land,
And in it is the germ of all
   That grows within the woodland.

O had I lived when song was great
   In days of old Amphion,
And ta'en my fiddle to the gate,
   Nor cared for seed or scion!
And had I lived when song was great,
   And legs of trees were limber,
And ta'en my fiddle to the gate,
   And fiddled in the timber!

'Tis said he had a tuneful tongue,
   Such happy intonation,
Wherever he sat down and sung
   He left a small plantation;
Wherever in a lonely grove
   He set up his forlorn pipes,
The gouty oak began to move,
   And flounder into hornpipes.

The mountain stirr'd its bushy crown,
  And, as tradition teaches,
Young ashes pirouetted down
  Coquetting with young beeches;
And briony-vine and ivy-wreath
  Ran forward to his rhyming,
And from the valleys underneath
  Came little copses climbing.

The linden broke her ranks and rent
  The woodbine wreaths that bind her,
And down the middle, buzz! she went
  With all her bees behind her.
The poplars, in long order due,
  With cypress promenaded,
The shock-head willows two and two
  By rivers gallopaded.

Came wet-shod alder from the wave,
  Came yews, a dismal coterie;
Each pluck'd his one foot from the grave,
  Poussetting with a sloe-tree:
Old elms came breaking from the vine,
  The vine stream'd out to follow,
And, sweating rosin, plump'd the pine
  From many a cloudy hollow.

And wasn't it a sight to see,
  When, ere his song was ended,
Like some great landslip, tree by tree,
  The country-side descended;
And shepherds from the mountain-eaves
  Look'd down, half-pleased, half-frighten'd
As dash'd about the drunken leaves
  The random sunshine lighten'd!

Oh, nature first was fresh to men
  And wanton without measure;
So youthful and so flexile then,
  You moved her at your pleasure.
Twang out, my fiddle! shake the twigs!
  And make her dance attendance
Blow, flute, and stir the stiff-set sprigs,
  And scirrhous roots and tendons.

'Tis vain! in such a brassy age
    I could not move a thistle;
The very sparrows in the hedge
    Scarce answer to my whistle;
Or at the most, when three-parts-sick
    With strumming and with scraping,
A jackass heehaws from the rick,
    The passive oxen gaping.

But what is that I hear? a sound
    Like sleepy counsel pleading:
O Lord! – 'tis in my neighbour's ground,
    The modern Muses reading.
They read Botanic Treatises,
    And Works on Gardening thro' there,
And Methods of transplanting trees,
    To look as if they grew there.

The wither'd Misses! how they prose
    O'er books of travell'd seamen,
And show you slips of all that grows
    From England to Van Diemen.
They read in arbours clipt and cut,
    And alleys, faded places,
By squares of tropic summer shut
    And warm'd in crystal cases.

But these, tho' fed with careful dirt,
    Are neither green nor sappy;
Half-conscious of the garden-squirt,
    The spindlings look unhappy.
Better to me the meanest weed
    That blows upon its mountain,
The vilest herb that runs to seed
    Beside its native fountain.

And I must work thro' months of toil,
    And years of cultivation,
Upon my proper patch of soil
    To grow my own plantation.
I'll take the showers as they fall,
    I will not vex my bosom:
Enough if at the end of all
    A little garden blossom.

Sir Galahad

My good blade carves the casques of men,
   My tough lance thrusteth sure,
My strength is as the strength of ten,
   Because my heart is pure.
The shattering trumpet shrilleth high,
   The hard brands shiver on the steel,
The splinter'd spear-shafts crack and fly,
   The horse and rider reel:
They reel, they roll in clanging lists,
   And when the tide of combat stands,
Perfume and flowers fall in showers,
   That lightly rain from ladies' hands.

How sweet are looks that ladies bend
   On whom their favours fall!
For them I battle till the end,
   To save from shame and thrall:
But all my heart is drawn above,
   My knees are bow'd in crypt and shrine:
I never felt the kiss of love,
   Nor maiden's hand in mine.
More bounteous aspects on me beam,
   Me mightier transports move and thrill;
So keep I fair thro' faith and prayer
   A virgin heart in work and will.

When down the stormy crescent goes,
   A light before me swims,
Between dark stems the forest glows,
   I hear a noise of hymns:
Then by some secret shrine I ride;
   I hear a voice, but none are there;
The stalls are void, the doors are wide,
   The tapers burning fair.
Fair gleams the snowy altar-cloth,
   The silver vessels sparkle clean,
The shrill bell rings, the censer swings,
   And solemn chaunts resound between.

Sometimes on lonely mountain-meres
   I find a magic bark;
I leap on board: no helmsman steers:
   I float till all is dark.
A gentle sound, an awful light!

Three angels bear the holy Grail:
With folded feet, in stoles of white,
    On sleeping wings they sail.
Ah, blessed vision! blood of God!
    My spirit beats her mortal bars,
As down dark tides the glory slides,
    And star-like mingles with the stars.

When on my goodly charger borne
    Thro' dreaming towns I go,
The cock crows ere the Christmas morn,
    The streets are dumb with snow.
The tempest crackles on the leads,
    And, ringing, springs from brand and mail;
But o'er the dark a glory spreads,
    And gilds the driving hail.
I leave the plain, I climb the height;
    No branchy thicket shelter yields;
But blessed forms in whistling storms
    Fly o'er waste fens and windy fields.

A maiden knight – to me is given
    Such hope, I know not fear;
I yearn to breathe the airs of heaven
    That often meet me here.
I muse on joy that will not cease,
    Pure spaces clothed in living beams,
Pure lilies of eternal peace,
    Whose odours haunt my dreams;
And, stricken by an angel's hand
    This mortal armour that I wear,
This weight and size, this heart and eyes,
    Are touch'd, are turn'd to finest air.

The clouds are broken in the sky,
    And thro' the mountain-walls
A rolling organ harmony
    Swells up, and shakes and falls.
Then move the trees, the copses nod,
    Wings flutter, voices hover clear
'O just and faithful knight of God!
    Ride on! the prize is near.'
So pass I hostel, hall, and grange;
    By bridge and ford, by park and pale,
All-arm'd I ride, whate'er betide,
    Until I find the holy Grail.

Edward Gray

Sweet Emma Moreland of yonder town
　　Met me walking on yonder way,
'And have you lost your heart?' she said;
　　'And are you married yet, Edward Gray?'

Sweet Emma Moreland spoke to me:
　　Bitterly weeping I turn'd away:
'Sweet Emma Moreland, love no more
　　Can touch the heart of Edward Gray

'Ellen Adair she loved me well,
　　Against her father's and mother's will:
To-day I sat for an hour and wept,
　　By Ellen's grave, on the windy hill

'Shy she was, and I thought her cold;
　　Thought her proud, and fled over the sea;
Fill'd I was with folly and spite,
　　When Ellen Adair was dying for me.

'Cruel, cruel the words I said!
　　Cruelly came they back to-day
"You're too slight and fickle," I said,
　　"To trouble the heart of Edward Gray"

'There I put my face in the grass –
　　Whisper'd, "Listen to my despair:
I repent me of all I did:
　　Speak a little, Ellen Adair!"

'Then I took a pencil, and wrote
　　On the messy stone, as I lay,
"Here lies the body of Ellen Adair;
　　And here the heart of Edward Gray!"

'Love may come, and love may go,
　　And fly, like a bird, from tree to tree
But I will love no more, no more,
　　Till Ellen Adair come back to me.

'Bitterly wept I over the stone:
　　Bitterly weeping I turn'd away:
There lies the body of Ellen Adair!
　　And there the heart of Edward Gray!'

Will Waterproof's Lyrical Monologue

Made at the Cock

O plump head-waiter at The Cock,
   To which I most resort,
How goes the time? 'Tis five o'clock.
   Go fetch a pint of port:
But let it not be such as that
   You set before chance-comers,
But such whose father-grape grew fat
   On Lusitanian summers.

No vain libation to the Muse,
   But may she still be kind,
And whisper lovely words, and use
   Her influence on the mind,
To make me write my random rhymes,
   Ere they be half-forgotten;
Nor add and alter, many times,
   Till all be ripe and rotten.

I pledge her, and she comes and dips
   Her laurel in the wine,
And lays it thrice upon my lips,
   These favour'd lips of mine;
Until the charm have power to make
   New lifeblood warm the bosom
And barren commonplaces break
   In full and kindly blossom.

I pledge her silent at the board;
   Her gradual fingers steal
And touch upon the master-chord
   Of all I felt and feel.
Old wishes, ghosts of broken plans,
   And phantom hopes assemble;
And that child's heart within the man's
   Begins to move and tremble.

Thro' many an hour of summer suns.
   By many pleasant ways,
Against its fountain upward runs
   The current of my days:
I kiss the lips I once have kiss'd;
   The gas-light wavers dimmer;
And softly, thro' a vinous mist,
   My college friendships glimmer.

I grow in worth, and wit, and sense,
   Unboding critic-pen,
Or that eternal want of pence,
   Which vexes public men,
Who hold their hands to all, and cry
   For that which all deny them –
Who sweep the crossings, wet or dry,
   And all the world go by them.

Ah yet, tho' all the world forsake,
   Tho' fortune clip my wings,
I will not cramp my heart, nor take
   Half-views of men and things.
Let Whig and Tory stir their blood;
   There must be stormy weather;
But for some true result of good
   All parties work together.

Let there be thistles, there are grapes;
   If old things, there are new;
Ten thousand broken lights and shapes,
   Yet glimpses of the true.
Let raffs be rife in prose and rhyme,
   We lack not rhymes and reasons,
As on this whirligig of Time
   We circle with the seasons.

This earth is rich in man and maid;
   With fair horizons bound:
This whole wide earth of light and shade
   Comes out, a perfect round.
High over roaring Temple-bar,
   And, set in Heaven's third story,
I look at all things as they are,
   But thro' a kind of glory.

*

Head-waiter, honour'd by the guest
   Half-mused, or reeling-ripe,
The pint, you brought me, was the best
   That ever came from pipe.
But tho' the port surpasses praise,
   My nerves have dealt with stiffer
Is there some magic in the place?
   Or do my peptics differ?

For since I came to live and learn,
    No pint of white or red
Had ever half the power to turn
    This wheel within my head,
Which bears a season'd brain about,
    Unsubject to confusion,
Tho' soak'd and saturate, out and out,
    Thro' every convolution.

For I am of a numerous house,
    With many kinsmen gay,
Where long and largely we carouse
    As who shall say me nay:
Each month, a birth-day coming on,
    We drink defying trouble,
Or sometimes two would meet in one,
    And then we drank it double;

Whether the vintage, yet unkept,
    Had relish fiery-new,
Or, elbow-deep in sawdust, slept,
    As old as Waterloo;
Or stow'd (when classic Canning died)
    In musty bins and chambers,
Had cast upon its crusty side
    The gloom of ten Decembers.

The Muse, the jolly Muse, it is!
    She answer'd to my call,
She changes with that mood or this,
    Is all-in-all to all:
She lit the spark within my throat,
    To make my blood run quicker,
Used all her fiery will, and smote
    Her life into the liquor.

And hence this halo lives about
    The waiter's hands, that reach
To each his perfect pint of stout,
    His proper chop to each.
He looks not like the common breed
    That with the napkin dally;
I think he came like Ganymede,
    From some delightful valley.

The Cock was of a larger egg
     Than modern poultry drop,
Stept forward on a firmer leg,
     And cramm'd a plumper crop;
Upon an ampler dunghill trod,
     Crow'd lustier late and early,
Sipt wine from silver, praising God,
     And raked in golden barley.

A private life was all his joy,
     Till in a court he saw
A something-pottle-bodied boy,
     That knuckled at the taw:
He stoop'd and clutch'd him, fair and good,
     Flew over roof and casement:
His brothers of the weather stood
     Stock-still for sheer amazement.

But he, by farmstead, thorpe and spire,
     And follow'd with acclaims,
A sign to many a staring shire,
     Came crowing over Thames.
Right down by smoky Paul's they bore,
     Till, where the street grows straiter,
One fix'd for ever at the door,
     And one became head-waiter.

                    *

But whither would my fancy go?
     How out of place she makes
The violet of a legend blow
     Among the chops and steaks!
'Tis but a steward of the can
     One shade more plump than common;
As just and mere a serving-man
     As any, born of woman.

I ranged too high: what draws me down
     Into the common day?
Is it the weight of that half-crown,
     Which I shall have to pay?
For, something duller than at first,
     Nor wholly comfortable,
I sit (my empty glass reversed),
     And thrumming on the table:

Half fearful that, with self at strife,
    I take myself to task;
Lest of the fullness of my life
    I leave an empty flask:
For I had hope, by something rare,
    To prove myself a poet;
But, while I plan and plan, my hair
    Is grey before I know it.

So fares it since the years began,
    Till they be gather'd up;
The truth, that flies the flowing can,
    Will haunt the vacant cup:
And others' follies teach us not,
    Nor much their wisdom teaches;
And most, of sterling worth, is what
    Our own experience preaches.

Ah, let the rusty theme alone!
    We know not what we know.
But for my pleasant hour, 'tis gone,
    'Tis gone, and let it go.
'Tis gone: a thousand such have slipt
    Away from my embraces,
And fall'n into the dusty crypt
    Of darken'd forms and faces.

Go, therefore, thou! thy betters went
    Long since, and came no more;
With peals of genial clamour sent
    From many a tavern-door,
With twisted quirks and happy hits,
    From misty men of letters;
The tavern-hours of mighty wits —
    Thine elders and thy betters.

Hours, when the Poet's words and looks
    Had yet their native glow:
Nor yet the fear of little books
    Had made him talk-for show;
But, all his vast heart sherris-warm'd,
    He flash'd his random speeches;
Ere days, that deal in ana, swarm'd
    His literary leeches.

So mix for ever with the past,
 Like all good things on earth!
For should I prize thee, couldst thou last,
 At half thy real worth?
I hold it good, good things should pass:
 With time I will not quarrel:
It is but yonder empty glass
 That makes me maudlin-moral.

*

Head-waiter of the chop-house here,
 To which I most resort,
I too must part: I hold thee dear
 For this good pint of port.
For this, thou shalt from all things suck
 Marrow of mirth and laughter;
And, wheresoe'er thou move, good luck
 Shall fling her old shoe after.

But thou wilt never move from hence,
 The sphere thy fate allots:
Thy latter days increased with pence
 Go down among the pots:
Thou battenest by the greasy gleam
 In haunts of hungry sinners,
Old boxes, larded with the steam
 Of thirty thousand dinners.

We fret, *we* fume, would shift our skins,
 Would quarrel with our lot;
Thy care is, under polish'd tins,
 To serve the hot-and-hot;
To come and go, and come again,
 Returning like the pewit,
And watch'd by silent gentlemen,
 That trifle with the cruet.

Live long, ere from thy topmost head
 The thick-set hazel dies;
Long, ere the hateful crow shall tread
 The corners of thine eyes:
Live long, nor feel in head or chest
 Our changeful equinoxes,
Till mellow Death, like some late guest,
 Shall call thee from the boxes.

But when he calls, and thou shalt cease
    To pace the gritted floor,
And, laying down an unctuous lease
    Of life, shalt earn no more;
No carved cross-bones, the types of Death,
    Shall show thee past to Heaven
But carved cross-pipes, and, underneath,
    A pint-pot, neatly graven.

Lady Clare

It was the time when lilies blow,
    And clouds are highest up in air,
Lord Ronald brought a lily-white doe
    To give his cousin, Lady Clare.

I trow they did not part in scorn:
    Lovers long-betroth'd were they:
They two will wed the morrow morn:
    God's blessing on the day!

'He does not love me for my birth,
    Nor for my lands so broad and fair;
He loves me for my own true worth,
    And that is well,' said Lady Clare.

In there came old Alice the nurse,
    Said, 'Who was this that went from thee?'
'It was my cousin,' said Lady Clare,
    'To-morrow he weds with me.'

'O God be thank'd!' said Alice the nurse,
    'That all comes round so just and fair:
Lord Ronald is heir of all your lands,
    And you are not the Lady Clare.'

'Are ye out of your mind, my nurse, my nurse?'
    Said Lady Clare, 'that ye speak so wild?'
'As God's above,' said Alice the nurse,
    'I speak the truth: you are my child.

'The old Earl's daughter died at my breast;
    I speak the truth, as I live by bread!
I buried her like my own sweet child,
    And put my child in her stead.'

'Falsely, falsely have ye done,
   O mother,' she said, 'if this be true,
To keep the best man under the sun
   So many years from his due.'

'Nay now, my child,' said Alice the nurse,
   'But keep the secret for your life,
And all you have will be Lord Ronald's
   When you are man and wife.'

'If I'm a beggar born,' she said,
   'I will speak out, for I dare not lie.
Pull off, pull off, the brooch of gold,
   And fling the diamond necklace by.'

'Nay now, my child,' said Alice the nurse,
   'But keep the secret all ye can.'
She said 'Not so: but I will know
   If there be any faith in man.'

'Nay now, what faith?' said Alice the nurse,
   'The man will cleave unto his right.'
'And he shall have it,' the lady replied,
   'Tho' I should die to-night.'

'Yet give one kiss to your mother dear!
   Alas, my child, I sinn'd for thee.'
'O mother, mother, mother,' she said,
   'So strange it seems to me.

'Yet here's a kiss for my mother dear,
   My mother dear, if this be so,
And lay your hand upon my head,
   And bless me, mother, ere I go.'

She clad herself in a russet gown,
   She was no longer Lady Clare:
She went by dale, and she went by down,
   With a single rose in her hair.

The lily-white doe Lord Ronald had brought
   Leapt up from where she lay,
Dropt her head in the maiden's hand,
   And follow'd her all the way.

Down stept Lord Ronald from his tower:
  'O Lady Clare, you shame your worth!
Why come you drest like a village maid,
  That are the flower of the earth?'

'If I come drest like a village maid,
  I am but as my fortunes are:
I am a beggar born,' she said,
  'And not the Lady Clare.'

'Play me no tricks,' said Lord Ronald
  'For I am yours in word and in deed.
Play me no tricks,' said Lord Ronald,
  'Your riddle is hard to read.'

O and proudly stood she up!
  Her heart within her did not fail:
She look'd into Lord Ronald's eyes,
  And told him all her nurse's tale.

He laugh'd a laugh of merry scorn:
  He turn'd and kiss'd her where she stood
'If you are not the heiress born,
  And I,' said he, 'the next in blood –

'If you are not the heiress born,
  And I,' said he, 'the lawful heir,
We two will wed to-morrow morn,
  And you shall still be Lady Clare.'

The Lord Burleigh

In her ear he whispers gaily,
  'If my heart by signs can tell,
Maiden, I have watch'd thee daily,
  And I think thou lov'st me well.'
She replies, in accents fainter,
  'There is none I love like thee.'
He is but a landscape-painter,
  And a village maiden she.
He to lips, that fondly falter,
  Presses his without reproof:
Leads her to the village altar,
  And they leave her father's roof.
'I can make no marriage present:

Little can I give my wife.
Love will make our cottage pleasant,
    And I love thee more than life.'
They by parks and lodges going
    See the lordly castles stand:
Summer woods, about them blowing,
    Made a murmur in the land.
From deep thought himself he rouses,
    Says to her that loves him well,
'Let us see these handsome houses
    Where the wealthy nobles dwell.'
So she goes by him attended,
    Hears him lovingly converse,
Sees whatever fair and splendid
    Lay betwixt his home and hers;
Parks with oak and chestnut shady,
    Parks and order'd gardens great,
Ancient homes of lord and lady,
    Built for pleasure and for state.
All he shows her makes him dearer:
    Evermore she seems to gaze
On that cottage growing nearer,
    Where they twain will spend their days.
O but she will love him truly!
    He shall have a cheerful home;
She will order all things duly,
    When beneath his roof they come.
Thus her heart rejoices greatly,
    Till a gateway she discerns
With armorial bearings stately,
    And beneath the gate she turns;
Sees a mansion more majestic
    Than all those she saw before:
Many a gallant gay domestic
    Bows before him at the door.
And they speak in gentle murmur,
    When they answer to his call,
While he treads with footstep firmer,
    Leading on from hall to hall.
And, while now she wonders blindly,
    Nor the meaning can divine,
Proudly turns he round and kindly,
    'All of this is mine and thine.'
Here he lives in state and bounty,
    Lord of Burleigh, fair and free,
Not a lord in all the county

Is so great a lord as he.
All at once the colour flushes
    Her sweet face from brow to chin:
As it were with shame she blushes,
    And her spirit changed within.
Then her countenance all over
    Pale again as death did prove:
But he clasp'd her like a lover,
    And he cheer'd her soul with love.
So she strove against her weakness,
    Tho' at times her spirit sank:
Shaped her heart with woman's meekness
    To all duties of her rank:
And a gentle consort made he,
    And her gentle mind was such
That she grew a noble lady,
    And the people loved her much.
But a trouble weigh'd upon her,
    And perplex'd her, night and morn,
With the burthen of an honour
    Unto which she was not born.
Faint she grew, and ever fainter,
    As she murmur'd, 'Oh, that he
Were once more that landscape-painter,
    Which did win my heart from me!'
So she droop'd and droop'd before him,
    Fading slowly from his side:
Three fair children first she bore him,
    Then before her time she died.
Weeping, weeping late and early,
    Walking up and pacing down,
Deeply mourn'd the Lord of Burleigh,
    Burleigh-house by Stamford-town.
And he came to look upon her,
    And he look'd at her and said,
'Bring the dress and put it on her,
    That she wore when she was wed.'
Then her people, softly treading,
    Bore to earth her body, drest
In the dress that she was wed in,
    That her spirit might have rest.

Sir Launcelot and Queen Guinevere

A Fragment

Like souls that balance joy and pain,
With tears and smiles from heaven again
The maiden Spring upon the plain
Came in a sun-lit fall of rain.
    In crystal vapour everywhere
Blue isles of heaven laugh'd between,
And, far in forest-deeps unseen,
The topmost elm-tree gather'd green
    From draughts of balmy air.

Sometimes the linnet piped his song:
Sometimes the throstle whistled strong:
Sometimes the sparhawk, wheel'd along,
Hush'd all the groves from fear of wrong:
    By grassy capes with fuller sound
In curves the yellowing river ran,
And drooping chestnut-buds began
To spread into the perfect fan,
    Above the teeming ground.

Then, in the boyhood of the year,
Sir Launcelot and Queen Guinevere
Rode thro' the coverts of the deer,
With blissful treble ringing clear.
    She seem'd a part of joyous Spring:
A gown of grass-green silk she wore,
Buckled with golden clasps before;
A light-green tuft of plumes she bore
    Closed in a golden ring.

Now on some twisted ivy-net,
Now by some tinkling rivulet,
In mosses mixt with violet
Her cream-white mule his pastern set:
    And fleeter now she skimm'd the plains
Than she whose elfin prancer springs
By night to eery warblings,
When all the glimmering moorland rings
    With jingling bridle-reins.

As she fled fast thro' sun and shade,
The happy winds upon her play'd,
Blowing the ringlet from the braid:
She look'd so lovely, as she sway'd
    The rein with dainty finger-tips,

A man had given all other bliss,
And all his worldly worth for this
To waste his whole heart in one kiss
   Upon her perfect lips.

A Farewell

Flow down, cold rivulet, to the sea,
   Thy tribute wave deliver:
No more by thee my steps shall be,
   For ever and for ever.

Flow, softly flow, by lawn and lea,
   A rivulet then a river:
No where by thee my stops shall be,
   For ever and for ever.

But here will sigh thine alder tree,
   And here thine aspen shiver;
And here by thee will hum the bee,
   For ever and for ever.

A thousand suns will stream on thee,
   A thousand moons will quiver;
But not by thee my steps shall be,
   For ever and for ever.

The Beggar Maid

Her arms across her breast she laid;
   She was more fair than words can say:
Bare-footed came the beggar maid
   Before the king Cophetua.
In robe and crown the king stept down,
   To meet and greet her on her way;
'It is no wonder,' said the lords,
   'She is more beautiful than day.'

As shines the moon in clouded skies,
   She in her poor attire was seen:
One praised her ankles, one her eyes,
   One her dark hair and lovesome mien.
So sweet a face, such angel grace,
   In all that land had never been:
Cophetua sware a royal oath:
   'This beggar maid shall be my queen!'

The Vision of Sin

I

I had a vision when the night was late:
A youth came riding toward a palace-gate.
He rode a horse with wings, that would have flown,
But that his heavy rider kept him down.
And from the palace came a child of sin,
And took him by the curls, and led him in,
Where sat a company with heated eyes,
Expecting when a fountain should arise:
A sleepy light upon their brows and lips —
As when the sun, a crescent of eclipse,
Dreams over lake and lawn, and isles and capes —
Suffused them, sitting, lying, languid shapes,
By heaps of gourds, and skins of wine, and piles of grapes.

II

Then methought I heard a mellow sound,
Gathering up from all the lower ground;
Narrowing in to where they sat assembled
Low voluptuous music winding trembled,
Wov'n in circles: they that heard it sigh'd,
Panted hand in hand with faces pale,
Swung themselves, and in low tones replied;
Till the fountain spouted, showering wide
Sleet of diamond-drift and pearly hail;
Then the music touch'd the gates and died;
Rose again from where it seem'd to fail,
Storm'd in orbs of song, a growing gale;
Till thronging in and in, to where they waited,
As 'twere a hundred-throated nightingale,
The strong tempestuous treble throbb'd and palpitated;
Ran into its giddiest whirl of sound,
Caught the sparkles, and in circles,
Purple gauzes, golden hazes, liquid mazes,
Flung the torrent rainbow round:
Then they started from their places,
Moved with violence, changed in hue,
Caught each other with wild grimaces,
Half-invisible to the view,
Wheeling with precipitate paces

To the melody, till they flew,
Hair, and eyes, and limbs, and faces,
Twisted hard in fierce embraces,

Like to Furies, like to Graces,
Dash'd together in blinding dew:
Till, kill'd with some luxurious agony,
The nerve-dissolving melody
Flutter'd headlong from the sky.

III

And then I look'd up toward a mountain-tract,
That girt the region with high cliff and lawn:
I saw that every morning, far withdrawn
Beyond the darkness and the cataract,
God made Himself an awful rose of dawn,
Unheeded: and detaching, fold by fold,
From those still heights, and, slowly drawing near,
A vapour heavy, hueless, formless, cold,
Came floating on for many a month and year,
Unheeded: and I thought I would have spoken,
And warn'd that madman ere it grew too late:
But, as in dreams, I could not. Mine was broken,
When that cold vapour touch'd the palace-gate,
And link'd again. I saw within my head
A grey and gap-tooth'd man as lean as death,
Who slowly rode across a wither'd heath,
And lighted at a ruin'd inn, and said:

IV

'Wrinkled ostler, grim and thin!
    Here is custom come your way;
Take my brute, and lead him in,
    Stuff his ribs with mouldy hay.

'Bitter barmaid, waning fast!
    See that sheets are on my bed;
What! the flower of life is past.
    It is long before you wed.

'Slip-shod waiter, lank and sour,
    At the Dragon on the heath!
Let us have a quiet hour,
    Let us hob-and-nob with Death.

'I am old, but let me drink;
    Bring me spices, bring me wine;
I remember, when I think,
    That my youth was half divine.

'Wine is good for shrivell'd lips,
    When a blanket wraps the day,
When the rotten woodland drips,
    And the leaf is stamp'd in clay.

'Sit thee down, and have no shame,
    Cheek by jowl, and knee by knee:
What care I for any name?
    What for order or degree?

'Let me screw thee up a peg:
    Let me loose thy tongue with wine:
Callest thou that thing a leg?
    Which is thinnest? thine or mine

'Thou shalt not be saved by works:
    Thou hast been a sinner too:
Ruin'd trunks on wither'd forks,
    Empty scarecrows, I and you!

'Fill the cup, and fill the can:
    Have a rouse before the morn:
Every moment dies a man,
    Every moment one is born.

'We are men of ruin'd blood;
    Therefore comes it we are wise.
Fish are we that love the mud,
    Rising to no fancy-flies.

'Name and fame! to fly sublime
    Thro' the courts, the camps, the schools,
Is to be the ball of Time,
    Bandied by the hands of fools.

'Friendship! – to be two in one –
    Let the canting liar pack!
Well I know, when I am gone,
    How she mouths behind my back

'Virtue! – to be good and just –
    Every heart, when sifted well,
Is a clot of warmer dust,
    Mix'd with cunning sparks of hell.

'O! we two as well can look
    Whited thought and cleanly life
As the priest, above his book
    Leering at his neighbour's wife.

'Fill the cup, and fill the can:
   Have a rouse before the morn:
Every moment dies a man,
   Every moment one is born.

'Drink, and let the parties rave:
   They are fill'd with idle spleen;
Rising, falling, like a wave,
   For they know not what they mean.

'He that roars for liberty
   Faster binds a tyrant's power;
And the tyrant's cruel glee
   Forces on the freer hour.

'Fill the can, and fill the cup:
   All the windy ways of men
Are but dust that rises up,
   And is lightly laid again.

'Greet her with applausive breath,
   Freedom, gaily doth she tread;
In her right a civic wreath,
   In her left a human head.

'No, I love not what is new;
   She is of an ancient house:
And I think we know the hue
   Of that cap upon her brows.

'Let her go! her thirst she slakes
   Where the bloody conduit runs:
Then her sweetest meal she makes
   On the first-born of her sons.

'Drink to lofty hopes that cool —
   Visions of a perfect State:
Drink we, last, the public fool,
   Frantic love and frantic hate.

'Chant me now some wicked stave,
   Till thy drooping courage rise,
And the glow-worm of the grave
   Glimmer in thy rheumy eyes.

'Fear not thou to loose thy tongue;
   Set thy hoary fancies free;
What is loathsome to the young
   Savours well to thee and me.

'Change, reverting to the years,
    When thy nerves could understand
What there is in loving tears,
    And the warmth of hand in hand.

'Tell me tales of thy first love —
    April hopes, the fools of chance;
Till the graves begin to move,
    And the dead begin to dance.

'Fill the can, and fill the cup:
    All the windy ways of men
Are but dust that rises up,
    And is lightly laid again.

'Trooping from their mouldy dens
    The chap-fallen circle spreads:
Welcome, fellow-citizens,
    Hollow hearts and empty heads!

'You are bones, and what of that?
    Every face, however full,
Padded round with flesh and fat,
    Is but modell'd on a skull.

'Death is king, and Vivat Rex!
    Tread a measure on the stones,
Madam — if I know your sex,
    From the fashion of your bones.

'No, I cannot praise the fire
    In your eye — nor yet your lip:
All the more do I admire
    Joints of cunning workmanship.

'Lo! God's likeness — the ground-plan —
    Neither modell'd, glazed, or framed:
Buss me, thou rough sketch of man,
    Far too naked to be shamed!

'Drink to Fortune, drink to Chance,
    While we keep a little breath!
Drink to heavy Ignorance!
    Hob-and-nob with brother Death!

'Thou art mazed, the night is long,
    And the longer night is near:
What! I am not all as wrong
    As a bitter jest is dear.

'Youthful hopes, by scores, to all,
    When the locks are crisp and curl'd:
Unto me my maudlin gall
    And my mockeries of the world.

'Fill the cup, and fill the can!
    Mingle madness, mingle scorn!
Dregs of life, and lees of man:
    Yet we will not die forlorn.'

v

The voice grew faint: there came a further change:
Once more uprose the mystic mountain-range:
Below were men and horses pierced with worms,
And slowly quickening into lower forms;
By shards and scurf of salt, and scum of dross,
Old plash of rains, and refuse patch'd with moss.
Then some one spake: 'Behold! it was a crime
Of sense avenged by sense that wore with time.'
Another answer'd 'But a crime of sense
Give him new nerves with old experience.'
Another said: 'The crime of sense became
The crime of malice, and is equal blame.'
And one: 'He had not wholly quench'd his power;
A little grain of conscience made him sour.'
At last I heard a voice upon the slope
Cry to the summit, 'Is there any hope?'
To which an answer peal'd from that high land,
But in a tongue no man could understand;
And on the glimmering limit far withdrawn
God made Himself an awful rose of dawn.

Move Eastward, Happy Earth

Move eastward, happy earth, and leave
    Yon orange sunset waning slow:
From fringes of the faded eve,
    O, happy planet, eastward go;
Till over thy dark shoulder glow
    Thy silver sister-world, and rise
To glass herself in dewy eyes
    That watch me from the glen below.

Ah, bear me with thee, smoothly borne,
    Dip forward under starry light,
And move me to my marriage-morn,
    And round again to happy night.

Break, Break, Break

Break, break, break,
   On thy cold grey stones, O Sea!
And I would that my tongue could utter
   The thoughts that arise in me.

O well for the fisherman's boy,
   That he shouts with his sister at play!
O well for the sailor lad,
   That he sings in his boat on the bay!

And the stately ships go on
   To their haven under the hill;
But O for the touch of a vanish'd hand,
   And the sound of a voice that is still!

Break, break, break,
   At the foot of thy crags, O Sea!
But the tender grace of a day that is dead
   Will never come back to me.

The Poet's Song

The rain had fallen, the Poet arose,
   He pass'd by the town and out of the street,
A light wind blew from the gates of the sun,
   And waves of shadow went over the wheat,
And he sat him down in a lonely place,
   And chanted a melody loud and sweet,
That made the wild-swan pause in her cloud,
   And the lark drop down at his feet.

The swallow stopt as he hunted the bee,
   The snake slipt under a spray,
The wild hawk stood with the down on his beak,
   And stared, with his foot on the prey,
And the nightingale thought, 'I have sung many songs,
   But never a one so gay,
For he sings of what the world will be
   When the years have died away.'

The Golden Year

Well, you shall have that song which Leonard wrote:
It was last summer on a tour in Wales:
Old James was with me: we that day had been
Up Snowdon; and I wish'd for Leonard there,
And found him in Llanberis: then we crost
Between the lakes, and clamber'd half way up
The counter side; and that same song of his
He told me; for I banter'd him, and swore
They said he lived shut up within himself,
A tongue-tied Poet in the feverous days,
That, setting the *how much* before the *how,*
Cry, like the daughters of the horseleech, 'Give,
Cram us with all,' but count not me the herd!

     To which 'They call me what they will,' he said:
'But I was born too late: the fair new forms,
That float about the threshold of an age,
Like truths of Science waiting to be caught –
Catch me who can, and make the catcher crown'd –
Are taken by the forelock. Let it be.
But if you care indeed to listen, hear
These measured words, my work of yestermorn.

     'We sleep and wake and sleep, but all things move
The Sun flies forward to his brother Sun;
The dark Earth follows wheel'd in her ellipse;
And human things returning on themselves
Move onward, leading up the golden year.

     'Ah, tho' the times, when some new' thought can bud,
Are but as poets' seasons when they flower,
Yet seas, that daily gain upon the shore,
Have ebb and flow conditioning their march,
And slow and sure comes up the golden year.

     'When wealth no more shall rest in mounded heaps,
But smit with freër light shall slowly melt
In many streams to fatten lower lands,
And light shall spread, and man be liker man
Thro' all the season of the golden year.

     'Shall eagles not be eagles? wrens be wrens?
If all the world were falcons, what of that?
The wonder of the eagle were the less,
But he not less the eagle. Happy days
Roll onward, leading up the golden year.

     'Fly, happy happy sails and bear the Press;
Fly happy with the mission of the Cross;
Knit land to land, and blowing havenward

With silks, and fruits, and spices, clear of toll,
Enrich the markets of the golden year.
    'But we grow old. Ah! when shall all men's good
Be each man's rule, and universal Peace
Lie like a shaft of light across the land,
And like a lane of beams athwart the sea,
Thro' all the circle of the golden year?'
    Thus far he flow'd, and ended; whereupon
'Ah, folly!' in mimic cadence answer'd James –
'Ah, folly! for it lies so far away,
Not in our time, nor in our children's time,
'Tis like the second world to us that live;
'Twere all as one to fix our hopes on Heaven
As on this vision of the golden year.'
    With that he struck his staff against the rocks
And broke it, – James, – you know him, – old, but full
Of force and choler, and firm upon his feet,
And like an oaken stock in winter woods,
O'erflourish'd with the hoary clematis:
Then added, all in heat:
                          'What stuff is this!
Old writers push'd the happy season back, –
The more fools they, – we forward: dreamers both:
You most, that in an age, when every hour
Must sweat her sixty minutes to the death
Live on, God love us, as if the seedsman, rapt
Upon the teeming harvest, should not plunge
His hand into the bag: but well I know
That unto him who works, and feels he works,
This same grand year is ever at the doors.'
    He spoke; and, high above, I heard them blast
The steep slate-quarry, and the great echo flap
And buffet round the hills from bluff to bluff.

After-Thought

Ah, God! the petty fools of rhyme,
    That shriek and sweat in pigmy wars
Before the stony face of Time
    And look'd at by the silent stars; –

That hate each other for a song,
    And do their little best to bite,
That pinch their brothers in the throng,
    And scratch the very dead for spite; –

And strain to make an inch of room
    For their sweet selves, and cannot hear
The sullen Lethe rolling doom
    On them and theirs, and all things here

When one small touch of Charity
    Could lift them nearer Godlike State,
Than if the crowded Orb should cry
    Like those that cried Diana great:

And I too talk, and lose the touch
    I talk of. Surely, after all,
The noblest answer unto such
    Is kindly silence when they brawl.

THE PRINCESS

A Medley

Prologue

Sir Walter Vivian all a summer's day
Gave his broad lawns until the set of sun
Up to the people: thither flock'd at noon
His tenants, wife and child, and thither half
The neighbouring borough with their Institute
Of which he was the patron. I was there
From college, visiting the son, – the son
A Walter too, – with others of our set,
Five others: we were seven at Vivian-place.

And me that morning Walter show'd the house,
Greek, set with busts: from vases in the hall
Flowers of all heavens, and lovelier than their names,
Grew side by side; and on the pavement lay
Carved stones of the Abbey-ruin in the park,
Huge Ammonites, and the first bones of Time
And on the tables every clime and age
Jumbled together; celts and calumets,
Claymore and snowshoe, toys in lava, fans
Of sandal, amber, ancient rosaries,
Laborious orient ivory sphere in sphere,
The cursed Malayan crease, and battle-clubs
From the isles of palm: and higher on the walls,
Betwixt the monstrous horns of elk and deer,
His own forefathers' arms and armour hung.

And 'this' he said 'was Hugh's at Agincourt;
And that was old Sir Ralph's at Ascalon:
A good knight he! we keep a chronicle
With all about him' – which he brought, and I
Dived in a hoard of tales that dealt with knights,
Half-legend, half-historic, counts and kings
Who laid about them at their wills and died;
And mixt with these, a lady, one that arm'd
Her own fair head, and sallying thro' the gate,
Had beat her foes with slaughter from her walls.

'O miracle of women,' said the book,
'O noble heart who, being strait-besieged

By this wild king to force her to his wish,
Nor bent, nor broke, nor shunn'd a soldier's death,
But now when all was lost or seem'd as lost –
Her stature more than mortal in the burst
Of sunrise, her arm lifted, eyes on fire –
Brake with a blast of trumpets from the gate,
And, falling on them like a thunderbolt,
She trampled some beneath her horses' heels,
And some were whelm'd with missiles of the wall,
And some were push'd with lances from the rock,
And part were drown'd within the whirling brook:
O miracle of noble womanhood!'

    So sang the gallant glorious chronicle;
And, I all rapt in this, 'Come out,' he said,
'To the Abbey: there is Aunt Elizabeth
And sister Lilia with the rest.' We went
(I kept the book and had my finger in it)
Down thro' the park: strange was the sight to me;
For all the sloping pasture murmur'd, sown
With happy faces and with holiday.
There moved the multitude, a thousand heads:
The patient leaders of their Institute
Taught them with facts. One rear'd a font of stone
And drew, from butts of water on the slope,
The fountain of the moment, playing now
A twisted snake, and now a rain of pearls,
Or steep-up spout whereon the gilded ball
Danced like a wisp: and somewhat lower down
A man with knobs and wires and vials fired
A cannon: Echo answer'd in her sleep
From hollow fields: and here were telescopes
For azure views; and there a group of girls
In circle waited, whom the electric shock
Dislink'd with shrieks and laughter: round the lake
A little clock-work steamer paddling plied
And shook the lilies: perch'd about the knolls
A dozen angry models jetted steam:
A petty railway ran: a fire-balloon
Rose gem-like up before the dusky groves
And dropt a fairy parachute and past:
And there thro' twenty posts of telegraph
They flash'd a saucy message to and fro
Between the mimic stations; so that sport
Went hand in hand with Science; otherwhere
Pure sport: a herd of boys with clamour bowl'd

And stump'd the wicket; babies roll'd about
Like tumbled fruit in grass; and men and maids
Arranged a country dance, and flew thro' light
And shadow, while the twangling violin
Struck up with Soldier-laddie, and overhead
The broad ambrosial aisles of lofty lime
Made noise with bees and breeze from end to end.

Strange was the sight and smacking of the time;
And long we gazed, but satiated at length
Came to the ruins. High-arch'd and ivy-claspt,
Of finest Gothic lighter than a fire,
Thro' one wide chasm of time and frost they gave
The park, the crowd, the house; but all within
The sward was trim as any garden lawn:
And here we lit on Aunt Elizabeth,
And Lilia with the rest, and lady friends
From neighbour seats: and there was Ralph himself,
A broken statue propt against the wall,
As gay as any. Lilia, wild with sport,
Half child half woman as she was, had wound
A scarf of orange round the stony helm,
And robed the shoulders in a rosy silk,
That made the old warrior from his ivied nook
Glow like a sunbeam: near his tomb a feast
Shone, silver-set; about it lay the guests,
And there we join'd them: then the maiden Aunt
Took this fair day for text, and from it preach'd
An universal culture for the crowd,
And all things great; but we, unworthier, told
Of college: he had climb'd across the spikes,
And he had squeezed himself betwixt the bars,
And he had breath'd the Proctor's dogs; and one
Discuss'd his tutor, rough to common men,
But honeying at the whisper of a lord;
And one the Master, as a rogue in grain
Veneer'd with sanctimonious theory.

But while they talk'd, above their heads I saw
The feudal warrior lady-clad; which brought
My book to mind: and opening this I read
Of old Sir Ralph a page or two that rang
With tilt and tourney; then the tale of her
That drove her foes with slaughter from her walls,
And much I praised her nobleness, and 'Where,'
Ask'd Walter, patting Lilia's head (she lay
Beside him) 'lives there such a woman now?'

Quick answer'd Lilia 'There are thousands now
Such women, but convention beats them down:
It is but bringing up; no more than that:
You men have done it: how I hate you all!
Ah, were I something great! I wish I were
Some mighty poetess, I would shame you then,
That love to keep us children! O I wish
That I were some great Princess, I would build
Far off from men a college like a man's,
And I would teach them all that men are taught;
We are twice as quick!' And here she shook aside
The hand that play'd the patron with her curls.

And one said smiling, 'Pretty were the sight
If our old halls could change their sex, and flaunt
With prudes for proctors, dowagers for deans,
And sweet girl-graduates in their golden hair.
I think they should not wear our rusty gowns,
But move as rich as Emperor-moths, or Ralph
Who shines so in the corner; yet I fear,
If there were many Lilias in the brood,
However deep you might embower the nest,
Some boy would spy it.'
                    At this upon the sward
She tapt her tiny silken-sandal'd foot:
'That's your light way; but I would make it death
For any male thing but to peep at us.'

Petulant she spoke, and at herself she laugh'd;
A rosebud set with little wilful thorns,
And sweet as English air could make her, she:
But Walter hail'd a score of names upon her
And 'petty Ogress,' and 'ungrateful Puss,'
And swore he long'd at college, only long'd,
All else was well, for she-society.
They boated and they cricketed; they talk'd
At wine, in clubs, of art, of politics;
They lost their weeks; they vext the souls of deans;
They rode; they betted; made a hundred friends
And caught the blossom of the flying terms,
But miss'd the mignonette of Vivian-place
The little hearth-flower Lilia. Thus he spoke,
Part banter, part affection.
                            'True,' she said,
'We doubt not that. O yes, you miss'd us much.
I'll stake my ruby ring upon it you did.'

She held it out; and as a parrot turns
Up thro' gilt wires a crafty loving eye,
And takes a lady's finger with all care,
And bites it for true heart and not for harm,
So he with Lilia's. Daintily she shriek'd
And wrung it. 'Doubt my word again!' he said.
'Come, listen! here is proof that you were miss'd:
We seven stay'd at Christmas up to read;
And there we took one tutor as to read:
The hard-grain'd Muses of the cube and square
Were out of season: never man, I think,
So moulder'd in a sinecure as he:
For while our cloisters echo'd frosty feet,
And our long walks were stript as bare as brooms,
We did but talk you over, pledge you all
In wassail; often, like as many girls –
Sick for the hollies and the yews of home –
As many little trifling Lilias – play'd
Charades and riddles as at Christmas here,
And *what's my thought* and *when* and *where* and *how*,
And often told a tale from mouth to mouth
As here at Christmas.'
               She remember'd that:
A pleasant game, she thought: she liked it more
Than magic music, forfeits, all the rest.
But these – what kind of tales did men tell men,
She wonder'd, by themselves?
               A half-disdain
Perch'd on the pouted blossom of her lips:
And Walter nodded at me; '*He* began,
The rest would follow, each in turn; and so
We forged a sevenfold story. Kind? what kind?
Chimeras, crotchets, Christmas solecisms,
Seven-headed monsters only made to kill
Time by the fire in winter.'
               'Kill him now,
The tyrant! kill him in the summer too.'
Said Lilia; 'Why not now?' the maiden Aunt.
'Why not a summer's as a winter's tale?
A tale for summer as befits the time,
And something it should be to suit the place,
Heroic, for a hero lies beneath,
Grave, solemn!'
               Walter warp'd his mouth at this
To something so mock-solemn, that I laugh'd
And Lilia woke with sudden-shrilling mirth

An echo like a ghostly woodpecker,
Hid in the ruins; till the maiden Aunt
(A little sense of wrong had touch'd her face
With colour) turn'd to me with 'As you will;
Heroic if you will, or what you will
Or be yourself your hero if you will.'

'Take Lilia, then, for heroine,' clamour'd he,
'And make her some great Princess, six feet high,
Grand, epic, homicidal; and be you
The Prince to win her!'
                              'Then follow me, the Prince,'
I answer'd, 'each be hero in his turn!
Seven and yet one, like shadows in a dream. –
Heroic seems our Princess as required –
But something made to suit with Time and place,
A Gothic ruin and a Grecian house,
A talk of college and of ladies' rights,
A feudal knight in silken masquerade,
And, yonder, shrieks and strange experiments
For which the good Sir Ralph had burnt them all –
This *were* a medley! we should have him back
Who told the 'Winter's tale' to do it for us.
No matter: we will say whatever comes.
And let the ladies sing us, if they will,
From time to time, some ballad or a song
To give us breathing-space.'
                              So I began,
And the rest follow'd: and the women sang
Between the rougher voices of the men,
Like linnets in the pauses of the wind:
And here I give the story and the songs.

I

A Prince I was, blue-eyed, and fair in face,
Of temper amorous as the first of May,
With lengths of yellow ringlets, like a girl,
For on my cradle shone the Northern star.

There lived an ancient legend in our house.
Some sorcerer, whom a far-off grandsire burnt
Because he cast no shadow, had foretold,
Dying, that none of all our blood should know
The shadow from the substance, and that one
Should come to fight with shadows and to fall.
For so, my mother said, the story ran.

And, truly, waking dreams were, more or less,
An old and strange affection of the house.
Myself too had weird seizures, Heaven knows what:
On a sudden in the midst of men and day,
And while I walk'd and talk'd as heretofore,
I seem'd to move among a world of ghosts,
And feel myself the shadow of a dream.
Our great court-Galen poised his gilt-head cane,
And paw'd his beard, and mutter'd 'catalepsy.'
My mother pitying made a thousand prayers;
My mother was as mild as any saint,
Half-canonized by all that look'd on her,
So gracious was her tact and tenderness:
But my good father thought a king a king;
He cared not for the affection of the house;
He held his sceptre like a pedant's wand
To lash offence, and with long arms and hands
Reach'd out, and pick'd offenders from the mass
For judgement.
           Now it chanced that I had been,
While life was yet in bud and blade, betroth'd
To one, a neighbouring Princess: she to me
Was proxy-wedded with a bootless calf
At eight years old; and still from time to time
Came murmurs of her beauty from the South,
And of her brethren, youths of puissance;
And still I wore her picture by my heart,
And one dark tress; and all around them both
Sweet thoughts would swarm as bees about their queen.

But when the days drew nigh that I should wed,
My father sent ambassadors with furs
And jewels, gifts, to fetch her: these brought back
A present, a great labour of the loom;
And therewithal an answer vague as wind:
Besides, they saw the king; he took the gifts;
He said there was a compact; that was true:
But then she had a will; was he to blame?
And maiden fancies; loved to live alone
Among her women; certain, would not wed.

That morning in the presence room I stood
With Cyril and with Florian, my two friends:
The first, a gentleman of broken means
(His father's fault) but given to starts and bursts
Of revel; and the last, my other heart,

And almost my half-self, for still we moved
Together, twinn'd as horse's ear and eye.

  Now, while they spake, I saw my father's face
Grow long and troubled like a rising moon,
Inflamed with wrath: he started on his feet,
Tore the king's letter, snow'd it down, and rent
The wonder of the loom thro' warp and woof
From skirt to skirt; and at the last he sware
That he would send a hundred thousand men,
And bring her in a whirlwind: then he chew'd
The thrice-turn'd cud of wrath, and cook'd his spleen,
Communing with his captains of the war.

    At last I spoke. 'My father, let me go.
It cannot be but some gross error lies
In this report, this answer of a king,
Whom all men rate as kind and hospitable:
Or, maybe, I myself, my bride once seen,
Whate'er my grief to find her less than fame,
May rue the bargain made.' And Florian said:
'I have a sister at the foreign court,
Who moves about the Princess; she, you know,
Who wedded with a nobleman from thence:
He, dying lately, left her, as I hear,
The lady of three castles in that land:
Thro' her this matter might be sifted clean.
And Cyril whisper'd: 'Take me with you too.'
Then laughing 'what, if these weird seizures come
Upon you in those lands, and no one near
To point you out the shadow from the truth!
Take me: I'll serve you better in a strait;
I grate on rusty hinges here:' but 'No!'
Roar'd the rough king, 'you shall not; we ourself
Will crush her pretty maiden fancies dead
In iron gauntlets: break the council up.'

    But when the council broke, I rose and past
Thro' the wild woods that hung about the town;
Found a still place, and pluck'd her likeness out;
Laid it on flowers, and watch'd it lying bathed
In the green gleam of dewy-tassell'd trees:
What were those fancies? wherefore break her troth?
Proud look'd the lips: but while I meditated
A wind arose and rush'd upon the South,
And shook the songs, the whispers, and the shrieks

Of the wild woods together; and a Voice
Went with it, 'Follow, follow, thou shalt win.'
Then, ere the silver sickle of that month
Became her golden shield, I stole from court
With Cyril and with Florian, unperceived,
Cat-footed thro' the town and half in dread
To hear my father's clamour at our backs
With Ho! from some bay-window shake the night;
But all was quiet: from the bastion'd walls
Like threaded spiders, one by one, we dropt,
And flying reach'd the frontier: then we crost
To a livelier land; and so by tilth and grange,
And vines, and blowing bosks of wilderness,
We gain'd the mother-city thick with towers,
And in the imperial palace found the king.

His name was Gama; crack'd and small his voice,
But bland the smile that like a wrinkling wind
On glassy water drove his cheek in lines;
A little dry old man, without a star,
Not like a king: three days he feasted us,
And on the fourth I spake of why we came,
And my betroth'd. 'You do us, Prince,' he said,
Airing a snowy hand and signet gem,
'All honour. We remember love ourselves
In our sweet youth: there did a compact pass
Long summers back, a kind of ceremony —
I think the year in which our olives fail'd.
I would you had her, Prince, with all my heart,
With my full heart: but there were widows here,
Two widows, Lady Psyche, Lady Blanche;
They fed her theories, in and out of place
Maintaining that with equal husbandry
The woman were an equal to the man.
They harp'd on this; with this our banquets rang;
Our dances broke and buzz'd in knots of talk;
Nothing but this; my very ears were hot
To hear them: knowledge, so my daughter held,
Was all in all: they had but been, she thought,
As children; they must lose the child, assume
The woman: then, Sir, awful odes she wrote,
Too awful, sure, for what they treated of,
But all she is and does is awful; odes
About this losing of the child; and rhymes
And dismal lyrics, prophesying change
Beyond all reason: these the women sang;

And they that know such things – I sought but peace;
No critic I – would call them masterpieces:
They master'd me. At last she begg'd a boon,
A certain summer-palace which I have
Hard by your father's frontier: I said no,
Yet being an easy man, gave it: and there,
All wild to found an University
For maidens, on the spur she fled; and more
We know not, – only this: they see no men
Not ev'n her brother Arac, nor the twins
Her brethren, tho' they love her, look upon her
As on a kind of paragon; and I
(Pardon me saying it) were much loath to breed
Dispute betwixt myself and mine: but since
(And I confess with right) you think me bound
In some sort, I can give you letters to her;
And yet, to speak the truth, I rate your chance
Almost at naked nothing.'
                              Thus the king;
And I, tho' nettled that he seem'd to slur
With garrulous ease and oily courtesies
Our formal compact, yet, not less (all frets
But chafing me on fire to find my bride)
Went forth again with both my friends. We rode
Many a long league back to the North. At last
From hills, that look'd across a land of hope,
We dropt with evening on a rustic town
Set in a gleaming river's crescent-curve,
Close at the boundary of the liberties;
There, enter'd an old hostel, call'd mine host
To council, plied him with his richest wines,
And show'd the late-writ letters of the king.

He with a long low sibilation, stared
As blank as death in marble; then exclaim'd
Averring it was clear against all rules
For any man to go: but as his brain
Began to mellow, 'If the king,' he said,
'Had given us letters, was he bound to speak?
The king would bear him out;' and at the last –
The summer of the vine in all his veins –
'No doubt that we might make it worth his while
She once had past that way; he heard her speak
She scared him; life! he never saw the like;
She look'd as grand as doomsday and as grave:
And he, he reverenced his liege-lady there;

He always made a point to post with mares;
His daughter and his housemaid were the boys:
The land, he understood, for miles about
Was till'd by women; all the swine were sows,
And all the dogs' –

               But while he jested thus,
A thought flash'd thro' me which I clothed in act,
Remembering how we three presented Maid,
Or Nymph, or Goddess, at high tide of feast,
In masque or pageant at my father's court.
We sent mine host to purchase female gear;
He brought it, and himself, a sight to shake
The midriff of despair with laughter, holp
To lace us up, till, each, in maiden plumes
We rustled: him we gave a costly bribe
To guerdon silence, mounted our good steeds,
And boldly ventured on the liberties.

  We follow'd up the river as we rode,
And rode till midnight when the college lights
Began to glitter firefly-like in copse
And linden alley: then we past an arch,
Whereon a woman-statue rose with wings
From four wing'd horses dark against the stars;
And some inscription ran along the front,
But deep in shadow: further on we gain'd
A little street half garden and half house;
But scarce could hear each other speak for noise
Of clocks and chimes, like silver hammers falling
On silver anvils, and the splash and stir
Of fountains spouted up and showering down
In meshes of the jasmine and the rose:
And all about us peal'd the nightingale,
Rapt in her song, and careless of the snare.

  There stood a bust of Pallas for a sign,
By two sphere lamps blazon'd like Heaven and Earth
With constellation and with continent,
Above an entry: riding in, we call'd;
A plump-arm'd Ostleress and a stable wench
Came running at the call, and help'd us down.
Then stept a buxom hostess forth, and sail'd,
Full-blown, before us into rooms which gave
Upon a pillar'd porch, the bases lost
In laurel: her we ask'd of that and this
And who were tutors. 'Lady Blanche' she said,

'And Lady Psyche.' 'Which was prettiest
Best-natured?' 'Lady Psyche.' 'Hers are we,'
One voice, we cried; and I sat down and wrote
In such a hand as when a field of corn
Bows all its ears before the roaring East;

'Three ladies of the Northern empire pray
Your Highness would enroll them with your own,
As Lady Psyche's pupils.'
                                    This I seal'd:
The seal was Cupid bent above a scroll,
And o'er his head Uranian Venus hung,
And raised the blinding bandage from his eyes:
I gave the letter to be sent with dawn;
And then to bed, where half in doze I seem'd
To float about a glimmering night, and watch
A full sea glazed with muffled moonlight, swell
On some dark shore just seen that it was rich.

*

> As thro' the land at eve we went,
>   And pluck'd the ripen'd ears,
> We fell out, my wife and I
> O we fell out I know not why,
>   And kiss'd again with tears.
> And blessings on the falling out
>   That all the more endears,
> When we fall out with those we love
>   And kiss again with tears!
> For when we came where lies the child
>   We lost in other years,
> There above the little grave,
> O there above the little grave,
>   We kiss'd again with tears.

II

At break of day the College Portress came:
She brought us Academic silks, in hue
The lilac, with a silken hood to each,
And zoned with gold; and now when these were on,
And we as rich as moths from dusk cocoons,
She, curtseying her obeisance, let us know
The Princess Ida waited: out we paced,
I first, and following thro' the porch that sang
All round with laurel, issued in a court
Compact with lucid marbles, boss'd with lengths

Of classic frieze, with ample awnings gay
Betwixt the pillars, and with great urns of flowers.
The Muses and the Graces, group'd in threes,
Enring'd a billowing fountain in the midst;
And here and there on lattice edges lay
Or book or lute; but hastily we past,
And up a flight of stairs into the hall.

There at a board by tome and paper sat,
With two tame leopards couch'd beside her throne,
All beauty compass'd in a female form,
The Princess; liker to the inhabitant
Of some clear planet close upon the Sun,
Than our man's earth; such eyes were in her head,
And so much grace and power, breathing down
From over her arch'd brows, with every turn
Lived thro' her to the tips of her long hands,
And to her feet. She rose her height, and said:

'We give you welcome: not without redound
Of use and glory to yourselves ye come,
The first-fruits of the stranger: aftertime,
And that full voice which circles round the grave,
Will rank you nobly, mingled up with me.
What! are the ladies of your land so tall?'
'We of the court' said Cyril. 'From the court'
She answer'd, 'then ye know the Prince?' and he:
'The climax of his age! as tho' there were
One rose in all the world, your Highness that,
He worships your ideal:' she replied:
'We scarcely thought in our own hall to hear
This barren verbiage, current among men,
Light coin, the tinsel clink of compliment.
Your flight from out your bookless wilds would seem
As arguing love of knowledge and of power;
Your language proves you still the child. Indeed,
We dream not of him: when we set our hand
To this great work, we purposed with ourself
Never to wed. You likewise will do well,
Ladies, in entering here, to cast and fling
The tricks, which make us toys of men, that so,
Some future time, if so indeed you will,
You may with those self-styled our lords ally
Your fortunes, justlier balanced, scale with scale.'

At those high words, we conscious of ourselves,

Perused the matting; then an officer
Rose up, and read the statutes, such as these:
Not for three years to correspond with home;
Not for three years to cross the liberties;
Not for three years to speak with any men;
And many more, which hastily subscribed,
We enter'd on the boards: and 'Now' she cried,
'Ye are green wood, see ye warp not. Look, our hall!
Our statues! – not of those that men desire,
Sleek Odalisques, or oracles of mode
Nor stunted squaws of West or East; but she
That taught the Sabine how to rule and she
The foundress of the Babylonian wail,
The Carian Artemisia strong in war,
The Rhodope, that built the pyramid,
Clelia, Cornelia, with the Palmyrene
That fought Aurelian, and the Roman brows
Of Agrippina. Dwell with these, and lose
Convention, since to look on noble forms
Makes noble thro' the sensuous organism
That which is higher. O lift your natures up:
Embrace our aims: work out your freedom. Girls,
Knowledge is now no more a fountain seal'd:
Drink deep, until the habits of the slave,
The sins of emptiness, gossip and spite
And slander, die. Better not be at all
Than not be noble. Leave us: you may go:
To-day the Lady Psyche will harangue
The fresh arrivals of the week before;
For they press in from all the provinces,
And fill the hive.'

                She spoke, and bowing waved
Dismissal: back again we crost the court
To Lady Psyche's: as we enter'd in,
There sat along the forms, like morning doves
That sun their milky bosoms on the thatch,
A patient range of pupils; she herself
Erect behind a desk of satin-wood,
A quick brunette, well-moulded, falcon-eyed,
And on the hither side, or so she look'd,
Of twenty summers. At her left, a child,
In shining draperies, headed like a star,
Her maiden babe, a double April old,
Aglaïa slept. We sat: the Lady glanced:
Then Florian, but no livelier than the dame
That whisper'd 'Asses' ears' among the sedge,

'My sister.' 'Comely, too, by all that's fair,'
Said Cyril. 'O hush, hush!' and she began.

'This world was once a fluid haze of light,
Till toward the centre set the starry tides,
And eddied into suns, that wheeling cast
The planets: then the monster, then the man;
Tattoo'd or woaded, winter-clad in skins,
Raw from the prime, and crushing down his mate;
As yet we find in barbarous isles, and here
Among the lowest.'
                              Thereupon she took
A bird's-eye-view of all the ungracious past;
Glanced at the legendary Amazon
As emblematic of a nobler age;
Appraised the Lycian custom, spoke of those
That lay at wine with Lar and Lucumo;
Ran down the Persian, Grecian, Roman lines
Of empire, and the woman's state in each,
How far from just; till warming with her theme
She fulmined out her scorn of laws Salique
And little-footed China, touch'd on Mahomet
With much contempt, and came to chivalry:
When some respect, however slight, was paid
To woman, superstition all awry:
However then commenced the dawn: a beam
Had slanted forward, falling in a land
Of promise; fruit would follow. Deep, indeed,
Their debt of thanks to her who first had dared
To leap the rotten pales of prejudice,
Disyoke their necks from custom, and assert
None lordlier than themselves but that which made
Woman and man. She had founded; they must build.
Here might they learn whatever men were taught:
Let them not fear: some said their heads were less:
Some men's were small; not they the least of men;
For often fineness compensated size:
Besides the brain was like the hand, and grew
With using; thence the man's, if more was more;
He took advantage of his strength to be
First in the field: some ages had been lost;
But woman ripen'd earlier, and her life
Was longer; and albeit their glorious names
Were fewer, scatter'd stars, yet since in truth
The highest is the measure of the man,
And not the Kaffir, Hottentot, Malay,

Nor those horn-handed breakers of the glebe,
But Homer, Plato, Verulam; even so
With woman: and in arts of government
Elizabeth and others; arts of war
The peasant Joan and others; arts of grace
Sappho and others vied with any man:
And, last not least, she who had left her place
And bow'd her state to them, that they might grow
To use and power on this Oasis, lapt
In the arms of leisure, sacred from the blight
Of ancient influence and scorn.
                              At last
She rose upon a wind of prophecy
Dilating on the future; 'everywhere
Two heads in council, two beside the hearth
Two in the tangled business of the world,
Two in the liberal offices of life,
Two plummets dropt for one to sound the abyss
Of science, and the secrets of the mind:
Musician, painter, sculptor, critic, more:
And everywhere the broad and bounteous Earth
Should bear a double growth of those rare souls,
Poets, whose thoughts enrich the blood of the world.'

    She ended here, and beckon'd us: the rest
Parted; and, glowing full-faced welcome, she
Began to address us, and was moving on
In gratulation, till as when a boat
Tacks, and the slacken'd sail flaps, all her voice
Faltering and fluttering in her throat, she cried,
'My brother!' 'Well, my sister.' 'O,' she said,
'What do you here? and in this dress? and these?
Why who are these? a wolf within the fold!
A pack of wolves! the Lord be gracious to me!
A plot, a plot, a plot, to ruin all!'
'No plot, no plot,' he answer'd. 'Wretched boy,
How saw you not the inscription on the gate,
LET NO MAN ENTER IN ON PAIN OF DEATH?'
'And if I had,' he answer'd, 'who could think
The softer Adams of your Academe, O sister,
Sirens tho' they be, were such
As chanted on the blanching bones of men?'
'But you will find it otherwise' she said.
'You jest: ill jesting with edge-tools! my vow
Binds me to speak, and O that iron will,
That axelike edge unturnable, our Head,

The Princess.' 'Well then, Psyche, take my life,
And nail me like a weasel on a grange
For warning: bury me beside the gate,
And cut this epitaph above my bones;
Here lies a brother by a sister slain
All for the common good of womankind.'
'Let me die too,' said Cyril, 'having seen
And heard the Lady Psyche.'
                                        I struck in:
'Albeit so mask'd, Madam, I love the truth;
Receive it; and in me behold the Prince
Your countryman, affianced years ago
To the Lady Ida: here, for here she was,
And thus (what other way was left) I came.'
'O Sir, O Prince, I have no country; none;
If any, this; but none. Whate'er I was
Disrooted, what I am is grafted here.
Affianced, Sir? love-whispers may not breathe
Within this vestal limit, and how should I,
Who am not mine, say, live: the thunderbolt
Hangs silent; out prepare: I speak; it falls.'
'Yet pause,' I said: 'for that inscription there,
I think no more of deadly lurks therein,
Than in a clapper clapping in a garth,
To scare the fowl from fruit: if more there be,
If more and acted on, what follows? war;
Your own work marr'd: for this your Academe,
Whichever side be Victor, in the halloo
Will topple to the trumpet down, and pass
With all fair theories only made to gild
A stormless summer.' 'Let the Princess judge
Of that' she said: 'farewell, Sir – and to you.
I shudder at the sequel, but I go.'

    'Are you that Lady Psyche,' I rejoin'd,
'The fifth in line from that old Florian,
Yet hangs his portrait in my father's hall
(The gaunt old Baron with his beetle brow
Sun-shaded in the heat of dusty fights)
As he bestrode my Grandsire, when he fell,
And all else fled? we point to it, and we say,
The loyal warmth of Florian is not cold,
But branches current yet in kindred veins.'
'Are you that Psyche,' Florian added, 'she
With whom I sang about the morning hills,
Flung ball, flew kite, and raced the purple fly,

And snared the squirrel of the glen? are you
That Psyche, wont to bind my throbbing brow,
To smoothe my pillow, mix the foaming draught
Of fever, tell me pleasant tales, and read
My sickness down to happy dreams? are you
That brother-sister Psyche, both in one?
You were that Psyche, but what are you now?'
'You are that Psyche,' Cyril said, 'for whom
I would be that for ever which I seem,
Woman, if I might sit beside your feet,
And glean your scatter'd sapience.'
                      Then once more
'Are you that Lady Psyche,' I began,
'That on her bridal morn before she past
From all her old companions, when the king
Kiss'd her pale cheek, declared that ancient ties
Would still be dear beyond the southern hills;
That were there any of our people there
In want or peril, there was one to hear
And help them? look! for such are these and I.'
'Are you that Psyche,' Florian ask'd, 'to whom,
In gentler days, your arrow-wounded fawn
Came flying while you sat beside the well?
The creature laid his muzzle on your lap,
And sobb'd, and you sobb'd with it, and the blood
Was sprinkled on your kirtle, and you wept.
That was fawn's blood, not brother's, yet you wept.
O by the bright head of my little niece,
You were that Psyche, and what are you now?'
'You are that Psyche,' Cyril said again,
'The mother of the sweetest little maid
That ever crow'd for kisses.'
                         'Out upon it!'
She answer'd, 'peace! and why should I not play
The Spartan Mother with emotion, be
The Lucius Junius Brutus of my kind?
Him you call great: he for the common weal,
The fading politics of mortal Rome,
As I might slay this child, if good need were,
Slew both his sons: and I, shall I, on whom
The secular emancipation turns
Of half this world, be swerved from right to save
A prince, a brother? a little will I yield.
Best so, perchance, for us, and well for you.
O hard, when love and duty clash! I fear
My conscience will not count me fleckless; yet –

Hear my conditions: promise (otherwise
You perish) as you came, to slip away,
To-day, to-morrow, soon: it shall be said,
These women were too barbarous, would not learn
They fled, who might have shamed us: promise, all.

    What could we else, we promised each; and she,
Like some wild creature newly-caged, commenced
A to-and-fro, so pacing till she paused
By Florian; holding out her lily arms
Took both his hands, and smiling faintly said:
'I knew you at the first: tho' you have grown
You scarce have alter'd: I am sad and glad
To see you, Florian. I give thee to death
My brother! it was duty spoke, not I.
My needful seeming harshness, pardon it.
Our mother, is she well?'
                          With that she kiss'd
His forehead, then, a moment after, clung
About him, and betwixt them blossom'd up
From out a common vein of memory
Sweet household talk, and phrases of the hearth,
And far allusion, till the gracious dews
Began to glisten and to fall: and while
They stood, so rapt, we gazing, came a voice,
'I brought a message here from Lady Blanche.'
Back started she, and turning round we saw
The Lady Blanche's daughter where she stood,
Melissa, with her hand upon the lock,
A rosy blonde, and in a college gown,
That clad her like an April daffodilly
(Her mother's colour) with her lips apart,
And all her thoughts as fair within her eyes,
As bottom agates seen to wave and float
In crystal currents of clear morning seas.

    So stood that same fair creature at the door.
Then Lady Psyche, 'Ah – Melissa – you!
You heard us?' and Melissa, 'O pardon me!
I heard, I could not help it, did not wish:
But, dearest Lady, pray you fear me not,
Nor think I bear that heart within my breast,
To give three gallant gentlemen to death.'
'I trust you,' said the other, 'for we two
Were always friends, none closer, elm and vine:
But yet your mother's jealous temperament –

Let not your prudence, dearest, drowse, or prove
The Danaid of a leaky vase, for fear
This whole foundation ruin, and I lose
My honour, these their lives.' 'Ah, fear me not'
Replied Melissa; 'no – I would not tell,
No, not for all Aspasia's cleverness,
No, not to answer, Madam, all those hard things
That Sheba came to ask of Solomon.'
'Be it so' the other, 'that we still may lead
The new light up, and culminate in peace,
For Solomon may come to Sheba yet.'
Said Cyril, 'Madam, he the wisest man
Feasted the woman wisest then, in halls
Of Lebanonian cedar: nor should you
(Tho', madam, *you* should answer, *we* would ask)
Less welcome find among us, if you came
Among us, debtors for our lives to you,
Myself for something more.' He said not what,
But 'Thanks,' she answer'd 'Go: we have been too long
Together: keep your hoods about the face;
They do so that affect abstraction here.
Speak little; mix not with the rest; and hold
Your promise: all, I trust, may yet be well.'

We turn'd to go, but Cyril took the child,
And held her round the knees against his waist,
And blew the swoll'n cheek of a trumpeter,
While Psyche watch'd them, smiling, and the child
Push'd her flat hand against his face and laugh'd
And thus our conference closed.
                              And then we stroll'd
For half the day thro' stately theatres
Bench'd crescent-wise. In each we sat, we heard
The grave Professor. On the lecture slate
The circle rounded under female hands
With flawless demonstration: follow'd then
A classic lecture, rich in sentiment,
With scraps of thundrous Epic lilted out
By violet-hooded Doctors, elegies
And quoted odes, and jewels five-words-long
That on the stretch'd forefinger of all Time
Sparkle for ever: then we dipt in all
That treats of whatsoever is, the state
The total chronicles of man, the mind,
The morals, something of the frame, the rock,
The star, the bird, the fish, the shell, the flower,

Electric, chemic laws, and all the rest,
And whatsoever can be taught and known;
Till like three horses that have broken fence,
And glutted all night long breast-deep in corn,
We issued gorged with knowledge, and I spoke:
'Why, Sirs, they do all this as well as we.'
'They hunt old trails' said Cyril 'very well;
But when did woman ever yet invent?'
'Ungracious!' answer'd Florian, 'have you learnt
No more from Psyche's lecture, you that talk'd
The trash that made me sick, and almost sad?'
'O trash' he said, 'but with a kernel in it.
Should I not call her wise, who made me wise?
And learnt? I learnt more from her in a flash,
Than if my brainpan were an empty hull,
And every Muse tumbled a science in.
A thousand hearts lie fallow in these halls,
And round these halls a thousand baby loves
Fly twanging headless arrows at the hearts
Whence follows many a vacant pang; but O
With me, Sir, enter'd in the bigger boy,
The Head of all the golden-shafted firm,
The long-limb'd lad that had a Psyche too;
He cleft me thro' the stomacher; and now
What think you of it, Florian? do I chase
The substance or the shadow? will it hold?
I have no sorcerer's malison on me,
No ghostly hauntings like his Highness. I
Flatter myself that always everywhere
I know the substance when I see it. Well,
Are castles shadows? Three of them? Is she
The sweet proprietress a shadow? If not,
Shall those three castles patch my tatter'd coat?
For dear are those three castles to my wants,
And dear is sister Psyche to my heart,
And two dear things are one of double worth,
And much I might have said, but that my zone
Unmann'd me: then the Doctors! O to hear
The Doctors! O to watch the thirsty plants
Imbibing! once or twice I thought to roar,
To break my chain, to shake my mane: but thou,
Modulate me, Soul of mincing mimicry!
Make liquid treble of that bassoon, my throat;
Abase those eyes that ever loved to meet
Star-sisters answering under crescent brows;
Abate the stride, which speaks of man, and loose

A flying charm of blushes o'er this cheek,
Where they like swallows coming out of time
Will wonder why they came: but hark the bell
For dinner, let us go!'
                              And in we stream'd
Among the columns, pacing staid and still
By twos and threes, till all from end to end
With beauties every shade of brown and fair
In colours gayer than the morning mist,
The long hall glitter'd like a bed of flowers.
How might a man not wander from his wits
Pierced thro' with eyes, but that I kept mine own
Intent on her, who rapt in glorious dreams,
The second-sight of some Astraean age,
Sat compass'd with professors: they, the while,
Discuss'd a doubt and tost it to and fro:
A clamour thicken'd, mixt with inmost terms
Of art and science: Lady Blanche alone
Of faded form and haughtiest lineaments,
With all her autumn tresses falsely brown,
Shot sidelong daggers at us, a tiger-cat
In act to spring.
                        At last a solemn grace
Concluded, and we sought the gardens: there
One walk'd reciting by herself, and one
In this hand held a volume as to read,
And smoothed a petted peacock down with that:
Some to a low song oar'd a shallop by,
Or under arches of the marble bridge
Hung, shadow'd from the heat: some hid and sought
In the orange thickets: others tost a ball
Above the fountain-jets, and back again
With laughter: others lay about the lawns,
Of the older sort, and murmur'd that their May
Was passing: what was learning unto them?
They wish'd to marry; they could rule a house
Men hated learned women: but we three
Sat muffled like the Fates; and often came
Melissa hitting all we saw with shafts
Of gentle satire, kin to charity,
That harm'd not: then day droopt; the chapel bells
Call'd us: we left the walks; we mixt with those
Six hundred maidens clad in purest white,
Before two streams of light from wall to wall,
While the great organ almost burst his pipes,
Groaning for power, and rolling thro' the court

A long melodious thunder to the sound
Of solemn psalms, and silver litanies
The work of Ida, to call down from Heaven
A blessing on her labours for the world.

*

Sweet and low, sweet and low,
   Wind of the western sea,
Low, low, breathe and blow,
   Wind of the western sea!
Over the rolling waters go
Come from the dying moon, and blow,
   Blow him again to me;
While my little one, while my pretty one, sleeps.

Sleep and rest, sleep and rest,
   Father will come to thee soon;
Rest, rest, on mother's breast,
   Father will come to thee soon;
Father will come to his babe in the nest,
Silver sails all out of the west
   Under the silver moon:
Sleep, my little one, sleep, my pretty one, sleep.

III

Morn in the white wake of the morning star
Came furrowing all the orient into gold.
We rose, and each by other drest with care
Descended to the court that lay three parts
In shadow, but the Muses' heads were touch'd
Above the darkness from their native East.

There while we stood beside the fount, and watch'd
Or seem'd to watch the dancing bubble, approach'd
Melissa, tinged with wan from lack of sleep,
Or grief, and glowing round her dewy eyes
The circled Iris of a night of tears;
'And fly,' she cried, 'O fly, while yet you may!
My mother knows:' and when I ask'd her 'how,'
'My fault!' she wept 'my fault! and yet not mine;
Yet mine in part. O hear me, pardon me.
My mother, 'tis her wont from night to night
To rail at Lady Psyche and her side.
She says the Princess should have been the Head,
Herself and Lady Psyche the two arms;
And so it was agreed when first they came;

But Lady Psyche was the right hand now,
And she the left, or not, or seldom used;
Hers more than half the students, all the love.
And so last night she fell to canvass you:
Her countrywomen! she did not envy her.
"Who ever saw such wild barbarians?
Girls? – more like men!" and at these words the snake,
My secret, seem'd to stir within my breast;
And oh, Sirs, could I help it, but my cheek
Began to burn and burn, and her lynx eye
To fix and make me hotter, till she laugh'd:
"O marvellously modest maiden, you!
Men! girls, like men! why, if they had been men
You need not set your thoughts in rubric thus
For wholesale comment." Pardon, I am shamed
That I must needs repeat for my excuse
What looks so little graceful: "men" (for still
My mother went revolving on the word)
"And so they are, – very like men indeed –
And with that woman closeted for hours!"
Then came these dreadful words out one by one,
"Why – these - are – men:" I shudder'd: "and you know it."
"O ask me nothing," I said: "And she knows too,
And she conceals it." So my mother clutch'd
The truth at once, but with no word from me;
And now thus early risen she goes to inform
The Princess: Lady Psyche will be crush'd;
But you may yet be saved, and therefore fly:
But heal me with your pardon ere you go.'

  'What pardon, sweet Melissa, for a blush?'
Said Cyril: 'Pale one, blush again: than wear
Those lilies, better blush our lives away.
Yet let us breathe for one hour more in Heaven'
He added, 'lest some classic Angel speak
In scorn of us, "They mounted, Ganymedes,
To tumble, Vulcans, on the second morn."
But I will melt this marble into wax
To yield us farther furlough:' and he went.

  Melissa shook her doubtful curls, and thought
He scarce would prosper. 'Tell us,' Florian ask'd,
'How grew this feud betwixt the right and left.'
'O long ago,' she said, 'betwixt these two
Division smoulders hidden; 'tis my mother,
Too jealous, often fretful as the wind

Pent in a crevice: much I bear with her:
I never knew my father, but she says
(God help her) she was wedded to a fool;
And still she rail'd against the state of things.
She had the care of Lady Ida's youth,
And from the Queen's decease she brought her up.
But when your sister came she won the heart
Of Ida: they were still together, grew
(For so they said themselves) inosculated;
Consonant chords that shiver to one note;
One mind in all things: yet my mother still
Affirms your Psyche thieved her theories,
And angled with them for her pupil's love:
She calls her plagiarist; I know not what:
But I must go: I dare not tarry' and light,
As flies the shadow of a bird, she fled.

Then murmur'd Florian gazing after her:
'An open-hearted maiden, true and pure.
If I could love, why this were she: how pretty
Her blushing was, and how she blush'd again,
As if to close with Cyril's random wish:
Not like your Princess cramm'd with erring pride,
Nor like poor Psyche whom she drags in tow.'

'The crane,' I said, 'may chatter of the crane,
The dove may murmur of the dove, but I
An eagle clang an eagle to the sphere.
My princess, O my princess! true she errs,
But in her own grand way: being herself
Three times more noble than three score of men,
She sees herself in every woman else,
And so she wears her error like a crown
To blind the truth and me: for her, and her,
Hebes are they to hand ambrosia, mix
The nectar; but – ah she – whene'er she moves
The Samian Here rises and she speaks
A Memnon smitten with the morning Sun.'

So saying from the court we paced, and gain'd
The terrace ranged along the Northern front,
And leaning there on those balusters, high
Above the empurpled champain, drank the gale
That blown about the foliage underneath,
And sated with the innumerable rose,
Beat balm upon our eyelids. Hither came

Cyril, and yawning 'O hard task,' he cried;
'No fighting shadows here! I forced a way
Thro' solid opposition crabb'd and gnarl'd.
Better to clear prime forests, heave and thump
A league of street in summer solstice down,
Than hammer at this reverend gentlewoman.
I knock'd and, bidden, enter'd; found her there
At point to move, and settled in her eyes
The green malignant light of coming storm.
Sir, I was courteous, every phrase well-oil'd,
As man's could be; yet maiden-meek I pray'd
Concealment: she demanded who we were,
And why we came? I fabled nothing fair,
But, your example pilot, told her all.
Up went the hush'd amaze of hand and eye.
But when I dwelt upon your old affiance,
She answer'd sharply that I talk'd astray.
I urged the fierce inscription on the gate,
And our three lives. True – we had limed ourselves
With open eyes, and we must take the chance.
But such extremes, I told her, well might harm
The woman's cause. "Not more than now," she said
"So puddled as it is with favouritism."
I tried the mother's heart. Shame might befall
Melissa, knowing, saying not she knew:
Her answer was "Leave me to deal with that."
I spoke of war to come and many deaths,
And she replied, her duty was to speak,
And duty duty, clear of consequences.
I grew discouraged, Sir; but since I knew
No rock so hard but that a little wave
May beat admission in a thousand years,
I recommenced; "Decide not ere you pause.
I find you here but in the second place,
Some say the third – the authentic foundress you.
I offer boldly: we will seat you highest:
Wink at our advent: help my prince to gain
His rightful bride, and here I promise you
Some palace in our land, where you shall reign
The head and heart of all our fair she-world,
And your great name flow on with broadening time
For ever." Well, she balanced this a little,
And told me she would answer us to-day
Meantime be mute: thus much, nor more I gain'd.'

He ceasing, came a message from the Head.

'That afternoon the Princess rode to take
The dip of certain strata to the North.
Would we go with her? we should find the land
Worth seeing; and the river made a fall
Out yonder:' then she pointed on to where
A double hill ran up his furrowy forks
Beyond the thick-leaved platans of the vale.

Agreed to, this, the day fled on thro' all
Its range of duties to the appointed hour.
Then summon'd to the porch we went. She stood
Among her maidens, higher by the head,
Her back against a pillar, her foot on one
Of those tame leopards. Kittenlike he roll'd
And paw'd about her sandal. I drew near;
I gazed. On a sudden my strange seizure came
Upon me, the weird vision of our house:
The Princess Ida seem'd a hollow show,
Her gay-furr'd cats a painted fantasy,
Her college and her maidens, empty masks,
And I myself the shadow of a dream
For all things were and were not. Yet I felt
My heart beat thick with passion and with awe;
Then from my breast the involuntary sigh
Brake, as she smote me with the light of eyes
That lent my knee desire to kneel, and shook
My pulses, till to horse we got, and so
Went forth in long retinue following up
The river as it narrow'd to the hills.

I rode beside her and to me she said:
'O friend, we trust that you esteem'd us not
Too harsh to your companion yestermorn;
Unwillingly we spake.' 'No – not to her,'
I answer'd, 'but to one of whom we spake
Your Highness might have seem'd the thing you say.'
'Again?' she cried, 'are you ambassadresses
From him to me? we give you, being strange,
A licence: speak, and let the topic die.'

I stammer'd that I knew him – could have wish'd –
'Our king expects – was there no precontract?
There is no truer-hearted – ah, you seem
All he prefigured, and he could not see
The bird of passage flying south but long'd
To follow: surely, if your Highness keep

Your purport, you will shock him ev'n to death.
Or baser courses, children of despair.'

'Poor boy,' she said, 'can he not read – no books?
Quoit, tennis, ball – no games? nor deals in that
Which men delight in, martial exercise?
To nurse a blind ideal like a girl;
Methinks he seems no better than a girl;
As girls were once, as we ourself have been:
We had our dreams; perhaps he mixt with them:
We touch on our dead self, nor shun to do it
Being other – since we learnt our meaning here,
To lift the woman's fall'n divinity
Upon an even pedestal with man.'

She paused, and added with a haughtier smile
'And as to precontracts, we move, my friend,
At no man's beck, but know ourself and thee,
O Vashti, noble Vashti! Summon'd out
She kept her state, and left the drunken king
To brawl at Shushan underneath the palms.'

'Alas your Highness breathes full East,' I said,
'On that which leans to you. I know the Prince,
I prize his truth: and then how vast a work
To assail this grey preeminence of man!
You grant me licence; might I use it? think;
Ere half be done perchance your life may fail;
Then comes the feebler heiress of your plan,
And takes and ruins all; and thus your pains
May only make that footprint upon sand
Which old-recurring waves of prejudice
Resmooth to nothing: might I dread that you,
With only Fame for spouse and your great deeds
For issue, yet may live in vain, and miss,
Meanwhile, what every woman counts her due,
Love, children, happiness?'
                              And she exclaim'd
'Peace, you young savage of the Northern wild!
What! tho' your Prince's love were like a God's,
Have we not made ourself the sacrifice?
You are bold indeed: we are not talk'd to thus:
Yet will we say for children, would they grew
Like field-flowers everywhere! we like them well:
But children die; and let me tell you, girl,
Howe'er you babble, great deeds cannot die;

They with the sun and moon renew their light
For ever, blessing those that look on them.
Children – that men may pluck them from our hearts
Kill us with pity, break us with ourselves –
O – children – there is nothing upon earth
More miserable than she that has a son
And sees him err: nor would we work for fame;
Tho' she perhaps might reap the applause of Great,
Who learns the one POU STO whence after-hands
May move the world, tho' she herself effect
But little: wherefore up and act, nor shrink
For fear our solid aim be dissipated
By frail successors. Would, indeed, we had been,
In lieu of many mortal flies, a race
Of giants living, each, a thousand years,
That we might see our own work out, and watch
The sandy footprint harden into stone.'

　　I answer'd nothing, doubtful in myself
If that strange Poet-princess with her grand
Imaginations might at all be won.
And she broke out interpreting my thoughts:

　　'No doubt we seem a kind of monster to you;
We are used to that: for women, up till this
Cramp'd under worse than South-sea-isle taboo,
Dwarfs of the gynaeceum, fail so far
In high desire, they know not, cannot guess
How much their welfare is a passion to us.
If we could give them surer, quicker proof –
Oh if our end were less achievable
By slow approaches, than by single act
Of immolation, any phase of death,
We were as prompt to spring against the pikes,
Or down the fiery gulf as talk of it,
To compass our dear sisters' liberties.'

　　She bow'd as if to veil a noble tear;
And up we came to where the river sloped
To plunge in cataract, shattering on black blocks
A breadth of thunder. O'er it shook the woods,
And danced the colour, and, below, stuck out
The bones of some vast bulk that lived and roar'd
Before man was. She gazed awhile and said,
'As these rude bones to us, are we to her
That will be.' 'Dare we dream of that,' I ask'd,

'Which wrought us, as the workman and his work
That practice betters?' 'How,' she cried, 'you love
The metaphysics! read and earn our prize,
A golden brooch: beneath an emerald plane
Sits Diotima, teaching him that died
Of hemlock; our devices wrought to the life,
She rapt upon her subject, he on her:
For there are schools for all.' 'And yet' I said
'Methinks I have not found among them all
One anatomic.' 'Nay, we thought of that,'
She answer'd, 'but it pleased us not: in truth
We shudder but to dream our maids should ape
Those monstrous males that carve the living hound,
And cram him with the fragments of the grave,
Or in the dark dissolving human heart,
And holy secrets of this microcosm,
Dabbling a shameless hand with shameful jest,
Encarnalize their spirits: yet we know
Knowledge is knowledge, and this matter hangs:
Howbeit ourself, foreseeing casualty,
Nor willing men should come among us, learnt,
For many weary moons before we came,
This craft of healing. Were you sick, ourself
Would tend upon you. To your question now,
Which touches on the workman and his work.
Let there be light and there was light: 'tis so:
For was, and is, and will be, are but is;
And all creation is one act at once,
The birth of light: but we that are not all,
As parts, can see but parts, now this, now that,
And live, perforce, from thought to thought, and make
One act a phantom of succession: thus
Our weakness somehow shapes the shadow, Time;
But in the shadow will we work, and mould
The woman to the fuller day.'
                                        She spake
With kindled eyes: we rode a league beyond,
And, o'er a bridge of pinewood crossing, came
On flowery levels underneath the crag,
Full of all beauty. 'O how sweet' I said
(For I was half-oblivious of my mask)
'To linger here with one that loved us.' 'Yea,'
She answer'd, 'or with fair philosophies
That lift the fancy; for indeed these fields
Are lovely, lovelier not the Elysian lawns,
Where paced the Demigods of old, and saw

The soft white vapour streak the crowned towers
Built to the Sun:' then, turning to her maids,
'Pitch our pavilion here upon the sward;
Lay out the viands.' At the word, they raised
A tent of satin, elaborately wrought
With fair Corinna's triumph; here she stood,
Engirt with many a florid maiden-cheek,
The woman-conqueror; woman-conquer'd there
The bearded Victor of ten-thousand hymns,
And all the men mourn'd at his side: but we
Set forth to climb; then, climbing, Cyril kept
With Psyche, with Melissa Florian, I
With mine affianced. Many a little hand
Glanced like a touch of sunshine on the rocks,
Many a light foot shone like a jewel set
In the dark crag: and then we turn'd, we wound
About the cliffs, the copses, out and in,
Hammering and clinking, chattering stony names
Of shale and hornblende, rag and trap and tuff,
Amygdaloid and trachyte, till the Sun
Grew broader toward his death and fell, and all
The rosy heights came out above the lawns.

*

 The splendour falls on castle walls
  And snowy summits old in story:
 The long light shakes across the lakes,
  And the wild cataract leaps in glory.
 Blow, bugle, blow, set the wild echoes flying,
 Blow, bugle; answer, echoes, dying, dying, dying.

 O hark, O hear! how thin and clear,
  And thinner, clearer, farther going!
 O sweet and far from cliff and scar
  The horns of Elfland faintly blowing!
 Blow, let we hear the purple glens replying:
 Blow, bugle; answer, echoes, dying, dying, dying.

 O love, they die in yon rich sky,
  They faint on hill or field or river:
 Our echoes roll from soul to soul,
  And grow for ever and for ever.
 Blow, bugle, blow, set the wild echoes flying,
 And answer, echoes, answer, dying, dying, dying.

IV

'There sinks the nebulous star we call the Sun
If that hypothesis of theirs be sound'
Said Ida; 'let us down and rest;' and we
Down from the lean and wrinkled precipices
By every coppice-feather'd chasm and cleft
Dropt thro' the ambrosial gloom to where below
No bigger than a glow-worm shone the tent
Lamp-lit from the inner. Once she lean'd on me,
Descending; once or twice she lent her hand
And blissful palpitations in the blood,
Stirring a sudden transport rose and fell.

But when we planted level feet, and dipt
Beneath the satin dome and enter'd in,
There leaning deep in broider'd down we sank
Our elbows: on a tripod in the midst
A fragrant flame rose, and before us glow'd:
Fruit, blossom, viand, amber wine, and gold.

Then she, 'Let some one sing to us: lightlier move
The minutes fledged with music:' and a maid,
Of those beside her, smote her harp, and sang.

> Tears, idle tears, I know not what they mean,
> Tears from the depth of some divine despair
> Rise in the heart, and gather to the eyes,
> In looking on the happy Autumn-fields,
> And thinking of the days that are no more.
>
> Fresh as the first beam glittering on a sail,
> That brings our friends up from the underworld,
> Sad as the last which reddens over one
> That sinks with all we love below the verge;
> So sad, so fresh, the days that are no more.
>
> Ah, sad and strange as in dark summer dawns
> The earliest pipe of half-awaken'd birds
> To dying ears, when unto dying eyes
> The casement slowly grows a glimmering square
> So sad, so strange, the days that are no more.
>
> Dear as remember'd kisses after death,
> And sweet as those by hopeless fancy feign'd
> On lips that are for others; deep as love,
> Deep as first love, and wild with all regret;
> O Death in Life, the days that are no more.

She ended with such passion that the tear,
She sang of, shook and fell, an erring pearl
Lost in her bosom: but with some disdain
Answer'd the Princess, 'If indeed there haunt
About the moulder'd lodges of the Past
So sweet a voice and vague, fatal to men,
Well needs it we should cram our ears with wool
And so pace by: but thine are fancies hatch'd
In silken-folded idleness; nor is it
Wiser to weep a true occasion lost,
But trim our sails, and let old bygones be,
While down the streams that float us each and all
To the issue, goes, like glittering bergs of ice,
Throne after throne, and molten on the waste
Becomes a cloud: for all things serve their time
Toward that great year of equal mights and rights,
Nor would I fight with iron laws, in the end
Found golden: let the past be past; let be
Their cancell'd Babels: tho' the rough kex break
The starr'd mosaic, and the beard-blown goat
Hang on the shaft, and the wild figtree split
Their monstrous idols, care not while we hear
A trumpet in the distance pealing news
Of better, and Hope, a poising eagle, burns
Above the unrisen morrow:' then to me;
'Know you no song of your own land,' she said,
'Not such as moans about the retrospect,
But deals with the other distance and the hues
Of promise; not a death's-head at the wine.'

Then I remember'd one myself had made,
What time I watch'd the swallow winging south
From mine own land, part made long since, and part
Now while I sang, and maidenlike as far
As I could ape their treble, did I sing.

> *O Swallow, Swallow, flying, flying South,*
> *Fly to her, and fall upon her gilded eaves,*
> *And tell her, tell her, what I tell to thee.*
>
> *O tell her, Swallow, thou that knowest each,*
> *That bright and fierce and fickle is the South,*
> *And dark and true and tender is the North.*
>
> *O Swallow, Swallow, if I could follow, and light*
> *Upon her lattice, I would pipe and trill,*
> *And cheep and twitter twenty million loves.*

O were I thou that the might take me in,
And lay me on her bosom, and her heart
Would rock the snowy cradle till I died.

Why lingereth she to clothe her heart with love,
Delaying as the tender ash delays
To clothe herself, when all the woods are green?

O tell her, Swallow, that thy brood is flown:
Say to her, I do but wanton in the South,
But in the North long since my nest is made.

O tell her, brief is life but love is long
And brief the sun of summer in the North
And brief the moon of beauty in the South.

O Swallow, flying from the golden woods
Fly to her, and pipe and woo her, and make her mine,
And tell her, tell her, that I follow thee.

I ceased, and all the ladies, each at each,
Like the Ithacensian suitors in old time,
Stared with great eyes, and laugh'd with alien lips,
And knew not what they meant; for still my voice
Rang false: but smiling 'Not for thee,' she said,
'O Bulbul, any rose of Gulistan
Shall burst her veil: marsh-divers, rather, maid
Shall croak thee sister, or the meadow-crake
Grate her harsh kindred in the grass: and this
A mere love-poem! O for such, my friend
We hold them slight: they mind us of the time
When we made bricks in Egypt. Knaves are men,
That lute and flute fantastic tenderness,
And dress the victim to the offering up
And paint the gates of Hell with Paradise,
And play the slave to gain the tyranny.
Poor soul! I had a maid of honour once;
She wept her true eyes blind for such a one,
A rogue of canzonets and serenades.
I loved her. Peace be with her. She is dead.
So they blaspheme the muse! But great is song
Used to great ends: ourself have often tried
Valkyrian hymns, or into rhythm have dash'd
The passion of the prophetess; for song
Is duer unto freedom, force and growth
Of spirit than to junketing and love.
Love is it? Would this same mock-love, and this
Mock-Hymen were laid up like winter bats,

Till all men grew to rate us at our worth,
Not vassals to be beat, nor pretty babes
To be dandled, no, but living wills, and sphered
Whole in ourselves and owed to none. Enough!
But now to leaven play with profit, you,
Know you no song, the true growth of your soil,
That gives the manners of your countrywomen?'

    She spoke and turn'd her sumptuous head with eyes
Of shining expectation fixt on mine.
Then while I dragg'd my brains for such a song,
Cyril, with whom the bell-mouth'd glass had wrought,
Or master'd by the sense of sport, began
To troll a careless, careless tavern-catch
Of Moll and Meg, and strange experiences
Unmeet for ladies. Florian nodded at him,
I frowning; Psyche flush'd and wann'd and shook;
The lilylike Melissa droop'd her brows
'Forbear,' the Princess cried; 'Forbear, Sir' I;
And heated thro' and thro' with wrath and love,
I smote him on the breast; he started up;
There rose a shriek as of a city sack'd;
Melissa clamour'd 'Flee the death;' 'To horse,'
Said Ida; 'home! to horse!' and fled, as flies
A troop of snowy doves athwart the dusk,
When some one batters at the dovecote-doors,
Disorderly the women. Alone I stood
With Florian, cursing Cyril, vext at heart,
In the pavilion: there like parting hopes
I heard them passing from me: hoof by hoof,
And every hoof a knell to my desires,
Clang'd on the bridge; and then another shriek,
'The Head, the Head, the Princess, O the Head!'
For blind with rage she miss'd the plank, and roll'd
In the river. Out I sprang from glow to gloom:
There whirl'd her white robe like a blossom'd branch
Rapt to the horrible fall: a glance I gave,
No more; but woman-vested as I was
Plunged; and the flood drew; yet I caught her; then
Oaring one arm, and bearing in my left
The weight of all the hopes of half the world,
Strove to buffet to land in vain. A tree
Was half-disrooted from his place and stoop'd
To drench his dark locks in tile gurgling wave
Mid channel. Right on this we drove and caught,
And grasping down the boughs I gain'd the shore.

There stood her maidens glimmeringly group'd
In the hollow bank. One reaching forward drew
My burthen from mine arms; they cried 'she lives:'
They bore her back into the tent: but I
So much a kind of shame within me wrought,
Not yet endured to meet her opening eyes,
Nor found my friends; but push'd alone on foot
(For since her horse was lost I left her mine)
Across the woods, and less from Indian craft
Than beelike instinct hiveward, found at length
The garden portals. Two great statues, Art
And Science, Caryatids, lifted up
A weight of emblem, and betwixt were valves
Of open-work in which the hunter rued
His rash intrusion, manlike, but his brows
Had sprouted, and the branches thereupon
Spread out at top, and grimly spiked the gates.

A little space was left between the horns,
Thro' which I clamber'd o'er at top with pain,
Dropt on the sward, and up the linden walks,
And, tost on thoughts that changed from hue to hue,
Now poring on the glowworm, now the star,
I paced the terrace, till the Bear had wheel'd
Thro' a great arc his seven slow suns.
                              A step
Of lightest echo, then a loftier form
Than female, moving thro' the uncertain gloom,
Disturb'd me with the doubt 'if this were she,'
But it was Florian. 'Hist O Hist,' he said,
'They seek us: out so late is out of rules.
Moreover "seize the strangers" is the cry.
How came you here?' I told him: 'I' said he,
'Last of the train, a moral leper, I,
To whom none spake, half-sick at heart, return'd.
Arriving all confused among the rest
With hooded brows I crept into the hall,
And, couch'd behind a Judith, underneath
The head of Holofernes peep'd and saw.
Girl after girl was call'd to trial: each
Disclaim'd all knowledge of us: last of all,
Melissa: trust me, Sir, I pitied her.
She, question'd if she knew us men, at first
Was silent; closer prest, denied it not:
And then, demanded if her mother knew,
Or Psyche, she affirm'd not, or denied:

From whence the Royal mind, familiar with her,
Easily gather'd either guilt. She sent
For Psyche, but she was not there; she call'd
For Psyche's child to cast it from the doors;
She sent for Blanche to accuse her face to face;
And I slipt out: but whither will you now?
And where are Psyche, Cyril? both are fled:
What, if together? that were not so well.
Would rather we had never come! I dread
His wildness, and the chances of the dark.'

'And yet,' I said, 'you wrong him more than I
That struck him: this is proper to the clown,
Tho' smock'd, or furr'd and purpled, still the clown,
To harm the thing that trusts him, and to shame
That which he says he loves: for Cyril, howe'er
He deal in frolic, as to-night – the song
Might have been worse and sinn'd in grosser lips
Beyond all pardon – as it is, I hold
These flashes on the surface are not he.
He has a solid base of temperament:
But as the waterlily starts and slides
Upon the level in little puffs of wind,
Tho' anchor'd to the bottom, such is he.

Scarce had I ceased when from a tamarisk near
Two Proctors leapt upon us, crying, 'Names:'
He, standing still, was clutch'd; but I began
To thrid the musky-circled mazes, wind
And double in and out the boles, and race
By all the fountains: fleet I was of foot;
Before me shower'd the rose in flakes; behind
I heard the puff'd pursuer, at mine ear
Bubbled the nightingale and heeded not
And secret laughter tickled all my soul.
At last I hook'd my ankle in a vine,
That claspt the feet of a Mnemosyne,
And falling on my face was caught and known.

They haled us to the Princess where she sat
High in the hall: above her droop'd a lamp,
And made the single jewel on her brow
Burn like the mystic fire on a mast-head
Prophet of storm: a handmaid on each side
Bow'd toward her, combing out her long black hair
Damp from the river; and close behind her stood

Eight daughters of the plough, stronger than men,
Huge women blowzed with health, and wind, and rain,
And labour. Each was like a Druid rock;
Or like a spire of land that stands apart
Cleft from the main, and wail'd about with mews.

   Then, as we came, the crowd dividing clove
An advent to the throne: and there beside,
Half-naked as if caught at once from bed
And tumbled on the purple footcloth, lay
The lily-shining child; and on the left,
Bow'd on her palms and folded up from wrong,
Her round white shoulder shaken with her sobs
Melissa knelt; but Lady Blanche erect
Stood up and spake, an affluent orator.

   'It was not thus, O Princess, in old days:
You prized my counsel, lived upon my lips:
I led you then to all the Castalies;
I fed you with the milk of every Muse;
I loved you like this kneeler, and you me
Your second mother: those were gracious times.
Then came your new friend: you began to change –
I saw it and grieved – to slacken and to cool;
Till taken with her seeming openness
You turn'd your warmer currents all to her,
To me you froze: this was my meed for all.
Yet I bore up in part from ancient love,
And partly that I hoped to win you back,
And partly conscious of my own deserts,
And partly that you were my civil head,
And chiefly you were born for something great,
In which I might your fellow-worker be,
When time should serve; and thus a noble scheme
Grew up from seed we two long since had sown;
In us true growth, in her a Jonah's gourd,
Up in one night and due to sudden sun:
We took this palace; but even from the first
You stood in your own light and darken'd mine.
What student came but that you planed her path
To Lady Psyche, younger, not so wise,
A foreigner, and I your countrywoman
I your old friend and tried, she new in all?
But still her lists were swell'd and mine were lean;
Yet I bore up in hope she would be known:
Then came these wolves: *they* knew her: *they* endured,

Long-closeted with her the yestermorn,
To tell her what they were, and she to hear:
And me none told: not less to an eye like mine,
A lidless watcher of the public weal,
Last night, their mask was patent, and my foot
Was to you: but I thought again: I fear'd
To meet a cold "We thank you, we shall hear of it
From Lady Psyche:" you had gone to her,
She told, perforce; and winning easy grace,
No doubt, for slight delay, remain'd among us
In our young nursery still unknown, the stem
Less grain than touchwood, while my honest heat
Were all miscounted as malignant haste
To push my rival out of place and power.
But public use required she should be known;
And since my oath was ta'en for public use,
I broke the letter of it to keep the sense.
I spoke not then at first, but watch'd them well,
Saw that they kept apart, no mischief done;
And yet this day (tho' you should hate me for it)
I came to tell you, found that you had gone,
Ridd'n to the hills she likewise: now, I thought,
That surely she will speak, if not, then I:
Did she? These monsters blazon'd what they were,
According to the coarseness of their kind,
For thus I hear; and known at last (my work)
And full of cowardice and guilty shame,
I grant in her some sense of shame, she flies;
And I remain on whom to wreak your rage,
I, that have lent my life to build up yours,
I that have wasted here health, wealth, and time,
And talents, I – you know it – I will not boast:
Dismiss me, and I prophesy your plan,
Divorced from my experience, will be chaff
For every gust of chance, and men will say
We did not know the real light, but chased
The wisp that flickers where no foot can tread.'

    She ceased: the Princess answer'd coldly, 'Good:
Your oath is broken: we dismiss you: go.
For this lost lamb (she pointed to the child)
Our mind is changed: we take it to ourself.'

    Thereat the Lady stretch'd a vulture throat,
And shot from crooked lips a haggard smile.
'The plan was mine. I built the nest' she said,

'To hatch the cuckoo. Rise!' and stoop'd to updrag
Melissa: she, half on her mother propt,
Half-drooping from her, turn'd her face, and cast
A liquid look on Ida, full of prayer,
Which melted Florian's fancy as she hung,
A Niobean daughter, one arm out,
Appealing to the bolts of Heaven; and while
We gazed upon her came a little stir
About the doors, and on a sudden rush'd
Among us, out of breath, as one pursued,
A woman-post in flying raiment. Fear
Stared in her eyes, and chalk'd her face, and wing'd
Her transit to the throne, whereby she fell
Delivering seal'd dispatches which the Head
Took half-amazed, and in her lion's mood
Tore open, silent we with blind surmise
Regarding, while she read, till over brow
And cheek and bosom brake the wrathful bloom
As of some fire against a stormy cloud,
When the wild peasant rights himself, the rick
Flames, and his anger reddens in the heavens;
For anger most it seem'd, while now her breast,
Beaten with some great passion at her heart,
Palpitated, her hand shook, and we heard
In the dead hush the papers that she held
Rustle: at once the lost lamb at her feet
Sent out a bitter bleating for its dam;
The plaintive cry jarr'd on her ire; she crush'd
The scrolls together, made a sudden turn
As if to speak, but, utterance failing her,
She whirl'd them on to me, as who should say
'Read,' and I read – two letters – one her sire's.

'Fair daughter, when we sent the Prince your way
We knew not your ungracious laws, which learnt,
We, conscious of what temper you are built,
Came all in haste to hinder wrong, but fell
Into his father's hands, who has this night,
You lying close upon his territory,
Slipt round and in the dark invested you,
And here he keeps me hostage for his son.'

The second was my father's running thus:
'You have our son: touch not a hair of his head:
Render him up unscathed: give him your hand:
Cleave to your contract: tho' indeed we hear

You hold the woman is the better man;
A rampant heresy, such as if it spread
Would make all women kick against their Lords
Thro' all the world, and which might well deserve
That we this night should pluck your palace down;
And we will do it, unless you send us back
Our son, on the instant, whole.'
                                    So far I read;
And then stood up and spoke impetuously.

    'O not to pry and peer on your reserve,
But led by golden wishes, and a hope
The child of regal compact, did I break
Your precinct; not a scorner of your sex
But venerator, zealous it should be
All that it might be: hear me, for I bear,
Tho' man, yet human, whatsoe'er your wrongs,
From the flaxen curl to the grey lock a life
Less mine than yours: my nurse would tell me of you;
I babbled for you, as babies for the moon,
Vague brightness; when a boy, you stoop'd to me
From all high places, lived in all fair lights,
Came in long breezes rapt from inmost south
And blown to inmost north; at eve and dawn
With Ida, Ida, Ida, rang the woods;
The leader wildswan in among the stars
Would clang it, and lapt in wreaths of glowworm light
The mellow breaker murmur'd Ida. Now,
Because I would have reach'd you, had you been
Sphered up with Cassiopëia, or the enthroned
Persephone in Hades, now at length,
Those winters of abeyance all worn out,
A man I came to see you: but, indeed,
Not in this frequence can I lend full tongue,
O noble Ida, to those thoughts that wait
On you, their centre: let me say but this,
That many a famous man and woman, town
And landskip, have I heard of, after seen
The dwarfs of presage: tho' when known, there grew
Another kind of beauty in detail
Made them worth knowing; but in you I found
My boyish dream involved and dazzled down
And master'd, while that after-beauty makes
Such head from act to act, from hour to hour,
Within me, that except you slay me here,
According to your bitter statute-book,

I cannot cease to follow you, as they say
The seal does music; who desire you more
Than growing boys their manhood; dying lips,
With many thousand matters left to do,
The breath of life; O more than poor men wealth,
Than sick men health – yours, yours, not mine – but half
Without you; with you, whole; and of those halves
You worthiest; and howe'er you block and bar
Your heart with system out from mine, I hold
That it becomes no man to nurse despair,
But in the teeth of clench'd antagonisms
To follow up the worthiest till he die:
Yet that I came not all unauthorized
Behold your father's letter.'
                    On one knee
Kneeling, I gave it, which she caught, and dash'd
Unopen'd at her feet: a tide of fierce
Invective seem'd to wait behind her lips,
As waits a river level with the dam
Ready to burst and flood the world with foam:
And so she would have spoken, but there rose
A hubbub in the court of half the maids
Gather'd together: from the illumined hall
Long lanes of splendour slanted o'er a press
Of snowy shoulders, thick as herded ewes,
And rainbow robes, and gems and gemlike eyes,
And gold and golden heads, they to and fro
Fluctuated, as flowers in storm, some red, some pale,
All open-mouth'd, all gazing to the light,
Some crying there was an army in the land,
And some that men were in the very walls,
And some they cared not; till a clamour grew
As of a new-world Babel, woman-built,
And worse-confounded: high above them stood
The placid marble Muses, looking peace.

Not peace she look'd, the Head: but rising up
Robed in the long night of her deep hair, so
To the open window moved, remaining there
Fixt like a beacon-tower above the waves
Of tempest, when the crimson-rolling eye
Glares ruin, and the wild birds on the light
Dash themselves dead. She stretch'd her arms and call'd
Across the tumult and the tumult fell.

'What fear ye, brawlers? am not I your Head?

On me, me, me, the storm first breaks: *I* dare
All these male thunderbolts: what is it ye fear?
Peace! there are those to avenge us and they come:
If not, – myself were like enough, O girls,
To urfurl the maiden banner of our rights,
And clad in iron burst the ranks of war,
Or, falling, protomartyr of our cause,
Die: yet I blame you not so much for fear;
Six thousand years of fear have made you that
From which I would redeem you: but for those
That stir this hubbub – you and you – I know
Your faces there in the crowd – to-morrow morn
We hold a great convention: then shall they
That love their voices more than duty, learn
With whom they deal, dismiss'd in shame to live
No wiser than their mothers, household stuff,
Live chattels, mincers of each other's fame,
Full of weak poison, turnspits for the clown,
The drunkard's football, laughing-stocks of Time,
Whose brains are in their hands and in their heels,
But fit to flaunt, to dress, to dance, to thrum,
To tramp, to scream, to burnish, and to scour,
For ever slaves at home and fools abroad.'

She, ending, waved her hands: thereat the crowd
Muttering, dissolved: then with a smile, that look'd
A stroke of cruel sunshine on the cliff,
When all the glens are drown'd in azure gloom
Of thunder-shower, she floated to us and said:

'You have done well and like a gentleman,
And like a prince: you have our thanks for all:
And you look well too in your woman's dress:
Well have you done and like a gentleman.
You saved our life: we owe you bitter thanks:
Better have died and spilt our bones in the flood –
Then men had said – but now – What hinders me
To take such bloody vengeance on you both? –
Yet since our father – Wasps in our good hive,
You would-be quenchers of the light to be,
Barbarians, grosser than your native bears –
O would I had his sceptre for one hour!
You that have dared to break our bound, and gull'd
Our servants, wrong'd and lied and thwarted us –
I wed with thee! *I* bound by precontract
Your bride, your bondslave! not tho' all the gold

That veins the world were pack'd to make your crown,
And every spoken tongue should lord you. Sir,
Your falsehood and yourself are hateful to us:
I trample on your offers and on you:
Begone: we will not look upon you more.
Here, push them out at gates.'
                              In wrath she spake
Then those eight mighty daughters of the plough
Bent their broad faces toward us and address'd
Their motion: twice I sought to plead my cause,
But on my shoulder hung their heavy hands,
The weight of destiny: so from her face
They push'd us, down the steps, and thro' the court,
And with grim laughter thrust us out at gates.

   We cross'd the street and gain'd a petty mound
Beyond it, whence we saw the lights and heard
The voices murmuring. While I listen'd, came
On a sudden the weird seizure and the doubt:
I seem'd to move among a world of ghosts;
The Princess with her monstrous woman-guard,
The jest and earnest working side by side,
The cataract and the tumult and the kings
Were shadows; and the long fantastic night
With all its doings had and had not been,
And all things were and were not.
                              This went by
As strangely as it came, and on my spirits
Settled a gentle cloud of melancholy
Not long; I shook it off; for spite of doubts
And sudden ghostly shadowings I was one
To whom the touch of all mischance but came
As night to him that sitting on a hill
Sees the midsummer, midnight, Norway sun
Set into sunrise; then we moved away.

                              *

   Thy voice is heard thro' rolling drums,
      That beat to battle where he stands;
   Thy face across his fancy comes,
      And gives the battle to his hands:
   A moment, while the trumpets blow,
      He sees his brood about thy knee;
   The next, like fire he meets the foe,
      And strikes him dead for thine and thee.

So Lilia sang: we thought her half-possess'd,
She struck such warbling fury thro' the words
And, after, feigning pique at what she call'd
The raillery, or grotesque, or false sublime –
Like one that wishes at a dance to change
The music – clapt her hands and cried for war,
Or some grand fight to kill and make an end:
And he that next inherited the tale
Half turning to the broken statue, said,
'Sir Ralph has got your colours: if I prove
Your knight, and fight your battle, what for me?'
It chanced, her empty glove upon the tomb
Lay by her like a model of her hand.
She took it and she flung it. 'Fight' she said
'And make us all we would be, great and good.'
He knightlike in his cap instead of casque,
A cap of Tyrol borrow'd from the hall,
Arranged the favour, and assumed the Prince.

V

Now, scarce three paces measured from the mound,
We stumbled on a stationary voice,
And 'Stand, who goes?' 'Two from the palace' I.
'The second two: they wait,' he said, 'pass on;
His Highness wakes:' and one, that clash'd in arms,
By glimmering lanes and walls of canvas, led
Threading the soldier-city, till we heard
The drowsy folds of our great ensign shake
From blazon'd lions o'er the imperial tent
Whispers of war.
                        Entering, the sudden light
Dazed me half-blind: I stood and seem'd to hear,
As in a poplar grove when a light wind wakes
A lisping of the innumerous leaf and dies,
Each hissing in his neighbour's ear; and then
A strangled titter, out of which there brake
On all sides, clamouring etiquette to death,
Unmeasured mirth; while now the two old kings
Began to wag their baldness up and down,
The fresh young captains flash'd their glittering teeth,
The huge bush-bearded Barons heaved and blew,
And slain with laughter roll'd the gilded Squire.

At length my Sire, his rough cheek wet with tears,
Panted from weary sides 'King, you are free!
We did but keep you surety for our son,
If this be he, – or a draggled mawkin, thou,

That tends her bristled grunters in the sludge:'
For I was drench'd with ooze, and torn with briers,
More crumpled than a poppy from the sheath,
And all one rag, disprinced from head to heel.
Then some one sent beneath his vaulted palm
A whisper'd jest to some one near him,'Look,
He has been among his shadows.' 'Satan take
The old women and their shadows! (thus the King
Roar'd) make yourself a man to fight with men.
Go: Cyril told us all.'
                    As boys that slink
From ferule and the trespass-chiding eye,
Away we stole, and transient in a trice
From what was left of faded woman-slough
To sheathing splendours and the golden scale
Of harness, issued in the sun, that now
Leapt from the dewy shoulders of the Earth,
And hit the Northern hills. Here Cyril met us,
A little shy at first, but by and by
We twain, with mutual pardon ask'd and given
For stroke and song, resolder'd peace, whereon
Follow'd his tale. Amazed he fled away
Thro' the dark land, and later in the night
Had come on Psyche weeping: 'then we fell
Into your father's hand, and there she lies,
But will not speak, nor stir.'
                    He show'd a tent
A stone-shot off: we enter'd in, and there
Among piled arms and rough accoutrements,
Pitiful sight, wrapp'd in a soldier's cloak,
Like some sweet sculpture draped from head to foot,
And push'd by rude hands from its pedestal,
All her fair length upon the ground she lay:
And at her head a follower of the camp,
A charr'd and wrinkled piece of womanhood,
Sat watching like a watcher by the dead.

  Then Florian knelt, and 'Come' he whisper'd to her,
'Lift up your head, sweet sister: lie not thus.
What have you done but right? you could not slay
Me, nor your prince: look up: be comforted:
Sweet is it to have done the thing one ought,
When fall'n in darker ways.' And likewise I:
'Be comforted: have I not lost her too,
In whose least act abides the nameless charm
That none has else for me?' She heard, she moved,

She moan'd, a folded voice; and up she sat,
And raised the cloak from brows as pale and smooth
As those that mourn half-shrouded over death
In deathless marble. 'Her,' she said, 'my friend –
Parted from her – betray'd her cause and mine –
Where shall I breathe? why kept ye not your faith?
O base and bad! what comfort? none for me!'
To whom remorseful Cyril, 'Yet I pray
Take comfort: live, dear lady, for your child!'
At which she lifted up her voice and cried.

'Ah me, my babe, my blossom, ah my child,
May one sweet child, whom I shall see no more!
For now will cruel Ida keep her back;
And either she will die from want of care,
Or sicken with ill-usage, when they say
The child is hers – for every little fault,
The child is hers; and they will beat my girl
Remembering her mother: O my flower!
Or they will take her, they will make her hard,
And she will pass me by in after-life
With some cold reverence worse than were she dead.
Ill mother that I was to leave her there,
To lag behind, scared by the cry they made,
The horror of the shame among them all:
But I will go and sit beside the doors,
And make a wild petition night and day,
Until they hate to hear me like a wind
Wailing for ever, till they open to me,
And lay my little blossom at my feet,
My babe, my sweet Aglaïa, my one child:
And I will take her up and go my way,
And satisfy my soul with kissing her:
Ah! what might that man not deserve of me,
Who gave me back my child?' 'Be comforted,'
Said Cyril, 'you shall have it:' but again
She veil'd her brows, and prone she sank, and so
Like tender things that being caught feign death,
Spoke not, nor stirr'd.
                              By this a murmur ran
Thro' all the camp and inward raced the scouts
With rumour of Prince Arac hard at hand.
We left her by the woman, and without
Found the grey kings at parle: and 'Look you' cried
My father 'that our compact be fulfill'd:
You have spoilt this child; she laughs at you and man:

She wrongs herself, her sex, and me, and him:
But red-faced war has rods of steel and fire;
She yields, or war.'
            Then Gama turn'd to me:
'We fear, indeed, you spent a stormy time
With our strange girl: and yet they say that still
You love her. Give us, then, your mind at large:
How say you, war or not?'
              'Not war, if possible,
O king,' I said, 'lest from the abuse of war,
The desecrated shrine, the trampled year,
The smouldering homestead, and the household flower
Torn from the lintel – all the common wrong –
A smoke go up thro' which I loom to her
Three times a monster: now she lightens scorn
At him that mars her plan, but then would hate
(And every voice she talk'd with ratify it,
And every face she look'd on justify it)
The general foe. More soluble is this knot,
By gentleness than war. I want her love.
What were I nigher this altho' we dash'd
Your cities into shards with catapults,
She would not love; – or brought her chain'd, a slave,
The lifting of whose eyelash is my lord,
Not ever would she love; but brooding turn
The book of scorn, till all my little chance
Were caught within the record of her wrongs
And crush'd to death: and rather, Sire, than this
I would the old God of war himself were dead,
Forgotten, rusting on his iron hills,
Rotting on some wild shore with ribs of wreck,
Or like an old-world mammoth bulk'd in ice,
Not to be molten out.'
               And roughly spake
My father, 'Tut, you know them not, the girls.
Boy, when I hear you prate I almost think
That idiot legend credible. Look you, Sir!
Man is the hunter; woman is his game:
The sleek and shining creatures of the chase,
We hunt them for the beauty of their skins;
They love us for it, and we ride them down.
Wheedling and siding with them! Out! for shame!
Boy, there's no rose that's half so dear to them
As he that does the thing they dare not do,
Breathing and sounding beauteous battle, comes
With the air of the trumpet round him, and leaps in

Among the women, snares them by the score
Flatter'd and fluster'd, wins, tho' dash'd with death
He reddens what he kisses: thus I won
Your mother, a good mother, a good wife,
Worth winning; but this firebrand – gentleness
To such as her! if Cyril spake her true,
To catch a dragon in a cherry net,
To trip a tigress with a gossamer,
Were wisdom to it.'

                'Yea but Sire,' I cried,
'Wild natures need wise curbs. The soldier? No:
What dares not Ida do that she should prize
The soldier? I beheld her, when she rose
The yesternight, and storming in extremes
Stood for her cause, and flung defiance down
Gagelike to man, and had not shunn'd the death,
No, not the soldier's: yet I hold her, king,
True woman: but you clash them all in one,
That have as many differences as we.
The violet varies from the lily as far
As oak from elm: one loves the soldier, one
The silken priest of peace, one this, one that,
And some unworthily; their sinless faith,
A maiden moon that sparkles on a sty,
Glorifying clown and satyr; whence they need
More breadth of culture: is not Ida right?
They worth it? truer to the law within?
Severer in the logic of a life?
Twice as magnetic to sweet influences
Of earth and heaven? and she of whom you speak,
My mother, looks as whole as some serene
Creation minted in the golden moods
Of sovereign artists; not a thought, a touch,
But pure as lines of green that streak the white
Of the first snowdrop's inner leaves; I say,
Not like the piebald miscellany, man,
Bursts of great heart and slips in sensual mire,
But whole and one: and take them all-in-all,
Were we ourselves but half as good, as kind,
As truthful, much that Ida claims as right
Had ne'er been mooted, but as frankly theirs
As dues of Nature. To our point: not war:
Lest I lose all.'

            'Nay, nay, you spake but sense,'
Said Gama. 'We remember love ourself
In our sweet youth; we did not rate him then

This red-hot iron to be shaped with blows.
You talk almost like Ida: *she* can talk;
And there is something in it as you say:
But you talk kindlier: we esteem you for it. —
He seems a gracious and a gallant Prince,
I would he had our daughter: for the rest,
Our own detention, why, the causes weigh'd,
Fatherly fears — you used us courteously —
We would do much to gratify your Prince —
We pardon it; and for your ingress here
Upon the skirt and fringe of our fair land,
You did but come as goblins in the night,
Nor in the furrow broke the ploughman's head,
Nor burnt the grange, nor buss'd the milking-maid,
Nor robb'd the farmer of his bowl of cream:
But let your Prince (our royal word upon it,
He comes back safe) ride with us to our lines,
And speak with Arac: Arac's word is thrice
As ours with Ida: something may be done —
I know not what — and ours shall see us friends.
You, likewise, our late guests, if so you will,
Follow us: who knows? we four may build some plan
Foursquare to opposition.'
                                    Here he reach'd
White hands of farewell to my sire, who growl'd
An answer which, half-muffled in his beard,
Let so much out as gave us leave to go.

    Then rode we with the old king across the lawns
Beneath huge trees, a thousand rings of Spring
In every bole, a song on every spray
Of birds that piped their Valentines, and woke
Desire in me to infuse my tale of love
In the old king's ears, who promised help, and oozed
All o'er with honey'd answer as we rode;
And blossom-fragrant slipt the heavy dews
Gather'd by night and peace, with each light air
On our mail'd heads: but other thoughts than Peace
Burnt in us, when we saw the embattled squares,
And squadrons of the Prince, trampling the flowers
With clamour: for among them rose a cry
As if to greet the king; they made a halt;
The horses yell'd; they clash'd their arms; the drum
Beat; merrily-blowing shrill'd the martial fife;
And in the blast and bray of the long horn
And serpent-throated bugle, undulated

The banner: anon to meet us lightly pranced
Three captains out; nor ever had I seen
Such thews of men: the midmost and the highest
Was Arac: all about his motion clung
The shadow of his sister, as the beam
Of the East, that play'd upon them, made them glance
Like those three stars of the airy Giant's zone,
That glitter burnish'd by the frosty dark;
And as the fiery Sirius alters hue,
And bickers into red and emerald, shone
Their morions, wash'd with morning, as they came

   And I that prated peace, when first I heard
War-music, felt the blind wildbeast of force,
Whose home is in the sinews of a man,
Stir in me as to strike: then took the king
His three broad sons; with now a wandering hand
And now a pointed finger, told them all:
A common light of smiles at our disguise
Broke from their lips, and, ere the windy jest
Had labour'd down within his ample lungs,
The genial giant, Arac, roll'd himself
Thrice in the saddle, then burst out in words.

   'Our land invaded, 'sdeath! and he himself
Your captive, yet my father wills not war:
And, 'sdeath! myself, what care I, war or no?
But then this question of your troth remains:
And there's a downright honest meaning in her;
She flies too high, she flies too high! and yet
She ask'd but space and fairplay for her scheme;
She prest and prest it on me – I myself,
What know I of these things? but, life and soul!
I thought her half-right talking of her wrongs;
I say she flies too high, 'sdeath! what of that?
I take her for the flower of womankind,
And so I often told her, right or wrong,
And, Prince, she can be sweet to those she loves,
And, right or wrong, I care not: this is all,
I stand upon her side: she made me swear it –
'Sdeath – and with solemn rites by candle-light –
Swear by St. something – I forget her name –
Her that talk'd down the fifty wisest men;
She was a princess too; and so I swore.
Come, this is all; she will not: waive your claim:
If not, the foughten field, what else, at once
Decides it, 'sdeath! against my father's will.'

I lagg'd in answer loath to render up
My precontract, and loath by brainless war
To cleave the rift of difference deeper yet;
Till one of those two brothers, half aside
And fingering at the hair about his lip,
To prick us on to combat 'Like to like!
The woman's garment hid the woman's heart.'
A taunt that clench'd his purpose like a blow!
For fiery-short was Cyril's counter-scoff,
And sharp I answer'd, touch'd upon the point
Where idle boys are cowards to their shame,
'Decide it here: why not? we are three to three.

Then spake the third 'But three to three? no more?
No more, and in our noble sister's cause?
More, more, for honour: every captain waits
Hungry for honour, angry for his king.
More, more, some fifty on a side, that each
May breathe himself, and quick! by overthrow
Of these or those, the question settled die.'

'Yea,' answer'd I, 'for this wild wreath of air,
This flake of rainbow flying on the highest
Foam of men's deeds – this honour, if ye will.
It needs must be for honour if at all:
Since, what decision? if we fail, we fail,
And if we win, we fail: she would not keep
Her compact.' ' 'Sdeath! but we will send to her,'
Said Arac, 'worthy reasons why she should
Bide by this issue: let our missive thro',
And you shall have her answer by the word.'

'Boys!' shriek'd the old king, but vainlier than a hen
To her false daughters in the pool; for none
Regarded; neither seem'd there more to say:
Back rode we to my father's camp, and found
He thrice had sent a herald to the gates,
To learn if Ida yet would cede our claim,
Or by denial flush her babbling wells
With her own people's life: three times he went:
The first, he blew and blew, but none appear'd:
He batter'd at the doors; none came: the next,
An awful voice within had warn'd him thence:
The third, and those eight daughters of the plough
Came sallying thro' the gates, and caught his hair,
And so belabour'd him on rib and cheek
They made him wild: not less one glance he caught
Thro' open doors of Ida station'd there

Unshaken, clinging to her purpose, firm
Tho' compass'd by two armies and the noise
Of arms; and standing like a stately Pine
Set in a cataract on an island-crag,
When storm is on the heights, and right and left
Suck'd from the dark heart of the long hills roll
The torrents, dash'd to the vale: and yet her will
Bred will in me to overcome it or fall.

But when I told the king that I was pledged
To fight in tourney for my bride, he clash'd
His iron palms together with a cry;
Himself would tilt it out among the lads:
But overborne by all his bearded lords
With reasons drawn from age and state, perforce
He yielded, wroth and red, with fierce demur:
And many a bold knight started up in heat,
And sware to combat for my claim till death.

All on this side the palace ran the field
Flat to the garden-wall: and likewise here,
Above the garden's glowing blossom-belts,
A column'd entry shone and marble stairs,
And great bronze valves, emboss'd with Tomyris
And what she did to Cyrus after fight,
But now fast barr'd: so here upon the flat
All that long morn the lists were hammer'd up,
And all that morn the heralds to and fro,
With message and defiance, went and came;
Last, Ida's answer, in a royal hand,
But shaken here and there, and rolling words
Oration-like. I kiss'd it and I read.

'O brother, you have known the pangs we felt,
What heats of indignation when we heard
Of those that iron-cramp'd their women's feet;
Of lands in which at the altar the poor bride
Gives her harsh groom for bridal-gift a scourge;
Of living hearts that crack within the fire
Where smoulder their dead despots; and of those, –
Mothers, – that, all prophetic pity, fling
Their pretty maids in the running flood, and swoops
The vulture, beak and talon, at the heart
Made for all noble motion: and I saw
That equal baseness lived in sleeker times
With smoother men: the old leaven leaven'd all:
Millions of throats would bawl for civil rights,

No woman named therefore I set my face
Against all men, and lived but for mine own.
Far off from men I built a fold for them
I stored it full of rich memorial:
I fenced it round with gallant institutes,
And biting laws to scare the beasts of prey,
And prosper'd; till a rout of saucy boys
Brake on us at our books, and marr'd our peace,
Mask'd like our maids, blustering I know not what
Of insolence and love, some pretext held
Of baby troth, invalid, since my will
Seal'd not the bond – the striplings! – for their sport! –
I tamed my leopards shall I not tame these?
Or you? or I? for since you think me touch'd
In honour – what, I would not aught of false –
Is not our cause pure? and whereas I know
Your prowess, Arac, and what mother's blood
You draw from, fight; you failing, I abide
What end soever: fail you will not. Still
Take not his life: he risk'd it for my own;
His mother lives: yet whatsoe'er you do,
Fight and fight well; strike and strike home
O dear Brothers, the woman's Angel guards you, you
The sole men to be mingled with our cause,
The sole men we shall prize in the after-time,
Your very armour hallow'd, and your statues
Rear'd, sung to, when, this gad-fly brush'd aside,
We plant a solid foot into the Time,
And mould a generation strong to move
With claim on claim from right to right, till she
Whose name is yoked with children's, know herself;
And Knowledge in our own land make her free,
And, ever following those two crowned twins,
Commerce and conquest, shower the fiery grain
Of freedom broadcast over all that orbs
Between the Northern and the Southern morn.'

    Then came a postscript dash'd across the rest.
See that there be no traitors in your camp:
We seem a nest of traitors – none to trust
Since our arms fail'd – this Egypt-plague of men!
Almost our maids were better at their homes
Than thus man-girdled here: indeed I think
Our chiefest comfort is the little child
Of one unworthy mother; which she left:
She shall not have it back: the child shall grow

To prize the authentic mother of her mind.
I took it for an hour in mine own bed
This morning: there the tender orphan hands
Felt at my heart, and seemed to charm from thence
The wrath I nursed against the world: farewell.'

    I ceased; he said: 'Stubborn, but she may sit
Upon a king's right hand in thunder-storms,
And breed up warriors! See now, tho' yourself
Be dazzled by the wildfire Love to sloughs
That swallow common sense, the spindling king,
This Gama swamp'd in lazy tolerance.
When the man wants weight, the woman takes it up,
And topples down the scales; but this is fixt
As are the roots of earth and base of all;
Man for the field and woman for the hearth:
Man for the sword and for the needle she:
Man with the head and woman with the heart:
Man to command and woman to obey;
All else confusion. Look you! the grey mare
Is ill to live with, when her whinny shrills
From tile to scullery, and her small goodman
Shrinks in his arm-chair while the fires of Hell
Mix with his hearth: but you – she's yet a colt –
Take, break her: strongly groom'd and straitly curb'd
She might not rank with those detestable
That let the bantling scald at home, and brawl
Their rights or wrongs like potherbs in the street.
They says she's comely; there's the fairer chance:
I like her none the less for rating at her!
Besides, the woman wed is not as we,
But suffers change of frame. A lusty brace
Of twins may weed her of her folly. Boy,
The bearing and the training of a child
Is woman's wisdom.'
                              Thus the hard old king:
I took my leave, for it was nearly noon:
I pored upon her letter which I held,
And on the little clause 'take not his life:'
I mused on that wild morning in the woods,
And on the 'Follow, follow, thou shalt win:'
I thought on all the wrathful king had said,
And how the strange betrothment was to end:
Then I remember'd that burnt sorcerer's curse
That one should fight with shadows and should fall;
And like a flash the weird affection came:

King, camp and college turn'd to hollow shows;
I seem'd to move in old memorial tilts,
And doing battle with forgotten ghosts,
To dream myself the shadow of a dream:
And ere I woke it was the point of noon,
The lists were ready. Empanoplied and plumed
We enter'd in, and waited, fifty there
Opposed to fifty, till the trumpet blared
At the barrier like a wild horn in a land
Of echoes, and a moment, and once more
The trumpet, and again: at which the storm
Of galloping hoofs bare on the ridge of spears
And riders front to front, until they closed
In conflict with the crash of shivering points,
And thunder. Yet it seem'd a dream, I dream'd
Of fighting. On his haunches rose the steed,
And into fiery splinters leapt the lance,
And out of stricken helmets sprang the fire.
Part sat like rocks: part reel'd but kept their seats:
Part roll'd on the earth and rose again and drew:
Part stumbled mixt with floundering horses. Down
From those two bulks at Arac's side, and down
From Arac's arm, as from a giant's flail,
The large blows rain'd, as here and everywhere
He rode the mellay, lord of the ringing lists,
And all the plain, — brand, mace. and shaft, and shield —
Shock'd, like an iron-clanging anvil bang'd
With hammers; till I thought, can this be he
From Gama's dwarfish loins? if this be so,
The mother makes us most — and in my dream
I glanced aside, and saw the palace-front
Alive with fluttering scarfs and ladies' eyes,
And highest, among the statues, statue-like,
Between a cymbal'd Miriam and a Jael,
With Psyche's babe, was Ida watching us,
A single band of gold about her hair,
Like a Saint's glory up in heaven: but she
No saint — inexorable — no tenderness —
Too hard, too cruel: yet she sees me fight,
Yea, let her see me fall! with that I drave
Among the thickest and bore down a Prince,
And Cyril, one. Yea, let me make my dream
All that I would. But that large-moulded man,
His visage all agrin as at a wake,
Made at me thro' the press, and, staggering back
With stroke on stroke the horse and horseman, came

As comes a pillar of electric cloud,
Flaying the roofs and sucking up the drains,
And shadowing down the champaign till it strikes
On a wood, and takes, and breaks, and cracks, and splits
And twists the grain with such a roar that Earth
Reels, and the herdsmen cry; for everything
Cave way before him: only Florian, he
That loved me closer than his own right eye,
Thrust in between; but Arac rode him down:
And Cyril seeing it, push'd against the Prince,
With Psyche's colour round his helmet, tough,
Strong, supple, sinew-corded, apt at arms;
But tougher, heavier, stronger, he that smote
And threw him: last I spurr'd; I felt my veins
Stretch with fierce heat; a moment hand to hand,
And sword to sword, and horse to horse we hung,
Till I struck out and shouted; the blade glanced;
I did but shear a feather, and dream and truth
Flow'd from me; darkness closed me; and I fell.

*

Home they brought her warrior dead:
She nor swoon'd, nor utter'd cry:
All her maidens, watching, said,
'She must weep or she will die.'

Then they praised him, soft and low,
Call'd him worthy to be loved,
Truest friend and noblest foe;
Yet she neither spoke nor moved.

Stole a maiden from her place,
Lightly to the warrior stept,
Took the face cloth from the face:
Yet she neither moved nor wept.

Rose a nurse of ninety years,
Set his child upon her knee —
Like summer tempest came her tears —
'Sweet my child, I live for thee.'

VI

My dream had never died or lived again.
As in some mystic middle state I lay;
Seeing I saw not, hearing not I heard:
Tho', if I saw not, yet they told me all
So often that I speak as having seen.

For so it seem'd, or so they said to me,
That all things grew more tragic and more strange;
That when our side was vanquish'd and my cause
For ever lost, there went up a great cry,
The Prince is slain. My father heard and ran
In on the lists, and there unlaced my casque
And grovell'd on my body, and after him
Came Psyche, sorrowing for Aglaïa.

But high upon the palace Ida stood
With Psyche's babe in arm: there on the roofs
Like that great dame of Lapidoth she sang.

    'Our enemies have fall'n, have fall'n: the seed,
    The little seed they laugh'd at in the dark,
    Has risen and cleft the soil, and grown a bulk
    Of spanless girth, that lays on every side
    A thousand arms and rushes to the Sun.

    'Our enemies have fall'n, have fall'n: they came;
    The leaves were wet with women's tears: they heard
    A noise of songs they would not understand:
    They mark'd it with the red cross to the fall,
    And would have strown it, and are fall'n themselves.

    'Our enemies have fall'n, have fall'n: they came,
    The woodmen with their axes: lo the tree!
    But we will make it faggots for the hearth,
    And shape it plank and beam for roof and floor,
    And boats and bridges for the use of men.

    'Our enemies have fall'n, have fall'n: they struck;
    With their own blows they hurt themselves, nor knew
    There dwelt an iron nature in the grain:
    The glittering axe was broken in their arms
    Their arms were shatter'd to the shoulder blade.

    'Our enemies have fall'n, but this shall grow
    A night of Summer from the heat, a breadth
    Of Autumn, dropping fruits of power; and roll'd
    With music in the growing breeze of Time,
    The tops shall strike from star to star, the fangs
    Shall move the stony bases of the world.

'And now, O maids, behold our sanctuary
Is violate, our laws broken: fear we not
To break them more in their behoof, whose arms
Champion'd our cause and won it with a day

Blanch'd in our annals, and perpetual feast,
When dames and heroines of the golden year
Shall strip a hundred hollows bare of Spring,
To rain an April of ovation round
Their statues, borne aloft, the three: but come,
We will be liberal, since our rights are won.
Let them not lie in the tents with coarse mankind,
Ill nurses; but descend, and proffer these
The brethren of our blood and cause, that there
Lie bruised and maim'd, the tender ministries
Of female hands and hospitality.'

She spoke, and with the babe yet in her arms,
Descending, burst the great bronze valves, and led
A hundred maids in train across the Park.
Some cowl'd, and some bare-headed, on they came,
Their feet in flowers, her loveliest: by them went
The enamour'd air sighing, and on their curls
From the high tree the blossom wavering fell,
And over them the tremulous isles of light
Slided, they moving under shade: but Blanche
At distance follow'd: so they came: anon
Thro' open field into the lists they wound
Timorously; and as the leader of the herd
That holds a stately fretwork to the Sun,
And follow'd up by a hundred airy does,
Steps with a tender foot, light as on air,
The lovely, lordly creature floated on
To where her wounded brethren lay; there stay'd;
Knelt on one knee, – the child on one, – and prest
Their hands, and call'd them dear deliverers,
And happy warriors, and immortal names,
And said 'You shall not lie in the tents but here,
And nursed by those for whom you fought, and served
With female hands and hospitality.'

Then, whether moved by this, or was it chance,
She past my way. Up started from my side
The old lion, glaring with his whelpless eye,
Silent; but when she saw me lying stark,
Dishelm'd and mute, and motionlessly pale,
Cold ev'n to her, she sigh'd; and when she saw
The haggard father's face and reverend beard
Of grisly twine, all dabbled with the blood
Of his own son, shudder'd, a twitch of pain
Tortured her mouth, and o'er her forehead past

A shadow, and her hue changed, and she said:
'He saved my life: my brother slew him for it.'
No more: at which the king in bitter scorn
Drew from my neck the painting and the tress
And held them up: she saw them, and a day
Rose from the distance on her memory,
When the good Queen, her mother, shore the tress
With kisses, ere the days of Lady Blanche:
And then once more she looked at my pale face:
Till understanding all the foolish work
Of Fancy, and the bitter close of all,
Her iron will was broken in her mind;
Her noble heart was molten in her breast;
She bow'd, she set the child on the earth; she laid
A feeling finger on my brows, and presently
'O Sire,' she said, 'he lives: he is not dead:
O let me have him with my brethren here
In our own palace: we will tend on him
Like one of these; if so, by any means,
To lighten this great clog of thanks, that make
Our progress falter to the woman's goal.'

     She said: but at the happy word 'he lives'
My father stoop'd, re-father'd o'er my wounds.
So those two foes above my fallen life,
With brow to brow like night and evening mixt
Their dark and grey, while Psyche ever stole
A little nearer, till the babe that by us
Half-lapt in glowing gauze and golden brede,
Lay like a new-fall'n meteor on the grass,
Uncared for, spied its mother and began
A blind and babbling laughter, and to dance
Its body, and reach its fatling innocent arms
And lazy lingering fingers. She the appeal
Brook'd not, but clamouring out 'Mine – mine – not yours,
It is not yours, but mine: give me the child'
Ceased all on tremble: piteous was the cry:
So stood the unhappy mother open-mouth'd,
And turn'd each face her way: wan was her cheek
With hollow watch, her blooming mantle torn,
Red grief and mother's hunger in her eye,
And down dead-heavy sank her curls, and half
The sacred mother's bosom, panting, burst
The laces toward her babe; but she nor cared
Nor knew it, clamouring on, till Ida heard,
Look'd up, and rising slowly from me, stood

Erect and silent, striking with her glance
The mother, me, the child; but he that lay
Beside us, Cyril, batter'd as he was,
Trail'd himself up on one knee: then he drew
Her robe to meet his lips, and down she look'd
At the arm'd man sideways, pitying, as it seem'd,
Or self-involved; but when she learnt his face,
Remembering his ill-omen'd song, arose
Once more thro' all her height, and o'er him grew
Tall as a figure lengthen'd on the sand
When the tide ebbs in sunshine, and he said
'O fair and strong and terrible! Lioness
That with your long locks play the Lion's mane!
But Love and Nature, these are two more terrible
And stronger. See, your foot is on our necks,
We vanquish'd, you the Victor of your will.
That would you more? give her the child! remain
Orb'd in your isolation: he is dead,
Or all as dead: henceforth we let you be:
Win you the hearts of women; and beware
Lest, where you seek the common love of these,
The common hate with the revolving wheel
Should drag you down, and some great Nemesis
Break from a darken'd future, crown'd with fire,
And tread you out for ever: but howsoe'er
Fix'd in yourself, never in your own arms
To hold your own, deny not hers to her,
Give her the child! O if, I say, you keep
One pulse that beats true woman, if you loved
The breast that fed or arm that dandled you,
Or own one part of sense not flint to prayer,
Give her the child! or if you scorn to lay it,
Yourself, in hands so lately claspt with yours,
Or speak to her, your dearest, her one fault
The tenderness, not yours, that could not kill,
Give *me* it: *I* will give it her.'

                              He said:
At first her eye with slow dilation roll'd
Dry flame, she listening; after sank and sank
And, into mournful twilight mellowing, dwelt
Full on the child; she took it: 'Pretty bud!
Lily of the vale! half open'd bell of the woods!
Sole comfort of my dark hour, when a world
Of traitorous friend and broken system made
No purple in the distance, mystery,
Pledge of a love not to be mine, farewell;

These men are hard upon us as of old,
We two must part: and yet how fain was I
To dream thy cause embraced in mine, to think
I might be something to thee, when I felt
Thy helpless warmth about my barren breast
In the dead prime: but may thy mother prove
As true to thee as false, false, false to me!
And, if thou needs must bear the yoke, I wish it
Gentle as freedom' – here she kiss'd it: then –
'All good go with thee! take it, Sir,' and so
Laid the soft babe in his hard-mailed hands,
Who turn'd half-round to Psyche as she sprang
To meet it, with an eye that swum in thanks;
Then felt it sound and whole from head to foot,
And hugg'd and never hugg'd it close enough,
And in her hunger mouth'd and mumbled it,
And hid her bosom with it; after that
Put on more calm and added suppliantly:

　'We two were friends: I go to mine own land
For ever: find some other: as for me
I scarce am fit for your great plans: yet speak to me,
Say one soft word and let me part forgiven.'

　But Ida spoke not, rapt upon the child.
Then Arac. 'Ida – 'sdeath! you blame the man;
You wrong yourselves – the woman is so hard
Upon the woman. Come, a grace to me!
I am your warrior: I and mine have fought
Your battle: kiss her; take her hand, she weeps:
'Sdeath! I would sooner fight thrice o'er than see it.'

　But Ida spoke not, gazing on the ground,
And reddening in the furrows of his chin,
And moved beyond his custom, Gama said:

　'I've heard that there is iron in the blood,
And I believe it. Not one word? not one?
Whence drew you this steel temper? not from me,
Not from your mother now a saint with saints.
She said you had a heart – I heard her say it –
"Our Ida has a heart" – just ere she died –
"But see that some one with authority
Be near her still" and I – I sought for one –
All people said she had authority –
The Lady Blanche: much profit! Not one word;

No! tho' your father sues: see how you stand
Stiff as Lot's wife, and all the good knights maim'd,
I trust that there is no one hurt to death,
For your wild whim: and was it then for this,
Was it for this we gave our palace up,
Where we withdrew from summer heats and state,
And had our wine and chess beneath the planes,
And many a pleasant hour with her that's gone,
Ere you were born to vex us? Is it kind?
Speak to her I say: is this not she of whom,
When first she came, all flush'd you said to me
Now had you got a friend of your own age
Now could you share your thought; now should men see
Two women faster welded in one love
Than pairs of wedlock; she you walk'd with, she
You talk'd with, whole nights long, up in the tower,
Of sine and arc, spheroid and azimuth,
And right ascension, Heaven knows what; and now
A word, but one, one little kindly word,
Not one to spare her out upon you, flint!
You love nor her, nor me, nor any; nay,
You shame your mother's judgement too. Not one?
You will not? well – no heart have you, or such
As fancies like the vermin in a nut
Have fretted all to dust and bitterness.'
So said the small king moved beyond his wont.

But Ida stood nor spoke, drain'd of her force
By many a varying influence and so long.
Down thro' her limbs a drooping languor wept:
Her head a little bent; and on her mouth
A doubtful smile dwelt like a clouded moon
In a still water: then brake out my sire,
Lifting his grim head from my wounds. 'O you,
Woman, whom we thought woman even now,
And were half fool'd to let you tend our son,
Because he might have wish'd it – but we see
The accomplice of your madness unforgiven,
And think that you might mix his draught with death,
When your skies change again: the rougher hand
Is safer: on to the tents take up the Prince.'

He rose, and while each ear was prick'd to attend
A tempest, thro' the cloud that dimm'd her broke
A genial warmth and light once more, and shone
Thro' glittering drops on her sad friend.

'Come hither,
O Psyche,' she cried out, 'embrace me, come,
Quick while I melt; make reconcilement sure
With one that cannot keep her mind an hour:
Come to the hollow heart they slander so!
Kiss and be friends, like children being chid!
I seem no more: I want forgiveness too:
I should have had to do with none but maids,
That have no links with men. Ah false but dear,
Dear traitor, too much loved, why? – why? – Yet see,
Before these kings we embrace you yet once more
With all forgiveness, all oblivion,
And trust, not love, you less.

                    And now, O Sire,
Grant me your son, to nurse, to wait upon him,
Like mine own brother. For my debt to him,
This nightmare weight of gratitude, I know it;
Taunt me no more: yourself and yours shall have
Free adit; we will scatter all our maids
Till happier times each to her proper hearth:
What use to keep them here – now? grant my prayer.
Help, father, brother, help; speak to the king:
Thaw this male nature to some touch of that
Which kills me with myself, and drags me down
From my fixt height to mob me up with all
The soft and milky rabble of womankind,
Poor weakling ev'n as they are.'

                    Passionate tears
Follow'd: the king replied not: Cyril said:
'Your brother, Lady, – Florian, – ask for him
Of your great head – for he is wounded too –
That you may tend upon him with the prince.'
'Aye so,' said Ida with a bitter smile,
'Our laws are broken: let him enter too.'
Then Violet, she that sang the mournful song,
And had a cousin tumbled on the plain,
Petition'd too for him. 'Aye so,' she said,
'I stagger in the stream: I cannot keep
My heart an eddy from the brawling hour:
We break our laws with ease, but let it be.'
'Aye so?' said Blanche: 'Amazed am I to hear
Your Highness: but your Highness breaks with ease
The law your Highness did not make: 'twas I.
I had been wedded-wife, I knew mankind,
And block'd them out; but these men came to woo
Your Highness – verily I think to win.'

So she, and turn'd askance a wintry eye:
But Ida with a voice, that like a bell
Toll'd by an earthquake in a trembling tower,
Rang ruin, answer'd full of grief and scorn.

'Fling our doors wide! all, all, not one, but all,
Not only he, but by my mother's soul,
Whatever man lies wounded, friend or foe,
Shall enter, if he will. Let our girls flit,
Till the storm die! but had you stood by us,
The roar that breaks the Pharos from his base
Had left us rock. She fain would sting us too,
But shall not. Pass, and mingle with your likes.
We brook no further insult but are gone.'

She turn'd; the very nape of her white neck
Was rosed with indignation: but the Prince
Her brother came; the king her father charm'd
Her wounded soul with words: nor did mine own
Refuse her proffer, lastly gave his hand.

Then us they lifted up, dead weights, and bare
Straight to the doors: to them the doors gave way
Groaning, and in the Vestal entry shriek'd
The virgin marble under iron heels:
And on they moved and gain'd the hall, and there
Rested: but great the crush was, and each base,
To left and right, of those tall columns drown'd
In silken fluctuation and the swarm
Of female whisperers: at the further end
Was Ida by the throne, the two great cats
Close by her, like supporters on a shield,
Bow-back'd with fear: but in the centre stood
The common men with rolling eyes; amazed
They glared upon the women, and aghast
The women stared at these, all silent, save
When armour clash'd or jingled, while the day,
Descending, struck athwart the hall, and shot
A flying splendour out of brass and steel,
That o'er the statues leapt from head to head,
Now fired an angry Pallas on the helm,
Now set a wrathful Dian's moon on flame,
And now and then an echo started up,
And shuddering fled from room to room, and died
Of fright in far apartments.
                              Then the voice
Of Ida sounded, issuing ordinance:
And me they bore up the broad stairs, and thro'

The long-laid galleries past a hundred doors
To one deep chamber shut from sound, and due
To languid limbs and sickness; left me in it;
And others otherwhere they laid; and all
That afternoon a sound arose of hoof
And chariot, many a maiden passing home
Till happier times; but some were left of those
Held sagest, and the great lords out and in,
From those two hosts that lay beside the walls,
Walk'd at their will, and everything was changed.

Ask me no more: the moon may draw the sea;
    The cloud may stoop from heaven and take the shape,
        With fold to fold, of mountain or of cape;
But O too fond, when have I answer'd thee?
            Ask me no more.

Ask me no more: what answer should I give?
    I love not hollow cheek or faded eye:
        Yet, O my friend, I will not have thee die!
Ask me no more, lest I should bid thee live;
            Ask me no more.

Ask me no more: thy fate and mine are seal'd
    I strove against the stream and all in vain:
        Let the great river take me to the main:
No more, dear love, for at a touch I yield;
            Ask me no more.

VII

So was their sanctuary violated,
So their fair college turn'd to hospital;
At first with all confusion: by and by
Sweet order lived again with other laws:
A kindlier influence reign'd; and everywhere
Low voices with the ministering hand
Hung round the sick: the maidens came, they talk'd,
They sang, they read: till she not fair, began
To gather light, and she that was, became
Her former beauty treble; and to and fro
With books, with flowers, with Angel offices,
Like creatures native unto gracious act,
And in their own clear element, they moved.

But sadness on the soul of Ida fell,
And hatred of her weakness, blent with shame.

Old studies fail'd; seldom she spoke; but oft
Clomb to the roofs, and gazed alone for hours
On that disastrous leaguer, swarms of men
Darkening her female field: void was her use;
And she as one that climbs a peak to gaze
O'er land and main, and sees a great black cloud
Drag inward from the deeps, a wall of night,
Blot out the slope of sea from verge to shore,
And suck the blinding splendour from the sand,
And quenching lake by lake and tarn by tarn
Expunge the world: so fared she gazing there;
So blacken'd all her world in secret, blank
And waste it seem'd and vain; till down she came,
And found fair peace once more among the sick.

  And twilight dawn'd; and morn by morn the lark
Shot up and shrill'd in flickering gyres, but I
Lay silent in the muffled cage of life:
And, twilight gloom'd; and broader-grown the bowers
Drew the great night into themselves, and Heaven,
Star after star, arose and fell; but I,
Deeper than those weird doubts could reach me, lay
Quite sunder'd from the moving Universe,
Nor knew what eye was on me, nor the hand
That nursed me, more than infants in their sleep.

  But Psyche tended Florian: with her oft,
Melissa came; for Blanche had gone, but left
Her child among us, willing she should keep
Court-favour: here and there the small bright head,
A light of healing, glanced about the cough,
Or thro' the parted silks the tender face
Peep'd, shining in upon the wounded man
With blush and smile, a medicine in themselves
To wile the length from languorous hours, and draw
The sting from pain; nor seem'd it strange that soon
He rose up whole, and those fair charities
Join'd at her side, nor stranger seem'd that hearts
So gentle, so employ'd, should close in love,
Than when two dewdrops on the petal shake
To the same sweet air, and tremble deeper down,
And slip at once all-fragrant into one.

  Less prosperously the second suit obtain'd
At first with Psyche. Not tho' Blanche had sworn
That after that dark night among the fields

She needs must wed him for her own good name;
Not tho' he built upon the babe restored;
Nor tho' she liked him, yielded she, but fear'd
To incense the Head once more; till on a day
When Cyril pleaded, Ida came behind
Seen but of Psyche: on her foot she hung
A moment, and she heard, at which her face
A little flush'd, and she past on; but each
Assumed from thence a half-consent involved
In stillness, plighted troth, and were at peace.

    Nor only these: Love in the sacred halls
Held carnival at will, and flying struck
With showers of random sweet on maid and man.
Nor did her father cease to press my claim
Nor did mine own now reconciled; nor yet
Did those twin brothers, risen again and whole;
Nor Arac, satiate with his victory.

    But I lay still, and with me oft she sat:
Then came a change; for sometimes I would catch
Her hand in wild delirium, gripe it hard,
And fling it like a viper off, and shriek,
'You are not Ida;' clasp it once again,
And call her Ida, tho' I knew her not,
And call her sweet, as if in irony,
And call her hard and cold which seem'd a truth:
And still she fear'd that I should lose my mind,
And often she believed that I should die:
Till out of long frustration of her care,
And pensive tendance in the all weary noons,
And watches in the dead, the dark, when clocks
Throbb'd thunder thro' the palace floors, or call'd
On flying Time from all their silver tongues –
And out of memories of her kindlier days,
And sidelong glances at my father's grief,
And at the happy lovers heart in heart –
And out of hauntings of my spoken love,
And lonely listenings to my mutter'd dream,
And often feeling of the helpless hands,
And wordless broodings on the wasted cheek –
From all a closer interest flourish'd up,
Tenderness touch by touch, and last, to these,
Love, like an Alpine harebell hung with tears
By some cold morning glacier; frail at first
And feeble, all unconscious of itself,
But such as gather'd colour day by day.

Last I woke sane, but wellnigh close to death
For weakness: it was evening: silent light
Slept on the painted walls, wherein were wrought
Two grand designs; for on one side arose
The women up in wild revolt, and storm'd
At the Oppian law. Titanic shapes, they cramm'd
The forum, and half-crush'd among the rest
A dwarf-like Cato cower'd. On the other side
Hortensia spoke against the tax; behind,
A train of dames: by axe and eagle sat,
With all their foreheads drawn in Roman scowls,
And half the wolf's-milk curdled in their veins,
The fierce triumvirs; and before them paused
Hortensia, pleading: angry was her face.

I saw the forms: I knew not where I was:
They did but look like hollow shows; nor more
Sweet Ida: palm to palm she sat: the dew
Dwelt in her eyes, and softer all her shape
And rounder seem'd: I moved: I sigh'd: a touch
Came round my wrist, and tears upon my hand:
Then all for languor and self-pity ran
Mine down my face, and with what life I had,
And like a flower that cannot all unfold,
So drench'd it is with tempest, to the sun,
Yet, as it may, turns toward him, I on her
Fixt my faint eyes, and utter'd whisperingly:

'If you be, what I think you, some sweet dream,
I would but ask you to fulfil yourself:
But if you be that Ida whom I knew,
I ask you nothing: only, if a dream,
Sweet dream, be perfect. I shall die to-night.
Stoop down and seem to kiss me ere I die.'

I could no more, but lay like one in trance,
That hears his burial talk'd of by his friends,
And cannot speak, nor move, nor make one sign,
But lies and dreads his doom. She turn'd; she paused;
She stoop'd; and out of languor leapt a cry;
Leapt fiery Passion from the brinks of death;
And I believed that in the living world
My spirit closed with Ida's at the lips;
Till back I fell, and from mine arms she rose
Glowing all over noble shame; and all
Her falser self slipt from her like a robe,

And left her woman, lovelier in her mood
Than in her mould that other, when she came
From barren deeps to conquer all with love;
And down the streaming crystal dropt; and she
Far-fleeted by the purple island-sides,
Naked, a double light in air and wave,
To meet her Graces, where they deck'd her out
For worship without end; nor end of mine,
Stateliest, for thee! but mute she glided forth,
Nor glanced behind her, and I sank and slept,
Fill'd thro' and thro' with Love, a happy sleep.

Deep in the night I woke: she, near me, held
A volume of the Poets of her land:
There to herself, all in low tones, she read.

> 'Now sleeps the crimson petal now the white;
> Nor waves the cypress in the palace walk;
> Nor winks the gold fin in the porphyry font:
> The fire-fly wakens: waken thou with me.
>
> Now droops the milkwhite peacock like a ghost,
> And like a ghost she glimmers on to me.
>
> Now lies the earth all Danaë to the stars,
> And all thy heart lies open unto me.
>
> Now slides the silent meteor on, and leaves
> A shining furrow, all thy thoughts in me.
>
> Now folds the lily all her sweetness up,
> And slips into tho bosom of the lake:
> So fold thyself, my dearest, thou, and slip
> Into my bosom and be lost in me.'

I heard her turn the page; she found a small
Sweet Idyl, and once more, as low, she read:

> 'Come down, O maid, from yonder mountain height:
> What pleasure lives in height (the shepherd sang)
> In height and cold, the splendour of the hills?
> But cease to move so near the Heavens, and cease
> To glide a sunbeam by the blasted Pine,
> To sit a star upon the sparkling spire;
> And come, for Love is of the valley, come,
> For Love is of the valley, come thou down

And find him; by the happy threshold, he,
Or hand in hand with Plenty in the maize
Or red with spirted purple of the vats,
Or foxlike in the vine, nor cares to walk
With Death and Morning on the silver horns,
Nor wilt thou snare him in the white ravine,
Nor find him dropt upon the firths of ice,
That huddling slant in furrow-cloven falls
To roll the torrent out of dusky doors:
But follow; let the torrent dance thee down
To find him in the valley; let the wild
Lean-headed Eagles yelp alone, and leave
The monstrous ledges there to slope, and spill
Their thousand wreaths of dangling water-smoke,
That like a broken purpose waste in air:
So waste not thou, but come, for all the vales
Await thee; azure pillars of the hearth
Arise to thee; the children call, and I
Thy shepherd pipe, and sweet is every sound,
Sweeter thy voice, but every sound is sweet;
Myriads of rivulets hurrying thro' the lawn,
The moan of doves in immemorial elms,
And murmuring of innumerable bees.'

  So she low-toned; while with shut eyes I lay
Listening; then look'd. Pale was the perfect face;
The bosom with long sighs labour'd; and meek
Seem'd the full lips, and mild the luminous eyes,
And the voice trembled and the hand. She said
Brokenly, that she knew it, she had fail'd
In sweet humility; had fail'd in all;
That all her labour was but as a block
Left in the quarry; but she still were loath,
She still were loath to yield herself to one
That wholly scorn'd to help their equal rights
Against the sons of men, and barbarous laws.
She pray'd me not to judge their cause from her
That wrong'd it, sought far less for truth than power
In knowledge: something wild within her breast,
A greater than all knowledge, beat her down.
And she had nursed me there from week to week:
Much had she learnt in little time. In part
It was ill counsel had misled the girl
To vex true hearts: yet was she but a girl –
'Ah fool, and made myself a Queen of farce!
When comes another such? never, I think,

Till the Sun drop dead from the signs.'
                                    Her voice
Choked, and her forehead sank upon her hands,
And her great heart thro' all the faultful Past
Went sorrowing in a pause I dared not break;
Till notice of a change in the dark world
Was lispt about the acacias, and a bird,
That early woke to feed her little ones,
Sent from a dewy breast a cry for light:
She moved, and at her feet the volume fell.

    'Blame not thyself too much,' I said, 'nor blame
Too much the sons of men and barbarous laws;
These were the rough ways of the world till now.
Henceforth thou hast a helper, me, that know
The woman's cause is man's: they rise or sink
Together, dwarf'd or godlike, bond or free:
For she that out of Lethe scales with man
The shining steps of Nature, shares with man
His nights, his days, moves with him to one goal,
Stays all the fair young planet in her hands –
If she be small, slight-natured, miserable,
How shall men grow? but work no more alone!
Our place is much: as far as in us lies
We two will serve them both in aiding her –
Will clear away the parasitic forms
That seem to keep her up but drag her down –
Will leave her space to burgeon out of all
Within her – let her make herself her own
To give or keep, to live and learn and be
All that not harms distinctive womanhood.
For woman is not undevelopt man,
But diverse: could we make her as the man,
Sweet Love were slain: his dearest bond is this,
Not like to like, but like in difference.
Yet in the long years liker must they grow;
The man be more of woman, she of man;
He gain in sweetness and in moral height
Nor lose the wrestling thews that throw the world;
She mental breadth, nor fail in childward care,
Nor lose the childlike in the larger mind;
Till at the last she set herself to man,
Like perfect music unto noble words;
And so these twain, upon the skirts of Time,
Sit side by side, full-summ'd in all their powers,
Dispensing harvest, sowing the To-be,

Self-reverent each and reverencing each,
Distinct in individualities,
But like each other ev'n as those who love.
Then comes the statelier Eden back to men:
Then reign the world's great bridals, chaste and calm:
Then springs the crowning race of humankind.
May these things be!'
                                    Sighing she spoke 'I fear
They will not.'
                        'Dear, but let us type them now
In our own lives, and this proud watchword rest
Of equal; seeing either sex alone
Is half itself, and in true marriage lies
Nor equal, nor unequal: each fulfils
Defect in each, and always thought in thought,
Purpose in purpose, will in will, they grow,
The single pure and perfect animal,
The two-cell'd heart beating, with one full stroke,
Life.'
                        And again sighing she spoke: 'A dream
That once was mine! what woman taught you this?'

   'Alone,' I said, 'from earlier than I know,
Immersed in rich foreshadowings of the world,
I loved the woman: he, that doth not, lives
A drowning life, besotted in sweet self,
Or pines in sad experience worse than death,
Or keeps his wing'd affections clipt with crime:
Yet was there one thro' whom I loved her, one
Not learned, save in gracious household ways,
Not perfect, nay, but full of tender wants,
No Angel, but a dearer being, all dipt
In Angel instincts, breathing Paradise,
Interpreter between the Gods and men,
Who look'd all native to her place, and yet
On tiptoe seem'd to touch upon a sphere
Too gross to tread, and all male minds perforce
Sway'd to her from their orbits as they moved,
And girdled her with music. Happy he
With such a mother! faith in womankind
Beats with his blood, and trust in all things high
Comes easy to him, and tho' he trip and fall
He shall not blind his soul with clay.'
                                    'But I,'
Said Ida, tremulously, 'so all unlike –
It seems you love to cheat yourself with words:

This mother is your model. I have heard
Of your strange doubts: they well might be: I seem
A mockery to my own self. Never, Prince;
You cannot love me.'
           'Nay but thee' I said
'From yearlong poring on thy pictured eyes,
Ere seen I loved, and loved thee seen, and saw
Thee woman thro' the crust of iron moods
That mask'd thee from men's reverence up, and forced
Sweet love on pranks of saucy boyhood: now,
Giv'n back to life, to life indeed, thro' thee,
Indeed I love: the new day comes, the light
Dearer for night, as dearer thou for faults
Lived over: lift thine eyes; my doubts are dead,
My haunting sense of hollow shows: the change,
This truthful change in thee has kill'd it. Dear,
Look up, and let thy nature strike on mine,
Like yonder morning on the blind half-world;
Approach and fear not; breathe upon my brows;
In that fine air I tremble, all the past
Melts mist-like into this bright hour, and this
Is morn to more, and all the rich to-come
Reels, as the golden Autumn woodland reels
Athwart the smoke of burning weeds.
Forgive me, I waste my heart in signs: let be. My bride,
My wife, my life. O we will walk this world,
Yoked in all exercise of noble end,
And so thro' those dark gates across the wild
That no man knows. Indeed I love thee: come,
Yield thyself up: my hopes and thine are one:
Accomplish thou my manhood and thyself;
Lay thy sweet hands in mine and trust to me.'

Conclusion

So closed our tale, of which I give you all
The random scheme as wildly as it rose:
The words are mostly mine; for when we ceased
There came a minute's pause, and Walter said,
'I wish she had not yielded!' then to me,
'What, if you drest it up poetically!'
So pray'd the men, the women: I gave assent:
Yet how to bind the scatter'd scheme of seven
Together in one sheaf? What style could suit?
The men required that I should give throughout

The sort of mock-heroic gigantesque,
With which we banter'd little Lilia first:
The women – and perhaps they felt their power,
For something in the ballads which they sang,
Or in their silent influence as they sat
Had ever seem'd to wrestle with burlesque,
And drove us, last, to quite a solemn close –
They hated banter, wish'd for something real,
A gallant fight, a noble princess – why
Not make her true-heroic – true-sublime?
Or all, they said, as earnest as the close?
Which yet with such a framework scarce could be.
Then rose a little feud betwixt the two,
Betwixt the mockers and the realists:
And I, betwixt them both, to please them both,
And yet to give the story as it rose,
I moved as in a strange diagonal,
And maybe neither pleased myself nor them.

But Lilia pleased me, for she took no part
In our dispute: the sequel of the tale
Had touch'd her; and she sat, she pluck'd the grass,
She flung it from her, thinking: last, she fixt
A showery glance upon her aunt, and said,
'You – tell us what we are' – who might have told,
For she was cramm'd with theories out of books,
But that there rose a shout: the gates were closed
At sunset, and the crowd were swarming now,
To take their leave, about the garden rails.

So I and some went out to these: we climb'd
The slope to Vivian-place, and turning saw
The happy valleys, half in light, and half
Far-shadowing from the west, a land of peace;
Grey halls alone among their massive groves;
Trim hamlets; here and there a rustic tower
Half-lost in belts of hop and breadths of wheat;
The shimmering glimpses of a stream; the seas;
A red sail, or a white; and far beyond, I
Imagined more than seen, the skirts of France.

'Look there, a garden!' said my college friend,
The Tory member's elder son,' and there!
God bless the narrow sea which keeps her off,
And keeps our Britain, whole within herself,
A nation yet, the rulers and the ruled –

Some sense of duty, something of a faith,
Some reverence for the laws ourselves have made,
Some patient force to change them when we will,
Some civic manhood firm against the crowd –
But yonder, whiff! there comes a sudden heat,
The gravest citizen seems to lose his head,
The king is scared, the soldier will not fight,
The little boys begin to shoot and stab,
A kingdom topples over with a shriek
Like an old woman, and down rolls the world
In mock heroics stranger than our own;
Revolts, republics, revolutions, most
No graver than a schoolboys' barring out;
Too comic for the solemn things they are,
Too solemn for the comic touches in them,
Like our wild Princess with as wise a dream
As some of theirs – God bless the narrow seas!
I wish they were a whole Atlantic broad.'

    'Have patience,' I replied, 'ourselves are full
Of social wrong; and maybe wildest dreams
Are but the needful preludes of the truth:
For me, the genial day, the happy crowd,
The sport half-science, fill me with a faith.
This fine old world of ours is but a child
Yet in the go-cart. Patience! Give it time
To learn its limbs: there is a hand that guides.'

    In such discourse we gain'd the garden rails,
And there we saw Sir Walter where he stood,
Before a tower of crimson holly-oaks,
Among six boys, head under head, and look'd
No little lily-handed Baronet he,
A great broad-shoulder'd genial Englishman,
A lord of fat prize-oxen and of sheep,
A raiser of huge melons and of pine,
A patron of some thirty charities,
A pamphleteer on guano and on grain,
A quarter-sessions chairman, abler none;
Fair-hair'd and redder than a windy morn;
Now shaking hands with him, now him, of those
That stood the nearest – now address'd to speech –
Who spoke few words and pithy, such as closed
Welcome, farewell, and welcome for the year
To follow: a shout rose again, and made
The long line of the approaching rookery swerve
From the elms, and shook the branches of the deer

From slope to slope thro' distant ferns, and rang
Beyond the bourn of sunset; O, a shout
More joyful than the city-roar that hails
Premier or king! Why should not these great Sirs
Give up their parks some dozen times a year
To let the people breathe? So thrice they cried
I likewise, and in groups they stream'd away.

But we went back to the Abbey, and sat on
So much the gathering darkness charm'd: we sat
But spoke not, rapt in nameless reverie,
Perchance upon the future man: the walls
Blacken'd about us, bats wheel'd, and owls whoop'd,
And gradually the powers of the night,
That range above the region of the wind,
Deepening the courts of twilight broke them up
Thro' all the silent spaces of the worlds,
Beyond all thought into the Heaven of Heavens.

Last little Lilia, rising quietly,
Disrobed the glimmering statue of Sir Ralph
From those rich silks, and home well-pleased we went.

To —
After Reading a Life and Letters

'Cursed be he that moves my bones'
                    Shakespeare's Epitaph

You might have won the Poet's name,
    If such be worth the winning now,
    And gain'd a laurel for your brow
Of sounder leaf than I can claim;

But you have made the wiser choice,
    A life that moves to gracious ends
    Thro' troops of unrecording friends,
A deedful life, a silent voice:

And you have miss'd the irreverent doom
    Of those that wear the Poet's crown:
    Hereafter, neither knave nor clown
Shall hold their orgies at your tomb.

For now the Poet cannot die,
    Nor leave his music as of old,
    But round him ere he scarce be cold
Begins the scandal and the cry:

'Proclaim the faults he would not show:
 Break lock and seal: betray the trust:
 Keep nothing sacred: 'tis but just
The many-headed beast should know.'

Ah shameless! for he did but sing
 A song that pleased us from its worth;
 No public life was his on earth,
No blazon'd statesman he, nor king.

He gave the people of his best:
 His worst he kept, his best he gave.
 My Shakespeare's curse on clown and knave
Who will not let his ashes rest!

Who make it seem more sweet to be
 The little life of bank and brier,
 The bird that pipes his lone desire
And dies unheard within his tree,

Than he that warbles long and loud
 And drops at Glory's temple-gates,
 For whom the carrion-vulture waits
To tear his heart before the crowd!

IN MEMORIAM A. H. H.

OBIIT MDCCCXXXIII

Strong Son of God, immortal Love,
    Whom we, that have not seen thy face,
    By faith, and faith alone, embrace,
Believing where we cannot prove;

Thine are these orbs of light and shade;
    Thou madest Life in man and brute;
    Thou madest Death; and lo, thy foot
Is on the skull which thou hast made.

Thou wilt not leave us in the dust:
    Thou madest man, he knows not why;
    He thinks he was not made to die;
And thou hast made him: thou art just.

Thou seemest human and divine,
    The highest, holiest manhood, thou:
    Our wills are ours, we know not how;
Our wills are ours, to make them thine.

Our little systems have their day;
    They have their day and cease to be:
    They are but broken lights of thee,
And thou, O Lord, art more than they.

We have but faith: we cannot know;
    For knowledge is of things we see;
    And yet we trust it comes from thee,
A beam in darkness: let it grow.

Let knowledge grow from more to more,
    But more of reverence in us dwell;
    That mind and soul, according well,
May make one music as before,

But vaster. We are fools and slight;
    We mock thee when we do not fear:
    But help thy foolish ones to bear;
Help thy vain worlds to bear thy light.

Forgive what seem'd my sin in me;
  What seem'd my worth since I began;
  For merit lives from man to man,
And not from man, O Lord, to thee.

Forgive my grief for one removed,
  Thy creature, whom I found so fair.
  I trust he lives in thee, and there
I find him worthier to be loved.

Forgive these wild and wandering cries,
  Confusions of a wasted youth;
  Forgive them where they fail in truth,
And ill thy wisdom make me wise.

I

I held it truth, with him who sings
  To one clear harp in divers tones,
  That men may rise on stepping-stones
Of their dead selves to higher things.

But who shall so forecast the years
  And find in loss a gain to match?
  Or reach a hand thro' time to catch
The far-off interest of tears?

Let Love clasp Grief lest both be drown'd,
  Let darkness keep her raven gloss:
  Ah, sweeter to be drunk with loss,
To dance with death, to beat the ground,

Than that the victor Hours should scorn
  The long result of love, and boast,
  'Behold the man that loved and lost,
But all he was is overworn.'

II

Old Yew, which graspest at the stones
  That name the under-lying dead,
  Thy fibres net the dreamless head,
Thy roofs are wrapt about the bones.

The seasons bring the flower again,
  And bring the firstling to the flock;
  And in the dusk of thee, the clock
Beats out the little lives of men.

O not for thee the glow, the bloom,
    Who changest not in any gale,
    Nor branding summer suns avail
To touch thy thousand years of gloom:

And gazing on thee, sullen tree,
    Sick for thy stubborn hardihood,
    I seem to fail from out my blood
And grow incorporate into thee.

III

O Sorrow, cruel fellowship,
    O Priestess in the vaults of Death,
    O sweet and bitter in a breath,
What whispers from thy lying lip?

'The stars,' she whispers, 'blindly run;
    A web is wov'n across the sky;
    From out waste places comes a cry,
And murmurs from the dying sun:

'And all the phantom, Nature, stands –
    With all the music in her tone,
    A hollow echo of my own, –
A hollow form with empty hands.'

And shall I take a thing so blind,
    Embrace her as my natural good;
    Or crush her, like a vice of blood,
Upon the threshold of the mind?

IV

To Sleep I give my powers away;
    My will is bondsman to the dark;
    I sit within a helmless bark,
And with my heart I muse and say:

O heart, how fares it with thee now,
    That thou should'st fail from thy desire,
    Who scarcely darest to inquire,
'What is it makes me beat so low?'

Something it is which thou hast lost,
    Some pleasure from thine early years.
    Break, thou deep vase of chilling tears,
That grief hath shaken into frost!

Such clouds of nameless trouble cross
    All night below the darken'd eyes;
    With morning wakes the will, and cries,
'Thou shalt not be the fool of loss.'

I sometimes hold it half a sin
    To put in words the grief I feel;
    For words, like Nature, half reveal
And half conceal the Soul within.

But, for the unquiet heart and brain,
    A use in measured language lies;
    The sad mechanic exercise,
Like dull narcotics, numbing pain.

In words, like weeds, I'll wrap me o'er,
    Like coarsest clothes against the cold;
    But that large grief which these enfold
Is given in outline and no more.

VI

One writes, that 'Other friends remain,'
    That 'Loss is common to the race' –
    And common is the commonplace,
And vacant chaff well meant for grain.

That loss is common would not make
    My own less bitter, rather more:
    Too common! Never morning wore
To evening, but some heart did break.

O father, wheresoe'er thou be,
    Who pledgest now thy gallant son;
    A shot, ere half thy draught be done,
Hath still'd the life that beat from thee.

O mother, praying God will save
    Thy sailor, – while thy head is bow'd,
    His heavy-shotted hammock-shroud
Drops in his vast and wandering grave.

Ye know no more than I who wrought
    At that last hour to please him well;
    Who mused on all I had to tell,
And something written, something thought;

Expecting still his advent home;
    And ever met him on his way
    With wishes, thinking, 'here to-day,'
Or 'here to-morrow will he come.'

O somewhere, meek unconscious dove,
    That sittest ranging golden hair,
    And glad to find thyself so fair,
Poor child, that waitest for thy love!

For now her father's chimney glows
    In expectation of a guest;
    And thinking 'this will please him best,'
She takes a riband or a rose;

For he will see them on to-night;
    And with the thought her colour burns;
    And, having left the glass, she turns
Once more to set a ringlet right;

And, even when she turn'd, the curse
    Had fallen, and her future Lord
    Was drown'd in passing thro' the ford,
Or kill'd in falling from his horse.

O what to her shall be the end?
    And what to me remains of good?
    To her, perpetual maidenhood,
And unto me no second friend.

VII

Dark house, by which once more I stand
    Here in the long unlovely street,
    Doors, where my heart was used to beat
So quickly, waiting for a hand,

A hand that can be clasp'd no more –
    Behold me, for I cannot sleep,
    And like a guilty thing I creep
At earliest morning to the door.

He is not here; but far away
    The noise of life begins again,
    And ghastly thro' the drizzling rain
On the bald street breaks the blank day.

VIII

A happy lover who has come
    To look on her that loves him well,
    Who 'lights and rings the gateway bell,
And learns her gone and far from home;

He saddens, all the magic light
    Dies off at once from bower and hall,
    And all the place is dark, and all
The chambers emptied of delight:

So find I every pleasant spot
    In which we two were wont to meet,
    The field, the chamber and the street,
For all is dark where thou art not.

Yet as that other, wandering there
    In those deserted walks, may find
    A flower beat with rain and wind,
Which once she foster'd up with care;

So seems it in my deep regret,
    O my forsaken heart, with thee
    And this poor flower of poesy
Which little cared for fades not yet.

But since it pleased a vanish'd eye,
    I go to plant it on his tomb,
    That if it can it there may bloom,
Or dying, there at least may die.

IX

Fair ship, that from the Italian shore
    Sailest the placid ocean-plains
    With my lost Arthur's loved remains,
Spread thy full wings, and waft him o'er.

So draw him home to those that mourn
    In vain; a favourable speed
    Ruffle thy mirror'd mast, and lead
Thro' prosperous floods his holy urn.

All night no ruder air perplex
    Thy sliding keel, till Phosphor, bright
    As our pure love, thro' early light
Shall glimmer on the dewy decks.

Sphere all your lights around, above;
    Sleep, gentle heavens, before the prow;
    Sleep, gentle winds, as he sleeps now,
My friend, the brother of my love;

My Arthur, whom I shall not see
    Till all my widow'd race be run;
    Dear as the mother to the son,
More than my brothers are to me.

X

I hear the noise about thy keel;
    I hear the bell struck in the night;
    I see the cabin-window bright;
I see the sailor at the wheel.

Thou bring'st the sailor to his wife,
    And travell'd men from foreign lands;
    And letters unto trembling hands;
And, thy dark freight, a vanish'd life.

So bring him: we have idle dreams:
    This look of quiet flatters thus
    Our home-bred fancies: O to us,
The fools of habit, sweeter seems

To rest beneath the clover sod,
    That takes the sunshine and the rains,
    Or where the kneeling hamlet drains
The chalice of the grapes of God;

Than if with thee the roaring wells
    Should gulf him fathom-deep in brine;
    And hands so often clasp'd in mine,
Should toss with tangle and with shells.

XI

Calm is the morn without a sound,
    Calm as to suit a calmer grief,
    And only thro' the faded leaf
The chestnut pattering to the ground:

Calm and deep peace on this high wold,
    And on these dews that drench the furze,
    And all the silvery gossamers
That twinkle into green and gold:

Calm and still light on yon great plain
    That sweeps with all its autumn bowers,
    And crowded farms and lessening towers,
To mingle with the bounding main:

Calm and deep peace in this wide air,
    These leaves that redden to the fall;
    And in my heart, if calm at all,
If any calm, a calm despair:

Calm on the seas, and silver sleep,
    And waves that sway themselves in rest,
    And dead calm in that noble breast
Which heaves but with the heaving deep.

XII

Lo, as a dove when up she springs
    To bear thro' Heaven a tale of woe,
    Some dolorous message knit below
The wild pulsation of her wings;

Like her I go; I cannot stay;
    I leave this mortal ark behind,
    A weight of nerves without a mind,
And leave the cliffs, and haste away

O'er ocean-mirrors rounded large,
    And reach the glow of southern skies,
    And see the sails at distance rise,
And linger weeping on the marge,

And saying; 'Comes he thus, my friend?
    Is this the end of all my care?'
    And circle moaning in the air:
'Is this the end? Is this the end?'

And forward dart again, and play
    About the prow, and back return
    To where the body sits, and learn
That I have been an hour away.

XIII

Tears of the widower, when he sees
    A late-lost form that sleep reveals,
    And moves his doubtful arms, and feels
Her place is empty, fall like these;

Which weep a loss for ever new,
    A void where heart on heart reposed;
    And, where warm hands have prest and closed,
Silence, till I be silent too.

Which weep the comrade of my choice,
    An awful thought, a life removed
    The human-hearted man I loved,
A Spirit, not a breathing voice.

Come Time, and teach me, many years,
    I do not suffer in a dream;
    For now so strange do these things seem,
Mine eyes have leisure for their tears;

My fancies time to rise on wing,
    And glance about the approaching sails,
    As tho' they brought but merchants' bales,
And not the burthen that they bring.

XIV

If one should bring me this report,
    That thou hadst touch'd the land to-day,
    And I went down unto the quay,
And found thee lying in the port;

And standing, muffled round with woe,
    Should see thy passengers in rank
    Come stepping lightly down the plank,
And beckoning unto those they know;

And if along with these should come
    The man I held as half-divine;
    Should strike a sudden hand in mine,
And ask a thousand things of home;

And I should tell him all my pain,
    And how my life had droop'd of late,
    And he should sorrow o'er my state
And marvel what possess'd my brain;

And I perceived no touch of change,
    No hint of death in all his frame,
    But found him all in all the same,
I should not feel it to be strange.

XV

To-night the winds begin to rise
    And roar from yonder dropping day:
    The last red leaf is whirl'd away,
The rooks are blown about the skies;

The forest crack'd, the waters curl'd,
    The cattle huddled on the lea;
    And wildly dash'd on tower and tree
The sunbeam strikes along the world:

And but for fancies, which aver
    That all thy motions gently pass
    Athwart a plane of molten glass,
I scarce could brook the strain and stir

That makes the barren branches loud;
    And but for fear it is not so,
    The wild unrest that lives in woe
Would dote and pore on yonder cloud

That rises upward always higher,
    And onward drags a labouring breast,
    And topples round the dreary west,
A looming bastion fringed with fire.

XVI

What words are these have fall'n from me?
    Can calm despair and wild unrest
    Be tenants of a single breast,
Or sorrow such a changeling be?

Or doth she only seem to take
    The touch of change in calm or storm;
    But knows no more of transient form
In her deep self, than some dead lake

That holds the shadow of a lark
    Hung in the shadow of a heaven?
    Or has the shock, so harshly given,
Confused me like the unhappy bark

That strikes by night a craggy shelf,
    And staggers blindly ere she sink?
    And stunn'd me from my power to think
And all my knowledge of myself;

And made me that delirious man
    Whose fancy fuses old and new,
    And flashes into false and true,
And mingles all without a plan?

XVII

Thou comest, much wept for: such a breeze
    Compell'd thy canvas, and my prayer
    Was as the whisper of an air
To breathe thee over lonely seas.

For I in spirit saw thee move
    Thro' circles of the bounding sky,
    Week after week: the days go by:
Come quick, thou bringest all I love.

Henceforth, wherever thou may'st roam,
    My blessing, like a line of light,
    Is on the waters day and night,
And like a beacon guards thee home.

So may whatever tempest mars
    Mid-ocean, spare thee, sacred bark;
    And balmy drops in summer dark
Slide from the bosom of the stars.

So kind an office hath been done,
    Such precious relics brought by thee;
    The dust of him I shall not see
Till all my widow'd race be run.

XVIII

'Tis well; 'tis something; we may stand
    Where he in English earth is laid,
    And from his ashes may be made
The violet of his native land.

'Tis little; but it looks in truth
    As if the quiet bones were blest
    Among familiar names to rest
And in the places of his youth.

Come then, pure hands, and bear the head
    That sleeps or wears the mask of sleep,
    And come, whatever loves to weep,
And hear the ritual of the dead.

Ah yet, ev'n yet, if this might be,
    I, falling on his faithful heart,
    Would breathing thro' his lips impart
The life that almost dies in me;

That dies not, but endures with pain,
    And slowly forms the firmer mind,
    Treasuring the look it cannot find,
The words that are not heard again.

XIX

The Danube to the Severn gave
    The darken'd heart that beat no more;
    They laid him by the pleasant shore,
And in the hearing of the wave.

There twice a day the Severn fills;
    The salt sea-water passes by,
    And hushes half the babbling Wye,
And makes a silence in the hills.

The Wye is hush'd nor moved along,
    And hush'd my deepest grief of all,
    When fill'd with tears that cannot fall,
I brim with sorrow drowning song.

The tide flows down, the wave again
    Is vocal in its wooded walls;
    My deeper anguish also falls,
And I can speak a little then.

XX

The lesser griefs that may be said,
    That breathe a thousand tender vows,
    Are but as servants in a house
Where lies the master newly dead;

Who speak their feeling as it is,
    And weep the fullness from the mind:
    'It will be hard,' they say, 'to find
Another service such as this.'

My lighter moods are like to these,
    That out of words a comfort win;
    But there are other griefs within,
And tears that at their fountain freeze;

For by the hearth the children sit,
    Cold in that atmosphere of Death,
    And scarce endure to draw the breath,
Or like to noiseless phantoms flit:

But open converse is there none,
    So much the vital spirits sink
    To see the vacant chair, and think,
'How good! how kind! and he is gone.'

XXI

I sing to him that rests below,
    And, since the grasses round me wave,
    I take the grasses of the grave,
And make them pipes whereon to blow.

The traveller hears me now and then,
    And sometimes harshly will he speak;
    'This fellow would make weakness weak,
And melt the waxen hearts of men.'

Another answers, 'Let him be,
    He loves to make parade of pain,
    That with his piping he may gain
The praise that comes to constancy.'

A third is wroth, 'Is this an hour
    For private sorrow's barren song,
    When more and more the people throng
The chairs and thrones of civil power?

'A time to sicken and to swoon,
    When Science reaches forth her arms
    To feel from world to world, and charms
Her secret from the latest moon?'

Behold, ye speak an idle thing:
    Ye never knew the sacred dust:
    I do but sing because I must,
And pipe but as the linnets sing:

And one is glad; her note is gay,
    For now her little ones have ranged;
    And one is sad; her note is changed,
Because her brood is stol'n away.

XXII

The path by which we twain did go,
     Which led by tracts that pleased us well,
     Thro' four sweet years arose and fell,
From flower to flower, from snow to snow:

And we with singing cheer'd the way,
     And, crown'd with all the season lent,
     From April on to April went,
And glad at heart from May to May:

But where the path we walk'd began
     To slant the fifth autumnal slope,
     As we descended following Hope,
There sat the Shadow fear'd of man;

Who broke our fair companionship,
     And spread his mantle dark and cold,
     And wrapt thee formless in the fold,
And dull'd the murmur on thy lip,

And bore thee where I could not see
     Nor follow, tho' I walk in haste,
     And think, that somewhere in the waste
The Shadow sits and waits for me.

XXIII

Now, sometimes in my sorrow shut,
     Or breaking into song by fits,
     Alone, alone, to where he sits,
The Shadow cloak'd from head to foot,

Who keeps the keys of all the creeds,
     I wander, often falling lame,
     And looking back to whence I came,
Or on to where the pathway leads;

And crying, How changed from where it ran
     Thro' lands where not a leaf was dumb;
     But all the lavish hills would hum
The murmur of a happy Pan:

When each by turns was guide to each,
     And Fancy light from Fancy caught,
     And Thought leapt out to wed with Thought
Ere Thought could wed itself with Speech;

And all we met was fair and good,
    And all was good that Time could bring,
    And all the secret of the Spring
Moved in the chambers of the blood;

And many an old philosophy
    On Argive heights divinely sang,
    And round us all the thicket rang
To many a flute of Arcady.

XXIV

And was the day of my delight
    As pure and perfect as I say?
    The very source and fount of Day
Is dash'd with wandering isles of night.

If all was good and fair we met
    This earth had been the Paradise
    It never look'd to human eyes
Since Adam left his garden yet.

And is it that the haze of grief
    Makes former gladness loom so great?
    The lowness of the present state,
That sets the past in this relief?

Or that the past will always win
    A glory from its being far;
    And orb into the perfect star
We saw not, when we moved therein?

XXV

I know that this was Life, – the track
    Whereon with equal feet we fared;
    And then, as now, the day prepared
The daily burden for the back.

But this it was that made me move
    As light as carrier-birds in air;
    I loved the weight I had to bear
Because it needed help of Love:

Nor could I weary, heart or limb,
    When mighty Love would cleave in twain
    The lading of a single pain,
And part it, giving half to him.

XXVI

Still onward winds the dreary way;
　　I with it; for I long to prove
　　No lapse of moons can canker Love,
Whatever fickle tongues may say.

And if that eye which watches guilt
　　And goodness, and hath power to see
　　Within the green the moulder'd tree,
And towers fall'n as soon as built —

Oh, if indeed that eye foresee
　　Or see (in Him is no before)
　　In more of life true life no more
And Love the indifference to be,

Then might I find, ere yet the morn
　　Breaks hither over Indian seas,
　　That Shadow waiting with the keys,
To shroud me from my proper scorn.

XXVII

I envy not in any moods
　　The captive void of noble rage,
　　The linnet born within the cage,
That never knew the summer woods:

I envy not the beast that takes
　　His licence in the field of time,
　　Unfetter'd by the sense of crime,
To whom a conscience never wakes;

Nor, what may count itself as blest,
　　The heart that never plighted troth
　　But stagnates in the weeds of sloth;
Nor any want-begotten rest.

I hold it true, whate'er befall;
　　I feel it, when I sorrow most;
　　'Tis better to have loved and lost
Than never to have loved at all.

XXVIII

The time draws near the birth of Christ:
　　The moon is hid; the night is still;
　　The Christmas bells from hill to hill
Answer each other in the mist.

Four voices of four hamlets round,
    From far and near, on mead and moor,
    Swell out and fail, as if a door
Were shut between me and the sound:

Each voice four changes on the wind,
    That now dilate, and now decrease,
    Peace and goodwill, goodwill and peace,
Peace and goodwill, to all mankind.

This year I slept and woke with pain,
    I almost wish'd no more to wake,
    And that my hold on life would break
Before I heard those bells again:

But they my troubled spirit rule
    For they controll'd me when a boy;
    They bring me sorrow touch'd with joy,
The merry merry bells of Yule.

XXIX

With such compelling cause to grieve
    As daily vexes household peace,
    And chains regret to his decease,
How dare we keep our Christmas-eve;

Which brings no more a welcome guest
    To enrich the threshold of the night
    With shower'd largess of delight,
In dance and song and game and jest?

Yet·go, and while the holly boughs
    Entwine the cold baptismal font,
    Make one wreath more for Use and Wont,
That guard the portals of the house;

Old sisters of a day gone by,
    Grey nurses, loving nothing new;
    Why should they miss their yearly due
Before their time? They too will die.

XXX

With trembling fingers did we weave
    The holly round the Christmas hearth;
    A rainy cloud possess'd the earth,
And sadly fell our Christmas-eve.

At our old pastimes in the hall
    We gambol'd, making vain pretence
    Of gladness, with an awful sense
Of one mute Shadow watching all.

We paused: the winds were in the beech:
    We heard them sweep the winter land;
    And in a circle hand-in-hand
Sat silent, looking each at each.

Then echo-like our voices rang,
    We sung, tho' every eye was dim,
    A merry song we sang with him
Last year: impetuously we sang:

We ceased: a gentler feeling crept
    Upon us: surely rest is meet:
    'They rest' we said, 'their sleep is sweet,'
And silence follow'd, and we wept.

Our voices took a higher range;
    Once more we sang: 'They do not die
    Nor lose their mortal sympathy,
Nor change to us, although they change;

Rapt from the fickle and the frail
    With gather'd power, yet the same,
    Pierces the keen seraphic flame
From orb to orb, from veil to veil.'

Rise, happy morn, rise, holy morn,
    Draw forth the cheerful day from night:
    O Father, touch the east, and light
The light that shone when Hope was born.

XXXI

When Lazarus left his charnel-cave,
    And home to Mary's house return'd,
    Was this demanded – if he yearn'd
To hear her weeping by his grave?

'Where wert thou, brother, those four days?'
    There lives no record of reply,
    Which telling what it is to die
Had surely added praise to praise.

From every house the neighbours met,
    The streets were fill'd with joyful sound,
    A solemn gladness even crown'd
The purple brows of Olivet.

Behold a man raised up by Christ!
    The rest remaineth unreveal'd;
    He told it not; or something seal'd
The lips of that Evangelist.

XXXII

Her eyes are homes of silent prayer,
    Nor other thought her mind admits
    But, he was dead, and there he sits,
And he that brought him back is there.

Then one deep love doth supersede
    All other, when her ardent gaze
    Roves from the living brother's face,
And rests upon the Life indeed.

All subtle thought, all curious fears,
    Borne down by gladness so complete,
    She bows, she bathes the Saviour's feet
With costly spikenard and with tears.

Thrice blest whose lives are faithful prayers,
    Whose loves in higher love endure;
    What souls possess themselves so pure,
Or is there blessedness like theirs?

XXXIII

O thou that after toil and storm
    Mayst seem to have reach'd a purer air,
    Whose faith has centre everywhere,
Nor cares to fix itself to form,

Leave thou thy sister when she prays,
    Her early Heaven, her happy views;
    Nor thou with shadow'd hint confuse
A life that leads melodious days.

Her faith thro' form is pure as thine,
    Her hands are quicker unto good:
    Oh, sacred be the flesh and blood
To which she links a truth divine!

See thou, that countest reason ripe
    In holding by the law within,
    Thou fail not in a world of sin,
And ev'n for want of such a type.

XXXIV

My own dim life should teach me this,
    That life shall live for evermore,
    Else earth is darkness at the core,
And dust and ashes all that is;

This round of green, this orb of flame,
    Fantastic beauty; such as lurks
    In some wild Poet, when he works
Without a conscience or an aim.

What then were God to such as I?
    'Twere hardly worth my while to choose
    Of things all mortal, or to use
A little patience ere I die;

'Twere best at once to sink to peace,
    Like birds the charming serpent draws,
    To drop head-foremost in the jaws
Of vacant darkness and to cease.

XXXV

Yet if some voice that man could trust
    Should murmur from the narrow house,
    'The cheeks drop in; the body bows;
Man dies: nor is there hope in dust:'

Might I not say? 'Yet even here,
    But for one hour, O Love, I strive
    To keep so sweet a thing alive:'
But I should turn mine eyes and hear

The moanings of the homeless sea
    The sound of streams that swift or slow
    Draw down Aeonian hills, and sow
The dust of continents to be;

And Love would answer with a sigh,
    'The sound of that forgetful shore
    Will change my sweetness more and more,
Half-dead to know that I shall die.'

O me, what profits it to put
    An idle case? If Death were seen
    At first as Death, Love had not been,
Or been in narrowest working shut,

Mere fellowship of sluggish moods,
    Or in his coarsest Satyr-shape
    Had bruised the herb and crush'd the grape,
And bask'd and batten'd in the woods.

XXXVI

Tho' truths in manhood darkly join,
    Deep-seated in our mystic frame,
    We yield all blessing to the name
Of Him that made them current coin;

For Wisdom dealt with mortal powers,
    Where truth in closest words shall fail,
    When truth embodied in a tale
Shall enter in at lowly doors.

And so the Word had breath, and wrought
    With human hands the creed of creeds
    In loveliness of perfect deeds,
More strong than all poetic thought;

Which he may read that binds the sheaf,
    Or builds the house, or digs the grave,
    And those wild eyes that watch the wave
In roarings round the coral reef.

XXXVII

Urania speaks with darken'd brow:
    'Thou pratest here where thou art least;
    This faith has many a purer priest,
And many an abler voice than thou.

'Go down beside thy native rill,
    On thy Parnassus set thy feet,
    And hear thy laurel whisper sweet
About the ledges of the hill.'

And my Melpomene replies,
    A touch of shame upon her cheek:
    'I am not worthy ev'n to speak
Of thy prevailing mysteries;

'For I am but an earthly Muse,
    And owning but a little art
    To lull with song an aching heart,
And render human love his dues;

'But brooding on the dear one dead,
    And all he said of things divine,
    (And dear to me as sacred wine
To dying lips is all he said),

'I murmur'd, as I came along
    Of comfort clasp'd in truth reveal'd;
    And loiter'd in the master's field,
And darken'd sanctities with song.'

XXXVIII

With weary steps I loiter on,
    Tho' always under alter'd skies
    The purple from the distance dies,
My prospect and horizon gone.

No joy the blowing season gives,
    The herald melodies of spring,
    But in the songs I love to sing
A doubtful gleam of solace lives.

If any care for what is here
    Survive in spirits render'd free,
    Then are these songs I sing of thee
Not all ungrateful to thine ear.

XXXIX

Old warder of these buried bones,
    And answering now my random stroke
    With fruitful cloud and living smoke,
Dark yew, that graspest at the stones

And dippest toward the dreamless head,
    To thee too comes the golden hour
    When flower is feeling after flower;
But Sorrow – fixt upon the dead,

And darkening the dark graves of men, –
    What whisper'd from her lying lips?
    Thy gloom is kindled at the tips,
And passes into gloom again.

XL

Could we forget the widow'd hour
    And look on Spirits breathed away,
    As on a maiden in the day
When first she wears her orange-flower!

When crown'd with blessing she doth rise
    To take her latest leave-of home,
    And hopes and light regrets that come
Make April of her tender eyes;

And doubtful joys the father move,
    And tears are on the mother's face,
    As parting with a long embrace
She enters other realms of love;

Her office there to rear, to teach,
    Becoming as is meet and fit
    A link among the days, to knit
The generations each with each;

And, doubtless, unto thee is given
    A life that bears immortal fruit
    In such great offices as suit
The full-grown energies of heaven.

Ay me, the difference I discern!
    How often shall her old fireside
    Be cheer'd with tidings of the bride,
How often she herself return,

And tell them all they would have told,
    And bring her babe, and make her boast,
    Till even those that miss'd her most
Shall count new things as dear as old:

But thou and I have shaken hands,
    Till growing winters lay me low;
    My paths are in the fields I know,
And thine in undiscover'd lands.

XLI

Thy spirit ere our fatal loss
    Did ever rise from high to higher;
    AB mounts the heavenward altar-fire,
As flies the lighter thro' the gross.

But thou art turn'd to something strange,
    And I have lost the links that bound
    Thy changes; here upon the ground,
No more partaker of thy change.

Deep folly! yet that this could be –
    That I could wing my will with might
    To leap the grades of life and light,
And flash at once, my friend, to thee:

For tho' my nature rarely yields
    To that vague fear implied in death;
    Nor shudders at the gulfs beneath,
The howlings from forgotten fields;

Yet oft when sundown skirts the moor
    An inner trouble I behold,
    A spectral doubt which makes me cold,
That I shall be thy mate no more,

Tho' following with an upward mind
    The wonders that have come to thee,
    Thro' all the secular to-be,
But evermore a life behind.

XLII

I vex my heart with fancies dim:
    He still outstript me in the race;
    It was but unity of place
That made me dream I rank'd with him.

And so may Place retain us still,
    And he the much-beloved again,
    A lord of large experience, train
To riper growth the mind and will:

And what delights can equal those
    That stir the spirit's inner deeps,
    When one that loves but knows not, reaps
A truth from one that loves and knows?

XLIII

If Sleep and Death be truly one,
    And every spirit's folded bloom
    Thro' all its intervital gloom
In some long trance should slumber on;

Unconscious of the sliding hour,
    Bare of the body, might it last,
    And silent traces of the past
Be all the colour of the flower:

So then were nothing lost to man;
    So that still garden of the souls
    In many a figured leaf enrolls
The total world since life began;

And love will last as pure and whole
    As when he loved me here in Time,
    And at the spiritual prime
Rewaken with the dawning soul.

XLIV

How fares it with the happy dead?
    For here the man is more and more
    But he forgets the days before
God shut the doorways of his head.

The days have vanish'd, tone and tint,
    And yet perhaps the hoarding sense
    Gives out at times (he knows not whence)
A little flash, a mystic hint;

And in the long harmonious years
    (If Death so taste Lethean springs)
    May some dim touch of earthly things
Surprise thee ranging with thy peers.

If such a dreamy touch should fall
    O turn thee round, resolve the doubt;
    My guardian angel will speak out
In that high place, and tell thee all.

XLV

The baby new to earth and sky,
    What time his tender palm is prest
    Against the circle of the breast,
Has never thought that 'this is I:'

But as he grows he gathers much,
    And learns the use of 'I,' and 'me,'
    And finds 'I am not what I see,
And other than the things I touch.'

So rounds he to a separate mind
    From whence clear memory may begin,
    As thro' the frame that binds him in
His isolation grows defined.

This use may lie in blood and breath,
    Which else were fruitless of their due,
    Had man to learn himself anew
Beyond the second birth of Death.

XLVI

We ranging down this lower track,
    The path we came by, thorn and flower,
    Is shadow'd by the growing hour,
Lest life should fail in looking back.

So be it: there no shade can last
    In that deep dawn behind the tomb,
    But clear from marge to marge shall bloom
The eternal landscape of the past;

A lifelong tract of time reveal'd;
    The fruitful hours of still increase;
    Days order'd in a wealthy peace,
And those five years its richest field.

O Love, thy province were not large,
    A bounded field, nor stretching far;
    Look also, Love, a brooding star,
A rosy warmth from marge to marge.

XLVII

That each, who seems a separate whole,
    Should move his rounds, and fusing all
    The skirts of self again, should fall
Remerging in the general Soul,

Is faith as vague as all unsweet:
    Eternal form shall still divide
    The eternal soul from all beside;
And I shall know him when we meet:

And we shall sit at endless feast,
    Enjoying each the other's good:
    What vaster dream can hit the mood
Of Love on earth? He seeks at least

Upon the last and sharpest height,
    Before the spirits fade away,
    Some landing-place, to clasp and say,
'Farewell! We lose ourselves in light.'

XLVIII

If these brief lays, of Sorrow born,
    Were taken to be such as closed
    Grave doubts and answers here proposed,
Then these were such as men might scorn:

Her care is not to part and prove;
    She takes, when harsher moods remit,
    What slender shade of doubt may flit,
And makes it vassal unto love:

And hence, indeed, she sports with words,
    But better serves a wholesome law,
    And holds it sin and shame to draw
The deepest measure from the chords:

Nor dare she trust a larger lay,
    But rather loosens from the lip
    Short swallow-flights of song, that dip
Their wings in tears, and skim away.

XLIX

From art, from nature, from the schools,
    Let random influences glance,
    Like light in many a shiver'd lance
That breaks about the dappled pools:

The lightest wave of thought shall lisp,
    The fancy's tenderest eddy wreathe,
    The slightest air of song shall breathe
To make the sullen surface crisp.

And look thy look, and go thy way,
    But blame not thou the winds that make
    The seeming-wanton ripple break,
The tender-pencil'd shadow play.

Beneath all fancied hopes and fears
    Ay me, the sorrow deepens down,
    Whose muffled motions blindly drown
The bases of my life in tears.

L

Be near me when my light is low,
    When the blood creeps, and the nerves prick
    And tingle; and the heart is sick,
And all the wheels of Being slow.

Be near me when the sensuous frame
    Is rack'd with pangs that conquer trust;
    And Time, a maniac scattering dust,
And Life, a Fury slinging flame.

Be near me when my faith is dry,
    And men the flies of latter spring,
    That lay their eggs, and sting and sing,
And weave their petty cells and die.

Be near me when I fade away,
    To point the term of human strife,
    And on the low dark verge of life
The twilight of eternal day.

LI

Do we indeed desire the dead
    Should still be near us at our side?
    Is there no baseness we would hide?
No inner vileness that we dread?

Shall he for whose applause I strove,
    I had such reverence for his blame,
    See with clear eye some hidden shame
And I be lessen'd in his love?

I wrong the grave with fears untrue:
    Shall love be blamed for want of faith?
    There must be wisdom with great Death.
The dead shall look me thro' and thro'.

Be near us when we climb or fall:
    Ye watch, like God, the rolling hours
    With larger other eyes than ours,
To make allowance for us all.

LII

I cannot love thee as I ought,
    For love reflects the thing beloved;
    My words are only words, and moved
Upon the topmost froth of thought.

'Yet blame not thou thy plaintive song,'
    The Spirit of true love replied;
    'Thou canst not move me from thy side,
Nor human frailty do me wrong.

'What keeps a spirit wholly true
    To that ideal which he bears?
    What record? not the sinless years
That breathed beneath the Syrian blue:

'So fret not, like an idle girl
    That life is dash'd with flecks of sin.
    Abide: thy wealth is gather'd in,
When Time hath sunder'd shell from pearl.'

LIII

How many a father have I seen,
    A sober man, among his boys,
    Whose youth was full of foolish noise,
Who wears his manhood hale and green:

And dare we to this fancy give,
    That had the wild oat not been sown,
    The soil, left barren, scarce had grown
The grain by which a man may live?

Or, if we held the doctrine sound
    For life outliving heats of youth,
    Yet who would preach it as a truth
To those that eddy round and round?

Hold thou the good: define it well:
    For fear divine Philosophy
    Should push beyond her mark, and be
Procuress to the Lords of Hell.

LIV

Oh yet we trust that somehow good
    Will be the final goal of ill,
    To pangs of nature, sins of will,
Defects of doubt, and taints of blood;

That nothing walks with aimless feet;
    That not one life shall be destroy'd,
    Or cast as rubbish to the void,
When God hath made the pile complete;

That not a worm is cloven in vain;
    That not a moth with vain desire
    Is shrivel'd in a fruitless fire,
Or but subserves another's gain.

Behold, we know not anything;
    I can but trust that good shall fall
    At last — far off — at last, to all,
And every winter change to spring.

So runs my dream: but what am I?
    An infant crying in the night:
    An infant crying for the light:
And with no language but a cry.

LV

The wish, that of the living whole
    No life may fail beyond the grave,
    Derives it not from what we have
The likest God within the soul?

Are God and Nature then at strife,
    That Nature lends such evil dreams?
    So careful of the type she seems,
So careless of the single life;

That I, considering everywhere
    Her secret meaning in her deeds,
    And finding that of fifty seeds
She often brings but one to bear,

I falter where I firmly trod,
    And falling with my weight of cares
    Upon the great world's altar-stairs
That slope thro' darkness up to God,

I stretch lame hands of faith, and grope,
    And gather dust and chaff, and call
    To what I feel is Lord of all,
And faintly trust the larger hope.

LVI

'So careful of the type?' but no.
    From scarped cliff and quarried stone
    She cries 'A thousand types are gone:
I care for nothing, all shall go.

'Thou makest thine appeal to me:
    I bring to life, I bring to death:
    The spirit does but mean the breath:
I know no more.' And he, shall he,

Man, her last work, who seem'd so fair,
    Such splendid purpose in his eyes,
    Who roll'd the psalm to wintry skies,
Who built him fanes of fruitless prayer,

Who trusted God was love indeed
    And love Creation's final law –
    Tho' Nature, red in tooth and claw
With ravine, shriek'd against his creed –

Who loved, who suffer'd countless ills,
    Who battled for the True, the Just,
    Be blown about the desert dust,
Or seal'd within the iron hills?

No more? A monster then, a dream,
    A discord. Dragons of the prime,
    That tare each other in their slime,
Were mellow music match'd with him.

O life as futile, then, as frail!
    O for thy voice to soothe and bless!
    What hope of answer, or redress?
Behind the veil, behind the veil.

LVII

Peace; come away: the song of woe
    Is after all an earthly song:
    Peace; come away: we do him wrong
To sing so wildly: let us go.

Come! let us go: your cheeks are pale;
    But half my life I leave behind:
    Methinks my friend is richly shrined;
But I shall pass; my work will fail.

Yet in these ears, till hearing dies
    One set slow bell will seem to toll
    The passing of the sweetest soul
That ever look'd with human eyes.

I hear it now, and o'er and o'er,
    Eternal greetings to the dead;
    And 'Ave, Ave, Ave,' said,
'Adieu, adieu' for evermore.

LVIII

In those sad words I took farewell:
    Like echoes in sepulchral halls,
    As drop by drop the water falls
In vaults and catacombs, they fell;

And, falling, idly broke the peace
    (Of hearts that beat from day to day,
    Half-conscious of their dying clay,
And those cold crypts where they shall cease.

The high Muse answer'd: 'Wherefore grieve
    Thy brethren with a fruitless tear?
    Abide a little longer here,
And thou shalt take a nobler leave.'

LIX

O Sorrow, wilt thou live with me
    No casual mistress, but a wife,
    My bosom-friend and half of life;
As I confess it needs must be;

O Sorrow, wilt thou rule my blood,
    Be sometimes lovely like a bride,
    And put thy harsher moods aside,
If thou wilt have me wise and good.

My centred passion cannot move,
    Nor will it lessen from to-day;
    But I'll have leave at times to play
As with the creature of my love;

And set thee forth, for thou art mine,
    With so much hope for years to come,
    That, howsoe'er I know thee, some
Could hardly tell what name were thine.

LX

He past; a soul of nobler tone:
    My spirit loved and loves him yet,
    Like some poor girl whose heart is set
On one whose rank exceeds her own.

He mixing with his proper sphere
  She finds the baseness of her lot,
  Half jealous of she knows not what,
And envying all that meet him there.

The little village looks forlorn;
  She sighs amid her narrow days,
  Moving about the household ways,
In that dark house where she was born.

The foolish neighbours come and go,
  And tease her till the day draws by:
  At night she weeps, 'How vain am I!
How should he love a thing so low?'

LXI

If, in thy second state sublime,
  Thy ransom'd reason change replies
  With all the circle of the wise,
The perfect flower of human time;

And if thou cast thine eyes below,
  How dimly character'd and slight,
  How dwarf'd a growth of cold and night,
How blanch'd with darkness must I grow!

Yet turn thee to the doubtful shore,
  Where thy first form was made a man;
  I loved thee, Spirit, and love, nor can
The soul of Shakespeare love thee more.

LXII

Tho' if an eye that's downward cast
  Could make thee somewhat blench or fail,
  Then be my love an idle tale,
And fading legend of the past;

And thou, as one that once declined,
  When he was little more than boy,
  On some unworthy heart with joy,
But lives to wed an equal mind;

And breathes a novel world, the while
  His other passion wholly dies,
  Or in the light of deeper eyes
Is matter for a flying smile.

LXIII

Yet pity for a horse o'er-driven,
    And love in which my hound has part,
    Can hang no weight upon my heart
In its assumptions up to heaven;

And I am so much more than these,
    As thou, perchance, art more than I,
    And yet I spare them sympathy,
And I would set their pains at ease.

So may'st thou watch me where I weep,
    As, unto vaster motions bound,
    The circuits of thine orbit round
A higher height, a deeper deep.

LXIV

Dost thou look back on what hath been,
    As some divinely gifted man,
    Whose life in low estate began
And on a simple village green;

Who breaks his birth's invidious bar,
    And grasps the skirts of happy chance,
    And breasts the blows of circumstance,
And grapples with his evil star;

Who makes by force his merit known
    And lives to clutch the golden keys,
    To mould a mighty state's decrees,
And shape the whisper of the throne;

And moving up from high to higher,
    Becomes on Fortune's crowning slope
    The pillar of a people's hope,
The centre of a world's desire;

Yet feels, as in a pensive dream,
    When all his active powers are still,
    A distant dearness in the hill,
A secret sweetness in the stream,

The limit of his narrower fate,
    While yet beside its vocal springs
    He play'd at counsellors and kings,
With one that was his earliest mate;

Who ploughs with pain his native lea
  And reaps the labour of his hands,
  Or in the furrow musing stands;
'Does my old friend remember me?'

LXV

Sweet soul, do with me as thou wilt;
  I lull a fancy trouble-tost
  With 'Love's too precious to be lost,
A little grain shall not be spilt.'

And in that solace can I sing,
  Till out of painful phases wrought
  There flutters up a happy thought,
Self-balanced on a lightsome wing:

Since we deserved the name of friends,
  And thine effect so lives in me,
  A part of mine may live in thee
And move thee on to noble ends.

LXVI

You thought my heart too far diseased;
  You wonder when my fancies play
  To find me gay among the gay,
Like one with any trifle pleased.

The shade by which my life was crost,
  Which makes a desert in the mind,
  Has made me kindly with my kind,
And like to him whose sight is lost;

Whose feet are guided thro' the land,
  Whose jest among his friends is free,
  Who takes the children on his knee,
And winds their curls about his hand:

He plays with threads, he beats his chair
  For pastime, dreaming of the sky;
  His inner day can never die,
His night of loss is always there.

LXVII

When on my bed the moonlight falls,
  I know that in thy place of rest
  By that broad water of the west,
There comes a glory on the walls:

Thy marble bright in dark appears,
   As slowly steals a silver flame
   Along the letters of thy name,
And o'er the number of thy years.

The mystic glory swims away;
   From off my bed the moonlight dies;
   And closing eaves of wearied eyes
I sleep till dusk is dipt in grey:

And then I know the mist is drawn
   A lucid veil from coast to coast,
   And in the dark church like a ghost
Thy tablet glimmers to the dawn.

LXVII

When in the down I sink my head,
   Sleep, Death's twin-brother, times my breath;
   Sleep, Death's twin-brother, knows not Death,
Nor can I dream of thee as dead:

I walk as ere I walk'd forlorn,
   When all our path was fresh with dew,
   And all the bugle breezes blew
Reveillée to the breaking morn.

But what is this? I turn about,
   I find a trouble in thine eye,
   Which makes me sad I know not why,
Nor can my dream resolve the doubt:

But ere the lark hath left the lea
   I wake, and I discern the truth;
   It is the trouble of my youth
That foolish sleep transfers to thee

LXIX

I dream'd there would be Spring no more,
   That Nature's ancient power was lost:
   The streets were black with smoke and frost,
They chatter'd trifles at the door:

I wander'd from the noisy town,
   I found a wood with thorny boughs:
   I took the thorns to bind my brows,
I wore them like a civic crown:

I met with scoffs, I met with scorns
    From youth and babe and hoary hairs:
    They call'd me in the public squares
The fool that wears a crown of thorns:

They call'd me fool, they call'd me child:
    I found an angel of the night;
    The voice was low, the look was bright;
He look'd upon my crown and smiled:

He reach'd the glory of a hand,
    That seem'd to touch it into leaf:
    The voice was not the voice of grief,
The words were hard to understand.

LXX

I cannot see the features right,
    When on the gloom I strive to paint
    The face I know; the hues are faint
And mix with hollow masks of night;

Cloud-towers by ghostly masons wrought,
    A gulf that ever shuts and gapes,
    A hand that points, and palled shapes
In shadowy thoroughfares of thought;

And crowds that stream from yawning doors,
    And shoals of pucker'd faces drive;
    Dark bulks that tumble half alive,
And lazy lengths on boundless shores;

Till all at once beyond the will
    I hear a wizard music roll,
    And thro' a lattice on the soul
Looks thy fair face and makes it still.

LXXI

Sleep, kinsman thou to death and trance
    And madness, thou hast forged at last
    A night-long Present of the Past
In which we went thro' summer France.

Hadst thou such credit with the soul?
    Then bring an opiate trebly strong,
    Drug down the blindfold sense of wrong
That so my pleasure may be whole;

While now we talk as once we talk'd
    Of men and minds, the dust of change,
    The days that grow to something strange,
In walking as of old we walk'd

Beside the river's wooded reach,
    The fortress, and the mountain ridge,
    The cataract flashing from the bridge,
The breaker breaking on the beach.

LXXII

Risest thou thus, dim dawn, again,
    And howlest, issuing out of night,
    With blasts that blow the poplar white
And lash with storm the streaming pane?

Day, when my crown'd estate begun
    To pine in that reverse of doom,
    Which sicken'd every living bloom,
And blurr'd the splendour of the sun;

Who usherest in the dolorous hour
    With thy quick tears that make the rose
    Pull sideways, and the daisy close
Her crimson fringes to the shower;

Who might'st have heaved a windless flame
    Up the deep East, or, whispering, play'd
    A chequer-work of beam and shade
Along the hills, yet look'd the same,

As wan, as chill, as wild as now;
    Day, mark'd as with some hideous crime,
    When the dark hand struck down thro' time,
And cancell'd nature's best: but thou,

Lift as thou may'st thy burthen'd brows
    Thro' clouds that drench the morning star,
    And whirl the ungarner'd sheaf afar,
And sow the sky with flying boughs,

And up thy vault with roaring sound
    Climb thy thick noon, disastrous day;
    Touch thy dull goal of joyless grey,
And hide thy shame beneath the ground.

LXXIII

So many worlds, so much to do,
    So little done, such things to be,
    How know I what had need of thee,
For thou wert strong as thou wert true?

The fame is quench'd that I foresaw,
    The head hath miss'd an earthly wreath:
    I curse not nature, no, nor death;
For nothing is that errs from law.

We pass; the path that each man trod
Is dim, or will be dim, with weeds:
What fame is left for human deeds
In endless age? It rests with God.

O hollow wraith of dying fame,
    Fade wholly, while the soul exults,
    And self-infolds the large results
Of force that would have forged a name.

LXXIV

As sometimes in a dead man's face,
    To those that watch it more and more,
    A likeness, hardly seen before,
Comes out – to some one of his race:

So, dearest, now thy brows are cold,
    I see thee what thou art, and know
    Thy likeness to the wise below,
Thy kindred with the great of old.

But there is more than I can see,
    And what I see I leave unsaid,
    Nor speak it, knowing Death has made
His darkness beautiful with thee.

LXXV

I leave thy praises unexpress'd
    In verse that brings myself relief,
    And by the measure of my grief
I leave thy greatness to be guess'd;

What practice howsoe'er expert
    In fitting aptest words to things,
    Or voice the richest-toned that sings,
Hath power to give thee as thou wert?

I care not in these fading days
    To raise a cry that lasts not long,
    And round thee with the breeze of song
To stir a little dust of praise.

Thy leaf has perish'd in the green,
    And, while we breathe beneath the sun,
    The world which credits what is done
Is cold to all that might have been.

So here shall silence guard thy fame;
    But somewhere, out of human view,
    Whate'er thy hands are set to do
Is wrought with tumult of acclaim.

LXXVI

Take wings of fancy, and ascend,
    And in a moment set thy face
    Where all the starry heavens of space
Are sharpen'd to a needle's end;

Take wings of foresight; lighten thro'
    The secular abyss to come,
    And lo, thy deepest lays are dumb
Before the mouldering of a yew;

And if the matin songs, that woke
    The darkness of our planet, last,
    Thine own shall wither in the vast,
Ere half the lifetime of an oak.

Ere these have clothed their branchy bowers
    With fifty Mays, thy songs are vain;
    And what are they when these remain
The ruin'd shells of hollow towers?

LXXVII

What hope is here for modern rhyme
    To him, who turns a musing eye
    On songs, and deeds, and lives, that lie
Foreshorten'd in the tract of time?

These mortal lullabies of pain
    May bind a book, may line a box,
    May serve to curl a maiden's locks;
Or when a thousand moons shall wane

A man upon a stall may find,
    And, passing, turn the page that tells
    A grief, then changed to something else,
Sung by a long-forgotten mind.

But what of that? My darken'd ways
    Shall ring with music all the same;
    To breathe my loss is more than fame,
To utter love more sweet than praise.

LXXVIII

Again at Christmas did we weave
    The holly round the Christmas hearth;
    The silent snow possess'd the earth,
And calmly fell our Christmas-eve:

The yule-clog sparkled keen with frost,
    No wing of wind the region swept,
    But over all things brooding slept
The quiet sense of something lost.

As in the winters left behind,
    Again our ancient games had place,
    The mimic picture's breathing grace,
And dance and song and hoodman-blind.

Who show'd a token of distress?
    No single tear, no mark of pain
    O sorrow, then can sorrow wane?
O grief, can grief be changed to less?

O last regret, regret can die!
    No – mixt with all this mystic frame,
    Her deep relations are the same,
But with long use her tears are dry.

LXXIX

'More than my brothers are to me' –
    Let this not vex thee, noble heart!
    I know thee of what force thou art
To hold the costliest love in fee.

But thou and I are one in kind,
    As moulded like in nature's mint;
    And hill and wood and field did print
The same sweet forms in either mind.

For us the same cold streamlet curl'd
 Thro' all his eddying coves; the same
 All winds that roam the twilight came
In whispers of the beauteous world.

At one dear knee we proffer'd vows,
 One lesson from one book we learn'd,
 Ere childhood's flaxen ringlet turn'd
To black and brown on kindred brows.

And so my wealth resembles thine,
 But he was rich where I was poor,
 And he supplied my want the more
As his unlikeness fitted mine.

LXXX

If any vague desire should rise,
 That holy Death ere Arthur died
 Had moved me kindly from his side,
And dropt the dust on tearless eyes;

Then fancy shapes, as fancy can,
 The grief my loss in him had wrought,
 A grief as deep as life or thought,
But stay'd in peace with God and man.

I make a picture in the brain;
 I hear the sentence that he speaks;
 He bears the burthen of the weeks,
But turns his burthen into gain.

His credit thus shall set me free;
 And, influence-rich to soothe and save,
 Unused example from the grave
Reach out dead hands to comfort me.

LXXXI

Could I have said while he was here,
 'My love shall now no further range;
 There cannot come a mellower change,
For now is love mature in ear.'

Love, then, had hope of richer store:
 What end is here to my complaint?
 This haunting whisper makes me faint,
'More years had made me love thee more.'

But Death returns an answer sweet:
    'My sudden frost was sudden gain,
    And gave all ripeness to the grain
It might have drawn from after-heat.'

LXXXII

I wage not any feud with Death
    For changes wrought on form and face,
    No lower life that earth's embrace
May breed with him, can fright my faith.

Eternal process moving on,
    From state to state the spirit walks;
    And these are but the shatter'd stalks,
Or ruin'd chrysalis of one.

Nor blame I Death, because he bare
    The use of virtue out of earth:
    I know transplanted human worth
Will bloom to profit, otherwhere.

For this alone on Death I wreak
    The wrath that garners in my heart;
    He put our lives so far apart
We cannot hear each other speak.

LXXXIII

Dip down upon the northern shore
    O sweet new-year delaying long;
    Thou doest expectant nature wrong;
Delaying long, delay no more.

What stays thee from the clouded noons,
    Thy sweetness from its proper place?
    Can trouble live with April days,
Or sadness in the summer moons?

Bring orchis, bring the foxglove spire,
    The little speedwell's darling blue,
    Deep tulips dash'd with fiery dew,
Laburnums, dropping-wells of fire.

O thou, new-year, delaying long,
    Delayest the sorrow in my blood,
    That longs to burst a frozen bud
And flood a fresher throat with song.

LXXXIV

When I contemplate all alone
    The life that had been thine below,
    And fix my thoughts on all the glow
To which thy crescent would have grown;

I see thee sitting crown'd with good,
    A central warmth diffusing bliss
    In glance and smile, and clasp and kiss,
On all the branches of thy blood;

Thy blood, my friend, and partly mine;
    For now the day was drawing on,
    When thou should'st link thy life with one
Of mine own house, and boys of thine

Had babbled 'Uncle' on my knee;
    But that remorseless iron hour
    Made cypress of her orange flower,
Despair of Hope, and earth of thee.

I seem to meet their least desire,
    To clap their cheeks, to call them mine.
    I see their unborn faces shine
Beside the never-lighted fire.

I see myself an honour'd guest,
    Thy partner in the flowery walk
    Of letters, genial table-talk,
Or deep dispute, and graceful jest;

While now thy prosperous labour fills
    The lips of men with honest praise,
    And sun by sun the happy days
Descend below the golden hills

With promise of a morn as fair;
    And all the train of bounteous hours
    Conduct by paths of growing powers,
To reverence and the silver hair;

Till slowly worn her earthly robe,
    Her lavish mission richly wrought,
    Leaving great legacies of thought,
Thy spirit should fail from off the globe;

What time mine own might also flee,
    As link'd with thine in love and fate,
    And, hovering o'er the dolorous strait
To the other shore, involved in thee,

Arrive at last the blessed goal,
    And He that died in Holy Land
    Would reach us out the shining hand,
And take us as a single soul.

What reed was that on which I leant?
    Ah, backward fancy, wherefore wake
    The old bitterness again, and break
The low beginnings of content.

LXXXV

This truth came borne with bier and pall,
    I felt it, when I sorrow'd most,
    'Tis better to have loved and lost,
Than never to have loved at all —

O true in word, and tried in deed,
    Demanding, so to bring relief
    To this which is our common grief,
What kind of life is that I lead;

And whether trust in things above
    Be dimm'd of sorrow, or sustain'd;
    And whether love for him have drain'd
My capabilities of love;

Your words have virtue such as draws
    A faithful answer from the breast,
    Thro' light reproaches, half exprest,
And loyal unto kindly laws.

My blood an even tenor kept,
    Till on mine ear this message falls,
    That in Vienna's fatal walls
Cod's finger touch'd him, and he slept.

The great Intelligences fair
    That range above our mortal state,
    In circle round the blessed gate
Received and gave him welcome there;

And led him thro' the blissful climes,
    And show'd him in the fountain fresh
    All knowledge that the sons of flesh
Shall gather in the cycled times.

But I remain'd, whose hopes were dim,
    Whose life, whose thoughts were little worth,
    To wander on a darken'd earth,
Where all things round me breathed of him.

O friendship, equal-poised control,
    O heart, with kindliest motion warm,
    O sacred essence, other form,
O solemn ghost, O crowned soul!

Yet none could better know than I,
    How much of act at human hands
    The sense of human will demands
By which we dare to live or die.

Whatever way my days decline,
    I felt and feel, tho' left alone,
    His being working in mine own,
The footsteps of his life in mine;

A life that all the Muses deck'd
    With gifts of grace, that might express
    All-comprehensive tenderness,
All-subtilizing intellect:

And so my passion hath not swerved
    To works of weakness, but I find
    An image comforting the mind,
And in my grief a strength reserved.

Likewise the imaginative woe,
    That loved to handle spiritual strife,
    Diffused the shock thro' all my life,
But in the present broke the blow.

My pulses therefore beat again
    For other friends that once I met;
    Nor can it suit me to forget
The mighty hopes that make us men.

I woo your love: I count it crime
    To mourn for any overmuch;
    I, the divided half of such
A friendship as had master'd Time;

Which masters Time indeed, and is
    Eternal, separate from fears:
    The all-assuming months and years
Can take no part away from this:

But Summer on the steaming floods,
    And Spring that swells the narrow brooks,
    And Autumn, with a noise of rooks,
That gather in the waning woods,

And every pulse of wind and wave
    Recalls, in change of light or gloom,
    My old affection of the tomb,
And my prime passion in the grave:

My old affection of the tomb,
    A part of stillness, yearns to speak:
    'Arise, and get thee forth and seek
A friendship for the years to come.

'I watch thee from the quiet shore;
    Thy spirit up to mine can reach;
    But in dear words of human speech
We two communicate no more.'

And I, 'Can clouds of nature stain
    The starry clearness of the free?
    How is it? Canst thou feel for me
Some painless sympathy with pain?'

And lightly does the whisper fall;
    ' 'Tis hard for thee to fathom this;
    I triumph in conclusive bliss,
And that serene result of all.'

So hold I commerce with the dead;
    Or so methinks the dead would say;
    Or so shall grief with symbols play,
And pining life be fancy-fed.

Now looking to some settled end,
    That these things pass, and I shall prove
    A meeting somewhere, love with love,
I crave your pardon, O my friend;

If not so fresh, with love as true,
    I, clasping brother-hands, aver
    I could not, if I would, transfer
The whole I felt for him to you.

For which be they that hold apart
    The promise of the golden hours?
    First love, first friendship, equal powers,
That marry with the virgin heart.

Still mine, that cannot but deplore,
    That beats within a lonely place,
    That yet remembers his embrace,
But at his footstep leaps no more,

My heart, tho' widow'd, may not rest
    Quite in the love of what is gone,
    But seeks to beat in time with one
That warms another living breast.

Ah, take the imperfect gift I bring,
    Knowing the primrose yet is dear,
    The primrose of the later year,
As not unlike to that of Spring.

LXXXVI

Sweet after showers, ambrosial air,
    That rollest from the gorgeous gloom
    Of evening over brake and bloom
And meadow, slowly breathing bare

The round of space, and rapt below
    Thro' all the dewy-tassell'd wood,
    And shadowing down the horned flood
In ripples, fan my brows and blow

The fever from my cheek, and sigh
    The full new life that feeds thy breath
    Throughout my frame, till Doubt and Death,
Ill brethren, let the fancy fly

From belt to belt of crimson seas
    On leagues of odour streaming far,
    To where in yonder orient star
A hundred spirits whisper 'Peace.'

LXXXVII

I past beside the reverend walls
    In which of old I wore the gown;
    I roved at random thro' the town,
And saw the tumult of the halls;

And heard once more in college fanes
    The storm their high-built organs make,
    And thunder-music, rolling, shake
The prophets blazon'd on the panes;

And caught once more the distant shout,
    The measured pulse of racing oars
    Among the willows; paced the shores
And many a bridge, and all about

The same grey flats again, and felt
    The same, but not the same; and last
    Up that long walk of limes I past
To see the rooms in which he dwelt.

Another name was on the door:
    I linger'd; all within was noise
    Of songs, and clapping hands, and boys
That crash'd the glass and beat the floor;

Where once we held debate, a band
    Of youthful friends, on mind and art,
    And labour, and the changing mart,
And all the framework of the land;

When one would aim an arrow fair,
    But send it slackly from the string;
    And one would pierce an outer ring,
And one an inner, here and there;

And last the master-bowman, he,
    Would cleave the mark. A willing ear
    We lent him. Who, but hung to hear
The rapt oration flowing free

From point to point, with power and grace
    And music in the bounds of law,
    To those conclusions when we saw
The God within him light his face,

And seem to lift the form, and glow
    In azure orbits heavenly-wise;
    And over those ethereal eyes
The bar of Michael Angelo.

LXXXVIII

Wild bird, whose warble, liquid sweet,
    Rings Eden thro' the budded quicks,
    O tell me where the senses mix,
O tell me where the passions meet,

Whence radiate: fierce extremes employ
    Thy spirits in the darkening leaf,
    And in the midmost heart of grief
Thy passion clasps a secret joy:

And I – my harp would prelude woe –
    I cannot all command the strings;
    The glory of the sum of things
Will flash along the chords and go.

LXXXIX

Witch-elms that counterchange the floor
    Of this flat lawn with dusk and bright;
    And thou, with all thy breadth and height
Of foliage, towering sycamore;

How often, hither wandering down,
    My Arthur found your shadows fair,
    And shook to all the liberal air
The dust and din and steam of town:

He brought an eye for all he saw;
    He mixt in all our simple sports;
    They pleased him, fresh from brawling courts
And dusty purlieus of the law.

O joy to him in this retreat
    Immantled in ambrosial dark,
    To drink the cooler air, and mark
The landscape winking thro' the heat:

O sound to rout the brood of cares,
 The sweep of scythe in morning dew,
 The gust that round the garden flew,
And tumbled half the mellowing pears!

O bliss, when all in circle drawn
 About him, heart and ear were fed
 To hear him, as he lay and read
The Tuscan poets on the lawn:

Or in the all-golden afternoon
 A guest, or happy sister, sung,
 Or here she brought the harp and flung
A ballad to the brightening moon:

Nor less it pleased in livelier moods
 Beyond the bounding hill to stray,
 And break the livelong summer day
With banquet in the distant woods;

Whereat we glanced from theme to theme,
 Discuss'd the books to love or hate,
 Or touch'd the changes of the state,
Or threaded some Socratic dream;

But if I praised the busy town,
 He loved to rail against it still,
 For ground in yonder social mill
We rub each other's angles down,

'And merge' he said 'in form and gloss
 The picturesque of man and man.'
 We talk'd: the stream beneath us ran,
The wine-flask lying couch'd in moss,

Or cool'd within the glooming wave;
 And last, returning from afar,
 Before the crimson-circled star
Had fall'n into her father's grave,

And brushing ankle-deep in flowers,
 We heard behind the woodbine veil
 The milk that bubbled in the pail,
And buzzings of the honied hours.

XC

He tasted love with half his mind,
　　Nor ever drank the inviolate spring
　　Where nighest heaven, who first could fling
This bitter seed among mankind;

That could the dead, whose dying eyes
　　Were closed with wail, resume their life,
　　They would but find in child and wife
An iron welcome when they rise:

'Twas well, indeed, when warm with wine,
　　To pledge them with a kindly tear,
　　To talk them o'er, to wish them here,
To count their memories half divine;

But if they came who past away,
　　Behold their brides in other hands;
　　The hard heir strides about their lands,
And will not yield them for a day.

Yea, tho' their sons were none of these,
　　Not less the yet-loved sire would make
　　Confusion worse than death, and shake
The pillars of domestic peace.

Ah dear, but come thou back to me:
　　Whatever change the years have wrought,
　　I find not yet one lonely thought
That cries against my wish for thee.

XCI

When rosy plumelets tuft the larch,
　　And rarely pipes the mounted thrush;
　　Or underneath the barren bush
Flits by the sea-blue bird of March;

Come, wear the form by which I know
　　Thy spirit in time among thy peers;
　　The hope of unaccomplish'd years
Be large and lucid round thy brow.

When summer's hourly-mellowing change
　　May breathe, with many roses sweet,
　　Upon the thousand waves of wheat,
That ripple round the lonely grange;

Come: not in watches of the night,
    But where the sunbeam broodeth warm,
    Come, beauteous in thine after form,
And like a finer light in light.

XCII

If any vision should reveal
    Thy likeness, I might count it vain
    As but the canker of the brain;
Yea, tho' it spake and made appeal

To chances where our lots were cast
    Together in the days behind,
    I might but say, I hear a wind
Of memory murmuring the past.

Yea, tho' it spake and bared to view
    A fact within the coming year;
    And tho' the months, revolving near,
Should prove the phantom-warning true,

They might not seem thy prophecies,
    But spiritual presentiments,
    And such refraction of events
As often rises ere they rise.

XCIII

I shall not see thee. Dare I say
    No spirit ever brake the band
    That stays him from the native land
Where first he walk'd when claspt in clay?

No visual shade of some one lost,
    But he, the Spirit himself, may come
    Where all the nerve of sense is numb;
Spirit to Spirit, Ghost to Ghost.

O, therefore from thy sightless range
    With gods in unconjectured bliss,
    O, from the distance of the abyss
Of tenfold-complicated change,

Descend, and touch, and enter; hear
    The wish too strong for words to name;
    That in this blindness of the frame
My Ghost may feel that thine is near.

XCIV

How pure at heart and sound in head,
    With what divine affections bold
    Should be the man whose thought would hold
An hour's communion with the dead.

In vain shalt thou, or any, call
    The spirits from their golden day,
    Except, like them, thou too canst say,
My spirit is at peace with all.

They haunt the silence of the breast,
    Imaginations calm and fair,
    The memory like a cloudless air,
The conscience as a sea at rest:

But when the heart is full of din,
    And doubt beside the portal waits,
    They can but listen at the gates,
And hear the household jar within.

XCV

By night we linger'd on the lawn,
    For underfoot the herb was dry;
    And genial warmth; and o'er the sky
The silvery haze of summer drawn;

And calm that let the tapers burn
    Unwavering: not a cricket chirr'd:
    The brook alone far-off was heard,
And on the board the fluttering urn:

And bats went round in fragrant skies,
    And wheel'd or lit the filmy shapes
    That haunt the dusk, with ermine capes
And woolly breasts and beaded eyes;

While now we sang old songs that peal'd
    From knoll to knoll, where, couch'd at ease,
    The white kine glimmer'd, and the trees
Laid their dark arms about the field.

But when those others, one by one,
    Withdrew themselves from me and night,
    And in the house light after light
Went out, and I was all alone,

A hunger seized my heart; I read
    Of that glad year which once had been,
    In those fall'n leaves which kept their green,
The noble letters of the dead:

And strangely on the silence broke
    The silent-speaking words, and strange
    Was love's dumb cry defying change
To test his worth; and strangely spoke

The faith, the vigour, bold to dwell
    On doubts that drive the coward back,
    And keen thro' wordy snares to track
Suggestion to her inmost cell.

So word by word, and line by line,
    The dead man touch'd me from the past,
    And all at once it seem'd at last
His living soul was flash'd on mine,

And mine in his was wound, and whirl'd
    About empyreal heights of thought,
    And came on that which is, and caught
The deep pulsations of the world,

Aeonian music measuring out
    The steps of Time – the shocks of Chance –
    The blows of Death. At length my trance
Was cancell'd, stricken thro' with doubt.

Vague words! but ah, how hard to frame
    In matter-moulded forms of speech,
    Or ev'n for intellect to reach
Thro' memory that which I became:

Till now the doubtful dusk reveal'd
    The knolls once more where, couch'd at ease,
    The white kine glimmer'd, and the trees
Laid their dark arms about the field:

And suck'd from out the distant gloom
    A breeze began to tremble o'er
    The large leaves of the sycamore,
And fluctuate all the still perfume,

And gathering freshlier overhead,
    Rock'd the full-foliaged elms, and swung
    The heavy-folded rose, and flung
The lilies to and fro, and said

'The dawn, the dawn,' and died away;
    And East and West, without a breath,
    Mixt their dim lights, like life and death,
To broaden into boundless day.

XCVI

You say, but with no touch of scorn,
    Sweet-hearted, you, whose light-blue eyes
    Are tender over drowning flies,
You tell me, doubt is Devil-born.

I know not: one indeed I knew
    In many a subtle question versed,
    Who touch'd a jarring lyre at first
But ever strove to make it true:

Perplext in faith, but pure in deeds,
    At last he beat his music out.
    There lives more faith in honest doubt,
Believe me, than in half the creeds.

He fought his doubts and gather'd strength,
    He would not make his judgement blind,
    He faced the spectres of the mind
And laid them: thus he came at length

To find a stronger faith his own;
    And Power was with him in the night,
    Which makes the darkness and the light,
And dwells not in the light alone,

But in the darkness and the cloud,
    As over Sinai's peaks of old,
    While Israel made their gods of gold,
Altho' the trumpet blew so loud.

XCVII

My love has talk'd with rocks and trees;
    He finds on misty mountain-ground
    His own vast shadow glory-crowned;
He sees himself in all he sees.

Two partners of a married life –
    I look'd on these and thought of thee
    In vastness and in mystery,
And of my spirit as of a wife.

These two – they dwelt with eye on eye,
    Their hearts of old have beat in tune,
    Their meetings made December June,
Their every parting was to die.

Their love has never past away;
    The days she never can forget
    Are earnest that he loves her yet,
Whate'er the faithless people say.

Her life is lone, he sits apart,
    He loves her yet, she will not weep,
    Tho' rapt in matters dark and deep
He seems to slight her simple heart.

He thrids the labyrinth of the mind,
    He reads the secret of the star,
    He seems so near and yet so far,
He looks so cold: she thinks him kind.

She keeps the gift of years before,
    A wither'd violet is her bliss:
    She knows not what his greatness is;
For that, for all, she loves him more.

For him she plays, to him she sings
    Of early faith and plighted vows;
    She knows but matters of the house,
And he, he knows a thousand things.

Her faith is fixt and cannot move,
    She darkly feels him great and wise,
    She dwells on him with faithful eyes,
'I cannot understand: I love.'

XCVIII

You leave us: you will see the Rhine,
    And those fair hills I sail'd below,
    When I was there with him; and go
By summer belts of wheat and vine

To where he breathed his latest breath,
    That City. All her splendour seems
    No livelier than the wisp that gleams
On Lethe in the eyes of Death.

Let her great Danube rolling fair
    Enwind her isles, unmark'd of me:
    I have not seen, I will not see
Vienna; rather dream that there,

A treble darkness, Evil haunts
    The birth, the bridal; friend from friend
    Is oftener parted, fathers bend
Above more graves, a thousand wants

Gnarr at the heels of men, and prey
    By each cold hearth, and sadness flings
    Her shadow on the blaze of kings:
And yet myself have heard him say,

That not in any mother town
    With statelier progress to and fro
    The double tides of chariots flow
By park and suburb under brown

Of lustier leaves; nor more content,
    He told me, lives in any crowd,
    When all is gay with lamps, and loud
With sport and song, in booth and tent,

Imperial halls, or open plain;
    And wheels the circled dance, and breaks
    The rocket molten into flakes
Of crimson or in emerald rain.

XCIX

Risest thou thus, dim dawn, again,
    So loud with voices of the birds,
    So thick with lowings of the herds,
Day, when I lost the flower of men;

Who tremblest thro' thy darkling red
    On yon swoll'n brook that bubbles fast
    By meadows breathing of the past,
And woodlands holy to the dead;

Who murmurest in the foliaged eaves
    A song that slights the coming care,
    And Autumn laying here and there
A fiery finger on the leaves;

Who wakenest with thy balmy breath
    To myriads on the genial earth,
    Memories of bridal, or of birth,
And unto myriads more, of death.

O wheresoever those may be,
    Betwixt the slumber of the poles,
    To-day they count as kindred souls;
They know me not, but mourn with me.

C

I climb the hill: from end to end
    Of all the landscape underneath,
    I find no place that does not breathe
Some gracious memory of my friend;

No grey old grange, or lonely fold,
    Or low morass and whispering reed,
    Or simple stile from mead to mead,
Or sheepwalk up the windy wold;

Nor hoary knoll of ash and haw
    That hears the latest linnet trill,
    Nor quarry trench'd along the hill
And haunted by the wrangling daw;

Nor runlet tinkling from the rock;
    Nor pastoral rivulet that swerves
    To left and right thro' meadowy curves,
That feed the mothers of the flock;

But each has pleased a kindred eye,
    And each reflects a kindlier day;
    And, leaving these, to pass away,
I think once more he seems to die.

CI

Unwatch'd, the garden bough shall sway,
    The tender blossom flutter down,
    Unloved, that beech will gather brown,
This maple burn itself away;

Unloved, the sun flower, shining fair,
    Ray round with flames her disk of seed,
    And many a rose-carnation feed
With summer spice tile humming air;

Unloved, by many a sandy bar,
    The brook shall babble down the plain,
    At noon or when the lesser wain
Is twisting round the polar star;

Uncared for, gird the windy grove,
    And flood the haunts of hem and crake,
    Or into silver arrows break
The sailing moon in creek and cove;

Till from the garden and the wild
    A fresh association blow,
    And year by year the landscape grow
Familiar to the stranger's child;

As year by year the labourer tills
    His wonted glebe, or lops the glades;
    And year by year our memory fades
From all the circle of the hills.

CII

We leave the well-beloved place
    Where first we gazed upon the sky;
    The roofs, that heard our earliest cry,
Will shelter one of stranger race.

We go, but ere we go from home,
    As down the garden-walks I move,
    Two spirits of a diverse love
Contend for loving masterdom.

One whispers, 'Here thy boyhood sung
    Long since its matin song, and heard
    The low love-language of the bird
In native hazels tassel-hung.'

The other answers, 'Yea, but here
    Thy feet have stray'd in after hours
    With thy lost friend among the bowers,
And this hath made them trebly dear.'

These two have striven half the day,
    And each prefers his separate claim,
    Poor rivals in a losing game,
That will not yield each other way.

I turn to go: my feet are set
    To leave the pleasant fields and farms;
    They mix in one another's arms
To one pure image of regret.

CIII

On that last night before we went
    From out the doors where I was bred:
    I dream'd a vision of the dead,
Which left my after-morn content.

Methought I dwelt within a hall,
    And maidens with me: distant hills
    From hidden summits fed with rills
A river sliding by the wall.

The hall with harp and carol rang.
    They sang of what is wise and good
    And graceful. In the centre stood
A statue veil'd, to which they sang;

And which, tho' veil'd, was known to me,
    The shape of him I loved, and love
    For ever: then flew in a dove
And brought a summons from the sea:

And when they learnt that I must go
    They wept and wail'd, but led the way
    To where a little shallop lay
At anchor in the flood below;

And on by many a level mead,
    And shadowing bluff that made the banks,
    We glided winding under ranks
Of iris, and the golden reed;

And still as vaster grew the shore,
    And roll'd the floods in grander space,
    The maidens gather'd strength and grace
And presence, lordlier than before;

And I myself, who sat apart
   And watch'd them, wax'd in every limb;
   I felt the thews of Anakim,
The pulses of a Titan's heart;

As one would sing the death of war,
   And one would chant the history
   Of that great race, which is to be,
And one the shaping of a star;

Until the forward-creeping tides
   Began to foam, and we to draw
   From deep to deep, to where we saw
A great ship lift her shining sides.

The man we loved was there on deck,
   But thrice as large as man he bent
   To greet us. Up the side I went,
And fell in silence on his neck:

Whereat those maidens with one mind
   Bewail'd their lot, I did them wrong:
   'We served thee here,' they said, 'so long,
And wilt thou leave us now behind?'

So rapt I was, they could not win
   An answer from my lips, but he
   Replying, 'Enter likewise ye
And go with us:' they enter'd in.

And while the wind began to sweep
   A music out of sheet and shroud,
   We steer'd her toward a crimson cloud
That landlike slept along the deep.

CIV

The time draws near the birth of Christ;
   The moon is hid, the night is still;
   A single church below the hill
Is pealing, folded in the mist.

A single peal of bells below,
   That wakens at this hour of rest
   A single murmur in the breast,
That these are not the bells I know.

Like strangers' voices here they sound,
    In lands where not a memory strays
    Nor landmark breathes of other days,
But all is new unhallow'd ground.

CV

To-night ungather'd let us leave
    This laurel, let this holly stand:
    We live within the stranger's land,
And strangely falls our Christmas-eve.

Our father's dust is left alone
    And silent under other snows:
    There in due time the woodbine blows,
The violet comes, but we are gone.

No more shall wayward grief abuse
    The genial hour with mask and mime;
    For change of place, like growth of time
Has broke the bond of dying use.

Let cares that petty shadows cast,
    By which our lives are chiefly proved,
    A little spare the night I loved,
And hold it solemn to the past.

But let no footstep beat the floor,
    Nor bowl of wassail mantle warm;
    For who would keep an ancient form
Thro' which the spirit breathes no more?

Be neither song, nor game, nor feast;
    Nor harp be touch'd, nor flute be blown;
    No dance, no motion, save alone
What lightens in the lucid east

Of rising worlds by yonder wood.
    Long sleeps the summer in the seed;
    Run out your measured arcs, and lead
The closing cycle rich in good.

CVI

Ring out, wild bells, to the wild sky,
    The flying cloud, the frosty light:
    The year is dying in the night;
Ring out, wild bells, and let him die.

Ring out the old, ring in the new,
    Ring, happy bells, across the snow:
    The year is going, let him go;
Ring out the false, ring in the true.

Ring out the grief that saps the mind,
    For those that here we see no more;
    Ring out the feud of rich and poor,
Ring in redress to all mankind.

Ring out a slowly dying cause,
    And ancient forms of party strife;
    Ring in the nobler modes of life,
With sweeter manners, purer laws.

Ring out the want, the care, the sin,
    The faithless coldness of the times;
    Ring out, ring out my mournful rhymes
But ring the fuller minstrel in.

Ring out false pride in place and blood,
    The civic slander and the spite;
    Ring in the love of truth and right,
Ring in the common love of good.

Ring out old shapes of foul disease;
    Ring out the narrowing lust of gold;
    Ring out the thousand wars of old,
Ring in the thousand years of peace.

Ring in the valiant man and free,
    The larger heart, the kindlier hand;
    Ring out the darkness of the land,
Ring in the Christ that is to be.

CVII

It is the day when he was born,
    A bitter day that early sank
    Behind a purple-frosty bank
Of valour, leaving night forlorn.

The time admits not flowers or leaves
    To deck the banquet. Fiercely flies
    The blast of North and East, and ice
Makes daggers at the sharpen'd eaves,

And bristles all the brakes and thorns
    To yon hard crescent, as she hangs
    Above the wood which grides and clangs
Its leafless ribs and iron horns

Together, in the drifts that pass
    To darken on the rolling brine
    That breaks the coast. But fetch the wine,
Arrange the board and brim the glass;

Bring in great logs and let them lie,
    To make a solid core of heat;
    Be cheerful-minded, talk and treat
Of all things ev'n as he were by;

We keep the day. With festal cheer,
    With books and music, surely we
    Will drink to him, whate'er he be,
And sing the songs he loved to hear.

CVIII

I will not shut me from my kind,
    And, lest I stiffen into stone,
    I will not eat my heart alone,
Nor feed with sighs a passing wind:

What profit lies in barren faith,
    And vacant yearning, tho' with might
    To scale the heaven's highest height,
Or dive below the wells of Death?

What find I in the highest place,
    But mine own phantom chanting hymns?
    And on the depths of death there swims
The reflex of a human face.

I'll rather take what fruit may be
    Of sorrow under human skies:
    'Tis held that sorrow makes us wise,
Whatever wisdom sleep with thee.

CIX

Heart-affluence in discursive talk
    From household fountains never dry;
    The critic clearness of an eye,
That saw thro' all the Muses' walk;

Seraphic intellect and force
    To seize and throw the doubts of man;
    Impassion'd logic, which outran
The hearer in its fiery course;

High nature amorous of the good,
    But touch'd with no ascetic gloom;
    And passion pure in snowy bloom
Thro' all the years of April blood;

A love of freedom rarely felt,
    Of freedom in her regal seat
    Of England; not the schoolboy heat,
The blind hysterics of the Celt;

And manhood fused with female grace
    In such a sort, the child would twine
    A trustful hand, unask'd, in thine,
And find his comfort in thy face;

All these have been, and thee mine eyes
    Have look'd on: if they look'd in vain,
    My shame is greater who remain,
Nor let thy wisdom make me wise.

CX

Thy converse drew us with delight,
    The men of rathe and riper years:
    The feeble soul, a haunt of fears,
Forgot his weakness in thy sight.

On thee the loyal-hearted hung,
    The proud was half disarm'd of pride,
    Nor cared the serpent at thy side
To flicker with his double tongue.

The stern were mild when thou wert by,
    The flippant put himself to school
    And heard thee, and the brazen fool
Was soften'd, and he knew not why;

While I, thy dearest, sat apart,
    And felt thy triumph was as mine;
    And loved them more, that they were thine,
The graceful tact, the Christian art;

Nor mine the sweetness or the skill,
    But mine the love that will not tire,
    And, born of love, the vague desire
That spurs an imitative will.

CXI

The churl in spirit, up or down
    Along the scale of ranks, thro' all,
    To him who grasps a golden ball,
By blood a king, at heart a clown;

The churl in spirit, howe'er he veil
    His want in forms for fashion's sake,
    Will let his coltish nature break
At seasons thro' the gilded pale:

For who can always act? but he,
    To whom a thousand memories call,
    Not being less but more than all
The gentleness he seem'd to be,

Best seem'd the thing he was, and join'd
    Each office of the social hour
    To noble manners, as the flower
And native growth of noble mind;

Nor ever narrowness or spite,
    Or villain fancy fleeting by,
    Drew in the expression of an eye,
Where God and Nature met in light;

And thus he bore without abuse
    The grand old name of gentleman,
    Defamed by every charlatan,
And soil'd with all ignoble use.

CXII

High wisdom holds my wisdom less,
    That I, who gaze with temperate eyes
    On glorious insufficiencies,
Set light by narrower perfectness.

But thou, that fillest all the room
    Of all my love, art reason why
    I seem to cast a careless eye
On souls, the lesser lords of doom.

For what wert thou? some novel power
    Sprang up for ever at a touch,
    And hope could never hope too much,
In watching thee from hour to hour,

Large elements in order brought,
    And tracts of calm from tempest made,
    And world-wide fluctuation sway'd
In vassal tides that follow'd thought.

CXIII

'Tis held that sorrow makes us wise;
    Yet how much wisdom sleeps with thee
    Which not alone had guided me,
But served the seasons that may rise;

For can I doubt, who knew thee keen
    In intellect, with force and skill
    To strive, to fashion, to fulfil –
I doubt not what thou wouldst have been:

A life in civic action warm,
    A soul on highest mission sent,
    A potent voice of Parliament,
A pillar steadfast in the storm,

Should licensed boldness gather force,
    Becoming, when the time has birth,
    A lever to uplift the earth
And roll it in another course,

With thousand shocks that come and go,
    With agonies, with energies,
    With overthrowings, and with cries,
And undulations to and fro.

CXIV

Who loves not Knowledge? Who shall rail
    Against her beauty? May she mix
    With men and prosper! Who shall fix
Her pillars? Let her work prevail.

But on her forehead sits a fire;
    She sets her forward countenance
    And leaps into the future chance,
Submitting all things to desire.

Half-grown as yet, a child, and vain –
 She cannot fight the fear of death.
 What is she, cut from love and faith,
But some wild Pallas from the brain

Of Demons? fiery-hot to burst
 All barriers in her onward race
 For power. Let her know her place;
She is the second, not the first.

A higher hand must make her mild,
 If all be not in vain; and guide
 Her footsteps, moving side by side
With wisdom, like the younger child:

For she is earthly of the mind,
 But Wisdom heavenly of the soul.
 O, friend, who camest to thy goal
So early, leaving me behind,

I would the great world grew like thee,
 Who grewest not alone in power
 And knowledge, but by year and hour
In reverence and in charity.

CXV

Now fades the last long streak of snow,
 Now burgeons every maze of quick
 About the flowering squares, and thick
By ashen roots the violets blow.

Now rings the woodland loud and long,
 The distance takes a lovelier hue,
 And drown'd in yonder living blue
The lark becomes a sightless song.

Now dance the lights on lawn and lea,
 The flocks are whiter down the vale,
 And milkier every milky sail
On winding stream or distant sea;

Where now the seamew pipes, or dives
 In yonder greening gleam, and fly
 The happy birds, that change their sky
To build and brood; that live their lives

From land to land; and in my breast
　　Spring wakens too; and my regret
　　Becomes an April violet,
And buds and blossoms like the rest.

CXVI

Is it, then, regret for buried time
　　That keenlier in sweet April wakes,
　　And meets the year, and gives and takes
The colours of the crescent prime?

Not all: the songs, the stirring air,
　　The life re-orient out of dust,
　　Cry thro' the sense to hearten trust
In that which made the world so fair.

Not all regret: the face will shine
　　Upon me, while I muse alone;
　　And that dear voice, I once have known,
Still speak to me of me and mine:

Yet less of sorrow lives in me
　　For days of happy commune dead;
　　Less yearning for the friendship fled,
Than some strong bond which is to be.

CXVII

O days and hours, your work is this,
　　To hold me from my proper place,
　　A little while from his embrace,
For fuller gain of after bliss:

That out of distance might ensue
　　Desire of nearness doubly sweet;
　　And unto meeting when we meet,
Delight a hundredfold accrue,

For every grain of sand that runs,
　　And every span of shade that steals,
　　And every kiss of toothed wheels,
And all the courses of the suns.

CXVIII

Contemplate all this work of Time,
　　The giant labouring in his youth;
　　Nor dream of human love and truth,
As dying Nature's earth and lime;

But trust that those we call the dead
    Are breathers of an ampler day
    For ever nobler ends. They say,
The solid earth whereon we tread

In tracts of fluent heat began,
    And grew to seeming-random forms,
    The seeming prey of cyclic storms,
Till at the last arose the man;

Who throve and branch'd from clime to clime,
    The herald of a higher race,
    And of himself in higher place.
If so he type this work of time

Within himself, from more to more;
    Or, crown'd with attributes of woe
    Like glories, move his course, and show
That life is not as idle ore,

But iron dug from central gloom,
    And heated hot with burning fears,
    And dipt in baths of hissing tears,
And batter'd with the shocks of doom

To shape and use. Arise and fly
    The reeling Faun, the sensual feast;
    Move upward, working out the beast,
And let the ape and tiger die.

CXIX

Doors, where my heart was used to beat
    So quickly, not as one that weeps
    I come once more; the city sleeps;
I smell the meadow in the street;

I hear a chirp of birds; I see
    Betwixt the black fronts long-withdrawn
    A light-blue lane of early dawn,
And think of early days and thee,

And bless thee, for thy lips are bland
    And bright the friendship of thine eye;
    And in my thoughts with scarce a sigh
I take the pressure of thine hand.

CXX

I trust I have not wasted breath:
   I think we are not wholly brain,
   Magnetic mockeries; not in vain,
Like Paul with beasts, I fought with Death;

Not only cunning casts in clay:
   Let Science prove we are, and then
   What matters Science unto men,
At least to me? I would not stay.

Let him, the wiser man who springs
   Hereafter, up from childhood shape
   His action like the greater ape,
But I was born to other things.

CXXI

Sad Hesper o'er the buried sun
   And ready, thou, to die with him,
   Thou watchest all things ever dim
And dimmer, and a glory done:

The team is loosen'd from the wain,
   The boat is drawn upon the shore;
   Thou listenest to the closing door,
And life is darken'd in the brain.

Bright Phosphor, fresher for the night,
   By thee the world's great work is heard
   Beginning, and the wakeful bird;
Behind thee comes the greater light:

The market boat is on the stream,
   And voices hail it from the brink;
   Thou hear'st the village hammer clink,
And see'st the moving of the team.

Sweet Hesper-Phosphor, double name
   For what is one, the first, the last,
   Thou, like my present and my past,
Thy place is changed; thou art the same.

CXXII

Oh, wast thou with me, dearest, then,
   While I rose up against my doom,
   And yearn'd to burst the folded gloom,
To bare the eternal Heavens again,

To feel once more, in placid awe,
    The strong imagination roll
    A sphere of stars about my soul,
In all her motion one with law;

If thou wert with me, and the grave
    Divide us not, be with me now,
    And enter in at breast and brow,
Till all my blood, a fuller wave,

Be quicken'd with a livelier breath,
    And like an inconsiderate boy,
    As in the former flash of joy,
I slip the thoughts of life and death;

And all the breeze of Fancy blows,
    And every dew-drop paints a bow,
    The wizard lightnings deeply glow,
And every thought breaks out a rose.

CXXIII

There rolls the deep where grew the tree.
    O earth, what changes hast thou seen!
    There where the long street roars, hath been
The stillness of the central sea.

The hills are shadows, and they flow
    From form to form, and nothing stands;
    They melt like mist, the solid lands,
Like clouds they shape themselves and go.

But in my spirit will I dwell,
    And dream my dream, and hold it true;
    For tho' my lips may breathe adieu,
I cannot think the thing farewell.

CXXIV

That which we dare invoke to bless;
    Our dearest faith; our ghastliest doubt;
    He, They, One, All; within, without;
The Power in darkness whom we guess;

I found Him not in world or sun,
    Or eagle's wing, or insect's eye;
    Nor thro' the questions men may try,
The petty cobwebs we have spun:

If e'er when faith had fall'n asleep,
    I heard a voice 'believe no more'
    And heard an ever-breaking shore
That tumbled in the Godless deep;

A warmth within the breast would melt
    The freezing reason's colder part,
    And like a man in wrath the heart
Stood up and answer'd 'I have felt.'

No, like a child in doubt and fear:
    But that blind clamour made me wise;
    Then was I as a child that cries,
But, crying, knows his father near;

And what I am beheld again
    What is, and no man understands;
    And out of darkness came the hands
That reach thro' nature, moulding men.

CXXV

Whatever I have said or sung,
    Some bitter notes my harp would give,
    Yea, tho' there often seem'd to live
A contradiction on the tongue,

Yet Hope had never lost her youth;
    She did but look through dimmer eyes;
    Or Love but play'd with gracious lies,
Because he felt so fix'd in truth:

And if the song were full of care,
    He breathed the spirit of the song;
    And if the words were sweet and strong
He set his royal signet there;

Abiding with me till I sail
    To seek thee on the mystic deeps,
    And this electric force, that keeps
A thousand pulses dancing, fail.

CXXVI

Love is and was my Lord and King,
    And in his presence I attend
    To hear the tidings of my friend,
Which every hour his couriers bring.

Love is and was my King and Lord,
        And will be, tho' as yet I keep
        Within his court on earth, and sleep
Encompass'd by his faithful guard,

And hear at times a sentinel
        Who moves about from place to place,
        And whispers to the worlds of space,
In the deep night, that all is well.

CXXVII

And all is well, tho' faith and form
        Be sunder'd in the night of fear;
        Well roars the storm to those that hear
A deeper voice across the storm,

Proclaiming social truth shall spread,
        And justice, ev'n tho' thrice again
        The red fool-fury of the Seine
Should pile her barricades with dead.

But ill for him that wears a crown,
        And him, the lazar, in his rags:
        They tremble, the sustaining crags;
The spires of ice are toppled down,

And molten up, and roar in flood;
        The fortress crashes from on high,
        The brute earth lightens to the sky,
And the great Aeon sinks in blood,

And compass'd by the fires of Hell;
        While thou, dear spirit, happy star,
        O'erlook'st the tumult from afar,
And smilest, knowing all is well.

CXXVIII

The love that rose on stronger wings,
        Unpalsied when he met with Death,
        Is comrade of the lesser faith
That sees the course of human things.

No doubt vast eddies in the flood
        Of onward time shall yet be made,
        And throned races may degrade;
Yet O ye mysteries of good,

Wild Hours that fly with Hope and Fear,
    If all your office had to do
    With old results that look like new;
If this were all your mission here,

To draw, to sheathe a useless sword,
    To fool the crowd with glorious lies,
    To cleave a creed in sects and cries,
To change the bearing of a word,

To shift an arbitrary power,
    To cramp the student at his desk,
    To make old bareness picturesque
And tuft with grass a feudal tower;

Why then my scorn might well descend
    On you and yours. I see in part
    That all, as in some piece of art,
Is toil cöoperant to an end.

CXXIX

Dear friend, far off, my lost desire,
    So far, so near in woe and weal;
    O loved the most, when most I feel
There is a lower and a higher;

Known and unknown; human, divine;
    Sweet human hand and lips and eye;
    Dear heavenly friend that canst not die,
Mine, mine, for ever, ever mine;

Strange friend, past, present, and to be;
    Loved deeplier, darklier understood;
    Behold, I dream a dream of good,
And mingle all the world with thee.

CXXX

Thy voice is on the rolling air;
    I hear thee where the waters run;
    Thou standest in the rising sun,
And in the setting thou art fair.

What art thou then? I cannot guess;
    But tho' I seem in star and flower
    To feel thee some diffusive power,
I do not therefore love thee less:

My love involves the love before;
    My love is vaster passion now;
    Tho' mix'd with God and Nature thou,
I seem to love thee more and more.

Far off thou art, but ever nigh;
    I have thee still, and I rejoice;
    I prosper, circled with thy voice;
I shall not lose thee tho' I die.

CXXXI

O living will that shalt endure
    When all that seems shall suffer shock,
    Rise in the spiritual rock,
Flow thro' our deeds and make them pure,

That we may lift from out of dust
    A voice as unto him that hears,
    A cry above the conquer'd years
To one that with us works, and trust,

With faith that comes of self-control,
    The truths that never can be proved
    Until we close with all we loved
And all we flow from, soul in soul.

*

O true and tried, so well and long,
    Demand not thou a marriage lay;
    In that it is thy marriage day
Is music more than any song.

Nor have I felt so much of bliss
    Since first he told me that he loved
    A daughter of our house; nor proved
Since that dark day a day like this;

Tho' I since then have number'd o'er
    Some thrice three years: they went and came,
    Remade the blood and changed the frame,
And yet is love not less, but more;

No longer caring to embalm
    In dying songs a dead regret,
    But like a statue solid-set,
And moulded in colossal calm.

Regret is dead, but love is more
　　Than in the summers that are flown,
　　For I myself with these have grown
To something greater than before;

Which makes appear the songs I made
　　As echoes out of weaker times,
　　As half but idle brawling rhymes,
The sport of random sun and shade.

But where is she, the bridal flower
　　That must be made a wife ere noon?
　　She enters, glowing like the moon
Of Eden on its bridal bower:

On me she bends her blissful eyes
　　And then on thee; they meet thy look
　　And brighten like the star that shook
Betwixt the palms of paradise.

O when her life was yet in bud,
　　He too foretold the perfect rose.
　　For thee she grew, for thee she grows
For ever, and as fair as good.

And thou art worthy; full of power;
　　As gentle; liberal-minded, great,
　　Consistent; wearing all that weight
Of learning lightly like a flower.

But now set out: the noon is near,
　　And I must give away the bride;
　　She fears not, or with thee beside
And me behind her, will not fear:

For I that danced her on my knee,
　　That watch'd her on her nurse's arm,
　　That shielded all her life from harm
At last must part with her to thee;

Now waiting to be made a wife,
　　Her feet, my darling, on the dead;
　　Their pensive tablets round her head,
And the most living words of life

Breathed in her ear. The ring is on,
    The 'wilt thou' answer'd, and again
    The 'wilt thou' ask'd, till out of twain
Her sweet 'I will' has made ye one.

Now sign your names, which shall be read,
    Mute symbols of a joyful morn,
    By village eyes as yet unborn;
The names are sign'd, and overhead

Begins the clash and clang that tells
    The joy to every wandering breeze;
    The blind wall rocks, and on the trees
The dead leaf trembles to the bells.

O happy hour, and happier hours
    Await them. Many a merry face
    Salutes them – maidens of the place,
That pelt us in the porch with flowers.

O happy hour, behold the bride
    With him to whom her hand I gave.
    They leave the porch, they pass the grave
That has to-day its sunny side.

To-day the grave is bright for me,
    For them the light of life increased,
    Who stay to share the morning feast,
Who rest to-night beside the sea.

Let all my genial spirits advance
    To meet and greet a whiter sun;
    My drooping memory will not shun
The foaming grape of eastern France.

It circles round, and fancy plays,
    And hearts are warm'd and faces bloom,
    As drinking health to bride and groom
We wish them store of happy days.

Nor count me all to blame if I
    Conjecture of a stiller guest,
    Perchance, perchance, among the rest,
And, tho' in silence, wishing joy.

But they must go, the time draws on,
 And those white-favour'd horses wait;
 They rise, but linger; it is late;
Farewell, we kiss, and they are gone.

A shade falls on us like the dark
 From little cloudlets on the grass,
 But sweeps away as out we pass
To range the woods, to roam the park,

Discussing how their courtship grew,
 And talk of others that are wed,
 And how she look'd, and what he said,
And back we come at fall of dew.

Again the feast, the speech, the glee,
 The shade of passing thought, the wealth
 Of words and wit, the double health,
Tho crowning cup, the three-times-three,

And last the dance; – till I retire:
 Dumb is that tower which spake so loud,
 And high in heaven the streaming cloud,
And on the downs a rising fire:

And rise, O moon, from yonder down,
 Till over down and over dale
 All night the shining vapour sail
And pass the silent-lighted town,

The white-faced halls, the glancing rills,
 And catch at every mountain head,
 And o'er the friths that branch and spread
Their sleeping silver thro' the hills;

And touch with shade the bridal doors,
 With tender gloom the roof, the wall;
 And breaking let the splendour fall
To spangle all the happy shores

By which they rest, and ocean sounds,
 And, star and system rolling past,
 A soul shall draw from out the vast
And strike his being into bounds,

And, moved thro' life of lower phase,
    Result in man, be born and think,
    And act and love, a closer link
Betwixt us and the crowning race

Of those that, eye to eye, shall look
    On knowledge; under whose command
    Is Earth and Earth's, and in their hand
Is Nature like an open book;

No longer half-akin to brute
    For all we thought and loved and did,
    And hoped, and suffer'd, is but seed
Of what in them is flower and fruit;

Whereof the man, that with me trod
    This planet, was a noble type
    Appearing ere the times were ripe,
That friend of mine who lives in God,

That God, which ever lives and loves,
    One God, one law, one element,
    And one far-off divine event,
To which the whole creation moves.

Edwin Morris; or The Lake

O me, my pleasant rambles by the lake,
My sweet, wild, fresh three quarters of a year
My one Oasis in the dust and drouth
Of city life! I was a sketcher then:
See here, my doing: curves of mountain, bridge,
Boat, island, ruins of a castle, built
When men knew how to build, upon a rock,
With turrets lichen-gilded like a rock:
And here, new-comers in an ancient hold,
New-comers from the Mersey, millionaires
Here lived the Hills – a Tudor-chimnied bulk
Of mellow brickwork on an isle of bowers.

  O me, my pleasant rambles by the lake
With Edwin Morris and with Edward Bull
The curate; he was fatter than his cure.

  But Edwin Morris, he that knew the names,
Long learned names of agaric, moss and fern,

Who forged a thousand theories of the rocks,
Who taught me how to skate, to row, to swim,
Who read me rhymes elaborately good,
His own – I call'd him Crichton, for he seem'd
All-perfect, finish'd to the finger nail.

    And once I ask'd him of his early life,
And his first passion; and he answer'd me;
And well his words became him: was he not
A full-cell'd honeycomb of eloquence
Stored from all flowers? Poet-like he spoke.

    'My love for Nature is as old as I;
But thirty moons, one honeymoon to that,
And three rich sennights more, my love for her.
My love for Nature and my love for her,
Of different ages, like twin-sisters grew
Twin-sisters differently beautiful.
To some full music rose and sank the sun,
And some full music seem'd to move and change
With all the varied changes of the dark,
And either twilight and the day between;
For daily hope fulfill'd, to rise again
Revolving toward fulfilment, made it sweet
To walk, to sit, to sleep, to wake, to breathe.'

    Or this or something like to this he spoke.
Then said the fat-faced curate Edward Bull,
    'I take it, God made the woman for the man,
And for the good and increase of the world.
A pretty face is well, and this is well
To have a dame indoors, that trims us up
And keeps us tight; but these unreal ways
Seem but the theme of writers, and indeed
Worn threadbare. Man is made of solid stuff.
I say, God made the woman for the man,
And for the good and increase of the world.'

    'Parson,' said I, 'you pitch the pipe too low:
But I have sudden touches, and can run
My faith beyond my practice into his:
Tho' if, in dancing after Letty Hill,
I do not hear the bells upon my cap,
I scarce hear other music: yet say on.
What should one give to light on such a dream?'
I ask'd him half-sardonically.

'Give?
Give all thou art,' he answer'd, and a light
Of laughter dimpled in his swarthy cheek;
'I would have hid her needle in my heart,
To save her little finger from a scratch
No deeper than the skin: my ears could hear
Her lightest breaths: her least remark was worth
The experience of the wise. I went and came;
Her voice fled always thro' the summer land;
I spoke her name alone. Thrice-happy days!
The flower of each, those moments when we met,
The crown of all, we met to part no more.'

Were not his words delicious, I a beast
To take them as I did? but something jarr'd;
Whether he spoke too largely; that there seem'd
A touch of something false, some self-conceit,
Or over-smoothness: howsoe'er it was,
He scarcely hit my humour, and I said:

'Friend Edwin, do not think yourself alone
Of all men happy. Shall not Love to me,
As in the Latin song I learnt at school,
Sneeze out a full God-bless-you right and left?
But you can talk: yours is a kindly vein: I have,
I think, – Heaven knows – as much within;
Have, or should have, but for a thought or two,
That like a purple beech among the greens
Looks out of place: 'tis from no want in her:
It is my shyness, or my self-distrust,
Or something of a wayward modern mind
Dissecting passion. Time will set me right.'

So spoke I knowing not the things that were.
Then said the fat-faced curate, Edward Bull:
'God made the woman for the use of man,
And for the good and increase of the world.'
And I and Edwin laugh'd, and now we paused
About the windings of the marge to hear
The soft wind blowing over meadowy holms
And alders, garden-isles; and now we left
The clerk behind us, I and he, and ran
By ripply shallows of the lisping lake,
Delighted with the freshness and the sound.

But, when the bracken rusted on their crags,
My suit had wither'd, nipt to death by him

That was a God, and is a lawyer's clerk,
The rentroll Cupid of our rainy isles.
'Tis true, we met; one hour I had, no more:
She sent a note, the seal an *Elle vous suit,*
The close 'Your Letty, only yours'; and this
Thrice underscored. The friendly mist of morn
Clung to the lake. I boated over, ran
My craft aground, and heard with beating heart
The Sweet-Gale rustle round the shelving keel;
And out I stept, and up I crept: she moved
Like Proserpine in Enna, gathering flowers:
Then low and sweet I whistled thrice; and she,
She turn'd, we closed, we kiss'd, swore faith, I breathed
In some new planet: a silent cousin stole
Upon us and departed: 'Leave,' she cried,
'O leave me!' 'Never, dearest, never: here
I brave the worst: 'And while we stood like fools
Embracing, all at once a score of pugs
And poodles yell'd within, and out they came
Trustees and Aunts and Uncles. 'What, with him!
Go!' (shrill'd the cotton-spinning chorus) 'him!'
I choked. Again they shriek'd the burthen 'Him!'
Again with hands of wild rejection 'Go! –
Girl, get you in!' She went – and in one month
They wedded her to sixty thousand pounds,
To lands in Kent and messuages in York,
And slight Sir Robert with his watery smile
And educated whisker. But for me,
They set an ancient creditor to work:
It seems I broke a close with force and arms:
There came a mystic token from the king
To greet the sheriff, needless courtesy!
I read, and fled by night, and flying turn'd:
Her taper glimmer'd in the lake below:
I turn'd once more, close-button'd to the storm;
So left the place, left Edwin, nor have seen
Him since, nor heard of her, nor cared to hear.

Nor cared to hear? perhaps: yet long ago
I have pardon'd little Letty, not indeed
It may be, for her own dear sake but this,
She seems a part of those fresh days to me;
For in the dust and drouth of London life
She moves among my visions of the lake,
While the prime swallow dips his wing, or then
While the gold-lily blows, and overhead
The light cloud smoulders on the summer crag.

Come not when I am Dead

Come not, when I am dead,
    To drop thy foolish tears upon my grave,
To trample round my fallen head,
    And vex the unhappy dust thou wouldst not save.
There let the wind sweep and the plover cry;
    But thou, go by.

Child, if it were thine error or thy crime
    I care no longer, being all unblest:
Wed whom thou wilt, but I am sick of Time,
    And I desire to rest.
Pass on, weak heart, and leave me where I lie:
    Go by, go by.

The Eagle

Fragment

He clasps the crag with crooked hands;
Close to the sun in lonely lands,
Ring'd with the azure world, he stands.

The wrinkled sea beneath him crawls;
He watches from his mountain walls,
And like a thunderbolt he falls.

Sonnet to W. C. Macready

Farewell, Macready, since to-night we part;
    Full-handed thunders often have confessed
    Thy power, well-used to move the public breast.
We thank thee with our voice, and from the heart.
Farewell, Macready, since this night we part.
    Go, take thine honours home; rank with the best,
    Garrick and statelier Kemble, and the rest
Who made a nation purer through their art.
Thine is it that our drama did not die,
    Nor flicker down to brainless pantomime,
    And those gilt gauds men-children swarm to see.
Farewell, Macready; moral, grave, sublime;
Our Shakespeare's bland and universal eye
    Dwells pleased, through twice a hundred years, on thee.

The Third of February 1852

My Lords, we heard you speak: you told us all
   That England's honest censure went too far;
That our free press should cease to brawl,
   Not sting the fiery Frenchman into war.
It was our ancient privilege, my Lords,
To fling whate'er we felt, not fearing, into words.

We love not this French God, the child of Hell,
   Wild War, who breaks the converse of the wise;
But though we love kind Peace so well,
   We dare not ev'n by silence sanction lies.
It might be safe our censures to withdraw;
And yet, my Lords, not well: there is a higher law.

As long as we remain, we must speak free
   Tho' all the storm of Europe on us break;
No little German state are we,
   But the one voice in Europe: we *must* speak;
That if to-night our greatness were struck dead,
There might be left some record of the things we said.

If you be fearful, then must we be bold.
   Our Britain cannot salve a tyrant o'er.
Better the waste Atlantic roll'd
   On her and us and ours for evermore.
What! have we fought for Freedom from our prime,
At last to dodge and palter with a public crime?

Shall we fear *him*? our own we never fear'd.
   From our first Charles by force we wrung our claims.
Prick'd by the Papal spur, we rear'd,
   We flung the burthen of the second James.
I say, we *never* fear'd! and as for these,
We broke them on the land, we drove them on the seas.

And you, my Lords, you make the people muse
   In doubt if you be of our Barons' breed –
Were those your sires who fought at Lewes
   Is this the manly strain of Runnymede?
O fall'n nobility, that, overawed,
Would lisp in honey'd whispers of this monstrous fraud!

We feel, at least, that silence here were sin,
   Not ours the fault if we have feeble hosts –

If easy patrons of their kin
   Have left the last free race with naked coasts!
They knew the precious things they had to guard:
For us, we will not spare the tyrant one hard word.

Tho' niggard throats of Manchester may bawl,
   What England was, shall her true sons forget?
We are not cotton-spinners all,
   But some love England and her honour yet.
And these in our Thermopylae shall stand,
And hold against the world this honour of the land.

Hands All Round

First drink a health, this solemn night,
   A health to England, every guest;
That man's the best cosmopolite
   Who loves his native country best.
May Freedom's oak for ever live
   With stronger life from day to day;
That man's the true Conservative,
   Who lops the moulder'd branch away.
      Hands all round!
      God the tyrant's hope confound!
    To this great cause of freedom drink, my friends,
     And the great name of England round and round.

A health to Europe's honest men!
   Heaven guard them from her tyrants' jails!
From wrong'd Poerio's noisome den,
   From iron'd limbs and tortured nails!
We curse the crimes of southern kings,
   The Russian whips and Austrian rods –
We, likewise, have our evil things;
   Too much we make our Ledgers, Gods,
      Yet hands all round!
      God the tyrant's cause confound!
    To Europe's better health we drink, my friends,
     And the great name of England round and round.

What health to France, if France be she,
   Whom martial prowess only charms?
Yet tell her – Better to be free
   Than vanquish all the world in arms.

Her frantic city's flashing heats
   But fire, to blast, the hopes of men.
Why change the titles of your streets?
   You fools, you'll want them all again.
       Yet hands all round!
        God their tyrant's cause confound!
     To France, the wiser France, we drink, my friends,
     And the great name of England round and round.

Gigantic daughter of the West,
   We drink to thee across the flood,
We know thee most, we love thee best,
   For art thou not of British blood?
Should war's mad blast again be blown,
   Permit not thou the tyrant powers
To fight thy mother here alone,
   But let thy broadsides roar with ours,
       Hands all round!
        God the tyrant's cause confound!
     To our great kinsmen of the West, my friends,
     And the great name of England round and round.

O rise, our strong Atlantic sons,
   When war against our freedom springs!
O speak to Europe thro' your guns!
   They *can* be understood by kings.
You must not mix our Queen with those
   That wish to keep their people fools;
Our freedom's foemen are her foes,
   She comprehends the race she rules.
       Hands all round!
        God the tyrant's cause confound!
     To our dear kinsmen of the West, my friends,
     And the great cause of freedom round and round.

Ode on the Death of the Duke of Wellington

I

Bury the Great Duke
   With an empire's lamentation,
Let us bury the Great Duke
   To the noise of the mourning of a mighty nation,
Mourning when their leaders fall,
Warriors carry the warrior's pall,
And sorrow darkens hamlet and hall.

II

Where shall we lay the man whom we deplore?
Here, in streaming London's central roar.
Let the sound of those he wrought for,
And the feet of those he fought for,
Echo round his bones for evermore.

III

Lead out the pageant: sad and slow,
As fits an universal woe,
Let the long long procession go,
And let the sorrowing crowd about it grow,
And let the mournful martial music blow:
The last great Englishman is low.

IV

Mourn, for to us he seems the last,
Remembering all his greatness in the Past
No more in soldier fashion will he greet
With lifted hand the gazer in the street.
O friends, our chief state-oracle is mute:
Mourn for the man of long-enduring blood,
The statesman-warrior, moderate, resolute,
Whole in himself, a common good.
Mourn for the man of amplest influence,
Yet clearest of ambitious crime,
Our greatest yet with least pretence,
Great in council and great in war,
Foremost captain of his time,
Rich in saving common-sense,
And, as the greatest only are,
In his simplicity sublime.
O good grey head which all men knew,
O voice from which their omens all men drew,
O iron nerve to true occasion true,
O fall'n at length that tower of strength
Which stood four-square to all the winds that blew!
Such was he whom we deplore.
The long self-sacrifice of life is o'er.
The great World-victor's victor will be seen no more.

V

All is over and done:
Render thanks to the Giver,
England, for thy son.
Let the bell be toll'd.
Render thanks to the Giver,

And render him to the mould.
Under the cross of gold
That shines over city and river,
There he shall rest for ever
Among the wise and the bold.
Let the bell be toll'd:
And a reverent people behold
The towering car, the sable steeds:
Bright let it be with its blazon'd deeds,
Dark in its funeral fold.
Let the bell be toll'd:
And a deeper knell in the heart be knoll'd;
And the sound of the sorrowing anthem roll'd
Thro' the dome of the golden cross;
And the volleying cannon thunder his loss;
He knew their voices of old.
For many a time in many a clime
His captain's-ear has heard them boom
Bellowing victory, bellowing doom:
When he with those deep voices wrought,
Guarding realms and kings from shame;
With those deep voices our dead captain taught
The tyrant, and asserts his claim
In that dread sound to the great name,
Which he has worn so pure of blame,
In praise and in dispraise the same,
A man of well-attemper'd frame.
O civic muse, to such a name,
To such a name for ages long,
To such a name
Preserve a broad approach of fame,
And ever-echoing avenues of song.

VI

Who is he that cometh, like an honour'd guest,
With banner and with music, with soldier and with priest,
With a nation weeping, and breaking on my rest?
Mighty Seaman, this is he
Was great by land as thou by sea.
Thine island loves thee well, thou famous man,
The greatest sailor since our world began.
Now, to the roll of muffled drums,
To thee the greatest soldier comes;
For this is he
Was great by land as thou by sea;
His foes were thine; he kept us free;
O give him welcome, this is he

Worthy of our gorgeous rites,
And worthy to be laid by thee;
For this is England's greatest son,
He that gain'd a hundred fights,
Nor ever lost an English gun;
This is he that far away
Against the myriads of Assaye
Clash'd with his fiery few and won,
And underneath another sun,
Warring on a later day,
Round affrighted Lisbon drew
The treble works, the vast designs
Of his labour'd rampart-lines,
Where he greatly stood at bay,
Whence he issued forth anew,
And ever great and greater grew
Beating from the wasted vines
Back to France her banded swarms,
Back to France with countless blows,
Till o'er the hills her eagles flew
Beyond the Pyrenean pines,
Follow'd up in valley and glen
With blare of bugle, clamour of men,
Roll of cannon and clash of arms,
And England pouring on her foes.
Such a war had such a close.
Again their ravening eagle rose
In anger, wheel'd on Europe-shadowing wings,
And barking for the thrones of kings;
Till one that sought but Duty's iron crown
On that loud sabbath shook the spoiler down;
A day of onsets of despair!
Dash'd on every rocky square
Their surging charges foam'd themselves away;
Last, the Prussian trumpet blew;
Thro' the long-tormented air
Heaven flash'd a sudden jubilant ray,
And down we swept and charged and overthrew.
So great a soldier taught us there,
What long-enduring hearts could do
In that world's-earthquake, Waterloo!
Mighty Seaman, tender and true,
And pure as he from taint of craven guile,
O saviour of the silver-coasted isle,
O shaker of the Baltic and the Nile,
If aught of things that here befall
Touch a spirit among things divine,

If love of country move thee there at all,
Be glad, because his bones are laid by thine!
And thro' the centuries let a people's voice
In full acclaim,
A people's voice,
The proof and echo of all human fame,
A people's voice, when they rejoice
At civic revel and pomp and game,
Attest their great commander's claim
With honour, honour, honour, honour to him,
Eternal honour to his name.

VII

A people's voice! we are a people yet.
Tho' all men else their nobler dreams forget,
Confused by brainless mobs and lawless Powers;
Thank Him who isled us here, and roughly set
His Briton in blown seas and storming showers,
We have a voice, with which to pay the debt
Of boundless love and reverence and regret
To those great men who fought, and kept it ours.
And keep it ours, O God, from brute control;
O Statesmen, guard us, guard the eye, the soul
Of Europe, keep our noble England whole,
And save the one true seed of freedom sown
Betwixt a people and their ancient throne,
That sober freedom out of which there springs
Our loyal passion for our temperate kings;
For, saving that, ye help to save mankind
Till public wrong be crumbled into dust,
And drill the raw world for the march of mind,
Till crowds at length be sane and crowns be just.
But wink no more in slothful overtrust.
Remember him who led your hosts;
He bad you guard the sacred coasts.
Your cannons moulder on the seaward walls:
His voice is silent in your council-hall
For ever; and whatever tempests lour
For ever silent; even if they broke
In thunder, silent; yet remember all
He spoke among you, and the Man who spoke;
Who never sold the truth to serve the hour,
Nor palter'd with Eternal God for power;
Who let the turbid streams of rumour flow
Thro' either babbling world of high and low;
Whose life was work, whose language rife

With rugged maxims hewn from life;
Who never spoke against a foe;
Whose eighty winters freeze with one rebuke
All great self-seekers trampling on the right:
Truth-teller was our England's Alfred named;
Truth-lover was our English Duke;
Whatever record leap to light
He never shall be shamed.

VIII

Lo, the leader in these glorious wars
Now to glorious burial slowly borne,
Follow'd by the brave of other lands,
He, on whom from both her open hands
Lavish Honour shower'd all her stars,
And affluent Fortune emptied all her horn.
Yea, let all good things await
Him who cares not to be great,
But as he saves or serves the state.
Not once or twice in our rough island-story,
The path of duty was the way to glory;
He that walks it, only thirsting
For the right, and learns to deaden
Love of self, before his journey closes,
He shall find the stubborn thistle bursting
Into glossy purples, which outredden
All voluptuous garden-roses.
Not once or twice in our fair island-story,
The path of duty was the way to glory:
He, that ever following her commands,
On with toil of heart and knees and hands,
Thro' the long gorge to the far light has won
His path upward, and prevail'd,
Shall find the toppling crags of Duty scaled
Are close upon the shining table-lands
To which our God Himself is moon and sun.
Such was he: his work is done,
But while the races of mankind endure,
Let his great example stand
Colossal, seen of every land,
And keep the soldier firm, the statesman pure:
Till in all lands and thro' all human story
The path of duty be the way to glory:
And let the land whose hearths he saved from shame
For many and many an age proclaim
At civic revel and pomp and game,

And when the long-illumined cities flame,
Their ever-loyal iron leader's fame,
With honour, honour, honour, honour to him,
Eternal honour to his name.

IX

Peace, his triumph will be sung
By some yet unmoulded tongue
Far on in summers that we shall not see:
Peace, it is a day of pain
For one about whose patriarchal knee
Late the little children clung:
O peace, it is a day of pain
For one, upon whose hand and heart and brain
Once the weight and fate of Europe hung.
Ours the pain, be his the gain!
More than is of man's degree
Must be with us, watching here
At this, our great solemnity.
Whom we see not we revere,
We revere, and we refrain
From talk of battles loud and vain,
And brawling memories all too free
For such a wise humility
As befits a solemn fane:
We revere, and while we hear
The tides of Music's golden sea
Setting toward eternity,
Uplifted high in heart and hope are we,
Until we doubt not that for one so true
There must be other nobler work to do
Than when he fought at Waterloo,
And Victor he must ever be.
For tho' the Giant Ages heave the hill
And break the shore, and evermore
Make and break, and work their will;
Tho' world on world in myriad myriads roll
Round us, each with different powers,
And other forms of life than ours,
What know we greater than the soul?
On God and Godlike men we build our trust.
Hush, the Dead March wails in the people's ears:
The dark crowd moves, and there are sobs and tears:
The black earth yawns: the mortal disappears;
Ashes to ashes, dust to dust;
He is gone who seem'd so great. —

Gone; but nothing can bereave him
Of the force he made his own
Being here, and we believe him
Something far advanced in State,
And that he wears a truer crown
Than any wreath that man can weave him.
Speak no more of his renown,
Lay your earthly fancies down,
And in the vast cathedral leave him.
God accept him, Christ receive him.

To E. L. on his Travels in Greece

Illyrian woodlands, echoing falls
  Of water, sheets of summer glass,
  The long divine Peneïan pass,
The vast Akrokeraunian walls,

Tomohrit, Athos, all things fair,
  With such a pencil, such a pen,
  You shadow forth to distant men,
I read and felt that I was there:

And trust me while I turn'd the page,
  And track'd you still on classic ground,
  I grew in gladness till I found
My spirits in the golden age.

For me the torrent ever pour'd
  And glisten'd – here and there alone
  The broad-limb'd Gods at random thrown
By fountain-urns; – and Naiads oar'd

A glimmering shoulder under gloom
  Of cavern pillars; on the swell
  The silver lily heaved and fell
And many a slope was rich in bloom

From him that on the mountain lea
  By dancing rivulets fed his flocks,
  To him who sat upon the rocks,
And fluted to the morning sea.

The Charge of the Light Brigade

I

Half a league, half a league,
  Half a league onward,
All in the valley of Death
  Rode the six hundred.
'Forward, the Light Brigade!
Charge for the guns!' he said;
Into the valley of Death
  Rode the six hundred.

II

'Forward, the Light Brigade!'
Was there a man dismay'd?
Not tho' the soldier knew
  Some one had blunder'd:
Their's not to make reply,
Their's not to reason why,
Their's but to do and die:
Into the valley of Death
  Rode the six hundred.

III

Cannon to right of them,
Cannon to left of them,
Cannon in front of them
  Volley'd and thunder'd;
Storm'd at with shot and shell,
Boldly they rode and well,
Into the jaws of Death,
Into the mouth of Hell
  Rode the six hundred.

IV

Flash'd all their sabres bare,
Flash'd as they turn'd in air,
Sabring the gunners there,
Charging an army, while
  All the world wonder'd:
Plunged in the battery-smoke
Right thro' the line they broke;
Cossack and Russian
Reel'd from the sabre-stroke
  Shatter'd and sunder'd.
Then they rode back, but not,
  Not the six hundred.

V

Cannon to right of them,
Cannon to left of them,
Cannon behind them
  Volley'd and thunder'd;
Storm'd at with shot and shell,
While horse and hero fell,
They that had fought so well
Came thro' the jaws of Death
Back from the mouth of Hell,
All that was left of them,
  Left of six hundred.

VI

When can their glory fade?
O the wild charge they made!
  All the world wonder'd.
Honour the charge they made!
Honour the Light Brigade,
  Noble six hundred!

MAUD, AND OTHER POEMS

Maud: Part 1

I

I

I hate the dreadful hollow behind the little wood,
Its lips in the field above are dabbled with blood-red heath,
The red-ribb'd ledges drip with a silent horror of blood,
And Echo there, whatever is ask'd her, answers 'Death.'

II

For there in the ghastly pit long since a body was found,
His who had given me life – O father! O God! was it well? –
Mangled, and flatten'd, and crush'd, and dinted into the ground:
There yet lies the rock that fell with him when he fell.

III

Did he fling himself down? who knows? for a vast speculation had
    fail'd,
And over he mutter'd and madden'd, and ever wann'd with despair,
And out he walk'd when the wind like a broken worldling wail'd,
And the flying gold of the ruin'd woodlands drove thro' the air.

IV

I remember the time, for the roots of my hair were stirr'd
By a shuffled step, by a dead weight trail'd, by a whisper'd fright,
And my pulses closed their gates with a shock on my heart as I heard
The shrill-edged shriek of a mother divide the shuddering night.

V

Villany somewhere! whose? One says, we are villains all.
Not he: his honest fame should at least by me be maintained:
But that old man, now lord of the broad estate and the Hall,
Dropt off gorged from a scheme that had left us flaccid and drain'd.

VI

Why do they prate of the blessings of Peace? we have made them a
    curse,
Pickpockets, each hand lusting for all that is not its own;
And lust of gain, in the spirit of Cain, is it better or worse
Than the heart of the citizen hissing in war on his own hearthstone?

VII

But these are the days of advance, the works of the men of mind,
When who but a fool would have faith in a tradesman's ware or his
    word?
Is it peace or war? Civil war, as I think, and that of a kind
The viler, as underhand, not openly bearing the sword.

VIII

Sooner or later I too may passively take the print
Of the golden age – why not? I have neither hope nor trust;
May make my heart as a millstone, set my face as a flint,
Cheat and be cheated, and die: who knows? we are ashes and dust.

IX

Peace sitting under her olive, and slurring the days gone by,
When the poor are hovell'd and hustled together, each sex, like swine,
When only the ledger lives, and when only not all men lie;
Peace in her vineyard – yes! – but a company forges the wine.

X

And the vitriol madness flushes up in the ruffian's head,
Till the filthy by-lane rings to the yell of the trampled wife,
And chalk and alum and plaster are sold to the poor for bread,
And the spirit of murder works in the very means of life,

XI

And Sleep must lie down arm'd, for the villainous centre-bits
Grind on the wakeful ear in the hush of the moonless nights,
While another is cheating the sick of a few last gasps, as he sits
To pestle a poison'd poison behind his crimson lights.

XII

When a Mammonite mother kills her babe for a burial fee,
And Timour-Mammon grins on a pile of children's bones,
Is it peace or war? better, war! loud war by land and by sea,
War with a thousand battles, and shaking a hundred thrones.

XIII

For I trust if an enemy's fleet came yonder round by the hill,
And the rushing battle-bolt sang from the three-decker out of the foam,
That the smooth-faced snubnosed rogue would leap from his counter
    and till,
And strike, if he could, were it but with his cheating yardwand, home.–

XIV

What! am I raging alone as my father raged in his mood?
Must *I* too creep to the hollow and dash myself down and die
Rather than hold by the law that I made, nevermore to brood
On a horror of shatter'd limbs and a wretched swindler's lie?

XV

Would there be sorrow for *me?* there was *love* in the passionate shriek,
Love for the silent thing that had made false haste to the grave –
Wrapt in a cloak, as I saw him, and thought he would rise and speak
And rave at the lie and the liar, ah God, as he used to rave.

XVI

I am sick of the Hall and the hill, I am sick of tho moor and the main.
Why should I stay? can a sweeter chance ever come to me here?
O, having the nerves of motion as well as the nerves of pain,
Were it not wise if I fled from the place and the pit and the fear?

XVII

Workmen up at the Hall! – they are coming back from abroad;
The dark old place will be gilt by the touch of a millionaire:
I have heard, I know not whence, of the singular beauty of Maud;
I play'd with the girl when a child; she promised then to be fair.

XVIII

Maud with her venturous climbings and tumbles and childish escapes,
Maud the delight of the village, the ringing joy of the Hall,
Maud with her sweet purse-mouth when my father dangled the grapes,
Maud the beloved of my mother, the moon-faced darling of all, –

XIX

What is she now? My dreams are bad. She may bring me a curse.
No, there is fatter game on the moor; she will let me alone.
Thanks, for the fiend best knows whether woman or man be the worse.
I will bury myself in myself, and the Devil may pipe to his own.

II

Long have I sigh'd for a calm: God grant I may find it at last!
It will never be broken by Maud, she has neither savour nor salt,
But a cold and clear-cut face, as I found when her carriage past
Perfectly beautiful: let it be granted her: where is the fault?
All that I saw (for her eyes were downcast, not to be seen)
Faultily faultless, icily regular, splendidly null,
Dead perfection, no more; nothing more, if it had not been
For a chance of travel, a paleness, an hour's defect of the rose,

Or an underlip, you may call it a little too ripe, too full,
Or the least little delicate aquiline curve in a sensitive nose,
From which I escaped heart-free, with the least little touch of spleen.

III

Cold and clear-cut face, why come you so cruelly meek,
Breaking a slumber in which all spleenful folly was drown'd,
Pale with the golden beam of an eyelash dead on the cheek,
Passionless, pale, cold face, star-sweet on a gloom profound;
Womanlike, taking revenge too deep for a transient wrong
Done but in thought to your beauty, and ever as pale as before
Growing and fading and growing upon me without a sound,
Luminous, gemlike, ghostlike, deathlike, half the night long
Growing and fading and growing, till I could bear it no more,
But arose, and all by myself in my own dark garden ground,
Listening now to the tide in its broad-flung shipwrecking roar,
Now to the scream of a madden'd beach dragg'd down by the wave,
Walk'd in a wintry wind by a ghastly glimmer, and found
The shining daffodil dead, and Orion low in his grave.

IV

I

A million emeralds break from the ruby-budded lime
In the little grove where I sit – ah, wherefore cannot I be
Like things of the season gay, like the bountiful season bland,
When the far-off sail is blown by the breeze of a softer clime,
Half-lost in the liquid azure bloom of a crescent of sea,
The silent sapphire-spangled marriage ring of the land?

II

Below me, there, is the village, and looks how quiet and small!
And yet bubbles o'er like a city, with gossip, scandal, and spite;
And Jack on his ale-house bench has as many lies as a Czar;
And here on the landward side, by a red rock, glimmers the Hall;
And up in the high Hall-garden I see her pass like a light;
But sorrow seize me if ever that light be my leading star!

III

When have I bow'd to her father, the wrinkled head of the race?
I met her to-day with her brother, but not to her brother I bow'd;
I bow'd to his lady-sister as she rode by on the moor;
But the fire of a foolish pride flash'd over her beautiful face.
O child, you wrong your beauty, believe it, in being so proud;
Your father has wealth well-gotten, and I am nameless and poor.

IV

I keep but a man and a maid, ever ready to slander and steal;
I know it, and smile a hard-set smile, like a stoic, or like
A wiser epicurean, and let the world have its way:
For nature is one with rapine, a harm no preacher can heal;
The Mayfly is torn by the swallow, the sparrow spear'd by the shrike,
And the whole little wood where I sit is a world of plunder and prey.

V

We are puppets, Man in his pride, and Beauty fair in her flower;
Do we move ourselves, or are moved by an unseen hand at a game
That pushes us off from the board, and others ever succeed?
Ah yet, we cannot be kind to each other here for an hour;
We whisper, and hint, and chuckle, and grin at a brother's shame;
However we brave it out, we men are a little bread.

VI

A monstrous eft was of old the Lord and Master of Earth,
For him did his high sun flame, and his river billowing ran,
And he felt himself in his force to be Nature's crowning race.
As nine months go to the shaping an infant ripe for his birth,
So many a million of ages have gone to the making of man:
Ho now is first, but is he the last? is he not too base?

VII

The man of science himself is fonder of glory, and vain,
An eye well-practised in nature, a spirit bounded and poor;
The passionate heart of the poet is whirl'd into folly and vice.
I would not marvel at either, but keep a temperate brain;
For not to desire or admire, if a man could learn it, were more
Than to walk all day like the sultan of old in a garden of spice.

VIII

For the drift of the Maker is dark, an Isis hid by the veil.
Who knows the ways of the world, how God will bring them about?
Our planet is one, the suns are many, the world is wide.
Shall I weep if a Poland fall? shall I shriek if a Hungary fail?
Or an infant civilization be ruled with rod or with knout?
I have not made the world, and He that made it will guide.

VIII

Be mine a philosopher's life in the quiet woodland ways,
Where if I cannot be gay let a passionless peace be my lot,
Far-off from the clamour of liars belied in the hubbub of lies;
From the long-neck'd geese of the world that are ever hissing dispraise
Because their natures are little, and, whether he heed it or not,
Where each man walks with his head in a cloud of poisonous flies.

X

And most of all would I flee from the cruel madness of love,
The honey of poison-flowers and all the measureless ill.
Ah Maud, you milkwhite fawn, you are all unmeet for a wife.
Your mother is mute in her grave as her image in marble above;
Your father is ever in London, you wander about at your will;
You have but fed on the roses, and lain in the lilies of life.

V

I

A voice by the cedar tree,
In the meadow under the Hall!
She is singing an air that is known to me,
A passionate ballad gallant and gay,
A martial song like a trumpet's call!
Singing alone in the morning of life,
In the happy morning of life and of May,
Singing of men that in battle array,
Ready in heart and ready in hand,
March with banner and bugle and fife
To the death, for their native land.

II

Maud with her exquisite face,
And wild voice pealing up to the sunny sky,
And feet like sunny gems on an English green,
Maud in the light of her youth and her grace,
Singing of Death, and of Honour that cannot die,
Till I well could weep for a time so sordid and mean,
And myself so languid and base.

III

Silence, beautiful voice!
Be still, for you only trouble the mind
With a joy in which I cannot rejoice,
A glory I shall not find.
Still!I will hear you no more,
For your sweetness hardly leaves me a choice
But to move to the meadow and fall before
Her feet on the meadow grass, and adore,
Not her, who is neither courtly nor kind,
Not her, not her, but a voice.

VI

I

Morning arises stormy and pale,
No sun, but a wannish glare
In fold upon fold of hueless cloud,
And the budded peaks of the wood are bow'd
Caught and cuff'd by the gale:
I had fancied it would be fair.

II

Whom but Maud should I meet
Last night, when the sunset burn'd
On the blossom'd gable-ends
At the head of the village street,
Whom but Maud should I meet?
And she touch'd my hand with a smile so sweet,
She made me divine amends
For a courtesy not return'd.

III

And thus a delicate spark
Of glowing and growing light
Thro' the livelong hours of the dark
Kept itself warm in the heart of my dreams,
Ready to burst in a colour'd flame;
Till at last when the morning came
In a cloud, it faded, and seems
But an ashen-grey delight.

IV

What if with her sunny hair,
And smile as sunny as cold,
She meant to weave me a snare
Of some coquettish deceit,
Cleopatra-like as of old
To entangle me when we met,
To have her lion roll in a silken net
And fawn at a victor's feet.

V

Ah, what shall I be at fifty
Should Nature keep me alive,
If I find the world so bitter
When I am but twenty-five?
Yet, if she were not a cheat,

If Maud were all that she seem'd,
And her smile were all that I dream'd,
Then the world were not so bitter
But a smile could make it sweet.

VI

What if tho' her eye seem'd full
Of a kind intent to me,
What if that dandy-despot, he,
That jewell'd mass of millinery,
That oil'd and curl'd Assyrian Bull
Smelling of musk and of insolence,
Her brother, from whom I keep aloof,
Who wants the finer politic sense
To mask, tho' but in his own behoof,
With a glassy smile his brutal scorn —
What if he had told her yestermorn
How prettily for his own sweet sake
A face of tenderness might be feign'd,
And a moist mirage in desert eyes,
That so, when the rotten hustings shake
In another month to his brazen lies,
A wretched vote may be gain'd.

VII

For a raven ever croaks, at my side,
Keep watch and ward, keep watch and ward,
Or thou wilt prove their tool.
Yea, too, myself from myself I guard,
For often a man's own angry pride
Is cap and bells for a fool.

VIII

Perhaps the smile and tender tone
Came out of her pitying womanhood,
For am I not, am I not, here alone
So many a summer since she died,
My mother, who was so gentle and good?
Living alone in an empty house,
Here half-hid in the gleaming wood,
Where I hear the dead at midday moan,
And the shrieking rush of the wainscot mouse,
And my own sad name in corners cried,
When the shiver of dancing leaves is thrown
About its echoing chambers wide,
Till a morbid hate and horror have grown

Of a world in which I have hardly mixt,
And a morbid eating lichen fixt
On a heart half-turn'd to stone.

IX

O heart of stone, are you flesh, and caught
By that you swore to withstand?
For what was it else within me wrought
But, I fear, the new strong wine of love,
That made my tongue so stammer and trip
When I saw the treasured splendour, her hand,
Come sliding out of her sacred glove,
And the sunlight broke from her lip?

X

I have play'd with her when a child;
She remembers it now we meet.
Ah well, well, well, I *may* be beguiled
By some coquettish deceit.
Yet, if she were not a cheat,
If Maud wore all that she seem'd,
And her smile had all that I dream'd,
Then the world were not so bitter
But a smile could make it sweet.

VII

I

Did I hear it half in a doze
    Long since, I know not where?
Did I dream it an hour ago,
    When asleep in this arm-chair?

II

Men were drinking together,
    Drinking and talking of me;
'Well, if it prove a girl, the boy
    Will have plenty: so let it be.'

III

Is it an echo of something
    Read with a boy's delight,
Viziers nodding together
    In some Arabian night?

IV

Strange, that I hear two men,
   Somewhere, talking of me;
'Well, if it prove a girl, my boy
   Will have plenty: so let it be.'

VIII

She came to the village church,
And sat by a pillar alone;
An angel watching an urn
Wept over her, carved in stone;
And once, but once, she lifted her eyes,
And suddenly, sweetly, strangely blush'd
To find they were met by my own;
And suddenly, sweetly, my heart beat stronger
And thicker, until I heard no longer
The snowy-banded, dilettante,
Delicate-handed priest intone;
And thought, is it pride, and mused and sigh'd
'No surely, now it cannot be pride.'

IX

I was walking a mile,
   More than a mile from the shore,
The sun look'd out with a smile
   Betwixt the cloud and the moor,
And riding at set of day
   Over the dark moor land,
Rapidly riding far away,
   She waved to me with her hand.
There were two at her side,
   Something flash'd in the sun,
Down by the hill I saw them ride,
   In a moment they were gone:
Like a sudden spark
   Struck vainly in the night,
Then returns the dark
   With no more hope of light.

X

I

Sick, am I sick of a jealous dread?
Was not one of the two at her side
This new-made lord, whose splendour plucks
The slavish hat from the villager's head?
Whose old grandfather has lately died,
Gone to a blacker pit, for whom
Grimy nakedness dragging his trucks
And laying his trams in a poison'd gloom
Wrought, till he crept from a gutted mine
Master of half a servile shire,
And left his coal all turn'd into gold
To a grandson, first of his noble line,
Rich in the grace all women desire,
Strong in the power that all men adore,
And simper and set their voices lower,
And soften as if to a girl, and hold
Awe-stricken breaths at a work divine,
Seeing his gewgaw castle shine,
New as his title, built last year,
There amid perky larches and pine,
And over the sullen-purple moor
(Look at it) pricking a cockney ear.

II

What, has he found my jewel out?
For one of the two that rode at her side
Bound for the Hall, I am sure was he:
Bound for the Hall, and I think for a bride.
Blithe would her brother's acceptance be.
Maud could be gracious too, no doubt,
To a lord, a captain, a padded shape,
A bought commission, a waxen face,
A rabbit mouth that is ever agape –
Bought? what is it he cannot buy?
And therefore splenetic, personal, base,
A wounded thing with a rancorous cry,
At war with myself and a wretched race,
Sick, sick to the heart of life, am I.

III

Last week came one to the county town,
To preach our poor little army down,
And play the game of the despot kings,

Tho' the state has done it and thrice as well:
This broad-brimm'd hawker of holy things,
Whose ear is cramm'd with his cotton, and rings
Even in dreams to the chink of his peace,
This huckster put down war! can he tell
Whether war be a cause or a consequence?
Put down the passions that make earth Hell!
Down with ambition, avarice, pride,
Jealousy, down! cut off from the mind
The bitter springs of anger and fear;
Down too, down at your own fireside,
With the evil tongue and the evil ear,
For each is at war with mankind.

IV

I wish I could hear again
The chivalrous battle-song
That she warbled alone in her joy!
I might persuade myself then
She would not do herself this great wrong,
To take a wanton dissolute boy
For a man and leader of men

V

Ah God, for a man with heart, head, hand,
Like some of the simple great ones gone
For ever and ever by,
One still strong man in a blatant land,
Whatever they call him, what care I,
Aristocrat, democrat, autocrat – one
Who can rule and dare not lie.

VI

And ah for a man to arise in me,
That the man I am may cease to be!

XI

I

O let the solid ground
    Not fail beneath my feet
Before my life has found
    What some have found so sweet;
Then let come what come may,
What matter if I go mad,
I shall have had my day.

II

Let the sweet heavens endure,
    Not close and darken above me
Before I am quite quite sure
    That there is one to love me;
Then let come what come may
To a life that has been so sad,
I shall have had my day.

XII

I

Birds in the high Hall-garden
    When twilight was falling,
Maud, Maud, Maud, Maud,
    They were crying and calling.

II

Where was Maud? in our wood;
    And I, who else, was with her,
Gathering woodland lilies,
    Myriads blow together.

III

Birds in our wood sang
    Ringing thro' the valleys,
Maud is here, here, here
    In among the lilies.

IV

I kiss'd her slender hand,
    She took the kiss sedately;
Maud is not seventeen,
    But she is tall and stately.

V

I to cry out on pride
    Who have won her favour!
O Maud were sure of Heaven
    If lowliness could save her.

VI

I know the way she went
    Home with her maiden posy,
For her feet have touch'd the meadows
    And left the daisies rosy.

VII

Birds in the high Hall-garden
   Were crying and calling to her,
Where is Maud, Maud, Maud?
   One is come to woo her.

VIII

Look, a horse at the door,
   And little King Charley snarling,
Go back, my lord, across the moor,
   You are not her darling.

XIII

I

Scorn'd, to be scorn'd by one that I scorn,
Is that a matter to make me fret?
That a calamity hard to be borne?
Well, he may live to hate me yet.
Fool that I am to be vext with his pride!
I past him, I was crossing his lands;
He stood on the path a little aside;
His face, as I grant, in spite of spite,
Has a broad-blown comeliness, red and white,
And six feet two, as I think, he stands;
But his essences turn'd the live air sick,
And barbarous opulence jewel-thick
Sunn'd itself on his breast and his hands.

II

Who shall call me ungentle, unfair,
I long'd so heartily then and there
To give him the grasp of fellowship;
But while I past he was humming an air,
Stopt, and then with a riding whip
Leisurely tapping a glossy boot,
And curving a contumelious lip
Gorgonized me from head to foot
With a stony British stare.

III

Why sits he here in his father's chair?
That old man never comes to his place:
Shall I believe him ashamed to be seen?
For only once, in the village street,

Last year, I caught a glimpse of his face,
A grey old wolf and a lean.
Scarcely, now, would I call him a cheat;
For then, perhaps, as a child of deceit,
She might by a true descent be untrue;
And Maud is as true as Maud is sweet:
Tho' I fancy her sweetness only due
To the sweeter blood by the other side;
Her mother has been a thing complete,
However she came to be so allied.
And fair without, faithful within,
Maud to him is nothing akin:
Some peculiar mystic grace
Made her only the child of her mother,
And heap'd the whole inherited sin
On that huge scapegoat of the race,
All, all upon the brother.

IV

Peace, angry spirit, and let him be!
Has not his sister smiled on me?

XIV

I

Maud has a garden of roses
And lilies fair on a lawn;
There she walks in her state
And tends upon bed and bower,
And thither I climb'd at dawn
And stood by her garden-gate;
A lion ramps at the top,
He is claspt by a passion-flower.

II

Maud's own little oak-room
(Which Maud, like a precious stone
Set in the heart of the carven gloom,
Lights with herself, when alone
She sits by her music and books,
And her brother lingers late
With a roystering company) looks
Upon Maud's own garden-gate:
And I thought as I stood, if a hand, as white
As ocean-foam in the moon, were laid

On the hasp of the window, and my Delight
Had a sudden desire, like a glorious ghost, to glide,
Like a beam of the seventh Heaven, down to my side,
There were but a step to be made.

III

The fancy flatter'd my mind,
And again seem'd overbold;
Now I thought that she cared for me,
Now I thought she was kind
Only because she was cold.

IV

I heard no sound where I stood
But the rivulet on from the lawn
Running, down to my own dark wood;
Or the voice of the long sea-wave as it swell'd
Now and then in the dim-grey dawn;
But I look'd, and round, all round the house I beheld
The death-white curtain drawn;
Felt a horror over me creep,
Prickle my skin and catch my breath,
Knew that the death-white curtain meant but sleep,
Yet I shudder'd and thought like a fool of the sleep of death.

XV

So dark a mind within me dwells,
    And I make myself such evil cheer,
That if I be dear to some one else,
    Then some one else may have much to fear;
But if I be dear to some one else,
Then I should be to myself more dear.
Shall I not take care of all that I think,
Yea ev'n of wretched meat and drink,
If I be dear,
If I be dear to some one else.

XVI

I

This lump of earth has left his estate
The lighter by the loss of his weight;
And so that he find what he went to seek,
And fulsome Pleasure clog him, and drown

His heart in the gross mud-honey of town,
He may stay for a year who has gone for a week:
But this is the day when I must speak,
And I see my Oread coming down,
O this is the day!
O beautiful creature, what am I
That I dare to look her way;
Think I may hold dominion sweet,
Lord of the pulse that is lord of her breast,
And dream of her beauty with tender dread,
From the delicate Arab arch of her feet
To the grace that, bright and light as the crest
Of a peacock, sits on her shining head,
And she knows it not: O, if she knew it,
To know her beauty might half undo it.
I know it the one bright thing to save
My yet young life in the wilds of Time,
Perhaps from madness, perhaps from crime,
Perhaps from a selfish grave.

II

What, if she be fasten'd to this fool lord,
Dare I bid her abide by her word?
Should I love her so well if she
Had given her word to a thing so low?
Shall I love her as well if she
Can break her word were it even for me?
I trust that it is not so.

III

Catch not my breath, O clamorous heart,
Let not my tongue be a thrall to my eye,
For I must tell her before we part,
I must tell her, or die.

XVII

Go not, happy day,
    From the shining fields,
Go not, happy day,
    Till the maiden yields.
Rosy is the West,
    Rosy is the South,
Roses are her cheeks,
    And a rose her mouth.

When the happy Yes
   Falters from her lips,
Pass and blush the news
   O'er the blowing ships.
Over blowing seas,
   Over seas at rest,
Pass the happy news,
   Blush it thro' the West;
Till the red man dance
   By his red cedar tree,
And the red man's babe
   Leap, beyond the sea.
Blush from West to East,
   Blush from East to West,
Till the West is East,
   Blush it thro' the West.
Rosy is the West,
   Rosy is the South,
Roses are her cheeks
   And a rose her mouth.

XVIII

I

I have led her home, my love, my only friend.
There is none like her, none.
And never yet so warmly ran my blood
And sweetly, on and on
Calming itself to the long-wish'd-for end,
Full to the banks, close on the promised good.

II

None like her, none.
Just now the dry-tongued laurels' pattering talk
Seem'd her light foot along the garden walk,
And shook my heart to think she comes once more;
But even then I heard her close the door,
The gates of Heaven are closed, and she is gone.

III

There is none like her, none.
Nor will be when our summers have deceased.
O, art thou sighing for Lebanon
In the long breeze that streams to thy delicious East,
Sighing for Lebanon,

Dark cedar, tho' thy limbs have here increased,
Upon a pastoral slope as fair,
And looking to the South, and fed
With honey'd rain and delicate air,
And haunted by the starry head
Of her whose gentle will has changed my fate,
And made my life a perfumed altar-flame;
And over whom thy darkness must have spread
With such delight as theirs of old, thy great
Forefathers of the thornless garden, there
Shadowing the snow-limb'd Eve from whom she came.

IV

Here will I lie, while these long branches sway,
And you fair stars that crown a happy day
Go in and out as if at merry play,
Who am no more so all forlorn,
As when it seem'd far better to be born
To labour and the mattock-harden'd hand,
Than nursed at ease and brought to understand
A sad astrology, the boundless plan
That makes you tyrants in your iron skies,
Innumerable, pitiless, passionless eyes,
Cold fires, yet with power to burn and brand
His nothingness into man.

V

But now shine on, and what care I,
Who in this stormy gulf have found a pearl
The countercharm of space and hollow sky,
And do accept my madness, and would die
To save from some slight shame one simple girl.

VI

Would die; for sullen-seeming Death may give
More life to Love than is or ever was
In our low world, where yet 'tis sweet to live.
Let no one ask me how it came to pass;
It seems that I am happy, that to me
A livelier emerald twinkles in the grass,
A purer sapphire melts into the sea.

VII

Not die; but live a life of truest breath,
And teach true life to fight with mortal wrongs.
O, why should Love, like men in drinking-songs,

Spice his fair banquet with the dust of death?
Make answer, Maud my bliss,
Maud made my Maud by that long lover's kiss,
Life of my life, wilt thou not answer this?
'The dusky strand of Death inwoven here
With dear Love's tie, makes Love himself more dear.'

VIII

Is that enchanted moan only the swell
Of the long waves that roll in yonder bay?
And hark the clock within, the silver knell
Of twelve sweet hours that past in bridal white,
And died to live, long as my pulses play;
But now by this my love has closed her sight
And given false death her hand, and stol'n away
To dreamful wastes where footless fancies dwell
Among the fragments of the golden day.
May nothing there her maiden grace affright!
Dear heart, I feel with thee the drowsy spell.
My bride to be, my evermore delight,
My own heart's heart and ownest own, farewell;
It is but for a little space I go:
And ye meanwhile far over moor and fell
Beat to the noiseless music of the night!
Has our whole earth gone nearer to the glow
Of your soft splendours that you look so bright?
I have climb'd nearer out of lonely Hell.
Beat, happy stars, timing with things below,
Beat with my heart more blest than heart can tell,
Blest, but for some dark undercurrent woe
That seems to draw – but it shall not be so:
Let all be well, be well.

XIX

I

Her brother is coming back to-night,
Breaking up my dream of delight.

II

My dream? do I dream of bliss?
I have walk'd awake with Truth.
O when did a morning shine
So rich in atonement as this
For my dark-dawning youth,

Darken'd watching a mother decline
And that dead man at her heart and mine:
For who was left to watch her but I?
Yet so did I let my freshness die.

III

I trust that I did not talk
To gentle Maud in our walk
(For often in lonely wanderings
I have cursed him even to lifeless things)
But I trust that I did not talk,
Not touch on her father's sin:
I am sure I did but speak
Of my mother's faded cheek
When it slowly grew so thin,
That I felt she was slowly dying
Vext with lawyers and harass'd with debt:
For how often I caught her with eyes all wet,
Shaking her head at her son and sighing
A world of trouble within!

IV

And Maud too, Maud was moved
To speak of the mother she loved
As one scarce less forlorn,
Dying abroad and it seems apart
From him who had ceased to share her heart,
And ever mourning over the feud,
The household Fury sprinkled with blood
By which our houses are torn:
How strange was what she said,
When only Maud and the brother
Hung over her dying bed –
That Maud's dark father and mine
Had bound us one to the other,
Betrothed us over their wine,
On the day when Maud was born;
Seal'd her mine from her first sweet breath.
Mine, mine by a right, from birth till death,
Mine, mine – our fathers have sworn.

V

But the true blood spilt had in it a heat
To dissolve the precious seal on a bond,
That, if left uncancell'd, had been so sweet:
And none of us thought of a something beyond,

A desire that awoke in the heart of the child,
As it were a duty done to the tomb,
To be friends for her sake, to be reconciled;
And I was cursing them and my doom,
And letting a dangerous thought run wild
While often abroad in the fragrant gloom
Of foreign churches – I see her there,
Bright English lily, breathing a prayer
To be friends, to be reconciled!

VI

But then what a flint is he!
Abroad, at Florence, at Rome,
I find whenever she touch'd on me
This brother had laugh'd her down,
And at last, when each came home,
He had darken'd into a frown,
Chid her, and forbid her to speak
To me, her friend of the years before;
And this was what had redden'd her cheek
When I bow'd to her on the moor.

VII

Yet Maud, altho' not blind
To the faults of his heart and mind,
I see she cannot but love him,
And says he is rough but kind,
And wishes me to approve him,
And tells me, when she lay
Sick once, with a fear of worse,
That he left his wine and horses and play,
Sat with her, read to her, night and day,
And tended her like a nurse.

VIII

Kind? but the deathbed desire
Spurn'd by this heir of the liar –
Rough but kind? yet I know
He has plotted against me in this.
That he plots against me still.
Kind to Maud? that were not amiss.
Well, rough but kind; why let it be so
For shall not Maud have her will?

IX

For, Maud, so tender and true,
As long as my life endures
I feel I shall owe you a debt,
That I never can hope to pay;
And if ever I should forget
That I owe this debt to you
And for your sweet sake to yours;
O then, what then shall I say? –
If ever I *should* forget,
May God make me more wretched
Than ever I have been yet!

X

So now I have sworn to bury
All this dead body of hate,
I feel so free and so clear
By the loss of that dead weight,
That I should grow light-headed, I fear,
Fantastically merry;
But that her brother comes, like a blight
On my fresh hope, to the Hall to-night.

XX

I

Strange, that I felt so gay,
Strange, that I tried to-day
To beguile her melancholy;
The Sultan, as we name him, –
She did not wish to blame him –
But he vext her and perplext her
With his worldly talk and folly:
Was it gentle to reprove her
For stealing out of view
From a little lazy lover
Who but claims her as his due?
Or for chilling his caresses
By the coldness of her manners,
Nay, the plainness of her dresses?
Now I know her but in two,
Nor can pronounce upon it
If one should ask me whether
The habit, hat, and feather,
Or the frock and gipsy bonnet

Be the neater and completer;
For nothing can be sweeter
Than maiden Maud in either.

II

But to-morrow, if we live
Our ponderous squire will give
A grand political dinner
To half the squirelings near;
And Maud will wear her jewels,
And the bird of prey will hover,
And the titmouse hope to win her
With his chirrup at her ear.

III

A grand political dinner
To the men of many acres,
A gathering of the Tory,
A dinner and then a dance
For the maids and marriage-makers,
And every eye but mine will glance
At Maud in all her glory.

IV

For I am not invited,
But, with the Sultan's pardon,
I am all as well delighted,
For I know her own rose-garden,
And mean to linger in it
Till the dancing will be over;
And then, oh then, come out to me
For a minute, but for a minute,
Come out to your own true lover,
That your true lover may see
Your glory also, and render
All homage to his own darling
Queen Maud in all her splendour.

XXI

Rivulet crossing my ground,
And bringing me down from the Hall
This garden-rose that I found,
Forgetful of Maud and me,
And lost in trouble and moving round

Here at the head of a tinkling fall,
    And trying to pass to the sea;
O Rivulet, born at the Hall,
    My Maud has sent it by thee
(If I read her sweet will right)
    On a blushing mission to me,
Saying in odour and colour, 'Ah, be
    Among the roses to-night.'

XXII

I

Come into the garden, Maud,
    For the black bat, night, has flown,
Come into the garden, Maud,
    I am here at the gate alone;
And the woodbine spices are wafted abroad,
    And the musk of the rose is blown.

II

For a breeze of morning moves,
    And the planet of Love is on high,
Beginning to faint in the light that she loves
    On a bed of daffodil sky,
To faint in the light of the sun she loves,
    To faint in his light, and to die.

III

All night have the roses heard
    The flute, violin, bassoon;
All night has the casement jessamine stirr'd
    To the dancers dancing in tune;
Till a silence fell with the waking bird,
    And a hush with the setting moon.

IV

I said to the lily, 'There is but one
    With whom she has heart to be gay.
When will the dancers leave her alone?
    She is weary of dance and play.'
Now half to the setting moon are gone,
    And half to the rising day;
Low on the sand and loud on the stone
    The last wheel echoes away.

V

I said to the rose, 'The brief night goes
    In babble and revel and wine.
O young lord-lover, what sighs are those,
    For one that will never be thine?
But mine, but mine,' so I sware to the rose,
    'For ever and ever, mine.'

VI

And the soul of the rose went into my blood,
    As the music clash'd in the hall;
And long by the garden lake I stood,
    For I heard your rivulet fall
From the lake to the meadow and on to the wood,
    Our wood, that is dearer than all;

VII

From the meadow your walks have left so sweet
    That whenever a March-wind sighs
He sets the jewel-print of your feet
    In violets blue as your eyes,
To the woody hollows in which we meet
    And the valleys of Paradise.

VIII

The slender acacia would not shake
    One long milk-bloom on the tree;
The white lake-blossom fell into the lake
    As the pimpernel dozed on the lea;
But the rose was awake all night for your sake,
    Knowing your promise to me;
The lilies and roses were all awake,
    They sigh'd for the dawn and thee.

IX

Queen rose of the rosebud garden of girls,
    Come hither, the dances are done,
In gloss of satin and glimmer of pearls,
    Queen lily and rose in one;
Shine out, little head, sunning over with curls,
    To the flowers, and be their sun.

X

There has fallen a splendid tear
    From the passion-flower at the gate.
She is coming, my dove, my dear;

She is coming, my life, my fate;
The red rose cries, 'She is near, she is near;'
  And the white rose weeps, 'She is late;'
The larkspur listens, 'I hear, I hear;'
  And the lily whispers, 'I wait.'

XI

She is coming, my own, my sweet;
  Were it ever so airy a tread,
My heart would hear her and beat,
  Were it earth in an earthy bed;
My dust would hear her and beat,
  Had I lain for a century dead;
Would start and tremble under her feet,
  And blossom in purple and red.

Maud: Part 2

I

i

'The fault was mine, the fault was mine' –
Why am I sitting here so stunn'd and still,
Plucking the harmless wild-flower on the hill? –
It is this guilty hand! –
And there rises ever a passionate cry
From underneath in the darkening land –
What is it, that has been done?
O dawn of Eden bright over earth and sky,
The fires of Hell brake out of thy rising sun,
The fires of Hell and of Hate;
For she, sweet soul, had hardly spoken a word
When her brother ran in his rage to the gate,
He came with the babe-faced lord;
Heap'd on her terms of disgrace,
And while she wept, and I strove to be cool,
He fiercely gave me the lie,
Till I with as fierce an anger spoke,
And he struck me, madman, over the face,
Struck me before the languid fool,
Who was gaping and grinning by:
Struck for himself an evil stroke;
Wrought for his house an irredeemable woe;
For front to front in an hour we stood,
And a million horrible bellowing echoes broke

From the red-ribb'd hollow behind the wood,
And thunder'd up into Heaven the Christless code,
That must have life for a blow.
Ever and ever afresh they seem'd to grow.
Was it he lay there with a fading eye?
'The fault was mine,' he whisper'd, 'fly!'
'Then glided out of the joyous wood
The ghastly Wraith of one that I know;
And there rang on a sudden a passionate cry,
A cry for a brother's blood:
It will ring in my heart and my ears, till I die, till I die.

II

Is it gone? my pulses beat –
What was it? a lying trick of the brain?
Yet I thought I saw her stand,
A shadow there at my feet,
High over the shadowy land.
It is gone; and the heavens fall in a gentle rain,
When they should burst and drown with deluging storms
The feeble vassals of wine and anger and lust,
The little hearts that know not how to forgive:
Arise, my God, and strike, for we hold Thee just,
Strike dead the whole weak race of venomous worms,
That sting each other here in the dust;
We are not worthy to live.

II

I

See what a lovely shell,
Small and pure as a pearl,
Lying close to my foot,
Frail, but a work divine,
Made so fairily well
With delicate spire and whorl,
How exquisitely minute miracle of design!

II

What is it? a learned man
Could give it a clumsy name.
Let him name it who can,
The beauty would be the same.

III

The tiny cell is forlorn,
Void of the little living will
That made it stir on the shore.
Did he stand at the diamond door
Of his house in a rainbow frill?
Did he push, when he was uncurl'd,
A golden foot or a fairy horn
Thro' his dim water-world?

IV

Slight, to be crush'd with a tap
Of my finger-nail on the sand,
Small, but a work divine,
Frail, but of force to withstand,
Year upon year, the shock
Of cataract seas that snap
The three-decker's oaken spine
Athwart the ledges of rock,
Here on the Breton strand!

V

Breton, not Briton; here
Like a shipwreck'd man on a coast
Of ancient fable and fear –
Plagued with a flitting to and fro,
A disease, a hard mechanic ghost
That never came from on high
Nor ever arose from below,
But only moves with the moving eye,
Flying along the land and the main –
Why should it look like Maud?
Am I to be overawed
By what I cannot but know
Is a juggle born of the brain?

VI

Back from the Breton coast,
Sick of a nameless fear,
Back to the dark sea-line
Looking, thinking of all I have lost;
An old song vexes my ear;
But that of Lamech is mine.

VII

For years, a measureless ill,
For years, for ever, to part –
But she, she would love me still;

And as long, O God, as she
Have a grain of love for me,
So long, no doubt, no doubt,
Shall I nurse in my dark heart,
However weary, a spark of will
Not to be trampled out.

VIII

Strange, that the mind, when fraught
With a passion so intense
One would think that it well
Might drown all life in the eye, –
That it should, by being so overwrought,
Suddenly strike on a sharper sense
For a shell, or a flower, little things
Which else would have been past by!
And now I remember, I,
When he lay dying there,
I noticed one of his many rings
(For he had many, poor worm) and thought
It is his mother's hair.

IX

Who knows if he be dead?
Whether I need have fled?
Am I guilty of blood?
However this may be,
Comfort her, comfort her, all things good,
While I am over the sea!
Let me and my passionate love go by,
But speak to her all things holy and high,
Whatever happen to me!
Me and my harmful love go by;
But come to her waking, find her asleep,
Powers of the height, Powers of the deep,
And comfort her tho' I die.

III

Courage, poor heart of stone!
I will not ask thee why
Thou canst not understand
That thou art left for ever alone:
Courage, poor stupid heart of stone. –
Or if I ask thee why,
Care not thou to reply:
She is but dead, and the time is at hand
When thou shalt more than die.

IV

I

O that 'twere possible
After long grief and pain
To find the arms of my true love
Round me once again!

II

When I was wont to meet her
In the silent woody places
By the home that gave me birth,
We stood tranced in long embraces
Mixt with kisses sweeter sweeter
Than any thing on earth.

III

A shadow flits before me,
Not thou, but like to thee;
Ah Christ, that it were possible
For one short hour to see
The souls we loved, that they might tell us
What and where they be.

IV

It leads me forth at evening,
It lightly winds and steals
In a cold white robe before me,
When all my spirit reels
At the shouts, the leagues of lights,
And the roaring of the wheels.

V

Half the night I waste in sighs,
Half in dreams I sorrow after
The delight of early skies;
In a wakeful doze I sorrow
For the hand, the lips, the eyes,
For the meeting of the morrow,
The delight of happy laughter,
The delight of low replies.

VI

Tis a morning pure and sweet,
And a dewy splendour falls
On the little flower that clings

To the turrets and the walls;
'Tis a morning pure and sweet,
And the light and shadow fleet;
She is walking in the meadow,
And the woodland echo rings;
In a moment we shall meet;
She is singing in the meadow,
And the rivulet at her feet
Ripples on in light and shadow
To the ballad that she sings.

VII

Do I hear her sing as of old,
My bird with the shining head,
My own dove with the tender eye?
But there rings on a sudden a passionate cry,
There is some one dying or dead,
And a sullen thunder is roll'd;
For a tumult shakes the city,
And I wake, my dream is fled;
In the shuddering dawn, behold,
Without knowledge, without pity,
By the curtains of my bed
That abiding phantom cold.

VIII

Get thee hence, nor come again,
Mix not memory with doubt
Pass, thou deathlike type of pain,
Pass and cease to move about!
'Tis the blot upon the brain
That *will* show itself without.

IX

Then I rise, the eavedrops fall,
And the yellow vapours choke
The great city sounding wide;
The day comes, a dull red ball
Wrapt in drifts of lurid smoke
On the misty river-tide.

X

Thro' the hubbub of the market
I steal, a wasted frame,
It crosses here, it crosses there,
Thro' all that crowd confused and loud,

The shadow still the same;
And on my heavy eyelids
My anguish hangs like shame.

XI

Alas for her that met me,
That heard me softly call,
Came glimmering thro' the laurels
At the quiet evenfall,
In the garden by the turrets
Of the old manorial hall.

XII

Would the happy spirit descend,
From the realms of light and song,
In the chamber or the street,
As she looks among the blest,
Should I fear to greet my friend
Or to say 'forgive the wrong,'
Or to ask her, 'take me, sweet,
To the regions of thy rest'?

XIII

But the broad light glares and beats,
And the shadow flits and fleets
And will not let me be;
And I loathe the squares and streets,
And the faces that one meets,
Hearts with no love for me:
Always I long to creep
Into some still cavern deep,
There to weep, and weep, and weep
My whole soul out to thee.

V

I

Dead, long dead,
Long dead!
And my heart is a handful of dust,
And the wheels go over my head,
And my bones are shaken with pain,
For into a shallow grave they are thrust,
Only a yard beneath the street,
And the hoofs of the horses beat, beat,
The hoofs of the horses beat,

Beat into my scalp and my brain,
With never an end to the stream of passing feet,
Driving, hurrying, marrying, burying,
Clamour and rumble, and ringing and clatter,
And here beneath it is all as bad,
For I thought the dead had peace, but it is not so;
To have no peace in the grave, is that not sad?
But up and down and to and fro,
Ever about me the dead men go;
And then to hear a dead man chatter
Is enough to drive one mad.

II

Wretchedest age, since Time began,
They cannot even bury a man;
And tho' we paid our tithes in the days that are gone,
Not a bell was rung, not a prayer was read;
It is that which makes us loud in the world of the dead;
There is none that does his work, not one;
A touch of their office might have sufficed,
But the churchmen fain would kill their church,
As the churches have kill'd their Christ.

III

See, there is one of us sobbing,
No limit to his distress;
And another, a lord of all things, praying
To his own great self, as I guess;
And another, a statesman there, betraying
His party-secret, fool, to the press;
And yonder a vile physician, blabbing
The case of his patient – all for what?
To tickle the maggot born in an empty head,
And wheedle a world that loves him not,
For it is but a world of the dead.

IV

Nothing but idiot gabble!
For the prophecy given of old
And then not understood,
Has come to pass as foretold;
Not let any man think for the public good,
But babble, merely for babble.
For I never whisper'd a private affair
Within the hearing of cat or mouse,
No, not to myself in the closet alone,

But I heard it shouted at once from the top of the house;
Everything came to be known:
Who told *him*, we were there?

V

Not that grey old wolf, for he came not back
From the wilderness, full of wolves, where he used to lie;
He has gather'd the bones for his o'ergrown whelp to crack;
Crack them now for yourself, and howl, and die.

VI

Prophet, curse me the blabbing lip,
And curse me the British vermin, the rat;
I know not whether he came in the Hanover ship,
But I know that he lies and listens mute
In an ancient mansion's crannies and holes:
Arsenic, arsenic, sure, would do it,
Except that now we poison our babes, poor souls!
It is all used up for that.

VII

Tell him now: she is standing here at my head;
Not beautiful now, not even kind;
He may take her now; for she never speaks her mind,
But is ever the one thing silent here.
She is not of us, as I divine;
She comes from another stiller world of the dead,
Stiller, not fairer than mine.

VIII

But I know where a garden grows,
Fairer than aught in the world beside,
All made up of the lily and rose
That blow by night, when the season is good,
To the sound of dancing music and flutes:
It is only flowers, they had no fruits,
And I almost fear they are not roses, but blood;
For the keeper was one, so full of pride,
He linkt a dead man there to a spectral bride;
For he, if he had not been a Sultan of brutes,
Would he have that hole in his side?

IX

But what will the old man say?
He laid a cruel snare in a pit
To catch a friend of mine one stormy day;

Yet now I could even weep to think of it;
For what will the old man say
When he comes to the second corpse in the pit?

X

Friend, to be struck by the public foe,
Then to strike him and lay him low,
That were a public merit, far,
Whatever the Quaker holds, from sin;
But the red life spilt for a private blow –
I swear to you, lawful and lawless war
Are scarcely even akin.

XI

O me, why have they not buried me deep enough?
Is it kind to have made me a grave so rough,
Me, that was never a quiet sleeper?
Maybe still I am but half-dead;
Then I cannot be wholly dumb;
I will cry to the steps above my head,
And somebody, surely, some kind heart will come
To bury me, bury me
Deeper, ever so little deeper.

Maud: Part 3

VI

I

My life has crept so long on a broken wing
Thro' cells of madness, haunts of horror and fear,
That I come to be grateful at last for a little thing:
My mood is changed, for it fell at a time of year
When the face of night is fair on the dewy downs,
And the shining daffodil dies, and the Charioteer
And starry Gemini hang like glorious crowns
Over Orion's grave low down in the west,
That like a silent lightning under the stars
She seem'd to divide in a dream from a band of the blest,
And spoke of a hope for the world in the coming wars –
'And in that hope, dear soul, let trouble have rest,
Knowing I tarry for thee,' and pointed to Mars
As he glow'd like a ruddy shield on the Lion's breast.

II

And it was but a dream, yet it yielded a dear delight
To have look'd, tho' but in a dream, upon eyes so fair,
That had been in a weary world my one thing bright;
And it was but a dream, yet it lighten'd my despair
When I thought that a war would arise in defence of the
    right,
That an iron tyranny now should bend or cease,
The glory of manhood stand on his ancient height,
Nor Britain's one sole God be the millionaire:
No more shall commerce be all in all, and Peace
Pipe on her pastoral hillock a languid note,
And watch her harvest ripen, her herd increase,
Nor the cannon-bullet rust on a slothful shore,
And the cobweb woven across the cannon's throat
Shall shake its threaded tears in the wind no more.

III

And as months ran on and rumour of battle grew,
'It is time, it is time, O passionate heart,' said I
(For I cleaved to a cause that I felt to be pure and true),
'It is time, O passionate heart and morbid eye,
That old hysterical mock-disease should die.'
And I stood on a giant deck and mix'd my breath
With a loyal people shouting a battle cry,
Till I saw the dreary phantom arise and fly
Far into the North, and battle, and seas of death.

IV

Let it go or stay, so I wake to the higher aims
Of a land that has lost for a little her lust of gold,
And love of a peace that was full of wrongs and shames,
Horrible, hateful, monstrous, not to be told;
And hail once more to the banner of battle unroll'd!
Tho' many a light shall darken, and many shall weep
For those that are crush'd in the clash of jarring claims,
Yet God's just wrath shall be wreak'd on a giant liar;
And many a darkness into the light shall leap,
And shine in the sudden making of splendid names,
And noble thought be freër under the sun,
And the heart of a people beat with one desire;
For the peace, that I deem'd no peace, is over and done,
And now by the side of the Black and the Baltic deep,
And deathful-grinning mouths of the fortress, flames
The blood-red blossom of war with a heart of fire.

v

Let it flame or fade, and the war roll down like a wind,
We have proved we have hearts in a cause, we are noble
    still,
And myself have awaked, as it seems, to the better mind;
It is better to fight for the good, than to rail at the ill;
I have felt with my native land, I am one with my kind,
I embrace the purpose of God, and the doom assign'd.

The Brook

An Idyl

'Here, by this brook, we parted; I to the East
And he for Italy – too late – too late:
One whom the strong sons of the world despise;
For lucky rhymes to him were scrip and share,
And mellow metres more than cent for cent;
Nor could he understand how money breeds,
Thought it a dead thing; yet himself could make
The thing that is not as the thing that is.
O had he lived! In our schoolbooks we say,
Of those that held their heads above the crowd,
They flourish'd then or then; but life in him
Could scarce be said to flourish, only touch'd
On such a time as goes before the leaf,
When all the wood stands in a mist of green,
And nothing perfect: yet the brook he loved,
For which, in branding summers of Bengal,
Or ev'n the sweet half-English Neilgherry air
I panted, seems, as I re-listen to it,
Prattling the primrose fancies of the boy,
To me that loved him; for "O brook," he says,
"O babbling brook," says Edmund in his rhyme,
"Whence come you?" and the brook, why not? replies.

I come from haunts of coot and hern,
    I make a sudden sally
And sparkle out among the fern,
    To bicker down a valley.

By thirty hills I hurry down
    Or slip between the ridges,
By twenty thorps, a little town,
    And half a hundred bridges.

> Till last by Philip's farm I flow
> > To join the brimming river,
> For men may come and men may go,
> > But I go on for ever.

'Poor lad, he died at Florence, quite worn out,
Travelling to Naples. There is Darnley bridge,
It has more ivy; there the river; and there
Stands Philip's farm where brook and river meet.

> I chatter over stony ways,
> > In little sharps and trebles,
> I bubble into eddying bays
> > I babble on the pebbles.

> With many a curve my banks I fret
> > By many a field and fallow,
> And many a fairy foreland set
> > With willow-weed and mallow.

> I chatter, chatter, as I flow
> > To join the brimming river,
> For men may come and men may go,
> > But I go on for ever.

'But Philip chatter'd more than brook or bird;
Old Philip; all about the fields you caught
His weary daylong chirping, like the dry
High-elbow'd grigs that leap in summer grass.

> I wind about, and in and out,
> > With here a blossom sailing,
> And here and there a lusty trout,
> > And here and there a grayling,

> And here and there a foamy flake
> > Upon me, as I travel
> With many a silvery waterbreak
> > Above the golden gravel,

> And draw them all along, and flow
> > To join the brimming river,
> For men may come and men may go,
> > But I go on for ever.

'O darling Katie Willows, his one child!
A maiden of our century, yet most meek;
A daughter of our meadows, yet not coarse;

Straight, but as lissome as a hazel wand;
Her eyes a bashful azure, and her hair
In gloss and hue the chestnut, when the shell
Divides threefold to show the fruit within.

'Sweet Katie, once I did her a good turn,
Her and her far-off cousin and betrothed,
James Willows, of one name and heart with her.
For here I came, twenty years back – the week
Before I parted with poor Edmund; crost
By that old bridge which, half in ruins then,
Still makes a hoary eyebrow for the gleam
Beyond it, where the waters marry – crost,
Whistling a random bar of Bonny Doon,
And push'd at Philip's garden-gate. The gate,
Half-parted from a weak and scolding hinge,
Stuck; and he clamour'd from a casement, "Run"
To Katie somewhere in the walks below,
"Run, Katie!" Katie never ran: she moved
To meet me, winding under woodbine bowers,
A little flutter'd, with her eyelids down,
Fresh apple-blossom, blushing for a boon.

'What was it? less of sentiment than sense
Had Katie, not illiterate; nor of those
Who dabbling in the fount of fictive tears,
And nursed by mealy-mouth'd philanthropies,
Divorce the Feeling from her mate the Deed.

'She told me. She and James had quarrell'd. Why?
What cause of quarrel? None, she said, no cause:
James had no cause: but when I prest the cause,
I learnt that James had flickering jealousies
Which anger'd her. Who anger'd James? I said.
But Katie snatch'd her eyes at once from mine,
And sketching with her slender pointed foot
Some figure like a wizard's pentagram
On garden gravel, let my query pass
Unclaim'd, in flushing silence, till I ask'd
If James were coming. "Coming every day,"
She answer'd, "ever longing to explain,
But evermore her father came across
With some long-winded tale, and broke him short;
And James departed vext with him and her."
How could I help her? "Would I – was it wrong?"
(Claspt hands and that petitionary grace

Of sweet seventeen subdued me ere she spoke)
"O would I take her father for one hour,
For one half-hour, and let him talk to me!"
And even while she spoke, I saw where James
Made toward us, like a wader in the surf,
Beyond the brook, waist-deep in meadow-sweet.

   'O Katie, what I suffer'd for your sake!
For in I went, and call'd old Philip out
To show the farm: full willingly he rose:
He led me thro' the short sweet-smelling lanes
Of his wheat-suburb, babbling as he went.
He praised his land, his horses, his machines;
He praised his ploughs, his cows, his hogs, his dogs;
He praised his hens, his geese, his guinea-hens;
His pigeons, who in session on their roofs
Approved him, bowing at their own deserts:
Then from the plaintive mother's teat he took
Her blind and shuddering puppies, naming each,
And naming those, his friends, for whom they were:
Then crost the common into Darnley chase
To show Sir Arthur's deer. In copse and fern
Twinkled the innumerable ear and tail.
Then, seated on a serpent-rooted beech,
He pointed out a pasturing colt, and said:
"That was the four-year-old I sold the Squire."
And there he told a long long-winded tale
Of how the Squire had seen the colt at grass,
And how it was the thing his daughter wish'd,
And how he sent the bailiff to the farm
To learn the price, and what the price he ask'd,
And how the bailiff swore that he was mad,
But he stood firm; and so the matter hung;
He gave them line: and five days after that
He met the bailiff at the Golden Fleece,
Who then and there had offer'd something more,
But he stood firm; and so the matter hung;
He knew the man; the colt would fetch its price;
He gave them line: and how by chance at last
(It may be May or April, he forgot,
The last of April or the first of May)
He found the bailiff riding by the farm
And, talking from the point, he drew him in,
And there he mellow'd all his heart with ale,
Until they closed a bargain, hand in hand.

'Then, while I breathed in sight of haven, he,
Poor fellow, could he help it? recommended,
And ran thro' all the coltish chronicle,
Wild Will, Black Bess, Tantivy, Tallyho,
Reform, White Rose, Bellerophon, the Jilt,
Arbaces, and Phenomenon, and the rest,
Till, not to die a listener, I arose,
And with me Philip, talking still; and so
We turn'd our foreheads from the falling sun,
And following our own shadows thrice as long
As when they follow'd us from Philip's door,
Arrived, and found the sun of sweet content
Re-risen in Katie's eyes, and all things well.

> I steal by lawns and grassy plots,
>   I slide by hazel covers;
> I move the sweet forget-me-nots
>   That grow for happy lovers.

> I slip, I slide, I gloom, I glance
>   Among my skimming swallows
> I make the netted sunbeam dance
>   Against my sandy shallows.

> I murmur under moon and stars
>   In brambly wildernesses;
> I linger by my shingly bars;
>   I loiter round my cresses;

> And out again I curve and flow
>   To join the brimming river,
> For men may come and men may go,
>   But I go on for ever.

Yes, men may come and go; and these are gone,
All gone. My dearest brother, Edmund, sleeps,
Not by the well-known stream and rustic spire,
But unfamiliar Arno, and the dome
Of Brunelleschi; sleeps in peace: and he,
Poor Philip, of all his lavish waste of words
Remains the lean P. W. on his tomb:
I scraped the lichen from it: Katie walks
By the long wash of Australasian seas
Far off, and holds her head to other stars,
And breathes in converse seasons. All are gone.'

So Lawrence Aylmer, seated on a stile
In the long hedge, and rolling in his mind
Old waifs of rhyme, and bowing o'er the brook
A tonsured head in middle age forlorn,
Mused, and was mute. On a sudden a low breath
Of tender air made tremble in the hedge
The fragile bindweed-bells and briony rings;
And he look'd up. There stood a maiden near,
Waiting to pass. In much amaze he stared
On eyes a bashful azure, and on hair
In gloss and hue the chestnut, when the shell
Divides threefold to show the fruit within:
Then, wondering, ask'd her 'Are you from the farm?'
'Yes,' answer'd she. 'Pray stay a little: pardon me;
What do they call you?' 'Katie.' 'That were strange.
What surname?' 'Willows.' 'No!' 'That is my name.'
'Indeed!' and here he look'd so self-perplext,
That Katie laugh'd, and laughing blush'd, till he
Laugh'd also, but as one before he wakes,
Who feels a glimmering strangeness in his dream.
Then looking at her; 'Too happy, fresh and fair,
Too fresh and fair in our sad world's best bloom.
To be the ghost of one who bore your name
About these meadows, twenty years ago.'

'Have you not heard?' said Katie, 'we came back.
We bought the farm we tenanted before.
Am I so like her? so they said on board.
Sir, if you knew her in her English days,
My mother, as it seems you did, the days
That most she loves to talk of, come with me.
My brother James is in the harvest-field:
But she – you will be welcome – O, come in!'

The Letters

I

Still on the tower stood the vane,
    A black yew gloom'd the stagnant air,
I peer'd athwart the chancel pane
    And saw the altar cold and bare.
A clog of lead was round my feet,
    A band of pain across my brow;
'Cold altar, Heaven and earth shall meet
    Before you hear my marriage vow.'

II

I turn'd and humm'd a bitter song
　　That mock'd the wholesome human heart,
And then we met in wrath and wrong,
　　We met, but only meant to part.
Full cold my greeting was and dry;
　　She faintly smiled, she hardly moved;
I saw with half-unconscious eye
　　She wore the colours I approved.

III

She took the little ivory chest,
　　With half a sigh she turn'd the key,
Then raised her head with lips comprest,
　　And gave my letters back to me.
And gave the trinkets and the rings,
　　My gifts, when gifts of mine could please;
As looks a father on the things
　　Of his dead son, I look'd on these.

IV

She told me all her friends had said;
　　I raged against the public liar;
She talk'd as if her love were dead,
　　But in my words were seeds of fire.
'No more of love; your sex is known:
　　I never will be twice deceived.
Henceforth I trust the man alone,
　　The woman cannot be believed.

V

'Thro' slander, meanest spawn of Hell
　　(And women's slander is the worst),
And you, whom once I loved so well,
　　Thro' you, my life will be accurst.'
I spoke with heart, and heat and force,
　　I shook her breast with vague alarms –
Like torrents from a mountain source
　　We rush'd into each other's arms.

VI

We parted: sweetly gleam'd the stars,
　　And sweet the vapour-braided blue,
Low breezes fann'd the belfry bars,
　　As homeward by the church I drew.
The very graves appear'd to smile,
　　So fresh they rose in shadow'd swells;
'Dark porch,' I said, 'and silent aisle,
　　There comes a sound of marriage bells.'

The Daisy

written at Edinburgh

O love, what hours were thine and mine,
In lands of palm and southern pine;
　　In lands of palm, of orange-blossom,
Of olive, aloe, and maize and vine.

What Roman strength Turbìa show'd
In ruin, by the mountain road;
　　How like a gem, beneath, the city
Of little Monaco, basking, glow'd.

How richly down the rocky dell
The torrent vineyard streaming fell
　　To meet the sun and sunny waters,
That only heaved with a summer swell.

What slender campanili grew
By bays, the peacock's neck in hue;
　　Where, here and there, on sandy beaches
A milky-bell'd amaryllis blew.

How young Columbus seem'd to rove,
Yet present in his natal grove,
　　Now watching high on mountain cornice,
And steering, now, from a purple cove,

Now pacing mute by ocean's rim;
Till, in a narrow street and dim,
　　I stay'd the wheels at Cogoletto,
And drank, and loyally drank to him.

Nor knew we well what pleased us most,
Not the clipt palm of which they boast;
　　But distant colour, happy hamlet,
A moulder'd citadel on the coast,

Or tower, or high hill-convent, seen
A light amid its olives green;
　　Or olive-hoary cape in ocean;
Or rosy blossom in hot ravine,

Where oleanders flush'd the bed
Of silent torrents, gravel-spread;
　　And, crossing, oft we saw the glisten
Of ice, far up on a mountain head.

We loved that hall, tho' white and cold,
Those niched shapes of noble mould,
   A princely people's awful princes,
The grave, severe Genovese of old.

At Florence too what golden hours,
In those long galleries, were ours;
   What drives about the fresh Cascinè,
Or walks in Boboli's ducal bowers.

In bright vignettes, and each complete,
Of tower or duomo, sunny-sweet,
   Or palace, how the city glitter'd,
Thro' cypress avenues, at our feet.

But when we crost the Lombard plain
Remember what a plague of rain;
   Of rain at Reggio, rain at Parma;
At Lodi, rain, Piacenza, rain.

And stern and sad (so rare the smiles
Of sunlight) look'd the Lombard piles;
   Porch-pillars on the lion resting,
And sombre, old, colonnaded aisles.

O Milan, O the chanting quires,
The giant windows' blazon'd fires,
   The height, the space, the gloom, the glory!
A mount of marble, a hundred spires!

I climb'd the roofs at break of day;
Sun-smitten Alps before me lay.
   I stood among the silent statues,
And statued pinnacles, mute as they.

How faintly-flush'd, how phantom-fair,
Was Monte Rosa, hanging there
   A thousand shadowy-pencill'd valleys
And snowy dells in a golden air.

Remember how we came at last
To Como; shower and storm and blast
   Had blown the lake beyond his limit,
And all was flooded; and how we past

From Como, when the light was grey,
And in my head, for half the day,
   The rich Virgilian rustic measure
Of Lari Maxume, all the way,

Like ballad-burthen music, kept,
As on The Lariano crept
   To that fair port below the castle
Of Queen Theodolind, where we slept;

Or hardly slept, but watch'd awake
A cypress in the moonlight shake,
   The moonlight touching o'er a terrace
One tall Agave above the lake.

What more? we took our last adieu,
And up the snowy Splugen drew,
   But ere we reach'd the highest summit
I pluck'd a daisy, I gave it you.

It told of England then to me,
And now it tells of Italy.
   O love, we two shall go no longer
To lands of summer across the sea;

So dear a life your arms enfold
Whose crying is a cry for gold:
   Yet here to-night in this dark city,
When ill and weary, alone and cold,

I found, tho' crush'd to hard and dry,
This nurseling of another sky
   Still in the little book you lent me,
And where you tenderly laid it by:

And I forgot the clouded Forth,
The gloom that saddens Heaven and Earth,
   The bitter east, the misty summer
And grey metropolis of the North.

Perchance, to lull the throbs of pain,
Perchance, to charm a vacant brain,
   Perchance, to dream you still beside me,
My fancy fled to the South again.

To the Rev. F. D. Maurice

Come, when no graver cares employ,
Godfather, come and see your boy:
   Your presence will be sun in winter,
Making the little one leap for joy.

For, being of that honest few,
Who give the Fiend himself his due,
   Should eighty-thousand college-councils
Thunder 'Anathema,' friend, at you;

Should all our churchmen foam in spite
At you, so careful of the right,
   Yet one lay-hearth would give you welcome
(Take it and come) to the Isle of Wight;

Where, far from noise and smoke of town,
I watch the twilight falling brown
   All round a careless-order'd garden
Close to the ridge of a noble down.

You'll have no scandal while you dine,
But honest talk and wholesome wine,
   And only hear the magpie gossip
Garrulous under a roof of pine:

For groves of pine on either hand,
To break the blast of winter, stand;
   And further on, the hoary Channel
Tumbles a breaker on chalk and sand;

Where, if below the milky steep
Some ship of battle slowly creep,
   And on thro' zones of light and shadow
Glimmer away to the lonely deep,

We might discuss the Northern sin
Which made a selfish war begin;
   Dispute the claims, arrange the chances;
Emperor, Ottoman, which shall win:

Or whether war's avenging rod
Shall lash all Europe into blood;
   Till you should turn to dearer matters,
Dear to the man that is dear to God;

How best to help the slender store,
How mend the dwellings, of the poor;
    How gain in life, as life advances,
Valour and charity more and more.

Come, Maurice, come: the lawn as yet
Is hoar with rime, or spongy-wet;
    But when the wreath of March has blossom'd,
Crocus, anemone, violet,

Or later, pay one visit here,
For those are few we hold as dear;
    Nor pay but one, but come for many,
Many and many a happy year.

Will

I

O well for him whose will is strong!
He suffers, but he will not suffer long;
He suffers, but he cannot suffer wrong:
For him nor moves the loud world's random mock,
Nor all Calamity's hugest waves confound,
Who seems a promontory of rock,
That, compass'd round with turbulent sound,
In middle ocean meets the surging shock,
Tempest-buffeted, citadel-crown'd.

II

But ill for him who, bettering not with time,
Corrupts the strength of heaven-descended Will,
And ever weaker grows thro' acted crime,
Or seeming-genial venial fault,
Recurring and suggesting still!
He seems as one whose footsteps halt,
Toiling in immeasurable sand,
And o'er a weary sultry land,
Far beneath a blazing vault,
Sown in a wrinkle of the monstrous hill,
The city sparkles like a grain of salt.

The War

There is a sound of thunder afar,
   Storm in the South that darkens the day,
Storm of battle and thunder of war,
   Well, if it do not roll our way.
      Storm! storm! Riflemen form!
      Ready, be ready to meet the storm!
      Riflemen, riflemen, riflemen form!

Be not deaf to the sound that warns!
   Be not gull'd by a despot's plea!
Are figs of thistles, or grapes of thorns?
   How should a despot set men free?
      Form! form! Riflemen form!
      Ready, be ready to meet the storm!
      Riflemen, riflemen, riflemen form!

Let your reforms for a moment go,
   Look to your butts and take good aims.
Better a rotten borough or so,
   Than a rotten fleet or a city in flames!
      Form! form! Riflemen form!
      Ready, be ready to meet the storm!
      Riflemen, riflemen, riflemen form!

Form, be ready to do or die!
   Form in Freedom's name and the Queen's!
True, that we have a faithful ally,
   But only the Devil knows what he means.
      Form! form! Riflemen form!
      Ready, be ready to meet the storm!
      Riflemen, riflemen, riflemen form!

IDYLLS OF THE KING

Dedication

These to His Memory – since he held them dear,
Perchance as finding there unconsciously
Some image of himself – I dedicate,
I dedicate, I consecrate with tears –
These Idylls.

        And indeed He seems to me
Scarce other than my own ideal knight,
'Who reverenced his conscience as his king;
Whose glory was, redressing human wrong;
Who spake no slander, no, nor listen'd to it;
Who loved one only and who clave to her – '
Her – over all whose realms to their last isle,
Commingled with the gloom of imminent war,
The shadow of His loss drew like eclipse,
Darkening the world. We have lost him: he is gone:
We know him now: all narrow jealousies
Are silent, and we see him as he moved,
How modest, kindly, all-accomplish'd, wise,
With what sublime repression of himself,
And in what limits, and how tenderly;
Not swaying to this faction or to that,
Not making his high place the lawless perch
Of wing'd ambitions, nor a vantage-ground
For pleasure, but thro' all this tract of years
Wearing the white flower of a blameless life,
Before a thousand peering littlenesses,
In that fierce light which beats upon a throne,
And blackens every blot: for where is he,
Who dares foreshadow for an only son
A lovelier life, a more unstain'd, than his?
Or how should England dreaming of *his* sons
Hope more for these than some inheritance
Of such a life, a heart, a mind as thine,
Thou noble Father of her Kings to be,
Laborious for her people and her poor –
Voice in the rich dawn of an ampler day –
Far-sighted summoner of War and Waste

To fruitful strifes and rivalries of peace –
Sweet nature gilded by the gracious gleam
Of letters, dear to Science, dear to Art,
Dear to thy land and ours, a Prince indeed,
Beyond all titles, and a household name,
Hereafter, thro' all times, Albert the Good.

Break not, O woman's-heart, but still endure,
Break not, for thou art Royal, but endure,
Remembering all the beauty of that star
Which shone so close beside Thee, that ye made
One light together, but has past and leaves
The Crown a lonely splendour.

                              May all love
His love, unseen but felt, o'ershadow Thee,
The love of all Thy sons encompass Thee,
The love of all Thy daughters cherish Thee,
The love of all Thy people comfort Thee,
Till God's love set Thee at his side again!

Enid

The brave Geraint, a knight of Arthur's court,
A tributary prince of Devon, one
Of that great order of the Table Round,
Had married Enid, Yniol's only child,
And loved her, as he loved the light of Heaven.
And as the light of Heaven varies, now
At sunrise, now at sunset, now by night
With moon and trembling stars, so loved Geraint
To make her beauty vary day by day,
In crimsons and in purples and in gems.
And Enid, but to please her husband's eye,
Who first had found and loved her in a state
Of broken fortunes, daily fronted him
In some fresh splendour; and the Queen herself
Grateful to Prince Geraint for service done
Loved her, and often with her own white hands
Array'd and deck'd her, as the loveliest,
Next after her own self, in all the court.
And Enid loved the Queen, and with true heart
Adored her, as the stateliest and the best
And loveliest of all women upon earth.

And seeing them so tender and so close,
Long in their common love rejoiced Geraint.
But when a rumour rose about the Queen,
Touching her guilty love for Lancelot,
Tho' yet there lived no proof, nor yet was heard
The world's loud whisper breaking into storm,
Not less Geraint believed it; and there fell
A horror on him, lest his gentle wife,
Thro' that great tenderness for Guinevere,
Had suffer'd, or should suffer any taint
In nature: wherefore going to the king,
He made this pretext, that, his princedom lay
Close on the borders of a territory,
Wherein were bandit earls, and caitiff knights,
Assassins, and all flyers from the hand
Of Justice, and whatever loathes a law:
And therefore, till the king himself should please
To cleanse this common sewer of all his realm,
He craved a fair permission to depart,
And there defend his marches; and the king
Mused for a little on his plea, but, last,
Allowing it, the Prince and Enid rode,
And fifty knights rode with them, to the shores
Of Severn, and they past to their own land;
Where, thinking, that if ever yet was wife
True to her lord, mine shall be so to me,
He compass'd her with sweet observances
And worship, never leaving her, and grew
Forgetful of his promise to the king,
Forgetful of the falcon and the hunt,
Forgetful of the tilt and tournament,
Forgetful of his glory and his name,
Forgetful of his princedom and its cares.
And this forgetfulness was hateful to her.
And by and by the people, when they met
In twos and threes, or fuller companies,
Began to scoff and jeer and babble of him
As of a prince whose manhood was all gone,
And molten down in mere uxoriousness.
And this she gather'd from the people's eyes:
This too the women who attired her head,
To please her, dwelling on his boundless love,
Told Enid, and they sadden'd her the more:
And day by day she thought to tell Geraint,
But could not out of bashful delicacy;
While he that watch'd her sadden, was the more

Suspicious that her nature had a taint.

    At last, it chanced that on a summer morn
(They sleeping each by other) the new sun
Beat thro' the blindless casement of the room,
And heated the strong warrior in his dreams;
Who, moving, cast the coverlet aside,
And bared the knotted column of his throat,
The massive square of his heroic breast,
And arms on which the standing muscle sloped,
As slopes a wild brook o'er a little stone,
Running too vehemently to break upon it.
And Enid woke and sat beside the couch,
Admiring him, and thought within herself,
Was ever man so grandly made as he?
Then, like a shadow, past the people's talk
And accusation of uxoriousness
Across her mind, and bowing over him,
Low to her own heart piteously she said:

   'O noble breast and all-puissant arms,
Am I the cause, I the poor cause that men
Reproach you, saying all your force is gone?
I *am* the cause because I dare not speak
And tell him what I think and what they say.
And yet I hate that he should linger here;
I cannot love my lord and not his name.
Far liefer had I gird his harness on him,
And ride with him to battle and stand by,
And watch his mightful hand striking great blows
At caitiffs and at wrongers of the world.
Far better were I laid in the dark earth,
Not hearing any more his noble voice,
Not to be folded more in these dear arms,
And darken'd from the high light in his eyes,
Than that my lord thro' me should suffer shame.
Am I so bold, and could I so stand by,
And see my dear lord wounded in the strife,
Or maybe pierced to death before mine eyes,
And yet not dare to tell him what I think,
And how men slur him, saying all his force
Is melted into mere effeminacy?
O me, I fear that I am no true wife.'

    Half inwardly, half audibly she spoke,
And the strong passion in her made her weep

True tears upon his broad and naked breast,
And these awoke him, and by great mischance
He heard but fragments of her later words,
And that she fear'd she was not a true wife.
And then he thought, 'In spite of all my care,
For all my pains, poor man, for all my pains,
She is not faithful to me, and I see her
Weeping for some gay knight in Arthur's hall.'
Then tho' he loved and reverenced her too much
To dream she could be guilty of foul act,
Right thro' his manful breast darted the pang
That makes a man, in the sweet face of her
Whom he loves most, lonely and miserable.
At this he hurl'd his huge limbs out of bed,
And shook his drowsy squire awake and cried,
'My charger and her palfrey,' then to her,
'I will ride forth into the wilderness;
For tho' it seems my spurs are yet to win,
I have not fall'n so low as some would wish.
And you, put on your worst and meanest dress
And ride with me.' And Enid ask'd, amazed,
'If Enid errs, let Enid learn her fault.'
But he, 'I charge you, ask not but obey.'
Then she bethought her of a faded silk,
A faded mantle and a faded veil
And moving toward a cedarn cabinet,
Wherein she kept them folded reverently
With sprigs of summer laid between the folds,
She took them, and array'd herself therein,
Remembering when first he came on her
Drest in that dress, and how he loved her in it,
And all her foolish fears about the dress,
And all his journey to her, as himself
Had told her, and their coming to the court.

    For Arthur on the Whitsuntide before
Held court at old Caerleon upon Usk.
There on a day, he sitting high in hall,
Before him came a forester of Dean,
Wet from the woods, with notice of a hart
Taller than all his fellows, milky-white,
First seen that day: these things he told the king.
Then the good king gave order to let blow
His horns for hunting on the morrow morn.
And when the Queen petition'd for his leave
To see the hunt, allow'd it easily.

So with the morning all the court were gone.
But Guinevere lay late into the morn,
Lost in sweet dreams, and dreaming of her love
For Lancelot, and forgetful of the hunt;
But rose at last, a single maiden with her,
Took horse, and forded Usk, and gain'd the wood;
There, on a little knoll beside it, stay'd
Waiting to hear the hounds; but heard instead
A sudden sound of hoofs, for Prince Geraint,
Late also, wearing neither hunting-dress
Nor weapon, save a golden-hilted brand,
Came quickly flashing thro' the shallow ford
Behind them, and so gallop'd up the knoll.
A purple scarf, at either end whereof
There swung an apple of the purest gold,
Sway'd round about him, as he gallop'd up
To join them, glancing like a dragon-fly
In summer suit and silks of holiday.
Low bow'd the tributary Prince, and she,
Sweetly and statelily, and with all grace
Of womanhood and queenhood, answer'd him:
'Late, late, Sir Prince,' she said, 'later than we!'
'Yea, noble Queen,' he answer'd, 'and so late
That I but come like you to see the hunt,
Not join it.' 'Therefore wait with me,' she said;
'For on this little knoll, if anywhere,
There is good chance that we shall hear the hounds:
Here often they break covert at our feet.'

    And while they listen'd for the distant hunt,
And chiefly for the baying of Cavall,
King Arthur's hound of deepest mouth, there rode
Full slowly by a knight, lady, and dwarf;
Whereof the dwarf lagg'd latest, and the knight
Had visor up, and show'd a youthful face,
Imperious, and of haughtiest lineaments.
And Guinevere, not mindful of his face
In the king's hall, desired his name, and sent
Her maiden to demand it of the dwarf;
Who being vicious, old and irritable,
And doubling all his master's vice of pride,
Made answer sharply that she should not know.
'Then will I ask it of himself,' she said.
'Nay, by my faith, thou shalt not,' cried the dwarf;
'Thou art not worthy ev'n to speak of him;'
And when she put her horse toward the knight,

Struck at her with his whip, and she return'd
Indignant to the Queen; at which Geraint
Exclaiming, 'Surely I will learn the name,'
Made sharply to the dwarf, and ask'd it of him,
Who answer'd as before; and when the Prince
Had put his horse in motion toward the knight,
Struck at him with his whip, and cut his cheek.
The Prince's blood spirted upon the scarf,
Dyeing it; and his quick, instinctive hand
Caught at the hilt, as to abolish him:
But he, from his exceeding manfulness
And pure nobility of temperament,
Wroth to be wroth at such a worm, refrain'd
From ev'n a word, and so returning said:

  'I will avenge this insult, noble Queen,
Done in your maiden's person to yourself:
And I will track this vermin to their earths:
For tho' I ride unarm'd, I do not doubt
To find, at some place I shall come at, arms
On loan, or else for pledge; and, being found,
Then will I fight him, and will break his pride,
And on the third day, will again be here,
So that I be not fall'n in fight. Farewell.'

  'Farewell, fair Prince,' answer'd the stately Queen.
'Be prosperous in this journey, as in all;
And may you light on all things that you love,
And live to wed with her whom first you love:
But ere you wed with any, bring your bride,
And I, were she the daughter of a king
Yea, tho' she were a beggar from the hedge,
Will clothe her for her bridals like the sun.'

  And Prince Geraint, now thinking that he heard
The noble hart at bay, now the far horn,
A little vext at losing of the hunt,
A little at the vile occasion, rode,
By ups and downs, thro' many a grassy glade
And valley, with fixt eye following the three.
At last they issued from the world of wood,
And climb'd upon a fair and even ridge,
And show'd themselves against the sky, and sank.
And thither came Geraint, and underneath
Beheld the long street of a little town
In a long valley, on one side of which

White from the mason's hand, a fortress rose;
And on one side a castle in decay,
Beyond a bridge that spann'd a dry ravine:
And out of town and valley came a noise
As of a broad brook o'er a shingly bed
Brawling, or like a clamour of the rooks
At distance, ere they settle for the night.

    And onward to the fortress rode the three,
And enter'd, and were lost behind the walls.
'So,' thought Geraint, 'I have track'd him to his earth.'
And down the long street riding wearily,
Found every hostel full, and everywhere
Was hammer laid to hoof, and the hot hiss
And bustling whistle of the youth who scour'd
His master's armour, and of such a one
He ask'd, 'What means the tumult in the town?'
Who told him, scouring still, 'The sparrow-hawk!'
Then riding close behind an ancient churl,
Who, smitten by the dusty sloping beam,
Went sweating underneath a sack of corn,
Ask'd yet once more what meant the huhbub here?
Who answer'd gruffly, 'Ugh! the sparrow-hawk.'
Then riding further past an armourer's,
Who, with back turn'd, and bow'd above his work,
Sat riveting a helmet on his knee,
He put the self-same query, but the man
Not turning round, nor looking at him, said:
'Friend, he that labours for the sparrow-hawk
Has little time for idle questioners.'
Whereat Geraint flash'd into sudden spleen:
'A thousand pips eat up your sparrow-hawk!
Tits, wrens and all wing'd nothings peck him dead!
Ye think the rustic cackle of your bourg
The murmur of the world! What is it to me?
O wretched set of sparrows, one and all,
Who pipe of nothing but of sparrow-hawks!
Speak, if you be not like the rest, hawk-mad,
Where can I get me harbourage for the night?
And arms, arms, arms to fight my enemy? Speak!'
At this the armourer turning all amazed
And seeing one so gay in purple silks,
Came forward with the helmet yet in hand
And answer'd, 'Pardon me, O stranger knight;

We hold a tourney here to-morrow morn
And there is scantly time for half the work.
Arms? truth! I know not: all are wanted here.
Harbourage? truth, good truth, I know not, save,
It may be, at Earl Yniol's, o'er the bridge
Yonder.' He spoke and fell to work again.

    Then rode Geraint, a little spleenful yet,
Across the bridge that spann'd the dry ravine.
There musing sat the hoary-headed Earl,
(His dress a suit of fray'd magnificence,
Once fit for feasts of ceremony) and said:
'Whither, fair son?' to whom Geraint replied,
'O friend, I seek a harbourage for the night.'
Then Yniol, 'Enter therefore and partake
The slender entertainment of a house
Once rich, now poor, but ever open-door'd.'
'Thanks, venerable friend,' replied Geraint;
'So that you do not serve me sparrow-hawks
For supper, I will enter, I will eat
With all the passion of a twelve hours' fast.'
Then sigh'd and smiled the hoary-headed Earl,
And answer'd, 'Graver cause than yours is mine
To curse this hedgerow thief, the sparrow-hawk:
But in go in; for save yourself desire it,
We will not touch upon him ev'n in jest.'

    Then rode Geraint into the castle court,
His charger trampling many a prickly star
Of sprouted thistle on the broken stones.
He look'd and saw that all was ruinous.
Here stood a shatter'd archway plumed with fern;
And here had fall'n a great part of a tower,
Whole, like a crag that tumbles from the cliff,
And like a crag was gay with wilding flowers:
And high above a piece of turret stair,
Worn by the feet that now were silent, wound
Bare to the sun, and monstrous ivy-stems
Claspt the grey walls with hairy-fibred arms,
And suck'd the joining of the stones, and look'd
A knot, beneath, of snakes, aloft, a grove.

    And while he waited in the castle court,
The voice of Enid, Yniol's daughter, rang
Clear thro' the open casement of the Hall,
Singing; and as the sweet voice of a bird,

Heard by the lander in a lonely isle,
Moves him to think what kind of bird it is
That sings so delicately clear, and make
Conjecture of the plumage and the form;
So the sweet voice of Enid moved Geraint;
And made him like a man abroad at morn
When first the liquid note beloved of men
Comes flying over many a windy wave
To Britain, and in April suddenly
Breaks from a coppice gemm'd with green and red,
And he suspends his converse with a friend,
Or it may be the labour of his hands,
To think or say, 'There is the nightingale;'
So fared it with Geraint who thought and said,
'Here, by God's grace, is the one voice for me.'

It chanced the song that Enid sang was one
Of Fortune and her wheel, and Enid sang:

'Turn, Fortune, turn thy wheel and lower the proud;
Turn thy wild wheel thro' sunshine, storm, and cloud;
Thy wheel and thee we neither love nor hate.

'Turn, Fortune, turn thy wheel with smile or frown;
With that wild wheel we go not up or down;
Our hoard is little, but our hearts are great.

'Smile and we smile, the lords of many lands,
Frown and we smile, the lords of our own hands,
For man is man and master of his fate.

'Turn, turn thy wheel above the staring crowd;
Thy wheel and thou are shadows in the cloud;
Thy wheel and thee we neither love nor hate.'

'Hark by the bird's song you may learn the nest,'
Said Yniol; 'Enter quickly.' Entering then,
Right o'er a mount of newly-fallen stones,
The dusky-rafter'd many-cobweb'd Hall,
He found an ancient dame in dim brocade;
And near her, like a blossom vermeil-white,
That lightly breaks a faded flower-sheath,
Moved the fair Enid, all in faded silk,
Her daughter. In a moment thought Geraint,
'Here by God's rood is the one maid for me.'
But none spake word except the hoary Earl:

'Enid, the good knight's horse stands in the court;
Take him to stall, and give him corn, and then
Go to the town and buy us flesh and wine;
And we will make us merry as we may.
Our hoard is little, but our hearts are great.'

He spake: the Prince, as Enid past him, fain
To follow, strode a stride, but Yniol caught
His purple scarf, and held, and said, 'Forbear!
Rest! the good house, tho' ruin'd, O my Son,
Endures not that her guest should serve himself.'
And reverencing the custom of the house
Geraint, from utter courtesy, forbore.

So Enid took his charger to the stall;
And after went her way across the bridge,
And reach'd the town, and while the Prince and Earl
Yet spoke together, came again with one,
A youth, that following with a costrel bore
The means of goodly welcome, flesh and wine.
And Enid brought sweet cakes to make them cheer,
And in her veil enfolded, manchet bread.
And then, because their hall must also serve
For kitchen, boil'd the-flesh, and spread the board,
And stood behind, and waited on the three.
And seeing her so sweet and serviceable,
Geraint had longing in him evermore
To stoop and kiss the tender little thumb,
That crost the trencher as she laid it down:
But after all had eaten, then Geraint,
For now the wine made summer in his veins,
Let his eye rove in following, or rest
On Enid at her lowly handmaid-work,
Now here, now there, about the dusky hall;
Then suddenly addrest the hoary Earl:

'Fair Host and Earl, I pray your courtesy
This sparrow-hawk, what is he, tell me of him.
His name? but no, good faith, I will not have it:
For if he be the knight whom late I saw
Ride into that new fortress by your town,
White from the mason's hand, then have I sworn
From his own lips to have it – I am Geraint
Of Devon – for this morning when the Queen
Sent her own maiden to demand the name,
His dwarf, a vicious under-shapen thing,
Struck at her with his whip, and she return'd

Indignant to the Queen; and then I swore
That I would track this caitiff to his hold,
And fight and break his pride, and have it of him.
And all unarm'd I rode, and thought to find
Arms in your town, where all the men are mad;
They take the rustic murmur of their bourg
For the great wave that echoes round the world;
They would not hear me speak: but if you know
Where I can light on arms, or if yourself
Should have them, tell me, seeing I have sworn
That I will break his pride and learn his name,
Avenging this great insult done the Queen.'

    Then cried Earl Yniol, 'Art thou he indeed,
Geraint, a name far-sounded among men
For noble deeds? and truly I, when first
I saw you moving by me on the bridge,
Felt you were somewhat, yea and by your state
And presence might have guess'd you one of those
That eat in Arthur's hall at Camelot.
Nor speak I now from foolish flattery;
For this dear child hath often heard me praise
Your feats of arms, and often when I paused
Hath ask'd again, and ever loved to hear;
So grateful is the noise of noble deeds
To noble hearts who see but acts of wrong:
O never yet had woman such a pair
Of suitors as this maiden; first Limours,
A creature wholly given to brawls and wine,
Drunk even when he woo'd; and be he dead
I know not, but he past to the wild land.
The second was your foe, the sparrow-hawk,
My curse, my nephew – I will not let his name
Slip from my lips if I can help it – he,
When I that knew him fierce and turbulent
Refused her to him, then his pride awoke;
And since the proud man often is the mean,
He sow'd a slander in the common ear,
Affirming that his father left him gold,
And in my charge, which was not render'd to him;
Bribed with large promises the men who served
About my person, the more easily
Because my means were somewhat broken into
Thro' open doors and hospitality;
Raised my own town against me in the night
Before my Enid's birthday, sack'd my house;

From mine own earldom foully ousted me;
Built that new fort to overawe my friends,
For truly there are those who love me yet;
And keeps me in this ruinous castle here,
Where doubtless he would put me soon to death,
But that his pride too much despises me:
And I myself sometimes despise myself;
For I have let men be, and have their way;
Am much too gentle, have not used my power:
Nor know I whether I be very base
Or very manful, whether very wise
Or very foolish; only this I know,
That whatsoever evil happen to me,
I seem to suffer nothing heart or limb,
But can endure it all most patiently.'

'Well said, true heart,' replied Geraint, 'but arms:
That if, as I suppose, your nephew fights
In next day's tourney I may break his pride.'

And Yniol answer'd, 'Arms, indeed, but old
And rusty, old and rusty, Prince Geraint,
Are mine, and therefore at your asking, yours.
But in this tournament can no man tilt,
Except the lady he loves best be there.
Two forks are fixt into the meadow ground,
And over these is laid a silver wand,
And over that is placed the sparrow-hawk,
The prize of beauty for the fairest there.
And this what knight soever be in field
Lays claim to for the lady at his side,
And tilts with my good nephew thereupon,
Who being apt at arms and big of bone
Has ever won it for the lady with him,
And toppling over all antagonism
Has earn'd himself the name of sparrow-hawk.
But you, that have no lady, cannot fight.'

To whom Geraint with eyes all bright replied,
Leaning a little toward him, 'Your leave!
Let *me* lay lance in rest, O noble host,
For this dear child, because I never saw,
Tho' having seen all beauties of our time,
Nor can see elsewhere, anything so fair.
And if I fall her name will yet remain
Untarnish'd as before; but if I live,

So aid me Heaven when at mine uttermost,
As I will make her truly my true wife.'

    Then, howsoever patient, Yniol's heart
Danced in his bosom, seeing better days.
And looking round he saw not Enid there,
(Who hearing her own name had slipt away)
But that old dame, to whom full tenderly
And fondling all her hand in his he said,
'Mother, a maiden is a tender thing
And best by her that bore her understood.
Go thou to rest, but ere thou go to rest
Tell her, and prove her heart toward the Prince.'

    So spake the kindly-hearted Earl, and she
With frequent smile and nod departing found,
Half disarray'd as to her rest, the girl;
Whom first she kiss'd on either cheek, and then
On either shilling shoulder laid a hand,
And kept her off and gazed upon her face,
And told her all their converse in the hall,
Proving her heart: but never light and shade
Coursed one another more on open ground
Beneath a troubled heaven, than red and pale
Across the face of Enid hearing her;
While slowly falling as a scale that falls,
When weight is added only grain by grain,
Sank her sweet head upon her gentle breast;
Nor did she lift an eye nor speak a word,
Rapt in the fear and in the wonder of it;
So moving without answer to her rest
She found no rest, and ever fail'd to draw
The quiet night into her blood, but lay
Contemplating her own unworthiness;
And when the pale and bloodless east began
To quicken to the sun, arose, and raised
Her mother too, and hand in hand they moved
Down to the meadow where the jousts were held,
And waited there for Yniol and Geraint.

    And thither came the twain, and when Geraint
Beheld her first in field, awaiting him,
He felt, were she the prize of bodily force
Himself beyond the rest pushing could move
The chair of Idris. Yniol's rusted arms
Were on his princely person, but thro' these
Princelike his bearing shone; and errant knights

And ladies came, and by and by the town
Flow'd in, and settling circled all the lists.
And there they fixt the forks into the ground,
And over these they placed a silver wand
And over that a golden sparrow-hawk.
Then Yniol's nephew, after trumpet blown
Spake to the lady with him and proclaim'd,
'Advance and take as fairest of the fair
For I these two years past have won it for thee,
The prize of beauty.' Loudly spake the Prince
'Forbear: there is a worthier,' and the knight
With some surprise and thrice as much disdain
Turn'd, and beheld the four, and all his face
Glow'd like the heart of a great fire at Yule,
So burnt he was with passion, crying out,
'Do battle for it then,' no more; and thrice
They clash'd together, and thrice they brake their spears.
Then each, dishorsed and drawing, lash'd at each
So often and with such blows, that all the crowd
Wonder'd, and now and then from distant walls
There came a clapping as of phantom hands.
So twice they fought, and twice they breathed, and still
The dew of their great labour, and the blood
Of their strong bodies, flowing, drain'd their force.
But either's force was match'd till Yniol's cry,
'Remember that great insult done the Queen,'
Increased Geraint's, who heaved his blade aloft,
And crack'd the helmet thro', and bit the bone,
And fell'd him, and set foot upon his breast,
And said, 'Thy name?' To whom the fallen man
Made answer, groaning, 'Edyrn, son of Nudd!
Ashamed am I that I should tell it thee.
My pride is broken: men have seen my fall.'
'Then, Edyrn, son of Nudd,' replied Geraint,
'These two things shalt thou do, or else thou diest.
First, thou thyself, thy lady, and thy dwarf,
Shalt ride to Arthur's court, and being there,
Crave pardon for that insult done the Queen,
And shalt abide her judgement on it; next,
Thou shalt give back their earldom to thy kin.
These two things shalt thou do, or thou shalt die.'
And Edyrn answer'd, 'These things will I do,
For I have never yet been overthrown,
And thou hast overthrown me, and my pride
Is broken down, for Enid sees my fall!'
And rising up, he rode to Arthur's court,

And there the Queen forgave him easily.
And being young, he changed himself, and grew
To hate the sin that seem'd so like his own
Of Modred, Arthur's nephew, and fell at last
In the great battle fighting for the king.

But when the third day from the hunting-morn
Made a low splendour in the world, and wings
Moved in her ivy, Enid, for she lay
With her fair head in the dim-yellow light,
Among the dancing shadows of the birds,
Woke and bethought her of her promise given
No later than last eve to Prince Geraint –
So bent he seem'd on going the third day,
He would not leave her, till her promise given –
To ride with him this morning to the court,
And there be made known to the stately Queen,
And there be wedded with all ceremony.
At this she cast her eyes upon her dress,
And thought it never yet had look'd so mean.
For as a leaf in mid-November is
To what it was in mid-October, seem'd
The dress that now she look'd on to the dress
She look'd on ere the coming of Geraint.
And still she look'd, and still the terror grew
Of that strange bright and dreadful thing, a court,
All staring at her in her faded silk:
And softly to her own sweet heart she said:

'This noble prince who won our earldom back,
So splendid in his acts and his attire,
Sweet heaven, how much I shall discredit him!
Would he could tarry with us here awhile!
But being so beholden to the Prince,
It were but little grace in any of us,
Bent as he seem'd on going this third day,
To seek a second favour at his hands.
Yet if he could but tarry a day or two,
Myself would work eye dim, and finger lame,
Far liefer than so much discredit him.'

And Enid fell in longing for a dress
All branch'd and flower'd with gold, a costly gift
Of her good mother, given her on the night
Before her birthday, three sad years ago,
That night of fire, when Edyrn sack'd their house,
And scatter'd all they had to all the winds:

For while the mother show'd it, and the two
Were turning and admiring it, the work
To both appear'd so costly, rose a cry
That Edyrn's men were on them, and they fled
With little save the jewels they had on,
Which being sold and sold had bought them bread:
And Edyrn's men had caught them in their flight,
And placed them in this ruin; and she wish'd
The Prince had found her in her ancient home;
Then let her fancy flit across the past,
And roam the goodly places that she knew;
And last bethought her how she used to watch,
Near that old home, a pool of golden carp
And one was patch'd and blurr'd and lustreless
Among his burnish'd brethren of the pool;
And half asleep she made comparison
Of that and these to her own faded self
And the gay court, and fell asleep again;
And dreamt herself was such a faded form
Among her burnish'd sisters of the pool;
But this was in the garden of a king;
And tho' she lay dark in the pool, she knew
That all was bright; that all about were birds
Of sunny plume in gilded trellis-work;
That all the turf was rich in plots that look'd
Each like a garnet or a turkis in it;
And lords and ladies of the high court went
In silver tissue talking things of state;
And children of the king in cloth of gold
Glanced at the doors or gambol'd down the walks;
And while she thought 'they will not see me,' came
A stately queen whose name was Guinevere,
And all the children in their cloth of gold
Ran to her, crying, 'If we have fish at all
Let them be gold; and charge the gardeners now
To pick the faded creature from the pool,
And cast it on the mixen that it die.'
And therewithal one came and seized on her,
And Enid started waking, with her heart
All overshadow'd by the foolish dream,
And lo! it was her mother grasping her
To get her well awake; and in her hand
A suit of bright apparel, which she laid
Flat on the couch, and spoke exultingly:

  'See here, my child, how fresh the colours look,

How fast they hold like colours of a shell
That keeps the wear and polish of the wave.
Why not? it never yet was worn, I trow:
Look on it, child, and tell me if you know it.'

    And Enid look'd, but all confused at first,
Could scarce divide it from her foolish dream:
Then suddenly she knew it and rejoiced,
And answer'd, 'Yea, I know it; your good gift,
So sadly lost on that unhappy night;
Your own good gift!' 'Yea, surely,' said the dame,
'And gladly given again this happy morn.
For when the jousts were ended yesterday,
Went Yniol thro' the town, and everywhere
He found the sack and plunder of our house
All scatter'd thro' the houses of the town;
And gave command that all which once was ours
Should now be ours again: and yester-eve
While you were talking sweetly with your Prince,
Came one with this and laid it in my hand,
For love or fear, or seeking favour of us,
Because we have our earldom back again.
And yester-eve I would not tell you of it,
But kept it for a sweet surprise at morn.
Yea, truly is it not a sweet surprise?
For I myself unwillingly have worn
My faded suit, as you, my child, have yours,
And howsoever patient, Yniol his.
Ah, dear, he took me from a goodly house,
With store of rich apparel, sumptuous fare,
And page, and maid, and squire, and seneschal,
And pastime both of hawk and hound, and all
That appertains to noble maintenance.
Yea, and he brought me to a goodly house;
But since our fortune slipt from sun to shade,
And all thro' that young traitor, cruel need
Constrain'd us, but a better time has come;
So clothe yourself in this, that better fits
Our mended fortunes and a Prince's bride:
For tho' you won the prize of fairest fair,
And tho' I heard him call you fairest fair,
Let never maiden think, however fair,
She is not fairer in new clothes than old.
And should some great court-lady say, the Prince
Hath pick'd a ragged-robin from the hedge,
And like a madman brought her to the court,

Then were you shamed, and, worse, might shame the Prince
To whom we are beholden; but I know,
When my dear child is set forth at her best,
That neither court nor country, tho' they sought
Thro' all the provinces like those of old
That lighted on Queen Esther, has her match.'

Here ceased the kindly mother out of breath;
And Enid listen'd brightening as she lay;
Then, as the white and glittering star of morn
Parts from a bank of snow, and by and by
Slips into golden cloud, the maiden rose,
And left her maiden couch, and robed herself,
Help'd by the mother's careful hand and eye,
Without a mirror, in the gorgeous gown;
Who, after, turn'd her daughter round, and said,
'She never yet had seen her half so fair;
And call'd her like that maiden in the tale,
Whom Gwydion made by glamour out of flowers,
And sweeter than the bride of Cassivelaun,
Flur, for whose love the Roman Caesar first
Invaded Britain, but we beat him back,
As this great prince invaded us, and we,
Not beat him back, but welcomed him with joy.
And I can scarcely ride with you to court,
For old am I, and rough the ways and wild;
But Yniol goes, and I full oft shall dream
I see my princess as I see her now,
Clothed with my gift, and gay among the gay.'

But while the women thus rejoiced, Geraint
Woke where he slept in the high hall, and call'd
For Enid, and when Yniol made report
Of that good mother making Enid gay
In such apparel as might well beseem
His princess, or indeed the stately queen,
He answer'd; 'Earl, entreat her by my love,
Albeit I give no reason but my wish,
That she ride with me in her faded silk.'
Yniol with that hard message went; it fell,
Like flaws in summer laying lusty corn:
For Enid, all abash'd she knew not why,
Dared not to glance at her good mother's face,
But silently, in all obedience,
Her mother silent too, nor helping her,
Laid from her limbs the costly-broider'd gift,

And robed them in her ancient suit again
And so descended. Never man rejoiced
More than Geraint to greet her thus attired;
And glancing all at once as keenly at her,
As careful robins eye the delver's toil
Made her cheek burn and either eyelid fall,
But rested with her sweet face satisfied;
Then seeing cloud upon the mother's brow,
Her by both hands he caught, and sweetly said,

'O my new mother, be not wroth or grieved
At your new son, for my petition to her.
When late I left Caerleon, our great Queen,
In words whose echo lasts, they were so sweet,
Made promise, that whatever bride I brought,
Herself would clothe her like the sun in Heaven.
Thereafter, when I reach'd this ruined hold,
Beholding one so bright in dark estate,
I vow'd that could I gain her, our kind Queen,
No hand but hers, should make your Enid burst
Sunlike from cloud – and likewise thought perhaps,
That service done so graciously would bind
The two together; for I wish the two
To love each other: how should Enid find
A nobler friend? Another thought I had;
I came among you here so suddenly,
That tho' her gentle presence at the lists
Might well have served for proof that I was loved,
I doubted whether filial tenderness,
Or easy nature, did not let itself
Be moulded by your wishes for her weal;
Or whether some false sense in her own self
Of my contrasting brightness, overbore
Her fancy dwelling in this dusky hall;
And such a sense might make her long for court
And all its dangerous glories: and I thought,
That could I someway prove such force in her
Link'd with such love for me, that at a word
(No reason given her) she could cast aside
A splendour dear to women, new to her,
And therefore dearer; or if not so new,
Yet therefore tenfold dearer by the power
Of intermitted custom; then I felt
That I could rest, a rock in ebbs and flows,
Fixt on her faith. Now, therefore, I do rest,
A prophet certain of my prophecy,

That never shadow of mistrust can cross
Between us. Grant me pardon for my thoughts:
And for my strange petition I will make
Amends hereafter by some gaudy-day,
When your fair child shall wear your costly gift
Beside your own warm hearth, with, on her knees,
Who knows? another gift of the high God,
Which, maybe, shall have learn'd to lisp you thanks.

   He spoke: the mother smiled, but half in tears,
Then brought a mantle down and wrapt her in it,
And claspt and kiss'd her, and they rode away.

   Now thrice that morning Guinevere had climb'd
The giant tower, from whose high crest, they say,
Men saw the goodly hills of Somerset,
And white sails flying on the yellow sea:
But not to goodly hill or yellow sea
Look'd the fair Queen, but up the vale of Usk,
By the flat meadow, till she saw them come;
And then descending met them at the gates,
Embraced her with all welcome as a friend,
And did her honour as the Prince's bride,
And clothed her for her bridals like the sun;
And all that week was old Caerleon gay,
For by the hands of Dubric, the high saint,
They twain were wedded with all ceremony.

   And this was on the last year's Whitsuntide.
But Enid ever kept the faded silk,
Remembering how first he came on her,
Drest in that dress, and how he loved her in it,
And all her foolish fears about the dress,
And all his journey toward her, as himself
Had told her, and their coming to the court.

   And now this morning when he said to her,
'Put on your worst and meanest dress,' she found
And took it, and array'd herself therein.

   O purblind race of miserable men,
How many among us at this very hour
Do forge a life-long trouble for ourselves,
By taking true for false, or false for true;
Here, thro' the feeble twilight of this world
Groping, how many, until we pass and reach

That other, where we see as we are seen!

So fared it with Geraint, who issuing forth
That morning, when they both had got to horse,
Perhaps because he loved her passionately,
And felt that tempest brooding round his heart,
Which, if he spoke at all, would break perforce
Upon a head so dear in thunder, said:
'Not at my side. I charge you ride before,
Ever a good way on before; and this
I charge you, on your duty as a wife,
Whatever happens, not to speak to me,
No, not a word!' and Enid was aghast;
And forth they rode, but scarce three paces on,
When crying out 'Effeminate as I am,
I will not fight my way with gilded arms,
All shall be iron;' he loosed a mighty purse,
Hung at his belt, and hurl'd it toward the squire.
So the last sight that Enid had of home
Was all the marble threshold flashing, strown
With gold and scatter'd coinage, and the squire
Chafing his shoulder: then he cried again,
'To the wilds!' and Enid leading down the tracks
Thro' which he bade her lead him on, they past
The marches, and by bandit-haunted holds,
Grey swamps and pools, waste places of the hern,
And wildernesses, perilous paths, they rode:
Round was their pace at first, but slacken'd soon:
A stranger meeting them had surely thought
They rode so slowly and they look'd so pale,
That each had suffer'd some exceeding wrong.
For he was ever saying to himself,
'O I that wasted time to tend upon her,
To compass her with sweet observances,
To dress her beautifully and keep her true' –
And there he broke the sentence in his heart
Abruptly, as a man upon his tongue
May break it, when his passion masters him.
And she was ever praying the sweet heavens
To save her dear lord whole from any wound.
And ever in her mind she cast about
For that unnoticed failing in herself,
Which made him look so cloudy and so cold;
Till the great plover's human whistle amazed
Her heart, and glancing round the waste she fear'd

In every wavering brake an ambuscade.
Then thought again, 'If there be such in me,
I might amend it by the grace of heaven,
If he would only speak and tell me of it.'

But when the fourth part of the day was gone,
Then Enid was aware of three tall knights
On horseback, wholly arm'd, behind a rock
In shadow, waiting for them, caitiffs all;
And heard one crying to his fellow, 'Look,
Here comes a laggard hanging down his head,
Who seems no bolder than a beaten hound;
Come, we will slay him and will have his horse
And armour, and his damsel shall be ours.'

Then Enid ponder'd in her heart, and said:
'I will go back a little to my lord,
And I will tell him all their caitiff talk;
For, be he wroth even to slaying me
Far liefer by his dear hand had I die,
Than that my lord should suffer loss or shame.'

Then she went back some paces of return,
Met his full frown timidly firm, and said:
'My lord, I saw three bandits by the rock
Waiting to fall on you, and heard them boast
That they would slay you, and possess your horse
And armour, and your damsel should be theirs.'

He made a wrathful answer. 'Did I wish
Your warning or your silence? one command
I laid upon you, not to speak to me,
And thus you keep it! Well then, look – for now,
Whether you wish me victory or defeat,
Long for my life, or hunger for my death,
Yourself shall see my vigour is not lost.'

Then Enid waited pale and sorrowful,
And down upon him bare the bandit three.
And at the midmost charging, Prince Geraint
Drave the long spear a cubit thro' his breast
And out beyond; and then against his brace
Of comrades, each of whom had broken on him
A lance that splinter'd like an icicle,
Swung from his brand a windy buffet out
Once, twice, to right, to left, and stunn'd the twain

Or slew them, and dismounting like a man
That skins the wild beast after slaying him,
Stript from the three dead wolves of woman born
The three gay suits of armour which they wore
And let the bodies lie, but bound the suits
Of armour on their horses, each on each,
And tied the bridle-reins of all the three
Together, and said to her, 'Drive them on
Before you;' and she drove them thro' the waste.

   He follow'd nearer: ruth began to work
Against his anger in him, while he watch'd
The being he loved best in all the world,
With difficulty in mild obedience
Driving them on: he fain had spoken to her,
And loosed in words of sudden fire the wrath
And smoulder'd wrong that burnt him all within;
But evermore it seem'd an easier thing
At once without remorse to strike her dead
Than to cry 'Halt,' and to her own bright face
Accuse her of the least immodesty:
And thus tongue-tied, it made him wroth the more
That she *could* speak whom his own ear had heard
Call herself false: and suffering thus he made
Minutes an age: but in scarce longer time
Than at Caerleon the full-tided Usk,
Before he turn to fall seaward again,
Pauses, did Enid, keeping watch, behold
In the first shallow shade of a deep wood,
Before a gloom of stubborn shafted oaks,
Three other horsemen waiting, wholly arm'd,
Whereof one seem'd far larger than her lord,
And shook her pulses, crying, 'Look, a prize!
Three horses and three goodly suits of arms,
And all in charge of whom? a girl: set on.'
'Nay,' said the second, 'yonder comes a knight.'
The third, 'A craven; how he hangs his head.'
The giant answer'd merrily, 'Yea, but one?
Wait here, and when he passes fall upon him.'

   And Enid ponder'd in her heart and said,
'I will abide the coming of my lord,
And I will tell him all their villany.
My lord is weary with the fight before,
And they will fall upon him unawares.
I needs must disobey him for his good;

How should I dare obey him to his harm?
Needs must I speak, and tho' he kill me for it,
I save a life dearer to me than mine.'

    And she abode his coming, and said to him
With timid firmness, 'Have I leave to speak?'
He said, 'You take it, speaking,' and she spoke.

    'There lurk three villains yonder in the wood,
And each of them is wholly arm'd, and one
Is larger-limb'd than you are, and they say
That they will fall upon you while you pass.'

    To which he flung a wrathful answer back:
'And if there were an hundred in the wood,
And every man were larger-limb'd than I,
And all at once should sally out upon me,
I swear it would not ruffle me so much
As you that not obey me. Stand aside,
And if I fall, cleave to the better man.'

    And Enid stood aside to wait the event,
Not dare to watch the combat, only breathe
Short fits of prayer, at every stroke a breath.
And he, she dreaded most, bare down upon him.
Aim'd at the helm, his lance err'd; but Geraint's,
A little in the late encounter strain'd,
Struck thro' the bulky bandit's corslet home,
And then brake short, and down his enemy roll'd,
And there lay still; as he that tells the tale,
Saw once a great piece of a promontory,
That had a sapling growing on it, slip
From the long shore-cliff's windy walls to the beach,
And there lie still, and yet the sapling grew:
So lay the man transfixt. His craven pair
Of comrades, making slowlier at the Prince,
When now they saw their bulwark fallen, stood;
On whom the victor, to confound them more,
Spurr'd with his terrible war-cry; for as one,
That listens near a torrent mountain-brook,
All thro' the crash of the near cataract hears
The drumming thunder of the huger fall
At distance, were the soldiers wont to hear
His voice in battle, and be kindled by it
And foemen scared, like that false pair who turn'd
Flying, but, overtaken, died the death
Themselves had wrought on many an innocent.

Thereon Geraint, dismounting, pick'd the lance
That pleased him best, and drew from those dead wolves
Their three gay suits of armour, each from each,
And bound them on their horses, each on each,
And tied the bridle-reins of all the three
Together, and said to her, 'Drive them on
Before you,' and she drove them thro' the wood.

He follow'd nearer still: the pain she had
To keep them in the wild ways of the wood,
Two sets of three laden with jingling arms,
Together, served a little to disedge
The sharpness of that pain about her heart:
And they themselves, like creatures gently born
But into bad hands fall'n, and now so long
By bandits groom'd, prick'd their light ears, and felt
Her low firm voice and tender government.

So thro' the green gloom of the wood they past,
And issuing under open heavens beheld
A little town with towers, upon a rock,
And close beneath, a meadow gemlike chased
In the brown wild, and mowers mowing in it:
And down a rocky pathway from the place
There came a fair-hair'd youth, that in his hand
Bare victual for the mowers: and Geraint
Had ruth again on Enid looking pale:
Then, moving downward to the meadow ground,
He, when the fair-hair'd youth came by him, said,
'Friend, let her eat; the damsel is so faint.'
'Yea, willingly,' replied the youth; 'and you,
My lord, eat also, tho' the fare is coarse,
And only meet for mowers;' then set down
His basket, and dismounting on the sward
They let the horses graze, and ate themselves.
And Enid took a little delicately,
Less having stomach for it than desire
To close with her lord's pleasure; but Geraint
Ate all the mowers' victual unawares
And when he found all empty, was amazed;
And 'Boy,' said he, 'I have eaten all, but take
A horse and arms for guerdon; choose the best.'
He, reddening in extremity of delight,
'My lord, you overpay me fifty-fold.'
'You will be all the wealthier,' cried the Prince.
'I take it as free gift, then,' said the boy,

'Not guerdon; for myself can easily,
While your good damsel rests, return, and fetch
Fresh victual for these mowers of our Earl;
For these are his, and all the field is his,
And I myself am his; and I will tell him
How great a man you are: he loves to know
When men of mark are in his territory:
And he will have you to his palace here,
And serve you costlier than with mowers' fare.'

    Then said Geraint, 'I wish no better fare:
I never ate with angrier appetite
Than when I left your mowers dinnerless.
And into no Earl's palace will I go. I know,
God knows, too much of palaces!
And if he want me, let him come to me.
But hire us some fair chamber for the night,
And stalling for the horses, and return
With victual for these men, and let us know.'

    'Yea, my kind lord,' said the glad youth, and went,
Held his head high, and thought himself a knight,
And up the rocky pathway disappear'd,
Leading the horse, and they were left alone.

    But when the Prince had brought his errant eyes
Home from the rock, sideways he let them glance
At Enid, where she droopt: his own false doom,
That shadow of mistrust should never cross
Betwixt them, came upon him, and he sigh'd;
Then with another humorous ruth remark'd
The lusty mowers labouring dinnerless,
And watch'd the sun blaze on the turning scythe,
And after nodded sleepily in the heat.
But she, remembering her old ruin'd hall,
And all the windy clamour of the daws
About her hollow turret, pluck'd the grass
There growing longest by the meadow's edge,
And into many a listless annulet,
Now over, now beneath her marriage ring,
Wove and unwove it, till the boy return'd
And told them of a chamber, and they went;
Where, after saying to her, 'If you will,
Call for the woman of the house,' to which
She answer'd, 'Thanks, my lord;' the two remain'd
Apart by all the chamber's width, and mute

As creatures voiceless thro' the fault of birth,
Or two wild men supporters of a shield,
Painted, who stare at open space, nor glance
The one at other, parted by the shield.

    On a sudden, many a voice along the street,
And heel against the pavement echoing, burst
Their drowse; and either started while the door,
Push'd from without, drave backward to the wall,
And midmost of a rout of roisterers,
Femininely fair and dissolutely pale,
Her suitor in old years before Geraint,
Enter'd, the wild lord of the place, Limours.
He moving up with pliant courtliness
Greeted Geraint full face, but stealthily,
In the mid-warmth of welcome and graspt hand,
Found Enid with the corner of his eye,
And knew her sitting sad and solitary.
Then cried Geraint for wine and goodly cheer
To feed the sudden guest, and sumptuously
According to his fashion, bad the host
Call in what men soever were his friends,
And feast with these in honour of their earl;
'And care not for the cost; the cost is mine.'

And wine and food were brought, and Earl Limours
Drank till he jested with all ease, and told
Free tales, and took the word and play'd upon it,
And made it of two colours; for his talk,
When wine and free companions kindled him,
Was wont to glance and sparkle like a gem
Of fifty facets; thus he moved the Prince
To laughter and his comrades to applause.
Then, when the Prince was merry, ask'd Limours,
'Your leave, my lord, to cross the room, and speak
To your good damsel there who sits apart,
And seems so lonely?' 'My free leave,' he said;
'Get her to speak: she does not speak to me.'
Then rose Limours and looking at his feet,
Like him who tries the bridge he fears may fail,
Crost and came near, lifted adoring eyes,
Bow'd at her side and utter'd whisperingly:

    'Enid, the pilot star of my lone life,
Enid, my early and my only love,
Enid, the loss of whom has turn'd me wild –

What chance is this? how is it I see you here?
You are in my power at last, are in my power.
Yet fear me not: I call mine own self wild,
But keep a touch of sweet civility
Here in the heart of waste and wilderness.
I thought, but that your father came between,
In former days you saw me favourably.
And if it were so do not keep it back:
Make me a little happier: let me know it:
Owe you me nothing for a life half-lost?
Yea, yea the whole dear debt of all you are.
And, Enid, you and he, I see it with joy –
You sit apart, you do not speak to him,
You come with no attendance, page or maid,
To serve you – does he love you as of old?
For, call it lovers' quarrels, yet I know
Tho' men may bicker with the things they love,
They would not make them laughable in all eyes,
Not while they loved them; and your wretched dress,
A wretched insult on you, dumbly speaks
Your story, that this man loves you no more.
Your beauty is no beauty to him now:
A common chance – right well I know it – pall'd –
For I know men: nor will you win him back,
For the man's love once gone never returns.
But here is one who loves you as of old;
With more exceeding passion than of old:
Good, speak the word: my followers ring him round:
He sits unarm'd; I hold a finger up;
They understand: no; I do not mean blood:
Nor need you look so scared at what I say:
My malice is no deeper than a moat,
No stronger than a wall: there is the keep;
He shall not cross us more; speak but the word:
Or speak it not; but then by Him that made me
The one true lover which you ever had,
I will make use of all the power I have.
O pardon me! the madness of that hour,
When first I parted from you, moves me yet.'

    At this the tender sound of his own voice
And sweet self-pity, or the fancy of it,
Made his eye moist; but Enid fear'd his eyes,
Moist as they were, wine-heated from the feast;
And answer'd with such craft as women use,
Guilty or guiltless, to stave off a chance

That breaks upon them perilously, and said:

'Earl, if you love me as in former years,
And do not practise on me, come with morn,
And snatch me from him as by violence;
Leave me to-night: I am weary to the death.'

Low at leave-taking, with his brandish'd plume
Brushing his instep, bow'd the all-amorous Earl,
And the stout Prince bad him a loud good-night.
He moving homeward babbled to his men,
How Enid never loved a man but him,
Nor cared a broken egg-shell for her lord.

But Enid left alone with Prince Geraint,
Debating his command of silence given,
And that she now perforce must violate it,
Held commune with herself, and while she held
He fell asleep, and Enid had no heart
To wake him, but hung o'er him, wholly pleased
To find him yet unwounded after fight,
And hear him breathing low and equally.
Anon she rose, and stepping lightly, heap'd
The pieces of his armour in one place,
All to be there against a sudden need;
Then dozed awhile herself, but overtoil'd
By that day's grief and travel, evermore
Seem'd catching at a rootless thorn, and then
Went slipping down horrible precipices,
And strongly striking out her limbs awoke;
Then thought she heard the wild Earl at the door,
With all his rout of random followers,
Sound on a dreadful trumpet, summoning her;
Which was the red cock shouting to the light,
As the grey dawn stole o'er the dewy world,
And glimmer'd on his armour in the room.
And once again she rose to look at it,
But touch'd it unawares: jangling, the casque
Fell, and he started up and stared at her.
Then breaking his command of silence given,
She told him all that Earl Limours had said,
Except the passage that he loved her not;
Nor left untold the craft herself had used;
But ended with apology so sweet,
Low-spoken, and of so few words, and seem'd
So justified by that necessity,

That tho' he thought 'was it for him she wept
In Devon?' he but gave a wrathful groan,
Saying, 'Your sweet faces make good fellows fools
And traitors. Call the host and bid him bring
Charger and palfrey.' So she glided out
Among the heavy breathings of the house,
And like a household Spirit at the walls
Beat, till she woke the sleepers, and return'd:
Then tending her rough lord, tho' all unask'd,
In silence, did him service as a squire;
Till issuing arm'd he found the host and cried,
'Thy reckoning, friend?' and ere he learnt it, 'Take
Five horses and their armours;' and the host,
Suddenly honest, answer'd in amaze,
'My lord, I scarce have spent the worth of one!'
''You will be all the wealthier,' said the Prince,
And then to Enid, 'Forward! and to-day
I charge you, Enid, more especially,
What thing soever you may hear, or see,
Or fancy (tho' I count it of small use
To charge you) that you speak not but obey.'

And Enid answer'd, 'Yea, my lord, I know
Your wish, and would obey; but riding first,
I hear the violent threats you do not hear,
I see the danger which you cannot see:
Then not to give you warning, that seems hard;
Almost beyond me: yet I would obey.'

'Yea so,' said he, 'do it: be not too wise;
Seeing that you are wedded to a man,
Not quite mismated with a yawning clown,
But one with arms to guard his head and yours,
With eyes to find you out however far,
And ears to hear you even in his dreams.'

With that he turn'd and look'd as keenly at her
As careful robins eye the delver's toil;
And that within her, which a wanton fool,
Or hasty judger would have call'd her guilt
Made her cheek burn and either eyelid fall.
And Geraint look'd and was not satisfied.

Then forward by a way which, beaten broad,
Led from the territory of false Limours
To the waste earldom of another earl,

Doorm, whom his shaking vassals call'd the Bull,
Went Enid with her sullen follower on.
Once she look'd back, and when she saw him ride
More near by many a rood than yestermorn,
It wellnigh made her cheerful; till Geraint
Waving an angry hand as who should say
'You watch me,' sadden'd all her heart again.
But while the sun yet beat a dewy blade,
The sound of many a heavily-galloping hoof
Smote on her ear, and turning round she saw
Dust, and the points of lances bicker in it.
Then not to disobey her lord's behest,
And yet to give him warning, for he rode
As if he heard not, moving back she held
Her finger up, and pointed to the dust.
At which the warrior in his obstinacy,
Because she kept the letter of his word,
Was in a manner pleased, and turning, stood.
And in the moment after, wild Limours,
Borne on a black horse, like a thunder-cloud
Whose skirts are loosen'd by the breaking storm,
Half ridden off with by the thing he rode,
And all in passion uttering a dry shriek,
Dash'd on Geraint, who closed with him, and bore
Down by the length of lance and arm beyond
The crupper, and so left him stunn'd or dead,
And overthrew the next that follow'd him,
And blindly rush'd on all the rout behind.
But at the flash and motion of the man
They vanish'd panic-stricken, like a shoal
Of darting fish, that on a summer morn
Adown the crystal dykes at Camelot
Come slipping o'er their shadows on the sand,
But if a man who stands upon the brink
But lift a shining hand against the sun,
There is not left the twinkle of a fin
Betwixt the cressy islets white in flower;
So, scared but at the motion of the man,
Fled all the boon companions of the Earl,
And left him lying in the public way;
So vanish friendships only made in wine.

Then like a stormy sunlight smiled Geraint,
Who saw the chargers of the two that fell
Start from their fallen lords, and wildly fly,
Mixt with the flyers. 'Horse and man,' he said,

'All of one mind and all right-honest friends!
Not a hoof left: and I methinks till now
Was honest – paid with horses and with arms;
I cannot steal or plunder, no nor beg:
And so what say you, shall we strip him there
Your lover? has your palfrey heart enough
To bear his armour? shall we fast, or dine?
No? – then do you, being right honest, pray
That we may meet the horsemen of Earl Doorm,
I too would still be honest.' Thus he said:
And sadly gazing on her bridle-reins,
And answering not one word, she led the way.

But as a man to whom a dreadful loss
Falls in a far land and he knows it not,
But coming back he learns it, and the loss
So pains him that he sickens nigh to death;
So fared it with Geraint, who being prick'd
In combat with the follower of Limours,
Bled underneath his armour secretly,
And so rode on, nor told his gentle wife
What ail'd him, hardly knowing it himself,
Till his eye darken'd and his helmet wagg'd;
And at a sudden swerving of the road,
Tho' happily down on a bank of grass,
The Prince, without a word, from his horse fell.

And Enid heard the clashing of his fall,
Suddenly came, and at his side all pale
Dismounting, loosed the fastenings of his arms,
Nor let her true hand falter, nor blue eye
Moisten, till she had lighted on his wound,
And tearing off her veil of faded silk
Had bared her forehead to the blistering sun,
And swathed the hurt that drain'd her dear lord's life.
Then after all was done that hand could do,
She rested, and her desolation came
Upon her, and she wept beside the way.

And many past, but none regarded her,
For in that realm of lawless turbulence,
A woman weeping for her murder'd mate
Was cared as much for as a summer shower:
One took him for a victim of Earl Doorm,
Nor dared to waste a perilous pity on him:
Another hurrying past, a man-at-arms,

Rode on a mission to the bandit Earl;
Half whistling and half singing a coarse song,
He drove the dust against her veilless eyes:
Another, flying from the wrath of Doorm
Before an ever-fancied arrow, made
The long way smoke beneath him in his fear;
At which her palfrey whinnying lifted heel,
And scour'd into the coppices and was lost,
While the great charger stood, grieved like a man.

But at the point of noon the huge Earl Doorm,
Broad-faced with under-fringe of russet beard,
Bound on a foray, rolling eyes of prey,
Came riding with a hundred lances up;
But ere he came, like one that hails a ship,
Cried out with a big voice, 'What, is he dead?'
'No, no, not dead!' she answer'd in all haste.
'Would some of your kind people take him up,
And bear him hence out of this cruel sun:
Most sure am I, quite sure, he is not dead.'

Then said Earl Doorm: 'Well, if he be not dead,
Why wail you for him thus? you seem a child.
And be he dead, I count you for a fool;
Your wailing will not quicken him: dead or not,
You mar a comely face with idiot tears.
Yet, since the face is comely – some of you,
Here, take him up, and bear him to our hall:
An if he live, we will have him of our band;
And if he die, why earth has earth enough
To hide him. See ye take the charger too,
A noble one.'
                        He spake, and past away,
But left two brawny spearmen, who advanced,
Each growling like a dog, when his good bone
Seems to be pluck'd at by the village boys
Who love to vex him eating, and he fears
To lose his bone, and lays his foot upon it,
Gnawing and growling: so the ruffians growl'd,
Fearing to lose, and all for a dead man,
Their chance of booty from the morning's raid;
Yet raised and laid him on a litter-bier,
Such as they brought upon their forays out
For those that might be wounded; laid him on it
All in the hollow of his shield, and took
And bore him to the naked hall of Doorm,

(His gentle charger following him unled)
And cast him and the bier in which he lay
Down on an oaken settle in the hall,
And then departed, hot in haste to join
Their luckier mates, but growling as before,
And cursing their lost time, and the dead man,
And their own Earl, and their own souls, and her.
They might as well have blest her: she was deaf
To blessing or to cursing save from one.

    So for long hours sat Enid by her lord,
There in the naked hall, propping his head,
And chafing his pale hands, and calling to him.
And at the last he waken'd from his swoon
And found his own dear bride propping his head,
And chafing his faint hands, and calling to him;
And felt the warm tears falling on his face;
And said to his own heart, 'She weeps for me:'
And yet lay still, and feign'd himself as dead,
That he might prove her to the uttermost,
And say to his own heart 'She weeps for me.'

    But in the falling afternoon return'd
The huge Earl Doorm with plunder to the hall.
His lusty spearmen follow'd him with noise:
Each hurling down a heap of things that rang
Against the pavement, cast his lance aside,
And doff'd his helm: and then there flutter'd in,
Half-bold, half-frighted, with dilated eyes,
A tribe of women, dress'd in many hues,
And mingled with the spearmen: and Earl Doorm
Struck with a knife's haft hard against the board,
And call'd for flesh and wine to feed his spears.
And men brought in whole hogs and quarter beeves,
And all the hall was dim with steam of flesh:
And none spake word, but all sat down at once,
And ate with tumult in the naked hall,
Feeding like horses when you hear them feed;
Till Enid shrank far back into herself,
To shun the wild ways of the lawless tribe.
But when Earl Doorm had eaten all he would,
He roll'd his eyes about the hall, and found
A damsel drooping in a corner of it.
Then he remember'd her, and how she wept;
And out of her there came a power upon him;
And rising on the sudden he said, 'Eat!

I never yet beheld a thing so pale.
God's curse, it makes me mad to see you weep.
Eat! Look yourself. Good luck had your good man,
For were I dead who is it would weep for me?
Sweet lady, never since I first drew breath
Have I beheld a lily like yourself.
And so there lived some colour in your cheek,
There is not one among my gentlewomen
Were fit to wear your slipper for a glove.
But listen to me, and by me be ruled,
And I will do the thing I have not done,
For you shall share my earldom with me, girl,
And we will live like two birds in one nest,
And I will fetch you forage from all fields,
For I compel all creatures to my will.'

He spoke: the brawny spearman let his cheek
Bulge with the unswallow'd piece, and turning stared;
While some, whose souls the old serpent long had drawn
Down, as the worm draws in the wither'd leaf
And makes it earth, hiss'd each at other's ear
What shall not be recorded – women they,
Women, or what had been those gracious things,
But now desired the humbling of their best,
Yea, would have help'd him to it: and all at once
They hated her, who took no thought of them,
But answer'd in low voice, her meek head yet
Drooping, 'I pray you of your courtesy,
He being as he is, to let me be.'

She spake so low he hardly heard her speak,
But like a mighty patron, satisfied
With what himself had done so graciously,
Assumed that she had thanked him, adding,
'Yea, Eat and be glad, for I account you mine.'

She answer'd meekly, 'How should I be glad
Henceforth in all the world at anything
Until my lord arise and look upon me?'

Here the huge Earl cried out upon her talk,
As all but empty heart and weariness
And sickly nothing; suddenly seized on her,
And bare her by main violence to the board,
And thrust the dish before her, crying, 'Eat.'

'No, no,' said Enid, vext, 'I will not eat,
Till yonder man upon the bier arise,
And eat with me.' 'Drink, then,' he answer'd. 'Here!'
(And fill'd a horn with wine and held it to her,)
'Lo! I, myself, when flush'd with fight, or hot,
God's curse, with anger – often I myself,
Before I well have drunken, scarce can eat:
Drink therefore and the wine will change your will.'

'Not so,' she cried, 'by Heaven, I will not drink,
Till my dear lord arise and bid me do it,
And drink with me; and if he rise no more,
I will not look at wine until I die.'

At this he turn'd all red and paced his hall,
Now gnaw'd his under, now his upper lip,
And coming up close to her, said at last;
'Girl, for I see you scorn my courtesies,
Take warning: yonder man is surely dead;
And I compel all creatures to my will.
Not eat nor drink? And wherefore wail for one,
Who put your beauty to this flout and scorn
By dressing it in rags? Amazed am I,
Beholding how you butt against my wish,
That I forbear you thus: cross me no more.
At least put off to please me this poor gown,
This silken rag, this beggar-woman's weed:
I love that beauty should go beautifully:
For see you not my gentlewomen here,
How gay, how suited to the house of one,
Who loves that beauty should go beautifully!
Rise therefore; robe yourself in this: obey.'

He spoke, and one among his gentlewomen
Display'd a splendid silk of foreign loom,
Where like a shoaling sea the lovely blue
Play'd into green, and thicker down the front
With jewels than the sward with drops of dew,
When all night long a cloud clings to the hill,
And with the dawn ascending lets the day
Strike where it clung: so thickly shone the gems.

But Enid answer'd, harder to be moved
Than hardest tyrants in their day of power,
With life-long injuries burning unavenged,
And now their hour has come; and Enid said:

'In this poor gown my dear lord found me first,
And loved me serving in my father's hall:
In this poor gown I rode with him to court,
And there the Queen array'd me like the sun:
In this poor gown he bade me clothe myself,
When now we rode upon this fatal quest
Of honour, where no honour can be gain'd:
And this poor gown I will not cast aside
Until himself arise a living man,
And bid me cast it. I have griefs enough:
Pray you be gentle, pray you let me be:
I never loved, can never love but him:
Yea, God, I pray you of your gentleness,
He being as he is, to let me be.'

Then strode the brute Earl up and down his hall,
And took his russet beard between his teeth;
Last, coming up quite close, and in his mood
Crying, 'I count it of no more avail,
Dame, to be gentle than ungentle with you;
Take my salute,' unknightly with flat hand,
However lightly, smote her on the cheek.

Then Enid, in her utter helplessness,
And since she thought, 'He had not dared to do it,
Except he surely knew my lord was dead,'
Sent forth a sudden sharp and bitter cry,
As of a wild thing taken in the trap,
Which sees the trapper coming thro' the wood.

This heard Geraint, and grasping at his sword,
(It lay beside him in the hollow shield),
Made but a single bound, and with a sweep of it
Shore thro' the swarthy neck, and like a ball
The russet-bearded head roll'd on the floor.
So died Earl Doorm by him he counted dead.
And all the men and women in the hall
Rose when they saw the dead man rise, and fled
Yelling as from a spectre, and the two
Were left alone together, and he said:

'Enid, I have used you worse than that dead man;
Done you more wrong: we both have undergone
That trouble which has left me thrice your own:
Henceforward I will rather die than doubt.
And here I lay this penance on myself,

Not, tho' mine own ears heard you yestermorn –
You thought me sleeping, but I heard you say,
I heard you say, that you were no true wife:
I swear I will not ask your meaning in it:
I do believe yourself against yourself,
And will henceforward rather die than doubt.'

And Enid could not say one tender word,
She felt so blunt and stupid at the heart:
She only prayed him, 'Fly, they will return
And slay you; fly, your charger is without,
My palfrey lost.' 'Then, Enid, shall you ride
Behind me.' 'Yea,' said Enid, 'let us go.'
And moving out they found the stately horse,
Who now no more a vassal to the thief,
But free to stretch his limbs in lawful fight,
Neigh'd with all gladness as they came, and stoop'd
With a low whinny toward the pair: and she
Kiss'd the white star upon his noble front,
Glad also; then Geraint upon the horse
Mounted, and reach'd a hand, and on his foot
She set her own and climb'd; he turn'd his face
And kiss'd her climbing, and she cast her arms
About him, and at once they rode away.

And never yet, since high in Paradise
O'er the four rivers the first roses blew,
Came purer pleasure unto mortal kind
Than lived thro' her, who in that perilous hour
Put hand to hand beneath her husband's heart,
And felt him hers again: she did not weep,
But o'er her meek eyes came a happy mist
Like that which kept the heart of Eden green
Before the useful trouble of the rain:
Yet not so misty were her meek blue eyes
As not to see before them on the path,
Right in the gateway of the bandit hold,
A knight of Arthur's court, who laid his lance
In rest, and made as if to fall upon him.
Then, fearing for his hurt and loss of blood
She, with her mind all full of what had chanced,
Shriek'd to the stranger, 'Slay not a dead man!'
'The voice of Enid,' said the knight; but she,
Beholding it was Edyrn son of Nudd,
Was moved so much the more, and shriek'd again,
'O cousin, slay not him who gave you life.'

And Edyrn moving frankly forward spake:
'My lord Geraint, I greet you with all love;
I took you for a bandit knight of Doorm;
And fear not, Enid, I should fall upon him,
Who love you, Prince, with something of the love
Wherewith we love the Heaven that chastens us.
For once, when I was up so high in pride
That I was halfway down the slope to Hell,
By overthrowing me you threw me higher.
Now, made a knight of Arthur's Table Round,
And since I knew this Earl, when I myself
Was half a bandit in my lawless hour,
I come the mouthpiece of our King to Doorm
(The King is close behind me) bidding him
Disband himself, and scatter all his powers,
Submit, and hear the judgement of the King.'

    'He hears the judgement of the King of Kings,'
Cried the wan Prince; 'and lo the powers of Doorm
Are scatter'd,' and he pointed to the field,
Where, huddled here and there on mound and knoll,
Were men and women staring and aghast,
While some yet fled; and then he plainlier told
How the huge Earl lay slain within his hall.
But when the knight besought him, 'Follow me,
Prince, to the camp, and in the King's own ear
Speak what has chanced; you surely have endured
Strange chances here alone;' that other flushed,
And hung his head, and halted in reply,
Fearing the mild face of the blameless King,
And after madness acted question ask'd:
Till Edyrn crying, 'If you will not go
To Arthur, then will Arthur come to you,'
'Enough,' he said, 'I follow,' and they went.
But Enid in their going had two fears,
One from the bandit scatter'd in the field,
And one from Edyrn. Every now and then
When Edyrn rein'd his charger at her side,
She shrank a little. In a hollow land,
From which old fires have broken, men may fear
Fresh fire and ruin. He, perceiving, said:
'Fair and dear cousin, you that most had cause
To fear me, fear no longer, I am changed.
Yourself were first the blameless cause to make
My nature's prideful sparkle in the blood
Break into furious flame; being repulsed

By Yniol and yourself, I schemed and wrought
Until I overturn'd him; then set up
(With one main purpose ever at my heart)
My haughty jousts, and took a paramour;
Did her mock-honour as the fairest fair,
And, toppling over all antagonism,
So wax'd in pride, that I believed myself
Unconquerable, for I was wellnigh mad:
And, but for my main purpose in these jousts,
I should have slain your father, seized yourself.
I lived in hope that sometime you would come
To these my lists with him whom best you loved;
And there, poor cousin, with your meek blue eyes,
The truest eyes that ever answer'd heaven,
Behold me overturn and trample on him.
Then, had you cried, or knelt, or pray'd to me,
I should not less have kill'd him. And you came, –
But once you came, – and with your own true eyes
Beheld the man you loved (I speak as one
Speaks of a service done him) overthrow
My proud self, and my purpose three years old,
And set his foot upon me, and give me life
There was I broken down; there was I saved:
Tho' thence I rode all-shamed, hating the life
He gave me, meaning to be rid of it.
And all the penance the Queen laid upon me
Was but to rest awhile within her court;
Where first as sullen as a beast new-caged,
And waiting to be treated like a wolf,
Because I knew my deeds were known, I found,
Instead of scornful pity or pure scorn,
Such fine reserve and noble reticence,
Manners so kind, yet stately, such a grace
Of tenderest courtesy, that I began
To glance behind me at my former life,
And find that it had been the wolf's indeed:
And oft I talk'd with Dubric, the high saint,
Who, with mild heat of holy oratory,
Subdued me somewhat to that gentleness,
Which, when it weds with manhood, makes a man.
And you were often there about the Queen,
But saw me not, or mark'd not if you saw;
Nor did I care or dare to speak with you,
But kept myself aloof till I was changed;
And fear not, cousin; I am changed indeed.'

He spoke, and Enid easily believed,
Like simple noble natures, credulous
Of what they long for, good in friend or foe,
There most in those who most have done them ill.
And when they reach'd the camp the King himself
Advanced to greet them, and beholding her
Tho' pale, yet happy, ask'd her not a word,
But went apart with Edyrn, whom he held
In converse for a little, and return'd,
And, gravely smiling, lifted her from horse,
And kiss'd her with all pureness, brother-like,
And show'd-an empty tent allotted her,
And glancing for a minute, till he saw her
Pass into it, turn'd to the Prince, and said:

'Prince, when of late you pray'd me for my leave
To move to your own land, and there defend
Your marches, I was prick'd with some reproof,
As one that let foul wrong stagnate and be,
By having look'd too much thro' alien eyes,
And wrought too long with delegated hands,
Not used mine own: but now behold me come
To cleanse this common sewer of all my realm,
With Edyrn and with others: have you look'd
At Edyrn? have you seen how nobly changed?
This work of his is great and wonderful.
His very face with change of heart is changed.
The world will not believe a man repents:
And this wise world of ours is mainly right.
Full seldom *does* a man repent, or use
Both grace and will to pick the vicious quitch
Of blood and custom wholly out of him,
And make all clean, and plant himself afresh.
Edyrn has done it, weeding all his heart
As I will weed this land before I go.
I, therefore, made him of our Table Round,
Not rashly, but have proved him everyway
One of our noblest, our most valorous,
Sanest and most obedient: and indeed
This work of Edyrn wrought upon himself
After a life of violence, seems to me
A thousand-fold more great and wonderful
Than if some knight of mine, risking his life,
My subject with my subjects under him,
Should make an onslaught single on a realm
Of robbers, tho' he slew them one by one,

And were himself nigh wounded to the death.'

   So spake the King; low bow'd the Prince, and felt
His work was neither great nor wonderful,
And past to Enid's tent; and thither came
The King's own leech to look into his hurt;
And Enid tended on him there; and there
Her constant motion round him, and the breath
Of her sweet tendance hovering over him,
Fill'd all the genial courses of his blood
With deeper and with ever deeper love,
As the south-west that blowing Bala lake
Fills all the sacred Dee. So past the days.

   But while Geraint lay healing of his hurt,
The blameless King went forth and cast his eyes
On whom his father Uther left in charge
Long since, to guard the justice of the King:
He look'd and found them wanting; and as now
Men weed the white horse on the Berkshire hills
To keep him bright and clean as heretofore,
He rooted out the slothful officer
Or guilty, which for bribe had wink'd at wrong,
And in their chairs set up a stronger race
With hearts and hands, and sent a thousand men
To till the wastes, and moving everywhere
Clear'd the dark places and let in the law,
And broke the bandit holds and cleansed the land.

   Then, when Geraint was whole again, they past
With Arthur to Caerleon upon Usk.
There the great Queen once more embraced her friend,
And clothed her in apparel like the day. And tho'
Geraint could never take again
That comfort from their converse which he took
Before the Queen's fair name was breathed upon,
He rested well content that all was well.
Thence after tarrying for a space they rode,
And fifty knights rode with them to the shores
Of Severn, and they past to their own land.
And there he kept the justice of the King
So vigorously yet mildly, that all hearts
Applauded, and the spiteful whisper died:
And being ever foremost in the chase,
And victor at the tilt and tournament,
They call'd him the great Prince and man of men.

But Enid, whom her ladies loved to call
Enid the Fair, a grateful people named
Enid the Good; and in their halls arose
The cry of children, Enids and Geraints
Of times to be; nor did he doubt her more
But rested in her fealty, till he crown'd
A happy life with a fair death, and fell
Against the heathen of the Northern Sea
In battle, fighting for the blameless King.

Vivien

A storm was coming, but the winds were still,
And in the wild woods of Broceliande,
Before an oak, so hollow, huge and old
It look'd a tower of ruin'd masonwork,
At Merlin's feet the wily Vivien lay.

The wily Vivien stole from Arthur's court:
She hated all the knights, and heard in thought
Their lavish comment when her name was named.
For once, when Arthur walking all alone,
Vext at a rumour rife about the Queen,
Had met her, Vivien, being greeted fair,
Would fain have wrought upon his cloudy mood
With reverent eyes mock-loyal, shaken voice,
And flutter'd adoration, and at last
With dark sweet hints of some who prized him more
Than who should prize him most; at which the King
Had gazed upon her blankly and gone by:
But one had watch'd, and had not held his peace:
It made the laughter of an afternoon
That Vivien should attempt the blameless King.
And after that, she set herself to gain
Him the most famous man of all those times,
Merlin, who knew the range of all their arts
Had built the King his havens, ships, and halls,
Was also Bard, and knew the starry heavens;
The people called him Wizard; whom at first
She play'd about with slight and sprightly talk,
And vivid smiles, and faintly-venom'd points
Of slander, glancing here and grazing there;
And yielding to his kindlier moods, the Seer
Would watch her at her petulance, and play,
Ev'n when they seem'd unlovable, and laugh

As those that watch a kitten; thus he grew
Tolerant of what he half disdain'd, and she,
Perceiving that she was but half disdain'd,
Began to break her sports with graver fits,
Turn red or pale, would often when they met
Sigh fully, or all-silent gaze upon him
With such a fixt devotion, that the old man,
Tho' doubtful, felt the flattery, and at times
Would flatter his own wish in age for love,
And half believe her true: for thus at times
He waver'd; but that other clung to him,
Fixt in her will, and so the seasons went.
Then fell upon him a great melancholy;
And leaving Arthur's court he gain'd the beach
There found a little boat, and stept into it;
And Vivien follow'd, but he mark'd her not.
She took the helm and he the sail; the boat
Crave with a sudden wind across the deeps,
And touching Breton sands, they disembark'd.
And then she follow'd Merlin all the way,
Ev'n to the wild woods of Broceliande.
For Merlin once had told her of a charm,
The which if any wrought on any one
With woven paces and with waving arms,
The man so wrought on ever seem'd to lie
Closed in the four walls of a hollow tower,
From which was no escape for evermore;
And none could find that man for evermore,
Nor could he see but him who wrought the charm
Coming and going, and he lay as dead
And lost to life and use and name and fame.
And Vivien ever sought to work the charm
Upon the great Enchanter of the Time,
As fancying that her glory would be great
According to his greatness whom she quench'd.

There lay she all her length and kiss'd his feet,
As if in deepest reverence and in love.
A twist of gold was round her hair; a robe
Of samite without price, that more exprest
Than hid her, clung about her lissome limbs,
In colour like the satin-shining palm
On sallows in the windy gleams of March:
And while she kiss'd them, crying, 'Trample me,
Dear feet, that I have follow'd thro' the world,
And I will pay you worship; tread me down

And I will kiss you for it;' he was mute:
So dark a forethought roll'd about his brain,
As on a dull day in an Ocean cave
The blind wave feeling round his long sea-hall
In silence: wherefore, when she lifted up
A face of sad appeal, and spake and said,
'O Merlin, do you love me?' and again,
'O Merlin, do you love me?' and once more
'Great Master, do you love me?' he was mute.
And lissome Vivien, holding by his heel,
Writhed toward him, slided up his knee and sat,
Behind his ankle twined her hollow feet
Together, curved an arm about his neck
Hung like a snake; and letting her left hand
Droop from his mighty shoulder, as a leaf,
Made with her right a comb of pearl to part
The lists of such a beard as youth gone out
Had left in ashes: then he spoke and said,
Not looking at her, 'Who are wise in love
Love most, say least,' and Vivien answer'd quick,
'I saw the little elf-god eyeless once
In Arthur's arras hall at Camelot:
But neither eyes nor tongue – O stupid child!
Yet you are wise who say it; let me think
Silence is wisdom: I am silent then
And ask no kiss;' then adding all at once,
'And lo, I clothe myself with wisdom,' drew
The vast and shaggy mantle of his beard
Across her neck and bosom to her knee,
And call'd herself a gilded summer fly
Caught in a great old tyrant spider's web,
Who meant to eat her up in that wild wood
Without one word. So Vivien call'd herself,
But rather seem'd a lovely baleful star
Veil'd in grey vapour; till he sadly smiled:
'To what request for what strange boon,' he said,
'Are these your pretty tricks and fooleries,
O Vivien, the preamble? yet my thanks,
For these have broken up my melancholy'

    And Vivien answer'd smiling saucily,
'What, O my Master, have you found your voice?
I bid the stranger welcome. Thanks at last!
But yesterday you never open'd lip,
Except indeed to drink: no cup had we:
In mine own lady palms I cull'd the spring

That gather'd trickling dropwise from the cleft,
And made a pretty cup of both my hands
And offer'd you it kneeling then you drank
And knew no more, nor gave me one poor word;
O no more thanks than might a goat have given
With no more sign of reverence than a beard.
And when we halted at that other well,
And I was faint to swooning, and you lay
Foot-gilt with all the blossom-dust of those
Deep meadows we had traversed, did you know
That Vivien bathed your feet before her own?
And yet no thanks and all thro' this wild wood
And all this morning when I fondled you:
Boon, yes, there was a boon, one not so strange –
How had I wrong'd you? surely you are wise,
But such a silence is more wise than kind.'

    And Merlin lock'd his hand in hers and said:
'O did you never lie upon the shore,
And watch the curl'd white of the coming wave
Glass'd in the slippery sand before it breaks?
Ev'n such a wave, but not so pleasurable,
Dark in the glass of some presageful mood,
Had I for three days seen, ready to fall.
And then I rose and fled from Arthur's court
To break the mood. You follow'd me unask'd;
And when I look'd, and saw you following still,
My mind involved yourself the nearest thing
In that mind-mist: for shall I tell you truth?
You seem'd that wave about to break upon me
And sweep me from my hold upon the world,
My use and name and fame. Your pardon, child.
Your pretty sports have brighten'd all again.
And ask your boon, for boon I owe you thrice,
Once for wrong done you by confusion, next
For thanks it seems till now neglected, last
For these your dainty gambols: wherefore ask;
And take this boon so strange and not so strange.

    And Vivien answer'd, smiling mournfully:
'O not so strange as my long asking it,
Nor yet so strange as you yourself are strange,
Nor half so strange as that dark mood of yours.
I ever fear'd you were not wholly mine;
And see, yourself have own'd you did me wrong.
The people call you prophet: let it be:

But not of those than can expound themselves.
Take Vivien for expounder; she will call
That three-days-long presageful gloom of yours
No presage, but the same mistrustful mood
That makes you seem less noble than yourself,
Whenever I have ask'd this very boon,
Now ask'd again: for see you not, dear love,
That such a mood as that, which lately gloom'd
Your fancy when you saw me following you,
Must make me fear still more you are not mine,
Must make me yearn still more to prove you mine,
And make me wish still more to learn this charm
Of woven paces and of waving hands,
Is proof of trust. O Merlin, teach it me.
The charm so taught will charm us both to rest
For, grant me some slight power upon your fate,
I, feeling that you felt me worthy trust,
Should rest and let you rest, knowing you mine.
And therefore be as great as you are named,
Not muffled round with selfish reticence.
How hard you look and how denyingly!
O, if you think this wickedness in me,
That I should prove it on you unawares,
To make you lose your use and name and fame,
That makes me most indignant; then our bond
Had best be loosed for ever: but think or not,
By Heaven that hears I tell you the clean truth
As clean as blood of babes, as white as milk:
O Merlin, may this earth, if ever I,
If these unwitty wandering wits of mine,
Ev'n in the jumbled rubbish of a dream,
Have tript on such conjectural treachery –
May this hard earth cleave to the Nadir hell
Down, down, and close again, and nip me flat,
If I be such a traitress. Yield my boon,
Till which I scarce can yield you all I am;
And grant my re-reiterated wish,
The great proof of your love: because I think,
However wise, you hardly know me yet.'

    And Merlin loosed his hand from hers and said,
'I never was less wise, however wise,
Too curious Vivien, tho' you talk of trust,
Than when I told you first of such a charm.
Yea, if you talk of trust I tell you this,
Too much I trusted, when I told you that,

And stirr'd this vice in you which ruin'd man
Thro' woman the first hour; for howsoe'er
In children a great curiousness be well,
Who have to learn themselves and all the world,
In you, that are no child, for still I find
Your face is practised, when I spell the lines,
I call it, – well, I will not call it vice:
But since you name yourself the summer fly,
I well could wish a cobweb for the gnat,
That settles, beaten back, and beaten back
Settles, till one could yield for weariness:
But since I will not yield to give you power
Upon my life and use and name and fame,
Why will you never ask some other boon?
Yea, by God's rood, I trusted you too much.'

    And Vivien, like the tenderest-hearted maid
That ever bided tryst at village stile,
Made answer, either eyelid wet with tears:
'Nay, master, be not wrathful with your maid;
Caress her: let her feel herself forgiven
Who feels no heart to ask another boon.
I think you hardly know the tender rhyme
Of "trust me not at all or all in all."
I heard the great Sir Lancelot sing it once,
And it shall answer for me. Listen to it.

    "In Love, if Love be Love, if Love be ours,
Faith and unfaith can ne'er be equal powers:
Unfaith in aught is want of faith in all.

    "It is the little rift within the lute,
That by and by will make the music mute,
And ever widening slowly silence all.

    "The little rift within the lover's lute,
Or little pitted speck in garner'd fruit,
That rotting inward slowly moulders all.

    "It is not worth the keeping: let it go:
But shall it? answer, darling, answer, no.
And trust me not at all or all in all."

O master, do you love my tender rhyme?'

    And Merlin look'd and half believed her true,

So tender was her voice, so fair her face,
So sweetly gleam'd her eyes behind her tears
Like sunlight on the plain behind a shower:
And yet he answer'd half indignantly.

'Far other was the song that once I heard
By this huge oak, sung nearly where we sit:
For here we met, some ten or twelve of us,
To chase a creature that was current then
In these wild woods, the hart with golden horns.
It was the time when first the question rose
About the founding of a Table Round,
That was to be, for love of God and men
And noble deeds, the flower of all the world.
And each incited each to noble deeds.
And while we waited, one, the youngest of us,
We could not keep him silent, out he flash'd,
And into such a song, such fire for fame,
Such trumpet-blowings in it, coming down
To such a stern and iron-clashing close,
That when he stopt we long'd to hurl together,
And should have done it; but the beauteous beast
Scared by the noise upstarted at our feet,
And like a silver shadow slipt away
Thro' the dim land; and all day long we rode
Thro' the dim land against a rushing wind,
That glorious roundel echoing in our ears,
And chased the flashes of his golden horns
Until they vanish'd by the fairy well
That laughs at iron – as our warriors did –
Where children cast their pins and nails, and cry,
"Laugh, little well," but touch it with a sword,
It buzzes wildly round the point; and there
We lost him: such a noble song was that.
But, Vivien, when you sang me that sweet rhyme,
I felt as tho' you knew this cursed charm,
Were proving it on me, and that I lay
And felt them slowly ebbing, name and fame.'

And Vivien answer'd smiling mournfully:
'O mine have ebb'd away for evermore,
And all thro' following you to this wild wood,
Because I saw you sad, to comfort you.
Lo now, what hearts have men! they never mount
As high as woman in her selfless mood.
And touching fame, howe'er you scorn my song,

Take one verse more – the lady speaks it – this:

"My name, once mine, now thine, is closelier mine,
For fame, could fame be mine, that fame were thine,
And shame, could shame be thine, that shame were mine.
So trust me not at all or all in all."

  'Says she not well? and there is more – this rhyme
Is like the fair pearl-necklace of the Queen,
That burst in dancing, and the pearls were spilt;
Some lost, some stolen, some as relics kept.
But nevermore the same two sister pearls
Ran down the silken thread to kiss each other
On her white neck – so is it with this rhyme:
It lives dispersedly in many hands,
And every minstrel sings it differently;
Yet is there one true line, the pearl of pearls;
"Man dreams of Fame while woman wakes to love."
True: Love, tho' Love were of the grossest, carves
A portion from the solid present, eats
And uses, careless of the rest; but Fame,
The Fame that follows death is nothing to us;
And what is Fame in life but half-disfame,
And counterchanged with darkness? you yourself
Know well that Envy calls you Devil's son,
And since you seem the Master of all Art,
They fain would make you Master of all Vice.'

  And Merlin lock'd his hand in hers and said,
'I once was looking for a magic weed,
And found a fair young squire who sat alone,
Had carved himself a knightly shield of wood,
And then was painting on it fancied arms,
Azure, an Eagle rising or, the Sun
In dexter chief; the scroll "I follow fame."
And speaking not, but leaning over him,
I took his brush and blotted out the bird,
And made a Gardener putting in a graff,
With this for motto, "Rather use than fame."
You should have seen him blush; but afterwards
He made a stalwart knight. O Vivien,
For you, methinks you think you love me well;
For me, I love you somewhat; rest: and Love
Should have some rest and pleasure in himself,
Not ever be too curious for a boon,
Too prurient for a proof against the grain

Of him you say you love: but Fame with men,
Being but ampler means to serve mankind,
Should have small rest or pleasure in herself,
But work as vassal to the larger love,
That dwarfs the petty love of one to one.
Use gave me Fame at first, and Fame again
Increasing gave me use. Lo, there my boon!
What other? for men sought to prove me vile,
Because I wish'd to give them greater minds:
And then did Envy call me Devil's son:
The sick weak beast seeking to help herself
By striking at her better, miss'd, and brought
Her own claw back, and wounded her own heart.
Sweet were the days when I was all unknown,
But when my name was lifted up, the storm
Broke on the mountain and I cared not for it.
Right well know I that Fame is half-disfame,
Yet needs must work my work. That other fame,
To one at least, who hath not children, vague,
The cackle of the unborn about the grave,
I cared not for it: a single misty star,
Which is the second in a line of stars
That seem a sword beneath a belt of three,
I never gazed upon it but I dreamt
Of some vast charm concluded in that star
To make fame nothing. Wherefore, if I fear,
Giving you power upon me thro' this charm,
That you might play me falsely, having power,
However well you think you love me now
(As sons of kings loving in pupillage
Have turn'd to tyrants when they came to power)
I rather dread the loss of use than fame;
If you – and not so much from wickedness,
As some wild turn of anger, or a mood
Of overstrain'd affection, it may be,
To keep me all to your own self, or else
A sudden spurt of woman's jealousy, –
Should try this charm on whom you say you love.'

    And Vivien answer'd smiling as in wrath,
Have I not sworn? I am not trusted. Good!
Well, hide it, hide it; I shall find it out;
And being found take heed of Vivien.
A woman and not trusted, doubtless I
Might feel some sudden turn of anger born
Of your misfaith; and your fine epithet

Is accurate too, for this full love of mine
Without the full heart back may merit well
Your term of overstrain'd. So used as I,
My daily wonder is, I love at all.
And as to woman's jealousy, O why not?
O to what end, except a jealous one,
And one to make me jealous if I love,
Was this fair charm invented by yourself?
I well believe that all about this world
You cage a buxom captive here and there,
Closed in the four walls of a hollow tower
From which is no escape for evermore.'

    Then the great Master merrily answered her:
'Full many a love in loving youth was mine,
I needed then no charm to keep them mine
But youth and love; and that full heart of yours
Whereof you prattle, may now assure you mine;
So live uncharm'd. For those who wrought it first,
The wrist is parted from the hand that waved,
The feet unmortised from their ankle-bones
Who paced it, ages back: but will you hear
The legend as in guerdon for your rhyme?

    'There lived a king in the most Eastern East,
Less old than I, yet older, for my blood
Hath earnest in it of far springs to be.
A tawny pirate anchor'd in his port,
Whose bark had plunder'd twenty nameless isles;
And passing one, at the high peep of dawn,
He saw two cities in a thousand boats
All fighting for a woman on the sea.
And pushing his black craft among them all,
He lightly scatter'd theirs and brought her off,
With loss of half his people arrow-slain;
A maid so smooth, so white, so wonderful,
They said a light came from her when she moved:
And since the pirate would not yield her up,
The King impaled him for his piracy;
Then made her Queen: but those isle-nurtur'd eyes
Waged such unwilling tho' successful war
On all the youth, they sicken'd; councils thinn'd,
And armies waned, for magnet-like she drew
The rustiest iron of old fighters' hearts;
And beasts themselves would worship; camels knelt
Unbidden, and the brutes of mountain back

That carry kings in castles, bow'd black knees
Of homage, ringing with their serpent hands,
To make her smile, her golden ankle-bells.
What wonder, being jealous, that he sent
His horns of proclamation out thro' all
The hundred under-kingdoms that he sway'd
To find a wizard who might teach the King
Some charm, which being wrought upon the Queen
Might keep her all his own: to such a one
He promised more than ever king has given,
A league of mountain full of golden mines,
A province with a hundred miles of coast,
A palace and a princess, all for him:
But on all those who tried and fail'd, the King
Pronounced a dismal sentence, meaning by it
To keep the list low and pretenders back,
Or like a king, not to be trifled with –
Their heads should moulder on the city gates.
And many tried and fail'd, because the charm
Of nature in her overbore their own:
And many a wizard brow bleach'd on the walls:
And many weeks a troop of carrion crows
Hung like a cloud above the gateway towers.'

    And Vivien breaking in upon him said:
'I sit and gather honey; yet, methinks,
Your tongue has tript a little: ask yourself.
The lady never made *unwilling* war
With those fine eyes: she had her pleasure in it,
And made her good man jealous with good cause.
And lived there neither dame nor damsel then
Wroth at a lover's loss? were all as tame,
I mean, as noble, as their Queen was fair?
Not one to flirt a venom at her eyes,
Or pinch a murderous dust into her drink,
Or make her paler with a poison'd rose?
Well, those were not our days: but did they find
A wizard? Tell me, was he like to thee?'

    She ceased, and made her lithe arm round his neck
Tighten, and then drew back, and let her eyes
Speak for her, glowing on him, like a bride's
On her new lord, her own, the first of men.

    He answer'd laughing, 'Nay, not like to me.
At last they found – his foragers for charms –

A little glassy-headed hairless man,
Who lived alone in a great wild on grass;
Read but one book, and ever reading grew
So grated down and filed away with thought,
So lean his eyes were monstrous; while the skin
Clung but to crate and basket, ribs and spine.
And since he kept his mind on one sole aim,
Nor ever touch'd fierce wine, nor tasted flesh,
Nor own'd a sensual wish, to him the wall
That sunders ghosts and shadow-casting men
Became a crystal, and he saw them thro' it,
And heard their voices talk behind the wall,
And learnt their elemental secrets, powers
And forces; often o'er the sun's bright eye
Drew the vast eyelid of an inky cloud,
And lash'd it at the base with slanting storm;
Or in the noon of mist and driving rain,
When the lake whiten'd and the pinewood roar'd,
And the cairn'd mountain was a shadow, sunn'd
The world to peace again: here was the man.
And so by force they dragg'd him to the King.
And then he taught the King to charm the Queen
In such-wise, that no man could see her more,
Nor saw she save the King, who wrought the charm,
Coming and going, and she lay as dead,
And lost all use of life: but when the King
Made proffer of the league of golden mines,
The province with a hundred miles of coast,
The palace and the princess, that old man
Went back to his old wild, and lived on grass,
And vanish'd, and his book came down to me.'

    And Vivien answer'd smiling saucily;
'You have the book: the charm is written in it:
Good: take my counsel: let me know it at once:
For keep it like a puzzle chest in chest,
With each chest lock'd and padlock'd thirty-fold,
And whelm all this beneath as vast a mound
As after furious battle turfs the slain
On some wild down above the windy deep,
I yet should strike upon a sudden means
To dig, pick, open, find and read the charm:
Then, if I tried it, who should blame me then?'

    And smiling as a Master smiles at one
That is not of his school, nor any school

But that where blind and naked Ignorance
Delivers brawling judgements, unashamed,
On all things all day long, he answer'd her.

'*You* read the book, my pretty Vivien!
O aye, it is but twenty pages long,
But every page having an ample marge,
And every marge enclosing in the midst
A square of text that looks a little blot,
The text no larger than the limbs of fleas;
And every square of text an awful charm,
Writ in a language that has long gone by.
So long, that mountains have arisen since
With cities on their flanks – *you* read the book!
And every margin scribbled, crost, and cramm'd
With comment, densest condensation, hard
To mind and eye; but the long sleepless nights
Of my long life have made it easy to me.
And none can read the text, not even I;
And none can read the comment but myself;
And in the comment did I find the charm.
O, the results are simple; a mere child
Might use it to the harm of any one,
And never could undo it: ask no more:
For tho' you should not prove it upon me,
But keep that oath you swore, you might, perchance
Assay it on some one of the Table Round,
And all because you dream they babble of you.'

And Vivien, frowning in true anger, said:
'What dare the full-fed liars say of me?
They ride abroad redressing human wrongs!
They sit with knife in meat and wine in horn.
They bound to holy vows of chastity!
Were I not woman, I could tell a tale.
But you are man, you well can understand
The shame that cannot be explain'd for shame.
Not one of all the drove should touch me: swine!'

Then answer'd Merlin careless of her words,
'You breathe but accusation vast and vague,
Spleen-born, I think, and proofless. If you know,
Set up the charge you know, to stand or fall!'

And Vivien answer'd frowning wrathfully:
'O aye, what say ye to Sir Valence, him

Whose kinsman left him watcher o'er his wife
And two fair babes, and went to distant lands;
Was one year gone, and on returning found
Not two but three: there lay the reckling, one
But one hour old! What said the happy sire?
A seven months' babe had been a truer gift.
Those twelve sweet moons confused his fatherhood.'

Then answer'd Merlin, 'Nay, I know the tale.
Sir Valence wedded with an outland dame:
Some cause had kept him sunder'd from his wife:
One child they had: it lived with her: she died:
His kinsman travelling on his own affair
Was charged by Valence to bring home the child.
He brought, not found it therefore: take the truth.'

'O aye,' said Vivien, 'overtrue a tale.
What say ye then to sweet Sir Sagramore,
That ardent man? "to pluck the flower in season;"
So says the song, "I trow it is no treason."
O Master, shall we call him overquick
To crop his own sweet rose before the hour?'

And Merlin answer'd, 'Overquick are you
To catch a loathly plume fall'n from the wing
Of that foul bird of rapine whose whole prey
Is man's good name: he never wrong'd his bride.
I know the tale. An angry gust of wind
Puff'd out his torch among the myriad-room'd
And many-corridor'd complexities
Of Arthur's palace: then he found a door
And darkling felt the sculptured ornament
That wreathen round it made it seem his own;
And wearied out made for the couch and slept,
A stainless man beside a stainless maid;
And either slept, nor knew of other there;
Till the high dawn piercing the royal rose
In Arthur's casement glimmer'd chastely down,
Blushing upon them blushing, and at once
He rose without a word and parted from her:
But when the thing was blazed about the court,
The brute world howling forced them into bonds,
And as it chanced they are happy, being pure.'

'O aye,' said Vivien, 'that were likely too.
What say ye then to fair Sir Percivale

And of the horrid foulness that he wrought,
The saintly youth, the spotless lamb of Christ,
Or some black wether of St. Satan's fold.
What, in the precincts of the chapel-yard,
Among the knightly brasses of the graves,
And by the cold Hic Jacets of the dead!'

    And Merlin answer'd careless of her charge,
'A sober man is Percivale and pure;
But once in life was fluster'd with new wine,
Then paced for coolness in the chapel-yard;
Where one of Satan's shepherdesses caught
And meant to stamp him with her master's mark;
And that he sinn'd is not believable;
For, look upon his face! – but if he sinn'd,
The sin that practice burns into the blood,
And not the one dark hour which brings remorse,
Will brand us, after, of whose fold we be:
Or else were he, the holy king, whose hymns
Are chanted in the minster, worse than all.
But is your spleen froth'd out, or have ye more?'

    And Vivien answer'd frowning yet in wrath:
'O aye; what say ye to Sir Lancelot, friend?
Traitor or true? that commerce with the Queen,
I ask you, is it clamour'd by the child,
Or whisper'd in the corner? do you know it?'

    To which he answer'd sadly, 'Yea, I know it.
Sir Lancelot went ambassador, at first,
To fetch her, and she took him for the King;
So fixt her fancy on him: let him be.
But have you no one word of loyal praise
For Arthur, blameless King and stainless man?'

    She answer'd with a low and chuckling laugh:
'Him? is he man at all, who knows and winks?
Sees what his fair bride is and does, and winks?
By which the good king means to blind himself,
And blinds himself and all the Table Round
To all the foulness that they work. Myself
Could call him (were it not for womanhood)
The pretty, popular name such manhood earns,
Could call him the main cause of all their crime;
Yea, were he not crown'd king, coward, and fool.'

Then Merlin to his own heart, loathing, said:
'O true and tender! O my liege and king!
O selfless man and stainless gentleman,
Who wouldst against thine own eye-witness fain
Have all men true and leal, all women pure;
How, in the mouths of base interpreters,
From over-fineness not intelligible
To things with every sense as false and foul
As the poach'd filth that floods the middle street,
Is thy white blamelessness accounted blame!'

But Vivien, deeming Merlin overborne
By instance, recommenced, and let her tongue
Rage like a fire among the noblest names,
Polluting, and imputing her whole self,
Defaming and defacing, till she left
Not even Lancelot brave, nor Galahad clean.

Her words had issue other than she will'd.
He dragg'd his eyebrow bushes down, and made
A snowy penthouse for his hollow eyes,
And mutter'd in himself, 'Tell *her* the charm!
So, if she had it, would she rail on me
To snare the next, and if she have it not,
So will she rail. What did the wanton say?
"Not mount as high;" we scarce can sink as low:
For men at most differ as Heaven and earth,
But women, worst and best, as Heaven and Hell.
I know the Table Round, my friends of old;
All brave, and many generous, and some chaste.
I think she cloaks the wounds of loss with lies;
I do believe she tempted them and fail'd,
She is so bitter: for fine plots may fail,
Tho' harlots paint their talk as well as face
With colours of the heart that are not theirs.
I will not let her know: nine tithes of times
Face-flatterers and backbiters are the same.
And they, sweet soul, that most impute a crime
Are pronest to it, and impute themselves,
Wanting the mental range; or low desire
Not to feel lowest makes them level all;
Yea, they would pare the mountain to the plain,
To leave an equal baseness; and in this
Are harlots like the crowd, that if they find
Some stain or blemish in a name of note,
Not grieving that their greatest are so small,

Inflate themselves with some insane delight,
And judge all nature from her feet of clay,
Without the will to lift their eyes, and see
Her godlike head crown'd with spiritual fire,
And touching other worlds. I am weary of her.'

    He spoke in words part heard, in whispers part,
Half-suffocated in the hoary fell
And many-winter'd fleece of throat and chin.
But Vivien, gathering somewhat of his mood,
And hearing 'harlot' mutter'd twice or thrice,
Leapt from her session on his lap, and stood
Stiff as a viper frozen; loathsome sight,
How from the rosy lips of life and love,
Flash'd the bare-grinning skeleton of death!
White was her cheek; sharp breaths of anger puff'd
Her fairy nostril out; her hand half-clench'd
Went faltering sideways downward to her belt,
And feeling; had she found a dagger there
For in a wink the false love turns to hate)
She would have stabb'd him; but she found it not:
His eye was calm, and suddenly she took
To bitter weeping like a beaten child,
A long, long weeping, not consolable.
Then her false voice made way broken with sobs.

    'O crueller than was ever told in tale,
Or sung in song! O vainly lavish'd love!
O cruel, there was nothing wild or strange,
Or seeming shameful, for what shame in love,
So love be true, and not as yours is – nothing
Poor Vivien had not done to win his trust
Who call'd her what he call'd her – all her crime,
All – all – the wish to prove him wholly hers.'

    She mused a little, and then clapt her hands
Together with a wailing shriek, and said:
'Stabb'd through the heart's affections to the heart!
Seeth'd like the kid in its own mother's milk!
Kill'd with a word worse than a life of blows!
I thought that he was gentle, being great:
O God, that I had loved a smaller man!
I should have found in him a greater heart.
O, I, that flattering my true passion, saw
The knights, the court, the king, dark in your light,
Who loved to make men darker than they are,
Because of that high pleasure which I had

To seat you sole upon my pedestal
Of worship – I am answer'd, and henceforth
The course of life that seem'd so flowery to me
With you for guide and master, only you,
Becomes the sea-cliff pathway broken short,
And ending in a ruin – nothing left,
But into some low cave to crawl, and there,
If the wolf spare me, weep my life away,
Kill'd with inutterable unkindliness.'

    She paused, she turn'd away, she hung her head,
The snake of gold slid from her hair, the braid
Slipt and uncoil'd itself, she wept afresh,
And the dark wood grew darker toward the storm
In silence, while his anger slowly died
Within him, till he let his wisdom go
For ease of heart, and half believed her true:
Call'd her to shelter in the hollow oak,
'Come from the storm,' and having no reply,
Gazed at the heaving shoulder, and the face
Hand-hidden, as for utmost grief or shame;
Then thrice essay'd, by tenderest-touching terms
To sleek her ruffled peace of mind, in vain.
At last she let herself be conquer'd by him,
And as the cageling newly flown returns,
The seeming-injured simple-hearted thing
Came to her old perch back and settled there.
There while she sat, half-falling from his knees,
Half-nestled at his heart, and since he saw
The slow tear creep from her closed eyelid yet,
About her, more in kindness than in love,
The gentle wizard cast a shielding arm.
But she dislink'd herself at once and rose,
Her arms upon her breast across, and stood
A virtuous gentlewoman deeply wrong'd,
Upright and flush'd before him: then she said:

    'There must be now no passages of love
Betwixt us twain henceforward evermore.
Since, if I be what I am grossly call'd,
What should be granted which your own gross heart
Would reckon worth the taking? I will go.
In truth, but one thing now – better have died
Thrice than have ask'd it once – could make me stay –
That proof of trust – so often ask'd in vain!
How justly, after that vile term of yours,

I find with grief! I might believe you then,
Who knows? once more. O, what was once to me
Mere matter of the fancy, now has grown
The vast necessity of heart and life.
Farewell; think kindly of me, for I fear
My fate or fault, omitting gayer youth
For one so old, must be to love you still.
But ere I leave you let me swear once more
That if I schemed against your peace in this,
May yon just heaven, that darkens o'er me, send
One flash, that, missing all things else, may make
My scheming brain a cinder, if I lie.'

Scarce had she ceased, when out of heaven a bolt
(For now the storm was close above them) struck,
Furrowing a giant oak, and javelining
With darted spikes and splinters of the wood
The dark earth round. He raised his eyes and saw
The tree that shone white-listed thro' the gloom.
But Vivien, fearing heaven had heard her oath,
And dazzled by the livid-flickering fork,
And deafen'd with the stammering cracks and claps
That follow'd, flying back and crying out,
'O Merlin, tho' you do not love me, save,
Yet save me!' clung to him and hugg'd him close;
And call'd him dear protector in her fright,
Nor yet forgot her practice in her fright,
But wrought upon his mood and hugg'd him close.
The pale blood of the wizard at her touch
Took gayer colours, like an opal warm'd.
She blamed herself for telling hearsay tales:
She shook from fear, and for her fault she wept
Of petulancy, she call'd him lord and liege,
Her seer, her bard, her silver star of eve,
Her God, her Merlin, the one passionate love
Of her whole life; and ever overhead
Bellow'd the tempest, and the rotten branch
Snapt in the rushing of the river-rain
Above them; and in change of glare and gloom
Her eyes and neck glittering went and came;
Till now the storm, its burst of passion spent,
Moaning and calling out of other lands,
Had left the ravaged woodland yet once more
To peace, and what should not have been had been,
For Merlin, overtalk'd and overworn,
Had yielded, told her all the charm, and slept.

Then, in one moment, she put forth the charm
Of woven paces and of waving hands,
And in the hollow oak he lay as dead,
And lost to life and use and name and fame.

Then crying 'I have made his glory mine,'
And shrieking out 'O fool!' the harlot leapt
Adown the forest, and the thicket closed
Behind her, and the forest echo'd 'fool.'

Elaine

Elaine the fair, Elaine the lovable,
Elaine, the lily maid of Astolat,
High in her chamber up a tower to the east
Guarded the sacred shield of Lancelot;
Which first she placed where morning's earliest ray
Might strike it, and awake her with the gleam;
Then fearing rust or soilure fashion'd for it
A case of silk, and braided thereupon
All the devices blazon'd on the shield
In their own tinct, and added, of her wit,
A border fantasy of branch and flower,
And yellow-throated nestling in the nest.
Nor rested thus content, but day by day,
Leaving her household and good father, climb'd
That eastern tower, and entering barr'd her door,
Stript off the case, and read the naked shield,
Now guess'd a hidden meaning in his arms,
Now made a pretty history to herself
Of every dint a sword had beaten in it,
And every scratch a lance had made upon it,
Conjecturing when and where: this cut is fresh;
That ten years back; this dealt him at Caerlyle;
That at Caerleon; this at Camelot:
And ah God's mercy, what a stroke was there!
And here a thrust that might have kill'd, but God
Broke the strong lance, and roll'd his enemy down,
And saved him: so she lived in fantasy.

How came the lily maid by that good shield
Of Lancelot, she that knew not ev'n his name?
He left it with her, when he rode to tilt
For the great diamond in the diamond jousts,
Which Arthur had ordain'd, and by that name

Had named them, since a diamond was the prize.

For Arthur when none knew from whence he came,
Long ere the people chose him for their king,
Roving the trackless realms of Lyonnesse,
Had found a glen, grey boulder and black tarn.
A horror lived about the tarn, and clave
Like its own mists to all the mountain side:
For here two brothers, one a king, had met
And fought together; but their names were lost.
And each had slain his brother at a blow,
And down they fell and made the glen abhorr'd:
And there they lay till all their bones were bleach'd,
And lichen'd into colour with the crags:
And he, that once was king, had on a crown
Of diamonds, one in front, and four aside.
And Arthur came, and labouring up the pass
All in a misty moonshine, unawares
Had trodden that crown'd skeleton, and the skull
Brake from the nape, and from the skull the crown
Roll'd into light, and turning on its rims
Fled like a glittering rivulet to the tarn:
And down the shingly scaur he plunged, and caught,
And set it on his head, and in his heart
Heard murmurs 'lo, thou likewise shalt be king.'

Thereafter, when a king, he had the gems
Pluck'd from the crown, and show'd them to his knights,
Saying 'these jewels, whereupon I chanced
Divinely, are the kingdom's not the king's –
For public use: henceforward let there be,
Once every year, a joust for one of these:
For so by nine years' proof we needs must learn
Which is our mightiest, and ourselves shall grow
In use of arms and manhood, till we drive
The Heathen, who, some say, shall rule the land
Hereafter, which God hinder.' Thus he spoke:
And eight years past, eight jousts had been, and still
Had Lancelot won the diamond of the year,
With purpose to present them to the Queen,
When all were won; but meaning all at once
To snare her royal fancy with a boon
Worth half her realm, had never spoken word.

Now for the central diamond and the last
And largest, Arthur, holding then his court

Hard on the river nigh the place which now
Is this world's hugest, let proclaim a joust
At Camelot, and when the time drew nigh
Spake (for she had been sick) to Guinevere:
'Are you so sick, my Queen, you cannot move
To these fair jousts?' 'Yea, lord,' she said, 'you know it.'
'Then will you miss,' he answer'd, 'the great deeds
Of Lancelot, and his prowess in the lists,
A sight you love to look on.' And the Queen
Lifted her eyes, and they dwelt languidly
On Lancelot, where he stood beside the King.
He thinking that he read her meaning there,
'Stay with me, I am sick; my love is more
Than many diamonds,' yielded, and a heart,
Love-loyal to the least wish of the Queen
(However much he yearn'd to make complete
The tale of diamonds for his destined boon)
Urged him to speak against the truth, and say,
'Sir King, mine ancient wound is hardly whole,
And lets me from the saddle;' and the King
Glanced first at him, then her, and went his way.
No sooner gone than suddenly she began.

    'To blame, my lord Sir Lancelot, much to blame.
Why go you not to these fair jousts? the knights
Are half of them our enemies, and the crowd
Will murmur, lo the shameless ones, who take
Their pastime now the trustful king is gone!'
Then Lancelot vext at having lied in vain:
'Are you so wise? you were not once so wise,
My Queen, that summer, when you loved me first.
Then of the crowd you took no more account
Than of the myriad cricket of the mead,
When its own voice clings to each blade of grass,
And every voice is nothing. As to knights,
Them surely can I silence with all ease.
But now my loyal worship is allow'd
Of all men: many a bard, without offence,
Has link'd our names together in his lay,
Lancelot, the flower of bravery, Guinevere,
The pearl of beauty: and our knights at feast
Have pledged us in this union, while the king
Would listen smiling. How then? is there more?
Has Arthur spoken aught? or would yourself,
Now weary of my service and devoir,
Henceforth be truer to your faultless lord?'

      She broke into a little scornful laugh.
'Arthur, my lord, Arthur, the faultless King,
That passionate perfection, my good lord –
But who can gaze upon the Sun in heaven?
He never spake word of reproach to me,
He never had a glimpse of mine untruth,
He cares not for me: only here to-day
There gleam'd a vague suspicion in his eyes:
Some meddling rogue has tamper'd with him – else
Rapt in this fancy of his Table Round,
And swearing men to vows impossible
To make them like himself: but, friend, to me
He is all fault who hath no fault at all:
For who loves me must have a touch of earth;
The low sun makes the colour: I am yours,
Not Arthur's, as you know, save by the bond.
And therefore hear my words: go to the jousts:
The tiny-trumpeting gnat can break our dream
When sweetest; and the vermin voices here
May buzz so loud – we scorn them, but they sting.'

      Then answer'd Lancelot, the chief of knights:
'And with what face, after my pretext made,
Shall I appear, O Queen, at Camelot, I
Before a king who honours his own word,
As if it were his God's?'
                              'Yea,' said the Queen,
'A moral child without the craft to rule,
Else had he not lost me: but listen to me,
If I must find you wit: we hear it said
That men go down before your spear at a touch
But knowing you are Lancelot; your great name,
This conquers: hide it therefore; go unknown:
Win! by this kiss you will: and our true king
Will then allow your pretext, O my knight,
As all for glory; for to speak him true,
You know right well, how meek soe'er he seem,
No keener hunter after glory breathes.
He loves it in his knights more than himself:
They prove to him his work: win and return.'

      Then got Sir Lancelot suddenly to horse,
Wroth at himself: not willing to be known,
He left the barren-beaten thoroughfare,
Chose the green path that show'd the rarer foot,
And there among the solitary downs,

Full often lost in fancy, lost his way;
Till as he traced a faintly-shadow'd track,
That all in loops and links among the dales
Ran to the Castle of Astolat, he saw
Fired from the west, far on a hill, the towers.
Thither he made and wound the gateway horn.
Then came an old, dumb, myriad-wrinkled man,
Who let him into lodging and disarm'd.
And Lancelot marvell'd at the wordless man;
And issuing found the Lord of Astolat
With two strong sons, Sir Torre and Sir Lavaine,
Moving to meet him in the castle court;
And close behind them stept the lily maid
Elaine, his daughter: mother of the house
There was not: some light jest among them rose
With laughter dying down as the great knight
Approach'd them: then the Lord of Astolat:
'Whence comest thou, my guest, and by what name
Livest between the lips? for by thy state
And presence I might guess thee chief of those,
After the king, who eat in Arthur's halls.
Him have I seen: the rest, his Table Round,
Known as they are, to me they are unknown.'

Then answer'd Lancelot, the chief of knights:
'Known am I, and of Arthur's hall, and known,
What I by mere mischance have brought, my shield.
But since I go to joust as one unknown
At Camelot for the diamond, ask me not,
Hereafter you shall know me – and the shield –
I pray you lend me one, if such you have,
Blank, or at least with some device not mine.'

Then said the Lord of Astolat, 'Here is Torre's:
Hurt in his first tilt was my son, Sir Torre.
And so, God wot, his shield is blank enough.
His you can have.' Then added plain Sir Torre,
'Yea, since I cannot use it, you may have it.'
Here laugh'd the father saying 'Fie, Sir Churl,
Is that an answer for a noble knight?
Allow him: but Lavaine, my younger here,
He is so full of lustihood, he will ride,
Joust for it, and win, and bring it in an hour
And set it in this damsel's golden hair,
To make her thrice as wilful as before.'

'Nay, father, nay good father, shame me not
Before this noble knight' said young Lavaine
'For nothing. Surely I but play'd on Torre:
He seem'd so sullen, vext he could not go:
A jest, no more: for, knight, the maiden dreamt
That some one put this diamond in her hand,
And that it was too slippery to be held,
And slipt and fell into some pool or stream,
The castle-well, belike; and then I said
That *if* I went and *if* I fought and won it
(But all was jest and joke among ourselves)
Then must she keep it safelier. All was jest.
But, father, give me leave, an if he will,
To ride to Camelot with this noble knight:
Win shall I not, but do my best to win:
Young as I am, yet would I do my best.'

'So you will grace me,' answer'd Lancelot,
Smiling a moment, 'with your fellowship
O'er these waste downs whereon I lost myself,
Then were I glad of you as guide and friend;
And you shall win this diamond – as I hear,
It is a fair large diamond, – if you may,
And yield it to this maiden, if you will.'
'A fair large diamond,' added plain Sir Torre,
'Such be for Queens and not for simple maids.'
Then she, who held her eyes upon the ground,
Elaine, and heard her name so tost about,
Flush'd slightly at the slight disparagement
Before the stranger knight, who, looking at her,
Full courtly, yet not falsely, thus return'd:
'If what is fair be but for what is fair,
And only Queens are to be counted so,
Rash were my judgement then, who deem this maid
Might wear as fair a jewel as is on earth,
Not violating the bond of like to like.'

He spoke and ceased: the lily maid Elaine,
Won by the mellow voice before she look'd,
Lifted her eyes, and read his lineaments.
The great and guilty love he bare the Queen,
In battle with the love he bare his lord,
Had marr'd his face, and mark'd it ere his time.
Another sinning on such heights with one,
The flower of all the west and all the world,
Had been the sleeker for it: but in him

His mood was often like a fiend, and rose
And drove him into wastes and solitudes
For agony, who was yet a living soul.
Marr'd as he was, he seem'd the goodliest man
That ever among ladies ate in hall,
And noblest, when she lifted up her eyes.
However marr'd, of more than twice her years,
Seam'd with an ancient swordcut on the cheek,
And bruised and bronzed, she lifted up her eyes
And loved him, with that love which was her doom.

Then the great knight, the darling of the court,
Loved of the loveliest, into that rude hall
Stept with all grace, and not with half disdain
Hid under grace, as in a smaller time,
But kindly man moving among his kind:
Whom they with meats and vintage of their best
And talk and minstrel melody entertain'd.
And much they ask'd of court and Table Round,
And ever well and readily answer'd he:
But Lancelot, when they glanced at Guinevere,
Suddenly speaking of the wordless man,
Heard from the Baron that, ten years before,
The heathen caught and reft him of his tongue.
'He learnt and warn'd me of their fierce design
Against my house, and him they caught and maim'd;
But I my sons and little daughter fled
From bonds or death, and dwelt among the woods
By the great river in a boatman's hut.
Dull days were those, till our good Arthur broke
The Pagan yet once more on Badon hill.'

'O there, great Lord, doubtless,' Lavaine said, rapt
By all the sweet and sudden passion of youth
Toward greatness in its elder, 'you have fought
O tell us – for we live apart – you know
Of Arthur's glorious wars.' And Lancelot spoke
And answer'd him at full, as having been
With Arthur in the fight which all day long
Rang by the white mouth of the violent Glem;
And in the four wild battles by the shore
Of Duglas; that on Bassa; then the war
That thunder'd in and out the gloomy skirts
Of Celidon the forest; and again
By castle Gurnion where the glorious King
Had on his cuirass worn our Lady's Head,

Carved of one emerald, center'd in a sun
Of silver rays, that lighten'd as he breathed;
And at Caerleon had he help'd his lord,
When the strong neighings of the wild white Horse
Set every gilded parapet shuddering;
And up in Agned Cathregonion too,
And down the waste sand-shores of Trath Treroit,
Where many a heathen fell; 'and on the mount
Of Badon I myself beheld the King
Charge at the head of all his Table Round
And all his legions crying Christ and him,
And break them; and I saw him, after, stand
High on a heap of slain, from spur to plume
Red as the rising sun with heathen blood,
And seeing me, with a great voice he cried
"They are broken, they are broken!" for the King,
However mild he seems at home, nor cares
For triumph in our mimic wars, the jousts –
For if his own knight cast him down, he laughs
Saying, his knights are better men than he –
Yet in this heathen war the fire of God
Fills him: I never saw his like: there lives
No greater leader.'
                            While he utter'd this,
Low to her own heart said the lily maid,
'Save your great self, fair lord,' and when he fell
From talk of war to traits of pleasantry –
Being mirthful he but in a stately kind –
She still took note that when the living smile
Died from his lips, across him came a cloud
Of melancholy severe, from which again,
Whenever in her hovering to and fro
The lily maid had striven to make him cheer,
There brake a sudden-beaming tenderness
Of manners and of nature: and she thought
That all was nature, all, perchance, for her.
And all night long his face before her lived,
As when a painter, poring on a face,
Divinely thro' all hindrance finds the man
Behind it, and so paints him that his face,
The shape and colour of a mind and life,
Lives for his children, ever at its best
And fullest; so the face before her lived,
Dark-splendid, speaking in the silence, full
Of noble things, and held her from her sleep.
Till rathe she rose, half-cheated in the thought

She needs must bid farewell to sweet Lavaine.
First as in fear, step after step, she stole
Down the long tower-stairs, hesitating:
Anon, she heard Sir Lancelot cry in the court,
'This shield, my friend, where is it?' and Lavaine
Past inward, as she came from out the tower.
There to his proud horse Lancelot turn'd, and smooth'd
The glossy shoulder, humming to himself.
Half-envious of the flattering hand, she drew
Nearer and stood. He look'd, and more amazed
Than if seven men had set upon him, saw
The maiden standing in the dewy light.
He had not dream'd she was so beautiful.
Then came on him a sort of sacred fear,
For silent, tho' he greeted her, she stood
Rapt on his face as if it were a God's.
Suddenly flash'd on her a wild desire,
That he should wear her favour at the tilt.
She braved a riotous heart in asking for it.
'Fair lord, whose name I know not – noble it is,
I well believe, the noblest – will you wear
My favour at this tourney?' 'Nay,' said he,
'Fair lady, since I never yet have worn
Favour of any lady in the lists.
Such is my wont, as those, who know me, know.'
'Yea, so,' she answer'd;' then in wearing mine
Needs must be lesser likelihood, noble lord,
That those who know should know you.' And he turn'd
Her counsel up and down within his mind,
And found it true, and answer'd, 'True, my child.
Well, I will wear it: fetch it out to me:
What is it?' and she told him 'A red sleeve
Broider'd with pearls,' and brought it: then he bound
Her token on his helmet, with a smile, Saying,
'I never yet have done so much
For any maiden living,' and the blood
Sprang to her face and fill'd her with delight;
But left her all the paler, when Lavaine
Returning brought the yet-unblazon'd shield,
His brother's; which he gave to Lancelot,
Who parted with his own to fair Elaine;
'Do me this grace, my child, to have my shield
In keeping till I come.' 'A grace to me,'
She answer'd, 'twice to-day. I am your Squire.'
Whereat Lavaine said, laughing, 'Lily maid,
For fear our people call you lily maid

In earnest, let me bring your colour back;
Once, twice, and thrice: now get you hence to bed:
'So kiss'd her, and Sir Lancelot his own hand
And thus they moved away: she stay'd a minute,
Then made a sudden step to the gate, and there –
Her bright hair blown about the serious face
Yet rosy-kindled with her brother's kiss –
Paused in the gateway, standing by the shield
In silence, while she watch'd their arms far-off
Sparkle, until they dipt below the downs.
Then to her tower she climb'd, and took the shield,
There kept it, and so lived in fantasy.

Meanwhile the new companions past away
Far o'er the long backs of the bushless downs,
To where Sir Lancelot knew there lived a knight
Not far from Camelot, now for forty years
A hermit, who had pray'd, labour'd and pray'd
And ever labouring had scoop'd himself
In the white rock a chapel and a hall
On massive columns, like a shorecliff cave,
And cells and chambers: all were fair and dry;
The green light from the meadows underneath
Struck up and lived along the milky roofs;
And in the meadows tremulous aspen-trees
And poplars made a noise of falling showers.
And thither wending there that night they bode.

But when the next day broke from underground,
And shot red fire and shadows thro' the cave,
They rose, heard mass, broke fast, and rode away:
Then Lancelot saying, 'Hear, but hold my name
Hidden, you ride with Lancelot of the Lake,'
Abash'd Lavaine, whose instant reverence,
Dearer to true young hearts than their own praise,
But left him leave to stammer, 'Is it indeed?'
And after muttering 'The great Lancelot,'
At last he got his breath and answer'd, 'One,
One have I seen – that other, our liege lord,
The dread Pendragon, Britain's king of kings,
Of whom the people talk mysteriously,
He will be there – then were I stricken blind
That minute, I might say that I had seen.'

So spake Lavaine, and when they reach'd the lists
By Camelot in the meadow, let his eyes

Run thro' the peopled gallery which half round
Lay like a rainbow fall'n upon the grass,
Until they found the clear-faced King, who sat
Robed in red samite, easily to be known,
Since to his crown the golden dragon clung,
And down his robe the dragon writhed in gold,
And from the carven-work behind him crept
Two dragons gilded, sloping down to make
Arms for his chair, while all the rest of them
Thro' knots and loops and folds innumerable
Fled ever thro' the woodwork, till they found
The new design wherein they lost themselves,
Yet with all ease, so tender was the work:
And, in the costly canopy o'er him set,
Blazed the last diamond of the nameless king.

Then Lancelot answer'd young Lavaine and said,
'Me you call great: mine is the firmer seat,
The truer lance: but there is many a youth
Now crescent, who will come to all I am
And overcome it; and in me there dwells
No greatness, save it be some far-off touch
Of greatness to know well I am not great:
There is the man.' And Lavaine gaped upon him
As on a thing miraculous, and anon
The trumpets blew; and then did either side,
They that assail'd, and they that held the lists,
Set lance in rest, strike spur, suddenly move,
Meet in the midst, and there so furiously
Shock, that a man far-off might well perceive,
If any man that day were left afield,
The hard earth shake, and a low thunder of arms.
And Lancelot bode a little, till he saw
Which were the weaker; then he hurl'd into it
Against the stronger: little need to speak
Of Lancelot in his glory: King, duke, earl
Count, baron – whom he smote, he overthrew.

But in the field were Lancelot's kith and kin,
Ranged with the Table Round that held the lists
Strong men, and wrathful that a stranger knight
Should do and almost overdo the deeds
Of Lancelot; and one said to the other,
'Lo! What is he? I do not mean the force alone,
The grace and versatility of the man –
Is it not Lancelot?' 'When has Lancelot worn

Favour of any lady in the lists?
Not such his wont, as we, that know him, know.'
'How then? Who then?' a fury seized on them,
A fiery family passion for the name
Of Lancelot, and a glory one with theirs.
They couch'd their spears and prick'd their steeds and thus,
Their plumes driv'n backward by the wind they made
In moving, all together down upon him
Bare, as a wild wave in the wide North-sea,
Green-glimmering toward the summit, bears, with all
Its stormy crests that smoke against the skies,
Down on a bark, and overbears the bark,
And him that helms it, so they overbore
Sir Lancelot and his charger, and a spear
Down-glancing lamed the charger, and a spear
Prick'd sharply his own cuirass, and the head
Pierced thro' his side, and there snapt, and remain'd.

    Then Sir Lavaine did well and worshipfully;
He bore a knight of old repute to the earth,
And brought his horse to Lancelot where he lay.
He up the side, sweating with agony, got,
But thought to do while he might yet endure,
And being lustily holpen by the rest,
His party, – tho' it seemed half-miracle
To those he fought with – drave his kith and kin,
And all the Table Round that held the lists,
Back to the barrier; then the heralds blew
Proclaiming his the prize, who wore the sleeve
Of scarlet, and the pearls; and all the knights,
His party, cried 'Advance, and take your prize
The diamond;' but he answer'd, 'Diamond me
No diamonds! for God's love, a little air!
Prize me no prizes, for my prize is death!
Hence will I, and I charge you, follow me not.'

    He spoke, and vanish'd suddenly from the field
With young Lavaine into the poplar grove.
There from his charger down he slid, and sat,
Gasping to Sir Lavaine, 'Draw the lance-head:'
'Ah my sweet lord Sir Lancelot,' said Lavaine,
'I dread me, if I draw it, you will die.'
But he, 'I die already with it: draw –
Draw,' – and Lavaine drew, and that other gave
A marvellous great shriek and ghastly groan,
And half his blood burst forth, and down he sank
For the pure pain, and wholly swoon'd away.

Then came the hermit out and bare him in,
There stanch'd his wound; and there, in daily doubt
Whether to live or die, for many a week
Hid from the wide world's rumour by the grove
Of poplars with their noise of falling showers,
And ever-tremulous aspen-trees, he lay.

But on that day when Lancelot fled the lists,
His party, knights of utmost North and West,
Lords of waste marches, kings of desolate isles,
Came round their great Pendragon, saying to him,
'Lo, Sire, our knight thro' whom we won the day
Hath gone sore wounded, and hath left his prize
Untaken, crying that his prize is death.'
'Heaven hinder,' said the King, 'that such an one,
So great a knight as we have seen to-day –
He seem'd to me another Lancelot –
Yea, twenty times I thought him Lancelot –
He must not pass uncared for. Gawain, rise,
My nephew, and ride forth and find the knight.
Wounded and wearied needs must he be near.
I charge you that you get at once to horse.
And, knights and kings, there breathes not one of you
Will deem this prize of ours is rashly given:
His prowess was too wondrous. We will do him
No customary honour: since the knight
Came not to us, of us to claim the prize,
Ourselves will send it after. Wherefore take
This diamond, and deliver it, and return,
And bring us what he is and how he fares,
And cease not from your quest, until you find.'

So saying, from the carven flower above,
To which it made a restless heart, he took,
And gave, the diamond: then from where he sat
At Arthur's right, with smiling face arose,
With smiling face and frowning heart, a Prince
In the mid might and flourish of his May,
Gawain, surnamed The Courteous, fair and strong
And after Lancelot, Tristram, and Geraint
And Lamorack, a good knight, but therewithal
Sir Modred's brother, of a crafty house,
Nor often loyal to his word, and now
Wroth that the king's command to sally forth
In quest of whom he knew not, made him leave
The banquet, and concourse of knights and kings.

So all in wrath he got to horse and went;
While Arthur to the banquet, dark in mood,
Past, thinking 'Is it Lancelot who has come
Despite the wound he spake of, all for gain
Of glory, and has added wound to wound,
And ridd'n away to die?' So fear'd the King,
And, after two days' tarriance there, return'd.
Then when he saw the Queen, embracing ask'd,
'Love, are you yet so sick?' 'Nay, Lord,' she said.
'And where is Lancelot?' Then the Queen amazed,
'Was he not with you? won he not your prize?'
'Nay, but one like him.' 'Why that like was he.'
And when the King demanded how she knew,
Said, 'Lord, no sooner had you parted from us,
Than Lancelot told me of a common talk
That men went down before his spear at a touch,
But knowing he was Lancelot; his great name
Conquer'd; and therefore would he hide his name
From all men, ev'n the King, and to this end
Had made the pretext of a hindering wound,
That he might joust unknown of all, and learn
If his old prowess were in aught decay'd:
And added, "our true Arthur, when he learns,
Will well allow my pretext, as for gain
Of purer glory." '
                       Then replied the King:
'Far lovelier in our Lancelot had it been,
In lieu of idly dallying with the truth,
To have trusted me as he has trusted you.
Surely his king and most familiar friend
Might well have kept his secret. True, indeed,
Albeit I know my knights fantastical,
So fine a fear in our large Lancelot
Must needs have moved my laughter: now remains
But little cause for laughter: his own kin –
Ill news, my Queen, for all who love him, these!
His kith and kin, not knowing, set upon him;
So that he went sore wounded from the field:
Yet good news too: for goodly hopes are mine
That Lancelot is no more a lonely heart.
He wore, against his wont, upon his helm
A sleeve of scarlet, broider'd with great pearls,
Some gentle maiden's gift.'
                               'Yea, lord,' she said,
'Your hopes are mine,' and saying that she choked,
And sharply turn'd about to hide her face,

Moved to her chamber, and there flung herself
Down on the great King's couch, and writhed upon it,
And clench'd her fingers till they bit the palm,
And shriek'd out 'Traitor' to the unhearing wall,
Then flash'd into wild tears, and rose again,
And moved about her palace, proud and pale.

Gawain the while thro' all the region round
Rode with his diamond, wearied of the quest,
Touch'd at all points, except the poplar grove,
And came at last, tho' late, to Astolat:
Whom glittering in enamell'd arms the maid
Glanced at, and cried 'What news from Camelot, lord?
What of the knight with the red sleeve?' 'He won.'
'I knew it,' she said. 'But parted from the jousts
Hurt in the side,' whereat she caught her breath
Thro' her own side she felt the sharp lance go;
Thereon she smote her hand: wellnigh she swoon'd:
And, while he gazed wonderingly at her, came
The lord of Astolat out, to whom the Prince
Reported who he was, and on what quest
Sent, that he bore the prize and could not find
The victor, but had ridden wildly round
To seek him, and was wearied of the search.
To whom the lord of Astolat, 'Bide with us,
And ride no longer wildly, noble Prince!
Here was the knight, and here he left a shield;
This will he send or come for: furthermore
Our son is with him; we shall hear anon,
Needs must we hear.' To this the courteous Prince
Accorded with his wonted courtesy,
Courtesy with a touch of traitor in it,
And stay'd; and cast his eyes on fair Elaine:
Where could be found face daintier? then her shape
From forehead down to foot perfect — again
From foot to forehead exquisitely turn'd:
'Well — if I bide, lo! this wild flower for me!'
And oft they met among the garden yews,
And there he set himself to play upon her
With sallying wit, free flashes from a height
Above her, graces of the court, and songs,
Sighs, and slow smiles, and golden eloquence
And amorous adulation, till the maid
Rebell'd against it, saying to him,
'Prince, O loyal nephew of our noble King,
Why ask you not to see the shield he left,

Whence you might learn his name? Why slight your King,
And lose the quest he sent you on, and prove
No surer than our falcon yesterday,
Who lost the hern we slipt him at, and went
To all the winds?' 'Nay, by mine head,' said he,
'I lose it, as we lose the lark in heaven,
O damsel, in the light of your blue eyes:
But an you will it let me see the shield.'
And when the shield was brought, and Gawain saw
Sir Lancelot's azure lions, crown'd with gold,
Ramp in the field, he smote his thigh, and mock'd;
'Right was the King! our Lancelot! that true man!'
'And right was I,' she answer'd merrily, 'I,
Who dream'd my knight the greatest knight of all.'
'And if I dream'd,' said Gawain, 'that you love
This greatest knight, your pardon! lo, you know it!
Speak therefore: shall I waste myself in vain?'
Full simple was her answer, 'What know I?
My brethren have been all my fellowship,
And I, when often they have talk'd of love,
Wish'd it had been my mother, for they talk'd,
Meseem'd, of what they knew not; so myself –
I know not if I know what true love is,
But if I know, then, if I love not him,
Methinks there is none other I can love.'
'Yea, by God's death,' said he, 'you love him well,
But would not, knew you what all others know,
And wham he loves.' 'So be it,' cried Elaine,
And lifted her fair face and moved away:
But he pursued her, calling 'Stay a little!
One golden minute's grace: he wore your sleeve:
Would he break faith with one I may not name?
Must our true man change like a leaf at last?
Nay – like enough: why then, far be it from me
To cross our mighty Lancelot in his loves!
And, damsel, for I deem you know full well
Where your great knight is hidden, let me leave
My quest with you; the diamond also: here!
For if you love, it will be sweet to give it;
And if he love, it will be sweet to have it
From your own hand and whether he love or not,
A diamond is a diamond. Fare you well
A thousand times! – a thousand times farewell!
Yet, if he love, and his love hold, we two
May meet at court hereafter: there, I think,
So you will learn the courtesies of the court,

We two shall know each other.'
                                   Then he gave,
And slightly kiss'd the hand to which he gave,
The diamond, and all wearied of the quest
Leapt on his horse, and carolling as he went
A true-love ballad, lightly rode away.

    Thence to the court he past; there told the King
What the King knew, 'Sir Lancelot is the knight.'
And added, 'Sire, my liege, so much I learnt;
But fail'd to find him tho' I rode all round
The region: but I lighted on the maid
Whose sleeve he wore; she loves him; and to her,
Deeming our courtesy is the truest law,
I gave the diamond: she will render it;
For by mine head she knows his hiding-place.'

    The seldom-frowning King frown'd, and replied,
'Too courteous truly! you shall go no more
On quest of mine, seeing that you forget
Obedience is the courtesy due to kings.'

    He spake and parted. Wroth but all in awe,
For twenty strokes of the blood, without a word,
Linger'd that other, staring after him;
Then shook his hair, strode off, and buzz'd abroad
About the maid of Astolat, and her love.
All ears were prick'd at once, all tongues were loosed:
'The maid of Astolat loves Sir Lancelot,
Sir Lancelot loves the maid of Astolat.'
Some read the King's face, some the Queen's, and all
Had marvel what the maid might be, but most
Predoom'd her as unworthy. One old dame
Came suddenly on the Queen with the sharp news.
She, that had heard the noise of it before,
But sorrowing Lancelot should have stoop'd so low,
Marr'd her friend's point with pale tranquillity.
So ran the tale like fire about the court,
Fire in dry stubble a nine days' wonder flared:
Till ev'n the knights at banquet twice or thrice
Forgot to drink to Lancelot and the Queen,
And pledging Lancelot and the lily maid
Smiled at each other, while the Queen who sat
With lips severely placid felt the knot
Climb in her throat, and with her feet unseen
Crush'd the wild passion out against the floor

Beneath the banquet, where the meats became
As wormwood, and she hated all who pledged.

But far away the maid in Astolat
Her guiltless rival, she that ever kept
The one-day-seen Sir Lancelot in her heart
Crept to her father, while he mused alone,
Sat on his knee, stroked his grey face and said,
'Father, you call me wilful, and the fault
Is yours who let me have my will, and now,
Sweet father, will you let me lose my wits?'
'Nay,' said he, 'surely.' 'Wherefore, let me hence,'
She answer'd, 'and find out our dear Lavaine.'
'You will not lose your wits for dear Lavaine:
Bide,' answer'd he: 'we needs must hear anon
Of him, and of that other.' 'Aye,' she said,
'And of that other, for I needs must hence
And find that other, wheresoe'er he be,
And with mine own hand give his diamond to him,
Lest I be found as faithless in the quest
As yon proud Prince who left the quest to me.
Sweet father, I behold him in my dreams
Gaunt as it were the skeleton of himself,
Death-pale, for lack of gentle maiden's aid.
The gentler-born the maiden, the more bound,
My father, to be sweet and serviceable
To noble knights in sickness, as you know,
When these have worn their tokens: let me hence
I pray you.' Then her father nodding said,
'Aye, aye, the diamond: wit you well, my child,
Right fain were I to learn this knight were whole,
Being our greatest: yea, and you must give it –
And sure I think this fruit is hung too high
For any mouth to gape for save a Queen's –
Nay, I mean nothing: so then, get you gone,
Being so very wilful you must go.'

Lightly, her suit allow'd, she slipt away,
And while she made her ready for her ride,
Her father's latest word humm'd in her ear,
'Being so very wilful you must go,'
And changed itself and echoed in her heart,
'Being so very wilful you must die.'
But she was happy enough and shook it off,
As we shake off the bee that buzzes at us;
And in her heart she answer'd it and said,

'What matter, so I help him back to life?'
Then far away with good Sir Torre for guide
Rode o'er the long backs of the bushless downs
To Camelot, and before the city-gates
Came on her brother with a happy face
Making a roan horse caper and curvet
For pleasure all about a field of flowers:
Whom when she saw, 'Lavaine,' she cried, 'Lavaine,
How fares my lord Sir Lancelot?' He amazed,
'Torre and Elaine! why here? Sir Lancelot!
How know you my lord's name is Lancelot?'
But when the maid had told him all her tale,
Then turn'd Sir Torre, and being in his moods
Left them, and under the strange-statued gate,
Where Arthur's wars were render'd mystically,
Past up the still rich city to his kin,
His own far blood, which dwelt at Camelot;
And her, Lavaine across the poplar grove
Led to the caves: there first she saw the casque
Of Lancelot on the wall: her scarlet sleeve,
Tho' carved and cut, and half the pearls away,
Stream'd from it still; and in her heart she laugh'd,
Because he had not loosed it from his helm,
But meant once more perchance to tourney in it.
And when they gain'd the cell in which he slept,
His battle-writhen arms and mighty hands
Lay naked on the wolfskin, and a dream
Of dragging down his enemy made them move.
Then she that saw him lying unsleek, unshorn,
Gaunt as it were the skeleton of himself,
Utter'd a little tender dolorous cry.
The sound not wonted in a place so still
Woke the sick knight, and while he roll'd his eyes
Yet blank from sleep, she started to him, saying,
'Your prize the diamond sent you by the King:'
His eyes glisten'd: she fancied 'Is it for me?'
And when the maid had told him all the tale
Of King and Prince, the diamond sent, the quest
Assign'd to her not worthy of it, she knelt
Full lowly by the corners of his bed,
And laid the diamond in his open hand.
Her face was near, and as we kiss the child
That does the task assign'd, he kiss'd her face.
At once she slipt like water to the floor.
'Alas,' he said, 'your ride has wearied you.
Rest must you have.' 'No rest for me,' she said;

'Nay, for near you, fair lord, I am at rest.'
What might she mean by that? his large black eyes,
Yet larger thro' his leanness, dwelt upon her,
Till all her heart's sad secret blazed itself
In the heart's colours on her simple face;
And Lancelot look'd and was perplext in mind,
And being weak in body said no more;
But did not love the colour; woman's love
Save one, he not regarded, and so turn'd
Sighing, and feign'd a sleep until he slept.

    Then rose Elaine and glided thro' the fields,
And past beneath the wildly-sculptured gates
Far up the dim rich city to her kin;
There bode the night: but woke with dawn, and past
Down thro' the dim rich city to the fields,
Thence to the cave: so day by day she past
In either twilight ghost-like to and fro
Gliding, and every day she tended him,
And likewise many a night: and Lancelot
Would, tho' he call'd his wound a little hurt
Whereof he should be quickly whole, at times
Brain-feverous in his heat and agony, seem
Uncourteous, even he: but the meek maid
Sweetly forbore him ever, being to him
Meeker than any child to a rough nurse,
Milder than any mother to a sick child,
And never woman yet, since man's first fall,
Did kindlier unto man, but her deep love
Upbore her; till the hermit, skill'd in all
The simples and the science of that time,
Told him that her fine care had saved his life.
And the sick man forgot her simple blush,
Would call her friend and sister, sweet Elaine,
Would listen for her coming and regret
Her parting step, and held her tenderly,
And loved her with all love except the love
Of man and woman when they love their best,
Closest and sweetest, and had died the death
In any knightly fashion for her sake.
And peradventure had he seen her first
She might have made this and that other world
Another world for the sick man; but now
The shackles of an old love straiten'd him,
His honour rooted in dishonour stood,
And faith unfaithful kept him falsely true.

Yet the great knight in his mid-sickness made
Full many a holy vow and pure resolve.
These, as but born of sickness, could not live:
For when the blood ran lustier in him again,
Full often the sweet image of one face,
Making a treacherous quiet in his heart,
Dispersed his resolution like a cloud.
Then if the maiden, while that ghostly grace
Beam'd on his fancy, spoke, he answer'd not,
Or short and coldly, and she knew right well
What the rough sickness meant, but what this meant
She knew not, and the sorrow dimm'd her sight,
And drave her ere her time across the fields
Far into the rich city, where alone
She murmur'd 'Vain, in vain: it cannot be.
He will not love me: how then? must I die?'
Then as a little helpless innocent bird,
That has but one plain passage of few notes,
Will sing the simple passage o'er and o'er
For all an April morning, till the ear
Wearies to hear it, so the simple maid
Went half the night repeating, 'Must I die?'
And now to right she turn'd, and now to left,
And found no ease in turning or in rest;
And 'him or death' she mutter'd, 'death or him,'
Again and like a burthen, 'him or death.'

But when Sir Lancelot's deadly hurt was whole,
To Astolat returning rode the three.
There morn by morn, arraying her sweet self
In that wherein she deem'd she look'd her best,
She came before Sir Lancelot, for she thought
'If I be loved, these are my festal robes,
If not, the victim's flowers before he fall.'
And Lancelot ever prest upon the maid
That she should ask some goodly gift of him
For her own self or hers, 'and do not shun
To speak the wish most near to your true heart;
Such service have you done me, that I make
My will of yours, and Prince and Lord am I
In mine own land, and what I will I can.'
Then like a ghost she lifted up her face,
But like a ghost without the power to speak.
And Lancelot saw that she withheld her wish,
And bode among them yet a little space
Till he should learn it; and one morn it chanced

He found her in among the garden yews,
And said, 'Delay no longer, speak your wish,
Seeing I must go to-day:' then out she brake;
'Going? and we shall never see you more.
And I must die for want of one bold word.'
'Speak: that I live to hear,' he said, 'is yours.'
Then suddenly and passionately she spoke:
'I have gone mad. I love you: let me die.'
'Ah, sister,' answer'd Lancelot, 'what is this?'
And innocently extending her white arms,
'Your love,' she said, 'your love – to be your wife.'
And Lancelot answer'd, 'Had I chos'n to wed,
I had been wedded earlier, sweet Elaine:
But now there never will be wife of mine.'
'No, no,' she cried, 'I care not to be wife,
But to be with you still to see your face,
To serve you, and to follow you thro' the world.'
And Lancelot answer'd, 'Nay, the world, the world,
All ear and eye, with such a stupid heart
To interpret ear and eye, and such a tongue
To blare its own interpretation – nay,
Full ill then should I quit your brother's love,
And your good father's kindness.' And she said,
'Not to be with you, not to see your face –
Alas for me then, my good days are done.'
'Nay, noble maid,' he answer'd, 'ten times nay!
This is not love: but love's first flash in youth,
Most common: yea, I know it of mine own self:
And you yourself will smile at your own self
Hereafter, when you yield your flower of life
To one more fitly yours, not thrice your age:
And then will I, for true you are and sweet
Beyond mine old belief in womanhood,
More specially should your good knight be poor,
Endow you with broad land and territory
Even to the half my realm beyond the seas,
So that would make you happy: furthermore,
Ev'n to the death, as tho' you were my blood,
In all your quarrels will I be your knight.
This will I do, dear damsel, for your sake,
And more than this I cannot.'
                              While he spoke
She neither blush'd nor shook, but deathly-pale
Stood grasping what was nearest, then replied;
'Of all this will I nothing;' and so fell,
And thus they bore her swooning to her tower.

Then spake, to whom thro' those black walls of yew
Their talk had pierced, her father. 'Aye, a flash,
I fear me, that will strike my blossom dead.
Too courteous are you, fair Lord Lancelot.
I pray you, use some rough discourtesy
To blunt or break her passion.'

Lancelot said,
'That were against me: what I can I will;'
And there that day remain'd, and toward even
Sent for his shield: full meekly rose the maid,
Stript off the case, and gave the naked shield;
Then, when she heard his horse upon the stones,
Unclasping flung the casement back, and look'd
Down on his helm, from which her sleeve had gone
And Lancelot knew the little clinking sound;
And she by tact of love was well aware
That Lancelot knew that she was looking at him.
And yet he glanced not up, nor waved his hand,
Nor bad farewell, but sadly rode away.
This was the one discourtesy that he used.

So in her tower alone the maiden sat:
His very shield was gone; only the case,
Her own poor work, her empty labour, left.
But still she heard him, still his picture form'd
And grew between her and the pictured wall.
Then came her father, saying in low tones,
'Have comfort,' whom she greeted quietly.
Then came her brethren saying, 'Peace to thee,
Sweet sister,' whom she answer'd with all calm.
But when they left her to herself again,
Death, like a friend's voice from a distant field
Approaching thro' the darkness, call'd, the owls
Wailing had power upon her, and she mixt
Her fancies with the sallow-rifted glooms
Of evening, and the moanings of the wind.

And in those days she made a little song
And call'd her song 'The Song of Love and Death,'
And sang it: sweetly could she make and sing.

'Sweet is true love tho' given in vain, in vain;
And sweet is death who puts an end to pain:
I know not which is sweeter, no, not I.

'Love, art thou sweet? then bitter death must be:
Love, thou art bitter; sweet is death to me.
O Love, if death be sweeter, let me die.

'Sweet love, that seems not made to fade away,
Sweet death, that seems to make us loveless clay,
I know not which is sweeter, no, not I.

'I fain would follow love, if that could be;
I needs must follow death, who calls for me;
Call and I follow, I follow! let me die.'

High with the last line scaled her voice, and this,
All in a fiery dawning wild with wind
That shook her tower, the brothers heard, and thought
With shuddering, 'Hark the Phantom of the house
That ever shrieks before a death,' and call'd
The father, and all three in hurry and fear
Ran to her, and lo! the blood-red light of dawn
Flared on her face, she shrilling 'Let me die!'

As when we dwell upon a word we know,
Repeating, till the word we know so well
Becomes a wonder and we know not why,
So dwelt the father on her face, and thought
'Is this Elaine?' till back the maiden fell
Then gave a languid hand to each, and lay,
Speaking a still good-morrow with her eyes.
At last she said, 'Sweet brothers, yesternight
I seem'd a curious little maid again,
As happy as when we dwelt among the woods,
And when you used to take me with the flood
Up the great river in the boatman's boat.
Only you would not pass beyond the cape
That has the poplar on it: there you fixt
Your limit, oft returning with the tide.
And yet I cried because you would not pass
Beyond it, and far up the shining flood
Until we found the palace of the king.
And yet you would not; but this night I dream'd
That I was all alone upon the flood,
And then I said "Now shall I have my will:"
And there I woke, but still the wish remain'd.
So let me hence that I may pass at last
Beyond the poplar and far up the flood,
Until I find the palace of the king.

There will I enter in among them all,
And no man there will dare to mock at me
But there the fine Gawain will wonder at me,
And there the great Sir Lancelot muse at me;
Gawain, who bad a thousand farewells to me,
Lancelot, who coldly went nor bad me one:
And there the King will know me and my love,
And there the Queen herself will pity me,
And all the gentle court will welcome me,
And after my long voyage I shall rest!'

'Peace,' said her father, 'O my child, you seem
Light-headed, for what force is yours to go,
So far, being sick? and wherefore would you look
On this proud fellow again, who scorns us all?'

Then the rough Torre began to heave and move,
And bluster into stormy sobs and say,
'I never loved him: an I meet with him,
I care not howsoever great he be,
Then will I strike at him and strike him down,
Give me good fortune, I will strike him dead,
For this discomfort he hath done the house.'

To which the gentle sister made reply,
'Fret not yourself, dear brother, nor be wroth,
Seeing it is no more Sir Lancelot's fault
Not to love me, than it is mine to love
Him of all men who seems to me the highest.'

'Highest?' the Father answer'd, echoing 'highest?'
(He meant to break the passion in her) 'nay,
Daughter, I know not what you call the highest;
But this I know, for all the people know it,
He loves the Queen, and in an open shame:
And she returns his love in open shame.
If this be high, what is it to be low?'

Then spake the lily maid of Astolat:
'Sweet father, all too faint and sick am I
For anger: these are slanders: never yet
Was noble man but made ignoble talk.
He makes no friend who never made a foe.
But now it is my glory to have loved
One peerless, without stain: so let me pass,
My father, howsoe'er I seem to you,

Not all unhappy, having loved God's best
And greatest, tho' my love had no return:
Yet, seeing you desire your child to live,
Thanks, but you work against your own desire,
For if I could believe the things you say
I should but die the sooner; wherefore cease,
Sweet father, and bid call the ghostly man
Hither, and let me shrive me clean, and die.'

So when the ghostly man had come and gone,
She with a face, bright as for sin forgiven,
Besought Lavaine to write as she devised
A letter, word for word; and when he ask'd
'Is it for Lancelot, is it for my dear lord?
Then will I bear it gladly;' she replied
'For Lancelot and the Queen and all the world,
But I myself must bear it.' Then he wrote
The letter she devised; which being writ
And folded, 'O sweet father, tender and true,
Deny me not,' she said – ' you never yet
Denied my fancies – this, however strange,
My latest: lay the letter in my hand
A little ere I die, and close the hand
Upon it; I shall guard it even in death.
And when the heat is gone from out my heart,
Then take the little bed on which I died
For Lancelot's love, and deck it like the Queen's
For richness, and me also like the Queen
In all I have of rich, and lay me on it.
And let there be prepared a chariot-bier
To take me to the river, and a barge
Be ready on the river, clothed in black.
I go in state to court, to meet the Queen.
There surely I shall speak for mine own self,
And none of you can speak for me so well.
And therefore let our dumb old man alone
Go with me, he can steer and row, and he
Will guide me to that palace, to the doors.'

She ceased: her father promised; whereupon
She grew so cheerful that they deem'd her death
Was rather in the fantasy than the blood.
But ten slow mornings past, and on the eleventh
Her father laid the letter in her hand,
And closed the hand upon it, and she died.
So that day there was dole in Astolat.

But when the next sun brake from underground,
Then, those two brethren slowly with bent brows
Accompanying, the sad chariot-bier
Past like a shadow thro' the field, that shone
Full-summer, to that stream whereon the barge,
Pall'd all its length in blackest samite, lay.
There sat the lifelong creature of the house,
Loyal, the dumb old servitor, on deck,
Winking his eyes, and twisted all his face.
So those two brethren from the chariot took
And on the black decks laid her in her bed,
Set in her hand a lily, o'er her hung
The silken case with braided blazonings,
And kiss'd her quiet brows, and saying to her
'Sister, farewell for ever,' and again
'Farewell, sweet sister,' parted all in tears.
Then rose the dumb old servitor, and the dead
Steer'd by the dumb went upward with the flood –
In her right hand the lily, in her left
The letter – all her bright hair streaming down –
And all the coverlid was cloth of gold
Drawn to her waist, and she herself in white
All but her face, and that clear-featured face
Was lovely, for she did not seem as dead
But fast asleep, and lay as tho' she smiled.

That day Sir Lancelot at the palace craved
Audience of Guinevere, to give at last
The price of half a realm, his costly gift,
Hard-won and hardly won with bruise and blow,
With deaths of others, and almost his own,
The nine-years-fought-for diamonds: for he saw
One of her house, and sent him to the Queen
Bearing his wish, whereto the Queen agreed
With such and so unmoved a majesty
She might have seem'd her statue, but that he,
Low-drooping till he wellnigh kiss'd her feet
For loyal awe, saw with a sidelong eye
The shadow of a piece of pointed lace,
In the Queen's shadow, vibrate on the walls
And parted, laughing in his courtly heart.

All in an oriel on the summer side,
Vine-clad, of Arthur's palace toward the stream,
They met, and Lancelot kneeling utter'd, 'Queen,
Lady, my liege, in whom I have my joy,

Take, what I had not won except for you,
These jewels, and make me happy, making them
An armlet for the roundest arm on earth,
Or necklace for a neck to which the swan's
Is tawnier than her cygnet's: these are words:
Your beauty is your beauty, and I sin
In speaking, yet O grant my worship of it
Words, as we grant grief tears. Such sin in words
Perchance, we both can pardon: but, my Queen,
I hear of rumours flying thro' your court.
Our bond, as not the bond of man and wife,
Should have in it an absoluter trust
To make up that defect: let rumours be:
When did not rumours fly? these, as I trust
That you trust me in your own nobleness,
I may not well believe that you believe.'

While thus he spoke, half turn'd away, the Queen
Brake from the vast oriel-embowering vine
Leaf after leaf, and tore, and cast them off,
Till all the place whereon she stood was green;
Then, when he ceased, in one cold passive hand
Received at once and laid aside the gems
There on a table near her, and replied:

'It may be, I am quicker of belief
Than you believe me, Lancelot of the Lake.
Our bond is not the bond of man and wife.
This good is in it, whatsoe'er of ill,
It can be broken easier. I for you
This many a year have done despite and wrong
To one whom ever in my heart of hearts
I did acknowledge nobler. What are these?
Diamonds for me! they had been thrice their worth
Being your gift, had you not lost your own.
To loyal hearts the value of all gifts
Must vary as the giver's. Not for me!
For her! for your new fancy. Only this
Grant me, I pray you: have your joys apart.
I doubt not that however changed, you keep
So much of what is graceful: and myself
Would shun to break those bounds of courtesy
In which as Arthur's queen I move and rule:
So cannot speak my mind. An end to this!
A strange one! yet I take it with Amen.
So pray you, add my diamonds to her pearls;

Deck her with these; tell her, she shines me down:
An armlet for an arm to which the Queen's
Is haggard, or a necklace for a neck
O as much fairer – as a faith once fair
Was richer than these diamonds – hers not mine –
Nay, by the mother of our Lord himself,
Or hers or mine, mine now to work my will –
She shall not have them.'
                                    Saying which she seized,
And, thro' the casement standing wide for heat,
Flung them, and down they flash'd, and smote the stream.
Then from the smitten surface flash'd, as it were,
Diamonds to meet them, and they past away.
Then while Sir Lancelot leant, in half disgust
At love, life, all things, on the window ledge,
Close underneath his eyes, and right across
Where these had fallen, slowly past the barge
Whereon the lily maid of Astolat
Lay smiling, like a star in blackest night.

    But the wild Queen, who saw not, burst away
To weep and wail in secret; and the barge,
On to the palace-doorway sliding, paused.
There two stood arm'd, and kept the door; to whom,
All up the marble stair, tier over tier,
Were added mouths that gaped, and eyes that ask'd
'What is it?' but that oarsman's haggard face,
As hard and still as is the face that men
Shape to their fancy's eye from broken rocks
On some cliff-side, appall'd them, and they said,
'He is enchanted, cannot speak – and she,
Look how she sleeps – the Fairy Queen, so fair!
Yea, but how pale! what are they? flesh and blood?
Or come to take the King to fairy land?
For some do hold our Arthur cannot die,
But that he passes into fairy land.'

    While thus they babbled of the King, the King
Came girt with knights: then turn'd the tongueless man
From the half-face to the full eye, and rose
And pointed to the damsel, and the doors.
So Arthur bad the meek Sir Percivale
And pure Sir Galahad to uplift the maid;
And reverently they bore her into hall.
Then came the fine Gawain and wonder'd at her,
And Lancelot later came and mused at her,

And last the Queen herself and pitied her:
But Arthur spied the letter in her hand,
Stoopt, took, brake seal, and read it; this was all.

    'Most noble lord, Sir Lancelot of the Lake,
I, sometime call'd the maid of Astolat,
Come, for you left me taking no farewell,
Hither, to take my last farewell of you.
I loved you, and my love had no return,
And therefore my true love has been my death.
And therefore to our lady Guinevere,
And to all other ladies, I make moan.
Pray for my soul, and yield me burial.
Pray for my soul thou too, Sir Lancelot,
As thou art a knight peerless.'
                              Thus he read,
And ever in the reading, lords and dames
Wept, looking often from his face who read
To hers which lay so silent, and at times,
So touch'd were they, half-thinking that her lips,
Who had devised the letter, moved again.

    Then freely spoke Sir Lancelot to them all:
'My lord liege Arthur, and all ye that hear,
Know that for this most gentle maiden's death
Right heavy am I; for good she was and true,
But loved me with a love beyond all love
In women, whomsoever I have known.
Yet to be loved makes not to love again;
Not at my years, however it hold in youth.
I swear by truth and knighthood that I gave
No cause, not willingly, for such a love:
To this I call my friends in testimony,
Her brethren, and her father, who himself
Besought me to be plain and blunt, and use,
To break her passion, some discourtesy
Against my nature: what I could, I did.
I left her and I bad her no farewell.
Tho', had I dreamt the damsel would have died,
I might have put my wits to some rough use,
And help'd her from herself.'
                              Then said the Queen
(Sea was her wrath, yet working after storm)
'You might at least have done her so much grace,
Fair lord, as would have help'd her from her death.'
He raised his head, their eyes met and hers fell,

He adding,

                   'Queen, she would not be content
Save that I wedded her, which could not be.
Then might she follow me thro' the world, she ask'd;
It could not be. I told her that her love
Was but the flash of youth, would darken down
To rise hereafter in a stiller flame
Toward one more worthy of her – then would I,
More specially were he, she wedded, poor,
Estate them with large land and territory
In mine own realm beyond the narrow seas,
To keep them in all joyance: more than this
I could not; this she would not, and she died.'

    He pausing, Arthur answer'd, 'O my knight,
It will be to your worship, as my knight,
And mine, as head of all our Table Round,
To see that she be buried worshipfully.'

    So toward that shrine which then in all the realm
Was richest, Arthur leading, slowly went
The marshall'd order of their Table Round,
And Lancelot sad beyond his wont, to see
The maiden buried, not as one unknown
Nor meanly, but with gorgeous obsequies,
And mass, and rolling music, like a Queen.
And when the knights had laid her comely head
Low in the dust of half-forgotten kings,
Then Arthur spake among them, 'Let her tomb
Be costly, and her image thereupon
And let the shield of Lancelot at her feet
Be carven, and her lily in her hand.
And let the story of her dolorous voyage
For all true hearts be blazon'd on her tomb
In letters gold and azure! 'which was wrought
Thereafter; but when now the lords and dames
And people, from the high door streaming, brake
Disorderly, as homeward each, the Queen,
Who mark'd Sir Lancelot where he moved apart,
Drew near, and sigh'd in passing, 'Lancelot,
Forgive me; mine was jealousy in love.'
He answer'd with his eyes upon the ground,
'That is love's curse; pass on, my Queen, forgiven.'
But Arthur, who beheld his cloudy brows,
Approach'd him, and with full affection flung
One arm about his neck, and spake and said.

'Lancelot, my Lancelot, thou in whom I have
Most joy and most affiance, for I know
What thou hast been in battle by my side,
And many a time have watch'd thee at the tilt
Strike down the lusty and long practised knight,
And let the younger and unskill'd go by
To win his honour and to make his name,
And loved thy courtesies and thee, a man
Made to be loved but now I would to God,
For the wild people say wild things of thee,
Thou could'st have loved this maiden, shaped, it seems,
By God for thee alone, and from her face,
If one may judge the living by the dead,
Delicately pure and marvellously fair,
Who might have brought thee, now a lonely man
Wifeless and heirless, noble issue, sons
Born to the glory of thy name and fame,
My knight, the great Sir Lancelot of the Lake.'

Then answer'd Lancelot, 'Fair she was, my King,
Pure, as you ever wish your knights to be.
To doubt her fairness were to want an eye,
To doubt her pureness were to want a heart —
Yea, to be loved, if what is worthy love
Could bind him, but free love will not be bound.'

'Free love, so bound, were freëst,' said the King.
'Let love be free; free love is for the best:
And, after heaven, on our dull side of death,
What should be best, if not so pure a love
Clothed in so pure a loveliness? yet thee
She fail'd to bind, tho' being, as I think,
Unbound as yet, and gentle, as I know.'

And Lancelot answer'd nothing, but he went,
And at the inrunning of a little brook
Sat by the river in a cove, and watch'd
The high reed wave, and lifted up his eyes
And saw the barge that brought her moving down,
Far-off, a blot upon the stream, and said
Low in himself, 'Ah simple heart and sweet,
You loved me, damsel, surely with a love
Far tenderer than my Queen's. Pray for thy soul?
Aye, that will I. Farewell too — now at last —
Farewell, fair lily. "Jealousy in love?"
Not rather dead love's harsh heir, jealous pride?

Queen, if I grant the jealousy as of love,
May not your crescent fear for name and fame
Speak, as it waves, of a love that wanes?
Why did the King dwell on my name to me?
Mine own name shames me, seeming a reproach,
Lancelot, whom the Lady of the Lake
Stole from his mother – as the story runs –
She chanted snatches of mysterious song
Heard on the winding waters, eve and morn
She kiss'd me saying "Thou art fair, my child,
As a king's son," and often in her arms
She bare me, pacing on the dusky mere.
Would she had drown'd me in it, where'er it be!
For what am I? what profits me my name
Of greatest knight? I fought for it, and have it:
Pleasure to have it, none; to lose it, pain;
Now grown a part of me: but what use in it?
To make men worse by making my sin known?
Or sin seem less, the sinner seeming great?
Alas for Arthur's greatest knight, a man
Not after Arthur's heart! I needs must break
These bonds that so defame me: not without
She wills it: would I, if she will'd it? nay,
Who knows? but if I would not, then may God
I pray him, send a sudden Angel down
To seize me by the hair and bear me far,
And fling me deep in that forgotten mere,
Among the tumbled fragments of the hills.'

  So groan'd Sir Lancelot in remorseful pain,
Not knowing he should die a holy man.

Guinevere

Queen Guinevere had fled the court, and sat
There in the holy house at Almesbury
Weeping, none with her save a little maid,
A novice: one low light betwixt them burn'd,
Blurr'd by the creeping mist, for all abroad,
Beneath a moon unseen albeit at full,
The white mist, like a face-cloth to the face,
Clung to the dead earth, and the land was still.

  For hither had she fled, her cause of flight
Sir Modred; he the nearest to the King,

His nephew, ever like a subtle beast
Lay couchant with his eyes upon the throne,
Ready to spring, waiting a chance: for this,
He chill'd the popular praises of the King
With silent smiles of slow disparagement;
And tamper'd with the Lords of the White Horse,
Heathen, the brood by Hengist left; and sought
To make disruption in the Table Round
Of Arthur, and to splinter it into feuds
Serving his traitorous end; and all his aims
Were sharpen'd by strong hate for Lancelot.

   For thus it chanced one morn when all the court,
Green-suited, but with plumes that mock'd the may,
Had been, their wont, a-maying and return'd,
That Modred still in green, all ear and eye,
Climb'd to the high top of the garden-wall
To spy some secret scandal if he might,
And saw the Queen who sat betwixt her best
Enid, and lissome Vivien, of her court
The wiliest and the worst; and more than this
He saw not, for Sir Lancelot passing by
Spied where he couch'd, and as the gardener's hand
Picks from the colewort a green caterpillar,
So from the high wall and the flowering grove
Of grasses Lancelot pluck'd him by the heel,
And cast him as a worm upon the way;
But when he knew the Prince tho' marr'd with dust,
He, reverencing king's blood in a bad man,
Made such excuses as he might, and these
Full knightly without scorn; for in those days
No knight of Arthur's noblest dealt in scorn;
But, if a man were halt or hunch'd, in him
By those whom God had made full-limb'd and tall,
Scorn was allow'd as part of his defect,
And he was answer'd softly by the King
And all his Table. So Sir Lancelot holp
To raise the Prince, who rising twice or thrice
Full sharply smote his knees, and smiled, and went:
But, ever after, the small violence done
Rankled in him and ruffled all his heart,
As the sharp wind that ruffles all day long
A little bitter pool about a stone
On the bare coast.
                    But when Sir Lancelot told
This matter to the Queen, at first she laugh'd

Lightly, to think of Modred's dusty fall,
Then shudder'd, as the village wife who cries
'I shudder, some one steps across my grave;'
Then laugh'd again, but faintlier, for indeed
She half-foresaw that he, the subtle beast,
Would track her guilt until he found, and hers
Would be for evermore a name of scorn.
Henceforward rarely could she front in Hall,
Or elsewhere, Modred's narrow foxy face,
Heart-hiding smile, and grey persistent eye:
Henceforward too, the Powers that tend the soul,
To help it from the death that cannot die,
And save it even in extremes, began
To vex and plague her. Many a time for hours,
Beside the placid breathings of the King,
In the dead night, grim faces came and went
Before her, or a vague spiritual fear —
Like to some doubtful noise of creaking doors,
Heard by the watcher in a haunted house,
That keeps the rust of murder on the walls —
Held her awake: or if she slept, she dream'd
An awful dream; for then she seem'd to stand
On some vast plain before a setting sun,
And from the sun there swiftly made at her
A ghastly something, and its shadow flew
Before it, till it touch'd her, and she turn'd —
When lo! her own, that broadening from her feet,
And blackening, swallow'd all the land, and in it
Far cities burnt, and with a cry she woke.
And all this trouble did not pass but grew;
Till ev'n the clear face of the guileless King,
And trustful courtesies of household life,
Became her bane; and at the last she said,
'O Lancelot, get thee hence to thine own land,
For if thou tarry we shall meet again,
And if we meet again, some evil chance
Will make the smouldering scandal break and blaze
Before the people, and our lord the King.'
And Lancelot ever promised, but remain'd,
And still they met and met. Again she said,
'O Lancelot, if thou love me get thee hence.'
And then they were agreed upon a night
(When the good King should not be there) to meet
And part for ever. Passion-pale they met
And greeted: hands in hands, and eye to eye,
Low on the border of her couch they sat

Stammering and staring: it was their last hour,
A madness of farewells. And Modred brought
His creatures to the basement of the tower
For testimony; and crying with full voice
'Traitor, come out, ye are trapt at last,' aroused
Lancelot, who rushing outward lionlike
Leapt on him, and hurl'd him headlong, and he fell
Stunn'd, and his creatures took and bare him off
And all was still: then she, 'the end is come
And I am shamed for ever;' and he said,
'Mine be the shame; mine was the sin: but rise
And fly to my strong castle overseas:
There will I hide thee, till my life shall end,
There hold thee with my life against the world.'
She answer'd, 'Lancelot, wilt thou hold me so?
Nay, friend, for we have taken our farewells.
Would God, that thou could'st hide me from myself!
Mine is the shame, for I was wife, and thou
Unwedded: yet rise now, and let us fly,
For I will draw me into sanctuary,
And bide my doom.' So Lancelot got her horse,
Set her thereon, and mounted on his own,
And then they rode to the divided way,
There kiss'd, and parted weeping: for he past,
Love-loyal to the least wish of the Queen,
Back to his land; but she to Almesbury
Fled all night long by glimmering waste and weald,
And heard the Spirits of the waste and weald
Moan as she fled, or thought she heard them moan:
And in herself she moan'd 'too late, too late!'
Till in the cold wind that foreruns the morn,
A blot in heaven, the Raven, flying high,
Croak'd, and she thought, 'He spies a field of death;
For now the Heathen of the Northern Sea,
Lured by the crimes and frailties of the court
Begin to slay the folk, and spoil the land.'

     And when she came to Almesbury she spake
There to the nuns, and said, 'Mine enemies
Pursue me, but, O peaceful Sisterhood,
Receive, and yield me sanctuary, nor ask
Her name, to whom ye yield it, till her time
To tell you:' and her beauty, grace and power,
Wrought as a charm upon them, and they spared
To ask it.
                         So the stately Queen abode

For many a week, unknown, among the nuns;
Nor with them mix'd, nor told her name, nor sought.
Wrapt in her grief, for housel or for shrift,
But communed only with the little maid,
Who pleased her with a babbling heedlessness
Which often lured her from herself, but now,
This night, a rumour wildly blown about
Came, that Sir Modred had usurp'd the realm,
And leagued him with the heathen, while the King
Was waging war on Lancelot: then she thought,
'With what a hate the people and the King
Must hate me,' and bow'd down upon her hands
Silent, until the little maid, who brook'd
No silence, brake it, uttering 'late! so late!
What hour, I wonder, now?' and when she drew
No answer, by and by began to hum
An air the nuns had taught her; 'late, so late!'
Which when she heard, the Queen look'd up, and said,
'O maiden, if indeed you list to sing
Sing, and unbind my heart that I may weep.'
Whereat full willingly sang the little maid.

'Late, late, so late! and dark the night and chill!
Late, late, so late! but we can enter still.
Too late, too late! ye cannot enter now.

'No light had we: for that we do repent;
And learning this, the bridegroom will relent.
Too late, too late! ye cannot enter now.

'No light: so late! and dark and chill the night!
O let us in, that we may find the light!
Too late, too late: ye cannot enter now.

'Have we not heard the bridegroom is so sweet?
O let us in, tho' late, to kiss his feet!
No, no, too late! ye cannot enter now.'

So sang the novice, while full passionately,
Her head upon her hands, remembering
Her thought when first she came, wept the sad Queen.
Then said the little novice prattling to her.

'O pray you, noble lady, weep no more;
But let my words, the words of one so small,
Who knowing nothing knows but to obey,

And if I do not there is penance given –
Comfort your sorrows; for they do not flow
From evil done; right sure am I of that,
Who see your tender grace and stateliness.
But weigh your sorrows with our lord the King's,
And weighing find them less; for gone is he
To wage grim war against Sir Lancelot there,
Round that strong castle where he holds the Queen;
And Modred whom he left in charge of all,
The traitor – Ah sweet lady, the King's grief
For his own self, and his own Queen, and realm,
Must needs be thrice as great as any of ours.
For me, I thank the saints, I am not great.
For if there ever come a grief to me
I cry my cry in silence, and have done:
None knows it, and my tears have brought me good:
But even were the griefs of little ones
As great as those of great ones, yet this grief
Is added to the griefs the great must bear,
That howsoever much they may desire
Silence, they cannot weep behind a cloud:
As even here they talk at Almesbury
About the good King and his wicked Queen,
And were I such a King with such a Queen
Well might I wish to veil her wickedness
But were I such a King, it could not be.'

    Then to her own sad heart mutter'd the Queen,
'Will the child kill me with her innocent talk?'
But openly she answer'd 'must not I,
If this false traitor have displaced his lord,
Grieve with the common grief of all the realm?'

    'Yea,' said the maid, 'this is all woman's grief,
That *she* is woman, whose disloyal life
Hath wrought confusion in the Table Round
Which good King Arthur founded, years ago,
With signs and miracles and wonders, there
At Camelot, ere the coming of the Queen.'

    Then thought the Queen within herself again,
'Will the child kill me with her foolish prate?'
But openly she spake and said to her,
'O little maid, shut in by nunnery walls,
What canst thou know of Kings and Tables Round,
Or what of signs and wonders, but the signs
And simple miracles of thy nunnery?'

To whom the little novice garrulously:
'Yea, but I know: the land was full of signs
And wonders ere the coming of the Queen.
So said my father, and himself was knight
Of the great Table — at the founding of it;
And rode thereto from Lyonnesse, and he said
That as he rode, an hour or maybe twain
After the sunset, down the coast, he heard
Strange music, and he paused and turning – there,
All down the lonely coast of Lyonnesse,
Each with a beacon-star upon his head,
And with a wild sea-light about his feet,
He saw them — headland after headland flame
Far on into the rich heart of the west:
And in the light the white mermaiden swam,
And strong man-breasted things stood from the sea,
And sent a deep sea-voice thro' all the land,
To which the little elves of chasm and cleft
Made answer, sounding like a distant horn.
So said my father — yea, and furthermore,
Next morning, while he past the dim-lit woods,
Himself beheld three spirits mad with joy
Come dashing down on a tall wayside flower,
That shook beneath them, as the thistle shakes
When three grey linnets wrangle for the seed:
And still at evenings on before his horse
The flickering fairy-circle wheel'd and broke
Flying, and link'd again, and wheel'd and broke
Flying, for all the land was full of life.
And when at last he came to Camelot,
A wreath of airy dancers hand-in-hand
Swung round the lighted lantern of the hall;
And in the hall itself was such a feast
As never man had dream'd; for every knight
Had whatsoever meat he long'd for served
By hands unseen; and even as he said
Down in the cellars merry bloated things
Shoulder'd the spigot, straddling on the butts
While the wine ran: so glad were spirits and men
Before the coming of the sinful Queen.'

Then spake the Queen and somewhat bitterly,
'Were they so glad? ill prophets were they all,
Spirits and men: could none of them foresee,
Not even thy wise father with his signs

And wonders, what has fall'n upon the realm?'

    To whom the novice garrulously again.
'Yea, one, a bard; of whom my father said,
Full many a noble war-song had he sung,
Ev'n in the presence of an enemy's fleet,
Between the steep cliff and the coming wave;
And many a mystic lay of life and death
Had chanted on the smoky mountain-tops,
When round him bent the spirits of the hills
With all their dewy hair blown back like flame:
So said my father – and that night the bard
Sang Arthur's glorious wars, and sang the King
As wellnigh more than man, and rail'd at those
Who call'd him the false son of Gorloïs:
For there was no man knew from whence he came;
But after tempest, when the long wave broke
All down the thundering shores of Bude and Bos,
There came a day as still as heaven, and then
They found a naked child upon the sands
Of dark Dundagil by the Cornish sea;
And that was Arthur; and they foster'd him
Till he by miracle was approven king:
And that his grave should be a mystery
From all men, like his birth; and could he find
A woman in her womanhood as great
As he was in his manhood, then, he sang,
The twain together well might change the world.
But even in the middle of his song
He falter'd, and his hand fell from the harp,
And pale he turn'd, and reel'd, and would have fall'n,
But that they stay'd him up; nor would he tell
His vision; but what doubt that he foresaw
This evil work of Lancelot and the Queen?'

    Then thought the Queen 'lo! they have set her on,
Our simple-seeming Abbess and her nuns,
To play upon me,' and bow'd her head nor spake.
Whereat the novice crying, with clasp'd hands,
Shame on her own garrulity garrulously,
Said the good nuns would check her gadding tongue
Full often, 'and, sweet lady, if I seem
To vex an ear too sad to listen to me,
Unmannerly, with prattling and the tales,
Which my good father told me, check me too:
Nor let me shame my father's memory, one

Of noblest manners, tho' himself would say
Sir Lancelot had the noblest; and he died,
Kill'd in a tilt, come next, five summers back,
And left me; but of others who remain,
And of the two first-famed for courtesy –
And pray you check me if I ask amiss –
But pray you, which had noblest, while you moved
Among them, Lancelot or our lord the King?'

    Then the pale Queen look'd up and answer'd her.
'Sir Lancelot, as became a noble knight,
Was gracious to all ladies, and the same
In open battle or the tilting-field
Forbore his own advantage, and the King
In open battle or the tilting-field
Forbore his, own advantage, and these two
Were the most nobly-manner'd men of all;
For manners are not idle, but the fruit
Of loyal nature, and of noble mind.'

    'Yea,' said the maid, 'be manners such fair fruit?
Then Lancelot's needs must be a thousand-fold
Less noble, being, as all rumour runs,
The most disloyal friend in all the world.'

    To which a mournful answer made the Queen:
'O closed about by narrowing nunnery-walls,
What knowest thou of the world, and all its lights,
And shadows, all the wealth and all the woe?
If ever Lancelot, that most noble knight,
Were for one hour less noble than himself,
Pray for him that he scape the doom of fire,
And weep for her, who drew him to his doom.'

    'Yea,' said the little novice, 'I pray for both;
But I should all as, soon believe that his,
Sir Lancelot's, were as noble as the King's,
As I could think, sweet lady, yours would be
Such as they are, were you the sinful Queen.'

    So she, like many another babbler, hurt
Whom she would soothe, and harm'd where she would heal;
For here a sudden flush of wrathful heat
Fired all the pale face of the Queen, who cried,
'Such as thou art be never maiden more
For ever! thou their tool, set on to plague

And play upon, and harry me, petty spy
And traitress.' When that storm of anger brake
From Guinevere, aghast the maiden rose,
White as her veil, and stood before the Queen
As tremulously as foam upon the beach
Stands in a wind, ready to break and fly,
And when the Queen had added 'Get thee hence,'
Fled frighted. Then that other left alone
Sigh'd, and began to gather heart again,
Saying in herself, 'The simple, fearful child
Meant nothing, but my own too-fearful guilt,
Simpler than any child, betrays itself.
But help me, heaven, for surely I repent.
For what is true repentance but in thought –
Not ev'n in inmost thought to think again
The sins that made the past so pleasant to us:
And I have sworn never to see him more,
To see him more.'
                              And ev'n in saying this,
Her memory from old habit of the mind
Went slipping back upon the golden days
In which she saw him first, when Lancelot came,
Reputed the best knight and goodliest man,
Ambassador, to lead her to his lord
Arthur, and led her forth, and far ahead
Of his and her retinue moving, they,
Rapt in sweet talk or lively, all on love
And sport and tilts and pleasure, (for the time
Was maytime, and as yet no sin was dream'd,)
Rode under groves that look'd a paradise
Of blossom, over sheets of hyacinth
That seem'd the heavens upbreaking thro' the earth,
And on from hill to hill, and every day
Beheld at noon in some delicious dale
The silk pavilions of King Arthur raised
For brief repast or afternoon repose
By couriers gone before; and on again,
Till yet once more ere set of sun they saw
The Dragon of the great Pendragonship,
That crown'd the state pavilion of the King,
Blaze by the rushing brook or silent well.

But when the Queen immersed in such a trance,
And moving thro' the past unconsciously,
Came to that point, when first she saw the King
Ride toward her from the city, sigh'd to find

Her journey done, glanced at him, thought him cold,
High, self-contain'd, and passionless, not like him,
'Not like my Lancelot' – while she brooded thus
And grew half-guilty in her thoughts again,
There rode an armed warrior to the doors.
A murmuring whisper thro' the nunnery ran,
Then on a sudden a cry, 'the King.' She sat
Stiff-stricken, listening; but when armed feet
Thro' the long gallery from the outer doors
Rang coming, prone from off her seat she fell,
And grovell'd with her face against the floor:
There with her milkwhite arms and shadowy hair
She made her face a darkness from the King:
And in the darkness heard his armed feet
Pause by her; then came silence, then a voice,
Monotonous and hollow like a Ghost's
Denouncing judgement, but tho' changed the King's.

  'Liest thou here so low, the child of one
I honour'd, happy, dead before thy shame?
Well is it that no child is born of thee.
The children born of thee are sword and fire,
Red ruin, and the breaking up of laws,
The craft of kindred and the Godless hosts
Of heathen swarming o'er the Northern Sea.
Whom I, while yet Sir Lancelot, my right arm,
The mightiest of my knights, abode with me,
Have everywhere about this land of Christ
In twelve great battles ruining overthrown.
And knowest thou now from whence I come – from him,
From waging bitter war with him: and he,
That did not shun to smite me in worse way,
Had yet that grace of courtesy in him left,
He spared to lift his hand against the King
Who made him knight: but many a knight was slain;
And many more, and all his kith and kin
Clave to him, and abode in his own land.
And many more when Modred raised revolt,
Forgetful of their troth and fealty, clave
To Modred, and a remnant stays with me.
And of this remnant will I leave a part,
True men who love me still, for whom I live,
To guard thee in the wild hour coming on,
Lest but a hair of this low head be harm'd.
Fear not: thou shalt be guarded till my death.
Howbeit I know, if ancient prophecies

Have err'd not, that I march to meet my doom.
Thou hast not made my life so sweet to me,
That I the King should greatly care to live;
For thou hast spoilt the purpose of my life.
Bear with me for the last time while I show,
Ev'n for thy sake, the sin which thou hast sinn'd.
For when the Roman left us, and their law
Relax'd its hold upon us, and the ways
Were fill'd with rapine, here and there a deed
Of prowess done redress'd a random wrong.
But I was first of all the kings who drew
The knighthood-errant of this realm and all
The realms together under me, their Head,
In that fair order of my Table Round,
A glorious company, the flower of men,
To serve as model for the mighty world,
And be the fair beginning of a time.
I made them lay their hands in mine and swear
To reverence the King, as if he were
Their conscience, and their conscience as their King,
To break the heathen and uphold the Christ,
To ride abroad redressing human wrongs,
To speak no slander, no, nor listen to it,
To lead sweet lives in purest chastity,
To love one maiden only, cleave to her,
And worship her by years of noble deeds,
Until they won her; for indeed I knew
Of no more subtle master under heaven
Than is the maiden passion for a maid,
Not only to keep down the base in man,
But teach high thought, and amiable words
And courtliness, and the desire of fame,
And love of truth, and all that makes a man.
And all this throve until I wedded thee!
Believing "lo mine helpmate, one to feel
My purpose and rejoicing in my joy."
Then came thy shameful sin with Lancelot;
Then came the sin of Tristram and Isolt;
Then others, following these my mightiest knights,
And drawing foul ensample from fair names
Sinn'd also, till the loathsome opposite
Of all my heart had destined did obtain,
And all thro' thee! so that this life of mine
I guard as God's high gift from scathe and wrong,
Not greatly care to lose; but rather think
How sad it were for Arthur, should he live,

To sit once more within his lonely hall,
And miss the wonted number of my knights,
And miss to hear high talk of noble deeds
As in the golden days before thy sin.
For which of us, who might be left, could speak
Of the pure heart, nor seem to glance at thee?
And in thy bowers of Camelot or of Usk
Thy shadow still would glide from room to room,
And I should evermore be vext with thee
In hanging robe or vacant ornament
Or ghostly footfall echoing on the stair.
For think not, tho' thou would'st not love thy lord,
Thy lord has wholly lost his love for thee.
I am not made of so slight elements.
Yet must I leave thee, woman, to thy shame.
I hold that man the worst of public foes
Who either for his own or children's sake
To save his blood from scandal, lets the wife
Whom he knows false, abide and rule the house:
For being thro' his cowardice allow'd
Her station, taken everywhere for pure,
She like a new disease, unknown to men,
Creeps, no precaution used, among the crowd,
Makes wicked lightnings of her eyes, and saps
The fealty of our friends, and stirs the pulse
With devil's leaps, and poisons half the young.
Worst of the worst were that man he that reigns!
Better the King's waste hearth and aching heart
Than thou reseated in thy place of light,
The mockery of my people, and their bane.'

    He paused, and in the pause she crept an inch
Nearer, and laid her hands about his feet.
Far off a solitary trumpet blew.
Then waiting by the doors the warhorse neigh'd
As at a friend's voice, and he spake again:

    'Yet think not that I come to urge thy crimes,
I did not come to curse thee, Guinevere,
I, whose vast pity almost makes me die
To see thee, laying there thy golden head,
My pride in happier summers, at my feet.
The wrath which forced my thoughts on that fierce law,
The doom of treason and the flaming death,
(When first I learnt thee hidden here) is past.
The pang – which while I weigh'd thy heart with one

Too wholly true to dream untruth in thee,
Made my tears burn – is also past, in part.
And all is past, the sin is sinn'd, and I,
Lo! I forgive thee, as Eternal God
Forgives: do thou for thine own soul the rest.
But how to take last leave of all I loved?
O golden hair, with which I used to play
Not knowing! O imperial-moulded form,
And beauty such as never woman wore,
Until it came a kingdom's curse with thee –
I cannot touch thy lips, they are not mine,
But Lancelot's: nay, they never were the King's.
I cannot take thy hand; that too is flesh,
And in the flesh thou hast sinn'd; and mine own flesh
Here looking down on thine polluted, cries
"I loathe thee:" yet not less, O Guinevere,
For I was ever virgin save for thee,
My love thro' flesh hath wrought into my life
So far, that my doom is, I love thee still.
Let no man dream but that I love thee still.
Perchance, and so thou purify thy soul,
And so thou lean on our fair father Christ,
Hereafter in that world where all are pure
We two may meet before high God, and thou
Wilt spring to me, and claim me thine, and know
I am thine husband – not a smaller soul,
Nor Lancelot, nor another. Leave me that,
I charge thee, my last hope. Now must I hence.
Thro' the thick night I hear the trumpet blow:
They summon me their King to lead mine hosts
Far down to that great battle in the west,
Where I must strike against my sister's son,
Leagued with the lords of the White Horse and knights
Once mine, and strike him dead, and meet myself
Death, or I know not what mysterious doom.
And thou remaining here wilt learn the event;
But hither shall I never come again,
Never lie by thy side, see thee no more:
Farewell!'
        And while she grovell'd at his feet,
She felt the King's breath wander o'er her neck,
And, in the darkness o'er her fallen head,
Perceived the waving of his hands that blest.

Then, listening till those armed steps were gone,
Rose the pale Queen, and in her anguish found

The casement: 'peradventure,' so she thought,
'If I might see his face, and not be seen.'
And lo, he sat on horseback at the door!
And near him the sad nuns with each a light
Stood, and he gave them charge about the Queen,
To guard and foster her for evermore.
And while he spake to these his helm was lower'd,
To which for crest the golden dragon clung
Of Britain; so she did not see the face,
Which then was as an angel's, but she saw,
Wet with the mists and smitten by the lights,
The Dragon of the great Pendragonship
Blaze, making all the night a steam of fire.
And even then he turn'd; and more and more
The moony vapour rolling round the King,
Who seem'd the phantom of a Giant in it,
Enwound him fold by fold, and made him grey
And greyer, till himself became as mist
Before her, moving ghostlike to his doom.

    Then she stretch'd out her arms and cried aloud
'Oh Arthur!' there her voice brake suddenly,
Then – as a stream that spouting from a cliff
Fails in mid air, but gathering at the base
Re-makes itself, and flashes down the vale –
Went on in passionate utterance.

                                'Gone – my lord!
Gone thro' my sin to slay and to be slain!
And he forgave me, and I could not speak.
Farewell? I should have answer'd his farewell.
His mercy choked me. Gone, my lord the King,
My own true lord! how dare I call him mine?
The shadow of another cleaves to me,
And makes me one pollution: he, the King,
Call'd me polluted: shall I kill myself?
What help in that? I cannot kill my sin,
If soul be soul; nor can I kill my shame;
No, nor by living can I live it down.
The days will grow to weeks, the weeks to months
The months will add themselves and make the years,
The years will roll into the centuries,
And mine will ever be a name of scorn.
I must not dwell on that defeat of fame.
Let the world be; that is but of the world.
What else? what hope? I think there was a hope,
Except he mock'd me when he spake of hope;

His hope he call'd it; but he never mocks,
For mockery is the fume of little hearts.
And blessed be the King, who hath forgiven
My wickedness to him, and left me hope
That in mine own heart I can live down sin
And be his mate hereafter in the heavens
Before high God. Ah great and gentle lord,
Who wast, as is the conscience of a saint
Among his warring senses, to thy knights –
To whom my false voluptuous pride, that took
Full easily all impressions from below,
Would not look up, or half-despised the height
To which I would not or I could not climb –
I thought I could not breathe in that fine air
That pure severity of perfect light –
I wanted warmth and colour which I found
In Lancelot – now I see thee what thou art,
Thou art the highest and most human too,
Not Lancelot, nor another. Is there none
Will tell the King I love him tho' so late?
Now – ere he goes to the great Battle? none:
Myself must tell him in that purer life,
But now it were too daring. Ah my God,
What might I not have made of thy fair world,
Had I but loved thy highest creature here?
It was my duty to have loved the highest:
It surely was my profit had I known:
It would have been my pleasure had I seen.
We needs must love the highest when we see it,
Not Lancelot, nor another.'
                                    Here her hand
Grasp'd, made her vail her eyes: she look'd and saw
The novice, weeping, suppliant, and said to her,
'Yea, little maid, for am I not forgiven?'
Then glancing up beheld the holy nuns
All round her, weeping; and her heart was loosed
Within her, and she wept with these and said:

    'Ye know me then, that wicked one, who broke
The vast design and purpose of the King.
O shut me round with narrowing nunnery-walls
Meek maidens, from the voices crying "shame."
I must not scorn myself: he loves me still.
Let no one dream but that he loves me still.
So let me, if you do not shudder at me
Nor shun to call me sister, dwell with you;

Wear black and white, and be a nun like you;
Fast with your fasts, not feasting with your feasts;
Grieve with your griefs, not grieving at your joys,
But not rejoicing; mingle with your rites;
Pray and be pray'd for; lie before your shrines;
Do each low office of your holy house;
Walk your dim cloister, and distribute dole
To poor sick people, richer in His eyes
Who ransom'd us, and haler too than I;
And treat their loathsome hurts and heal mine own;
And so wear out in almsdeed and in prayer
The sombre close of that voluptuous day,
Which wrought the ruin of my lord the King.'

She said: they took her to themselves; and she
Still hoping, fearing 'is it yet too late?'
Dwelt with them, till in time their Abbess died.
Then she, for her good deeds and her pure life,
And for the power of ministration in her,
And likewise for the high rank she had borne,
Was chosen Abbess, there, an Abbess, lived
For three brief years, and there, an Abbess, past
To where beyond these voices there is peace.

The Grandmother

I

And Willy, my eldest-born, is gone, you say, little Anne?
Ruddy and white, and strong on his legs, he looks like a man.
And Willy's wife has written: she never was overwise,
Never the wife for Willy: he wouldn't take my advice.

II

For, Annie, you see, her father was not the man to save,
Hadn't a head to manage, and drank himself into his grave.
Pretty enough, very pretty! but I was against it for one.
Eh! – but he wouldn't hear me – and Willy, you say, is gone.

III

Willy, my beauty, my eldest-born, the flower of the flock;
Never a man could fling him: for Willy stood like a rock.
'Here's a leg for a babe of a week!' says doctor; and he would be
    bound,
There was not his like that year in twenty parishes round.

IV

Strong of his hands, and strong on his legs, but still of his tongue!
I ought to have gone before him: I wonder he went so young.
I cannot cry for him, Annie: I have not long to stay;
Perhaps I shall see him the sooner, for he lived far away.

V

Why do you look at me, Annie? you think I am hard and cold;
But all my children have gone before me, I am so old:
I cannot weep for Willy, nor can I weep for the rest;
Only at your age, Annie, I could have wept with the best.

VI

For I remember a quarrel I had with your father, my dear,
All for a slanderous story, that cost me many a tear.
I mean your grandfather, Annie: it cost me a world of woe,
Seventy years ago, my darling, seventy years ago.

VII

For Jenny, my cousin, had come to the place, and I knew right well
That Jenny had tript in her time: I knew, but I would not tell.
And she to be coming and slandering me, the base little liar!
But the tongue is a fire as you know, my dear, the tongue is a fire.

VIII

And the parson made it his text that week, and he said likewise,
That a lie which is half a truth is ever the blackest of lies,
That a lie which is all a lie may be met and fought with outright,
But a lie which is part a truth is a harder matter to fight.

IX

And Willy had not been down to the farm for a week and a day;
And all things look'd half-dead, tho' it was the middle of May.
Jenny, to slander me, who knew what Jenny had been!
But soiling another, Annie, will never make oneself clean.

X

And I cried myself wellnigh blind, and all of an evening late
I climb'd to the top of the garth, and stood by the road at the gate.
The moon like a rick on fire was rising over the dale,
And whit, whit, whit, in the bush beside me chirrupt the nightingale.

XI

All of a sudden he stopt: there past by the gate of the farm,
Willy, – he didn't see me, – and Jenny hung on his arm.
Out into the road I started, and spoke I scarce knew how;
Ah, there's no fool like the old one – it makes me angry now.

XII

Willy stood up like a man, and look'd the thing that he meant;
Jenny, the viper, made me a mocking curtsy and went.
And I said, 'Let us part: in a hundred years it'll all be the same,
You cannot love me at all, if you love not my good name.'

XIII

And he turn'd, and I saw his eyes all wet, in the sweet moonshine:
'Sweetheart, I love you so well that your good name is mine.
And what do I care for Jane, let her speak of you well or ill;
But marry me out of hand: we two shall be happy still'

XIV

'Marry you, Willy!.' said I, 'but I needs must speak my mind,
And I fear you'll listen to tales, be jealous and hard and unkind.'
But he turn'd and claspt me in his arms, and answer'd, 'No, love, no;'
Seventy years ago, my darling, seventy years ago.

XV

So Willy and I were wedded: I wore a lilac gown;
And the ringers rang with a will, and he gave the ringers a crown.
But the first that ever I bare was dead before he was born,
Shadow and shine is life, little Annie, flower and thorn.

XVI

That was the first time, too, that ever I thought of death.
There lay the sweet little body that never had drawn a breath.
I had not wept, little Anne, not since I had been a wife;
But I wept like a child that day, for the babe had fought for his life.

XVII

His dear little face was troubled, as if with anger or pain:
I look'd at the still little body – his trouble had all been in vain.
For Willy I cannot weep, I shall see him another morn:
But I wept like a child for the child that was dead before he was born.

XVIII

But he cheer'd me, my good man, for he seldom said me nay:
Kind, like a man, was he; like a man, too, would have his way:
Never jealous – not he: we had many a happy year;
And he died, and I could not weep – my own time seem'd so near.

XIX

But I wish'd it had been God's will that I, too, then could have died:
I began to be tired a little, and fain had slept at his side.
And that was ten years back, or more, if I don't forget:
But as to the children, Annie, they're all about me yet.

XX

Pattering over the boards, my Annie who left me at two,
Patter she goes, my own little Annie, an Annie like you:
Pattering over the boards, she comes and goes at her will,
While Harry is in the five-acre and Charlie ploughing the hill.

XXI

And Harry and Charlie, I hear them too – they sing to their team:
Often they come to the door in a pleasant kind of a dream.
They come and sit by my chair, they hover about my bed –
I am not always certain if they be alive or dead.

XXII

And yet I know for a truth, there's none of them left alive;
For Harry went at sixty, your father at sixty-five:
And Willy, my eldest born, at nigh threescore and ten;
I knew them all as babies, and now they're elderly men.

XXIII

For mine is a time of peace, it is not often I grieve;
I am oftener sitting at home in my father's farm at eve:
And the neighbours come and laugh and gossip, and so do I;
I find myself often laughing at things that have long gone by.

XXIV

To be sure the preacher says, our sins should make us sad:
But mine is a time of peace, and there is Grace to be had;
And God, not man, is the Judge of us all when life shall cease;
And in this Book, little Annie, the message is one of Peace.

XXV

And age is a time of peace, so it be free from pain,
And happy has been my life; but I would not live it again.
I seem to be tired a little, that's all, and long for rest;
Only at your age, Annie, I could have wept with the best.

XXVI

So Willy has gone, my beauty, my eldest-born, my flower;
But how can I weep for Willy, he has but gone for an hour, –
Gone for a minute, my son, from this room into the next;
I, too, shall go in a minute. What time have I to be vext?

XXVII

And Willy's wife has written, she never was overwise.
Get me my glasses, Annie: thank God that I keep my eyes.
There is but a trifle left you, when I shall have past away.
But stay with the old woman now: you cannot have long to stay.

Sea Dreams

A city clerk, but gently born and bred;
His wife, an unknown artist's orphan child –
One babe was theirs, a Margaret, three years old:
They, thinking that her clear germander eye
Droopt in the giant-factoried city-gloom,
Came, with a month's leave given them, to the sea:
For which his gains were dock'd, however small:
Small were his gains, and hard his work; besides,
Their slender household fortunes (for the man
Had risk'd his little) like the little thrift,
Trembled in perilous places o'er a deep:
And oft, when sitting all alone, his face
Would darken, as he cursed his credulousness,
And that one unctuous mouth which lured him, rogue,
To buy strange shares in some Peruvian mine.
Now seaward-bound for health they gain'd a coast,
All sand and cliff and deep-inrunning cave,
At close of day; slept, woke, and went the next,
The Sabbath, pious variers from the church,
To chapel; where a heated pulpiteer,
Not preaching simple Christ to simple men,
Announced the coming doom, and fulminated
Against the scarlet woman and her creed:
For sideways up he swung his arms, and shriek'd
'Thus, thus with violence,' ev'n as if he held
The Apocalyptic millstone, and himself
Were that great Angel; 'Thus with violence
Shall Babylon be cast into the sea;
Then comes the close.' The gentle-hearted wife
Sat shuddering at the ruin of a world;
He at his own; but when the wordy storm
Had ended, forth they came and paced the shore,
Ran in and out the long sea-framing caves,
Drank the large air, and saw, but scarce believed
(The sootflake of so many a summer still
Clung to their fancies) that they saw, the sea.
So now on sand they walk'd, and now on cliff,
Lingering about the thymy promontories,
Till all the sails were darken'd in the west,
And rosed in the east: then homeward and to bed:
Where she, who kept a tender Christian hope
Haunting a holy text, and still to that
Returning, as the bird returns, at night,
'Let not the sun go down upon your wrath,'

Said, 'Love, forgive him:' but he did not speak;
And silenced by that silence lay the wife,
Remembering her dear Lord who died for all,
And musing on the little lives of men,
And how they mar this little by their feuds.

    But while the two were sleeping, a full tide
Rose with ground-swell, which, on the foremost rocks
Touching, upjetted in spirts of wild sea-smoke,
And scaled in sheets of wasteful foam, and fell
In vast sea-cataracts – ever and anon
Dead claps of thunder from within the cliffs
Heard thro' the living roar. At this the babe,
Their Margaret cradled near them, wail'd and woke
The mother, and the father suddenly cried,
'A wreck, a wreck!' then turn'd, and groaning said,

    'Forgive! How many will say, "forgive," and find
A sort of absolution in the sound
To hate a little longer! No; the sin
That neither God nor man can well forgive,
Hypocrisy, I saw it in him at once.
Is it so true that second thoughts are best?
Not first, and third, which are a riper first?
Too ripe, too late! they come too late for use.
Ah love, there surely lives in man and beast
Something divine to warn them of their foes:
And such a sense, when first I fronted him,
Said, "trust him not;" but after, when I came
To know him more, I lost it, knew him less;
Fought with what seem'd my own uncharity;
Sat at his table; drank his costly wines;
Made more and more allowance for his talk;
Went further, fool! and trusted him with all,
All my poor scrapings from a dozen years
Of dust and deskwork: there is no such mine,
None; but a gulf of ruin, swallowing gold,
Not making. Ruin'd! ruin'd! the sea roars
Ruin: a fearful night!'

                              'Not fearful; fair,'
Said the good wife, 'if every star in heaven
Can make it fair: you do but hear the tide.
Had you ill dreams?'

                    'O yes,' he said, 'I dream'd

Of such a tide swelling toward the land,
And I from out the boundless outer deep
Swept with it to the shore, and enter'd one
Of those dark caves that run beneath the cliffs.
I thought the motion of the boundless deep
Bore through the cave, and I was heaved upon it
In darkness: then I saw one lovely star
Larger and larger. "What a world," I thought,
"To live in!" but in moving on I found
Only the landward exit of the cave,
Bright with the sun upon the stream beyond:
And near the light a giant woman sat,
All over earthy, like a piece of earth,
A pickaxe in her hand: then out I slipt
Into a land all sun and blossom, trees
As high as heaven, and every bird that sings:
And here the night-light flickering in my eyes
Awoke me.'

   'That was then your dream,' she said,
'Not sad, but sweet.'

              'So sweet, I lay,' said he,
'And mused upon it, drifting up the stream
In fancy, till I slept again, and pieced
The broken vision; for I dream'd that still
The motion of the great deep bore me on,
And that the woman walk'd upon the brink:
I wonder'd at her strength, and ask'd her of it:
"It came," she said, "by working in the mines:"
O then to ask her of my shares, I thought;
And ask'd; but not a word; she shook her head.
And then the motion of the current ceased,
And there was rolling thunder; and we reach'd
A mountain, like a wall of burs and thorns;
But she with her strong feet up the steep hill
Trod out a path: I follow'd; and at top
She pointed seaward: there a fleet of glass,
That seem'd a fleet of jewels under me,
Sailing along before a gloomy cloud
That not one moment ceased to thunder, past
In sunshine: right across its track there lay,
Down in the water, a long reef of gold,
Or what seem'd gold: and I was glad at first
To think that in our often-ransack'd world
Still so much gold was left; and then I fear'd

Lest the gay navy there should splinter on it,
And fearing waved my arm to warn them off;
An idle signal, for the brittle fleet
(I thought I could have died to save it) near'd,
Touch'd, clink'd, and clash'd, and vanish'd, and
I woke, I heard the clash so clearly. Now I see
My dream was Life; the woman honest Work;
And my poor venture but a fleet of glass
Wreck'd on a reef of visionary gold.'

    'Nay,' said the kindly wife to comfort him,
'You raised your arm, you tumbled down and broke
The glass with little Margaret's medicine in it;
And, breaking that, you made and broke your dream:
A trifle makes a dream, a trifle breaks.'

    'No trifle,' groan'd the husband; 'yesterday
I met him suddenly in the street, and ask'd
That which I ask'd the woman in my dream.
Like her, he shook his head. "Show me the books!"
He dodged me with a long and loose account.
"The books, the books!" but he, he could not wait,
Bound on a matter he of life and death:
When the great Books (see Daniel seven and ten)
Were open'd, I should find he meant me well;
And then began to bloat himself, and ooze
All over with the fat affectionate smile
That makes the widow lean. "My dearest friend,
Have faith, have faith! We live by faith," said he;
"And all things work together for the good
Of those" – it makes me sick to quote him – last
Gript my hand hard, and with God-bless-you went.
I stood like one that had received a blow:
I found a hard friend in his loose accounts,
A loose one in the hard grip of his hand,
A curse in his God-bless-you: then my eyes
Pursued him down the street, and far away,
Among the honest shoulders of the crowd,
Read rascal in the motions of his back,
And scoundrel in the supple-sliding knee.'

    'Was he so bound, poor soul?' said the good wife;
'So are we all: but do not call him, love,
Before you prove him, rogue, and proved, forgive.
His gain is loss; for he that wrongs his friend
Wrongs himself more, and ever bears about

A silent court of justice in his breast,
Himself the judge and jury, and himself
The prisoner at the bar, ever condemn'd:
And that drags down his life: then comes what comes
Hereafter: and he meant, he said he meant,
Perhaps he meant, or partly meant, you well.'

' "With all his conscience and one eye askew"—
Love, let me quote these lines, that you may learn
A man is likewise counsel for himself,
Too often, in that silent court of yours —
"With all his conscience and one eye askew,
So false, he partly took himself for true;
Whose pious talk, when most his heart was dry,
Made wet the crafty crowsfoot round his eye;
Who, never naming God except for gain,
So never took that useful name in vain;
Made Him his catspaw and the Cross his tool,
And Christ the bait to trap his dupe and fool;
Nor deeds of gift, but gifts of grace he forged,
And snakelike slimed his victim ere he gorged;
And oft at Bible meetings, o'er the rest
Arising, did his holy oily best,
Dropping the too rough H in Hell and Heaven,
To spread the Word by which himself had thriven."
How like you this old satire?'

                              'Nay,' she said,
'I loathe it: he had never kindly heart,
Nor ever cared to better his own kind,
Who first wrote satire, with no pity in it.
But will you hear my dream, for I had one
That altogether went to music? Still
 It awed me.'

                    Then she told it, having dream'd
Of that same coast.

                    — But round the North, a light,
A belt, it seem'd, of luminous vapour, lay,
And ever in it a low musical note
Swell'd up and died; and, as it swell'd, a ridge
Of breaker issued from the belt, and still
Grew with the growing note, and when the note
Had reach'd a thunderous fullness, on those cliffs
Broke, mixt with awful light (the same as that
Living within the belt) whereby she saw
That all those lines of cliffs were cliffs no more,

But huge cathedral fronts of every age,
Grave, florid, stern, as far as eye could see,
One after one: and then the great ridge drew,
Lessening to the lessening music, back,
And past into the belt and swell'd again
Slowly to music: ever when it broke
The statues, king or saint, or founder fell;
Then from the gaps and chasms of ruin left
Came men and women in dark clusters round,
Some crying, 'Sot them up! they shall not fall!'
And others 'Let them lie, for they have fall'n.'
And still they strove and wrangled: and she grieved
In her strange dream, she knew not why, to find
Their wildest wailings never out of tune
With that sweet note; and ever as their shrieks
Ran highest up the gamut, that great wave
Returning, while none mark'd it, on the crowd
Broke, mixt with awful light, and show'd their eyes
Glaring, and passionate looks, and swept away
The men of flesh and blood, and men of stone,
To the waste deeps together.

     'Then I fixt
My wistful eyes on two fair images,
Both crown'd with stars and high among the stars, –
The Virgin Mother standing with her child
High up on one of those dark minster-fronts –
Till she began to totter, and the child
Clung to the mother, and sent out a cry
Which mixt with little Margaret's, and I woke,
And my dream awed me: – well – but what are dreams?
Yours came but from the breaking of a glass,
And mine but from the crying of a child.'

 'Child? No!' said he, 'but this tide's roar, and his,
Our Boanerges with his threats of doom,
And loud-lung'd Antibabylonianisms
(Altho' I grant but little music there)
Went both to make your dream: but if there were
A music harmonizing our wild cries,
Sphere-music such as that you dream'd about,
Why, that would make our passions far too like
The discords dear to the musician. No –
One shriek of hate would jar all the hymns of heaven:
True Devils with no ear, they howl in tune
With nothing but the Devil!'

' "True" indeed!
One of our town, but later by an hour
Hero than ourselves, spoke with me on the shore;
While you were running down the sands, and made
The dimpled flounce of the sea-furbelow flap,
Good man, to please the child. She brought strange news.
Why were you silent when I spoke to-night?
I had set my heart on your forgiving him
Before you knew. We *must* forgive the dead.'

    'Dead! who is dead?'

                    'The man your eye pursued.
A little after you had parted with him,
He suddenly dropt dead of heart-disease.'

    'Dead? he? of heart-disease? what heart had he
To die of? dead!'

                    'Ah, dearest, if there be
A devil in man, there is an angel too,
And if he did that wrong you charge him with,
His angel broke his heart. But your rough voice
(You spoke so loud) has roused the child again.
Sleep, little birdie, sleep! will she not sleep
Without her "little birdie"? well then, sleep,
And I will sing you "birdie."'

                            Saying this,
The woman half turn'd round from him she loved,
Left him one hand, and reaching thro' the night
Her other, found (for it was close beside)
And half embraced the basket cradle-head
With one soft arm, which, like the pliant bough
That moving moves the nest and nestling, sway'd
The cradle, while she sang this baby song.

    What does little birdie say
    In her nest at peep of day?
    Let me fly, says little birdie,
    Mother, let me fly away.
    Birdie, rest a little longer,
    Till the little wings are stronger.
    So she rests a little longer,
    Then she flies away.

What does little baby say,
In her bed at peep of day?
Baby says, like little birdie,
Let me rise and fly away.
Baby, sleep a little longer,
Till the little limbs are stronger.
If she sleeps a little longer,
Baby too shall fly away.

'She sleeps: let us too, let all evil, sleep.
He also sleeps – another sleep than ours.
He can do no more wrong: forgive him, dear,
And I shall sleep the sounder!'

       Then the man,
'His deeds yet live, the worst is yet to come.
Yet let your sleep for this one night be sound:
I do forgive him!'

       'Thanks, my love,' she said,
'Your own will be the sweeter,' and they slept.

Tithonus

The woods decay, the woods decay and fall,
The vapours weep their burthen to the ground,
Man comes and tills the field and lies beneath,
And after many a summer dies the swan.
Me only cruel immortality
Consumes: I wither slowly in thine arms,
Here at the quiet limit of the world,
A white-hair'd shadow roaming like a dream
The ever silent spaces of the East,
Far-folded mists, and gleaming halls of morn.

Alas! for this grey shadow, once a man –
So glorious in his beauty and thy choice,
Who madest him thy chosen, that he seem'd
To his great heart none other than a God!
I ask'd thee, 'Give me immortality.'
Then didst thou grant mine asking with a smile,
Like wealthy men who care not how they give.
But thy strong Hours indignant work'd their wills,
And beat me down and marr'd and wasted me,
And tho' they could not end me, left me maim'd .

To dwell in presence of immortal youth,
Immortal age beside immortal youth,
And all I was, in ashes. Can thy love,
Thy beauty, make amends, tho' even now,
Close over us, the silver star, thy guide,
Shines in those tremulous eyes that fill with tears
To hear me? Let me go: take back thy gift:
Why should a man desire in any way
To vary from the kindly race of men,
Or pass beyond the goal of ordinance
Where all should pause, as is most meet for all?

   A soft air fans the cloud apart; there comes
A glimpse of that dark world where I was born.
Once more the old mysterious glimmer steals
From thy pure brows, and from thy shoulders pure,
And bosom beating with a heart renew'd.
Thy cheek begins to redden thro' the gloom,
Thy sweet eyes brighten slowly close to mine,
Ere yet they blind the stars, and the wild team
Which love thee, yearning for thy yoke, arise,
And shake the darkness from their loosen'd manes,
And beat the twilight into flakes of fire.

   Lo! ever thus thou growest beautiful
In silence, then before thine answer given
Departest, and thy tears are on my cheek.

   Why wilt thou ever scare me with thy tears,
And make me tremble lest a saying learnt,
In days far-off, on that dark earth, be true?
'The Gods themselves cannot recall their gifts.'

   Ay me! ay me! with what another heart
In days far-off, and with what other eyes
I used to watch – if I be he that watch'd –
The lucid outline forming round thee; saw
The dim curls kindle into sunny rings;
Changed with thy mystic change, and felt my blood
Glow with the glow that slowly crimson'd all
Thy presence and thy portals, while I lay,
Mouth, forehead, eyelids, growing dewy-warm
With kisses balmier than half-opening buds
Of April, and could hear the lips that kiss'd
Whispering I knew not what of wild and sweet,
Like that strange song I heard Apollo sing,

While Ilion like a mist rose into towers.

Yet hold me not for ever in thine East:
How can my nature longer mix with thine?
Coldly thy rosy shadows bathe me, cold
Are all thy lights, and cold my wrinkled feet
Upon thy glimmering thresholds, when the steam
Floats up from those dim fields about the homes
Of happy men that have the power to die,
And grassy barrows of the happier dead.
Release me, and restore me to the ground;
Thou seëst all things, thou wilt see my grave:
Thou wilt renew thy beauty morn by morn;
I earth in earth forget these empty courts,
And thee returning on thy silver wheels.

The Sailor Boy

He rose at dawn and, fired with hope
   Shot o'er the seething harbour-bar,
And reach'd the ship and caught the rope,
   And whistled to the morning star.

And while he whistled long and loud
   He heard a fierce mermaiden cry,
'O boy, tho' thou art young and proud,
   I see the place where thou wilt lie.

'The sands and yeasty surges mix
   In caves about the dreary bay,
And on thy ribs the limpet sticks,
   And in thy heart the scrawl shall play.'

'Fool,' he answer'd, 'death is sure
   To those that stay and those that roam,
But I will nevermore endure
   To sit with empty hands at home.

'My mother clings about my neck,
   My sisters crying "stay for shame;"
My father raves of death and wreck,
   They are all to blame, they are all to blame.

'God help me! save I take my part
   Of danger on the roaring sea,
A devil rises in my heart,
   Far worse than any death to me.'

Ode for the Opening of the International Exhibition, 1862

Uplift a thousand voices full and sweet,
   In this wide hall with earth's invention stored,
   And praise th' invisible universal Lord,
Who lets once more in peace the nations meet,
   Where Science, Art, and Labour have outpour'd
Their myriad horns of plenty at our feet.

   O silent father of our Kings to be,
   Mourn'd in this golden hour of jubilee,
   For this, for all, we weep our thanks to thee!

      The world-compelling plan was thine,
      And, lo! the long laborious miles
      Of Palace; lo! the giant aisles,
      Rich in model and design;
      Harvest-tool and husbandry,
      Loom, and wheel, and engin'ry,
      Secrets of the sullen mine,
      Steel and gold, and corn and wine,
      Fabric rough, or fairy-fine,
      Sunny tokens of the Line,
      Polar marvels, and a feast
      Of wonder, out of West and East,
      And shapes and hues of Art divine!
      All of beauty, all of use,
      That one fair planet can produce,
      Brought from under every star,
    Blown from over every main,
    And mixt, as life is mixt with pain,
      The works of peace with works of war.

        Is the goal so far away?
        Ear, how far no tongue can say,
        Let us dream our dream to-day.

O ye, the wise who think, the wise who reign,
From growing commerce loose her latest chain,
And let the fair white-winged peacemaker fly
To happy havens under all the sky,
And mix the seasons and the golden hours,
Till each man find his own in all men's good,
And all men work in noble brotherhood,
Breaking their mailed fleets and armed towers,
And ruling by obeying nature's powers,
And gathering all the fruits of earth and crown'd with all her
    flowers.

A Welcome to Alexandra

March 7 1863

Sea-Kings' daughter from over the sea,
                Alexandra!
Saxon and Norman and Dane are we,
But all of us Danes in our welcome of thee,
                Alexandra!
Welcome her, thunders of fort and of fleet!
Welcome her, thundering cheer of the street!
Welcome her, all things youthful and sweet,
Scatter the blossom under her feet!
Break, happy land, into earlier flowers!
Make music, O bird, in the new-budded bowers!
Blazon your mottoes of blessing and prayer!
Welcome her, welcome her, all that is ours!
Warble, O bugle, and trumpet, blare!
Flags, flutter out upon turrets and towers!
Flames, on the windy headland flare!
Utter your jubilee, steeple and spire!
Clash, ye bells, in the merry March air!
Flash, ye cities, in rivers of fire!
Rush to the roof, sudden rocket, and higher
Melt into stars for the land's desire!
Roll and rejoice, jubilant voice,
Roll as a ground-swell dash'd on the strand,
Roar as the sea when he welcomes the land,
And welcome her, welcome the land's desire,
The sea-kings' daughter as happy as fair,
Blissful bride of a blissful heir,
Bride of the heir of the kings of the sea —
O joy to the people and joy to the throne,
Come to us, love us and make us your own:
For Saxon or Dane or Norman we,
Teuton or Celt, or whatever we be,
We are each all Dane in our welcome of thee,
                Alexandra!

Attempts at Classic Metres in Quantity

TRANSLATIONS OF HOMER

Hexameters and Pentameters

These lame hexameters the strong-wing'd music of Homer!
   No – but a most burlesque barbarous experiment.
When was a harsher sound ever heard, ye Muses, in England?
   When did a frog coarser croak upon our Helicon?
Hexameters no worse than daring Germany gave us,
   Barbarous experiment, barbarous hexameters!

MILTON

Alcaics

O mighty-mouth'd inventor of harmonies,
O skill'd to sing of Time or Eternity,
    God-gifted organ-voice of England,
       Milton, a name to resound for ages;
Whose Titan angels, Gabriel, Abdiel,
Starr'd from Jehovah's gorgeous armouries,
    Tower, as the deep-domed empyrëan
       Rings to the roar of an angel onset –
Me rather all that bowery loneliness,
The brooks of Eden mazily murmuring,
    And bloom profuse and cedar arches
       Charm, as a wanderer out in ocean,
Where some refulgent sunset of India
Streams o'er a rich ambrosial ocean isle
    And crimson-hued the stately palmwoods
       Whisper in odorous heights of even.

Hendecasyllabics

O you chorus of indolent reviewers,
Irresponsible, indolent reviewers,
Look, I come to the test, a tiny poem
All composed in a metre of Catullus,
All in quantity, careful of my motion,
Like the skater on ice that hardly bears him,
Lest I fall unawares before the people,
Waking laughter in indolent reviewers.

Should I flounder awhile without a tumble
Thro' this metrification of Catullus,
They should speak to me not without a welcome,
All that chorus of indolent reviewers.
Hard, hard, hard is it, only not to tumble,
So fantastical is the dainty metre.
Wherefore slight me not wholly, nor believe me
Too presumptuous, indolent reviewers.
O blatant Magazines, regard me rather —
Since I blush to belaud myself a moment —
As some rare little rose, a piece of inmost
Horticultural art, or half coquette-like
Maiden, not to be greeted unbenignly.

Specimen of a Translation of the Iliad in Blank Verse

So Hector said, and sea-like roar'd his host;
Then loosed their sweating horses from the yoke,
And each beside his chariot bound his own;
And oxen from the city, and goodly sheep
In haste they drove, and honey-hearted wine
And bread from out the houses brought, and heap'd
Their firewood, and the winds from off the plain
Roll'd the rich vapour far into the heaven.
And these all night upon the bridge of war
Sat glorying; many a fire before them blazed:
As when in heaven the stars about the moon
Look beautiful, when all the winds are laid,
And every height comes out, and jutting peak
And valley, and the immeasurable heavens
Break open to their highest, and all the stars
Shine, and the Shepherd gladdens in his heart:
So many a fire between the ships and stream
Of Xanthus blazed before the towers of Troy
A thousand on the plain; and close by each
Sat fifty in the blaze of burning fire;
And champing golden grain, the horses stood
Hard by their chariots, waiting for the dawn.

ENOCH ARDEN, AND OTHER POEMS

Enoch Arden

Long lines of cliff breaking have left a chasm;
And in the chasm are foam and yellow sands;
Beyond, red roofs about a narrow wharf
In cluster; then a moulder'd church; and higher
A long street climbs to one tall-tower'd mill;
And high in heaven behind it a grey down
With Danish barrows; and a hazelwood,
By autumn nutters haunted, flourishes
Green in a cuplike hollow of the down.

Here on this beach a hundred years ago,
Three children of three houses, Annie Lee,
The prettiest little damsel in the port,
And Philip Ray the miller's only son,
And Enoch Arden, a rough sailor's lad
Made orphan by a winter shipwreck, play'd
Among the waste and lumber of the shore,
Hard coils of cordage, swarthy fishing-nets,
Anchors of rusty fluke, and boats updrawn;
And built their castles of dissolving sand
To watch them overflow'd, or following up
And flying the white breaker, daily left
The little footprint daily wash'd away.

A narrow cave ran in beneath the cliff:
In this the children play'd at keeping house.
Enoch was host one day, Philip the next,
While Annie still was mistress; but at times
Enoch would hold possession for a week:
'This is my house and this my little wife.'
'Mine too's aid Philip 'turn and turn about:'
When, if they quarrell'd, Enoch stronger-made
Was master: then would Philip, his blue eyes
All flooded with the helpless wrath of tears,
Shriek out 'I hate you, Enoch,' and at this
The little wife would weep for company,
And pray them not to quarrel for her sake,
And say she would be little wife to both.

But when the dawn of rosy childhood past,
And the new warmth of life's ascending sun

Was felt by either, either fixt his heart
On that one girl; and Enoch spoke his love,
But Philip loved in silence; and the girl
Seem'd kinder unto Philip than to him;
But she loved Enoch; tho' she knew it not,
And would if ask'd deny it. Enoch set
A purpose evermore before his eyes,
To hoard all savings to the uttermost,
To purchase his own boat, and make a home
For Annie: and so prosper'd that at last
A luckier or a bolder fisherman,
A carefuller in peril, did not breathe
For leagues along that breaker-beaten coast
Than Enoch. Likewise had he served a year
On board a merchantman, and made himself
Full sailor; and he thrice had pluck'd a life
From the dread sweep of the down-streaming seas:
And all men look'd upon him favourably:
And ere he touch'd his one-and-twentieth May
He purchased his own boat, and made a home
For Annie, neat and nestlike, halfway up
The narrow street that clamber'd toward the mill.

    Then, on a golden autumn eventide,
The younger people making holiday,
With bag and sack and basket, great and small,
Went nutting to the hazels. Philip stay'd
(His father lying sick and needing him)
An hour behind; but as he climb'd the hill,
Just where the prone edge of the wood began
To feather toward the hollow, saw the pair,
Enoch and Annie, sitting hand-in-hand,
His large grey eyes and weather-beaten face
All-kindled by a still and sacred fire,
That burn'd as on an altar. Philip look'd,
And in their eyes and faces read his doom;
Then, as their faces drew together, groan'd,
And slipt aside, and like a wounded life
Crept down into the hollows of the wood;
There, while the rest were loud in merrymaking,
Had his dark hour unseen, and rose and past
Bearing a lifelong hunger in his heart.

    So these were wed, and merrily rang the bells,
And merrily ran the years, seven happy years,
Seven happy years of health and competence,

And mutual love and honourable toil;
With children; first a daughter. In him woke,
With his first babe's first cry, the noble wish
To save all earnings to the uttermost,
And give his child a better bringing-up
Than his had been, or hers; a wish renew'd,
When two years after came a boy to be
The rosy idol of her solitudes,
While Enoch was abroad on wrathful seas,
Or often journeying landward; for in truth
Enoch's white horse, and Enoch's ocean-spoil
In ocean-smelling osier, and his face
Rough-redden'd with a thousand winter gales,
Not only to the market-cross were known,
But in the leafy lanes behind the down,
Far as the portal-warding lion-whelp,
And peacock-yewtree of the lonely Hall,
Whose Friday fare was Enoch's ministering.

      Then came a, change, as all things human change.
Ten miles to northward of the narrow port
Open'd a larger haven: thither used
Enoch at times to go by land or sea;
And once when there and clambering on a mast
In harbour, by mischance he slipt and fell:
A limb was broken when they lifted him;
And while he lay recovering there, his wife
Bore him another son, a sickly one:
Another hand crept too across his trade
Taking her bread and theirs: and on him fell,
Altho' a grave and staid God-fearing man,
Yet lying thus inactive, doubt and gloom.
He seem'd, as in a nightmare of the night,
To see his children leading evermore
Low miserable lives of hand-to-mouth,
And her, he loved, a beggar: then he pray'd
'Save them from this, whatever comes to me.'
And while he pray'd, the master of that ship
Enoch had served in, hearing his mischance,
Came, for he knew the man and valued him,
Reporting of his vessel China-bound,
And wanting yet a boatswain. Would he go?
There yet were many weeks before she sail'd,
Sail'd from this port. Would Enoch have the place?
And Enoch all at once assented to it,
Rejoicing at that answer to his prayer.

So now that shadow of mischance appear'd
No graver than as when some little cloud
Cuts off the fiery highway of the sun,
And isles a light in the offing: yet the wife –
When he was gone – the children – what to do?
Then Enoch lay long-pondering on his plans;
To sell the boat – and yet he loved her well –
How many a rough sea had he weather'd in her!
He knew her, as a horseman knows his horse –
And yet to sell her – then with what she brought
Buy goods and stores – set Annie forth in trade
With all that seamen needed or their wives –
So might she keep the house while he was gone
Should he not trade himself out yonder? go
This voyage more than once? yea twice or thrice –
As oft as needed – last, returning rich,
Become the master of a larger craft
With fuller profits lead an easier life,
Have all his pretty young ones educated,
And pass his days in peace among his own.

    Thus Enoch in his heart determined all:
Then moving homeward came on Almie pale,
Nursing the sickly babe, her latest-born.
Forward she started with a happy cry,
And laid the feeble infant in his arms;
Whom Enoch took, and handled all his limbs,
Appraised his weight and fondled fatherlike,
But had no heart to break his purposes
To Annie, till the morrow, when he spoke.

    Then first since Enoch's golden ring had girt
Her finger, Annie fought against his will:
Yet not with brawling opposition she,
But manifold entreaties, many a tear,
Many a sad kiss by day by night renew'd
(Sure that all evil would come out of it)
Besought him, supplicating, if he cared
For her or his dear children, not to go.
He not for his own self caring but her,
Her and her children, let her plead in vain;
So grieving held his will, and bore it thro'.

    For Enoch parted with his old sea-friend,
Bought Annie goods and stores, and set his hand
To fit their little streetward sitting-room

With shelf and corner for the goods and stores.
So all day long till Enoch's last at home,
Shaking their pretty cabin, hammer and axe,
Auger and saw, while Annie seem'd to hear
Her own death-scaffold raising, shrill'd and rang,
Till this was ended, and his careful hand, –
The space was narrow, – having order'd all
Almost as neat and close as Nature packs
Her blossom or her seedling, paused; and he,
Who needs would work for Annie to the last,
Ascending tired, heavily slept till morn.

    And Enoch faced this morning of farewell
Brightly and boldly. All his Annie's fears,
Save, as his Annie's, were a laughter to him.
Yet Enoch as a brave God-fearing man
Bow'd himself down, and in that mystery
Where God-in-man is one with man-in-God,
Pray'd for a blessing on his wife and babes
Whatever came to him: and then he said
'Annie, this voyage by the grace of God
Will bring fair weather yet to all of us.
Keep a clean hearth and a clear fire for me,
For I'll be back, my girl, before you know it.'
Then lightly rocking baby's cradle 'and he,
This pretty, puny, weakly little one, –
Nay – for I love him all the better for it –
God bless him, he shall sit upon my knees
And I will tell him tales of foreign parts
And make him merry, when I come home again
Come Annie, come, cheer up before I go.'

    Him running on thus hopefully she heard,
And almost hoped herself; but when he turn'd
The current of his talk to graver things
In sailor fashion roughly sermonizing
On providence and trust in Heaven, she heard,
Heard and not heard him; as the village girl,
Who sets her pitcher underneath the spring,
Musing on him that used to fill it for her,
Hears and not hears, and lets it overflow.

    At length she spoke 'O Enoch, you are wise;
And yet for all your wisdom well know I
That I shall look upon your face no more.'

'Well then,' said Enoch, 'I shall look on yours.
Annie, the ship I sail in passes here
(He named the day) get you a seaman's glass,
Spy out my face, and laugh at all your fears.'

But when the last of those last moments came,
'Annie, my girl, cheer up, be comforted,
Look to the babes, and till I come again
Keep everything shipshape, for I must go.
And fear no more for me; or if you fear
Cast all your cares on God; that anchor holds
Is He not yonder in those uttermost
Parts of the morning? if I flee to these
Can I go from Him? and the sea is His,
The sea is His: He made it.'

                      Enoch rose,
Cast his strong arms about his drooping wife,
And kiss'd his wonder-stricken little ones;
But for the third, the sickly one, who slept
After a night of feverous wakefulness,
When Annie would have raised him Enoch said
'Wake him not; let him sleep; how should the child
Remember this?' and kiss'd him in his cot
But Annie from her baby's forehead clipt
A tiny curl, and gave it: this he kept
Thro' all his future; but now hastily caught
His bundle, waved his hand, and went his way.

She when the day, that Enoch mention'd, Game,
Borrow'd a glass, but all in vain perhaps
She could not fix the glass to suit her eye;
Perhaps her eye was dim, hand tremulous;
She saw him not and while he stood on deck
Waving, the moment and the vessel past.

Ev'n to the last dip of the vanishing sail
She watch'd it, and departed weeping for him;
Then, tho' she mourn'd his absence as his grave,
Set her sad will no less to chime with his,
But throve not in her trade, not being bred
To barter, nor compensating the want
By shrewdness, neither capable of lies,
Nor asking overmuch and taking less,
And still foreboding 'what would Enoch say?'
For more than once, in days of difficulty
And pressure, had she sold her wares for less

Than what she gave in buying what she sold
She fail'd and sadden'd knowing it; and thus,
Expectant of that news which never came
Gain'd for her own a scanty sustenance,
And lived a life of silent melancholy.

Now the third child was sickly-born and grew
Yet sicklier, tho' the mother cared for it
With all a mother's care nevertheless,
Whether her business often call'd her from it,
Or thro' the want of what it needed most,
Or means to pay the voice who best could tell
What most it needed – howsoe'er it was,
After a lingering, – ere she was aware, –
Like the caged bird escaping suddenly,
The little innocent soul flitted away.

In that same week when Annie buried it,
Philip's true heart, which hunger'd for her peace
(Since Enoch left he had not look'd upon her),
Smote him, as having kept aloof so long.
'Surely' said Philip 'I may see her now,
May be some little comfort;' therefore went,
Past thro' the solitary room in front,
Paused for a moment at an inner door,
Then struck it thrice, and, no one opening,
Enter'd; but Annie, seated with her grief,
Fresh from the burial of her little one,
Cared not to look on any human face,
But turn'd her own toward the wall and wept.
Then Philip standing up said falteringly
'Annie, I came to ask a favour of you.'

He spoke; the passion in her moan'd reply
'Favour from one so sad and so forlorn
As I am!' half abash'd him; yet unask'd,
His bashfulness and tenderness at war,
He set himself beside her, saying to her:

'I came to speak to you of what he wish'd,
Enoch, your husband: I have ever said
You chose the best among us – a strong man:
For where he fixt his heart he set his hand
To do the thing he will'd, and bore it thro'.
And wherefore did he go this weary way,
And leave you lonely? not to see the world –

For pleasure? – nay, but for the wherewithal
To give his babes a better bringing-up
Than his had been, or yours: that was his wish.
And if he come again, vext will he be
To find the precious morning hours were lost.
And it would vex him even in his grave,
If he could know his babes were running wild
Like colts about the waste. So, Annie, now –
Have we not known each other all our lives?
I do beseech you by the love you bear
Him and his children not to say me nay –
For, if you will, when Enoch comes again
Why then he shall repay me – if you will
Annie – for I am rich and well-to-do.
Now let me put the boy and girl to school:
This is the favour that I came to ask.'

    Then Annie with her brows against the wall
Answer'd 'I cannot look you in the face;
I seem so foolish and so broken down.
When you came in my sorrow broke me down;
And now I think your kindness breaks me down;
But Enoch lives; that is borne in on me:
He will repay you: money can be repaid;
Not kindness such as yours.'

               And Philip ask'd
'Then you will let me, Annie?'

               There she turn'd,
She rose, and fixt her swimming eyes upon him,
And dwelt a moment on his kindly face,
Then calling down a blessing on his head
Caught at his hand, and wrung it passionately,
And past into the little garth beyond.
So lifted up in spirit he moved away.

    Then Philip put the boy and girl to school,
And bought them needful books, and everyway,
Like one who does his duty by his own,
Made himself theirs; and tho' for Annie's sake,
Fearing the lazy gossip of the port,
He oft denied his heart his dearest wish,
And seldom crost her threshold, yet he sent
Gifts by the children, garden-herbs and fruit,
The late and early roses from his wall,

Or conies from the down, and now and then
With some pretext of fineness in the meal
To save the offence of charitable, flour
From his tall mill that whistled on the waste.

    But Philip did not fathom Annie's mind:
Scarce could the woman when he came upon her,
Out of full heart and boundless gratitude
Light on a broken word to thank him with.
But Philip was her children's all-in-all;
From distant corners of the street they ran
To greet his hearty welcome heartily;
Lords of his house and of his mill were they;
Worried his passive ear with petty wrongs
Or pleasures, hung upon him, play'd with him
And call'd him Father Philip. Philip gain'd
As Enoch lost; for Enoch seem'd to them
Uncertain as a vision or a dream,
Faint as a figure seen in early dawn
Down at the far end of an avenue,
Going we know not where: and so ten years,
Since Enoch left his hearth and native land,
Fled forward, and no news of Enoch came.

    It chanced one evening Annie's children long'd
To go with others, nutting to the wood,
And Annie would go with them; then they begg'd
For Father Philip (as they call'd him) too:
Him, like the working bee in blossom-dust,
Blanch'd with his mill, they found; and saying to him
'Come with us, Father Philip' he denied;
But when the children pluck'd at him to go,
He laugh'd, and yielded readily to their wish,
For was not Annie with them? and they went.

    But after scaling half the weary down,
Just where the prone edge of the wood began
To feather toward the hollow, all her force
Fail'd her; and sighing 'let me rest' she said:
So Philip rested with her well-content;
While all the younger ones with jubilant cries
Broke from their elders and tumultuously
Down thro' the whitening hazels made a plunge
To the bottom, and dispersed, and bent or broke
The lithe reluctant boughs to tear away
Their tawny clusters, crying to each other

And calling, here and there, about the wood.

But Philip sitting at her side forgot
Her presence, and remember'd one dark hour
Here in this wood, when like a wounded life
He crept into the shadow: at last he said,
Lifting his honest forehead, 'Listen, Annie,
How merry they are down yonder in the wood.
Tired, Annie?' for she did not speak a word.
'Tired?' but her face had fall'n upon her hands;
At which, as with a kind of anger in him,
'The ship was lost' he said, 'the ship was lost!
No more of that! why should you kill yourself
And make them orphans quite?' And Annie said
'I thought not of it: but – I know not why –
Their voices make me feel so solitary.'

Then Philip coming somewhat closer spoke.
'Annie, there is a thing upon my mind,
And it has been upon my mind so long,
That tho' I know not when it first came there,
I know that it will out at last. O Annie,
It is beyond all hope, against all chance,
That he who left you ten long years ago
Should still be living; well then – let me speak:
I grieve to see you poor and wanting help:
I cannot help you as I wish to do
Unless – they say that women are so quick –
Perhaps you know what I would have you know –
I wish you for my wife. I fain would prove
A father to your children: I do think
They love me as a father: I am sure
That I love them as if they were mine own;
And I believe, if you were fast my wife,
That after all these sad uncertain years,
We might be still as happy as God grants
To any of His creatures. Think upon it:
For I am well-to-do – no kin, no care,
No burthen, save my care for you and yours:
And we have known each other all our lives,
And I have loved you longer than you know.'

Then answer'd Annie; tenderly she spoke:
'You have been as God's good angel in our house.
God bless you for it, God reward you for it,
Philip, with something happier than myself.

Can one love twice? can you be ever loved
As Enoch was? what is it that you ask?'
'I am content' he answer'd 'to be loved
A little after Enoch.' 'O' she cried,
Scared as it were, 'dear Philip, wait a while:
If Enoch comes – but Enoch will not come –
Yet wait a year, a year is not so long:
Surely I shall be wiser in a year:
O wait a little!' Philip sadly said,
'Annie, as I have waited all my life
I well may wait a little.' 'Nay,' she cried,
'I am bound: you have my promise – in a year:
Will you not bide your year as I bide mine?'
And Philip answer'd, 'I will bide my year.'

    Here both were mute, till Philip glancing up
Beheld the dead flame of the fallen day
Pass from the Danish barrow overhead;
Then fearing night and chill for Annie rose,
And sent his voice beneath him thro' the wood.
Up came the children laden with their spoil;
Then all descended to the port, and there
At Annie's door he paused and gave his hand,
Saying gently 'Annie, when I spoke to you,
That was your hour of weakness. I was wrong.
I am always bound to you, but you are free.'
Then Annie weeping answer'd 'I am bound.'

    She spoke; and in one moment as it were,
While yet she went about her household ways,
Ev'n as she dwelt upon his latest words,
That he had loved her longer than she knew,
That autumn into autumn flash'd again,
And there he stood once more before her face,
Claiming her promise. 'Is it a year?' she ask'd.
'Yes, if the nuts' he said 'be ripe again:
Come out and see.' But she – she put him off –
So much to look to – such a change – a month –
Give her a month – she knew that she was bound –
A month – no more. Then Philip with his eyes
Full of that lifelong hunger, and his voice
Shaking a little like a drunkard's hand,
'Take your own time, Annie, take your own time.'
And Annie could have wept for pity of him;
And yet she held him on delayingly
With many a scarce-believable excuse,

Trying his truth and his long-sufferance,
Till half-another year had slipt away.

  By this the lazy gossips of the port,
Abhorrent of a calculation crost,
Began to chafe as at a personal wrong.
Some thought that Philip did but trifle with her;
Some that she but held off to draw him on;
And others laugh'd at her and Philip too,
As simple folk that knew not their own minds;
And one, in whom all evil fancies clung
Like serpent eggs together, laughingly
Would hint at worse in either. Her own son
Was silent, tho' he often look'd his wish;
But evermore the daughter prest upon her
To wed the man so dear to all of them
And lift the household out of poverty;
And Philip's rosy face contracting grew
Careworn and wan; and all these things fell on her
Sharp as reproach.

          At last one night it chanced
That Annie could not sleep, but earnestly
Pray'd for a sign 'my Enoch is he gone?'
Then compass'd round by the blind wall of night
Brook'd not the expectant terror of her heart,
Started from bed, and struck herself a light,
Then desperately seized the holy Book,
Suddenly set it wide to find a sign,
Suddenly put her finger on the text,
'Under a palmtree.' That was nothing to her:
No meaning there: she closed the Book and slept:
When lo! her Enoch sitting on a height,
Under a palmtree, over him the Sun:
'He is gone,' she thought, 'he is happy, he is singing
Hosanna in the highest: yonder shines
The Sun of Righteousness, and these be palms
Whereof the happy people strowing cried,
"Hosanna in the highest!" ' Here she woke,
Resolved, sent for him and said wildly to him,
'There is no reason why we should not wed.'
'Then for God's sake,' he answer'd, 'both our sakes,
So you will wed me, let it be at once.'

  So these were wed and merrily rang the bells,
Merrily rang the bells and they were wed.

But never merrily beat Annie's heart.
A footstep seem'd to fall beside her path,
She knew not whence; a whisper on her ear,
She knew not what; nor loved she to be left
Alone at home, nor ventured out alone.
What ail'd her then, that ere she enter'd, often
Her hand dwelt lingeringly on the latch,
Fearing to enter: Philip thought he knew:
Such doubts and fears were common to her state,
Being with child: but when her child was born,
Then her new child was as herself renew'd,
Then the new mother came about her heart,
Then her good Philip was her all-in-all,
And that mysterious instinct wholly died.

    And where was Enoch? prosperously sail'd
The ship 'Good Fortune,' tho' at setting forth
The Biscay, roughly ridging eastward, shook
And almost overwhelm'd her, yet unvext
She slipt across the summer of the world,
Then after a long tumble about the Cape
And frequent interchange of foul and fair,
She passing thro' the summer world again,
The breath of heaven came continually
And sent her sweetly by the golden isles,
Till silent in her oriental haven.

    There Enoch traded for himself, and bought
Quaint monsters for the market of those times,
A gilded dragon, also, for the babes.

    Less lucky her home-voyage: at first indeed
Thro' many a fair sea-circle, day by day,
Scarce-rocking, her full-busted figure-head
Stared o'er the ripple feathering from her bows:
Then follow'd calms, and then winds variable,
Then baffling, a long course of them; and last
Storm, such as drove her under moonless heavens
Till hard upon the cry of 'breakers' came
The crash of ruin, and the loss of all
But Enoch and two others. Half the night,
Buoy'd upon floating tackle and broken spars,
These drifted, stranding on an isle at morn
Rich, but the loneliest in a lonely sea.

    No want was there of human sustenance,

Soft fruitage, mighty nuts, and nourishing roots;
Nor save for pity was it hard to take
The helpless life so wild that it was tame.
There in a seaward-gazing mountain-gorge
They built, and thatch'd with leaves of palm, a hut,
Half hut, half native cavern. So the three
Set in this Eden of all plenteousness
Dwelt with eternal summer, ill-content.

For one, the youngest, hardly more than boy,
Hurt in that night of sudden ruin and wreck,
Lay lingering out a three-years' death-in-life.
They could not leave him. After he was gone,
The two remaining found a fallen stem;
And Enoch's comrade, careless of himself,
Fire-hollowing this in Indian fashion, fell
Sun-stricken, and that other lived alone.
In those two deaths he read God's warning 'wait.'

The mountain wooded to the peak, the lawns
And winding glades high up like ways to Heaven,
The slender coco's drooping crown of plumes,
The lightning flash of insect and of bird,
The lustre of the long convolvuluses
That coil'd around the stately stems, and ran
Ev'n to the limit of the land, the glows
And glories of the broad belt of the world,
All these he saw; but what he fain had seen
He could not see, the kindly human face,
Nor ever hear a kindly voice, but heard
The myriad shriek of wheeling ocean-fowl,
The league-long roller thundering on the reef,
The moving whisper of huge trees that branch'd
And blossom'd in the zenith, or the sweep
Of some precipitous rivulet to the wave,
As down the shore he ranged, or all day long
Sat often in the seaward-gazing gorge,
A shipwreck'd sailor, waiting for a sail:
No sail from day to day, but every day
The sunrise broken into scarlet shafts
Among the palms and ferns and precipices;
The blaze upon the waters to the east;
The blaze upon his island overhead;
The blaze upon the waters to the west;
Then the great stars that globed themselves in Heaven
The hollower-bellowing ocean, and again

The scarlet shafts of sunrise – but no sail.

There often as he watch'd or seem'd to watch,
So still, the golden lizard on him paused,
A phantom made of many phantoms moved
Before him haunting him, or he himself
Moved haunting people, things and places, known
Far in a darker isle beyond the line;
The babes, their babble, Annie, the small house,
The climbing street, the mill, the leafy lanes,
The peacock-yewtree and the lonely Hall,
The horse he drove, the boat he sold, the chill
November dawns and dewy-glooming downs,
The gentle shower, the smell of dying leaves,
And the low moan of leaden-colour'd seas.

Once likewise, in the ringing of his ears,
Tho' faintly, merrily – far and far away –
He heard the pealing of his parish bells;
Then, tho' he knew not wherefore, started up
Shuddering, and when the beauteous hateful isle
Return'd upon him, had not his poor heart
Spoken with That, which being everywhere
Lets none, who speaks with Him, seem all alone,
Surely the man had died of solitude.

Thus over Enoch's early-silvering head
The sunny and rainy seasons came and went
Year after year. His hopes to see his own,
And pace the sacred old familiar fields
Not yet had perish'd, when his lonely doom
Came suddenly to an end. Another ship
(She wanted water) blown by baffling winds,
Like the Good Fortune, from her destined course,
Stay'd by this isle, not knowing where she lay:
For since the mate had seen at early dawn
Across a break on the mist-wreathen isle
The silent water slipping from the hills,
They sent a crew that landing burst away
In search of stream or fount, and fill'd the shores
With clamour. Downward from his mountain gorge
Stept the long-hair'd long-bearded solitary,
Brown, looking hardly human, strangely clad,
Muttering and mumbling, idiotlike it seem'd,
With inarticulate rage, and making signs
They knew not what: and yet he led the way

To where the rivulets of sweet water ran;
And ever as he mingled with the crew,
And heard them talking, his long-bounden tongue
Was loosen'd, till he made them understand;
Whom, when their casks were fill'd they took aboard:
And there the tale he utter'd brokenly,
Scarce credited at first but more and more,
Amazed and melted all who listen'd to it;
And clothes they gave him and free passage home;
But oft he work'd among the rest and shook
His isolation from him. None of these
Came from his county, or could answer him,
If question'd, aught of what he cared to know.
And dull the voyage was with long delays,
The vessel scarce sea-worthy; but evermore
His fancy fled before the lazy wind
Returning, till beneath a clouded moon
He like a lover down thro' all his blood
Drew in the dewy meadowy morning-breath
Of England, blown across her ghostly wall:
And that same morning officers and men
Levied a kindly tax upon themselves,
Pitying the lonely man, and gave him it:
Then moving up the coast they landed him,
Ev'n in that harbour whence he sail'd before.

There Enoch spoke no word to any one,
But homeward – home – what home? had he a home?
His home, he walk'd. Bright was that afternoon,
Sunny but chill; till drawn thro' either chasm,
Where either haven open'd on the deeps,
Roll'd a sea-haze and whelm'd the world in grey;
Cut off the length of highway on before,
And left but narrow breadth to left and right
Of wither'd holt or tilth or pasturage.
On the nigh-naked tree the Robin piped
Disconsolate, and thro' the dripping haze
The dead weight of the dead leaf bore it down:
Thicker the drizzle grew, deeper the gloom;
Last, as it seem'd, a great mist-blotted light
Flared on him, and he came upon the place.

Then down the long street having slowly stolen,
His heart foreshadowing all calamity,
His eyes upon the stones, he reach'd the home
Where Annie lived and loved him, and his babes

In those far-off seven happy years were born;
But finding neither light nor murmur there
(A bill of sale gleam'd thro' the drizzle) crept
Still downward thinking 'dead or dead to me!'

Down to the pool and narrow wharf he went
Seeking a tavern which of old he knew,
A front of timber-crost antiquity,
So propt, worm-eaten, ruinously old,
He thought it must have gone; but he was gone
Who kept it; and his widow, Miriam Lane,
With daily-dwindling profits held the house;
A haunt of brawling seamen once, but now
Stiller, with yet a bed for wandering men.
There Enoch rested silent many days.

But Miriam Lane was good and garrulous,
Nor let him be, but often breaking in,
Told him, with other annals of the port,
Not knowing – Enoch was so brown, so bow'd,
So broken – all the story of his house.
His baby's death, her growing poverty,
How Philip put her little ones to school,
And kept them in it, his long wooing her,
Her slow consent, and marriage, and the birth
Of Philip's child: and o'er his countenance
No shadow past, nor motion: any one,
Regarding, well had deem'd he felt the tale
Less than the teller: only when she closed
'Enoch, poor man, was cast away and lost'
He, shaking his grey head pathetically,
Repeated muttering 'cast away and lost;'
Again in deeper inward whispers 'lost!'

But Enoch yearn'd to see her face again;
'If I might look on her sweet face again
And know that she is happy.' So the thought
Haunted and harass'd him, and drove him forth,
At evening when the dull November day
Was growing duller twilight, to the hill.
There he sat down gazing on all below;
There did a thousand memories roll upon him,
Unspeakable for sadness. By and by
The ruddy square of comfortable light,
Far-blazing from the rear of Philip's house,
Allured him, as the beacon-blaze allures

The bird of passage, till he madly strikes
Against it, and beats out his weary life.

　　For Philip's dwelling fronted on the street,
The latest house to landward; but behind,
With one small gate that open'd on the waste,
Flourish'd a little garden square and wall'd:
And in it throve an ancient evergreen,
A yewtree, and all round it ran a walk
Of shingle, and a walk divided it:
But Enoch shunn'd the middle walk and stole
Up by the wall, behind the yew; and thence
That which he better might have shunn'd, if griefs
Like his have worse or better, Enoch saw.

　　For cups and silver on the burnish'd board
Sparkled and shone; so genial was the hearth:
And on the right hand of the hearth he saw
Philip, the slighted suitor of old times,
Stout, rosy, with his babe across his knees;
And o'er her second father stoopt a girl,
A later but a loftier Annie Lee,
Fair-hair'd and tall, and from her lifted hand
Dangled a length of ribbon and a ring
To tempt the babe, who rear'd his creasy arms,
Caught at and ever miss'd it, and they laugh'd:
And on the left hand of the hearth he saw
The mother glancing often toward her babe,
But turning now and then to speak with him,
Her son, who stood beside her tall and strong,
And saying that which pleased him, for he smiled.

　　Now when the dead man come to life beheld
His wife his wife no more, and saw the babe
Hers, yet not his, upon the father's knee,
And all the warmth, the peace, the happiness
And his own children tall and beautiful,
And him, that other, reigning in his place,
Lord of his rights and of his children's love, –
Then he, tho' Miriam Lane had told him all,
Because things seen are mightier than things heard,
Stagger'd and shook, holding the branch, and fear'd
To send abroad a shrill and terrible cry,
Which in one moment, like the blast of doom,
Would shatter all the happiness of the hearth.

He therefore turning softly like a thief,
Lest the harsh shingle should grate underfoot,
And feeling all along the garden-wall,
Lest he should swoon and tumble and be found,
Crept to the gate, and open'd it, and closed,
As lightly as a sick man's chamber-door,
Behind him, and came out upon the waste.

And there he would have knelt, but that his knees
Were feeble, so that falling prone he dug
His fingers into the wet earth, and pray'd.

'Too hard to bear! why did they take me thence?
O God Almighty, blessed Saviour, Thou
That didst uphold me on my lonely isle.
Uphold me, Father, in my loneliness
A little longer! aid me, give me strength
Not to tell her, never to let her know.
Help me not to break in upon her peace.
My children too! must I not speak to these?
They know me not. I should betray myself.
Never: no father's kiss for me – the girl
So like her mother, and the boy, my son.'

There speech and thought and nature fail'd a little,
And he lay tranced; but when he rose and paced
Back toward his solitary home again,
All down the long and narrow street he went
Beating it in upon his weary brain,
As tho' it were the burthen of a song,
'Not to tell her, never to let her know.'

He was not all unhappy. His resolve
Upbore him, and firm faith, and evermore
Prayer from a living source within the will,
And beating up thro' all the bitter world
Like fountains of sweet water in the sea
Kept him a living soul. 'This miller's wife'
He said to Miriam 'that you told me of,
Has she no fear that her first husband lives?'
'Aye, aye, poor soul's aid Miriam, 'fear enow!
If you could tell her you had seen him dead,
Why, that would be her comfort;' and he thought
'After the Lord has call'd me she shall know,
I wait His time,' and Enoch set himself,
Scorning an alms, to work whereby to live.

Almost to all things could he turn his hand.
Cooper he was and carpenter, and wrought
To make the boatmen fishing-nets, or help'd
At lading and unlading the tall barks,
That brought the stinted commerce of those days;
Thus earn'd a scanty living for himself:
Yet since he did but labour for himself,
Work without hope, there was not life in it
Whereby the man could live; and as the year
Roll'd itself round again to meet the day
When Enoch had return'd, a languor came
Upon him, gentle sickness, gradually
Weakening the man, till he could do no more,
But kept the house, his chair, and last his bed.
And Enoch bore his weakness cheerfully.
For sure no gladlier does the stranded wreck
See thro' the grey skirts of a lifting squall
The boat that bears the hope of life approach
To save the life despair'd of, than he saw
Death dawning on him, and the close of all.

    For thro' that dawning gleam'd a kindlier hope
On Enoch thinking 'after I am gone
Then may she learn I loved her to the last.'
He call'd aloud for Miriam Lane and said,
'Woman, I have a secret – only swear
Before I tell you – swear upon the book
Not to reveal it, till you see me dead.'
'Dead,' clamour'd the good woman, 'hear him talk!
I warrant, man, that we shall bring you round.'
'Swear,' added Enoch sternly, 'on the book.'
And on the book, half-frighted, Miriam swore.
Then Enoch rolling his grey eyes upon her,
'Did you know Enoch Arden of this town?'
'Know him?' she said 'I knew him far away.
Aye, aye, I mind him coming down the street;
Held his head high, and cared for no man, he.'
Slowly and sadly Enoch answer'd her:
'His head is low, and no man cares for him.
I think I have not three days more to live;
I am the man.' At which the woman gave
A half-incredulous, half-hysterical cry.
'You Arden, you I nay, – sure he was a foot
Higher than you be.' Enoch said again,
'My God has bow'd me down to what I am;
My grief and solitude have broken me;

Nevertheless, know you that I am he
Who married – but that name has twice been changed –
I married her who married Philip Ray.
Sit, listen.' Then he told her of his voyage
His wreck, his lonely life, his coming back,
His gazing in on Annie, his resolve,
And how he kept it. As the woman heard,
Fast flow'd the current of her easy tears,
While in her heart she yearn'd incessantly
To rush abroad all round the little haven,
Proclaiming Enoch Arden and his woes;
But awed and promise-bounden she forbore,
Saying only 'See your bairns before you go!
Eh, let me fetch 'em, Arden.' and arose
Eager to bring them down, for Enoch hung
A moment on her words, but then replied.

   'Woman, disturb me not now at the last,
But let me hold my purpose till I die.
Sit down again; mark me and understand,
While I have power to speak. I charge you now,
When you shall see her, tell her that I died
Blessing her, praying for her, loving her;
Save for the bar between us, loving her
As when she laid her head beside my own.
And tell my daughter Annie, whom I saw
So like her mother, that my latest breath
Was spent in blessing her and praying for her.
And tell my son that I died blessing him.
And say to Philip that I blest him too;
He never meant us any thing but good.
But if my children care to see me dead,
Who hardly knew me living, let them come,
I am their father; but she must not come,
For my dead face would vex her after-life.
And now there is but one of all my blood
Who will embrace me in the world-to-be.
This hair is his: she cut it off and gave it,
And I have borne it with me all these years,
And thought to bear it with me to my grave;
But now my mind is changed, for I shall see him.
My babe in bliss: wherefore when I am gone,
Take, give her this, for it may comfort her:
It will moreover be a token to her,
That I am he.'

He ceased; and Miriam Lane
Made such a voluble answer promising all,
That once again he roll'd his eyes upon her
Repeating all he wish'd, and once again
She promised.

Then the third night after this,
While Enoch slumber'd motionless and pale,
And Miriam watch'd and dozed at intervals,
There came so loud a calling of the sea,
That all the houses in the haven rang.
He woke, he rose, he spread his arms abroad
Crying with a loud voice 'a sail! a sail!
I am saved'; and so fell back and spoke no more.

So past the strong heroic soul away.
And when they buried him the little port
Had seldom seen a costlier funeral.

Aylmer's Field

1793

Dust are our frames; and, gilded dust, our pride
Looks only for a moment whole and sound;
Like that long-buried body of the king,
Found lying with his urns and ornaments,
Which at a touch of light, an air of heaven,
Slipt into ashes and was found no more.

Here is a story which in rougher shape
Came from a grizzled cripple, whom I saw
Sunning himself in a waste field alone –
Old, and a mine of memories – who had served,
Long since, a bygone Rector of the place,
And been himself a part of what he told.

SIR AYLMER AYLMER, that almighty man,
The county God – in whose capacious hall,
Hung with a hundred shields, the family tree
Sprang from the midriff of a prostrate king –
Whose blazing wyvern weathercock'd the spire,
Stood from his walls and wing'd his entry-gates
And swang besides on many a windy sign –
Whose eyes from under a pyramidal head

Saw from his windows nothing save his own –
What lovelier of his own had he than her,
His only child, his Edith, whom he loved
As heiress and not heir regretfully?
But 'he that marries her marries her name'
This fiat somewhat soothed himself and wife,
His wife a faded beauty of the Baths,
Insipid as the Queen upon a card;
Her all of thought and bearing hardly more
Than his own shadow in a sickly sun.

A land of hops and poppy-mingled corn,
Little about it stirring save a brook!
A sleepy land where under the same wheel
The same old rut would deepen year by year;
Where almost all the village had one name;
Where Aylmer follow'd Aylmer at the Hall
And Averill Averill at the Rectory
Thrice over; so that Rectory and Hall,
Bound in an immemorial intimacy,
Were open to each other; tho' to dream
That Love could bind them closer well had made
The hoar hair of the Baronet bristle up
With horror, worse than had he heard his priest
Preach an inverted scripture, sons of men
Daughters of God; so sleepy was the land.

And might not Averill, had he will'd it so,
Somewhere beneath his own low range of roofs,
Have also set his many-shielded tree?
There was an Aylmer-Averill marriage once,
When the red rose was redder than itself,
And York's white rose as red as Lancaster's,
With wounded peace which each had prick'd to death.
'Not proven' Averill said, or laughingly
'Some other race of Averills' – prov'n or no,
What cared he? what, if other or the same?
He lean'd not on his fathers but himself.
But Leolin, his brother, living oft
With Averill, and a year or two before
Call'd to the bar, but ever call'd away
By one low voice to one dear neighbourhood,
Would often, in his walks with Edith, claim
A distant kinship to the gracious blood
That shook the heart of Edith hearing him.

Sanguine he was: a but less vivid hue
Than of that islet in the chestnut-bloom
Flamed in his cheek; and eager eyes, that still
Took joyful note of all things joyful, beam'd,
Beneath a manelike mass of rolling gold,
Their best and brightest, when they dwelt on hers,
Edith, whose pensive beauty, perfect else,
But subject to the season or the mood,
Shone like a mystic star between the less
And greater glory varying to and fro,
We know not wherefore; bounteously made,
And yet so finely, that a troublous touch
Thinn'd, or would seem to thin her in a day,
A joyous to dilate, as toward the light.
And these had been together from the first.
Leolin's first nurse was, five years after, hers:
So much the boy foreran; but when his date
Doubled her own, for want of playmates, he
(Since Averill was a decade and a half
His elder, and their parents underground)
Had tost his ball and flown his kite, and roll'd
His hoop to pleasure Edith, with her dipt
Against the rush of the air in the prone swing,
Made blossom-ball or daisy-chain, arranged
Her garden, sow'd her name and kept it green
In living letters, told her fairy-tales,
Show'd her the fairy footings on the grass,
The little dells of cowslip, fairy palms,
The petty marestail forest, fairy pines,
Or from the tiny pitted target blew
What look'd a flight of fairy arrows aim'd
All at one mark, all hitting: make-believes
For Edith and himself: or else he forged,
But that was later, boyish histories
Of battle, bold adventure, dungeon, wreck,
Flights, terrors, sudden rescues, and true love
Crown'd after trial; sketches rude and faint,
But where a passion yet unborn perhaps
Lay hidden as the music of the moon
Sleeps in the plain eggs of the nightingale.
And thus together, save for college-times
Or Temple-eaten terms, a couple, fair
As ever painter painted, poet sang,
Or Heav'n in lavish bounty moulded, grew.
And more and more, the maiden woman-grown,
He wasted hours with Averill; there, when first

The tented winter-field was broken up
Into that phalanx of the summer spears
That soon should wear the garland; there again
When burr and bine were gather'd; lastly there
At Christmas, ever welcome at the Hall,
On whose dull sameness his full tide of youth
Broke with a phosphorescence cheering even
My lady; and the Baronet yet had laid
No bar between them: dull and self-involved,
Tall and erect, but bending from his height
With half-allowing smiles for all the world,
And mighty courteous in the main – his pride
Lay deeper than to wear it as his ring –
He, like an Aylmer in his Aylmerism,
Would care no more for Leolin's walking with her
Than for his old Newfoundland's, when they ran
To loose him at the stables, for he rose
Twofooted at the limit of his chain,
Roaring to make a third: and how should Love,
Whom the cross-lightnings of four chance-met eyes
Flash into fiery life from nothing, follow
Such dear familiarities of dawn?
Seldom, but when he does, Master of all.

So these young hearts not knowing that they loved,
Not she at least, nor conscious of a bar
Between them, nor by plight or broken ring
Bound, but an immemorial intimacy,
Wander'd at will, but oft accompanied
By Averill his, a brother's love, that hung
With wings of brooding shelter o'er her peace,
Might have been other, save for Leolin's –
Who knows? but so they wander'd, hour by hour
Gather'd the blossom that rebloom'd, and drank
The magic cup that fill'd itself anew.

A whisper half reveal'd her to herself.
For out beyond her lodges, where the brook
Vocal, with here and there a silence, ran
By sallowy rims, arose the labourers' homes,
A frequent haunt of Edith, on low knolls
That dimpling died into each other, huts
At random scatter'd, each a nest in bloom
Her art, her hand, her counsel all had wrought
About them here was one that, summer-blanch'd,
Was parcel-bearded with the traveller's-joy

In Autumn, parcel ivy-clad; and here
The warm-blue breathings of a hidden hearth
Broke from a bower of vine and honeysuckle:
One look'd all rosetree, and another wore
A close-set robe of jasmine sown with stars:
This had a rosy sea of gillyflowers
About it; this, a milky-way on earth,
Like visions in the Northern dreamer's heavens,
A lily-avenue climbing to the doors;
One, almost to the martin-haunted eaves
A summer burial deep in hollyhocks;
Each, its own charm; and Edith's everywhere;
And Edith ever visitant with him,
He but less loved than Edith, of her poor:
For she – so lowly-lovely and so loving,
Queenly responsive when the loyal hand
Rose from the clay it work'd in as she past,
Not sowing hedgerow texts and passing by,
Nor dealing goodly counsel from a height
That makes the lowest hate it, but a voice
Of comfort and an open hand of help,
A splendid presence flattering the poor roofs
Revered as theirs, but kindlier than themselves
To ailing wife or wailing infancy
Or old bedridden palsy, – was adored;
He, loved for her and for himself. A grasp
Having the warmth and muscle of the heart,
A childly way with children, and a laugh
Ringing like proven golden coinage true,
Were no false passport to that easy realm,
Where once with Leolin at her side the girl,
Nursing a child, and turning to the warmth
The tender pink five-beaded baby-soles,
Heard the good mother softly whisper, 'Bless,
God bless 'em: marriages are made in Heaven.'

A flash of semi-jealousy clear'd it to her.
My lady's Indian kinsman unannounced
With half a score of swarthy faces came.
His own, tho' keen and bold and soldierly,
Sear'd by the close ecliptic, was not fair;
Fairer his talk, a tongue that ruled the hour,
Tho' seeming boastful: so when first he dash'd
Into the chronicle of a deedful day,
Sir Aylmer half forgot his lazy smile
Of patron 'Good! my lady's kinsman! good!'

My lady with her fingers interlock'd,
And rotatory thumbs on silken knees,
Call'd all her vital spirits into each ear
To listen: unawares they flitted off,
Busying themselves about the flowerage
That stood from out a stiff brocade in which,
The meteor of a splendid season, she,
Once with this kinsman, ah so long ago,
Stept thro' the stately minuet of those days:
But Edith's eager fancy hurried with him
Snatch'd thro' the perilous passes of his life:
Till Leolin ever watchful of her eye
Hated him with a momentary hate.
Wife-hunting, as the rumour ran, was he:
I know not, for he spoke not, only shower'd
His oriental gifts on everyone
And most on Edith: like a storm he came.
And shook the house, and like a storm he went.

Among the gifts he left her (possibly
He flow'd and ebb'd uncertain, to return
When others had been tested) there was one,
A dagger, in rich sheath with jewels on it
Sprinkled about in gold that branch'd itself
Fine as ice-ferns on January panes
Made by a breath. I know not whence at first,
Nor of what race, the work; but as he told
Tho story, storming a hill-fort of thieves
He got it; for their captain after fight,
His comrades having fought their last below,
Was climbing up the valley; at whom he shot:
Down from the beetling crag to which he clung
Tumbled the tawny rascal at his feet,
This dagger with him, which when now admired
By Edith whom his pleasure was to please,
At once the costly Sahib yielded to her.

And Leolin, coming after he was gone,
Tost over all her presents petulantly:
And when she show'd the wealthy scabbard, saying
'Look what a lovely piece of workmanship!'
Slight was his answer 'Well – I care not for it:'
Then playing with the blade he prick'd his hand,
'A gracious gift to give a lady, this!'
'But would it be more gracious' ask'd the girl
'Were I to give this gift of his to one

That is no lady?' 'Gracious? No' said he.
'Me? – but I cared not for it. O pardon me,
I seem to be ungraciousness itself.'
'Take it' she added sweetly, 'tho' his gift;
For I am more ungracious ev'n than you,
I care not for it either;' and he said
'Why then I love it:' but Sir Aylmer past,
And neither loved nor liked the thing he heard.

    The next day came a neighbour. Blues and reds
They talk'd of: blues were sure of it, he thought:
Then of the latest fox – where started – kill'd
In such a bottom: 'Peter had the brush,
My Peter, first': and did Sir Aylmer know
That great pock-pitten fellow had been caught?
Then made his pleasure echo, hand to hand,
And rolling as it were the substance of it
Between his palms a moment up and down –
'The birds were warm, the birds were warm upon him;
We have him now:' and had Sir Aylmer heard –
Nay, but he must – the land was ringing of it –
This blacksmith-border marriage – one they knew –
Raw from the nursery – who could trust a child?
That cursed France with her egalities!
And did Sir Aylmer (deferentially
With nearing chair and lower'd accent) think –
For people talk'd – that it was wholly wise
To let that handsome fellow Averill walk
So freely with his daughter? people talk'd –
The boy might get a notion into him;
The girl might be entangled ere she knew.
Sir Aylmer Aylmer slowly stiffening spoke:
'The girl and boy, Sir, know their differences!'
'Good' said his friend, 'but watch! 'and he 'enough,
More than enough, Sir! I can guard my own.'
They parted, and Sir Aylmer Aylmer watch'd.

    Pale, for on her the thunders of the house
Had fallen first, was Edith that same night;
Pale as the Jephtha's daughter, a rough piece
Of early rigid colour, under which
Withdrawing by the counter door to that
Which Leolin open'd, she cast back upon him
A piteous glance, and vanish'd. He, as one
Caught in a burst of unexpected storm,
And pelted with outrageous epithets,

Turning beheld the Powers of the House
On either side the hearth, indignant, her
Cooling her false cheek with a featherfan,
Him glaring, by his own stale devil spurr'd,
And, like a beast hard-ridden, breathing hard.
'Ungenerous, dishonourable, base,
Presumptuous! trusted as he was with her,
The sole succeeder to their wealth, their lands,
The last remaining pillar of their house,
The one transmitter of their ancient name,
Their child.' 'Our child!' 'Our heiress!' 'Ours!' for still,
Like echoes from beyond a hollow, came
Her sicklier iteration. Last he said
'Boy, mark me! for your fortunes are to make.
I swear you shall not make them out of mine.
Now inasmuch as you have practised on her
Perplext her, made her half forget herself,
Swerve from her duty to herself and us –
Things in an Aylmer deem'd impossible,
Far as we track ourselves – I say that this –
Else I withdraw favour and countenance
From you and yours for ever – shall you do.
Sir, when you see her – but you shall not see her –
No, you shall write, and not to her, but me:
And you shall say that having spoken with me,
And after look'd into yourself, you find
That you meant nothing – as indeed you know
That you meant nothing. Such a match as this!
Impossible, prodigious!' These were words,
As meted by his measure of himself
Arguing boundless forbearance: after which,
And Leolin's horror-stricken answer, 'I
So foul a traitor to myself and her,
Never oh never,' for about as long
As the wind-hover hangs in balance, paused
Sir Aylmer reddening from the storm within,
Then broke all bonds of courtesy, and crying
'Boy, should I find you by my doors again,
My men shall lash you from them like a dog;
Hence!' with a sudden execration drove
The footstool from before him, and arose;
So, stammering 'scoundrel' out of teeth that ground
As in a dreadful dream, while Leolin still
Retreated half-aghast, the fierce old man
Follow'd, and under his own lintel stood
Storming with lifted hands, a hoary face

Meet for the reverence of the hearth, but now,
Beneath a pale and unimpassion'd moon,
Vext with unworthy madness, and deform'd.

Slowly and conscious of the rageful eye
That watch'd him, till he heard the ponderous door
Close, crashing with long echoes thro' the land,
Went Leolin; then, his passions all in flood
And masters of his motion, furiously
Down thro' the bright lawns to his brother's ran,
And foam'd away his heart at Averill's ear:
Whom Averill solaced as he might, amazed:
The man was his, had been his father's, friend:
He must have seen, himself had seen it long;
He must have known, himself had known: besides,
He never yet had set his daughter forth
Here in the woman-markets of the west,
Where our Caucasians let themselves be sold.
Some one, he thought, had slander'd Leolin to him.
'Brother, for I have loved you more as son
Than brother, let me tell you: I myself –
What is their pretty saying? jilted, is it?
Jilted I was: I say it for your peace.
Pain'd, and, as bearing in myself the shame
The woman should have borne, humiliated,
I lived for years a stunted sunless life;
Till after our good parents past away
Watching your growth, I seem'd again to grow.
Leolin, I almost sin in envying you:
The very whitest lamb in all my fold
Loves you: I know her: the worst thought she has
Is whiter even than her pretty hand:
She must prove true: for, brother, where two fight
The strongest wins, and truth and love are strength,
And you are happy: let her parents be.'

But Leolin cried out the more upon them –
Insolent, brainless, heartless! heiress, wealth,
Their wealth, their heiress! wealth enough was theirs
For twenty matches. Were he lord of this,
Why twenty boys and girls should marry on it,
And forty blest ones bless him, and himself
Be wealthy still, ay wealthier. He believed
This filthy marriage-hindering Mammon made
The harlot of the cities: nature crost
Was mother of the foul adulteries

That saturate soul with body. Name, too! name
Their ancient name! they *might* be proud; its worth
Was being Edith's. Ah how pale she had look'd
Darling, to-night! they must have rated her
Beyond all tolerance. These old pheasant-lords,
These partridge-breeders of a thousand years,
Who had mildew'd in their thousands, doing nothing
Since Egbert – why, the greater their disgrace!
Fall back upon a name! rest, rot in that!
Not *keep* it noble, make it nobler? fools,
With such a vantage-ground for nobleness!
He had known a man, a quintessence of man,
The life of all – who madly loved – and he,
Thwarted by one of these old father-fools,
Had rioted his life out, and made an end.
He would not do it! her sweet face and faith
Held him from that: but he had powers, he knew it:
Back would he to his studies, make a name,
Name, fortune too: the world should ring of him
To shame these mouldy Aylmers in their graves:
Chancellor, or what is greatest would he be –
'O brother, I am grieved to learn your grief –
Give me my fling, and let me say my say.'

    At which, like one that sees his own excess,
And easily forgives it as his own.
He laugh'd; and then was mute; but presently
Wept like a storm: and honest Averill seeing
How low his brother's mood had fallen, fetch'd
His richest beeswing from a binn reserved
For banquets, praised the waning red, and told
The vintage – when *this* Aylmer came of age –
Then drank and past it; till at length the two,
Tho' Leolin flamed and fell again, agreed
That much allowance must be made for men.
After an angry dream this kindlier glow
Faded with morning, but his purpose held.

    Yet once by night again the lovers met,
A perilous meeting under the tall pines
That darken'd all the northward of her Hall.
Him, to her meek and modest bosom prest
In agony, she promised that no force,
Persuasion, no, nor death could alter her:
He, passionately hopefuller, would go,
Labour for his own Edith, and return

In such a sunlight of prosperity
He should not be rejected. 'Write to me,
They loved me, and because I love their child
They hate me: there is war between us, dear,
Which breaks all bonds but ours; we must remain
Sacred to one another.' So they talk'd,
Poor children, for their comfort: the wind blew;
The rain of heaven, and their own bitter tears,
Tears, and the careless rain of heaven, mixt
Upon their faces, as they kiss'd each other
In darkness, and above them roar'd the pine.

So Leolin went, and as we task ourselves
To learn a language known but smatteringly
In phrases here and there at random, toil'd
Mastering the lawless science of our law,
That codeless myriad of precedent,
That wilderness of single instances,
Thro' which a few, by wit or fortune led,
May beat a pathway out to wealth and fame.
The jests, that flash'd about the pleader's room,
Lightning of the hour, the pun, the scurrilous tale, –
Old scandals buried now seven decads deep
In other scandals that have lived and died,
And left the living scandal that shall die –
Were dead to him already; bent as he was
To make disproof of scorn, and strong in hopes.
And prodigal of all brain-labour he,
Charier of sleep, and wine, and exercise,
Except when for a breathing-while at eve,
Some niggard fraction of an hour, he ran
Beside the river-bank: and then indeed
Harder the times were, and the hands of power
Were bloodier, and the according hearts of men
Seem'd harder too- but the soft river-breeze,
Which fann'd the gardens of that rival rose
Yet fragrant in a heart remembering
His former talks with Edith, on him breathed
Far purelier in his rushings to and fro,
After his books, to flush his blood with air,
Then to his books again. My lady's cousin,
Half-sickening of his pension'd afternoon,
Drove in upon the student once or twice,
Ran a Malayan muck against the times,
Had golden hopes for France and all mankind,
Answer'd all queries touching those at home

With a heaved shoulder and a saucy smile,
And fain had haled him out into the world,
And air'd him there: his nearer friend would say
'Screw not the chord too sharply lest it snap.'
Then left alone he pluck'd her dagger forth
From where his worldless heart had kept it warm,
Kissing his vows upon it like a knight.
And wrinkled benchers often talk'd of him
Approvingly, and prophesied his rise:
For heart, I think, help'd head: her letters too,
Tho' far between, and coming fitfully
Like broken music, written as she found
Or made occasion, being strictly watch'd,
Charm'd him thro' every labyrinth till he saw
An end, a hope, a light breaking upon him.

But they that cast her spirit into flesh,
Her worldly-wise begetters, plagued themselves
To sell her, those good parents, for her good.
Whatever eldest-born of rank or wealth
Might lie within their compass, him they lured
Into their net made pleasant by the baits
Of gold and beauty, wooing him to woo.
So month by month the noise about their doors,
And distant blaze of those dull banquets, made
The nightly wirer of their innocent hare
Falter before he took it. All in vain.
Sullen, defiant, pitying, wroth, return'd
Leolin's rejected rivals from their suit
So often, that the folly taking wings
Slipt o'er those lazy limits down the wind
With rumour, and became in other fields
A mockery to the yeomen over ale,
And laughter to their lords: but those at home,
As hunters round a hunted creature draw
The cordon close and closer toward the death,
Narrow'd her goings out and comings in;
Forbad her first the house of Averill,
Then closed her access to the wealthier farms,
Last from her own home-circle of the poor
They barr'd her: yet she bore it: yet her cheek
Kept colour: wondrous! but, O mystery!
What amulet drew her down to that old oak,
So old, that twenty years before, a part
Falling had let appear the brand of John –
Once grovelike, each huge arm a tree, but now

The broken base of a black tower, a cave
Of touchwood, with a single flourishing spray.
There the manorial lord too curiously
Raking in that millennial touchwood-dust:
Found for himself a bitter treasure-trove;
Burst his own wyvern on the seal, and read
Writhing a letter from his child, for which
Came at the moment Leolin's emissary
A crippled lad, and coming turn'd to fly,
But scared with threats of jail and halter gave
To him that fluster'd his poor parish wits
The letter which he brought, and swore besides
To play their go-between as heretofore
Nor let them know themselves betray'd; and then,
Soul-stricken at their kindness to him, went
Hating his own lean heart and miserable.

Thenceforward oft from out a despot dream
The father panting woke, and oft, as dawn
Aroused the black republic on his elms,
Sweeping the frothfly from the fescue brush'd
Thro' the dim meadow toward his treasure-trove,
Seized it, took home, and to my lady, – who made
A downward crescent of her minion mouth,
Listless in all despondence, – read; and tore,
As if the living passion symbol'd there
Were living nerves to feel the rent; and burnt,
Now chafing at his own great self defied,
Now striking on huge stumbling-blocks of scorn
In babyisms, and dear diminutives
Scatter'd all over the vocabulary
Of such a love as like a chidden child,
After much wailing, hush'd itself at last
Hopeless of answer: then tho' Averill wrote
And bad him with good heart sustain himself –
All would be well – the lover heeded not,
But passionately restless came and went,
And rustling once at night about the place,
There by a keeper shot at, slightly hurt,
Raging return'd: nor was it well for her
Kept to the garden now, and grove of pines,
Watch'd even there, and one was set to watch
The watcher, and Sir Aylmer watch'd them all,
Yet bitterer from his readings: once indeed,
Warm'd with his wines, or taking pride in her,
She look'd so sweet, he kiss'd her tenderly

Not knowing what possess'd him: that one kiss
Was Leolin's one strong rival upon earth;
Seconded, for my lady follow'd suit,
Seem'd hope's returning rose: and then ensued
A Martin's summer of his faded love,
Or ordeal by kindness; after this
He seldom crost his child without a sneer;
The mother flow'd in shallower acrimonies:
Never one kindly smile, one kindly word:
So that the gentle creature shut from all
Her charitable use, and face to face
With twenty months of silence, slowly lost
Nor greatly cared to lose, her hold on life.
Last, some low fever ranging round to spy
The weakness of a people or a house,
Like flies that haunt a hound, or deer, or men,
Or almost all that is, hurting the hurt –
Save Christ as we believe him – found the girl
And flung her down upon a couch of fire,
Where careless of the household faces near,
And crying upon the name of Leolin,
She, and with her the race of Aylmer, past.

Star to star vibrates light: may soul to soul
Strike thro' a finer element of her own?
So, – from afar, – touch as at once? or why
That night, that moment, when she named his name,
Did the keen shriek 'yes love, yes Edith, yes,'
Shrill, till the comrade of his chambers woke,
And came upon him half-arisen from sleep,
With a weird bright eye, sweating and trembling,
His hair as it were crackling into flames,
His body half flung forward in pursuit,
And his long arms stretch'd as to grasp a flyer:
Nor knew he wherefore he had made the cry;
And being much befool'd and idioted
By the rough amity of the other, sank
As into sleep again. The second day,
My lady's Indian kinsman rushing in,
A breaker of the bitter news from home,
Found a dead man, a letter edged with death
Beside him, and the dagger which himself
Gave Edith, redden'd with no bandit's blood:
'From Edith' was engraven on the blade.

Then Averill went and gazed upon his death.

And when he came again, his flock believed –
Beholding how the years which are not Time's
Had blasted him – that many thousand days
Were clipt by horror from his term of life.
Yet the sad mother, for the second death
Scarce touch'd her thro' that nearness of the first,
And being used to find her pastor texts,
Sent to the harrow'd brother, praying him
To speak before the people of her child,
And fixt the Sabbath. Darkly that day rose:
Autumn's mock sunshine of the faded woods
Was all the life of it; for hard on these,
A breathless burthen of low-folded heavens
Stifled and chill'd at once: but every roof
Sent out a listener: many too had known
Edith among the hamlets round, and since
The parents' harshness and the hapless loves
And double death were widely murmur'd, left
Their own grey tower, or plain-faced tabernacle,
To hear him; all in mourning these, and those
With blots of it about them, ribbon, grove
Or kerchief; while the church, – one night, except
For greenish glimmerings thro' the lancets, – made
Still paler the pale head of him, who tower'd
Above them, with his hopes in either grave.

Long o'er his bent brows linger'd Averill,
His face magnetic to the hand from which
Livid he pluck'd it forth, and labour'd thro'
His brief prayer-prelude, gave the verse 'Behold,
Your house is left unto you desolate!'
But lapsed into so long a pause again
As half amazed half frighted all his flock:
Then from his height and loneliness of grief
Bore down in flood, and dash'd his angry heart
Against the desolations of the world.

Never since our bad earth became one sea,
Which rolling o'er the palaces of the proud,
And all but those who knew the living God –
Eight that were left to make a purer world –
When since had flood, fire, earthquake, thunder, wrought
Such waste and havoc as the idolatries,
Which from the low light of mortality
Shot up their shadows to the Heaven of Heavens,
And worshipt their own darkness as the Highest?

'Gash thyself, priest, and honour thy brute Baäl,
And to thy worst self sacrifice thyself,
For with thy worst self hast thou clothed thy God.
Then came a Lord in no wise like to Baäl.
The babe shall lead the lion. Surely now
The wilderness shall blossom as the rose.
Crown thyself, worm, and worship thine own lusts! —
No coarse and blockish God of acreage
Stands at thy gate for thee to grovel to —
Thy God is far diffused in noble groves
And princely halls, and farms, and flowing lawns,
And heaps of living gold that daily grow,
And title-scrolls and gorgeous heraldries.
In such a shape dost thou behold thy God.
Thou wilt not gash thy flesh for *him;* for thine
Fares richly, in fine linen, not a hair
Ruffled upon the scarfskin, even while
The deathless ruler of thy dying house
Is wounded to the death that cannot die;
And tho' thou numberest with the followers
Of One who cried "leave all and follow me."
Thee therefore with His light about thy feet
Thee with His message ringing in thine ears,
Thee shall thy brother man, the Lord from Heaven,
Born of a village girl, carpenter's son,
Wonderful, Prince of peace, the Mighty God,
Count the more base idolater of the two;
Crueller: as not passing thro' the fire
Bodies, but souls — thy children's — thro' the smoke,
The blight of low desires — darkening thine own
To thine own likeness; or if one of these,
Thy better born unhappily from thee,
Should, as by miracle, grow straight and fair —
Friends, I was bid to speak of such a one
By those who most have cause to sorrow for her —
Fairer than Rachel by the palmy well,
Fairer than Ruth among the fields of corn,
Fair as the Angel that said "hail" she seem'd,
Who entering fill'd the house with sudden light.
For so mine own was brighten'd: where indeed
The roof so lowly but that beam of Heaven
Dawn'd sometime thro' the doorway? whose the babe
Too ragged to be fondled on her lap,
Warm'd at her bosom? The poor child of shame,
The common care whom no one cared for, leapt
To greet her, wasting his forgotten heart,

As with the mother he had never known,
In gambols; for her fresh and innocent eyes
Had such a star of morning in their blue
That all neglected places of the field
Broke into nature's music when they saw her.
Low was her voice, but won mysterious way
Thro' the seal'd ear to which a louder one
Was all but silence – free of alms her hand –
The hand that robed your cottage-walls with flowers
Has often toil'd to clothe your little ones;
How often placed upon the sick man's brow
Cool'd it, or laid his feverous pillow smooth!
Had you one sorrow and she shared it not?
One burthen and she would not lighten it?
One spiritual doubt she did not soothe?
Or when some heat of difference sparkled out,
How sweetly would she glide between your wraths,
And steal you from each other! for she walk'd
Wearing the light yoke of that Lord of love,
Who still'd the rolling wave of Galilee!
And one – of him I was not bid to speak –
Was always with her, whom you also knew.
Him too you loved, for he was worthy love.
And these had been together from the first;
They might have been together till the last.
Friends, this frail bark of ours, when sorely tried,
May wreck itself without the pilot's guilt,
Without the captain's knowledge: hope with me.
Whose shame is that, if he went hence with shame?
Nor mine the fault, if losing both of these
I cry to vacant chairs and widow'd walls,
"My house is left unto me desolate." '

While thus he spoke, his hearers wept; but some,
Sons of the glebe, with other frowns than those
That knit themselves for summer shadow, scowl'd
At their great lord. He, when it seem'd he saw
No pale sheet-lightnings from afar, but fork'd
Of the near storm, and aiming at his head,
Sat anger-charm'd from sorrow, soldierlike,
Erect: but when the preacher's cadence flow'd
Softening thro' all the gentle attributes
Of his lost child, the wife, who watch'd his face,
Paled at a sudden twitch of his iron mouth;
And 'O pray God that he hold up' she thought
'Or surely I shall shame myself and him.'

'Nor yours the blame – for who beside your hearths
Can take her place – if echoing me you cry
"Our house is left unto us desolate"?
But thou, O thou that killest, hadst thou known,
O thou that stonest, hadst thou understood
The things belonging to thy peace and ours!
Is there no prophet but the voice that calls
Doom upon kings, or in the waste "Repent "?
Is not our own child on the narrow way
Who down to those that saunter in the broad
Cries "come up hither,'' as a prophet to us?
Is there no stoning save with flint and rock?
Yes, as the dead we weep for testify –
No desolation but by sword and fire?
Yes, as your moanings witness, and myself
Am lonelier, darker, earthlier for my loss.
Give me your prayers, for he is past your prayers,
Not past the living fount of pity in Heaven.
But I that thought myself long-suffering, meek,
Exceeding "poor in spirit" – how the words
Have twisted back upon themselves, and mean
Vileness, we are grown so proud – I wish'd my voice
A rushing tempest of the wrath of God
To blow these sacrifices thro' the world –
Sent like the twelve-divided concubine
To inflame the tribes: but there – out yonder – earth
Lightens from her own central Hell – O there
The red fruit of an old idolatry –
The heads of chiefs and princes fall so fast,
They cling together in the ghastly sack –
The land all shambles – naked marriages
Flash from the bridge, and ever-murder'd France,
By shores that darken with the gathering wolf,
Runs in a river of blood to the sick sea.
Is this a time to madden madness then?
Was this a time for these to flaunt their pride?
May Pharaoh's darkness, folds as dense as those
Which hid the Holiest from the people's eyes
Ere the great death, shroud this great sin from all!
Doubtless our narrow world must canvass it:
O rather pray for those and pity them,
Who thro' their own desire accomplish'd bring
Their own grey hairs with sorrow to the grave –
Who broke the bond which they desired to break,
Which else had link'd their race with times to come –
Who wove coarse webs to snare her purity,

Grossly contriving their dear daughter's good –
Poor souls, and knew not what they did, but sat
Ignorant, devising their own daughter's death!
May not that earthly chastisement suffice?
Have not our love and reverence left them bare?
Will not another take their heritage?
Will there be children's laughter in their hall
For ever and for ever, or one stone
Left on another, or is it a light thing
That I their guest, their host, their ancient friend,
I made by these the last of all my race
Must cry to these the last of theirs, as cried
Christ ere His agony to those that swore
Not by the temple but the gold, and made
Their own traditions God, and slew the Lord,
And left their memories a world's curse – "Behold,
Your house is left unto you desolate"?'

   Ended he had not, but she brook'd no more:
Long since her heart had beat remorselessly,
Her crampt-up sorrow pain'd her, and a sense
Of meanness in her unresisting life.
Then their eyes vext her; for on entering
He had cast the curtains of their seat aside –
Black velvet of the costliest – she herself
Had seen to that: fain had she closed them now,
Yet dared not stir to do it, only near'd
Her husband inch by inch, but when she laid,
Wifelike, her hand in one of his, he veil'd
His face with the other, and at once, as falls
A creeper when the prop is broken, fell
The woman shrieking at his feet, and swoon'd.
Then her own people bore along the nave
Her pendent hands, and narrow meagre face
Seam'd with the shallow cares of fifty years:
And her the Lord of all the landscape round
Ev'n to its last horizon, and of all
Who peer'd at him so keenly, follow'd out
Tall and erect, but in the middle aisle
Reel'd, as a footsore ox in crowded ways
Stumbling across the market to his death,
Unpitied; for he groped as blind, and seem'd
Always about to fall, grasping the pews
And oaken finials till he touch'd the door;
Yet to the lychgate, where his chariot stood,
Strode from the porch, tall and erect again.

But nevermore did either pass the gate
Save under pall with bearers. In one month,
Thro' weary and yet ever wearier hours,
The childless mother went to seek her child;
And when he felt the silence of his house
About him, and the change and not the change,
And those fixt eyes of painted ancestors
Staring for ever from their gilded walls
On him their last descendant, his own head
Began to droop, to fall; the man became
Imbecile; his one word was 'desolate';
Dead for two years before his death was he;
But when the second Christmas came, escaped
His keepers, and the silence which he felt,
To find a deeper in the narrow gloom
By wife and child, nor wanted at his end
The dark retinue reverencing death
At golden thresholds; nor from tender hearts,
And those who sorrow'd o'er a vanish'd race,
Pity, the violet on the tyrant's grave.
Then the great Hall was wholly broken down,
And the broad woodland parcell'd into farms;
And where the two contrived their daughter's good,
Lies the hawk's cast, the mole has made his run,
The hedgehog underneath the plantain bores,
The rabbit fondles his own harmless face,
The slow-worm creeps, and the thin weasel there
Follows the mouse, and all is open field.

Northern Farmer

Old Style

I

Wheer 'asta beän saw long and meä liggin' 'ere aloän?
Noorse? thoort nowt o' a noorse: whoy, Doctor's abeän an' agoän:
Says that I moänt 'a naw moor yaäle: but I beänt a fool:
Git ma my yaäle, for I beänt a-gooin' to breäk my rule.

II

Doctors, they knaws nowt, for a says what's nawways true:
Naw soort o' koind o' use to saäy the things that a do.
I've 'ed my point o' yaäle ivry noight sin' I bean 'ere,
An' I've 'ed my quart ivry market-noight for foorty year.

III

Parson's a beän loikewoise, an' a sittin' 'ere o' my bed.
'The amoighty's a taäkin o' you to 'issén, my friend,' a said,
An' a towd ma my sins, an's toithe were due, an' I gied it in hond;
I done my duty by un, as I 'a done by the lond.

IV

Larn'd a ma' beä. I reckons I 'annot sa mooch to larn.
But a cost oop, thot a did, 'boot Bessy Marris's barn.
Thof a knaws I hallus voäted wi' Squoire an' choorch an' staäte,
An' i' the woost o' toimes I wur niver agin the raäte.

V

An' I hallus comed to 's choorch afoor moy Sally wur deäd,
An' 'eerd un a bummin' awaäy loike a buzzard-clock ower my yeäd,
An' I niver knaw'd whot a meän'd but I thowt a 'ad summut to saäy,
An I thowt a said whot a owt to 'a said an' I comed awaäy.

VI

Bessy Marris's barn! tha knaws she laäid it to meä.
Mowt 'a beän, mayhap, for she wur a bad un, sheä.
'Siver, I kep un, I kep un, my lass, tha mun understond;
I done my duty by un as I 'a done by the lond.

VII

But Parson a comes an' a goos, an' a says it eäsy an' freeä
'The amoighty's a taäkin o' you to 'issén, my friend,' says 'eä.
I weänt saäy men be loiars, thof summun said it in 'aäste:
But a reäds wonn sarmin a weeäk, an' I 'a stubb'd Thornaby waäste.

VIII

D'ya moind the waäste, my lass? naw, naw, tha was not born then;
Theer wur a boggle in it, I often 'eerd un mysen;
Moäst loike a butter-bump, for I 'eerd un aboot an' aboot,
But I stubb'd un oop wi' the lot, an' raäved an' rembled un oot.

IX

Keäper's it wur; fo' they fun un theer a-laäid on 'is faäce
Doon i' the woild 'enemies afoor I comed to the plaäce.
Noäks or Thimbleby — toner'ed shot un as deäd as a naäil.
Noäks wur 'ang'd for it oop at 'soize — but git ma my yaäle.

X

Dubbut looäk at the waäste: theer warn't not feäd for a cow:
Nowt at all but bracken an' fuzz, an' looäk at it now —
Warnt worth nowt a haäcre, an' now theer's lots o' feäd,
Fourscore yows upon it an' some on it doon in seäd.

XI

Nobbut a bit on it's left, an' I meän'd to 'a stubb'd it at fall,
Done it ta-year I meän'd, an' runn'd plow thruff it an' all,
If godamoighty an' parson 'ud nobbut let ma aloän.
Meä, wi' haäte oonderd haäcre o' Squoire's, an' lond o' my oän.

XII

Do godamoighty knaw what a's doing a-taäkin' o' meä?
I beänt wonn as saws 'ere a beän an' yonder a peä;
An' Squoire 'ull be sa mad an' all – a' dear a' dear!
And I 'a monaged for Squoire come Michaelmas thirty year.

XIII

A mowt 'a taäken Joänes, as 'ant 'aäpoth o' sense,
Or a mowt 'a taäken Robins – a niver mended a fence:
But godamoighty a moost taäke meä an' taäke ma now
Wi 'auf the cows to cauve an' Thornaby holms to plow!

XIV

Looäk 'ow quoloty smoiles when they sees ma a passin' by,
Says to thessén naw doot, what a mon a beä sewer-ly!
For they knaws what I beän to Squoire sin fust a comed to the 'All;
I done my duty by Squoire an' I done my duty by all.

XV

Squoire's in Lunnon, an' summun I reckons 'ull 'a to wroite,
For who's to howd the lond ater meä thot muddles ma quoit;
Sartin-sewer I beä, thot a weänt niver give it to Joänes,
Noither a moänt to Robins – a niver rembles the stoäns.

XVI

But summun 'ull come ater meä mayhap wi' 'is kittle o' steam
Huzzin' an' maäzin' the blessed feälds wi' the Divil's oän teäm.
Gin I mun doy I mun doy, an' loife they says is sweet,
But gin I mun doy I mun doy, for I couldn abear to see it.

XVII

What atta stannin' theer for, an' doesn bring ma the yaäle?
Doctor's a 'tottler, lass, an a 's hallus i' the owd taäle;
I weänt breäk rules for Doctor, a knaws naw moor nor a floy;
Git ma my yaäle I tell tha, an' gin I mun doy I mun doy.

The Voyage

I

We left behind the painted buoy
    That tosses at the harbour-mouth;
And madly danced our hearts with joy,
    As fast we fleeted to the South:
How fresh was every sight and sound
    On open main or winding shore!
We knew the merry world was round,
    And we might sail for evermore.

II

Warm broke the breeze against the brow,
    Dry sang the tackle, sang the sail:
The Lady's-head upon the prow
    Caught the shrill salt, and sheer'd the gale.
The broad seas swell'd to meet the keel,
    And swept behind: so quick the run,
We felt the good ship shake and reel,
    We seem'd to sail into the Sun!

III

How oft we saw the Sun retire,
    And burn the threshold of the night,
Fall from his Ocean-lane of fire,
    And sleep beneath his pillar'd light!
How oft the purple-skirted robe
    Of twilight slowly downward drawn,
As thro' the slumber of the globe
    Again we dash'd into the dawn!

IV

New stars all night above the brim
    Of waters lighten'd into view,
They climb'd as quickly, for the rim
    Changed every moment as we flew,
Far ran the naked moon across
    The houseless ocean's heaving field,
Or flying shone, the silver boss
    Of her own halo's dusky shield;

V

The peaky islet shifted shapes,
    High towns on hills were dimly seen,
We past long lines of Northern capes

And dewy Northern meadows green.
We came to warmer waves, and deep
   Across the boundless east we drove,
Where those long swells of breaker sweep
   The nutmeg rocks and isles of clove

VI

By peaks that flamed, or, all in shade,
   Gloom'd the low coast and quivering brine
With ashy rains, that spreading made
   Fantastic plume or sable pine;
By sands and steaming flats, and floods
   Of mighty mouth, we scudded fast,
And hills and scarlet-mingled woods
   Glow'd for a moment as we past.

VII

O hundred shores of happy climes,
   How swiftly stream'd ye by the bark!
At times the whole sea burn'd, at times
   With wakes of fire we tore the dark;
At times a carven craft would shoot
   From havens hid in fairy bowers,
With naked limbs and flowers and fruit,
   But we nor paused for fruit nor flowers.

VIII

For one fair Vision ever fled
   Down the waste waters day and night,
And still we follow'd where she led,
   In hope to gain upon her flight.
Her face was evermore unseen,
   And fixt upon the far sea-line;
But each man murmur'd 'O my Queen,
   I follow till I make thee mine'

IX

And now we lost her, now she gleam'd
   Like Fancy made of golden air,
Now nearer to the prow she seem'd
   Like Virtue firm, like Knowledge fair,
Now high on waves that idly burst
   Like Heavenly Hope she crown'd the sea,
And now, the bloodless point reversed,
   She bore the blade of Liberty.

X

And only one among us – him
　　We pleased not – he was seldom pleased:
He saw not far: his eyes were dim:
　　But ours he swore were all diseased.
'A ship of fools' he shriek'd in spite,
　　'A ship of fools' he sneer'd and wept.
And overboard one stormy night
　　He cast his body, and on we swept.

XI

And never sail of ours was furl'd,
　　Nor anchor dropt at eve or morn;
We loved the glories of the world,
　　But laws of nature were our scorn;
For blasts would rise and rave and cease,
　　But whence were those that drove the sail
Across the whirlwind's heart of peace,
　　And to and thro' the counter-gale?

XII

Again to colder climes we came,
　　For still we follow'd where she led:
Now mate is blind and captain lame,
　　And half the crew are sick or dead.
But blind or lame or sick or sound
　　We follow that which flies before:
We know the merry world is round,
　　And we may sail for evermore.

In the Valley of Cauteretz

All along the valley, stream that flashest white,
Deepening thy voice with the deepening of the night,
All along the valley, where thy waters flow,
I walk'd with one I loved two and thirty years ago.
All along the valley while I walk'd to-day,
The two and thirty years were a mist that rolls away;
For all along the valley, down thy rocky bed
Thy living voice to me was as the voice of the dead,
And all along the valley, by rock and cave and tree,
The voice of the dead was a living voice to me.

The Flower

Once in a golden hour
   I cast to earth a seed.
Up there came a flower,
   The people said, a weed.

To and fro they went
   Thro' my garden-bower,
And muttering discontent
   Cursed me and my flower.

Then it grew so tall
   It wore a crown of light,
But thieves from o'er the wall
   Stole the seed by night.

Sow'd it far and wide
   By every town and tower,
Till all the people cried
   'Splendid is the flower.'

Read my little fable:
   He that runs may read.
Most can raise the flowers now,
   For all have got the seed.

And some are pretty enough,
   And some are poor indeed;
And now again the people
   Call it but a weed.

Requiescat

Fair is her cottage in its place,
   Where yon broad water sweetly slowly glides.
It sees itself from thatch to base
   Dream in the sliding tides.

And fairer she, but ah how soon to die!
   Her quiet dream of life this hour may cease.
Her peaceful being slowly passes by
   To some more perfect peace.

The Islet

'Whither, O whither love, shall we go,
For a score of sweet little summers or so?'
The sweet little wife of the singer said,
On the day that follow'd the day she was wed,
'Whither, O whither, love, shall we go?'
And the singer shaking his curly head
Turn'd as he sat, and struck the keys
There at his right with a sudden crash,
Singing, 'and shall it be over the seas
With a crew that is neither rude nor rash,
But a bevy of Eroses apple-cheek'd,
In a shallop of crystal ivory-beak'd,
With a satin sail of a ruby glow,
To a sweet little Eden on earth that I know,
A mountain islet pointed and peak'd;
Waves on a diamond shingle dash,
Cataract brooks to the ocean run,
Fairily-delicate palaces shine
Mixt with myrtle and clad with vine,
And overstream'd and silvery-streak'd
With many a rivulet high against the Sun
The facets of the glorious mountain flash
Above the valleys of palm and pine.'

'Thither, O thither, love, let us go.'

'No, no, no! For in all that exquisite isle, my dear,
There is but one bird with a musical throat,
And his compass is but of a single note,
That it makes one weary to hear.'

'Mock me not! mock me not! love, let us go.'

'No, love, no.
For the bud ever breaks into bloom on the tree,
And a storm never wakes on the lonely sea,
And a worm is there in the lonely wood,
That pierces the liver and blackens the blood,
And makes it a sorrow to be.'

A Dedication

Dear, near and true – no truer Time himself
Can prove you, tho' he make you evermore
Dearer and nearer, as the rapid of life
Shoots to the fall – take this and pray that he,
Who wrote it, honouring your sweet faith in him,
May trust himself; and spite of praise and scorn,
As one who feels the immeasurable world,
Attain the wise indifference of the wise;
And after Autumn past – if left to pass
His autumn into seeming-leafless days –
Draw toward the long frost and longest night,
Wearing his wisdom lightly, like the fruit
Which in our winter woodland looks a flower.

Boädicea

While about the shore of Mona those Neronian legionaries
Burnt and broke the grove and altar of the Druid and Druidess,
Far in the East Boädicéa, standing loftily charioted,
Mad and maddening all that heard her in her fierce volubility,
Girt by half the tribes of Britain, near the colony Cámulodúne,
Yell'd and shriek'd between her daughters o'er a wild confederacy.

'They that scorn the tribes and call us Britain's barbarous populaces,
Did they hear me, would they listen, did they pity me supplicating?
Shall I heed them in their anguish? shall I brook to be supplicated?
Hear Icenian, Catieuchlanian, hear Coritanian, Trinobant!
Must their ever-ravening eagle's beak and talon annihilate us?
Tear the noble heart of Britain, leave it gorily quivering?
Bark an answer, Britain's raven! bark and blacken innumerable,
Blacken round the Roman carrion, make the carcass a skeleton,
Kite and kestrel, wolf and wolfkin, from the wilderness, wallow in it,
Till the face of Bel be brighten'd, Taranis be propitiated.
Lo their colony half-defended! lo their colony, Cámulodúne!
There the horde of Roman robbers mock at a barbarous adversary.
There the hive of Roman liars worship a gluttonous emperor-idiot.
Such is Rome, and this her deity: hear it, Spirit of Cassivëlaún!

'Hear it, Gods! the Gods have heard it, O Icenian, O Coritanian!
Doubt not ye the Gods have answer'd, Catieuchlanian, Trinobant.
These have told us all their anger in miraculous utterances,
Thunder, a flying fire in heaven, a murmur heard aërially,
Phantom sound of blows descending, moan of an enemy massacred,
Phantom wail of women and children, multitudinous agonies.

Bloodily flow'd the Tamesa rolling phantom bodies of horses and men;
Then a phantom colony smoulder'd on the refluent estuary;
Lastly yonder yester-even, suddenly giddily tottering –
There was one who watch'd and told me – down their statue of Victory
    fell.
Lo their precious Roman bantling, lo the colony Cámulodúne,
Shall we teach it a Roman lesson? shall we care to be pitiful?
Shall we deal with it as an infant? shall we dandle it amorously?

   'Hear Icenian, Catieuchlanian, hear Coritanian, Trinobant!
While I roved about the forest, long and bitterly meditating,
There I heard them in the darkness, at the mystical ceremony,
Loosely robed in flying raiment, sang the terrible prophetesses.
"Fear not, isle of blowing woodland, isle of silvery parapets!
Tho' the Roman eagle shadow thee, tho' the gathering enemy narrow
    thee,
Thou shalt wax and he shall dwindle, thou shalt be the mighty one yet!
Thine the liberty, thine the glory, thine the deeds to be celebrated,
Thine the myriad-rolling ocean, light and shadow illimitable,
Thine the lands of lasting summer, many-blossoming Paradises,
Thine the North and thine the South and thine the battle-thunder of
    God."
So they chanted: how shall Britain light upon auguries happier?
So they chanted in the darkness, and there cometh a victory now.

   'Hear Icenian, Catieuchlanian, hear Coritanian, Trinobant!
Me the wife of rich Prasutagus, me the lover of liberty,
Me they seized and me they tortured, me they lash'd and humiliated,
Me the sport of ribald Veterans, mine of ruffian violators!
See they sit, they hide their faces, miserable in ignominy!
Wherefore in me burns an anger, not by blood to be satiated.
Lo the palaces and the temple, lo the colony Cámulodúne!
There they ruled, and thence they wasted all the flourishing territory,
Thither at their will they haled the yellow-ringleted Britoness –
Bloodily, bloodily fall the battle-axe, unexhausted, inexorable.
Shout Icenian, Catieuchlanian, shout Coritanian, Trinobant,
Till the victim hear within and yearn to hurry precipitously
Like the leaf in a roaring whirlwind, like the smoke in a hurricane
    whirl'd.
Lo the colony, there they rioted in the city of Cúnobelíne!
There they drank in cups of emerald, there at tables of ebony lay,
Rolling on their purple couches in their tender effeminacy.
There they dwelt and there they rioted; there – there – they dwell no
    more.
Burst the gates, and burn the palaces, break the works of the statuary,
Take the hoary Roman head and shatter it, hold it abominable,
Cut the Roman boy to pieces in his lust and voluptuousness,

Lash the maiden into swooning, me they lash'd and humiliated,
Chop the breasts from off the mother, dash the brains of the little one
    out,
Up my Britons, on my chariot, on my chargers, trample them under
    us.'

So the Queen Boädicéa, standing loftily charioted,
Brandishing in her hand a dart and rolling glances lionesslike,
Yell'd and shrieked between her daughters in her fierce volubility.
Till her people all around the royal chariot agitated,
Madly dash'd the darts together, writhing barbarous lineäments,
Made the noise of frosty woodlands, when they shiver in January,
Roar'd as when the rolling breakers boom and blanch on the
    precipices,
Yell'd as when the winds of winter tear an oak on a promontory.
So the silent colony hearing her tumultuous adversaries
Clash the darts and on the buckler beat with rapid unanimous hand,
Thought on all her evil tyrannies, all her pitiless avarice,
Till she felt the heart within her fall and flutter tremulously,
Then her pulses at the clamouring of her enemy fainted away.
Out of evil evil flourishes, out of tyranny tyranny buds.
Ran the land with Roman slaughter, multitudinous agonies.
Perish'd many a maid and matron, many a valorous legionary.
Fell the colony, city, and citadel, London, Verulam, Cámulodúne.

The Captain

A Legend of the Navy

He that only rules by terror
    Doeth grievous wrong.
Deep as Hell I count his error.
    Let him hear my song.
Brave the Captain was: the seamen
    Made a gallant crew,
Gallant sons of English freemen,
    Sailors bold and true.
But they hated his oppression,
    Stern he was and rash;
So for every light transgression
    Doom'd them to the lash.
Day by day more harsh and cruel
    Seem'd the Captain's mood.
Secret wrath like smother'd fuel
    Burnt in each man's blood.

Yet he hoped to purchase glory,
    Hoped to make the name
Of his vessel great in story,
    Wheresoe'er he came.
So they past by capes and islands,
    Many a harbour-mouth,
Sailing under palmy highlands
    Far within the South.
On a day when they were going
    O'er the lone expanse,
In the north, her canvas flowing,
    Rose a ship of France.
Then the Captain's colour heighten'd,
    Joyful came his speech:
But a cloudy gladness lighten'd
    In the eyes of each.
'Chase,' he said: the ship flew forward,
    And the wind did blow;
Stately, lightly, went she Norward,
    Till she near'd the foe.
Then they look'd at him they hated,
    Had what they desired:
Mute with folded arms they waited –
    Not a gun was fired.
But they heard the foeman's thunder
    Roaring out their doom;
All the air was torn in sunder,
    Crashing went the boom,
Spars were splinter'd, decks were shatter'd,
    Bullets fell like rain;
Over mast and deck were scatter'd
    Blood and brains of men.
Spars were splinter'd; decks were broken:
    Every mother's son –
Down they dropt – no word was spoken –
    Each beside his gun.
On the decks as they were lying,
    Were their faces grim.
In their blood, as they lay dying,
    Did they smile on him.
Those, in whom he had reliance
    For his noble name,
With one smile of still defiance
    Sold him unto shame.
Shame and wrath his heart confounded,
    Pale he turn'd and red,

Till himself was deadly wounded
    Falling on the dead.
Dismal error! fearful slaughter!
    Years have wander'd by,
Side by side beneath the water
    Crew and Captain lie;
There the sunlit ocean tosses
    O'er them mouldering,
And the lonely seabird crosses
    With one waft of the wing.

Three Sonnets to a Coquette

I

Caress'd or chidden by the dainty hand,
    And singing airy trifles this or that,
Light Hope at Beauty's call would perch and stand,
    And run thro' every change of sharp and flat;
    And Fancy came and at her pillow sat,
When Sleep had bound her in his rosy band,
    And chased away the still-recurring gnat,
And woke her with a lay from fairy land.
But now they live with Beauty less and less,
    For Hope is other Hope and wanders far,
        Nor cares to lisp in love's delicious creeds;
And Fancy watches in the wilderness,
    Poor Fancy sadder than a single star,
        That sets at twilight in a land of reeds.

II

The form, the form alone is eloquent!
    A nobler yearning never broke her rest
    Than but to dance and sing, be gaily drest,
And win all eyes with all accomplishment:
Yet in the waltzing-circle as we went,
    My fancy made me for a moment blest
    To find my heart so near the beauteous breast
That once had power to rob it of content.
A moment came the tenderness of tears,
    The phantom of a wise, that once could move,
        A ghost of passion that no smiles restore —
For ah! the slight coquette, she cannot love,
And if you kissed her feet a thousand years,
        She still would take the praise, and care no more.

III

Wan Sculptor, weepest thou to take the cast
   Of those dead lineaments that near thee lie?
Or sorrowest thou, pale Painter, for the past,
   In painting some dead friend from memory?
Weep on: beyond his object Love can last:
   His object lives: more cause to weep have I:
My tears, no tears of love, are flowing fast,
   No tears of love, but tears that Love can die.
I pledge her not in any cheerful cup,
   Nor care to sit beside her where she sits –
     Ah pity – hint it not in human tones,
But breathe it into earth and close it up
    With secret death for ever, in the pits
     Which some green Christmas crams with weary bones.

On a Mourner

I

Nature, so far as in her lies,
   Imitates God, and turns her face
To every land beneath the skies,
   Counts nothing that she meets with base,
   But lives and loves in every place;

II

Fills out the homely quickset-screens,
   And makes the purple lilac ripe,
Steps from her airy hill, and greens
   The swamp, where hums the dropping snipe,
   With moss and braided marish-pipe;

III

And on thy heart a finger lays,
   Saying, 'Beat quicker, for the time
Is pleasant, and the woods and ways
   Are pleasant, and the beech and lime
   Put forth and feel a gladder clime.'

IV

And murmurs of a deeper voice,
   Going before to some far shrine,
Teach that sick heart the stronger choice,
   Till all thy life one way incline
With one wide will that closes thine.

V

And when the zoning eve has died
    Where yon dark valleys wind forlorn,
Come Hope and Memory, spouse and bride,
    From out the borders of the morn,
    With that fair child betwixt them born.

VI

And when no mortal motion jars
    The blackness round the tombing sod,
Thro' silence and the trembling stars
    Comes Faith from tracts no feet have trod,
    And Virtue, like a household god

VII

Promising empire; such as those
    That once at dead of night did greet
Troy's wandering prince, so that he rose
    With sacrifice, while all the fleet
    Had rest by stony hills of Crete.

The Victim

I

A plague upon the people fell,
    A famine after laid them low,
Then thorpe and byre arose in fire,
    For on them brake the sudden foe;
So thick they died the people cried
    'The Gods are moved against the land.'
The Priest in horror about his altar
    To Thor and Odin lifted a hand.
        'Help us from famine
        And plague and strife!
        What would you have of us?
        Human life?
        Were it our nearest,
        Were it our dearest,
        (Answer, O answer)
        We give you his life.'

II

But still the foeman spoil'd and burn'd,
    And cattle died, and deer in wood,
And bird in air, and fishes turn'd

And whiten'd all the rolling flood;
And dead men lay all over the way,
Or down in a furrow scathed with flame:
And ever and ay the Priesthood moan'd
Till at last it seem'd that an answer came:
The King is happy
In child and wife;
Take you his nearest,
Take you his dearest,
Give us a life.'

III

The Priest went out by heath and hill;
The King was hunting in the wild;
They found the mother sitting still;
She cast her arms about the child.
The child was only eight summers old,
His beauty still with his years increased,
His face was ruddy, his hair was gold,
He seem'd a victim due to the priest.
The Priest exulted,
And cried with joy,
'Here is his nearest,
Here is his dearest,
We take the boy.'

IV

The King returned from out the wild,
He bore but little game in hand;
The mother said 'They have taken the child,
To spill his blood and heal the land:
The land is sick, the people diseased,
And blight and famine on all the lea:
The holy Gods, they must be appeased,
So I pray you tell the truth to me.
They have taken our son,
They will have his life,
Is *he* your nearest?
Is *he* your dearest?
(Answer, O answer)
Or I, the wife?'

V

The King bent low, with hand on brow,
He stay'd his arms upon his knee:
'O wife, what use to answer now?

For now the Priest has judged for me.'
The King was shaken with holy fear;
    'The Gods,' he said, 'would have chosen well
Yet both are near, and both are dear,
    And which the dearest I cannot tell!'
            But the Priest was happy,
            His victim won,
            'We have his nearest,
            We have his dearest,
            His only son!'

                    VI

The rites prepared, the victim bared,
    The knife uprising toward the blow,
To the altar-stone she sprang alone,
    'Me, me, not him, my darling, no!'
He caught her away with a sudden cry;
    Suddenly from him brake the wife,
And shrieking 'I am his dearest, I –
    I am his dearest!' rush'd on the knife.
            And the Priest was happy,
            'O, Father Odin,
            We give you a life.
            Which was his nearest?
            Which was his dearest?
            The Gods have answered:
            We give them the wife!'

On a Spiteful Letter

Here, it is here – the close of the year,
    And with it a spiteful letter.
My name in song has done him much wrong,
    For himself has done much better.

O foolish bard, is your lot so hard,
    If men neglect your pages?
I think not much of yours or of mine:
    I hear the roll of the ages.

This fallen leaf, isn't fame as brief?
    My rhymes may have been the stronger,
Yet hate me not, but abide your lot:
    I last but a moment longer.

O faded leaf, isn't fame as brief?
    What room is here for a hater?
Yet the yellow leaf hates the greener leaf,
    For it hangs one moment later.

Greater than I – isn't that your cry?
    And I shall live to see it.
Well, if it be so, so it is, you know;
    And if it be so – so be it!

O summer leaf, isn't fame as brief?
    But this is the time of hollies.
And my heart, my heart is an evergreen:
    I hate the spites and the follies.

Wages

Glory of warrior, glory of orator, glory of song,
    Paid with a voice flying by to be lost on an endless sea –
Glory of Virtue, to fight, to struggle, to right the wrong –
    Nay, but she aim'd not at glory, no lover of glory she:
Give her the glory of going on, and still to be.

The wages of sin is death: if the wages of Virtue be dust,
    Would she have heart to endure for the life of the worm and
        the fly?
She desires no isles of the blest, no quiet seats of the just,
    To rest in a golden grove, or to bask in a summer sky:
Give her the wages of going on, and not to die.

Lucretius

Lucilia, wedded to Lucretius, found
Her master cold; for when the morning flush
Of passion and the first embrace had died
Between them, tho' he loved her none the less,
Yet often when the woman heard his foot
Return from pacings in the field, and ran
To greet him with a kiss, the master took
Small notice, or austerely, for – his mind
Half buried in some weightier argument,
Or fancy-borne perhaps upon the rise
And long roll of the Hexameter – he past
To turn and ponder those three hundred scrolls

Left by the Teacher whom he held divine.
She brook'd it not; but wrathful, petulant
Dreaming some rival, sought and found a witch
Who brew'd the philtre which had power, they said,
To lead an errant passion home again.
And this, at times, she mingled with his drink,
And this destroy'd him; for the wicked broth
Confused the chemic labour of the blood,
And tickling the brute brain within the man's
Made havock among those tender cells, and check'd
His power to shape: he loath'd himself; and once
After a tempest woke upon a morn
That mock'd him with returning calm, and cried,

  'Storm in the night! for thrice I heard the rain
Rushing; and once the flash of a thunderbolt –
Methought I never saw so fierce a fork –
Struck out the streaming mountain-side, and show'd
A riotous confluence of watercourses
Blanching and billowing in a hollow of it,
Where all but yester-eve was dusty-dry.

  'Storm, and what dreams, ye holy Gods, what dreams!
For thrice I waken'd after dreams.
Perchance We do but recollect the dreams that come
Just ere the waking: terrible! for it seem'd
A void was made in Nature; all her bonds
Crack'd; and I saw the flaring atom-streams
And torrents of her myriad universe,
Ruining along the illimitable inane,
Fly on to clash together again, and make
Another and another frame of things
For ever: that was mine, my dream, I knew it –
Of and belonging to me, as the dog
With inward yelp and restless forefoot plies
His function of the woodland: but the next!
I thought that all the blood by Sylla shed
Came driving rainlike down again on earth,
And where it dash'd the reddening meadow, sprang
No dragon warriors from Cadmean teeth,
For these I thought my dream would show to me,
But girls, Hetairai, curious in their art,
Hired animalisms, vile as those that made
The mulberry-faced Dictator's orgies worse
Than aught they fable of the quiet Gods.
And hands they mixt, and yell'd and round me drove
In narrowing circles till I yell'd again

Half-suffocated, and sprang up, and saw –
Was it the first beam of my latest day?

    'Then, then, from utter gloom stood out the breasts,
The breasts of Helen, and hoveringly a sword
Now over and now under, now direct,
Pointed itself to pierce, but sank down shamed
At all that beauty; and as I stared, a fire,
The fire that left a roofless Ilion,
Shot out of them, and scorch'd me that I woke.

    'Is this thy vengeance, holy Venus, thine,
Because I would not one of thine own doves,
Not ev'n a rose, were offer'd to thee? thine,
Forgetful how my rich proœmion makes
Thy glory fly along the Italian field,
In lays that will outlast thy Deity?

    'Deity? nay, thy worshippers. My tongue
Trips, or I speak profanely. Which of these
Angers thee most, or angers thee at all?
Not if thou be'st of those who far aloof
From envy, hate and pity, and spite and scorn,
Live the great life which all our greatest fain
Would follow, center'd in eternal calm.

    'Nay, if thou can'st, O Goddess, like ourselves
Touch, and be touch'd, then would I cry to thee
To kiss thy Mavors, roll thy tender arms
Round him, and keep him from the lust of blood
That makes a steaming slaughter-house of Rome.

    'Aye, but I meant not thee; I meant not her,
Whom all the pines of Ida shook to see
Slide from that quiet heaven of hers, and tempt
The Trojan, while his neat-herds were abroad;
Nor her that o'er her wounded hunter wept
Her Deity false in human-amorous tears;
Nor whom her beardless apple-arbiter
Decided fairest. Rather, O ye Gods,
Poet-like, as the great Sicilian called
Calliope to grace his golden verse –
Aye, and this Kypris also – did I take
That popular name of thine to shadow forth
The all-generating powers and genial heat
Of Nature, when she strikes through the thick blood
Of cattle, and light is large and lambs are glad
Nosing the mother's udder, and the bird

Makes his heart voice amid the blaze of flowers:
Which things appear the work of mighty Gods.

   'The Gods! and if I go *my* work is left
Unfinish'd – *if* I go. The Gods, who haunt
The lucid interspace of world and world,
Where never creeps a cloud, or moves a wind,
Nor ever falls the least white star of snow,
Nor ever lowest roll of thunder moans,
Nor sound of human sorrow mounts to mar
Their sacred everlasting calm! and such,
Not all so fine, nor so divine a calm,
Not such, nor all unlike it, man may gain
Letting his own life go. The Gods, the Gods!
If all be atoms, how then should the Gods
Being atomic not be dissoluble,
Not follow the great law? My master held
That Gods there are, for all men so believe.
I prest my footsteps into his, and meant
Surely to lead my Memmius in a train
Of flowery clauses onward to the proof
That Gods there are, and deathless. Meant? I meant?
I have forgotten what I meant: my mind
Stumbles, and all my faculties are lamed.

   'Look where another of our Gods, the Sun,
Apollo, Delius, or of older use
All-seeing Hyperion – what you will –
Has mounted yonder; since he never sware,
Except his wrath were wreak'd on wretched man,
That he would only shine among the dead
Hereafter; tales! for never yet on earth
Could dead flesh creep, or bits of roasting ox
Moan round the spit – nor knows he what he sees;
King of the East altho' he seem, and girt
With song and flame and fragrance, slowly lifts
His golden feet on those empurpled stairs
That climb into the windy halls of heaven:
And here he glances on an eye new-born,
And gets for greeting but a wail of pain;
And here he stays upon a freezing orb
That fain would gaze upon him to the last:
And here upon a yellow eyelid fall'n
And closed by those who mourn a friend in vain,
Not thankful that his troubles are no more.
And me, altho' his fire is on my face
Blinding, he sees not, nor at all can tell

Whether I mean this day to end myself,
Or lend an ear to Plato where he says,
That men like soldiers may not quit the post
Allotted by the Gods: but he that holds
The Gods are careless, wherefore need he care
Greatly for them, nor rather plunge at once,
Being troubled, wholly out of sight, and sink
Past earthquake – aye, and gout and stone, that break
Body toward death, and palsy, death-in-life,
And wretched age – and worst disease of all.
These prodigies of myriad nakednesses,
And twisted shapes of lust, unspeakable,
Abominable, strangers at my hearth
Not welcome, harpies miring every dish
The phantom husks of something foully done,
And fleeting thro' the boundless universe,
And blasting the long quiet of my breast
With animal heat and dire insanity.

    'How should the mind, except it loved them, clasp
These idols to herself? or do they fly
Now thinner, and now thicker, like the flakes
In a fall of snow, and so press in, perforce
Of multitude, as crowds that in an hour
Of civic tumult jam the doors, and bear
The keepers down, and throng, their rags and they,
The basest, far into that council-hall
Where sit the best and stateliest of the land?

    'Can I not fling this horror off me again,
Seeing with how great ease Nature can smile,
Balmier and nobler from her bath of storm,
At random ravage? and how easily
The mountain there has cast his cloudy slough,
Now towering o'er him in serenest air,
A mountain o'er a mountain, aye, and within
All hollow as the hopes and fears of men.

'But who was he, that in the garden snared
Picus and Faunus, rustic Gods? a tale
To laugh at – more to laugh at in myself –
For look! what is it? there? yon arbutus
Totters; a noiseless riot underneath
Strikes through the wood, sets all the tops quivering –
The mountain quickens into Nymph and Faun;
And here an Oread, and this way she runs
Before the rest – A satyr, a satyr, see –

Follows; but him I proved impossible;
Twy-natured is no nature: yet he draws
Nearer and nearer, and I scan him now
Beastlier than any phantom of his kind
That ever butted his rough brother-brute
For lust or lusty blood or provender:
I hate, abhor, spit, sicken at him; and she
Loathes him as well; such a precipitate heel,
Fledged as it were with Mercury's ankle-wing,
Whirls her to me: but will she fling herself,
Shameless upon me? Catch her, goatfoot: nay,
Hide, hide them, million-myrtled wilderness,
And cavern-shadowing laurels, hide! do I wish –
What? – that the bush were leafless? or to whelm
All of them in one massacre? O ye Gods,
I know you careless, yet, behold, to you
From childly wont and ancient use I call –
I thought I lived securely as yourselves –
No lewdness, narrowing envy, monkey-spite,
No madness of ambition, avarice, none:
No larger feast than under plane or pine
With neighbours laid along the grass, to take
Only such cups as left us friendly-warm,
Affirming each his own philosophy –
Nothing to mar the sober majesties
Of settled, sweet, Epicurean life.
But now it seems some unseen monster lays
His vast and filthy hands upon my will,
Wrenching it backward into his; and spoils
My bliss in being; and it was not great;
For save when shutting reasons up in rhythm,
Or Heliconian honey in living words,
To make a truth less harsh, I often grew
Tired of so much within our little life,
Or of so little in our little life –
Poor little life that toddles half an hour
Crown'd with a flower or two, and there an end –
And since the nobler pleasure seems to fade,
Why should I, beastlike as I find myself,
Not manlike end myself? – our privilege –
What beast has heart to do it? And what man,
What Roman would be dragg'd in triumph thus?
Not I; not he, who bears one name with her,
Whose death-blow struck the dateless doom of kings,
When, brooking not the Tarquin in her veins,
She made-her blood in sight of Collatine

And all his peers, flushing the guiltless air,
Spout from the maiden fountain in her heart.
And from it sprang the Commonwealth, which breaks
As I am breaking now!

           'And therefore now
Let her, that is the womb and tomb of all,
Great Nature, take, and forcing far apart
Those blind beginnings that have made me man,
Dash them anew together at her will
Through all her cycles – into man once more,
Or beast or bird or fish, or opulent flower –
But till this cosmic order everywhere
Shatter'd into one earthquake in one day
Cracks all to pieces, – and that hour perhaps
Is not so far when momentary man
Shall seem no more a something to himself,
But he, his hopes and hates, his homes and fanes,
And even his bones long laid within the grave,
The very sides of the grave itself shall pass,
Vanishing, atom and void, atom and void,
Into the unseen for ever, – till that hour,
My golden work in which I told a truth
That stays the rolling Ixionian wheel,
And numbs the Fury's ringlet-snake, and plucks
The mortal soul from out immortal hell,
Shall stand: aye, surely: then it fails at last
And perishes as I must; for O Thou,
Passionless bride, divine Tranquillity,
Yearn'd after by the wisest of the wise,
Who fail to find thee, being as thou art
Without one pleasure and without one pain,
Howbeit I know thou surely must be mine
Or .soon or late, yet out of season, thus
I woo thee roughly, for thou carest not
How roughly men may woo thee so they win –
Thus – thus: the soul flies out and dies in the air.'

   With that he drove the knife into his side:
She heard him raging, heard him fall; ran in,
Beat breast, tore hair, cried out upon herself
As having fail'd in duty to him, shriek'd
That she but meant to win him back, fell on him,
Clasp'd, kiss'd him, wail'd: he answer'd, 'Care not thou!
What matters? All is over: Fare thee well!'

INDEX OF POEMS

INDEX OF FIRST LINES